D0684910

Freedom in the World

The findings of the *Comparative Survey of Freedom* and the Map of Freedom include events up to January 1, 1999.

Freedom in the World
The Annual Survey of Political Rights & Civil Liberties 1998-1999

Freedom House Survey Team

Adrian Karatnycky
Editor and Survey Coordinator

Aili Piano
Research Coordinator

Martin Edwin Andersen
Charles Graybow
Kristen Guida
Marshall Freeman Harris
William Kramer
Thomas R. Lansner
Jason Muse
Arch Puddington
Leonard R. Sussman
George Zarycky

Faranak Rofeh
General Editor

Mark Wolkenfeld
Production Coordinator

Academic Advisers
David Becker
Daniel Brumberg
Larry Diamond
Charles Gati
Jeane J. Kirkpatrick
Seymour Martin Lipset
Alexander J. Motyl
Joshua Muravchik
Daniel Pipes
Robert Scalapino
Ashutosh Varshney
Arthur Waldron

Cover Design by Anne Green

ISSN: 0732-6610
ISBN: 0-7658-0012-8 (Cloth); 0-7658-0675-4 (paper)
Printed in the United States of America

The Library of Congress has catalogued this serial title as follows:

Freedom in the world / —1978-
New York : Freedom House, 1978-
v. : map; 25 cm.—(Freedom House Book)
Annual.
ISSN 0732-6610=Freedom in the World.
1. Civil rights—Periodicals. I. R. Adrian Karatnycky, et al.   I. Series.
JC571.F66   323.4'05-dc 19   82-642048
AACR 2   MARC-S
Library of Congress   [84101]

Contents

Foreword   1

The Comparative Survey of Freedom, 1998-1999

A Good Year for Freedom   *Adrian Karatnycky*   3

Regional Essays
Does America Have a   *Arch Puddington*   17
  Human Rights Problem?
Democracy and "Failed States"   *Timothy D. Sisk*   24
"Multilateralism and Its Discontents"   *Peter W. Rodman*   35

Survey of Press Freedom
The News of the Century   *Leonard R. Sussman*   43

Country Reports
Introduction   53
The Reports   55

Related Territories Reports   509

Survey Methodology   546

Tables and Ratings
Table of Independent Countries—Comparative Measures of Freedom   554
Table of Related Territories—Comparative Measures of Freedom   556
Table of Disputed Territories—Comparative Measures of Freedom   557
Table of Social and Economic Indicators   558
Combined Average Ratings, Independent Countries   560
Combined Average Ratings, Related and Disputed Territories   561
Table of Electoral Democracies   562

Sources   564
The Map of Freedom—1998   567

Foreword

The *Comparative Survey of Freedom* is an institutional effort by Freedom House to monitor the progress and decline of political rights and civil liberties in 191 nations and 61 related and disputed territories. These year-end reviews of freedom began in 1955, when they were called the *Balance Sheet of Freedom* and, still later, the *Annual Survey of the Progress of Freedom*. This program was expanded in the early 1970s, and has appeared in *Freedom Review* since 1973. It has also been issued in a more developed context as a yearbook since 1978.

Since 1989, the *Survey* project has been a year-long effort produced by our regional experts, consultants, and human rights specialists. The *Survey* derives its information from a wide range of sources. Most valued of these are the many human rights activists, journalists, editors, and political figures around the world who keep us informed of the human rights situation in their countries.

The Survey team is grateful to the considerable advice and input of our Survey of Freedom Advisory Board, consisting of Prof. David Becker, Prof. Daniel Brumberg, Dr. Larry Diamond, Prof. Charles Gati, Prof. Jeane J. Kirkpatrick, Dr. Seymour Martin Lipset, Prof. Alexander Motyl, Dr. Joshua Muravchik, Dr. Daniel Pipes, Prof. Robert Scalapino, Prof. Ashutosh Varshney, and Prof. Arthur Waldron.

Throughout the year, Freedom House personnel regularly conduct fact-finding missions to gain more in-depth knowledge of the vast political transformations affecting our world. During these investigations, we make every effort to meet a cross-section of political parties and associations, human rights monitors, religious figures, representatives of both the private sector and trade union movement, academics and journalists.

During the past year, Freedom House staff traveled to Argentina, Austria, Azerbaijan, Belarus, Bosnia-Herzegovina, Bulgaria, China, Croatia, Czech Republic, Cuba, Ecuador, Egypt, Estonia, Georgia, Hungary, India, Italy, Latvia, Lithuania, Mexico, Peru, Poland, Romania, Russia, Slovakia, Turkey, Ukraine, and Yugoslavia. The *Survey* project team also consults a vast array of published source materials, ranging from the reports of other human rights organizations to often rare, regional newspapers and magazines.

This year's *Survey* team includes project coordinator Adrian Karatnycky, Mick Andersen, Charles Graybow, Kristen Guida, Marshall Harris, William Kramer, Thomas R. Lansner, Jason Muse, Aili Piano, Arch Puddington, Leonard R. Sussman, and George Zarycky. The general editor of *Freedom in the World* is Faranak Rofeh. The proofreader is Trish Fox. The production coordinator is Mark Wolkenfeld. The cover was designed by Anne Green.

Principal support for the *Comparative Survey of Freedom* has been generously provided by the Lynde and Harry Bradley Foundation and the Smith Richardson Foundation.

The Comparative Survey of Freedom 1989-1999

A Good Year for Freedom

Adrian Karatnycky

More Free Countries Than Ever

Despite a year that saw violent civil war in the Republic of the Congo, attempts at ethnic cleansing in Kosovo, ethnic and political violence in Indonesia, and severe economic turbulence in many of the world's emerging markets, freedom made significant strides in 1998. As the year drew to a close, 88 of the world's 191 countries (46 percent) were rated as Free, meaning that they maintain a high degree of political and economic freedom and respect basic civil liberties. This was the largest number of Free countries on record, and represented a net gain of seven from last year—the second-largest increase in the 26-year history of the *Survey*. Another 53 countries (28 percent of the world total) were rated as Partly Free, enjoying more limited political rights and civil liberties, often in a context of corruption, weak rule of law, ethnic strife, or civil war. This represented a drop of four from the previous year. Finally, 50 countries (26 percent of the world total) that deny their citizens basic rights and civil liberties were rated as Not Free. This represented a drop of three from the previous year.

There were seven new entrants into the ranks of Free countries in 1998, including India, which had been rated as Partly Free since 1991, a year that saw the killing of former prime minister Rajiv Gandhi, intense labor strife, and an escalation of intercommunal violence resulting in thousands of deaths. India's return to the ranks of Free countries was the consequence of greater internal stability, fewer instances of intercommunal violence, and the peaceful democratic transfer of power to an opposition-led government. Other entrants into the ranks of Free countries were the Dominican Republic, where a democratically elected government has made efforts to strengthen the administration of justice; Ecuador, which recently concluded free and fair elections; Nicaragua, where improved relations between civilian authorities and a military formerly dominated by the Sandinistas contributed to the strengthening of democratic stability and where greater attention was paid to the problems of indigenous peoples on the country's Atlantic coast; Papua New Guinea, which saw a January 1998 peace agreement put an end to a destabilizing nine-year secessionist rebellion on Bougainville Island; Slovakia, where free and fair elections brought to power a government dominated by reformers; and Thailand, where the government of Prime Minister Chuan Leekpai has fostered increasing political accountability.

In addition, three countries formerly ranked as Not Free—Indonesia, Nigeria, and Sierra Leone—made tangible progress and are now rated as Partly Free. In Indonesia, the downfall of Suharto has led to the reemergence of political parties and civic groups and the promise of free elections. Although the country's economic crisis has sparked ethnic violence targeting the Chinese minority (and some violence has occurred during

Freedom in the World—1998-1999

The population of the world this year is estimated at 5,908.7 million persons, who reside in 191 sovereign states and 61 related and disputed territories—a total of 252 entities. The level of political rights and civil liberties as shown comparatively by the Freedom House Survey is:

Free: 2,354.0 million (39.84 percent of the world's population) live in 88 of the states and in 44 of the related and/or disputed territories.

Partly Free: 1,570.6 million (26.59 percent of the world's population) live in 53 of the states and 4 of the related and/or disputed territories.

Not Free: 1,984.1 million (33.58 percent of the world's population) live in 50 of the states and 13 of the related and/or disputed territories.

A Record of the Survey
(population in millions)

SURVEY DATE	FREE		PARTLY FREE		NOT FREE		WORLD POPULATION
January '81	1,613.0	(35.90%)	970.9	(21.60%)	1,911.9	(42.50%)	4,495.8
January '83	1,665.4	(36.32%)	918.8	(20.04%)	2,000.2	(43.64%)	4,584.1
January '85	1,671.4	(34.85%)	1,117.4	(23.30%)	2,007.0	(41.85%)	4,795.8
January '87	1,842.5	(37.10%)	1,171.5	(23.60%)	1,949.9	(39.30%)	4,963.9
January '89	1,992.8	(38.86%)	1,027.9	(20.05%)	2,107.3	(41.09%)	5,128.0
January '90	2,034.4	(38.87%)	1,143.7	(21.85%)	2,055.9	(39.28%)	5,234.0
January '91*	2,088.2	(39.23%)	1,485.7	(27.91%)	1,748.7	(32.86%)	5,322.6
January '92 (a)	1,359.3	(25.29%)	2,306.6	(42.92%)	1,708.2	(31.79%)	5,374.2
January '93	1,352.2	(24.83%)	2,403.3	(44.11%)	1,690.4	(31.06%)	5,446.0
January '94	1,046.2	(19.00%)	2,224.4	(40.41%)	2,234.6	(40.59%)	5,505.2
January '95	1,119.7	(19.97%)	2,243.4	(40.01%)	2,243.9	(40.02%)	5,607.0
January '96	1,114.5	(19.55%)	2,365.8	(41.49%)	2.221.2	(38.96%)	5.701.5
January '97	1,250.3	(21.67%)	2,260.1	(39.16%)	2,260.6	(39.17%)	5,771.0
January '98	1,266.0	(21.71%)	2,281.9	(39.12%)	2,284.6	(39.17%)	5,832.5
January '99 (b)	2,354.0	(39.84%)	1,570.6	(26.59%)	1,984.1	(33.58%)	5,908.7

(a) The large shift in the population figure between 1991 and 1992 is due to India's change from Free to Partly Free.

(b) The large shift in the population figure between 1998 and 1999 is due to India's change from Partly Free to Free.

student demonstrations), some political controls have loosened, political parties and movements have begun to gain strength, and the media have become more outspoken. In Nigeria, the death of military dictator Sani Abacha has led to a political opening that holds out the promise of multiparty elections and already has seen the reemergence of public debate, a resurgence of political parties, the return of exiled leaders, relatively free and fair local elections, and the rise of an increasingly vibrant press. In Sierra Leone, the defeat of a military coup has put an end to chaos and violence and restored power to the country's democratically elected civilian authorities.

More Free People Than Ever

As a result of the gains in freedom in 1998—especially in India, the world's most populous democracy—2.354 billion people (40 percent of the world's population) now live in Free societies, 1.570 billion (26.5 percent) live in countries that are Partly Free, and 1.984 billion (33.5 percent) live in Not Free countries. The proportion of the world's population living in freedom is the highest in the history of the Survey.

In addition to these shifts from one category to another, the 1998 survey recorded more modest improvements in freedom in 21 countries. Not all trends for the year were positive. The survey registered more modest declines in freedom in ten countries. These changes are reflected by upward or downward arrows, signifying improvements or declines in a country's score on the freedom scale. One country which registered worrying trends was Argentina, which suffered from the destabilizing effects of political sex scandals and efforts to blackmail political leaders.

Thirteen countries were judged to be the world's most repressive and have received Freedom House's lowest rating: scores of 7 for political rights and 7 for civil liberties. In these states, basic political rights and civil liberties are nonexistent, there is no free press, and independent civic life is suppressed. The most repressive countries, the "world's worst" in terms of freedom, include Iraq, North Korea, Cuba, and Sudan. The others are Afghanistan, Burma, Equatorial Guinea, Libya, Saudi Arabia, Somalia, Syria, Turkmenistan, and Vietnam. It is notable that of the 13 least free states, three are one-party Marxist-Leninist states and eight are predominantly Islamic. The number of countries that received Freedom House's lowest rating (7,7) has declined from 21 at the close of 1994.

The *Survey of Freedom* also found that at the end of 1998 there were 117 electoral democracies, representing over 61 percent of the world's countries and nearly 55 percent of its population. The Freedom House roster of electoral democracies is based on a stringent standard requiring that all elected national authority must be the product of free and fair electoral processes. Thus, in the estimation of the *Survey*, neither Mexico (whose 1997 national legislative elections were judged free and fair, but whose last national presidential elections failed to meet that standard) nor Malaysia (whose governing United Malays National Organization enjoys huge and unfair advantages in national elections) qualifies as an electoral democracy. After a period in which electoral democracies increased dramatically from 69 in 1987, their number has remained stagnant at 117 since 1995.

The survey team identified five events that represented important gains for freedom in 1988 and five which signaled setbacks for freedom.

The Global Trend			
	Free	**Partly Free**	**Not Free**
1988-1989	61	39	68
1993-1994	72	63	55
1998-1999	88	53	50

Tracking Democracy	
Number of Democracies	
1988-1989	69
1993-1994	108
1998-1999	117

Top Five Gains for Freedom in 1998

1. *NIGERIA*: Developments have moved in a promising direction since the death of the tyrannical General Abacha, with many civil liberties restored, political parties legalized, and national elections pledged for 1999. A good omen was the holding of local elections which were deemed free and fair.

2. *INDONESIA*: President Suharto's resignation has been accompanied by indications of changes towards electoral democracy and enhanced civil liberties. On the negative side has been mounting violence against the Chinese minority and bloody clashes between students and the army.

3. *CORRUPTION ALERT*: The governments of the United States and other leading

democracies, along with the World Bank, are focusing increased attention on the role of corruption in undermining political and economic reform in transitional societies. A positive sign: demands for improvements in the rule of law are increasingly being incorporated into decisions on foreign assistance.

4. *FREEDOM ON THE NET*: Several years ago China and other authoritarian regimes announced plans to control the Internet's political content. Those efforts have failed. In the future, the Internet will play a growing role in linking democratic forces within repressive societies and in building a global network of freedom activists.

5. *DICTATORS BEWARE*: Both current and former dictators had reason for concern. Though controversial, the effort to bring General Pinochet to justice sent a chilling message to tyrants around the world. Yugoslavia's Milosevic was under

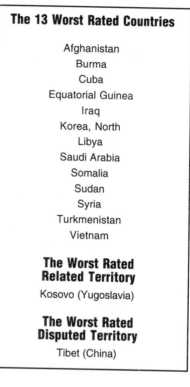

The 13 Worst Rated Countries

Afghanistan
Burma
Cuba
Equatorial Guinea
Iraq
Korea, North
Libya
Saudi Arabia
Somalia
Sudan
Syria
Turkmenistan
Vietnam

The Worst Rated Related Territory

Kosovo (Yugoslavia)

The Worst Rated Disputed Territory

Tibet (China)

increased pressure, Indonesia's Suharto resigned, and Congo's Kabila traveled abroad only after securing assurance that he would not be arrested.

Top Five Setbacks for Freedom in 1998

1. *RUSSIA*: The assassination of democracy advocate Galina Staravoitova was the most tragic development in a bad year for Russian reformers. With President Yeltsin enfeebled, a coalition of neo-Communists and hardline nationalists gained increased influence, and succeeded in bringing down a reformist government. A new government, dominated by former Communists, made little progress in stemming corruption or reviving the economy.

2. *MALAYSIA*: President Mahathir Mohamad responded to his country's economic decline in all the wrong ways: repressing political critics, tightening political control, and placing restrictions on the economy. Here is a prime example of everything that is wrong with "Asian values."

3. *CONGO*: Events moved from bad to worse in the Democratic Republic of Congo. President Kabila showed no sign of relaxing his repressive policies. Much of the country remained contested territory, with forces from a half dozen African nations pillaging the countryside and terrorizing the populace.

4. *RELIGIOUS PERSECUTION*: The persecution of religious minorities, especially

Christians, remained a serious problem in a number of countries. Among the worst violators: Pakistan, Egypt, China, and Iran. Persecution was most serious in Sudan, where Christians and animists in the southern regions were killed, starved, and forced into exile by forces of the Moslem North.

5. *NUCLEAR PROLIFERATION*: The detonation of nuclear devices by India and Pakistan was a jolting reminder of the menace still posed by weapons of mass destruction. Other reasons to worry included Iraq's determination to rebuild its nuclear, chemical, and biological arsenal, North Korea's nuclear saber-rattling, and the role of Russian scientists in the development of weapons for Iran and other states.

Electoral Democracy and Freedom

Despite the emergence of electoral democracy as the world's predominant form of government, major violations of human rights and civil liberties remain the norm in a majority of countries containing some three-fifths of the world's population. This disjunction arises from the fact that many electoral democracies fall short of being Free. In an influential 1997 article in *Foreign Affairs*, Fareed Zakaria drew on Freedom House data underlining this fact to suggest that the world had entered an era characterized by "The Rise of Illiberal Democracy." Yet there are signs that electoral democracy eventually does have a positive effect on freedom. Particularly notable in the 1998 Survey was the growing respect for civil liberties in a number of electoral democracies. In fact, it appears that the trend to which political scientists were pointing had peaked in the first half of the 1990s—a period of rapid democratic expansion in the wake of the collapse of Marxist-Leninist regimes.

Freedom House's most current data suggest that, as the 1990s draw toward a close, we are observing a decline in the number of "illiberal democracies" and an increase in the number and proportion of the world's electoral democracies that are also liberal (i.e., Free) democracies. In 1995, for example, the *Survey* found there were 117 electoral democracies, of which 76 were rated Free (64.9 percent), 40 were judged to be Partly Free (over 34 percent), and one—war-ravaged Bosnia-Herzegovina—was Not Free. Today, out of 117 electoral democracies, 88 (over 75 percent) are Free, while the remaining 29 are Partly Free.

Since 1995, the electoral democracies that have seen a deepening climate of respect for political rights and civil liberties and thus have entered the ranks of Free countries include the Dominican Republic, El Salvador, Honduras, India, Mali, Nicaragua, Papua New Guinea, the Philippines, Romania, Taiwan, and Thailand. These gains have been partly offset by setbacks in some formerly Free electoral democracies, for a net gain of ten Free countries. Ecuador, Slovakia, and Venezuela have oscillated between the Free and Partly Free categories since 1995.

While electoral democracy allows space to emerge for competing political interests and holds out the promise of greater freedom and respect for human rights, the record of some electoral democracies remains marred by political restrictions and violations of civil liberties. Not all these Partly Free democracies suffer from an identical set of problems: Some have weak governments incapable of guaranteeing basic civil liberties in the face of violent political movements (Colombia and Georgia); others must contend with powerful and politically influential militaries (Turkey and Paraguay), or internal security forces that can act with impunity (Brazil). Some are plagued by powerful oligarchic forces and/or the weak rule of law (Russia and Ukraine); in other cases, democratically elected leaders seek to centralize their power or to exercise power arbitrarily. Yet these phenomena should not obscure the overall global record: Most democratically elected leaders function within the context of effective checks and balances on their power, and most are able to marshal democratic legitimacy in their efforts to govern effectively and responsibly.

At the close of 1998, the Partly Free democracies were 29 in number. The record of the *Survey* in recent years shows that precisely these flawed, Partly Free electoral democracies hold the greatest potential for the expansion of freedom. For where there is free electoral competition among political parties, there is also the possibility for open criticism of government policies and the airing of alternative viewpoints. Many new democracies are just beginning the arduous process of institutionalizing the rule of law; creating a vibrant civil society; instituting procedures that protect minority rights; fostering a sense of moderation and tolerance among competing political forces; developing economically and politically independent broadcast media; and ensuring effective civilian control over the police and the military. All this takes time. It should therefore come as no surprise that most new democracies make more rapid progress in the areas of political processes and political rights than in the area of civil liberties. Nonetheless, though complete freedom may be long in coming, citizens of Partly Free electoral democracies can at least engage in serious debate over public policy—a right rarely, if ever, enjoyed in nondemocratic regimes. Some critics have suggested that electoral democracy leads to bad governance, increases instability, places ethnic minorities at peril, and legitimizes efforts to suppress political opponents. But the record suggests otherwise. There are 88 electoral democracies that successfully protect a broad range of political and civil rights. Moreover, even the 29 electoral democracies that Freedom House rates as only Partly Free are not states that brutally suppress basic freedoms. Rather, they are generally countries in which civic institutions are weak, poverty is rampant, and intergroup tensions are acute. This is not surprising, as many such fragile democracies are emerging from protracted periods of intense civil strife, and some are building new states.

The *Survey* shows evidence of improvements in civil liberties in countries that had previously established democratic electoral practices. This sequence makes sense because free and fair elections take less time to implement than the more complex processes that produce the rule of law and a strong civil society. As the Freedom House data suggest, illiberal democracy tends toward liberal democracy so long as there is internal or external pressure for further reform. Moreover, the regular transfer of power between competing political elites, or even the prospect of such a transfer, appears to improve the chances for the deepening of civil liberties.

Clearly, some Partly Free (or illiberal) democracies lack respect for the rule of law, checks and balances among the branches of government, and protections for the rights of minorities. It is also true that in some circumstances (especially in multiethnic settings) open electoral processes can be occasions for the emergence of political demagogy directed against ethnic minorities. Indeed, almost three in ten electoral democracies fail adequately to safeguard basic freedoms for these sorts of reasons. At the same time, the *Survey of Freedom* suggests that, over the last 20 years, the emergence of electoral democracies has been the best indicator of subsequent progress in the areas of civil liberties and human rights.

Ethnicity and Nationalism

The Freedom House data also suggest that countries without a predominant ethnic majority are less successful in establishing open and democratic societies than ethnically homogeneous countries. For the purposes of making this comparison, we define countries in which over two-thirds of the population belong to a single ethnic group as mono-ethnic, and those without such a two-thirds majority as multiethnic.

According to this definition, 66 of the 88 Free countries (75 percent) are mono-ethnic, while 22 (25 percent) are multiethnic. Of the 114 countries in the world that possess a dominant ethnic group, 66 (58 percent) are Free, 22 (19 percent) are Partly Free, and 26 (23 percent) are Not Free. By contrast, among multiethnic countries only 22 of 77 (29 percent) are Free, 31 (40 percent) are Partly Free, and 24 (31 percent) are Not Free. A mono-ethnic country, therefore, is twice as likely to be Free as a multiethnic one.

A similar pattern can be found among the 117 electoral democracies, which include 77 mono-ethnic and 40 multiethnic countries. Of the 77 mono-ethnic democracies, 66 (86 percent) are Free, and 11 (14 percent) are Partly Free. Among multiethnic democracies, 22 (55 percent) are Free and 18 are Partly Free (45 percent). Thus multiethnic democracies are nearly two-and-a-half times more likely to be only Partly Free than are mono-ethnic ones.

In the face of ethnic conflicts in Africa, the former Yugoslavia, and elsewhere, many analysts have recently focused on the destructive power of contemporary nationalism. Yet the fact that nation-states appear to provide the most durable basis for political freedom and respect for civil liberties deserves greater attention. At the same time, while the survey suggests that democracies are more likely to be Free if they do not face significant ethnic cleavages, there also is compelling evidence that multiethnic societies can preserve a broad array of political and civil freedoms. Successful multiethnic societies include established democracies like Canada, Belgium, and Switzerland, as well as such new democracies as Estonia, Latvia, Mali, Namibia, and South Africa. India's return to the ranks of Free countries is an indication that, even in an ethnically charged environment, it is possible for multiethnic societies to establish a climate and framework of significant respect for personal freedoms, the rule of law, and the rights of religious and ethnic minorities.

The set of 40 multiethnic electoral democracies merits closer investigation. Are there common characteristics among the Free multiethnic democracies? Is there a significant correlation between certain patterns of population distribution in multiethnic societies and greater freedom? Are homogeneous concentrations of particular ethnic groups more or less conducive to stability and freedom? Is the dispersion of ethnic minorities throughout a country more compatible with democratic stability and the expansion of freedom? Do different forms of state organization contribute to a higher degree of freedom? Are federal arrangements more or less conducive to the development of freedom? When are federal arrangements successful and when do they provoke ethnic conflict or separatism? Under what circumstances do federal arrangements break down? What is the effect of external diasporas and the forces of irredentism on the political development of multiethnic states?

It is clear that in some settings political appeals based on ethnicity make it impossible for democratic systems that feature a regular transfer of power to function. Yet the example of numerous free and democratic multiethnic societies shows that it is possible to transcend ethnic appeals in politics, to avert the permanent disenfranchisement of ethnic minorities, and to establish durable democracies.

In the aftermath of the Cold War, nationalism has come to be identified with violence and intolerance. The *Survey* makes clear, however, that nation-states—many of which are the products of nationalist ideas of state organization—tend to be more compatible with stable democratic rule and political freedom. Indeed, in the 1980s and 1990s, most successful ethnic struggles for national self-determination and even nationhood have been peaceful, involving mass protests, independent civic organization, strikes, and other forms of opposition activity. In the former Soviet bloc, such activism contributed to the downfall of oppressive regimes and the creation of a number of free and democratic states. Where nationalism has led to violence and bloody warfare, another factor has often been present—that of irredentism.

In several instances, ethnic and national aspirations to autonomy or independence have received military support from neighboring nation-states ruled by the very ethnic group that is seeking sovereignty or separation. In such cases (for example, Bosnia's Serb Republic; ethnically Armenian Nagorno-Karabakh in Azerbaijan; the Transdniester Republic in Moldova; to a lesser but considerable degree, the Kosovo Liberation Army; and the Rwandan-aided rebellions in the Republic of the Congo), what is at work may be support provided by an existing state seeking to extend its borders rather than the aspiration to create a new nation-state.

Regional Variations

Democracy and freedom have been on the upswing since the mid-1970s. Clearly, this trend has been visible across all continents and in most cultures, underscoring that human liberty and democracy are not Western constructs, but universal aspirations. Yet while the expansion of democracy and freedom has been global, it has not everywhere proceeded at the same pace. There have been important geographical and cultural variations that deserve attention and deeper understanding.

At the close of 1998, democracy and freedom are the dominant trends in Western and East-Central Europe, in the Americas, and increasingly in the Asian-Pacific region. In the former Soviet Union the picture is decidedly more mixed, with the growth of freedom stalled and a number of countries evolving into dictatorships. In Africa, too, Free societies and electoral democracies remain a distinct minority. Moreover, there are no democracies or Free societies within the Arab world, and few in other predominantly Muslim societies.

Of the 53 countries in Africa, 9 are Free (17 percent), 21 are Partly Free (40 percent) and 23 are Not Free (43 percent). Only 17 African countries (less than one-third) are electoral democracies. As of the end of 1998, Lesotho's democracy fell, while at the same time, the Survey noted positive trends in Nigeria and Sierra Leone.

In Asia, 19 of the region's 38 countries are Free (50 percent), 9 are Partly Free (24 percent), and 10 are Not Free (26 percent). Despite the looming presence of Communist China and the rhetoric of "Asian values," 24 (63 percent) of the region's polities are electoral democracies.

In East-Central Europe and the former USSR, there are growing signs of a deepening chasm. In Central Europe and parts of Eastern Europe, including the Baltic states, democracy and freedom prevail; in the former USSR, however, progress toward the emergence of open societies has stalled or failed. Overall, 19 of the 27 post-Communist countries of East-Central Europe and the former USSR are electoral democracies. Ten of the regions states are Free, 11 are Partly Free, and 6 are Not Free. Of the 12 non-Baltic former Soviet republics, 7 countries are Partly Free, 5 are Not Free, and none are Free.

Among the 35 countries in the Americas, 31 are electoral democracies. Twenty-five states are rated as Free, 9 are Partly Free, and 1—Cuba—is Not Free.

In the Middle East (excluding North Africa), the roots of democracy and freedom are weakest. In this region there is only one Free country, Israel; there are three Partly Free states, Jordan, Kuwait, and Turkey; and there are ten countries that are Not Free. Israel and Turkey are the region's only two electoral democracies.

Western Europe is the preserve of Free countries and democracies, with all 24 states both free and democratic.

In addition to these regional breakdowns, Freedom House has examined the state of freedom and democracy in the Arab world. Among the 16 states with an Arab majority, there are no Free countries. Three predominantly Arab states—Jordan, Kuwait, and Morocco—are Partly Free. There are no electoral democracies in the Arab world.

The *Survey* also reveals some interesting patterns in the relationship between cultures and political development. While there are broad differences within civilizations, and while democracy and human rights find expression in a wide array of cultures and beliefs, the *Survey* shows some important variations in the relationship between religious belief or tradition and political freedom.

Of the 88 countries that are rated Free, 79 are majority Christian by tradition or belief. Of the nine Free countries that are not majority Christian, one is Israel, often considered part of a Judeo-Christian tradition, and two others, Mauritius and South Korea, have significant Christian communities representing at least a third of their population. Of the six remaining Free countries, Mali is predominantly Muslim; nearly half of Taiwan's population is Buddhist; Mongolia and Thailand are chiefly Buddhist; Japan has a majority that observes both Buddhist and Shinto traditions; and India is predominantly Hindu.

While 79 of the 88 Free countries are predominantly Christian, just 11 of the 67 countries with the poorest record in terms of political rights and civil liberties are predominantly Christian. By this indicator, a predominantly Christian country is nearly five-and-a-half times as likely to be Free and democratic as it is to be repressive and non-democratic. There is also a strong correlation between electoral democracy and Hinduism (India, Mauritius, and Nepal), and there are a significant number of Free countries among traditionally Buddhist societies and societies in which Buddhism is the most widespread faith (Japan, Mongolia, Taiwan, and Thailand).

At the close of the twentieth century, the Islamic world remains most resistant to the spread of democracy and civil liberties, especially the Arab countries. Only one country with a Muslim majority—Mali—is Free, 14 are Partly Free, and 28 are Not Free. Six countries with a predominantly Muslim population are electoral democracies: Albania, Bangladesh, Kyrgyzstan, Mali, Pakistan, and Turkey. Yet the year's trends also showed that the Islamic world is not completely resistant to the expansion of freedom. There was limited progress in Indonesia, the world's most populous Islamic country, and in Nigeria, where half the population is Muslim, there was momentum toward a democratic political opening.

Although we tend to think of civilizations and cultures as fixed and stable entities, it should be kept in mind that political transformations within civilizations can spread rapidly. For example, before the Third Wave of democratization was launched in the 1970s, the majority of predominantly Catholic countries were tyrannies; they included Latin America's oligarchies and military dictatorships, East-Central Europe's Marxist-Leninist states, Iberia's authoritarian-corporatist systems, and the Philippine dictatorship of Ferdinand Marcos. Social scientists speculated about the influence that Catholicism's hierarchical system of church authority might have on Catholic attitudes toward politics. Today, of course, most Catholic countries have become Free and democratic, and some would argue that it was precisely the internal discipline of the Catholic church which made possible the rapid spread of pro-democratic values following Vatican II and under the papacy of John Paul II.

The Global Expansion of Freedom

The last quarter century has seen a rapid expansion of democratic governance along with a more gradual expansion of civil society and civil liberties. There is little question that the *Survey*'s findings reflect significant gains for human freedom at the dawn of a new millennium. Still, many of the new electoral democracies and newly Free countries remain fragile, and political reversals cannot be excluded. Moreover, there appears to be little forward momentum for democratic change and freedom in many of the Not Free countries. In particular, there is little evidence of progress toward democracy in the Arab world and in the world's remaining Marxist-Leninist states.

The global expansion of political and civic freedoms has coincided with the expansion of market-based economies. Indeed, on the basis of the Freedom House *Survey* and parallel efforts to monitor and assess global economic change, there is growing empirical evidence of the links between economic freedom and political freedom.[1]

Not only does economic freedom help establish the conditions for political freedom by promoting the growth of prosperous middle and working classes, but successful market economies appear to require political freedom as a barrier against economic cronyism, rent seeking, and other anticompetitive and inefficient practices. Open and democratically accountable societies and economies have also shown themselves capable of weathering economic setbacks—a likely consequence of their political legitimacy (rooted in democratic accountability) and economic legitimacy (rooted in property rights). Moreover, while open societies are not immune to corruption scandals, they have strong instruments for combating graft and bribery, including a free press, the separation of powers, alternations in power between various political elites, and independent judicial systems.

While the *Survey* can be used to examine broad trends, it is important that such trends not be equated with iron laws of history or be interpreted one-dimensionally. For example, while the *Survey*'s findings show that liberal economic change at times leads to liberal political reform, there are also numerous other cases where political openings lead the way to economic liberalization. The more careful conclusion from an examination of the 26-year record of the *Survey* is that both trends manifest themselves in close proximity to one another. Opposition to the dominance of the state in economic life is usually accompanied by opposition to the dominance of the state in personal life and in the life of civil society. Certainly, there appears to be growing awareness of this relationship, as indicated by the growing emphasis on democracy promotion in the foreign assistance policies of the advanced industrial democracies, and by the stress on issues of good governance and effective anticorruption regimes by multilateral donors like the World Bank.

Policy Implications

What challenges issue from the *Survey*'s findings? What are the policy implications?

The Freedom House findings make it clear that the world is becoming more free. This trend is mainly the consequence of the strengthening of the rule of law, of improvements in civilian control over militaries and police, the successful management of divisive group conflicts, and the growing effectiveness of civil society.

Most of this progress toward respect for political rights and civil liberties is unfolding in countries which have already undergone more limited democratic openings. The *Survey* finds that such societies over time grow receptive to a further deepening of freedom. This suggests that U.S. and international efforts to promote democratic transitions and to give some priority to material and technical assistance to democratic regimes are having a positive effect. But it also means that most progress is occurring in already Partly Free countries. This year, only a small number of Not Free countries registered meaningful progress. Moreover, after a decade of the rapid expansion of electoral democracies, the number of democracies in 1998, 117, is the same as the figure for 1994.

Yet while there is an extremely active and intelligently conceived U.S. policy to promote democratic transitions once limited political openings have occurred, far fewer resources are being directed at promoting democratic openings in the most repressive societies. For example, USAID efforts in closed societies focus mainly on limited technical assistance in support of modest economic reforms, rather than on support for democratic forces in these closed societies. Moreover, USAID does not devote significant resources to promoting political openings in closed societies. Such efforts are are primarily undertaken by the independent, Congressionally funded National Endowment for Democracy.

While the U.S. has something approaching a consistent policy with regard to several rogue and pariah states that also violate basic human rights on a massive scale—Burma, Cuba, Iran, Iraq, Libya, and North Korea specifically—that policy mainly seeks to isolate these countries, and few resources are devoted to efforts that might actively promote change within them.

In the cases of some of the world's most important countries in which basic freedoms are broadly suppressed, U.S. policy consists of occasional—and at times muted—criticism of human rights violations and general expectations that the forces of economic change and trade will somehow inevitably lead to improvements in political and civil liberties. Among the countries in which there is little effort to promote democratic change are China, Vietnam, and—with the exception of the Palestinian National Authority—the Arab world.

Admittedly, some of the world's most closed societies (for example, North Korea) may be impervious to US and other efforts to promote democratic ideas and foster the emergence of democratic movements. But the example of the collapse of communism in Central and Eastern Europe shows that totalitarian societies cannot forever withstand the pressures of an increasingly open and interdependent world.

Moreover, new technologies and the force of modest market-oriented change in some of the most repressive countries suggest that the capacity of the state to exert day-to-day control over information and private life is lessening, even if repression of political dissent is not.

Opening Up Closed Societies

A comprehensive strategy to open up closed societies should be developed in cooperation with the nongovernmental sector. The mission of USAID should be expanded to allow it to be more active in fostering the development of the nongovernmental sector in closed countries. Aid and assistance for radio broadcasting, book publishing, contact with independent civic forces, and the transfer of information through the Internet should be expanded.

Protecting Against Reversals

While 1998 saw the expansion of freedom in many parts of the world, forward momentum appears to have stalled in the 12 non-Baltic former republics of the Soviet Union, including Russia and Ukraine. Setbacks for reform and the weakening of reformist voices is likely a temporary phenomenon. It should not be seen as a signal to scale back drastically U.S. engagement. Rather, it requires a more efficient and precise deployment of resources oriented around assisting reformers in their efforts to win the political battle of ideas.

Reversals of democratic progress should meet with active diplomatic and nongovernmental initiatives. In a period of some economic turmoil and social difficulties in transitional societies, the preservation of gains for civil liberties and political rights must be an urgent priority for U.S. policymakers and the international democratic community.

Economic Freedom and Political Liberty

The economic crisis that rocked emerging markets in 1998 has not resulted in a reversal of progress toward greater political and economic freedom. Indeed, economic difficulties have not led to a worldwide resurgence of statism. On the contrary, economic failures have rightly been identified with a lack of transparency, cronyism, and corruption. In short, the case for a link between more open and democratically accountable government and economic success is gaining greater credence. The acknowledgment of such a relationship appears to have played a key role in the political openings in Indonesia and Nigeria. The ability of democratic states like the Philippines, Thailand, South Korea, and Brazil to implement policies to address the looming economic crisis have also done much to convince the international financial community that democratic accountability and legitimacy of rule is an important instrument for political reform.

But international donors and financial institutions need to take more resolute policy steps to act on these trends. The changing attitude of some international financial and aid organizations is a positive sign. The World Bank, in particular, has been innovative in its efforts to introduce issues of governance, corruption, and transparency into its programming and to begin to reach out to civil society and nongovernmental groups.

There is growing understanding among some policymakers of the link between the functioning of an effective rule of law system—a system that requires the checks and balances of a free society, a free press, and democratic accountability—and effective economic performance.

International Structures

In 1998, the fiftieth anniversary of the Universal Declaration of Human Rights was celebrated and efforts were made to intensify international action against basic rights violations. There were welcome efforts to arrest and prosecute those guilty of genocide and war crimes, including those guilty of atrocities in Rwanda and in Bosnia.

Many countries—though not the U.S., which, for convincing reasons, was opposed—voted to adopt a charter for a far-reaching International Criminal Court. Yet while international action to eradicate rights abuses can be helpful, it must be limited in scope. Above all, international structures should not jeopardize or weaken the ability of democratic states to act to preserve or to protect freedom. Regrettably, many of the provisions in the proposed Criminal Court would have just such an effect.

As the Freedom House findings suggest, freedom is making important gains around the world. Nevertheless, the majority of mankind still lives in societies in which many or all basic freedoms are violated, and in a majority of countries the rule of law is absent or weak. Any body that emerges from an international consensus that includes undemocratic and unfree states is likely to be problematic in its composition. Adequate safeguards must exist to prevent such a court from acting capriciously. The U.S. is right to object to the current form of the proposed International Criminal Court. A far better policy would be the promotion of new structures made up of the growing community of free and democratic countries that could coordinate cooperation on behalf of human rights and against genocide and war crimes.

Conclusions

The remarkable expansion of human freedom recorded in the 26 years of the *Survey* of Freedom has not proceeded in a straight line. It has featured reversals as well as gains. Therefore, nothing in the findings should suggest that the expansion of democracy and freedom is inevitable. Indeed, much of the progress the *Survey* has recorded is the byproduct of a growing and systematic collaboration between established and new democracies, between democracies and countries in transition, and between established civic groups operating in the context of freedom and their pro-democratic counterparts seeking to promote change in closed societies. The findings of the *Survey* in future years will depend in no small measure on the success of such collaboration and on the elaboration of effective U.S. government policies to extend freedom to parts of the world where it is largely absent.

NOTES

1. Recent comparisons of the relationship between political freedom and economic liberty conducted by Freedom House (Adrian Karatnycky, Alexander Motyl, and Charles Graybow, eds., *Nations in Transit 1998*, New Brunswick, N.J.: Transaction Books, 1998) and the Heritage Foundation (Bryan T. Johnson, "Comparing Economic Freedom and Political Freedom," in Bryan T. Johnson, Kim R. Homes, and Melanie Kirkpatrick, eds., *1999 Index of Economic Freedom*, Washington, D.C.: The Heritage Foundation and Dow Jones Company, Inc., 1999: 29-34), respectively, have found a high correlation between the two variables. According to the authors of *Nations in Transit 1998*, post-Communist countries that are consolidated democracies also tend to have consolidated their market economies. When these countries' performance with respect to political and economic freedom is related to economic growth, the study found that consolidated democracies

and market economies averaged a growth rate of 4.7 percent in 1997, transitional polities and economies registered an average growth rate of 1.4 percent, and consolidated autocracies and statist economies in the region averaged close to a 3 percent drop in GDP. The study similarly found high correlations between more open political systems and lower levels of corruption. Moreover, societies with lower levels of corruption were significantly more successful in generating economic growth. The region's least corrupt countries, for example, grew at an average rate of 4.7 percent in 1997, while states registering high levels of corruption averaged a decline of nearly 1 percent. Researchers at the Heritage Foundation found a high degree of correlation between political rights and civil liberties (as measured by Freedom House) and economic freedom (as measured by the Heritage Foundation's surveys).

Adrian Karatnycky is President of Freedom House.

Does America Have A Human Rights Problem?

Arch Puddington

Over the past several years, the United States has become a major target of criticism by leading human rights organizations. Both Amnesty International and Human Rights Watch have issued a series of reports which castigate America for its treatment of minority groups, women, prisoners, immigrants, asylum seekers, and criminal defendants. Amnesty International has gone so far as to enlist its millions of members in a worldwide campaign against human rights abuses in the United States; at the 1999 session of the United Nations Commission on Human Rights, Amnesty International listed the U.S. as a major human rights priority, along with Algeria, Cambodia, Turkey, and the Great Lakes region of Africa, which embraces Rwanda, Burundi, and the Democratic Republic of Congo.

What accounts for this upsurge of concern over the American record? Ordinarily, human rights organizations issue reports in response to clear and verifiable patterns of human rights abuses, such as the imprisonment of democracy advocates in China or the massacre of Christians in India. Or they may shine the spotlight on a particular country because of a generalized deterioration in a broad range of human rights, as has been the case in Belarus. Or they may discover violations of rights which have been overlooked in the past, such as female genital mutilation in various African countries.

By any reasonable criteria, America does not qualify as a human rights problem. Like all societies, the United States suffers its share of social ills. Nevertheless, its record of protecting the rights of society's most vulnerable groups ranks with the best in the world. Layer upon layer of laws, administrative regulations, and court decrees exist to promote the fair treatment of racial minorities, immigrants, the handicapped, women, children, the elderly, the mentally ill, and religious believers (and non-believers as well). Although homosexuals are not extended the protection of most federal civil rights laws, the states have increasingly included gays and lesbians in the roster of classes protected by anti-discrimination legislation.

Yet to its critics, the U.S. is not a country where special rights have been adopted for those who might conceivably suffer discrimination, but a cheerless place where the individual is at the mercy of a pitiless market economy and a brutal police regime. True enough, while in America all manner of rights are protected, this is also a society where heavy demands are placed on the individual. Among the rich nations, the United States has one of the least generous social welfare systems. Unemployment benefits are limited, and there is no national health insurance system for ordinary workers, as in many European countries. Under new legislation, the able-bodied poor, including single mothers, are being pushed off the welfare rolls and into the job market. Furthermore, America has become highly integrated into the global economy, something which has accelerated the decline of the older industrial base, disrupted the lives of millions of displaced workers, and led to the decline of once-vibrant cities.

It is this second, highly distorted, image of America—an America where, critics contend, the rich get richer and more powerful at the expense of everyone else—which seems to predominate among the major human rights organizations. The Amnesty International report speaks of the U.S. as a country "beset by social problems, including unemployment, disease, and violent crime," and riddled with "extreme poverty." That Amnesty International is wrong on every point in its assessment of America's socio-economic condition is beside the point. If human rights organizations believe that America's political leaders treat the economic plight of the poor and vulnerable with extreme indifference, then it is only logical that they would expect America to violate the constitutional and human rights of its citizens as well.

Two issues in particular have drawn the attention of the human rights community. The first involves the methods America has chosen to wage its war on crime. The second is discrimination against nonwhites or, to place the matter in a broader and more appropriate context, the country's efforts to build a successful multinational society.

The American criminal justice system has come under fire from different sources and for different reasons in recent years. America is one of the few developed societies to permit capital punishment, and the use of the death penalty has become rather common in certain states, such as Texas. America has one of the highest rates of incarceration in the world, and in many states, those convicted of violent crimes or drug-related offenses are being handed lengthy sentences with stipulations that most or all of the sentence must be served. Much of the increase in the prison population is due to the war on drugs, a controversial subject even within the law enforcement profession. Critics claim that sentencing petty drug dealers to years in the penitentiary is unjust and even discriminatory, since a high proportion of drug crime defendants are black. There is also the question of police abuse. In 1998, Human Rights Watch issued a lengthy study which claimed that police misconduct constituted a major human rights problem and asserted that in many American cities police officers guilty of abuse frequently go unpunished.

Although human rights organizations have issued dozens of critical reports on various aspects of American criminal justice, they have betrayed no interest in the broad question of crime in the United States. This may be because of their position that the context of a human rights violation is immaterial, and the question of how best to wage the war against crime is the responsibility of law enforcement professionals. This is a purist, and ultimately insufficient, argument. If we have learned anything over the past thirty years, it is that high levels of crime, or the public perception that crime is out of control, can present an even greater threat to democracy, the rule of law, and human rights than the abuse of power by the authorities or draconian sentencing policies.

The impact of violent crime on American democracy was an important theme of Haynes Johnson's 1994 book, *Divided We Fall.* After having spent months touring the country and testing the mood of the people, Johnson concluded:

> No subject generates more concern than violent crime, none touches
> people more deeply and personally, none triggers more emotion.
> More than any issue, including jobs and education, the growing
> specter of violence leads people to think that something
> fundamental has been broken in America....

> When people are asked what they think can be done about "it,"
> the answer that invariably comes back is either "I don't know"

or "Nothing!" Crime is believed to be beyond the society's
capacity to eliminate.

Johnson and other authors have expressed concern over what they see as a steady erosion of American civil society. They point to a weakening of the broad institutions, such as the public schools, which gave Americans the sense of belonging to a single nation. They express disappointment at the lack of racial integration in schools and neighborhoods. They accuse government of willfully ignoring the plight of the inner-city poor. They lament the abandonment of urban America by the middle class.

The role of violent crime in each of these problems, and many more, is central. Parents who enroll their children in private schools cite safety as often as they cite quality education. They do not find the presence of metal detectors or security guards reassuring; if the public schools find it necessary to take such extreme steps, they would prefer to move to the suburbs and a safer environment or send their children to non-public schools, despite the expense.

Security has also played a major role in the rise of "gated communities." Critics who regard America as a society in decline often point to the expansion of apartment complexes or residential developments which feature high-tech security devices and private security guards as clear evidence that the rich are walling themselves off from the rest of society. But while there may be a complex series of motives in the creation of gated communities, logic suggests that fear of criminals and lack of faith in the criminal justice system is the most important consideration.

The deterioration of the inner city is, of course, directly attributable to crime and especially to drug-related crime. The failure of schools, businesses, the abandonment of housing, the flight of entrepreneurs and potential community leaders—all reflect the impact of high crime rates in minority neighborhoods over the past three decades.

And, of course, crime has had a major impact on American politics. Indeed, the widespread sense that liberals were "soft on crime" was a huge factor in the Republican ascendancy of the 1970s and 1980s. With some justification, liberals became identified with such notions as that the "root causes" of crime were more important than controlling crime, that ensuring the rights of criminal defendants was a higher priority than getting criminals off the streets, and that to call for a war on crime was to appeal to the racial prejudices of the white electorate. With liberals unwilling to confront the public's distress over rising crime rates, the way was paved for the rise of demagogues like George Wallace, whose presidential campaign siphoned off many blue-collar Democratic votes, and Frank Rizzo, the tough-talking mayor of Philadelphia.

The perception that the state was incapable of dealing with the upsurge of violent crime also eroded the public's confidence in the core institutions of democracy. Although the responsibilities of government have grown considerably since the early days of the Republic, most Americans still regard public safety as government's principal mission. Americans can hardly be blamed for believing that something fundamental in the democratic fabric had given way when high law enforcement officials were expressing doubts over winning the war on crime. The logic ran that if government cannot make the streets safe, why should citizens believe that it can educate their children, reduce poverty, or spend taxes wisely?

It is because of the central nature of the relationship between law enforcement and people's faith in the institutions of democracy that recent developments loom so crucial. For, in fact, there is mounting evidence that through a combination of public policies and new policing techniques, crime has undergone a substantial decrease in practically every major city of the United States. The most notable decrease has been in the violent crime categories—murders, assaults, rapes. Americans are still concerned about violent crime, and may continue to express skepticism about government's ability to bring peace to the streets. Yet when asked about their greatest concerns, Americans no longer list crime as issue number one; they are more likely to rank crime below education, Social Security, medical care, and other domestic issues.

There are a number of reasons for the decrease in violent crime that has been recorded in each of the past seven years. Perhaps the most important is the trend toward lengthy prison sentences, which has ensured that, at any given moment, many potentially violent offenders are off the streets and behind bars. But certainly another factor is the implementation of a new law enforcement strategy known generally as "zero tolerance" policing. Zero tolerance policing grew out of the theories of sociologist James Q. Wilson, who wrote some years ago that the failure to prosecute those who commit relatively minor, quality-of-life crimes would inevitably lead to an escalation of criminality until a condition is reached where events begin to spin out of control and neighborhood deterioration sets in.

The principal laboratory for the implementation of zero tolerance policing has been New York City during the administration of Mayor Rudolph Giuliani. A former federal prosecutor, Giuliani ran on a tough-on-crime platform, and has instituted a number of initiatives designed to make New York safer and "more livable." None has generated more controversy than mass arrests for quality-of life misdemeanors: drinking or smoking marijuana in public, urinating in the street, subway fare beating, trespassing, reckless bicycle riding, and the like.

Zero tolerance is credited with the revival of several New York neighborhoods that had been plagued by an environment notable for drug use, drug sales, public intoxication, and groups of menacing young men—all out in the open with no intervention by the police. Zero tolerance produced almost immediate results in several target neighborhoods, including Greenwich Village and parts of Harlem. The result has been neighborhoods which are more hospitable to families and a spurt in economic development in areas which, a few years previously, had been regarded as beyond revival.

There is, of course, a cost to zero tolerance and other new urban police techniques, which stems from the rather substantial increase in encounters between the police and the public. In New York, hundreds of arrests are made each night for misdemeanors such as public drinking and fare beating. The accused are taken to the local precinct, booked, and often taken to the central holding area where they may remain overnight, after which they are arraigned before a judge who will ordinarily hand down a small fine, community service, or simply dismiss the case. Another aspect of zero tolerance is the arrest of petty drug dealers. Unlike the quality-of-life misdemeanors, drug sales of even a small amount can be a serious matter; small-time drug dealers make up a sizeable proportion of the American prison population.

Civil libertarians take a dim view of zero tolerance and are actively opposed to the war on drugs, objecting to the jailing of petty dealers and fretting over the preponderance of blacks arrested on drug counts. Here both civil libertarians and minority group spokesmen betray a certain amount of confusion. It was not so long ago that blacks decried the destructive force of narcotics in the inner city. Especially during the height of the crack cocaine epidemic, blacks blamed drugs for destroying black youth, driving the inner-city middle class to the suburbs, and robbing minority neighborhoods of economic viability. True, black leaders were divided on the proper anti-drug strategy. Some called for a massive police drive against drug use, while others, uncomfortable with an arrest-and-punish approach, talked about ways of dealing with the "root causes" of crime. The problem with this latter approach is that the root causes—poverty, lack of jobs and economic development—will resist all efforts at betterment unless crime itself is brought under control.

Furthermore, the root causes argument has been weakened somewhat by recent experiences in Europe. Despite its elaborate social welfare protection and social democratic economic policies, Europe has undergone an increase in crime to the point where in countries like France, violent crime rates surpass those in the United States. Much of the increase in criminality is attributed to unemployed, alienated nonwhite immigrant youths. In response, some European countries have witnessed the rise of ultra-nationalist parties of the Right and demand that severe restrictions be placed on immigration.

The United States has been spared this phenomenon. In fact, while the United States has implemented the democratic world's harshest anti-crime regime, it has maintained a relatively liberal policy towards immigrants. Despite calls by a special commission on immigration chaired by the late Barbara Jordan for a modest reduction in the number of legal immigrants, America has maintained the same, relatively high immigration level through periods of both boom and recession. Proposals to change the immigration balance, which now overwhelmingly favors Hispanics and Asians, to encourage a higher proportion of European immigrants, have been rejected, as have proposals to adjust immigration criteria to favor the educated and highly skilled.

Thus the charge advanced by one well-known human rights organization that the U.S. is undergoing a wave of anti-immigrant sentiment is patently false. In 1994, California voters adopted a measure which denied certain rights to illegal immigrants. Again, the proposition affected only illegal aliens, and the effect of the measure has been minimized by various court decisions. Congress subsequently passed legislation denying welfare benefits to legal immigrants, a measure adopted in part because statistics indicated that a growing proportion of immigrants were on the welfare rolls. There is a good chance that this restriction will be lifted, since both President Clinton and a number of Republicans have spoken in favor of removing a measure which singled out immigrants for special treatment.

If America has not become hostile to legal immigrants, it is also true that many people are concerned over evidence that some of the newer immigrant groups were resisting assimilation into the broader American culture. Many immigrants seemed to regard American citizenship with indifference, and developed an interest in the naturalization process only after the adoption of restrictions on immigrants' access to welfare. The notion that some immigrant groups were resistant to becoming "American" was fortified by immigrant constituency organizations, which sometimes spoke disparagingly of assimilation and pressed for government policies which would encourage immigrants to retain their cultural identities. Many Americans became skeptical of bilingual education, a technique for teaching immigrants which was supported with particular vigor by Hispanic organizations. To many, bilingual education was a prime example of a policy of dubious educational merit which was kept in place for political reasons.

Immigrants bring many benefits to a society such as the United States. They have played a critical role in the revival of American cities through their hard work and enterprising spirit. Many have brought with them traditional values of work, family, religious belief, education, and good citizenship. But high levels of immigration are not cost free, especially when the immigrants are ethnically and culturally different from the majority. Furthermore, our current level of mass immigration takes place at a time of unprecedented expansion in the rights of minorities, with immigrants themselves quick to identify new and special "rights." Thus, some have decried the policy of eliminating remedial courses at the City University of New York system as a violation of the rights of immigrants. Similarly, some see measures to roll back bilingual education as a violation of the right to an equal education, while others decry the roll-back of affirmative action as the denial of the rights of blacks, Hispanics, and even relatively prosperous Asian groups.

Thus, at the core of the debate over the American condition is a conflict between those who believe that society's strength lies in an elaborate and constantly expanding series of rights and those who understand that a safe and successful multinational democracy requires hard decisions and trade-offs between individual rights, the protection of minorities, and the requirements of the broader society. Most societies would not support the high levels of culturally diverse immigrants that the United States allows in each year. But even in America, the welcome mat would be withdrawn if high percentages of immigrants were on welfare or if immigrants were a major contributor to uncontrolled violent crime. Likewise, the resistance to neighborhood or school integration will remain a substantial problem as long as high rates of crime prevail in minority neighborhoods. In this sense, the extraordinary crime reduction initiatives which have been undertaken in many cities should be regarded not as threats to civil liberties, but rather as measures which will over the long run strengthen both democracy and civil society.

While the U.S. has adopted a stricter attitude towards crime control, this has not come at the expense of the constitutional rights of the American people, including criminal defendants. Most of the procedural safeguards set down by the Supreme Court during the 1960s remain in place. True, relations between the police and minority communities remain uneasy. But urban police departments are racially integrated, and a number of cities have appointed black officers as police chiefs. Although bigoted police officers remain an unfortunate reality, the fact is that most deadly encounters between the police and black civilians involve black officers. Most police departments require better educated police officers than in the past, and new recruits are usually given extensive training in crowd control, community relations, and similarly sensitive subjects. Veterans of the criminal justice field overwhelmingly say that police abuse is much less prevalent today than at any time in the past, and police racism is much less a problem than in the pre-civil rights period.

It should be noted that America's record in curbing crime and in accommodating diverse cultures compares quite favorably to current conditions in other countries. In societies such as Russia and Mexico, uncontrolled crime ranks as the greatest threat to democracy, political stability, and prosperity. Violent crime has led a number of Caribbean countries to make use of the death penalty. In Europe, robberies, assaults, and murders are on the rise in a number of countries, fueling demands to limit or cut off the flow of immigrants from Africa and the Middle East. European elites often express shock at the rough justice meted out by American courts, are appalled by America's use of the death penalty, and continue to regard America as incurably racist 35 years after the abolition of legal segregation. Now, however, it is Europe which is confronting the challenge of cultural diversity, and while the proportion of non-European immigrants in France, Germany, and elsewhere does not compare with American figures, Europe is finding the experience a painful one. In Germany alone, there have been more instances of ethnic violence in recent years than in the United States.

Finally, no assessment of human rights in the U.S. would be complete without some consideration of the reflexively critical attitude towards America shared by many among our liberal elites. A half-century ago, the U.S. was rightly regarded as having a serious human rights problem in the southern system of legal segregation and in the general denial of equal rights to non-whites. Ironically, America's racial record was chastised much more severely *after* it had taken steps to dismantle segregation and other legal obstacles to equality. Indeed, the more America changed, the more tenaciously many critics, both here and abroad, held to the view of a society dominated by bigotry and "institutional racism."

During the latter stages of the Cold War, America was also accused of blocking popular revolution in Asia, Africa, and Latin America. Although the major human rights organizations did not join with those who branded America as the nerve center of world imperialism, they did criticize the U.S. for its support of El Salvador and other repressive Third World regimes. At the same time, some advocates of human rights resisted the idea that democracy was a precondition for the full flowering of personal liberty. To accept the democracy argument, they claimed, would be to side with one of the contending sides in the Cold War, the West, and to automatically adopt a critical stance towards the Communist world, where democracy was unknown.

The end of the Cold War, with its sudden and totally unexpected collapse of Soviet Communism, caught the critics of America off-guard. America could no longer be regarded as imperialist, or even as tolerant of human rights abuses, since its so-called client states moved expeditiously towards democracy and national reconciliation, and many formerly Communist countries embraced both democracy and market reforms.

It was predictable that the U.S. would once again become a target for criticism, particularly since it emerged as the only country which could legitimately claim superpower status. Although America no longer can be accused of supporting "reactionary" regimes in Central America, it can, and is, derided for its failure to sign certain international covenants, such as the International Criminal Court. And since America cannot be criticized seriously for supporting repression abroad, it is increasingly attacked for tolerating official persecution of its own citizens at home.

No society, and certainly not the U.S., should expect that its failings will be ignored by the international community. At the same time, America should not be judged by a more rigorous standard than is applied elsewhere. During the postwar period America has forged an impressive record in promoting the spread of democracy and the respect for individual rights throughout the world, and in expanding human rights and civil liberties among its own people. America's record is all the more impressive because of its success in building a peaceful and relatively integrated multinational society in an era in which ethnic diversity is more often a source of division than of strength. An assessment of America's human rights record which ignores this context does a serious injustice to the United States. More to the point, it ultimately does a disservice to the principles on which the human rights movement has been built.

Arch Puddington is vice president for research at Freedom House.

Deeply Divided and Failed States: Democratization in Unfavorable Circumstances

Timothy D. Sisk

In the post-Cold War period, armed conflict within states, rather than wars between sovereign states, has posed the principal threat to life, freedom, and personal security.

These conflicts and civil wars have occurred overwhelmingly in ethnically divided societies. Of the 33 armed conflicts in 1998, all but one—India and Pakistan's annual summer border clash high in the Himalayas—took place essentially within the boundaries of a sovereign state. And all featured disputes over ethnicity, religion, or language and the relationships between these identities and the legitimacy, territory, and policies of the state.

In the most extreme instances, internal violence has led to the near-complete collapse of a state. On other occasions, a severe weakening of central authority has occurred. Often, governments have contributed to their own incapacitation through acts of repression. For example, longstanding discrimination against Tigreans, Oromos, and others in Ethiopia during the brutal regime of Mengistu Haile Meriam led to powerful guerrilla movements that toppled the dictatorship in May 1991.

The suppression of ethnic grievances has also damaged the legitimacy and reputation of otherwise strong states. Turkey's stature as a European power and as an Islamic democracy has been weakened by its conflict with its Kurdish minority; similarly China's international credibility has suffered because of its repression of Tibet.

Elsewhere, we have seen cases in which the erosion of state authority has led to anarchy and violence, the breakdown of effective government, and the rise of warlords and petty fiefdoms. Somalia's central government collapsed in 1990 after years of sclerotic dictatorship by Siad Barre. Somalia, the ultimate "failed state" of the 1990s, lacks a functioning central authority to this day despite myriad international efforts to mediate a settlement among the warring clan-based militias. The consequences of imploding states like Somalia are hundreds of thousands of lives lost, millions of refugees and internally displaced persons, and widespread suffering, starvation, and homelessness.

The international community has long agonized over how to create sustainable peace in these deeply divided multiethnic societies. In the long run, democracy would seem the only lasting solution. Ironically, most divided and failed states do not, by definition, enjoy the presumed prerequisites of democracy: social cohesion, economic development, as well as a broad-based middle class, a vibrant, independent civil society, and tolerance. Nevertheless, there is a general consensus among the international community—as reflected in international organizations, norms, and policies—that the basis of long term domestic peace in divided societies is democratic governance and market-based economic development. Democracy and development ideally advance together hand in glove; good governance appears to be a prerequisite for development, and economic development facilitates the creation of middle class interests that transcend ethnic and other ascriptive divisions. The alternatives to democratization as a long-term solution to managing conflict in multiethnic states—authoritarianism or partition—are not solutions at all, but rather prescriptions for more hatred, division, and killing.

Although its response to civil strife has been fitful and tardy, the international community does seem to regard democratization as an important strategy in resolving conflict and preventing violence. Democratic elections are considered a necessary step in reestablishing the legitimacy of the state even when conditions on the ground are unambiguously unfavorable to elections and other features of democracy. Coupled with the advocacy of democratization is the promotion of inclusive government, or power sharing, in which all major interests are included in the governing coalition. The international community has thus been promoting a policy of democratization as conflict management, even in cases like Bosnia, where power sharing does not reflect a desire for reconciliation. The nationalist leadership of Bosnia's political parties share power because the international pressures to maintain the country's territorial integrity are so intense.

There are inherent contradictions at work here. In some countries, democracy is being promoted even though many doubt its viability, and the warring parties themselves have no desire to live together peacefully. Nevertheless, international policy makers have concluded that there is no feasible alternative to inclusive democratic governance as a means of attaining sustainable peace, even though the failures may well outnumber the successes.

Patterns of Internal Violence

There is no single pattern to the conflicts which raged during the 1990s. Some continue to flare with a high degree of violence, some have been resolved, and some have settled into a tenuous "peace process" that explicitly marries democratization and conflict management.

- Several remaining "hot" civil wars—Algeria, Afghanistan, Democratic Republic of the Congo, Sri Lanka, Turkey, and Sudan—have seen more than 1,000 battle-related deaths during the past the year.

- In other instances, militarily victorious regimes are seeking to build postwar legitimacy, such as in Ethiopia, Rwanda, and Chechnya (which legally remains within Russia). Some victorious rulers have sought to legitimize their rule through elections, as in Ethiopia, whereas others, such as Rwanda's government, have rejected the ballot box.

- Some countries, such as Angola, Cambodia, Sierra Leone, and Liberia, while struggling to revive after years of violent conflict, remain perched on the edge of the abyss, with the ever-present possibility of a return to violence, anarchy, and strife. Still others, such as Bosnia, Israel-Palestine, Northern Ireland, and South Africa, are slowly but steadily implementing negotiated peace agreements in conditions of protracted conflict, where compliance with agreements continues but progress toward reconciliation is difficult to measure. In each case, elections have been held to ratify or implement a peace agreement.

Interestingly, Swedish researchers Peter Wallensteen and Margarita Sollenberg report in the *Journal of Peace Research* (July 1998) that the number of armed conflicts reached a peak in 1992, when there were 55 active conflicts, after which there has been a gradual decrease in their frequency. This trend holds true in all regions. The number of serious conflicts, civil wars in which more than 1,000 die in political violence in a given year, dropped precipitously in 1994, from 20 in 1992, to 14 in 1993, to 7 in 1994, to 6 in 1998.

Despite the broader trend indicating that internal armed conflict is on the wane, violent internal conflicts can be expected to recur over time. A country which experiences one instance of civil strife is usually fated to experience further outbreaks of violence in the future. This means that the problem of internal conflict remains acute and will likely dominate the international security agenda into the twenty-first century.

Violence, Intractability, and Collapse

Most of the new internal wars of the 1990s (as opposed to those which had Cold War roots) erupted as an inept authoritarian regime decayed, state authority collapsed, and a struggle for power ensued. This was the case in Siad Barre's Somalia in 1990 and in Mobutu Sese Seko's Zaire (now Democratic Republic of Congo, DRC) in 1997. Bosnia collapsed as a state from 1992-1995 after old-style Yugoslav political leaders on all sides fanned the flames of ethnic hatred.

As in faltering Yugoslavia in the early 1990s, a clear and seemingly ever-present underlying cause of social divisions and state collapse is the ambition of political leaders who instigate ethnic violence. A 1995 Human Rights Watch report, *Playing the Communal Card*, places blame directly at the feet of state officials, arguing that "communal tensions per se are not the immediate cause of many of today's violence and persistent communal conflicts. While deep-seated communal tensions are obviously a necessary ingredient of an explosive mix, they are not sufficient to unleash widespread violence. Most multiethnic societies live in peace. Rather, time after time, the proximate cause of violence is governmental exploitation of communal differences."

Other underlying causes of internal violence are complex and usually not amenable to generalization. In many instances, however, a central cause is found in the legacy of decolonization. In Africa, Asia, and the Middle East, colonial boundaries left many disputed territories with arbitrary borders that bear little resemblance to demography or geography. States in this "global south" invariably encompass a diverse ethnic mix of peoples that initially lack the shared values and common identities that yield a cohesive nationalism loyal to the central state.

Demands for self-determination by aggrieved ethnic groups within such states often lead to group mobilization, to counter-mobilization by other groups and by the state, and eventually lead to violence. Group claims for self-determination often clash with state claims for territorial integrity. An example of the intractability of internal conflicts when the parties refuse to compromise is the still-unresolved conflict in Cyprus, in which earlier efforts at power sharing broke down in violence in 1974.

Many post-colonial situations and many cases of disintegrated empires, such as the successor states to the Soviet Union, lack internal legitimacy. Particularly for minority groups once dominant in a broader state in which they enjoyed majority status, such as the Russian-speaking peoples in the Baltics, Caucasus, and Central Asia, new grievances have emerged over language and citizenship rights. These grievances weaken the ability of the new states to forge a cohesive national identity and legitimate government. Thus, the eminent scholar of ethnic conflict, Donald Horowitz, argues in *Ethnic Groups in Conflict* (University of California Press, 1985), that it is not necessarily absolute deprivation that prompts interethnic strife, but the relative status of one group *vis a vis* others. This relative sense of deprivation or "group worth" may include not only economic disparities and advantages, but perceptions of group standing as well. Conflict is often triggered when previously dominant groups' hold on power begins to slip, or when disadvantaged groups gain influence and authority.

Some leaders suggest that democracy itself is to blame for the inculcation of deep social divisions and the weakening of state authority. Political leaders in Kenya, Uganda, and Indonesia prior to the of fall Suharto in 1998, for example, argue that multiparty electoral competition stimulates ethnic rivalry and polarization; the antidote is a single party or no-party democracy, or "soft authoritarianism." Yet, as the problems of these states show, such policies tend to suppress ethnic differences and postpone or contain problems, but not to resolve them. Larry Diamond notes that in Kenya, "ethnic hatred, land grabs, and violence have been deliberately fostered by the regime of President Daniel Arap Moi in a desperate bid to divide the people and thereby cling to power" (*Promoting Democracy in the 1990s,* Carnegie Commission on Preventing Deadly Conflict, 1995).

Understanding the causes of conflict is but half of the challenge. The other is finding a way to de-escalate the violence once it begins. Ethnic violence is particularly difficult to manage for two important reasons. First, the issues at stake are not easily divisible in a split-the-difference compromise. When the inalienable rights of group self-determination (often defined as group entitlement to state sovereignty) and the sanctity of state territorial integrity collide, the parties perceive their options in zero-sum, win or lose, terms.

Moreover, the dynamics of internal conflicts don't lend themselves to cool-headed compromise. Mobilization by one group yields counter-mobilization by another, violence begets violence, and the parties become trapped in a set of mutually destructive relationships. This was the pattern in the renewal of Burundi's civil war following a shaky peace agreement in 1993, which collapsed in 1995 leading to a civil war that defies myriad international efforts at a settlement. A similar dynamic stands in the way of meaningful peace talks in Algeria and Sri Lanka.

Whether war precedes state collapse or collapse leads to war, the consequences for freedom are deadly. State collapse implies that the central authorities can no longer manage social differences, and power withers and is seized by independent militias and warlords, or by the police or military acting autonomously. At the extreme end of the spectrum, many wars in the 1990s which occurred in collapsed and deeply divided states featured crimes against humanity: genocide, ethnic cleansing, forced migration, mass starvation, and group persecution.

The struggle between Albanian separatist forces (led by the Kosovo Liberation Army) and the Serb-dominated Yugoslav federation's army and police forces in 1998 reflects the sad truth that the "international community" remains hamstrung in efforts to prevent massive human rights violations in internal conflicts. Ethnic cleansing and genocidal repression occurred as the world watched and international diplomacy achieved inconclusive results. Only after horrendous human rights violations had occurred did western powers acting through the North Atlantic Treaty Organization, and without a clear UN Security council mandate, broker a cease-fire using the threat of air strikes against the Yugoslav government forces as leverage. The Kosovo cease-fire of October 1998 managed to stop the fighting for a while and allowed for initial humanitarian relief to the displaced, but it did not definitively resolve the underlying question of the disputed province's status within the larger Yugoslav federation. Sadly, efforts to achieve a broader political settlement failed despite intense diplomatic efforts in early 1999. The collapse of diplomacy prompted a NATO bombing campaign, after which the Milosevic regime unleashed a campaign of ethnic cleansing which effectively cleared the disputed territory of much of its Albanian population.

New Authoritarianism

How are deeply divided states and failed states resuscitated after violent internal conflict? It must first be understood that there is little room for maneuvering when war ends. Roy Licklider sums up the problem when he notes that, unlike war between sovereign states, in internal conflicts the combatants "must live side by side and work together in a common government to make the country work. . . . How do groups of people who have been killing one another with considerable enthusiasm and success come together to form a common government?"[1]

One possibility is the rise of a new authoritarianism. In Rwanda, after the minority Tutsi Rwandan Patriotic Front militarily defeated the Hutu-majority militias, it formed a new, narrow-based minority government that established its authority through force. Given the suffering of Rwanda's Tutsis, the government also gained international sympathy and won recognition. Although Rwanda remained a highly weakened and vulnerable state, basic order was reestablished under the new authoritarian regime. Similarly, when Mobutu's Zaire collapsed, rebel forces under Laurent Kabila eventually took the capital Kinshasa, and a new regime was inaugurated. Neither the RPF regime in Rwanda nor Kabila's coalition of rebels entertained any serious pretense of establishing a new democracy, focusing instead on short-term security imperatives.

These examples, however, highlight the fleeting nature of the "strongman" solution to divided and collapsed states. The imposition of a narrowly based, non-democratic regime will eventually trigger new grievances and precipitate another round of violent encounters. Today, Rwanda's government finds itself increasingly vulnerable to Hutu rebels, and its forces are embroiled in military engagements in neighboring Congo. The long-term prognosis for Tutsi rule in majority-Hutu Rwanda is not positive.

In Kabila's Congo, relative domestic tranquility lasted all of 18 months before a new civil war emerged. The Kabila regime never established control of its vast territory, nor did it quiet the many voices of opposition to its dictatorial and incompetent rule. New authoritarianism may be a common outcome of violence in deeply divided and failed states, but it is not a sustainable one.

Partition

Partition may be another answer. When groups cannot coexist, why should the international community force the perpetuation of an artificial state? Clearly in some situations partition may be desirable, particularly if previous peace agreements have broken down and power sharing seems unlikely. In Sudan, many believe that the differences between the more Arab, Islamist regime in Khartoum and the forces of the more African, Christian, and animist south are—after decades of civil war—irreconcilable. Partition may be a desirable solution, especially in light of the collapsed autonomy regime for the south that was established in the 1972 Addis Ababa accords, which broke down in 1983.

Some advocate partition for situations like Bosnia in which the progress of post-war reconciliation is halting at best, nonexistent at worst.[2] The power sharing system for Bosnia that was created by the 1995 Dayton peace accord is untenable, in this view. The brutal civil war in Bosnia creates such enmity that the Bosniac (Muslim), Croat, and Serb communities cannot live together. Some argue that these groups will go back to war as soon as NATO's peacekeeping operation withdraws. Similarly, advocates of partition consider the October 1998 peace agreement in Kosovo calling for the revival of autonomy for the troubled province as bound to fail, and they foresee future problems for other multiethnic states in the Balkans. Political scientist John Mearsheimer writes in *The New York Times* (October 19, 1998) that,

> It is hard for Americans to understand that the breakup of large countries into smaller states can sometimes lead to stability. But unless we intend to intervene in Kosovo and to occupy Bosnia and Macedonia forever, the only way to stop the spread of violence and civil war is to help the antagonists find the best ways to divorce.

Yet even after the Serb reign of terror in Kosovo, policy makers seem to prefer some form of international protectorate which would amount to something less than independence as opposed to establishing the precedent that new states can be created following bloody civil conflict. There are, however, a number of problems inherent in most partition arrangements. First, partition rarely produces a definitive solution to the problems of multinational societies. Partition solutions simply rearrange the pattern of minorities and majorities, creating new grievances and establishing new dynamics of conflict. If Yugoslavia were to be further partitioned and Kosovo recognized as an independent state, the problem of an Albanian minority in Yugoslavia might be solved. However, a new problem, an aggrieved Serb minority within a newly sovereign, Albanian-majority Kosovo, would be created. The only way to definitively resolve this problem is forced migration, a solution that is in violation of international norms.

The second problem is the "moral hazard" or demonstration effect that partition encourages. If the international community allows partition by force in Bosnia or Kosovo, how could it deny the claims for sovereignty through arms by Abkhaz in Georgia, Chechens in Russia, Tamils in Sri Lanka, Republicans in Northern Ireland, Oromo in Ethiopia, Timorese in Indonesia, Kashmiris in India, Turks in Cyprus, Kurds in Iraq and Turkey, and so on?

Unless the international community can develop consistent criteria on the dissolution of existing states by force and can draft specific norms and conditions under which new states will be recognized, *ad hoc* recognition of new, ethnically based states will simply encourage violence elsewhere. More importantly, the further division of the former Yugoslavia, for example, would award the territorial spoils of war to those who committed war crimes in the name of ethnic purity in violation of international covenants on the prevention and punishment of genocide.

Partition may be a solution in some circumstances, such as in the former Czechoslovakia, where agreement to separate was reached nonviolently, or in Eritrea, where independence was related to botched decolonization in a previous era. It also makes sense when empires such as the Soviet Union collapse, a situation more analogous to the decolonization of the 1960s than to the problems of established multiethnic states of the 1990s.

Some situations are ambiguous. Should "Somaliland," a traditionally administered territory that is now *de facto* independent of the rest of Somalia (a country that has lacked a functioning central government for nearly a decade) be recognized? Is the Israeli-Palestinian dispute, which appears to be inevitably struggling toward partition, an exception in international affairs or a model partition scheme applicable to other seemingly intractable conflicts?

For the most part, partition is likely to be an impractical and violent enterprise. Partition plans will yield more killing, as the central powers resist the dismemberment of their country. Partition may occasionally bring peace; more often, it fails to resolve the problems of state collapse and indeed may lead to a widening of ethnic and national conflict.

Democratization as Conflict Management

The diminution of internal conflicts since 1992 shows that many countries are able to make the transition from war to peace and from war to democracy while avoiding partition. In several notable cases, progress toward democratization has gone hand in hand with peaceful conflict management, building a more sustainable basis for long-term peace and the creation of new mechanisms for the protection and advancement of human rights and freedoms.

Among the more successful instances of democratization as conflict management in the 1990s are El Salvador, Northern Ireland, Mozambique, and South Africa. In each case, success has not eliminated social conflict. In many societies emerging from armed conflict, political violence is replaced by alarmingly high levels of criminal violence. Both El Salvador and South Africa have suffered dramatic crime waves in the wake of peace.

Nonetheless, these examples confirm that democracy can be a powerful tool in managing seemingly intractable ethnic or political conflicts. Transitions from war to peace offer the opportunities for constitution-making and the reestablishment of legitimacy through elections. "Peace processes" encourage consensus building and the creation of a political system that allows for power sharing arrangements and such basic structural reforms as the integration of the police and land redistribution.

In recent years, focus has been placed on the new institutions that emerge from negotiated transitions and the implications of appropriate institutional choices for the establishment of a sustainable democracy in divided societies. With a threefold increase of democratic institutions in the "third wave" of democracy from the 1970s to the early 1990s, special attention has been paid to how political institutions in divided societies can simultaneously promote democratization and conflict management.

Analysts were delighted to learn, for example, that wise institutional choices may have helped consolidate the peace process in Northern Ireland. Following the April 1998 Good Friday Agreement that established a power sharing executive in the disputed territory, elections were held for representatives to the new leadership positions. The rules for Northern Ireland's elections were designed in part to foster voting across sectarian lines by allowing voters to indicate not just their first party or candidate preference, but their second and third preferences as well. The "subsequent" preference votes could be transferred among parties and candidates. Politicians, then, had a real inducement to moderate their appeals to reach across lines of traditional antagonisms. Exit polls in the June 1998 voting showed that voters responded by voting across the religious divide and electing more moderate voices to the new government in Ulster.

Democratic institutions in divided societies need special features, such as carefully considered electoral systems. The choice of the wrong political institutions can contribute to the collapse of weak and divided societies. This is especially true of elections that took place under ill-considered rules, especially winner-take-all systems, or elections which were poorly timed. For example:

> • Algeria's military-backed government aborted an election in January 1992 when it appeared Islamists were about to gain a majority in the national assembly. The country plummeted into a brutal war that has seen more than 30,000 deaths.

> • Angola's presidential election in November 1992 fell apart when rebel forces returned to the battlefield rather than accept a junior role in government after the presidential candidate, Jonas Savimbi, was poised to lose a run-off. More than 300,000 Angolans have died in that deadly civil war.

> • A referendum on independence in Bosnia in June 1992 precipitated the slide into civil war, as Serbs feared becoming a minority in the majority Bosniac and Croat country.

> • In Burundi's 1993 election, a Hutu-majority party won the majority of seats, after which the Tutsi minority-backed military staged a coup and prevented the formation of a new government. Despite efforts to share power, the country eventually succumbed to renewed civil war.

These conflict-inducing elections are illustrative of a broader problem with democracy in divided societies, namely the problem of ethnic voting and the systematic exclusion of minorities. Under some election systems, even significant minorities can be permanently excluded from power if votes are cast along exclusively ethnic lines. Ethnic voting patterns can also encourage the dominant ethnic group to form highly nationalistic parties which identify their group interest with the power of the state and base their appeal on the exclusion of other groups from government.

The permanent exclusion of vulnerable minorities or disadvantaged majorities is a recipe for conflict and violence. Minority exclusion in Northern Ireland was a root cause of violence; majority exclusion in South Africa precipitated decades of bloodshed. If an aggrieved group is denied the parliamentary path to power, what options, other than a turn to violence, does it have to make its claims heard?

Increasingly, lessons are being learned about appropriate democratic institutions for divided societies. In the electoral sphere, successful elections have been held in Bosnia, Northern Ireland, and South Africa under forms of proportional representation, in which the number of seats won roughly parallels the proportion of the popular vote. Under these systems, majorities and minorities alike are all but guaranteed a voice in government, and under certain conditions, voters can be persuaded to cross ethnic lines and back multiethnic political parties.

Coupled with an emphasis on inclusive election systems, territorial arrangements may also promote peace and foster democracy in divided societies. In relatively more successful divided societies, such as India and Malaysia, federalism has been an important mechanism for the accommodation of diverse communities. Autonomy arrangements, too, have helped mitigate conflict in Mindanao in the Philippines and Tatarstan in Russia.

The Russian example also dramatizes the difficulties of moving toward a democratic federal system as a means of managing ethnic conflict in rapidly changing societies. Russia's emerging system of "asymmetric federalism" means that some provinces such as Chechnya or Tatarstan have special relationships with the center that other provinces may not enjoy, for example differential rates of collecting value-added tax. These special relationships encourage other ethnic groups in Russia, such as Dagestanis or Ossetians, to make claims against the state.

Autonomy is a potentially useful strategy towards resolving many of today's conflicts, such as Sri Lanka's civil war between Tamil separatists and the mostly Sinhalese Buddhist government, or the long-simmering dispute over East Timor in Indonesia. In these cases, as in Northern Ireland, autonomy may help blur lines of sovereignty and allow the advocates of self-determination and territorial integrity to claim success. When coupled with regional integration, such as the broader context of European integration in which Northern Ireland's changing status takes place, autonomy solutions appear even more attractive.

Least Likely Cases

The international community must remain sober about the prospects of promoting democracy in deeply divided and collapsed states. The challenges of building democracy in unfavorable conditions of social tension and ethnic strife cannot be underestimated. In countries with a history of violence and intergroup enmity, where economies are devastated, where recently demobilized military forces are a potential threat, and where the wounds of war have not yet healed, it is too much to expect that democratic values can be quickly inculcated and fragile democratic institutions can manage conflicts nonviolently.

Still, the international community has promoted elections in the very least likely candidates for democracy, such as the impoverished and socially ravaged countries of Sierra Leone and Liberia. In conjunction with negotiated peace accords, the United Nations has stepped in to facilitate transitional elections to reconstitute a government. It appears impossible to establish some semblance of legitimate, post-war government without an election.

The results of such elections are invariably tenuous. In Sierra Leone, unfortunately, peace has been shattered as the democratically elected government of President Kabbah has come under siege from rebel forces (including renegade factions of the country's army). Liberia's voting resulted in the presidential election of one of the principal warlords, Charles Taylor, portending a shaky start in a country sorely in need of inclusive government, reconciliation, and reconstruction. Few would be surprised if Liberia's war begins anew.

In other situations, elections have been a vehicle for reestablishing minimum conditions for peace and democracy. Despite widespread criticism, the Organization for

Security and Cooperation in Europe pressed ahead for early elections in post-war Bosnia in 1996, barely a year after the guns had fallen silent. The elections were decried for strengthening the hand of the nationalist parties that had prosecuted the war. Elections in 1998 in Bosnia, however, witnessed the very initial emergence of more moderate voices. While multiethnic democracy and sustained peace remain distant goals, international mediators appear in hindsight to have been right by promoting power sharing through the ballot box.

The choice for divided societies should not be whether to rely on democratic institutions to mediate inter-group conflict. Without democratic institutions and consensus-oriented decision making, over time some degree of violent conflict seems likely. Instead, the question is how and when to embrace democratization as conflict management, even in the most divided societies, that appear to offer infertile ground for democracy and the protection of human rights and freedoms.

A short decade ago, in 1988, South Africa seemed a poor candidate for democracy and conflict management. An embattled white minority regime, with a nuclear-capable military force, faced an aggrieved, abused, and angry majority black population. Yet today, South Africa enjoys a fully enfranchised population, a popularly elected government, a new constitution and model bill of rights, and a leadership and citizenry which is tackling the challenge of creating a multiethnic democracy with enthusiasm.

South Africa also indicates the importance of creating democratically inspired human rights instruments in divided societies. Institutions such as the constitutional court, the human rights commission, and commissions on gender equality help to interpret and implement constitutional norms that require the state to accommodate diverse cultures, traditions, religions, languages, and groups.

Democracy Promotion in Divided Societies

South Africa demonstrates that the promotion of democratization as conflict management can help reconstruct failing states. Such remarkable cases affirm that democratic development in divided societies can be the key to long-term conflict management. It is also the most effective long-term structural means for the prevention of deadly conflict in multiethnic states that have not yet deteriorated into violence.

Promoting democracy in deeply divided societies entails significant risks, particularly in advocating elections that reinforce, rather than mitigate, conflict. Yet the necessity of elections even in the most unfavorable circumstances remains imperative.

International norms on the promotion of democracy in divided societies evolved rapidly in the 1990s, and their further development is critical to maintaining peace in today's multiethnic societies. In 1992, the United Nations General Assembly adopted a resolution on the fair treatment of minorities and indigenous groups. The Organization for Security and Cooperation in Europe established a High Commissioner for National Minorities, which seeks to prevent the eruption of ethnic violence in Europe through quiet diplomacy, particularly in the newly democratic states of the former Eastern Bloc. Electoral assistance is now readily available from the United Nations, the Commonwealth, regional organizations, and a plethora of nongovernmental groups. Conditionalities, too, are used by Western governments, international financial institutions, and regional organizations; political aid is tied to progress toward democratic rights and freedoms.

Most policymakers recognize that democracy cannot save many of today's failed states, at least in the short run. And few deeply conflicted multiethnic societies will become consolidated democracies in the near term. In most instances, efforts to promote democracy after war and state failure will be thwarted by lingering enmities and structural barriers to peace, such as entrenched economic inequality.

Yet the imperatives of managing today's security threats and group conflicts demand that the efforts to promote democracy in deeply divided societies must proceed. The alternatives are few and unattractive. Sustained peace in deeply divided societies requires a formula for the recognition and tolerance of ethnic differences, strong legal protections for individual and group rights, and political institutions that encourage bargaining and inclusive coalitions. These necessary ingredients of sustained peace can only be achieved through democracy. In today's world, the promotion of democracy must remain high on the global agenda—even in divided and failed states where the conditions for democracy are unfavorable.

Notes

1. Licklider, Roy, ed. 1993. *Stopping the Killing*. New York: New York University Press, p. 3.

2. For example, Kaufman, Chaim. "Possible and Impossible Solutions to Ethnic Civil Wars," *International Security* 20 (Spring 1996): 136-175.

Timothy D. Sisk is senior research associate at the Graduate School of International Studies, University of Denver. He is the author of Power Sharing and International Mediation in Ethnic Conflicts.

"Multilateralism and Its Discontents"

Peter W. Rodman

When President George Bush organized the Gulf War coalition in 1990-91, it was a euphoric moment in international affairs. The President spoke of a "new world order," and so it seemed to be. With the U.S.-Soviet rivalry fading, there seemed to be unprecedented possibilities for collaboration among the world's nations, especially the major powers. In the early '90s, an unusual degree of consensus was apparent among the five permanent members of the United Nations Security Council—reflected most dramatically of all, of course, in the mandates that the Security Council gave to the U.S.-led coalition in the Gulf War. Given the conciliatory posture of Soviet foreign policy at the time—and the hopes that could only grow once the USSR was replaced on the world stage by a democratic Russia—we seemed indeed to be entering an era of great-power harmony unlike anything seen since the end of the nineteenth century. It was a great-power harmony, moreover, that seemed quite content to follow the U.S. tune.

While these hopes were widely shared, the Bush Administration's private calculations were in fact more sober. The Bush concept of a "new world order" was never really fleshed out; it was more of an optimistic slogan than a grand design.[1] It is also clear now that President Bush was prepared to go to war to liberate Kuwait with or without a UN mandate. If a Security Council endorsement proved unobtainable, the United States was prepared to pursue its course with whatever "coalition of the willing" could be cobbled together, invoking the inherent right of collective defense recognized in Article 51 of the UN Charter.[2] The supportive Security Council resolutions that were obtained only made the American task of coalition-building that much easier.

In the decade since then, much has changed, both in the state of relations among the major powers and in the American attitude toward multilateral action. But, perversely, these changes have pulled in opposite directions. Among the major powers, many disagreements and tensions now characterize the policy discourse on such important issues as Iraq, Bosnia and Kosovo, the Arab-Israeli dispute, and proliferation questions. Harmony no longer seems so automatic. And in the same period, the Bush Administration has given way to a Clinton Administration that has had much more of a moral and psychological investment in the United Nations and in the principle of multilateralism. The result is an increasing frustration in American diplomacy and a period of intellectual confusion about what role multilateralism can and should play in American foreign policy.

The Clinton Administration and Multilateralism

The Clinton Administration's philosophy of international engagement has reflected the Wilsonian strain in American foreign policy thinking. A humanitarian emphasis, rather than a focus on strategic national interest, has characterized its approach. In this framework, collaboration with other nations has taken on an ideological and not merely instrumental purpose.

In 1993, Madeleine Albright, then our Permanent Representative to the United Nations, spoke of an "assertive multilateralism" as a hallmark of our foreign policy. It included, in her definition, multilateral engagement with other nations in the world community and prevention of crises through American leadership in international organizations.[3] But there seemed to be the implication that multilateralism offered not only the practical benefit of spreading the burden of international security, but also a legitimization of American actions. Morton Halperin, one of the administration's leading intellectuals, wrote in the summer of 1993 (before joining the government) that U.S. military intervention, if not a matter of self-defense in the strictest sense, was not legitimate unless blessed by the UN or other international organizations:

> The United States should explicitly surrender the right to intervene unilaterally in the internal affairs of other countries by overt military means or by covert operations. Such self-restraint would bar interventions like those in Grenada and Panama, unless the United States first gained the explicit consent of the international community acting through the Security Council or a regional organization. [4]

American unilateralism was the principal sin to be avoided, as if to atone for a shameful past. Indeed, many in the administration (including the President) had begun their careers actively opposing U.S. involvement in Indochina.

In the post-Cold War era, moreover, it was believed that humanitarian interventions and peacekeeping operations were in any case the principal kinds of military actions that were likely. Most American military involvement was thus expected to be in the service of others, rather than for any selfish American strategic interest. Accordingly, when the United States intervened in force in Haiti in September 1994 to replace the rightist government, the Halperin prescription was followed: The United States did so with the prior endorsement of a UN Security Council resolution[5]—an historic innovation for U.S. military engagement in the Western Hemisphere.

The failed international interventions in Bosnia and Somalia in 1993-94, however, eventually led the Clinton Administration to distance itself from the United Nations somewhat in the military sphere, at least in operational terms.[6] In Bosnia, the inadequacies of UN involvement in military command and control quickly gave way to a NATO operation, a procedure followed in Kosovo in 1999. In Somalia, in October 1993, after the U.S. military contingent was turned over to a UN command, a deadly firefight killed 18 American GIs, and the corpse of one was dragged publicly through the streets of Mogadishu. But even before that disaster, the casualties suffered in the Somalia exercise were undermining American public support for such multilateral endeavors. A Presidential Decision Directive working its way through the bureaucracy in 1993 to formalize the more central role of the United Nations in peacekeeping ran into a barrage of public criticism. In his UN General Assembly address of September 1993, President Clinton was forced into the rather embarrassing posture of warning against the excesses of UNophilia that his own administration had been fostering. "The United Nations simply cannot become engaged in every one of the world's conflicts," a chastened President cautioned. "If the American people are to say yes to UN peacekeeping, the United Nations must know when to say no."[7]

By the time the administration came forth in May 1994 with its formal policy statement on the U.S. role in UN peacekeeping, it had absorbed the lesson that such operations within the UN framework must be seen as "one useful tool to advance American national interests and pursue our national security objectives."[8] Likewise, the administration took pains to stress that the President would never relinquish his command authority over U.S. troops.[9] But the damage was done: A pledge never to permit U.S. troops to serve under UN command became a prominent part of the Republicans' "Contract with America," the platform that is thought to have contributed to the Republican capture of the House of Representatives in November 1994.[10]

If the Administration has reined in its initial exuberance over UN peacekeeping, it has continued to place great stress on the UN Security Council as a forum for diplomacy. Witness the extraordinary fact that more than one-third of all the UN Security Council resolutions in the history of the UN since 1945 have occurred in the Clinton Administration.[11] It is as if the United States has found it most comfortable, on a wide range of international issues, to speak in the language of UN Security Council resolutions rather than in its own voice. Yet, as consensus among the major powers becomes more difficult on the most important issues, the commitment to multilateralism promises to be more and more a source of frustration for such an American approach. It only heightens the dilemmas of American policymaking, as we are more frequently required to choose between maintaining an international consensus or decisively shaping events.

A World Transformed

The Clinton Administration's multilateralist impulse, alas, has run up against a retrograde trend in international politics in the last decade. To some extent it was probably inevitable that the euphoric afterglow of the Cold War's end would prove temporary. History moves on. But there was also another effect: The collapse of the Soviet Union and the United States' emergence as the sole superpower have led other nations— even friendly ones—to see the new unipolar world as unbalanced. Classical balance-of-power principles have led others to see an interest in leaning against the sole superpower to one degree or another, building counterweights against American dominance rather than cheerily following America's moral lead. It is the revenge of history, and somewhat of a shock to a Wilsonian administration that identifies its goals with universal principles. For much of the rest of the world, restoring "multipolarity" to the international system has become a major goal of foreign policy.

Russia and China, in particular, have made it a staple of their own strategic relations that "hegemonism" (meaning American dominance) was a principal danger to world peace and that promoting "multipolarity" (meaning resistance to American dominance) was a principal task of their foreign policies. When Russian President Boris Yeltsin visited Beijing in April 1996, for example, the communiqué of his summit with President Jiang Zemin declared bluntly that:

> [T]he world is far from being tranquil. Hegemonism, power politics and repeated imposition of pressures on other countries have continued to occur. [12]

Therefore, the goal of their own strategic partnership was to counter this, as stated in their next summit statement in December 1996:

> [A] partnership of equal rights and trust between Russia and China aimed at strategic cooperation in the 21st century promotes the formation of a multipolar world. [13]

The Europeans have expressed similar views. One of the purposes behind the current push for monetary union and a common European foreign and security policy is "to counterbalance the United States," Dutch Prime Minister Wim Kok has stated bluntly. [14] And similarly, French Foreign Minister Herbert Vedrine, at a conference of French ambassadors in August 1997:

> Today there is one sole great power—the United States of America— ...When I speak of its power, I state a fact...without acrimony....But this power carries in itself, to the extent that there is no counterweight, especially today, a unilateralist temptation...and the risk of hegemony. [15]

Therefore, according to Vedrine, Europe's role is:

> to contribute...to the emergence of several poles in the world capable of constituting a factor of balance...Europe is an actor, a means of influence that is absolutely necessary for this multipolar world to arrive. [16]

It is not surprising, therefore, that these powers see the UN Security Council as especially important as a restraint on American unilateralism. This explains the insistence of France (and some other allies) that NATO military actions other than collective defense be under the authority of the Security Council. This featured prominently in the debate over the Alliance's new "Strategic Concept" in advance of the April 1999 NATO Summit. [17] Even more explicitly, the Russian-Chinese summit communiqué in November 1998 stressed at length the Security Council's value as a guarantor of "multipolarity":

> UN action can display more fully and prominently the increasing multipolar potential of the world. The United Nations is gradually excluding unilateral or narrow nationalist moves in international affairs....Any attempt to bypass the Security Council will lead to damage to the existing peacekeeping mechanism and to chaos in international affairs....The most ideal way is to seek unanimity through consultation among all member states of the United Nations. [18]

Dilemmas of U.S. Policy

In short, we have come a long way in this decade, from a view of multilateralism in 1990-91 as something that enhanced American leadership and multiplied America's effectiveness, to a view of multilateralism today (at least in the minds of the other major powers) that it is useful most of all as a restraint on American action. This has posed a conceptual problem that is particularly difficult for the Clinton Administration, which came into office more than half-believing that restraints on American unilateralism were a good thing. Toward the end of its term, however, the Administration has found itself frustrated in the pursuit of its own goals by the resistance of others.

One example, already mentioned, was the debate over the new NATO "Strategic Concept." The Administration believed that in the post-Cold War era, NATO needed to demonstrate its value by taking on new challenges besides the military defense of NATO territory. In the U.S. view, ethnic violence elsewhere in Europe, terrorism, and proliferation of weapons of mass destruction were serious potential threats to common

NATO interests. And, while the United States was prepared to consider UN involve-ment on a case-by-case basis, it was *not* prepared to establish the blanket principle that a UN Security Council mandate was required for all such activities.[19] The allies, the administration believed, were going much too far in insisting on this. (NATO's inter-vention in Kosovo in 1999 seemed to validate the U.S. position, in that the issue was kept out of the Security Council, where Russia would have exercised its veto.)

Another chastening example was the Anti-Personnel Land Mine Treaty, signed in Ottawa by scores of nations at the end of 1997. The ban on land mines was enormously popular around the world—it emerged out of a grassroots movement that was later awarded the Nobel Peace Prize and even enlisted the Princess of Wales as an advo-cate. The United States had long committed itself to using only self-destructing land mines and to taking responsibility for mine clearing, and was prepared to share its mine clearing expertise widely. It sought in this negotiation only a limited exemption for the use of land mines in dangerous areas like the Korean peninsula, where U.S. and allied forces faced a deadly threat. It also sought a delay before the treaty's entry into force. The international community rebuffed these U.S. requests, and the administration was forced to withhold its signature from the treaty.

Yet another example was the multilateral negotiation to establish a permanent In-ternational Criminal Court to try crimes against humanity and war crimes. The admin-istration strongly supported this negotiation when it began, seeing in it a great advance for international law. Yet, again, when the negotiation produced a treaty in July 1998, the international community had pushed it further than the United States felt it could safely go. The administration wanted to assure that U.S. personnel involved in peace-keeping operations—in which we, after all, were bearing a disproportionate burden—would have some protection against such prosecutions, especially since our own mili-tary code provides a credible and sufficient basis for enforcing these civilized prin-ciples.

The United States had two even more fundamental problems with the treaty on the International Criminal Court. One was the treaty's bald assertion of "universal juris-diction," meaning that the United States and its nationals could be subject to the new court's criminal jurisdiction even if the United States did not sign the treaty. This was "contrary to the most fundamental principles of treaty law,"[20] which had held for cen-turies that states could be bound only if they gave their consent. Beyond this, there was a serious constitutional problem for the United States, in that the creation of "instant customary international law," as the founders of this new court were attempting, could not override subsequent U.S. statutory law or the sovereignty of the U.S. Constitution. No treaty could override the Constitution; even less a treaty we had not signed. The protests of the court's advocates could not be accepted, as John Bolton has argued:

> One must be wary of any theory of international law so quick to declare the world's strongest and freest representative democracy to be in con-stant flagrant violation, simply for adhering to its own constitution. One should be especially concerned when that constitution happens to be used as a model by liberal democracies around the world.[21]

But perhaps the most frustrating challenge to the administration's faith in multilateralism has been the continuing confrontation with Iraq. The Clinton Administration had set great store by the Security Council consensus that, until the end of 1998, had supported the continued inspection activity of the UN Special Commission (UNSCOM) that monitored Iraq's weapons of mass destruction. The President shied away from military action in several of the various diplomatic confrontations with Iraq in deference to the lack of enthusiasm for it in the Security Council—as, for example, in the crisis in February 1998 which culminated in UN Secretary-General Kofi Annan's negotiated agreement with Saddam Hussein. While the United States and Britain attacked Iraq in December 1998 without seeking additional Security Council authorization—a rare step for this administration—they then found themselves facing renewed pressures from other members of the Security Council (Russia, China, France) to weaken the sanctions and inspection regime.

The United States, in the future, will be forced more and more to choose between its convictions on what is essential to spare the Middle East from weapons of mass destruction in the hands of Saddam Hussein, on the one hand, and deference to the more assertive resistance of other major powers that either do not share the U.S. alarm or are driven by other motives. Iraq may turn out to be multilateralism's last hurrah.

The Kosovo intervention raised a different kind of problem. It was a collective NATO endeavor, so no ally could accuse the United States of "unilateralism." But the outcome may in fact encourage some Europeans to distance themselves from America in future conflicts. At bottom, the key to multilateralism is not what one thinks of the United Nations but what one thinks of the United States. Those who believe the United States guilty of too many sins in the past—and these include some Americans—will be eager to see restraints on American unilateral action. Those who believe that global freedom and peace and the cause of human rights have more often than not been advanced if not sustained by the United States, acting out of some combination of its own self-interest and a general interest, will find multilateralism a potential source of paralysis. In the face of a deadly threat like Saddam's weapons of mass destruction, such paralysis is no service to world peace.

The dilemma will not go away, for any American administration. Congress makes clear with increasing vehemence its desire that we share our burdens with others. The United States can be far more effective (as in the Gulf War) if we succeed in building a coalition to join us. Isolationism is no option for the United States, and unilateralism sometimes hazards important relationships that we should value.

But our friends abroad, too, should see the problem as a dilemma. A turbulent history, to be sure, has taught them to be wary of any dominant power. They are entitled to their own views and interests; especially those that are our allies are entitled to a relationship of mutuality, consultation, and trust. But our allies, especially, cannot possibly have a stake in American paralysis. And America's moral self-assurance is at the core of its motivation for international engagement. As Kim Holmes has argued:

> Much of the will and stamina which America musters to shoulder the burden of global leadership rests on its own perceived moral authority as a leader of the West. Hamstringing and weakening U.S. global leadership by insisting on UN mandates for every overseas military operation or other multilateral action could undermine the will of the United States to lead.[22]

An America that does not believe in itself cannot lead. The passing of the early post-

Cold War euphoria only signals that we are entering a period of new uncertainties and perils. Many of those abroad now complaining of American exuberance would soon enough discover the dangers to themselves in a world from which America had abdicated. The United States needs to temper its enthusiasms with concern for the views and interests of those it wishes to lead, especially among its democratic allies. But it cannot escape its responsibility, even if occasionally it must face it alone.

Notes

1. Don Oberdorfer, "Bush's Talk of a 'New World Order': Foreign Policy Tool or Mere Slogan?" *Washington Post*, May 26, 1991, p. A31.

2. George Bush and Brent Scowcroft, *A World Transformed.* (New York: Knopf, 1998), pp. 355-356.

3. Amb. Madeleine Albright, statement before the Subcommittee on International Security, International Organizations, and Human Rights, Committee on Foreign Affairs, U.S. House of Representatives, June 24, 1993.

4. Morton H. Halperin, "Guaranteeing Democracy", *Foreign Policy*, Summer 1993, p.120.

5. UN Security Council Resolution 940 (31 July 1994)

6. See John Hillen, *Blue Helmets: The Strategy of UN Military Operations.* (Washington: Brassey's 1998). esp. Chapters 6 and 7.

7. President Bill Clinton, "Confronting the Challenges of a Broader World," address to the UN General Assembly, New York City, September 27, 1993.

8. U.S. Department of State, *The Clinton Administration's Policy on Reforming Multilateral Peace Operations*, Department of State Publication No.10161 (Washington: Department of State, May 1994), p.15.

9. Ibid., p.9.

10. Ed Gillespie and Bob Schellhas, eds., *Contract With America* (New York: Times Books, 1994), pp.10, 101-106.

11. Just before the Clinton Administration took over, the total number of UN Security Council resolutions had reached 801. At this writing, the number is 1231.

12. Russian-Chinese Joint Statement on President Boris Yeltsin's Summit Visit to Beijing, April 25, 1996.

13. Russian-Chinese Joint Statement on Premier Li Peng's Summit visit to Moscow, December 18, 1996.

14. Wim Kok quoted in *Der Standard* (Vienna), October 27, 1998, p.2.

15. Remarks of Minister of Foreign Affairs Hubert Vedrine at Conference of Ambassadors, Paris, August 28, 1997.

16. Ibid.

17. E.g., Foreign Minister Hubert Vedrine, intervention at North Atlantic Council meeting, Brussels, December 8, 1998.

18. Russian-Chinese Joint Statement on President Jiang Zemin's Summit visit to Moscow, November 23, 1998.

19. See Secretary of state Madeleine Albright's intervention at the North Atlantic Council meeting, Brussels, December 8, 1998.

20. Amb. David Scheffer, Ambassador-at-large for War Crimes Issues, testimony before the Committee on Foreign Relations, U.S. Senate, July 23, 1998.

21. John R. Bolton, "The Global Prosecutors: Hunting for Criminals in the Name of Utopia," *Foreign Affairs,* January/February 1999, p. 164.

22. Kim R. Holmes, "U.S.-European Strategic Bargains: Old and New," *Heritage Lectures,* No. 627, November 13, 1998, p. 5.

Peter W. Rodman, a former White House and State Department official, is Director of National Security Programs at the Nixon Center and a trustee of Freedom House.

The News of the Century

Leonard R. Sussman

This century, particularly the past decade, has seen remarkable gains for freedom of the press throughout the world. One hundred years ago, press freedom barely existed outside North America and a few Western European countries, and no one expected that things would change. There were no serious efforts to expand the reach of a free press to the 95 percent of the world's population which experienced censored or controlled information, or had no free press whatsoever. Three European countries controlled all the news flowing into and out of Africa, Asia, and much of Latin America.

Not until the fall of the Berlin Wall in 1989 did those areas of the world under Communist domination begin to experience some freedom of the news media. And even today, press freedom in much of the world is weakened by inexperienced journalists and news media still tied to partisan interests. In 1998, even as political freedom enjoyed important gains around the globe, global press freedom suffered a minor setback.

The muzzling of journalists was increasingly accomplished by more subtle, legalistic methods than through violence or outright repression. But the decline was real and journalists redoubled their efforts to develop strategies and organizations for self-protection. Our Freedom House press study of 186 nations rates 68 (36 percent) with free print and broadcast media, 52 (28 percent) partly free, and 66 (36 percent) with news media that are not free. The survey places only 1.2 billion people in countries with a free press (20 percent of the world's population), 2.4 billion (40 percent) with a partly free press, and 2.4 billion living in nations with a press that is not free.

Press limitations continue even when there is improvement in a country's political and civil rights; India is an example. The latest Freedom House survey of governance raises India's rating from partly free to free. The country remains, however. in the partly free press category. State-run Doordarshan television still controls the world's largest electronic network, delivering news and views to 80 percent of India's population. All-India radio controls almost all radio stations. On the positive side, an estimated 35 million Indians watch satellite TV, which is less partisan than normal broadcast programming. Video and audio cassettes (mostly pirated) are popular. There is a steady increase in cable TV and a robust print press in many languages. But the bulk of news reaching the public favors government interests.

In the United States, as the twentieth century winds down, freedom of the press remains secure because of the Supreme Court's commitment to First Amendment principles. For its part, the American public has increasingly come to question the media's judgment and fairness. The freest press in world history suffers from the very freedom a democracy requires.

As the century closes, our annual press freedom analysis deserves a 100-year retrospective. Never in history has the Word been as widely heard or seen; never has it been as rapidly or as distantly conveyed, or have ideas as diversified and compelling been transmitted. Never has human ingenuity built machines that clone human memory and creativity. And never has communication been put to baser destructiveness or cruder inhumanity.

In the first years of this century, President Theodore Roosevelt used to call a few journalists to his office. Reporters would stand before Roosevelt, notebooks and pencils in hand. When he concluded, they would race to the few bulky telephones to dial their offices and dictate brief reports. Developed by rewrite men, reports were transmitted by telegraph. Shorter versions might be sent overseas by the new wireless. Thus went the forerunner of today's televised press conference.

Today, reporters travel everywhere with the president. Portable satellite feeds place words and pictures online for instantaneous reception and re-transmission within seconds. The president's words are taped as he speaks. His every motion is photographed and sent by digital camera for instantaneous use. Even in authoritarian societies, facsimile machines and computers linked to telephone lines bypass the censor and challenge the political structure. In November 1998, with U.S. planes in the air about to bomb Iraq, the commercial Cable News Network (CNN)—not the CIA—reported Saddam Hussein was yielding, causing President Clinton to recall the bombers. Technology has transformed communication. But the crucial question remains: To what purpose?

A millennial retrospective would parallel the century's, revealing both retrogression and progress. Straight-line projections never accurately depict the history of press freedom. That is both the lesson of the past and the warning for the future.

Since the first reporters used smoke signals, stone carvings, or writing on papyrus, they encountered hurdles similar to those which now afflict mass-media presses, multimedia broadcasters, and the ubiquitous Internet. In the past, the church or the state held the key to the instruments of communication. Today, commercial managers vie with the state to sustain the information flows. All rulers, even democrats, seek to manage the news. Since entrepreneurs do not have the police power of the state, a major degree of press freedom is possible, provided commercially supported journalism reflects the diversity of ideas and plurality of ownership needed to assure freedom of the news media.

At the opening of the twentieth century, new technologies such as speedier printing presses, the telegraph, and the telephone facilitated communication. In the U.S., the new transcontinental railroads delivered newspapers and magazines promptly, creating a new mass market for advertising. Photographs began to appear in the press.

But the tightly controlled British, French, and German press cartel monopolized coverage of these countries' colonial outposts and other vast areas of the world in which they retained control. The American wire service, the Associated Press, was prevented by the cartel from covering news outside the United States. The foreign agencies, Reuters in England and Havas in France, were subsidized by their governments and carried reports that served official policies.

In the U.S., muckrakers—early investigative journalists—revealed political corruption ("the shame of the cities"), upset the Standard Oil monopoly, publicized horrors in Chicago's stockyards, and spurred federal reform laws. Before long, however, the First World War disrupted news flows and put military censors at the elbows of journalists. A censorship board was established, and the Espionage Act revoked the mailing privilege of many alternative, mainly Socialist, newspapers.

In 1920, commercial radio opened a new channel of mass communication. At first, news was secondary, although a feature of that first year was election night coverage of the Harding-Cox presidential race. By 1927, regulation of the airwaves was legislated, and in 1934, it expanded to create the Federal Communication Commission. Unlike newspapers, which were kept free of government intervention, radio stations were licensed "in the public interest," but their programs suffered little interference. Later, radio stations were made to comply with the "fairness doctrine," which insisted that broadcasts of controversial subjects must include the airing of an alternate view. The doctrine was rarely invoked, though it did provide special interest groups a lever to gain airtime. The doctrine was withdrawn by the FCC in 1987.

Between the world wars, newspapers and magazines in a relatively small number of countries were free of overt governmental control, though ruling parties or oligarchs did influence political coverage. There were thus varying degrees of press freedom in England, France, Germany, Scandinavia, Australia, New Zealand, and several countries in Latin America and the Caribbean. But in virtually every nation, the radio networks were state-owned and run, and served as mouthpieces for the views of government or regime. The U.S. radio networks, which were privately owned, and the domestic arm of the British Broadcasting Corporation (BBC) were the exceptions.

Then came the dictators: Hitler in Germany, Mussolini in Italy, Franco in Spain, Salazar in Portugal, the militarists in Japan, military juntas in Latin America. In those countries where dictatorship prevailed, "news" was mainly propaganda.

American radio, on the other hand, came of age in the 1930s. It produced reporters and commentators who covered the increasingly dangerous developments abroad. To project his broad domestic reform program, President Franklin D. Roosevelt employed radio "fireside chats" as a means of bypassing the newspapers, whose editorials were often hostile to the New Deal. Several stridently racist broadcasters clouded the airwaves, and isolationist editorialists weakened U.S. defense preparation as another world war neared. Yet newsreels in movie theaters and "The March of Time," a dramatic reenactment of current news heard on radio, projected threatening military preparations in Europe and Asia.

A bright spot for press freedom came in 1931. The U.S. Supreme Court ruled in *Near v. Minnesota* that prior restraint (in effect, censorship) is permitted only in extraordinary situations. This decision, after 142 years, established the First Amendment's fundamental protection for press freedom.

World War II weakened press freedom in much of the world. But in Britain and America, the press could still discuss wartime measures with some freedom, provided military deployment and casualties were not publicized. When the Japanese attacked the United States in December 1941, the Espionage Act and the Trading With The Enemy Act of 1917 were still on the statute books. But they were enforced mainly to block distribution of fascist publications.

The Code of Wartime Practices for the American Press (and radio), issued in 1942, restricted coverage of troop movements, war production, and the weather. The Office of Censorship examined mail, cables, and radio communications between the U.S. and other countries.

The most effective wartime reporters were Ernie Pyle, the syndicated Scripps-Howard columnist who traveled with frontline troops and wrote first-person accounts of the GIs' courage under inhuman battlefield conditions; and Edward R. Murrow, the CBS radio commentator who appeared on British rooftops during Nazi bombing raids and calmly intoned, "London calling," before describing the day's air battles.

Once the war ended, American wire services and newspaper correspondents clearly dominated the reporting of international news. But prospects for enhanced press liberty were dashed by the spread of communism throughout the Soviet Union, Eastern Europe, and China. Nor did decolonization bring significant gains for a free press. In Africa, journalists who under colonialism had been staunch advocates of press freedom imposed strict censorship after they or their allies took over the reins of power.

The Cold War would influence most domestic and international news flows for the next 45 years. Most American correspondents abroad would fashion news reports in the context of the latest event's influence on Cold War geopolitics. Sometimes the attempt to fit every story into a Cold War context gave the reader an over-simplified interpretation of global events. But as elite Western European newspapers recovered pre-war freedoms, they provided generally more sophisticated reportage, particularly on international issues.

American participation in the Korean War in 1950 did not trigger censorship except in the actual fighting arena. But the assault by Communist North Korea did partly spark inflammatory anti-Communist hearings in legislative chambers of several states, and particularly in the U.S. Senate. Senator Joseph McCarthy discovered the soft underbelly of U.S. journalism: the press's commitment to "objectivity" and its reliance on an informed source. McCarthy himself became the major news source by revealing the presence of "Communists" high in the State Department and other offices of government. The press lavished coverage on McCarthy, usually without asking serious questions about the accuracy of his charges. His successful publicity campaign, timed for the evening television programs, produced a daily flurry of new accusations against the army as well as other government agencies.

His Senate investigations dominated the press for months. Reporters and editors took McCarthy at his word; his claims, unchallenged by the press, blackened the names of hundreds of citizens. But in the end, McCarthy was brought down by his own excesses and by the work of a few courageous journalists, notably Edward R. Murrow.

The press learned that objectivity requires balance, a questioning mind, and multiple sources. But the fabric of American society had been torn. In a perverse way, press freedom had been exploited by a demagogue.

In the 1960s, the role of the press and its relationship to government officials, including the president, became a burning issue because of controversy over coverage of the Vietnam War. Ironically, that war was the least censored of any in modern times. But claims put forth from the White House, largely for domestic U.S. purposes, were often at odds with events in the field. And even though Communist forces suffered massive losses during the 1968 Tet offensive, the press generally termed the attack an enemy victory because it had taken the U.S. defenders by surprise. Virtually no press favored the president's war policy thereafter, though Vietnam coverage had begun with almost unanimous press support.

The U.S. press had transformed itself from informal advocate to adversary of official policy, and remained so for several decades. A new generation of journalists would emerge more cynical of official pronouncements.

The Watergate scandals exacerbated the rupture between government and press, as did President Nixon's appeal to the Supreme Court to block publication of the Pentagon Papers. The court ruled, 6-3, in favor of continued publication, relying on *Near v. Minnesota* and other precedents. This victory for press freedom nevertheless revealed the fragility of the court's commitment to wide ranging press freedom. One justice said

PRESS FREEDOM VIOLATIONS — 1998
(and cumulative figures since 1982)

	1998	1982-98
A. Killed	35 [19]*	844
B. Kidnapped, Disappeared, Abducted	11 [6]	388
C. Arrested/Detained	335 [56]	4082
D. Expelled	25 [9]	468

A. Afghanistan 1; Angola 1; Bangladesh 1; Brazil 2; Canada 1; Colombia 7; Congo (Brazzaville)1; Ethiopia 1; Georgai 1; India 1; Mexico 4; Nigeria 2; Peru 2; Philippines 2; Russia 4; Rwanda 1; Sierra Leone 1; Tajikistan 1; Thailand 1.

B. Afghanistan 1; Colombia 3; Congo, DR 1; Iran 2; Kenya 1; Yugoslavia 3.

C. Algeria 3; Angola 2; Argentina 3; Azerbaijan 11; Bangladesh 6; Belarus 4; Benin 1; Bosnia 3; Burma 3; Cameroon 6; Chad 1; China 2; Colombia 3; Congo, Dem. Rep. 41; Cuba 11; Czech Republic 1;Djibouti 4; Egypt 1;Ethiopia 19; France 7; Gabon 3; Gambia 7; Ghana 4; Guinea 2; India 1; Indonesia 7; Iran 11; Iraq 1; Italy 5; Jordan 5; Kenya 2; Korea, S. 2; Liberia 3; Malawi 2; Namibia 3; Nepal 5; Niger 3; Nigeria 23; Pakistan 8; Palestinian Authority 23; Peru 5; Romania 1; Russia 1; Sierra Leone 21; Slovakia 1; Somalia 3; Sri Lanka 4; Tanzania 9; Togo 5; Tunisia 1; Turkey 15; Uganda 3; Ukraine 1; Yemen 5; Yugoslavia 6; Zambia 6.

D. Burma 5; China 2; Congo, DR 2; Equatorial Guinea 8; Gambia 1; Guinea 2; Indonesia 3; South Africa 1; Yugoslavia 1.

	1998	1987-97
E. Charged, Sentenced, Fined	175 [48]	980
F. Beaten, Assaulted, Tortured	269 [53]	1898
G. Wounded in Attack	17 [4]	399
H. Threatened	39 [16]	769
I. Robbery, Confiscation of Materials or Credentials	46 [24]	776
J. Barred from Entry or Travel	41 [16]	493
K. Harassed	121 [40]	1524
L. Publication or Program Shut Down	39 [16]	721
M. Publication or Program Banned, Censored, or Suspended.	190 [41]	1076
N. Home Bombed, Burned, Raided, or Occupied	25 [16]	149
O. Publication or Program Bombed, Burned, Raided or Occupied	49 [25]	390

* [ ] indicates the number of countries in which the violation occurred.

that if the government had made a better case that publication would harm American interests by threatening the safety of troops or risking a diplomatic crisis, the decision might have been reversed.

U.S. military forays in the 1980s further deepened the press-government rift. After reporters were prohibited from accompanying troops during the brief invasion of Grenada, the press pleaded for representation "next time." When that time came during the U.S. landing in Panama, reporters were again excluded during the initial phases of the operation. On both occasions, public opinion polls showed support for the military, not the news media. When announcing the subsequent U.S. attack on Iraq in 1991, President Bush declared that the "lessons of Vietnam" had been learned. Among the lessons: the press must not be allowed free rein. Military handlers accompanied interviewers; live television briefings were seen simultaneously by the public and the press; and press reports were examined by censors before being dispatched. Again, the public generally approved of military censorship in wartime.

Public regard for the credibility of American news media remained low through 1998 and the prolonged debates over the impeachment of President Clinton. The press was accused of sensationalizing the sexual aspects of the charges, though the most sex-oriented television and print reports earned high ratings.

As the century draws to a close, American journalism can boast the greatest freedom it has ever enjoyed. But, today, if it were put to a vote, a clearly dissatisfied public might not entirely endorse the press freedom guarantee of the First Amendment.

Abroad, meanwhile, the level of press freedom has changed dramatically since the century opened. In the century's first half, the European colonial powers controlled most of the world's news flows. During the Cold War (1945-1991), the vast Soviet bloc controlled what the public could and could not read or hear in roughly half the world. Under pressure of economic deterioration in the Soviet Union and its need to introduce modern communication technologies, the blanket of complete censorship was lifted. Dissidents in the Soviet Union and other Communist countries exploited the relaxation. The destruction of the Berlin wall and other "velvet revolutions"—including "the wind blowing from the East" into some African and Asian nations—gave great impetus to the spread of Western-style journalism. A free press, however, would prove an elusive goal in countries without a tradition of civil freedoms, without a market economy to support diversified journalism, and where writers were polemicists, either for or against the deposed Communist regimes.

The Asian financial debacle of the late 1990s revealed the pitfalls of state-directed journalism. The crisis illustrated the destructive consequences that result from a lack of transparency in public and economic affairs.

The decade-long debates in UNESCO and other international forums over the proposed "new world information and communications order" also collapsed. In their place, UNESCO held regional conferences to support press freedom, aided journalists in trouble in many countries, and designated May 3 World Press Freedom Day.

In the turmoil over dramatic political, economic, and social changes, and the striving for freer news delivery systems, the role of journalists in many countries became at once more hopeful and more endangered. The news media in many nations were regarded as active players in either advancing or restraining political change.

To record this developing phenomenon, Freedom House began the annual Press Freedom Survey in 1978.

In 1979, of 161 countries studied, only 51 (31 percent) had free news media. Even in those nations the broadcast media were Free in only 37 countries (24 percent). Partly Free media were found in 54 countries (34 percent); 56 nations had Not Free media. Some 83 countries (54 percent of the world) had broadcast media that were Not Free. Thus, in three-fourths of the world in 1979, governments had a dominant voice in determining what did or did not appear in the media. In 1937, there were 39 news services in 28 countries, of which 70 percent were nominally independent of governments. By 1979, however, 68 percent of all governments had a state-run news agency: 81 percent of the Not Free countries, 68 percent of the Partly Free countries, and 57 percent of the Free countries. Of nations with the lowest freedom rating, 95 percent operated state news agencies. Some of these agencies assigned themselves monopoly power over domestic news for distribution inside or outside the country. They also edited incoming international news for home consumption.

Ten years later, in 1989, political tremors that splintered the Soviet bloc led to a freer press throughout Eastern Europe. News and data flows suffered, however, in Latin America and China. Physical assaults on the press worldwide were the highest yet recorded, though the number of unfree press systems diminished. Physical attacks and harassment of the news media often accompany domestic turmoil when strict censorship and other governmental controls are relaxed. Sixty-three journalists in 22 countries were killed on the job in 1989, 17 more than the year before. More than half were murdered in Latin America, half of those by guerrillas and half by drug traffickers.

Of 159 countries examined in 1989, 56 (35 percent) were in the free-press category, 29 (18 percent) had a partly free press, and 74 (47 percent) not-free news media.

A decade later, at the beginning of 1999, the statistics for press freedom showed more gains throughout the world. Of 186 countries examined, 68 nations (36 percent) were placed in the free-press category—barely a 1 percent improvement over the decade before. But the partly-free-press group had grown to 52 countries (28 percent)—a two-thirds improvement. Sixty-six countries (36 percent) were still in the not-free-press category, a significant decline.

Developments in 1998

Peru's media declined from Partly Free to Not Free. The nation's newspapers and magazines felt increasing pressure from President Fujimori, who many believe is planning to run for a constitutionally-prohibited third term. Since 1992, many print and broadcast journalists have been pressured into self-censorship. Others have been intimidated by libel suits, detention, house arrest, and in one famous case, the revocation of a TV station owner's citizenship. Last year, 2 journalists were killed, 12 received death threats, 10 were beaten or otherwise attacked, 5 were arrested, and others were charged with various offenses.

Ghana slipped into the Not Free category by one point in a rating system of 100 points. Despite the constitutional guarantee of press freedom, the government last year found ways to circumvent the basic press law. The privately owned press frequently suffered crackdowns in which journalists were imprisoned for "insulting" officials and allegedly breaching national security. Radio stations engaged in self-censorship rather than risk the penalties that may be incurred for critical coverage of politics.

Namibia, listed in 1997 as Free but at the very cusp of Partly Free, moved over the line in 1998 to Partly Free. The regime and ruling party attempted to restrict critical reporting of their policies. TV reporters were twice assaulted, one program was dismissed for "libelous and malicious" stories, a journalist was arrested for not revealing his sources, and two defamation suits were brought by government ministers. The state owns and operates the radio and TV systems, which give prominent and favorable coverage to officials, but generally allow some criticism of the government.

Among Asian states, the press was rated Not Free in Malaysia and Singapore, yet Partly Free in the governance survey. The financial crisis that provoked riots last year in Malaysia caused the government to criticize and censor foreign journalists and exert additional pressures on the domestic press. Authorities say they will permit the free flow of information if it is done in a "proper manner." An information official threatened to imprison journalists without trial if, in the authority's judgment, they undermine the country's leadership. In Singapore, the broadcast media are Free in principle but subject to stringent governmental controls, as are domestic and foreign print media.

Press freedom diminished last year in Russia. Communists in parliament called for greater censorship but President Boris Yeltsin vowed late in December to protect the press and fight censorship. "We will use all our strength to defend freedom of the press," said the ailing Yeltsin, "I promise you this as president and as guarantor of the constitution." Nevertheless, the Russian print and broadcast press are increasingly subject to control by Russian plutocrats who own practically all major media, as well as by political forces. A Russian press-defense committee has been created to monitor the state of press freedom and lobby the government on behalf of journalistic independence.

Fifteen years ago, the press everywhere paid little organized attention to its own survival. Now there are active press-freedom monitoring organizations on all continents. Many of them are linked in the International Freedom of Expression Exchange (IFEX), an electronic network, and issue protests when a journalist is arrested or otherwise persecuted. Thus, technology provides journalists with the means to combat state controls in the most repressive countries even as democratic openings force governments to find more subtle means of repression.

Both Canada and the United States enjoy a free press, but both saw their press freedom ratings decline slightly in 1998. Canada's was lowered several points despite its tradition of broad press freedom. It permitted surveillance of a broadcast reporter investigating police corruption. Two newspaper reporters were kidnapped by the police. One newspaper in Quebec was harassed over the language issue. A CBC reporter had his home broken into after reporting on Hell's Angels. And one reporter, critical of the Sikhs, was killed.

The U.S. rating dropped one point. Though the Supreme Court declared unconstitutional the 1996 law banning pornography on the Internet, Congress continued to draft bills to control Internet content. Sensational and saturated coverage of the presidential scandals in 1998 reduced the credibility of journalists and their institutions, a negative sign in a democratic society.

When allowed its freedom, the press has been an educator, an entertainer, sensationalist, propagandist, sustainer of civil discourse, reformer, biased, politically courageous; it has been a supporter of commerce, photography, scientific development, exploration (of the universe and its occupants, and beyond), community development, and political mischief.

Amid the century of turmoil, the press has also provided sound analysis of the social and political structures on which a country is based. And courage: some 135 press photographers died filming the Vietnam war. Another 844 journalists have been murdered on the job since 1982.

The twentieth century has avoided a nuclear holocaust. The twenty-first century has no smaller challenge than permitting the spirit of human freedom, finally, to prevail through communication. Despite decades of destructive wars, conspiracies, dictatorships, and censorship, the survival of humanity and the urge to seek the freer exchange of ideas has never been stronger.

Leonard R. Sussman is senior scholar in international communication of Freedom House, and adjunct professor of journalism and mass communication at New York University. His forthcoming book is a history of press freedom. He was assisted in this survey by Kristen Guida.

1999 Press Freedom Survey of Freedom House

(186 countries: 68 Free press; 52 Partly Free; 66 Not Free.
Shown by numbered ratings within categories.)

FREE 1-15 (19)

Australia
Austria
Bahamas
Belgium
Denmark
. Finland
Germany
Iceland
Jamaica
Luxembourg
Marshall Is.
Nauru
Netherlands
New Zealand
Norway
St. Lucia
Sweden
Switzerland
United States

FREE 16-30 (49)

Barbados
Belize
Benin
Bolivia
Botswana
Canada
Chile
Costa Rica
Cyprus
Czech Rep.
Dominica
Dominican Rep.
Estonia
France
Greece
Grenada
Guyana
Hungary
Ireland
Israel
Italy
Japan
Kiribati
Korea, S.
Latvia
Ltihuania
Mali
Malta
Mauritius

Micronesia
Mongolia
Panama
Papua New Guinea
Philippines
Poland
Portugal
St. Kitts-Nevis
St. Vincent &
Grenadines
Sao Tome & Principe
Slovakia
Slovenia
Solomon Is.
South Africa
Spain
Taiwan
Thailand
Trinidad & Tobago
United Kingdom
Uruguay

PARTLY FREE 31-45 (22)

Argentina
Brazil
Bulgaria
Burkina Faso
Cape Verde
Comoros
Ecuador
India
Kuwait
Macedonia
Madagascar
Malawi
Namibia
Nicaragua
Romania
Samoa
Senegal
Suriname
Tonga
Uganda
Vanuatu
Venezuela

PARTLY FREE 46-60 (30)

Albania
Antigua-Barbuda

Armenia
Bangladesh
Bosnia-Herzegovina
Central African Rep.
Colombia
El Salvador
Fiji
Gabon
Georgia
Guatemala
Guinea-Bissau
Haiti
Honduras
Indonesia
Lesotho
Mexico
Moldova
Morocco
Mozambique
Nepal
Nigeria
Pakistan
Paraguay
Russia
Seychelles
Sri Lanka
Tanzania
Ukraine

NOT FREE 61-75 (42)

Angola
Azerbaijan
Bahrain
Brunei
Cambodia
Chad
Congo Brazzaville
Cote d'Ivoire
Croatia
Djibouti
Egypt
Eritrea
Ethiopia
Gambia
Guinea
Israel Occ. Terr.
Jordan
Kazakhstan
Kenya
Krygzstan

Laos
Lebanon
Malaysia
Maldives
Mauritania
Niger
Oman
Peru
Qatar
Rwanda
Singapore
Swaziland
Syria
Togo
Tunisia
Turkey
Vietnam
Yemen
Zambia
Zimbabwe

NOT FREE 76-100 (24)

Afghanistan
Algeria
Belarus
Bhutan
Burma
Burundi
Cameroon
China
Congo, Dem. Rep.
Cuba
Equatorial Guinea
Iran
Iraq
Korea, N.
Libya
Saudi Arabia
Sierra Leone
Somalia
Sudan
Tajikistan
Turkmenistan
United Arab
Republic
Uzbekistan
Yugoslavia

Introduction to Country and Related Territory Reports

The *Freedom in the World 1998-1999 Survey* contains reports on 191 countries and 17 related and disputed territories. Each report includes basic political, economic, and social data arranged in the following categories: **polity**, **economy**, **population**, **purchasing power parities (PPP)**, **life expectancy**, **ethnic groups**, **capital**, **political rights** [numerical rating], **civil liberties** [numerical rating], and **status** [Free, Partly Free, or Not Free]. For countries or territories which received a numerical ratings change or trend arrow this year, a brief explanatory sentence is included. An explanation of the methods used to determine the *Survey*'s ratings is contained in the chapter on methodology.

The **polity** category contains an encapsulated description of the dominant centers of freely chosen or unelected political power in each country or territory. Most of the descriptions are self-explanatory, such as Communist one-party for China or parliamentary democracy for Ireland. Such nonparliamentary democracies as the United States of America are designated as presidential-legislative democracies. European democratic countries with constitutional monarchs are designated as parliamentary democracies, because the elected body is the center of most real political power. Only countries with powerful monarchs (e.g., the Sultan of Brunei) warrant a reference to the monarchy in the polity description. Dominant-party polities are systems in which the ruling party (or front) dominates the government, but allows other parties to organize or compete, short of taking control of the government. Other types of polities include various military or military-influenced or dominated regimes, transitional systems, and several unique polities, such as Iran's clergy-dominated presidential-parliamentary system. Countries with genuine federalism contain the word "federal" in their polity description.

The reports contain a brief description of the **economy** of each country or territory. Non-industrial economies are called traditional or pre-industrial. Developed market economies and Third World economies with a modern market sector have the designation capitalist. Mixed capitalist countries combine private enterprise with substantial government involvement in the economy for social welfare purposes. Capitalist-statist economies have both large market sectors and government-owned productive enterprises, due either to elitist economic policies or state dependence on key natural resource industries. Mixed capitalist-statist economies have the characteristics of capitalist-statist economies, as well as major social welfare programs. Statist economies have the goal of placing the entire economy under direct or indirect government control. Mixed statist economies are primarily government-controlled, but also have significant private enterprise. Developing Third World economies with a government-directed modern sector belong in the statist category. Economies in transition between statist and capitalist forms may have the word "transitional" in their economy description.

The **population** and **life expectancy** figures were obtained from the "1998 World Population Data Sheet" of the Population Reference Bureau.

The **purchasing power parities (PPP)** show per capita gross domestic product (GDP) in terms of international dollars in order to account for real buying power. These figures were obtained from the *1998 United Nations Development Program Human Development Report*. However, for some countries, especially tiny island countries, this information was not available.

Information about the **ethnic groups** in a country or territory is provided in order to assist with the understanding of certain issues, including minority rights, addressed by the *Survey*. Sources used to obtain this information included *The World Almanac and Book of Facts, 1999* and the CIA *1998 World Factbook*.

The **political rights** and **civil liberties** categories contain numerical ratings between 1 and 7 for each country or territory rated, with 1 representing the most free and 7 the least free. The **status** designation of "Free," "Partly Free," or "Not Free," which is determined by the combination of the political rights and civil liberties ratings, indicates the general state of freedom in a country or territory. The ratings of countries or territories which have improved or declined since the previous survey are indicated by upward or downward arrows, respectively. Positive or negative trends which do not warrant a ratings change since the previous year may be indicated by upward or downward trend arrows, which are located next to the name of the country or territory. A brief explanation of ratings changes or trend arrows is provided for each country or territory as required.

Following the section on political, economic, and social data, each country report is divided into two parts: an **overview** and an analysis of **political rights and civil liberties**. The overview provides a brief historical background and a description of current political events. The political rights and civil liberties section summarizes each country or territory's degree of respect for the rights and liberties which Freedom House uses to evaluate freedom in the world.

Reports on related and disputed territories follow the country reports. In most cases, these reports are comparatively brief and contain fewer categories of information than do the country essays. In this year's *Survey*, reports are included for 17 related and disputed territories, although ratings are provided for all 61 territories.

Afghanistan

Polity: Competing
warlords, traditional
rulers, and local councils
Economy: Mixed-statist
Population: 24,800,000
PPP: na
Life Expectancy: 46

Political Rights: 7
Civil Liberties: 7
Status: Not Free

Ethnic Groups: Pashtun (38 percent), Tajik (25 percent),
Hazara (19 percent), Uzbek (6 percent)
Capital: Kabul

Overview:

Two years after the Taliban captured Kabul and imposed the strict, centuries-old social code of isolated, mountain villages on more progressive urban areas, life in Afghanistan has returned to a pre-modern, Hobbesian form: nasty, short, and brutish. The Taliban's violent, arbitrary rule has imposed order through terror. Its dehumanization of women and girls has turned educated women into beggars; left widows, mothers, and daughters to die of illnesses that have been treatable for decades; and denied a generation of girls access to basic education.

Following a nineteenth century Anglo-Russian contest for domination, Britain recognized Afghanistan as an independent monarchy in 1921. King Zahir Shah ruled from 1933 until he was deposed in a 1973 coup. Since a Communist coup in 1978, Afghanistan has been in continuous civil conflict. In 1979, the Soviet Union invaded to install a pro-Moscow Communist faction. More than 100,000 Soviet troops faced fierce resistance from U.S.-backed, ethnic-based mujahideen guerrillas before withdrawing in 1989.

After overthrowing the Communist government in 1992, the mujahideen, backed by neighboring countries and regional powers, battled for control of Kabul and, by 1994, had reduced the city to rubble. Today, the main ethnic divide is between the rural-based Pashtuns, who form a near majority and have ruled for most of the past 250 years, and the large Tajik minority.

The Taliban, a new, Pashtun-based militia organized around theology students, began its conquest of the country in mid-1994. In 1996, it ousted the nominal Kabul government led by Burhanuddin Rabbani and his Tajik-dominated Jamiat-i-Islami (Islamic Association). Later that year, Ahmad Shah Masood, the ethnic Tajik military commander of the Rabbani government, and Uzbek warlord Rashid Dostum formed an anti-Taliban alliance.

In May 1997, Abdul Malik Pahlawan and other ethnic Uzbek commanders ousted Dostum and allowed the Taliban to control five key northern provinces under a power-sharing deal. The Taliban reneged, and northern troops quickly pushed back the Islamic militia. In November, Dostum's troops forced Pahwalan to flee to Iran.

In August and September 1998, the Taliban captured Mazar-i-Sharif and much of central Bamian province. While taking Mazar-i-Sharif, the Taliban massacred what are believed to be thousands of civilians, mainly ethnic Hazaras. The last major area remaining outside of the Taliban's control is the Panjshir Valley in the north, where Masood's Tajik troops continue to launch attacks against Taliban positions north of Kabul.

Political Rights and Civil Liberties: There are no democratic processes in Afghanistan. The Taliban, whose regime is recognized by only three foreign governments, control 90 percent of the country. The remainder is held by three main militias comprising the self-styled United Front: Tajik-based forces under Masood, Uzbek-based forces under Dostum's National Islamic Front faction, and a small Hazara Shiite-based Hezb-i-Wahadat militia led by Karim Khalili in central Afghanistan.

While eliminating banditry, the Taliban have largely neglected most government functions and have relied on the United Nations and foreign nongovernmental organizations (NGOs) to provide basic services. An inner circle of clerics issues strictly enforced decrees to regulate social affairs. Appointed local *shura* (councils) also rule by decree.

The judiciary consists of tribunals in which clerics with little legal training issue rulings based on Pashtun customs and the Taliban's interpretation of Shari'a law. Proceedings are brief, and defendants lack the right to legal counsel, due process, and appeal. Sentences are often carried out in public stadiums. Families of murder victims have the option of executing court-imposed death sentences or granting clemency. Victims' relatives have killed murderers on several occasions, and authorities have bulldozed alleged sodomists under walls, stoned adulterers to death, and amputated the hands of thieves.

Religious police have publicly beaten and otherwise humiliated hundreds of women for violating Taliban dress codes, which include wearing the *burqa*, a one-piece garment that covers the entire body. Soldiers, militiamen, and renegades abduct and rape scores of women each year.

The Taliban arbitrarily detain and torture thousands of men, particularly Hazaras and other ethnic minorities. Many have been killed or disappeared. Prison conditions are inhumane.

The Taliban have made the rural Islamic custom of *purdah*, under which women are isolated from men who are not relatives and cannot leave home unless escorted by a close male relative, mandatory even in urban areas. The Taliban also ban women from working, thereby curtailing not only income, but also female-based relief services. In 1997, the Taliban largely banned female medical workers from working in Kabul's hospitals and restricted female patients, who must be accompanied by a close male relative to be treated, to a few poorly equipped hospitals. As a result, most women in Kabul have little or no access to health care.

A 1997 Taliban decree that aid to women is to be provided only through male relatives has sharply curtailed foreign-funded food-for-work programs, which had supported approximately 35,000 war widows in Kabul. After girls were banned from attending school, unemployed teachers formed privately funded, underground "home schools" for girls. In June 1998, the Taliban ordered the closure of more than 100 home schools, as well as vocational centers for widows and other women in Kabul. Education is also poor for boys. Teachers are paid infrequently, and many fired female teachers have not been replaced.

Freedoms of speech, press, and association are sharply restricted. The Taliban closed the only television station in 1996, but air propaganda and issue decrees over Radio Voice of Shari'a. In July, the Taliban banned televisions, videocassette recorders, videos, and satellite dishes and began to destroy those found in shops. There are few, if any, civic institutions and no known trade unions.

The Taliban sharply restrict religious freedom and force men to grow beards and pray in mosques. The Hazara Shiite minority has faced particularly harsh treatment. In 1998, Afghanistan's warring parties killed scores of civilians through indiscriminate rocket and artillery attacks. Years of civil conflict have also internally displaced tens of thousands of people, including Tajiks and other ethnic minorities forcibly relocated by the Taliban since 1996. Approximately 1.2 million Afghans are refugees in Pakistan.

In areas beyond the Taliban's control, the rule of law is also non-existent. Justice is administered arbitrarily according to Shari'a and traditional customs. Rival groups torture and kill opponents and suspected sympathizers. In March, United Front soldiers killed at least eight people attending a peace rally in Mazar-i-Sharif. Opposition groups operate radio stations and publish propaganda newspapers.

Albania

Polity: Presidential-parliamentary democracy
Economy: Mixed statist (transitional)
Population: 3,300,000
PPP: $2,853
Life Expectancy: 72
Political Rights: 4
Civil Liberties: 5*
Status: Partly Free

Ethnic Groups: Albanians (95 percent), Greeks (3 percent), others, including Vlachs, Gypsies, Serbs and Bulgarians (2 percent)
Capital: Tirana
Ratings Change: Albania's civil liberties rating changed from 4 to 5 due to increased civil unrest and corruption.

Overview:

In September, Prime Minister Fatos Nano abruptly resigned amid civic unrest sparked by the assassination of Azem Hajdari, a leading member of the opposition Democratic Party (PD). The ruling Socialist Party elected Pandeli Majko, a former student leader, to form a new government. The Majko government faced debate over adoption of a post-Communist constitution and continued instability in the north and in the neighboring Yugoslav province of Kosovo.

Albania gained independence in 1912 after 450 years of Ottoman rule. Following the country's annexation by Italy in 1939, a one-party Communist regime was established in 1946 under World War II partisan Enver Hoxha, who died in office in 1985. In 1990, Ramiz Alia, the Socialist Party leader and Hoxha's successor as first secretary of the Albanian Party of Labor (Communist), was elected president. The PD won the 1992 elections, and the parliament elected PD leader Sali Berisha as president. The defeat of a government-backed constitution by referendum in 1994 and the passage in 1995 of the "genocide law" to bar former senior Communists from office until 2002 led to opposition charges that Berisha and the PD were becoming more authoritarian.

In 1997, anti-government riots erupted in Tirana as pyramid schemes that promised gullible savers monthly interest rates of 50 percent began to collapse. Months of escalating violence and unrest, particularly in the south, made the country virtually ungovernable and led to the deployment of an Italian-led 6,500-member international peacekeeping force. President Berisha, re-elected by parliament in March, was forced to call for new parliamentary elections. The June election campaign was marred by violence, especially in the south, where PD candidates were often attacked. Factional fighting continued through election day, when the Socialists and their allies won 119 of 155 seats. International observers nevertheless called the vote "adequate and acceptable." In July, Berisha resigned. As expected, the new parliament named Nano to lead the government and elected Rexhep Mejdani as president.

Despite massive foreign aid in 1998, the country's infrastructure remained in ruins, corruption was rife, criminal gangs operated with impunity, and government administration was weak or nonexistent. The PD boycotted parliament after the government decided to prosecute six Berisha government officials for allegedly using lethal gas to quell protests in 1997. The PD then mounted street protests and vowed to bring down the government. In September, the assassination of Hajdari, a top Berisha aide, led to days of rioting. After consultations with President Mejdani, Prime Minister Nano resigned and was replaced by Majko.

After consultations in October with the PS's coalition members, which included the Social Democratic Party, the Human Rights Party, and the Agrarian Party, a new government was inaugurated. Unlike the Nano cabinet, which only had one member from the south, Berisha's stronghold, the new government included four ministers from the region. Majko vowed that the government would begin talks with the opposition, restore public order, and pass a new constitution.

With a two-thirds majority, the PS-dominated parliament approved a new constitution. In a November 22 referendum, 93 percent of voters approved the constitution. Despite PD calls for a boycott, the Central Voting Commission announced that turnout was above the 50 percent required to make the vote valid. Beginning in March, the conflict in Kosovo led to a large influx of refugees, thereby adding to instability in the north.

Political Rights and Civil Liberties:

Albanians can elect their government democratically. Civil unrest forced the resignation of Prime Minister Fatos Nano in September 1998. The 1997 parliamentary elections, called after civil war ended President Sali Berisha's tenure, were marred by violence, fraud, and other serious irregularities.

In late 1998, the new Socialist government approved a new constitution that was approved by referendum. The Western-style constitution, supported by the OSCE, would allow Albanians legally to change their religion and the government to expropriate land deemed to be of national interest.

The Penal Code criminalizes defamation. Persons can face fines and imprisonment from three months to five years for denigrating the president or the nation and its symbols or for printing "false information." Few such cases arose in 1998. Several journalists were arrested during the civil unrest in September. Most of the print media are privately owned, as political parties, unions, and various societies publish their own papers. Approximately 250 newspapers, magazines, and journals are registered, but many are issued sporadically due to economic constraints, high taxation, and limited print facilities.

Albanian Radio-Television controls all electronic broadcasting. Its structure and leadership became a major political issue during the year. In October, parliament amended the law to restructure the radio and television agency as a public company with no single shareholder in any national radio or television station holding more than 33 percent of the shares. In January, the offices of SHIJAK-TV, a private station, were ransacked, allegedly by government supporters.

Religious activity is unrestricted in this predominantly Muslim country, which also has Orthodox Christian and Roman Catholic minorities. In August, in response to official U.S. and European concerns about terrorism, the government launched a broad crackdown on Arab and Islamic groups and missionaries.

Freedom of assembly is subject to government restrictions. Workers have the right to form independent unions. The umbrella Independent Confederation of Trade Unions of Albania has an estimated 280,000 members. The Confederation of Unions, a federation that is linked to the Socialist Party and that succeeded the official Communist-era entity, represents some workers in the education, petroleum, and telecommunications industries.

Albania's judiciary has been hampered by political pressure, insufficient resources, and corruption. The High Council of Justice, headed by the president, appoints and dismisses all other judges, and prosecutors serve at the pleasure of the Council. The Council has broad powers to fire, demote, transfer, and otherwise discipline district and appeals courts. In January, eight judges launched a hunger strike to protest their actual or impending dismissals.

A climate of lawlessness pervades much of the country, and citizens have no legal recourse due to ineffective or nonexistent police and other government institutions. Corruption is endemic at all levels of government, private business, state enterprises, and the civil service. Property rights are guaranteed by law, but the issue of restitution to owners whose property was seized by the Communists remains unresolved.

Algeria

Polity: Civilian-military **Political Rights:** 6
Economy: Statist **Civil Liberties:** 5*
Population: 30,200,000 **Status:** Not Free
PPP: $5,618
Life Expectancy: 67
Ethnic Groups: Arabs and Berber (99 percent),
European (1 percent)
Capital: Algiers
Ratings Change: Algeria's civil liberties rating changed
from 6 to 5 due to a slight easing of repression in the country.

Overview: Algerians suffered a seventh year of bloody civil conflict marked by horrific and often random violence that has claimed as many as 70,000 lives. The conflict between Islamist radicals and the country's military-dominated regime began in 1992 when the regime cancelled elections that Islamic parties appeared poised to win. Comprehension of the conflict is clouded by heavy official censorship and an Islamist murder campaign which has killed approximately 70 journalists and forced many into exile. While Islamist radical groups are primarily responsible for the vicious massacres of men, women, and children, government-backed militias have also apparently committed some mass killings. Human rights groups have also charged government forces with thousands of "disappearances," torture, and other excesses against alleged militants and their suspected supporters. The overall security situation improved in 1998, but daily killings continued in several parts of the country. In addition, new laws mandating the use of Arabic throughout the country has inflamed the minority Berber community, which has been a staunch foe of the Islamists.

President and former Major-General Lamine Zeroual announced in September that the next presidential elections would be advanced by over a year to early 1999 and that he would not be a candidate. Despite the slow reconstruction of representative institutions in Algeria, the army remains dominant, and Zeroual's successor will likely be determined by infighting between military factions long before any voter reaches the polls. Two leading contenders are Army Chief of Staff General Mohammad Lamari and Zeroual's top advisor, former military intelligence chief General Mohammad Betchine. There is no prospect for an early end to the war. The Islamic Salvation Front (FIS) has called for a ceasefire, but the extremist Armed Islamic Group (GIA) and other radical armed elements are unlikely to abandon the use of force unless they gain outright power, an outcome that the military will go to any lengths to prevent.

International policies towards Algeria are shaped both by revulsion over the ongoing violence and many countries' strong opposition to the extreme Islamist thrust for power. In July, the United Nations Human Rights Commission issued a report harshly critical of the Algerian regime's human rights record. In September, a report by a top-level UN mission to the country expressed qualified support for the Algerian authorities' efforts to quash the rebellion. According to the *Washington Post*, Western governments believe that this position reflected the "distasteful necessity of supporting an imperfect and intractable government seeking to thwart the much greater menace of an Islam-driven revolution only a few miles across the Mediterranean from Western Europe."

After a bloody liberation struggle convinced France to abandon its 130 years of colonial rule, Algeria achieved independence in 1962. The National Liberation Front (FLN) ruled as an effective one-party regime until the political system was reformed in 1989. Algeria's army canceled the second round of 1992 parliamentary elections in which the FIS had achieved a commanding lead. FIS's avowed aim to install theocratic rule under *Shari'a* law would have ended many constitutional protections, yet corruption, housing shortages, unemployment, and other severe economic and social problems had increased anti-government sentiment and convinced Algerians to vote for change. In 1993, Major General Lamine Zeroual was appointed president after President Chadli Benjedid was forced from office.

Political Rights and Civil Liberties: Algerians' right to choose their government freely in democratic elections has never been honored. The country has effectively been under martial law since the cancellation of the 1992 polls. The government-backed National Democratic Rally party scored a sweeping win in June 1997 legislative polls that excluded the main Islamic opposition groups and that were conducted under severe restrictions of freedom of expression and association. International observers found the parliamentary vote to be seriously flawed. A November 1995 presidential election victory gave Zeroual limited legitimacy in a vote that was restricted to regime-approved candidates and that drew a 75 percent turnout. A new constitution that was approved in a 1996 referendum expands presidential powers and bans Islamic-based parties. The declared emergency and an anti-terrorist decree give the regime almost unlimited power.

Human rights violations are rife, and the rule of law is seldom respected by any of the sides to the conflict. Members of the security forces and government officials are among the fundamentalists' favorite targets, but all of civil society and, increasingly, the civilian population are under threat. Unveiled women, Christians, foreigners, and other individuals not fully committed to an Islamist state are marked for execution. Many murders are committed in a calculatedly cruel manner to maximize their terrorist impact. Government security forces have responded brutally as well. Extrajudicial killings are allegedly common, even beyond the thousands of militants who have died in armed clashes. Many suspected militants and supporters are detained without trial, and reports of torture are common.

The civil war has drastically curtailed freedom of expression. Journalists, especially employees of state broadcast media, have been particular targets for Islamists. The regime is also unrelenting in its efforts to restrict and direct reporting. The state controls broadcast media and some newspapers and has repeatedly threatened and arrested reporters and editors and closed newspapers. Government censors must approve all war reports. These conditions have caused extensive self-censorship by the country's media. Approximately 500 Algerian journalists have fled the country, but more than 20 newspapers still publish and offer a lively, if circumscribed, forum for political debate.

Both Islamist terror and government strictures constrain public debate. Public assemblies other than those that support the government are rarely permitted, although legal opposition parties technically need no permission to hold meetings. Nongovernmental organizations must be licensed. The Algerian League for the Defense of Human Rights has offered harsh public criticism of human rights abuses. Matoub Lounes, a popular singer, leading figure of the minority Berber community, and public critic of both sides in the civil war, was murdered by Islamists in July. The Berber, who predominate in the northeastern Kabylie region, are targeted by extreme fundamentalists because of their more liberal interpretations of Islamic practice. They are also now in near rebellion because of strict new laws imposing Arabic as Algeria's only official language and downgrading the Berbers' native Tamazight language and related dialects.

Constitutionally guaranteed religious freedom is under threat by the fundamentalists. The GIA has publicly declared Christians, Jews, and polytheists to be targets. The *Shari'a*-based 1984 family code, other laws, and many traditional practices discriminate against women. Trade union rights are protected, and nearly two-thirds of the labor force is unionized. An FIS-allied union has been banned, but strikes and other union activity are legal. In September, the one-million-strong umbrella Algerian General Workers Union won concessions, including the limiting of factory closings, in a pact with the regime.

Algeria's economy is burdened with more than $30 billion in foreign debt, but foreign investment in oil exploration and production continues. Extractive industries produce few local jobs, however, and unemployment remains a serious problem. Privatization plans have been expanded, but the largest state-owned enterprises are not yet on offer.

Andorra

Polity: Parliamentary democracy
Economy: Capitalist
Population: 100,000
PPP: na
Life Expectancy: 79
Ethnic Groups: Spanish (61 percent), Andorran (30 percent), French (6 percent), other (3 percent)
Capital: Andorra la Vella

Political Rights: 1
Civil Liberties: 1
Status: Free

Overview:

Andorra became a sovereign parliamentary democracy and a member of the United Nations in 1993. Since 1278, its six parishes, under the joint control of France and the bishop of Urgel in Spain, had existed as an unwritten democracy without official borders. Since 1868, the General Council (parliament) has functioned in various legislative and executive capacities under the supervision of co-princes.

In 1990, the Council of Europe recommended that the principality adopt a modern constitution in order to achieve full integration into the European Union (EU). French President Francois Mitterrand and Bishop Joan Marti I Alanis agreed to grant full sovereignty to Andorra. Under the constitution, the French president and the bishop of Urgel, as co-princes, continue as heads of state, but they are represented locally by officials known as *veguers*. The head of government retains executive power.

Andorran politics are dominated by five major parties. Four of them governed in coalition until early 1997, at which time the Unio Liberal party won 18 of 28 General Council seats. Eighty-two percent of the country's eligible 10,837 voters cast ballots.

Andorra has no national currency, circulating French *francs* and Spanish *pesetas* instead. The country's duty-free status attracts large numbers of tourists, although the EU limits duty-free allowances, which has curtailed this source of revenue in recent years.

Under pressure from the EU, the government is continuing its efforts to modernize and liberalize the economy. Due to increasing debt and falling revenues from duty-free sales and tourism, Prime Minister Marc Forne Molne has vowed to streamline Andorra's relations with the EU and to open the country to more foreign investment.

Political Rights and Civil Liberties:

Andorrans can change their government democratically. The Sindic (President), subsindic, and the 28 members of the General Council are elected in general elections held every four years. The new constitution mandates that half of its representatives be elected by parish and half selected from nationwide lists.

The country's independent judiciary is based on the French and Spanish civil codes.

Citizens enjoy the right to due process, the presumption of innocence, and the right to legal council, including free counsel for the indigent.

The constitution proclaims respect for the promotion of liberty, equality, justice, tolerance, and the defense of human rights and human dignity. Torture and the death penalty are outlawed. There have been no documented cases of police brutality.

The constitution prohibits discrimination on the basis of birth, race, sex, origin, religion, disability, opinion, language, or any other "personal or social condition." Many rights and privileges, however, are granted only to Andorran citizens. Citizenship is attained through lineage, marriage, birth, or after 30 years of living and working in the country. Dual citizenship is prohibited, and immigrant workers are not entitled to social benefits. Noncitizens are allowed to own 33 percent of the shares of a company. Freedom of assembly, association, and religion is guaranteed. The 1993 constitution legalized trade unions for the first time, although no labor unions currently exist.

The constitution guarantees freedom of expression, communication, and information, but allows for laws regulating the right of reply, correction, and professional confidentiality. The domestic press consists of two daily and several weekly newspapers. There are two radio stations, one state-owned and the other privately owned, as well as six television stations. Several radio stations can be received from France and Spain.

The Roman Catholic Church is guaranteed the "preservation of the relations of special cooperation with the State in accordance with the Andorran tradition." The Church, however, is not subsidized by the government. The practice of other religions is respected, but subject to limitations "in the interests of public safety, order, health, or morals, or for the protection of the fundamental rights and freedoms of others."

There are no restrictions on domestic or foreign travel, emigration, or repatriation. Andorra has a tradition of providing asylum for refugees, although it has no formal asylum policy. Requests are considered on an individual basis.

Women were granted full suffrage in 1970, and there are no legal barriers to their political participation, although social conservatism continues to limit their involvement in politics.

Angola

Polity: Presidential-legislative
Economy: Statist
Population: 12,000,000
PPP: $1,839
Life Expectancy: 47
Ethnic Groups: Ovimbundu (37 percent), Kimbundu (25 percent), Bakongo (13 percent), mestico (2 percent), European (1 percent), other (22 percent)
Capital: Luanda

Political Rights: 6
Civil Liberties: 6
Status: Not Free

Overview:
Renewed large-scale warfare began at year's end as forces of the ruling Popular Movement for the Liberation of Angola (MPLA) and the rebel National Union for Total Independence

of Angola (UNITA) battled in December over several strategic provincial cities. Each side hoped to benefit from turmoil in the neighboring Democratic Republic of Congo. In an effort to defeat a rebel advance on Kinshasa in September, Angolan government forces once again intervened on behalf of Congo President Laurent Kabila. UNITA leader Jonas Savimbi was reportedly backing rebel forces in order to regain supply routes and staging areas long provided to him by Congo's former regime. Neither side has ever fully complied with the 1994 Lusaka Accords, which were meant to end nearly three decades of devastating warfare in Angola. The coalition Government of Unity and National Reconciliation installed in April 1997 now survives in name only. Its UNITA members split from Savimbi in August and have no genuine political base. Both sides have reportedly resumed laying land mines, although UNITA's loss of diamond-producing areas in northeastern Angola has seriously reduced its ability to wage a pro-tracted war. In addition, Savimbi's regional and international support is eroding. In September, the United Nations warned Savimbi that any further delay in compliance with the peace accords would result in his official exclusion from the process. In October, Southern African states pledged to aid the government militarily if UNITA resumes the war.

Increased oil production from offshore wells off the northern enclave of Cabinda, where a separatist movement continued to wage a bush war, provides 90 percent of the country's exports. Most Angolans remain desperately poor, however, because government revenues only feed the ongoing war. In August, the government reportedly reached an agreement to trade diamonds to Russia for weapons.

Angola achieved independence in November 1975 after 14 years of anti-colonial bush war and five centuries of Portuguese presence. The country immediately became a cockpit for a surrogate Cold War struggle, however, and 15 more years of fighting followed. During this time, Angola's ethnic-based rivals were armed by East and West, with Cuban and South African involvement on opposing sides. Massive covert American aid bolstered UNITA's fortunes, but produced no clear victor. The United Nations became deeply involved in the Angola peace process only with the Cold War's end. U.N.-supervised elections in September 1992 were described by international observers as generally free and fair despite many irregularities, but failed to end the long-running war. When MPLA leader Jose Eduardo dos Santos nearly won a majority in the first round of voting, UNITA leader and presidential candidate Savimbi rejected his defeat and resumed the guerrilla war.

By the time of the 1994 peace accord, as many as a half million people had died in combat and from starvation and disease in 20 years of war. Continuing uncertainty hinders economic reconstruction for the country's 12 million people.

Political Rights and Civil Liberties: Angolans freely elected their own representatives for the only time in 1992 presidential and legislative elections. The second round runoff required when neither presidential candidate won an outright majority was canceled when UNITA returned to war, but President dos Santos nevertheless assumed office. The MPLA dominates the 220-member national assembly.

The political process has been subsumed by the military contest between the MPLA and UNITA. Broader popular participation, especially from the rural areas where the vast majority of Angolans live, therefore remains problematic. New elections have been provisionally scheduled for 2000, but it is not certain that the Angolan people will yet be free to change their government through the ballot box.

In 1998, serious human rights abuses by both government security forces and UNITA were reported, including torture and extrajudicial executions. Local courts rule on civil matters and petty crime in some areas, but an overall lack of training and infrastructure inhibit judicial proceedings, which are also heavily influenced by the government. Many prisoners were detained for long periods while awaiting trial in life-threatening conditions.

In October, renewed fighting between government forces and secessionist guerrilla groups, most of which are offshoots of the *Frente para a Libertação do Enclave de Cabinda* (Front for the Liberation of the Enclave of Cabinda), was reported in the oil-rich and little-developed northern enclave of Cabinda. In April, Amnesty International stated that it had received many credible reports of torture and killings of civilians by security forces in the territory. Several attempts at negotiation have produced offers of limited revenue-sharing by the central government. It is inconceivable that any Angolan government would allow more than limited autonomy to an area in which oil exports bring approximately $700 million to the central treasury each year.

Scant media freedom exists in areas controlled by either the government or UNITA. Harassment of journalists is common, and the few newspapers that appear regularly practice self-censorship. A government committee exercises formal censorship. The government maintains a tight rein on its own daily newspaper and the broadcast media, although some critical independent newsletters are distributed in Luanda. In October, the government dropped some of the UN programming carried on state radio after a top UN peacekeeper criticized the government. The January 1995 murder of independent journalist Ricardo de Mello in Luanda and the October 1996 killing of state television journalist Antonio Casmiro in Cabinda remain unsolved. Freedom of association is constitutionally guaranteed, but is often not respected in practice.

Despite legal protections, de facto societal discrimination against women remains strong, particularly in rural areas. Religious freedom is generally respected. Constitutional guarantees protect labor rights, although implementing legislation and administrative procedures are lacking. Some independent unions are functioning, but all organized labor activities are in Angola's cities. The vast majority of rural agricultural workers remain outside of the modern economic sector.

Official claims of a per capita income of approximately $300 grossly overestimate the average Angolan's income. Most export income from oil and diamonds goes to the country's small elite and for military spending. The state is still deeply involved in the country's limited economic activity, and genuine development is unlikely without a durable peace. Corruption and black market activities are widespread. Proposed limited privatization will likely be slowed by the political elite's stake in government holdings.

Antigua and Barbuda

Polity: Dominant party
Economy: Capitalist-statist
Population: 100,000
PPP: $9,131
Life Expectancy: 74
Ethnic Groups: Black (89 percent), other, including British, Protuguese, Lebanese, and Syrian (11 percent)
Capital: St. John's

Political Rights: 4
Civil Liberties: 3
Status: Partly Free

Overview:

International suspicions regarding the real purposes of dozens of low profile businesses established by Russian investors in the Caribbean have focused on offshore banks and trust and insurance companies in Antigua and Barbuda. Concerns that these enterprises may be laundering the proceeds from crime syndicates in the former Soviet Union have led the government of Prime Minister Lester Bird to begin to restrict the influx of Russian capital and monitor financial operations.

Antigua and Barbuda is a member of the British Commonwealth. The British monarchy is represented by a governor-general. The islands gained independence in 1981. Under the constitution, the political system is a parliamentary democracy, with a bicameral parliament consisting of an appointed senate and a 17-member House of Representatives elected for five years. In the House, there are 16 seats for Antigua and one for Barbuda. Eleven senators are appointed by the prime minister, four by the parliamentary opposition leader, one by the Barbuda Council, and one by the governor-general.

Antigua and Barbuda has been dominated by the Bird family and the Antigua Labour Party (ALP) for decades. Rule has been based more on power and the abuse of authority than on law. The constitution has been consistently disregarded.

In 1994 Vere Bird, the patriarch of the most prominent family, resigned as prime minister in favor of his son Lester. Prior to the 1994 elections, three opposition parties united to form the United Progressive Party (UPP). Labor activist Baldwin Spencer became UPP leader, and Tim Hector, editor of the outspoken weekly *Outlet*, became deputy leader. The UPP campaigned on a social democratic platform that emphasized rule of law and good governance. In the election, the ALP won 11 parliamentary seats, down from 15 in 1989. The UPP won 5 , up from 1 in 1989. The Barbuda People's Movement retained the Barbuda seat, thereby giving the opposition a total of six seats. Despite unfair campaign conditions, the UPP opted to accept the outcome because it believed that political momentum was now on its side.

After taking office as prime minister, Lester Bird promised cleaner, more efficient government, but his administration continued to be dogged by scandals and corruption. In 1997, a U.S. State Department report took aim at the "inadequate regulation and vetting" of the 57 banks that have opened on the islands in the last ten years. In 1998, Antigua and Barbuda's offshore industry was rocked by the disclosure of what the U.S. Customs Service called the biggest non-narcotics money laundering racket that it had ever uncovered.

The Bird government still clearly hopes to diversify the tourist-dependent economy through offshore banking. In December, it issued new legislation on international corporate structures. The new law includes oversight mechanisms, but does not mandate cooperation with foreign tax investigations.

Political Rights and Civil Liberties: Constitutionally, citizens are able to change their government by democratic means. Political parties, labor unions, and civic organizations are free to organize. The 1994 elections, however, were neither free nor fair. The balloting system did not guarantee a secret vote, the ruling party dominated the broadcast media and excluded the opposition, the voter registration system was deficient, and the voter registry was inflated by as much as 30 percent with names of people who had died or left the country.

The judiciary is nominally independent, but weak and subject to political manipulation by the ruling party. It has been nearly powerless to address corruption in the executive branch. Legislation allows for the issuance of Internet casino licenses that, like those of offshore banks, promise minimum regulation, maximum discretion, and no taxation. The police generally respect human rights, but basic police reporting statistics are confidential.

The ALP government and the Bird family control the country's television, cable, and radio outlets. During the 1994 elections, the opposition was allowed to purchase broadcast time only to announce its campaign events. The government barred the UPP from the broadcast media through a strict interpretation of the country's archaic electoral law, which prohibits broadcast of any item for the "purpose of promoting or procuring the election of any candidate or of any political party." Meanwhile, the ALP launched a concerted political campaign thinly disguised as news about the government.

The government, the ruling party, and the Bird family also control four newspapers, including *Antigua Today*, an expensively produced weekly established in 1993 as an election vehicle for Lester Bird. The opposition counts solely on *Outlet*, which the government attempts to thwart through intimidation and libel suits, and the *Daily Observer*, a small but vocal publication.

Freedom of religion is respected. An industrial court mediates labor disputes, but public sector unions tend to be influenced by the ruling party. Demonstrators are occasionally subject to harassment by the police, who are politically linked to the ruling party.

Argentina

Polity: Federal presiden- **Politic Rights:** 3*
tial-legislative democracy **Civil Liberties:** 3
Economy: Capitalist **Status:** Free
Population: 36,100,000
PPP: $8,498
Life Expectancy: 72
Ethnic Groups: European [mostly Spanish and Italian],
(85 percent), mestizo, Amerindian, and other nonwhites (15 percent)
Capital: Buenos Aires
Ratings Change: Argentina's political rights rating changed from 2 to 3 due to government spying on, and the extortion of, political leaders, including the videotaping of consensual sexual acts between adults; gross indifference to official corruption; the "packing" of the Argentine senate by the ruling party; and a public campaign waged by the president against independent federal prosecutors.

Overview:　In 1998, President Carlos Menem's hopes of winning legal sanction for a third consecutive term ebbed despite strong-arm tactics employed against a usually compliant judiciary. Public opinion surveys continued to cite rampant official corruption and lack of public safety as major concerns. Corruption scandals involving Menem cabinet ministers and senior police officials, intelligence agency extortion of business and political leaders secretly filmed in a gay bordello, and the unseemly suicides of three key witnesses in earlier government corruption cases fueled public unease.

The Argentine Republic was established after independence from Spain in 1816. Democratic rule was often interrupted by military coups. The end of Juan Peron's authoritarian rule in 1955 led to a series of right-wing military dictatorships, and left-wing and nationalist violence. Argentina returned to elected civilian rule in 1983 after seven years of vicious repression of suspected leftist guerrillas and other dissidents.

As amended in 1994, the 1853 constitution provides for a president elected for four years with the option of re-election to one additional term. Presidential candidates must win 45 percent of the vote to avoid a runoff vote. The legislature consists of a 257-member Chamber of Deputies elected for six years, with half of the seats renewable every three years, and a 72-member Senate nominated by elected provincial legislatures for nine-year terms, with one-third of the seats renewable every three years. Two senators are directly elected in the newly autonomous Buenos Aires federal district.

Provincial governor Menem, running on an orthodox Peronist platform of nationalism and state intervention in the economy, won a six-year presidential term in 1989. After the election, he discarded statist Peronist traditions by implementing, mostly by decree, an economic liberalization program. In 1995, he handily won re-election, and his Peronist party also won a narrow majority in both houses of Congress.

In October1997, Menem's Peronists experienced their first nationwide defeat in a decade. An alliance of the Radical Party and the center-left Front for a Country in Solidarity won nearly 46 percent of the vote. Menem's party won 36 percent. In November 1998. Buenos Aires Mayor and Radical Party leader Fernando de la Rua won a contested primary to become the alliance's presidential candidate in 1999. Fears of an impending opposition victory led Menem to direct a campaign against federal prosecutors investigating government corruption. He also orchestrated the packing of the Argentine senate with two members of his ruling party in an effort to prevent corruption inquiries until at least 2001.

Political Rights and Civil Liberties: Citizens can change their government through elections. Constitutional guarantees regarding freedom of religion and the right to organize political parties, civic organizations, and labor unions are generally respected. Under Menem, legislative authority has been circumvented by the use of more "necessity and urgency" decrees than by all other previous civilian and military regimes combined.

Journalists and human rights groups are generally allowed to operate freely, but both have been subject to anonymous threats and various forms of intimidation, including more than 1,000 beatings, kidnappings, and telephone death threats during Menem's rule. International pressure has prevented the government from passing a series of restrictive press laws.

Labor is dominated by Peronist unions. Union influence has diminished, however, due to corruption scandals, internal divisions, and restrictions on public sector strikes decreed by Menem to pave the way for his privatization program. In 1998, a deadlocked parliament approved a government-sponsored labor "flexiblization' initiative after a parliamentary deputy allegedly filmed by state intelligence agents in a gay bordello changed political positions and voted for the measure.

Menem's authoritarian practices and manipulation of the judiciary have undermined the country's separation of powers and the rule of law. In 1990, Menem obtained passage in the Peronist-controlled Senate of a bill that allowed him to stack the Supreme Court with an additional four members and to fill the judiciary with politically loyal judges.

Menem has used the Supreme Court to uphold decrees removing the comptroller general and other officials mandated to probe government wrongdoing. In general, the judicial system is politicized, inefficient, and riddled with the corruption endemic to all branches of government. In 1998, as Menem's re-election fortunes appeared to wane, some members of the judiciary appeared to take a somewhat more independent course. Menem nevertheless spearheaded an effort to derail an investigation into official misconduct in international arms trafficking by seeking to discredit the federal prosecutor leading the probe.

In 1990, Menem pardoned military officers convicted of human rights violations committed during the country's so-called "dirty war," in which the guerrilla threat was vastly exaggerated in order to justify a 1976 coup. In 1998, the courts ruled that five former military junta leaders released by Menem should stand trial for the kidnapping of the children of dissidents murdered by the regime.

Police misconduct, often apparently promoted by senior government officials, has resulted in a number of allegedly extrajudicial executions by law enforcement officers. In 1998, the federal police high command was purged after press reports of bribery and other wrongdoing. Arbitrary arrests and mistreatment by police are rarely punished in civil courts due to intimidation of witnesses and judges. Criminal court judges are frequent targets of anonymous threats. The investigation of a 1994 car bombing of a Jewish organization has languished in part due to poor police work at the crime scene, but also reportedly in part due to complicity by members of the security forces with the terrorists.

The country's Roman Catholic majority enjoys freedom of religious expression. The 250,000-strong Jewish community is a frequent target of anti-Semitic vandalism. Neo-Nazi organizations and other anti-Semitic groups remain active.

Armenia

Polity: Presidential-
parliamentary democracy
Economy: Mixed statist
(transitional)
Population: 3,800,000
PPP: $2,208
Life Expectancy: 73

Political Rights: 4*
Civil Liberties: 4
Status: Partly Free

Ethnic Groups: Armenian (93 percent), Azeri (3 percent), Russian (2 percent), Kurd and others (2 percent)
Capital: Yerevan
Ratings change: Armenia's political rights rating changed from 5 to 4 due to the legalization of the leading opposition party and reasonably free presidential elections.

Overview:
President Levon Ter Petrosian, who had led Armenia since independence from the Soviet Union in 1991, resigned in February. The move followed mass defections from his ruling Armenian National Movement (ANM)-led coalition and the resignation of key officials in protest against his gradualist approach in negotiations over control of Nagorno-Karabakh, the Armenian enclave in Azerbaijan. In March, Prime Minister Robert Kocharian, who was appointed by Petrosian in 1997 and formerly served as president of Nagorno-Karabakh, was elected president with the support of the formerly banned Armenian Revolutionary Federation (ARF-Dashnak).

The landlocked, predominantly Christian Transcaucus republic of Armenia was ruled at various times by Macedonians, Romans, Persians, Mongols, and others. Prior to their defeat in World War I, Ottoman Turks controlled a western region and, between 1894 and 1915, engaged in a systematic genocide. The Russian region came under Communist control and was designated a Soviet republic in 1922 after western Armenia was returned to Turkey. Armenia declared its independence from the Soviet Union in September 1991.

Prior to 1995 parliamentary elections, ARF-Dashnak and eight other parties were banned, thereby ensuring the dominance of Petrosian's ruling ANM coalition. Petrosian's Republican bloc won control of two-thirds of the seats. Approximately 25 percent of the ballots were declared invalid. Approximately 68 percent of voters approved the government-backed constitution, which provides for a weak legislature and a strong presidency.

In the 1996 presidential election, Petrosian defeated former Prime Minister Vazgen Manukian, who ran on a promarket, anti-corruption platform. The state-appointed central and regional electoral commissions, which included 160 Petrosian loyalists among their 240 members, announced that the president had won 51 percent of the vote, thereby avoiding a runoff election. The results sparked three days of mass protests in Yerevan. Western observers responded by urging the government to investigate irregularities.

In campaigning for the March 1998 presidential elections, the newly legalized ARF-Dashnak and the Yerkrapah bloc led the Justice and Unity Alliance, a five-party coalition, in support of Prime Minister Kocharian. Kocharian defeated Karen Demirchian, who ruled Soviet Armenia from 1974 to 1988, with 60 percent of a second-round vote. Western observers noted irregularities in the first round, but found that they did not affect the outcome. The second round was deemed an improvement, but some observers cited significant flaws. In April, President Kocharian appointed former Finance and Economy Minister Armen Darbinian as prime minister. Several key opposition figures were named as presidential advisors.

In April, President Kocharian appointed a special commission to amend the constitution to define relations between the branches of government more clearly. The National Democratic Union (NDU) and other groups maintained that the current constitution was adopted by a fraudulent referendum in 1995 and was therefore illegitimate. The constitutional commission, dominated by government officials, rejected an NDU demand for a transition to a parliamentary republic.

In Nagorno-Karabakh, the cease-fire in force since 1994 continued to be largely observed, but no major progress was registered in international peace negotiations. Armenia continued to insist that Nagorno-Karabakh abandon its goal of outright independence from Azerbaijan and that Baku drop its insistence on a conventional autonomous status for the disputed region.

Political Rights and Civil Liberties: Democracy was seriously undermined by the 1995 parliamentary and 1996 presidential elections, which were fraught with irregularities. In 1995, the government banned nine parties, including the ARF- Dashnak. International monitors characterized the 1998 presidential election as "deeply flawed."

All print, radio, and television media must register with the ministry of justice. Papers routinely permit government censors to review material, and self-censorship is common to avoid suspension. Scores of private newspapers operate independently, however, or in open affiliation with opposition political parties. Libel laws have been used to intimidate the media. In June, parliamentary speaker Khosrov Harutiunian filed libel charges against the editor of the newspaper *Iravunk* for remarking on a national television show that parliament was "95 percent criminal." More than 120 television and radio stations are registered. There are two state-owned television channels and a number of private cable broadcasters. There are also two independent radio stations and five independent news agencies in Yerevan. In August, the Snark news agency complained that it was being excluded from presidential events by the Kocharian administration. In May, several media groups wrote to Kocharian to protest that the country's media were being hindered by economic conditions, a shortage of equipment, high production costs, and a continuing monopoly on distribution.

Freedom of religion in this overwhelmingly Christian country is generally respected, but the government has periodically launched campaigns against Protestant sects.

Freedom of assembly is generally respected, although permits are needed for demonstrations. The constitution enshrines the right to form and join trade unions, most of which are holdovers from the Soviet era and operate under the umbrella of the Confederation of Labor Unions. The Federation of Independent Labor Unions was founded in 1997 to compete with the confederation. Professional organizations, community groups, and other nongovernmental organizations function without undue government interference.

The judiciary is not independent, with the president appointing all judges. A constitutionally mandated Judicial Council is chaired by the president and includes two legal scholars, nine judges, and three prosecutors, all of whom are appointed by the president. It prepares lists of judges and prosecutors to be considered for appointments, promotions, or dismissals. In July, the chairman of the parliamentary commission on state and legal issues announced that a new judicial and legal system would take effect in January 1999. Corruption and bribery of judges, particularly in cases involving business crimes, remain pervasive.

The right to private property is enshrined in the constitution. While citizens have the right to establish businesses under several laws, regulation and an inefficient and sometimes corrupt bureaucracy and court system hinder operations. Key industries remain in the hands of oligarchs and influential clans who received preferential treatment in the early stages of privatization.

Employers are prohibited by law from discriminating against women. The law is frequently violated in practice, however, and women face obstacles to advancement in business and government.

Australia

Polity: Federal parliamentary democracy
Economy: Capitalist
Population: 18,700,000
PPP: $19,632
Life Expectancy: 78
Ethnic Groups: Caucasian (92 percent), Asian (7 percent), Aboriginal [including mixed] (1 percent)
Capital: Canberra

Political Rights: 1
Civil Liberties: 1
Status: Free

Overview:

Buffeted by divisive social and economic issues, Premier John Howard's conservative governing coalition withstood a strong challenge by the resurgent Labor Party in October 1998 elections. Rural farmers and townspeople, stung by globalization, signaled their disillusionment with traditional parties by giving 8.4 percent of the vote to a far-right party.

The British claimed Australia in 1770. In 1901, six states gained independence as the Commonwealth of Australia. The Northern Territory and the capital territory of Canberra were added as territorial units in 1911. The Queen of England is the nominal head of state in this parliamentary democracy. The directly elected bicameral parliament consists of a 76-member Senate and a 148-member House of Representatives.

Power is vested in a cabinet headed by a prime minister whose party or coalition commands the most support in the House.

Since World War II, political power has alternated between the center-left Labor Party and the center-right coalition of the Liberal Party and the smaller, rural-based National Party. Beginning in 1983, the Labor Party under Bob Hawke and Paul Keating began to cut tariffs and deregulate financial markets to hone the economy for global competition. A decade of restructuring took its toll on ordinary Australians, however, and many viewed Keating as indifferent to the country's high unemployment. In the 1996 elections, the Liberal-National coalition won power with 94 seats. The Labor Party won 49 seats.

In his first term, Howard faced divisive issues that sharpened cleavages over Australia's rural-urban divide and cultural identity. In June 1998, MP Pauline Hanson's far-right One Nation Party, in its first campaign, won 23 percent of the vote in Queensland state elections. One Nation's anti-Aboriginal land rights, anti-Asian immigration, and protectionist platform tapped into rising job insecurity among economically marginalized farmers and townspeople in this conservative, largely rural state. In July, Howard satisfied demands of farmers and miners by winning passage of controversial legislation restricting Aboriginal claims to pastoral lands. Wary that Asia's economic crisis could slow the Australian economy, Howard called an early election for October 3, 1998. The Liberal-National coalition won 70 seats (64 and 16, respectively). The Labor Party won 66. One Nation won 8.39 percent of the popular vote, but Hanson lost her seat. The party's only victory was one Senate seat.

Political Rights and Civil Liberties:

Australians can change their government democratically. Fundamental freedoms are respected. The judiciary is independent, although the official Law Reform Commission reported in the mid-1990s that women face discrimination in the legal system.

Australia's main human rights problem is the treatment of its indigenous population of approximately 386,000 Aborigines and Torres Straits Islanders. Aborigines face arbitrary arrest, systemic discrimination, and mistreatment by police. They are incarcerated at higher rates than whites, often because they cannot afford a fine or are denied bail for minor offenses, and die in custody at far higher rates than whites. A 1997 Amnesty International report found that mistreatment, a systemic lack of care, and inadequate investigations into Aboriginal deaths still characterize the penal system. Gaps in health indicators between the indigenous and white populations are among the highest for developed countries. Aborigines also face societal discrimination and inferior educational opportunities. The government is generally responsive to these concerns, and the 1999 budget boosted Aboriginal healthcare funding.

A landmark 1992 High court ruling formally recognized that, from a legal standpoint, Aborigines inhabited Australia prior to the British arrival. Native title could thus still be valid where Aboriginal groups maintained a connection to the land. The 1993 Native Title Act required the government to compensate groups with valid claims to state land, but left unclear the status of pastoral land (state land leased to farmers and miners), which represents approximately 42 percent of Australian territory. In 1996, the High Court ruled that native title can coexist with pastoral leases, although pastoral rights would take precedence over native title claims. In 1998, farmers and mining companies successfully lobbied for legislation curbing Aboriginal rights to claim title over pastoral land.

In May, the official Human Rights Commission criticized the practice of detaining asylum seekers pending resolution of their claims. Most are Asian boat people, and the strain of detention for up to five years has led to several suicides. Domestic violence is common.

Australian trade unions are independent and active, although recent labor legislation has caused union rolls to decline. The 1994 Industrial Relations Reform Act encouraged the use of workplace contracts linked to productivity rather than industry-wide collective bargaining. The 1997 Workplace Relations Act restricted the right to strike to periods when contracts are being negotiated, abolished closed shops, and limited redress for unfair dismissal. In March 1998, the International Labor Organization (ILO) ruled that the Workplace Relations Act breaches ILO conventions because it does not promote collective bargaining.

Austria

Polity: Federal parliamentary democracy
Economy: Mixed capitalist
Population: 8,100,000
PPP: $21,322
Life Expectancy: 77
Ethnic Groups: German (99 percent), other, including Slovene, Croat (1 percent)
Capital: Vienna

Political Rights: 1
Civil Liberties: 1
Status: Free

Overview:

In July, Austria assumed the presidency of the European Union (EU), thereby leading a major international institution for the first time since the end of the Hapsburg empire 70 years ago. This public role, however, also brought greater exposure to rifts in Austria's coalition government. Chancellor Victor Klima, who replaced Franz Vranitzky in 1997, and his Social Democratic Party (SPO), which has dominated national political life for 28 years, seek to maintain Austria's traditional neutrality and claim that there is insufficient popular support for the country to seek NATO membership. At the same time, Foreign Minister Wolfgang Schussel, the leader of the SPO's junior coalition partner, the Christian Democratic Austrian People's Party (OVP), argues that Austria should join NATO, just as it joined the EU, and influence the policy of an organization that clearly affects events in Austria. The SPO and the OVP have governed in coalition for twelve years.

Klima, whose mantra has been "politics must intervene to ensure justice," attempted to force the EU to focus as much on reducing unemployment as on creating monetary stability.

Meanwhile, the nationalist Freedom Party and its anti-Semitic leader, Jorg Haider, continued to gain political influence. The party, which is the largest far-right party in Europe, now commands the support of approximately one-fourth of the electorate and is the second largest party on Vienna's city council. Its popularity, however, may be affected by a financial scandal involving deputy party leader Peter Rosenstingl, who fled to Brazil with nearly $50 million in party and public funds.

The Republic of Austria was established in 1918 after the collapse of the Austro-Hungarian Empire, and was reborn in 1945, seven years after its annexation by Nazi Germany. Occupation by the Western allies and the Soviet Union ended in 1955 under the Austrian State Treaty, which guaranteed Austrian neutrality and restored national sovereignty.

Political Rights and Civil Liberties:

Austrians can change their government democratically. The country's provinces possess considerable latitude in local administration and can check federal power by electing members of the upper house of parliament. Voting is compulsory in some provinces. The independent judiciary is headed by a Supreme Court and includes both constitutional and administrative courts.

A 1955 treaty prohibits Nazis from exercising freedom of assembly or association. Nazi organizations are illegal, but Nazis are welcomed in the Freedom Party. In 1992, public denial of the Holocaust and justification of approval of Nazi crimes against humanity were outlawed. In general, Austrian police enforce these anti-Nazi statutes more enthusiastically when extremists attract international attention.

Austrian media are free. Legal restrictions on press freedom on the grounds of public morality or national security are rarely invoked. The Austrian Broadcasting Company, which controls radio and television, is state-owned, but protected from political interference by a broadcasting law.

Women hold approximately 10 percent of Federal Assembly seats and approximately 20 percent of provincial seats. They are prohibited by law from working at night in most occupations. Nurses, taxi drivers, and a few other occupations are exempted from this ban. Women generally earn 20 percent less than men and are not allowed to serve in the military. The ruling SPO party has pledged to begin to address gender biases by ensuring that women occupy 40 percent of all party and government posts by 2003.

Under the informal *proporz* system, many state and private sector appointments—including those of senior teachers in state schools—are made on the basis of affiliation with the two main political parties.

Trade unions retain an important independent voice in Austria's political, social, and economic life. Fifty-two percent of workers are organized in 14 national unions, all of which belong to the Austrian Trade Union Federation and which are managed by supporters of the country's traditional political parties.

Although not explicitly guaranteed in the constitution or national legislation, the right to strike is universally recognized.

↓ Azerbaijan

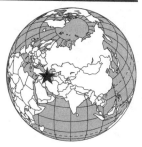

Polity: Presidential (dominant party)
Political Rights: 6
Civil Liberties: 4
Status: Partly Free
Economy: Mixed statist (transitional)
Population: 7,700,000
PPP: $1,463
Life Expectancy: 70
Ethnic Groups: Azeri (90 percent), Dagestani Peoples (3 percent), Russian (3 percent), Armenian (2 percent), other (2 percent)
Capital: Baku
Trend Arrow: Azerbaijan receives a downward trend arrow due to unfair presidential elections, a renewed crackdown on the opposition, and corruption.

Overview:

Haydar Aliev, a former KGB general and Soviet-era politburo member, was re-elected president of Azerbaijan on October 11, 1998. The election was boycotted by leading opposition parties and characterized by international monitors as fraught with irregularities. During the year, leading issues included securing new oil deals with foreign companies, completing a pipeline route, resolving the conflict over the secessionist Armenian enclave of Nagorno-Karabakh, and narrowing the gulf between a wealthy, corrupt elite and an impoverished citizenry that has not seen the benefits of the country's highly profitable oil and gas exploration.

Persia and the Ottoman Empire competed for Azeri territory in the sixteenth century, with the former gaining control in 1603. The northern sector, ceded to Russia in the early 1800s, briefly joined Armenia and Georgia in the Transcaucasia Federation after the 1917 Bolshevik Revolution. It proclaimed its independence the following year, but was subdued by the Red Army in 1920. In 1922, it entered the Soviet Union as part of the Transcaucasian Soviet Federal Republic. It became a separate Soviet Socialist republic in 1936. Azerbaijan declared independence from the Soviet Union after a referendum in 1991.

The key political issue in 1998 was the presidential election and indications that some segments of the ruling Yeni Azerbaijan were dissatisfied with official corruption and the grooming of President Aliyev's son as successor. In February, Foreign Minister Hasan Hasanov was forced to resign after an investigation by a special corruption commission found that he had diverted a Turkish loan to finance a luxury hotel and casino complex in Baku. In June, Nizami Suleymanov, the chairman of Yeni Azerbaijan, announced that he would run for president and pledged to introduce reforms and combat corruption.

In March, the opposition Azerbaijan Popular Front, Musavat, Liberal, and Democratic parties formed a coalition to ensure that the presidential elections were fair. It announced a boycott, however, after a new election law allowed President Aliyev and the rubber-stamp parliament to appoint the Central Election Commission and permitted police and security forces to monitor voting at polling stations. In addition to Suleymanov, President Aliyev was challenged by Etibar Mamedov, whose pro-government Democratic Party of Independence of Azerbaijan had split in 1997, and four other candidates.

The Central Election Commission announced that President Aliyev received 72 percent of the vote, more than the two-thirds necessary to avoid a runoff election. Mamedov finished second with 11 percent. Western observers reported "serious irregularities."

At year's end, international mediation efforts over control of the disputed enclave of Nagorno-Karabakh remained inconclusive. Azerbaijan continued to support a phased approach through which Armenia would return occupied Azeri territory, the blockade of Armenia would be lifted, and refugees would be returned prior to a final decision on the enclave's status.

Political Rights and Civil Liberties: Azerbaijan's citizens cannot change their government democratically. President Aliyev has imposed a totalitarian regime while building a cult of personality. The 1995 constitution gives the president control over the government, legislature, and judiciary.

While a 1992 media law and the 1995 constitution enshrine the principles of press freedom, in reality the print media in Azerbaijan are subject to harassment, and the state-run electronic media are firmly in the hands of the government and President Aliyev. In August, President Aliyev signed a decree abolishing *Glavlit*, the main department for protection of state secrets in the press. In June, the *Chag* daily accused the government of intimidation after its offices were searched, equipment confiscated, and several journalists briefly detained. Several articles in the criminal code limit criticism of government officials. Forty-seven radio and television companies are registered with the government, but only eight are operating. Most private newspapers operate with precarious finances and depend on government-controlled printing and distribution facilities.

Most Azeris are Shiite Muslims. The Russian and Jewish minorities can worship freely. There have been reports of continued persecution of the small Kurdish minority and the Lezhgin people. Most Armenian Christians outside of Nagorno-Karabakh were expelled during ethnic tensions in the early 1990s.

Freedom of assembly and association have been curtailed. Scores of demonstrators were arrested during several rallies in September, but most were subsequently released.

More than 45 parties applied for official registration prior to the 1995 parliamentary vote, but only 32 were recognized by the Ministry of Justice. Since 1996, several parties and opposition organizations have been banned. In March, the Ministry of Justice threatened to take legal action against the opposition Brotherhood, Evolution, and Moderan Turan Party for engaging in "illegal acts and activities."

The largest labor organization is the government-subsidized, post-Communist Azerbaijan Labor Federation. The largest independent union is the oil workers' union, which represents approximately 80 percent of the industry's workers. In August, the Committee for the Protection of Oilmen's Rights charged that foreign oil companies pay local workers less than foreign workers for the same work and deprive local workers of benefits such as sick leave.

The constitution provides for a judicial system of limited independence. A 1997 judicial reform law created regional appellate courts and an appellate Supreme Court. With parliamentary approval, the president appoints Supreme Court and Constitutional Court judges. The judicial system is subject to the influence of executive authorities and is inefficient and corrupt. In July, former prime minister Suret Huseynov, who was extradited from Russia in 1997, was tried for treason for his part in a failed 1994 coup.

The constitution enshrines the right to property and freedom of enterprise and business. Privatization has led to a rise in small businesses, mostly in the retail and service sectors, and a significant segment of urban housing has been privatized. Bureaucratic hurdles and rampant corruption at all levels of government and services are common. Significant parts of the economy remain in the hands of a corrupt nomenklatura, including many individuals from President Aliyev's native Nakichevan region. These factors severely limit equality of opportunity. Most Azeris, particularly refugees from Nagorno-Karabakh, live in privation.

Cultural traditions often impede resolution of social problems and perpetuate discrimination and violence against women.

Bahamas

Polity: Parliamentary democracy
Economy: Capitalist-statist
Population: 300,000
PPP: $15,738
Life Expectancy: 72
Ethnic Groups: Black (85 percent), white [British, Canadian, U.S.] (15 percent)
Capital: Nassau

Political Rights: 1
Civil Liberties: 2
Status: Free

Overview: In 1998, reformist Prime Minister Hubert Ingraham, whose re-election victory in 1997 marked a generational shift in Bahamian politics, began to honor his commitment to wage a tough campaign against crime.

The Commonwealth of the Bahamas, a 700-island nation in the Caribbean, is a member of the British Commonwealth. It was granted independence in 1973. The British monarchy is represented by a governor-general. Under the 1973 constitution, the country's bicameral parliament consists of a House of Assembly directly elected for five years and a 16-member Senate with nine members appointed by the prime minister, four by the leader of the parliamentary opposition, and three by the governor-general. The prime minister is the leader of the party that commands a majority in the House.

After 25 years in office, Lynden Pindling's Progressive Liberal Party (PLP) was ousted by Ingraham and the Free National Movement (FNM) in 1992 elections. The PLP had been dogged by years of allegations of corruption and official involvement in narcotics trafficking. Ingraham, a lawyer and former cabinet official, had been expelled by the PLP in 1986 for his outspoken attacks on corruption. He became leader of the FNM in 1990 and vowed to bring honesty, efficiency, and accountability to government. Pindling, at the time the Western hemisphere's longest-serving head of government, relied on his image as the father of the nation's independence. With 90 percent of the electorate voting, the FNM won 32 seats in the House of Assembly. The PLP won 17. Pindling held his own seat and became the official opposition leader.

Upon taking office, Ingraham appointed a Commission of Inquiry to investigate the Pindling government. In 1995 the commission detailed widespread mismanagement and malpractice in the national telephone and airline companies. In the 1997 election, Ingraham and the FNM claimed credit for revitalizing the economy by attracting foreign investment and won 34 of the parliament's 40 seats. In April 1997, Pindling resigned as opposition leader and was replaced by Perry Christie, who had served in the PLP cabinet until he denounced government corruption in the wake of a drug probe.

In 1998, Ingraham commuted the death sentences of 17 prisoners who had spent more than five years on death row. The commutation was in keeping with a limit set by the Privy Council, the highest court for several current and former British colonies. In September, Ingraham announced that his government would limit the right of appeal in capital cases. He also began the process of hiring 200 more police officers in an effort to combat violent crime.

Political Rights and Civil Liberties:

Citizens can change their government democratically. Constitutional guarantees regarding the right to organize political parties, civic organizations, and labor unions are generally respected, as is the free exercise of religion.

The judicial system is headed by a Supreme Court and a Court of Appeal, with the right of appeal under certain circumstances to the Privy Council in London. There are also local courts. On the outer islands, local commissioners have magisterial powers. Despite anti-drug legislation and a 1987 agreement with the United States to suppress the drug trade, there is evidence of drug-related corruption and money laundering, although less than during the Pindling years.

Violent crime is a growing concern, particularly in Nassau. Nongovernmental organizations have documented the increase in recent years of violent crime and police brutality. Human rights groups have also criticized the "subhuman conditions" and overcrowding in the nation's prisons. The Fox Hill prison remains filled to more than twice its intended capacity. In 1996, Ingraham reinstated the death penalty for murder. In 1998, two of the 30 prisoners on death row were executed.

Full freedom of expression is constrained by strict libel laws. Unlike its predecessor, the Ingraham government has not made use of these laws against independent newspapers. It has amended media laws to allow for private ownership of broadcasting outlets.

In 1998, the government denied asylum requests and deported scores of Cuban refugees held in detention centers. Among those repatriated were three Cuban national baseball team members, who were returned despite an asylum offer from the government of Nicaragua. Bahamian authorities responded to criticism of the deportations by noting that they were complying with the terms of a 1996 memorandum of understanding with Cuba.

Labor, business, and professional organizations are generally free. Unions have the right to strike, and collective bargaining is prevalent. As many as 40,000 Haitians reside illegally in the Bahamas. Tight citizenship laws and a strict work permit system leave them with few rights. The influx has created social tension due to the strain on government services. In November, law enforcement authorities disbanded an international "flesh cartel" that was trafficking in illegal Asian immigrants by supplying U.S. businesses with cheap labor.

Bahrain

Polity: Traditional monarchy
Economy: Capitalist-statist
Population: 600,000
PPP: $16,751
Life Expectancy: 69

Political Rights: 7
Civil Liberties: 6
Status: Not Free

Ethnic Groups: Bahraini (63 percent), Asian (13 percent), other Arab (10 percent), Iranian (8 percent), other (6 percent)
Capital: Manama

Overview:

Violent civil unrest continued in 1998 as the government cracked down on *Shi'ite* Muslim-led dissidents campaigning for the restoration of Bahrain's National Assembly, the return of exiles, and the release of political prisoners. Opposition activists have been summarily arrested, tortured, and expelled by government security forces since popular uprisings began in 1994.

An archipelago of 35 islands located between Qatar and Saudi Arabia, Bahrain has been ruled by the Al Khalifa family since 1782. The country was a British protectorate from 1861 until 1971, when British forces withdrew after years of Arab nationalist disturbances. The emir retained a virtual monopoly on power until the adoption in 1973 of a constitution that provided for a partially elected National Assembly. Describing Bahrain's new legislative body as "obstructionist," the emir ordered its dissolution in 1975.

With the Iranian revolution in 1979 and the accompanying spread of Islamic fundamentalism, resentment among Bahrain's majority Shi'ite population against its Sunni rulers intensified. The government faced an opposition which had grown to include not only leftist and secular elements, but religious ones as well. Religious and secular opposition activists were arrested and exiled in large numbers in the 1980s and 1990s.

The emir, Sheikh 'Isa ibn Salman Al Khalifa, assumed power in 1961 and rules with his brother, Prime Minister Khalifa ibn Salman Al Khalifa, and his son, Crown Prince Hamad ibn 'Isa Al Khalifa. In 1993, the emir responded to international calls for political liberalization by appointing a consultative council of 30 business and religious leaders. The council has little legislative power.

On December 5, 1994, Shi'ite cleric Sheikh 'Ali Salman and several Sunni former members of parliament were arrested for petitioning for the reinstatement of parliament and the release of political detainees. The resulting protests and street clashes marked the beginning of the current conflict. To date, over 40 people have been killed in the civil unrest. According to international human rights groups, the Bahraini government has arrested thousands of people, sentenced hundreds to jail terms, and expelled some 500 citizens and their families. Homes are routinely raided by security forces, and their inhabitants beaten and arrested. The government rejects all criticism of its human rights record and blames Iran for fomenting civil unrest. Political analysts and private sector businessmen, however, blame the government's failure to resolve widespread economic and social disparity, and particularly unemployment, which stands at around 30 percent in the majority Shi'a community.

In turn, social unrest and repression have worsened Bahrain's economy, which is already suffering the effects of lower oil prices, a lack of private sector investment, failure to diversify, and rampant corruption. Shi'ites, who comprise 70 percent of the national population, often lack means of education and training. They are further disadvantaged because wealthy Bahrainis prefer to hire foreigners, who they say will work longer hours in harsher conditions for less money. The government, which claims that it tries to meet the needs of the poor, introduced a job counseling system this year which aims to increase the number of Bahraini workers in business.

Political Rights and Civil Liberties:

Bahrainis cannot change their government democratically. Political parties are prohibited, and all opposition leaders are currently either imprisoned or exiled. The emir rules by decree and appoints all government officials, including the 15-member cabinet, the 40-member *majlis al-shura* (parliament), the urban municipal councils, and the rural *mukhtars* (local councils). The only political recourse for citizens is to submit petitions to the government and to appeal to the emir and officials at *majlises*, or regularly scheduled audiences.

The interior ministry maintains informal control over most activities through pervasive informant networks. Agents can search homes without warrants and have used this power frequently against Shi'ites. In 1998, the Bahrain Freedom Movement, a London-based opposition group, reported dozens of cases in which security forces raided homes in Shi'ite areas; destroyed belongings; severely beat men, women, and children; and arrested entire families.

The 1974 State Security Act allows the government to detain individuals accused of "anti-government activity," which may and often does include participation in peaceful demonstrations and membership in outlawed organizations, for up to three years without trial. According to human rights groups, defendants are subject to torture, forced confessions, arbitrary arrest, incommunicado detention, and inadequate prison conditions. An estimated 1,500 people are currently detained without trial.

Freedom of speech and the press are sharply restricted. Privately owned newspapers refrain from criticizing the regime, while radio and television are government owned and only broadcast official propaganda.

Freedom of association is also highly restricted. Political parties and organizations are prohibited. Some professional societies and social or sports clubs have traditionally served as forums for political discussion, but they are restricted by law from engaging in political activity. In January, the prime minister dissolved the bar society, which was the only association exempt from the ban on political activity. Bahrainis are not permitted to demonstrate, and even peaceful protests are met with intimidation.

Women face fewer restrictions in Bahrain than in other Islamic countries. *Shari'a* law governs their legal rights. Women of either sect may own and inherit property and represent themselves in public and legal matters. Laws for Shi'a and Sunni differ in matters of inheritance. A non-Bahraini woman will automatically lose custody of her children if she divorces their Bahraini father. Women may obtain passports and leave the country without the permission of a male relative, work outside of the home, drive cars without escorts, and wear the clothing of their choice. The Labor Law does not discriminate against women, although there is discrimination in the workplace, including inequality of wages and denial of opportunity for advancement.

Islam is the state religion, but Christians, Hindus, Jews, and others are generally permitted to worship freely. The 1963 Bahraini citizenship act denies full citizenship to Persian-origin Shi'as, or *bidoon* (those without). Bidoon are restricted in business activities and have difficulty obtaining passports and government loans.

No independent labor unions exist. Workers do not have the right to bargain collectively. The law restricts strikes deemed damaging to worker-employer relations or the national interest, and few strikes occur.

Bangladesh

Polity: Parliamentary democracy
Economy: Capitalist-statist
Population: 123,400,000
PPP: $1,382
Life Expectancy: 59
Ethnic Groups: Bengali (98 percent), Bihari, tribals (2 percent)
Capital: Dhaka

Political Rights: 2
Civil Liberties: 4
Status: Partly Free

Overview:

In a landmark court ruling in November 1998, 15 former army officers were sentenced to death for killing the country's independence leader in a 1975 coup, an event that continues to polarize Bangladeshi politics.

Bangladesh won independence in 1971 after a brief war with occupying West Pakistan. After 15 years of often turbulent rule by a succession of generals, the country's democratic transition began with the resignation of General H. M. Ershad in 1990 in the wake of prodemocracy demonstrations.

Elections in 1991 brought the centrist Bangladesh Nationalist Party (BNP) to power under Khaleda Zia. A national referendum then transformed the powerful presidency into a largely ceremonial head of state in a parliamentary system.

In 1994, the center-left opposition Awami League boycotted the parliament to protest alleged official corruption and a rigged by-election, thereby triggering two years of crippling general strikes and partisan violence. The Awami League boycotted the February 1996 elections, which the BNP won handily, but then forced Zia's resignation. In June 1996 elections, which were held with a 73 percent turnout, the Awami League won 146 of 300 parliamentary seats. (Thirty additional seats are reserved for women.) The BNP won 113 seats, while Ershad's Jatiya Party won 33. The Awami League's Sheikh Hasina Wajed formed a government initially backed by the Jatiya Party.

In August 1997, the BNP quit parliament to protest alleged harassment of its workers and a proposed treaty giving India transit rights through Bangladesh. Despite constant tensions, the Awami League and the BNP differ little on domestic policy. Their disputes mainly reflect the intense personal rivalry between Sheikh Hasina, the daughter of assassinated independence leader Sheikh Mujibar Rahman, and Zia, the widow of an army general implicated in the coup that toppled Sheikh Mujib in 1975. In March 1998, the BNP returned to parliament after the government pledged to enforce parliamentary rules evenly and permit BNP street rallies in Dhaka.

In the summer, Bangladesh's worst flooding ever caused approximately 1,500 deaths, left millions of people homeless, and caused more than $4.3 billion in losses in agriculture, industry, and infrastructure. Many Bangladeshis appeared to welcome the November court decision, which could result in the public execution of the four officers who were in the country for the trial.

Political Rights and Civil Liberties:

Bangladeshis can change their government through elections. The 1996 elections, the freest in Bangladesh's history despite some violence and irregularities, were the first under a March 1996 constitutional amendment requiring a caretaker government to conduct elections. The military's influence in politics continues to diminish. Frequent parliamentary boycotts by both major parties have undermined the legislative process.

Political institutions are weak. Politics are frequently conducted through strikes and demonstrations that are marred by violence and clashes between party activists and police.

The judiciary is independent, but lower courts are plagued by corruption, severe backlogs, and lengthy pretrial detentions. In practice, poor people have limited recourse through the courts. Torture, rape, and other abuse of suspects and prisoners are routine, widespread, and rarely punished.

Both the Zia and Hasina governments have used the 1974 Special Powers Act, which allows authorities to detain suspects without charge for up to 120 days, against political opponents. Human rights advocates have sharply criticized the practice of "safe custody" detention, whereby judges have ostensibly protected female victims of rape, kidnapping, and trafficking by imprisoning them for up to four years.

The print media is diverse, outspoken, and under pressure. In April, the Paris-based Reporters Sans Frontieres reported that at least five journalists had been arrested in recent months and that at least seven had been harassed by police since the beginning of the year. In March, a court sentenced three journalists from the weekly *Benapole Barta* to one year's imprisonment, pending appeal, for defamation. Party activists and Islamic fundamentalists also harass journalists. Unknown assailants killed the editor of an outspoken newspaper in Jessore in August. Political considerations influence the apportionment of government advertising revenue and subsidized newsprint, on which most publications are dependent. Broadcast media are state-owned, and coverage favors the ruling party.

Rape, dowry-related assaults, acid throwing, and other violent acts against women are apparently increasing, with minimal police intervention. A law requiring rape victims to file police reports and obtain medical certificates within 24 hours of the crime in order to press charges prevents most rape cases from reaching the courts. Police also accept bribes not to register cases. In April, parliament approved the death penalty for rape, murder, trafficking, and other crimes against women. Yet the 1995 Women Repression Law and similar laws are weakly enforced, and it remains to be seen whether this measure will have much effect. In rural areas, religious leaders arbitrarily impose floggings and other punishments on women accused of violating strict moral codes.

Women face discrimination in health care, education, and employment. In September, Taslima Nasreen, a feminist writer who fled Bangladesh in 1994 following death threats by Islamic fundamentalists, returned to the country to care for her ailing mother and received new death threats. She was also ordered to appear in court to respond to two blasphemy suits.

Organized networks, operating with the complicity of local authorities, send approximately 15,000 women and children each year to Pakistan and other countries for prostitution and other forced labor. Domestic child prostitution remains a problem.

Islam is the official religion. Hindus, Christians, and other minorities worship freely, but face societal discrimination. All but 21,000 of the 250,000 Rohingya refugees who fled from Burma in 1991 and 1992 to escape forced labor and other abuses have been repatriated. The remaining Rohingyas refuse to return, citing fear of further abuse by the Burmese army.

Union formation is hampered by a 30 percent employee approval requirement and restrictions on organizing by unregistered unions. Workers suspected of union activities can be legally transferred or fired. Unions are largely prohibited in the two export processing zones. The Bangladesh Independent Garment Workers Union is one of the few effective nonpartisan unions. In low-wage industries, working conditions are poor, and anti-union harassment and discrimination are prevalent. Child labor is widespread.

Barbados

Polity: Parliamentary democracy
Economy: Capitalist
Population: 300,000
PPP: $11,306
Life Expectancy: 75
Ethnic Groups: Black (80 percent), white (4 percent), other (16 percent)
Capital: Bridgetown

Political Rights: 1
Civil Liberties: 1
Status: Free

Overview:
Relations with the United States and Britain dominated the Barbadian political debate in 1998. In December, a government-appointed constitutional commission recommended that the country change from a monarchy to a republic and remove the Queen of England as the official head of state. Earlier, the island nation announced that it would replace the British Privy Council with a regional court of last resort. Prime Minister Owen Arthur, the architect of plans to diversify the island nation's economy, suggested to parliament that Caribbean island nations not renew their anti-drug maritime agreements with the United States until the dispute over the U.S. trade position on bananas was resolved.

A member of the British Commonwealth, Barbados achieved independence in 1966. The British monarchy is represented by a governor-general. The government is a parliamentary democracy with a bicameral legislature and a party system based on universal adult suffrage. The Senate is comprised of 21 members, all of whom are appointed by the governor-general. Twelve are appointed on the advice of the prime minister, two on the advice of the leader of the opposition, and the remaining seven at the discretion of the governor-general. A 28-member House of Assembly is elected for a five-year term. Executive authority is vested in the prime minister, who is the leader of the political party commanding a majority in the House.

Since independence, power has alternated between two centrist parties, the Democratic Labor Party (DLP) under Errol Barrow and the Barbados Labor Party (BLP) under Tom Adams. Adams led the BLP from 1976 until his death in 1985. Adams was succeeded by Bernard St. John, but the BLP was defeated. This returned Barrow to power in 1986. Barrow died in 1987 and was succeeded by Erskine Sandiford, who led the DLP to victory in the 1991 elections.

Under Sandiford, Barbados suffered a prolonged economic recession as revenues from sugar and tourism declined. In 1994, Sandiford lost a no-confidence vote in parliament. The DLP elected David Thompson, the government's young finance minister, to replace him. In the 1994 election campaign, Owen Arthur, an economist elected in 1993 to head the BLP, promised to build a "modern, technologically dynamic economy," create jobs, and restore investor confidence. The BLP won 19 seats, while the DLP won eight. The New Democratic Party (NDP), a disaffected DLP offshoot formed in 1989, won one seat.

Arthur has combined a technocratic approach to revitalizing the economy with savvy politics. He has appointed a number of promising young cabinet officials. By mid-1995, unemployment had decreased to 20.5 percent, the lowest level since 1990. It has remained at approximately that level since then.

Political Rights and Civil Liberties:

Citizens can change their government through democratic elections. Constitutional guarantees regarding freedom of religion and the right to organize political parties, labor unions, and civic organizations are respected.

The judicial system is independent and includes a Supreme Court that encompasses a High Court and a Court of Appeal. Lower court officials are appointed on the advice of the Judicial and Legal Service Commission. The government provides free legal aid to the indigent. In 1992, the Court of Appeals outlawed the public flogging of criminals. The prison system is antiquated and overcrowded, with more than 800 inmates held in a building built for 350.

In 1999, Barbados is expected to become a charter member of the Caribbean Court of Justice, which will replace the British Privy Council as the region's court of last resort. The English court has come under increasing criticism for seeking to regulate capital punishment. In early 1998, Barbados Attorney General David Simmons charged that it had "bound regional governments hand and foot" and had imposed "Eurocentric notions and values totally at variance with the notions of the [Caribbean] people."

Human rights organizations operate freely. The high crime rate, fueled by an increase in drug abuse and trafficking, has given rise to human rights concerns. On occasion, the police allegedly use excessive force during arrests and interrogation. A counternarcotics agreement signed between the United States and Barbados in late 1996 will provide funding for the Barbados police force, the coast guard, customs, and other ministries for a broad array of programs to combat drug-related crimes. Barbados has also entered into an updated extradition treaty and a maritime law enforcement agreement with the United States.

Freedom of expression is fully respected. Public opinion expressed through the news media, which are free of censorship and government control, has a powerful influence on policy. Newspapers are privately owned, and there are two major dailies. Private and government radio stations operate. The single television station, operated by the government-owned Caribbean Broadcasting Corporation, presents a wide range of political viewpoints.

In 1992, a domestic violence law was passed to give police and judges greater powers to protect women. Women constitute approximately half of the workforce. There are two major labor unions and various smaller ones that are politically active.

Belarus

Polity: Presidential-dictatorship
Economy: Statist
Population: 10,200,000
PPP: $4,398
Life Expectancy: 68
Ethnic Groups: Belarusian (78 percent), Russian (13 percent), Polish (4 percent), Ukrainian (3 percent), other (2 percent)
Capital: Minsk

Political Rights: 6
Civil Liberties: 6
Status: Not Free

Overview:

Harsher press restrictions, the possibility of food shortages, threats to evict foreign diplomats from their residences, and renewed calls for the re-creation of the Soviet Union marked the 1998 rule of President Alyaksandr Lukashenka. Since assuming power in 1994, Lukashenka has harassed and expelled dissidents, repressed the news media, reintroduced a command economy, and obtained passage of a constitution to strengthen his one-man rule.

Belarus was part of the tenth century Kievan realm. After a lengthy period of Lithuanian rule, it merged with Poland in the 1500s. It became part of the Russian Empire after Poland was partitioned in the 1700s and became a constituent republic of the Soviet Union in 1922. With the collapse of the Soviet Union in 1991, nationalist leader Stanislaw Shushkevich became head of state. A pro-Russian parliament ousted Shushkevich in 1994, and the newly created post of president was won by Lukashenka, a former state farm director and chairman of the parliament's anti-corruption committee. After his election, Lukashenka gradually reintroduced censorship and Soviet-era textbooks and national symbols, banned independent trade unions, ignored the Supreme Court when it overturned his decrees, limited the rights of candidates in parliamentary elections, and sought reintegration with Russia. In 1996, Lukashenka extended his term and amended the country's constitution by referendum to enable the president to annul decisions of local councils, set election dates, call parliamentary sessions, and dissolve parliament. Parliament was restructured into a bicameral legislature consisting of a house of representatives with 110 deputies and a senate, with the president appointing one-third of the senators.

In 1998, the government implemented new restrictions on media and free expression. In June, it announced that it would evict diplomats from 22 houses in the Drozdy compound outside Minsk in order to conduct urgent repairs. The dispute led Britain, France, Germany, Greece, Italy, and the United States to recall their ambassadors. In October, Lukashenka called for direct elections to the parliament of the Russian-Belarus Union and for single citizenship within the union. Russian President Boris Yeltsin and Lukashenka signed a union agreement for a single state in December.

Political Rights and Civil Liberties:

The citizens of Belarus cannot change their government democratically. President Lukashenka has instituted de facto presidential rule.

Freedom of the press is strictly curtailed. In 1998, greater restrictions were introduced to limit access to government officials and documents, and prison terms were introduced for defaming the president. Under a 1997 law, the State Committee for the Press has the right to suspend the activity of a media organ for a period of three months to one year without judicial recourse. The law also bars the importation of newspapers that "include reports that may do harm to the political and economic interests" of the country. The law was aimed at several major opposition newspapers that had been forced to move their printing operations to Lithuania in 1995. In June, the independent news agency Belapan was denied accreditation during the visit of the Russian prime minister. The State Press Committee also warned the weekly *Zdravy Smysl* for reporting on the edict banning government officials from providing edicts to independent media. The State Committee on Television and Radio controls broadcasting. A number of small, local, privately owned television stations broadcast entertainment programming.

Freedom of religion is guaranteed by law and usually respected in practice. Roman Catholics and Jews have complained of governmental delays in returning church property and synagogues. Even though 80 percent of the population is ethnic Belarusian, the Belarusian-language educational system is being dismantled. Russian was restored as an official language in 1995. In September 1998, approximately 200 parents and public activists rallied in Minsk to protest the increasing use of Russian as the primary language for educating children.

Public rallies and demonstrations require government approval. A 1997 presidential decree curtailed freedom of assembly. In 1998, several unsanctioned demonstrations were halted by police, and marchers were detained.

There are nearly 2,000 nongovernmental organizations registered in Belarus, including educational, women's, cultural, environmental, and business groups. Even charitable organizations have faced government pressure. Arbitrary and contradictory tax policies have led several international humanitarian groups to cease operations in Belarus.

In 1995, the president banned the Independent Free Trade Union of Belarus, the Minsk Metro Trade Union, and the Railroad and Transport Facilities Workers' Union. In response to international pressure in 1997, the government ordered the Ministry of Justice to reregister the Free Trade Union of Belarus and register the Congress of Democratic Trade Unions (CDTU), which had earlier been denied registration. The Federation of Trade Unions of Belarus, a successor to the Soviet-era federation, claims five million members. In June 1998, the CDTU held an authorized rally to protest reduced living standards and price increases.

The judicial system is essentially the same three-tiered structure that existed during the Soviet era. Judges continue to be influenced by the political leadership. They are dependent on the Ministry of Justice for sustaining court infrastructure and on local executive branch officials for providing their personal housing. The president appoints the chairman and five other members of the Constitutional Court. The remaining six members are appointed by the Council of the Republic, which itself is composed partly of presidential appointees and partly of loyalists chosen by the Minsk City Council and six oblast councils, which are pro-government. The Criminal Code includes many provisions that are susceptible to political abuse, including a host of anti-state activities. In 1997, parliament approved new codes on criminal procedure and corrective labor. The Corrective Labor Code introduced a new form of punishment called "arrest," which allows a suspect to be held for 30 days without charge. Security forces routinely enter homes without warrants, tap telephones, and conduct unauthorized searches.

All citizens must still carry internal passports, which serve as primary identity documents and are required for travel, permanent housing, and hotel registration. While protected by law, the right to choose one's place of residence remains restricted in practice. All citizens are required to register their places of residence and may not change them without official permission.

The constitution guarantees property rights, but land ownership, with few exceptions, is not allowed. There are no legal restrictions on the participation of women in government, business, or education.

Belgium

Polity: Federal parliamentary democracy
Economy: Capitalist
Population: 10,200,000
PPP: $21,548
Life Expectancy: 77
Ethnic Groups: Fleming (55 percent), Walloon (33 percent), mixed and others, including Moroccan, Turkish and other immigrant groups (12 percent)
Capital: Brussels

Political Rights: 1
Civil Liberties: 2
Status: Free

Overview:
Belgium continued to be plagued by political scandals, ethnic tensions, and decreased confidence in its government, judiciary, and police forces. Two ministers in the government of Prime Minister Jean-Luc Dehaene resigned over the brief escape of Marc Dutroux, the country's most notorious criminal. Dutroux's escape, however, did prompt the four center-left government coalition parties and four major opposition parties to agree to restructure the criminal justice system. Under their agreement, the federal police will

be unified, and a single police force will operate at the district level. Other police units will be abolished.

In September, 12 politicians and businessmen, including former NATO Secretary General Willy Claes and two other Socialist Party ministers, were put on trial for corruption. Italian and French aircraft companies are alleged to have won lucrative Belgian military contracts by making large cash "gifts" to the Socialist Party. Belgium had outlawed corporate contributions to political parties five years earlier.

At the same time, the country faced increased ethnic and linguistic tensions between its Walloons, who worry that they are losing their identity, and Flemings, who are calling for a confederate or separate state. In September, Standard and Poor's warned that political uncertainty caused by these tensions poses short-term risks to Belgium's economy.

Modern Belgium dates from 1830, when the territory broke away from the Netherlands and formed a constitutional monarchy. Today, the largely ceremonial monarchy symbolizes the weakness of Belgian unity. Ethnic and linguistic antagonism during the 1960s prompted a series of constitutional amendments, in 1970-71 and 1993, that devolved power to regional councils at the expense of the central government in Brussels. A 1993 amendment formally transformed the country into a federation of Flanders, Wallonia, and bilingual Brussels, with the German-speaking area accorded cultural autonomy. Also in 1993, parliament adopted an amendment establishing three directly elected regional assemblies with primary responsibility for housing, transportation, public works, education, culture and the environment. The weak central government continues to oversee foreign policy, defense, justice, monetary policy, taxation, and the management of the budget deficit.

Political parties are split along linguistic lines, with both Walloon and Flemish parties ranging across the political spectrum. Numerous small ethnic parties and special interest groups have emerged, leading to a decline in the dominance of the three major groupings of Social Democrats, Christian Democrats, and Liberals.

Political Rights and Civil Liberties:

Belgians can change their government democratically. Non-voters are subject to fines. Political parties generally organize along ethnic lines, with different factions of the leading parties subscribing to a common platform for general elections. Each ethnic group has autonomy in its region, but constitutional disputes arise when members of one group elected to office in a different territory refuse to take competency tests in the dominant language of that region.

The country's judiciary is independent, but has continued to experience criticism due to the country's ongoing political and criminal scandals.

While freedom of speech and the press is guaranteed, Belgian law prohibits some forms of pornography as well as incitements to violence. Libel laws have some minor restraining effects on the press, and restrictions on the right of civil servants to criticize the government may constitute a slight reduction of the right of civil speech. Autonomous public boards govern the state television and radio networks and ensure that public broadcasting is linguistically pluralistic. The state has permitted and licensed independent radio stations since 1985.

Belgians enjoy freedom of religion and association. Christian, Jewish, and Muslim institutions are state subsidized in this overwhelmingly Roman Catholic country, and other faiths are not restricted. Immigrants and linguistic minorities argue that linguistic zoning limits opportunity.

Belgium has enacted measures to promote sexual equality, including the prohibition of sexual harassment. Legislation mandates that, in the next general parliamentary election, 33 percent of the candidates be women. Approximately 60 percent of the work force are members of labor unions, which have the right to strike—one that they frequently exercise—even in "essential" services.

Belize

Polity: Parliamentary democracy
Economy: Capitalist
Population: 200,000
PPP: $5,623
Life Expectancy: 72
Ethnic Groups: Mestizo (44 percent), Creole (30 percent), Maya (11 percent), Garifuna (7 percent), other (8 percent)
Capital: Belmopan

Political Rights: 1
Civil Liberties: 1
Status: Free

Overview:
In August, opposition leader and former Attorney General Said Musa was elected prime minister. Musa, whose People's United Party (BUP) won 26 of 29 seats in parliament, ran on an anti-tax, pro-jobs platform and pledged to make Belize party to international treaties on the rights of women and indigenous people.

Belize is a member of the British Commonwealth. The British monarchy is represented by a governor-general. Formerly British Honduras, the name was changed to Belize in 1973. Independence was granted in 1981. Belize is a parliamentary democracy with a bicameral National Assembly. The House of Representatives is elected for a five-year term. Members of the Senate are appointed: five by the governor-general on the advice of the prime minister, two by the leader of the parliamentary opposition, and one by the Belize Advisory Council. Since independence, the control of the government has alternated three times between the center-right United Democratic Party (UDP) and the center-left BUP. In the 1993 elections, the UDP and the National Alliance for Belizean Rights formed a coalition and won 16 of the 29 seats in the House of Representatives.

The 1998 elections proved to be a referendum on Prime Minister Manuel Esquivel's largely unfulfilled pledge that his UDP would create jobs. Esquivel was successful, however, in resisting a regional trend towards currency devaluation. Among Musa's early initiatives were the creation of a national health service and curbs on the powers of cabinet ministers.

Political Rights and Civil Liberties:
Citizens can change their government democratically in peaceful, fair, and open elections. Since independence, each election in racially diverse Belize has resulted in the incum-

bent party being ousted. In the 1998 elections, 78 percent of eligible voters cast their ballots. The incumbent UDP was heavily outspent in the campaign. There are no restrictions on the right to organize political parties. Civil society is well established, with a large number of nongovernmental organizations working on social, economic, and environmental issues.

In general, the judiciary is independent and nondiscriminatory, and the rule of law is respected. Judges and the director of public prosecutions, however, must negotiate the renewal of their employment contracts, thereby rendering them vulnerable to political influence. Prison conditions do not meet minimum standards.

Belizeans have suffered from an increase in violent crime, much of it related to drug trafficking and gang conflict. In 1996, the U.S. government added Belize to its list of major drug transit countries. In 1997, Belizean officials, who fear a possible influx of European and other criminal elements, are believed to have rebuffed three efforts by Russian firms to open banks in the country.

The Belize Human Rights Commission is independent and effective. Human rights concerns include the plight of migrant workers and refugees from neighboring Central American countries and charges of labor abuses by Belizean employers. Most of the estimated 40,000 Spanish-speakers who have immigrated since the 1980s do not have legal status. Some have registered under an amnesty program implemented in cooperation with the UN High Commissioner for Refugees.

There are six privately owned newspapers, three of which are subsidized by major political parties. The press is free to publish a variety of political viewpoints, including those critical of the government, and there are Spanish-language media. Belize has a literacy rate of more than 90 percent. Radio and television are saturated with political advertising during elections. Fourteen private television stations operate, including four cable systems. There is an independent board to oversee operations of the government-owned outlets.

Freedom of religion is respected, and the government actively discourages racial and ethnic discrimination. The Esquivel government, however, did not recognize aboriginal land rights and took actions that threatened the survival of the Maya Indian communities. More than half of the 21,000 Belize Maya live in the Toledo district, where they form nearly two-thirds of the population. Despite their claim to be the original inhabitants of Belize, they have no secure title to their ancestral lands, which have been targeted by Malaysian and other foreign investors. For thousands of years, this land has provided Maya Indians food, medicinal plants, building materials, and hunting grounds. In 1996, the Maya Indians organized demonstrations and took legal steps to block government-negotiated logging contracts. They also opposed the paving of a major road to afford business access to the area. Land claims continue to be contested in the courts.

Workers have the right to strike. Labor unions are independent, but only 11 percent of workers, who earn two to three times more than their counterparts in neighboring countries, are unionized. Disputes are adjudicated by official boards of inquiry, and businesses are penalized for failing to abide by the labor code.

Benin

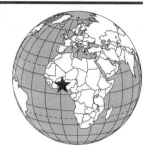

Polity: Presidential-parliamentary democracy
Economy: Mixed statist
Population: 6,000,000
PPP: $1,800
Life Expectancy: 54
Ethnic Groups: African [42 ethnic groups, including Fon, Adja, Bariba, Yoruba] (99 percent)
Capital: Porto-Novo

Political Rights: 2
Civil Liberties: 2
Status: Free

Overview:

Benin's recent status as one of Africa's most open societies was tested in 1998 by political infighting, labor unrest, and a sharp rise in violent crime. The country's fledgling democratic institutions were threatened by extreme partisanship and potential manipulation. Legislative polls scheduled for March 1999 could recast the political landscape. They will be conducted under a new election commission, created in September by a unanimous vote in the usually fractious parliament. Former Marxist military dictator Mathieu Kerekou, who returned to power in March 1996 presidential elections, may be reverting to authoritarian practices. In a mid-year cabinet reshuffle, several hardliners from his previous military regimes were installed in government positions. The president of the Constitutional Court was removed and replaced by a Kerekou loyalist. Kerekou has respected parliamentary action and court decisions, however, and the media remain generally free. The proliferation of the country's estimated 100 small political parties, which are primarily based on personality and ethnicity rather than issues, could threaten democratic consolidation. Repeated strikes by civil servants and other workers have hindered economic growth, and privatization has proceeded slowly.

After six decades of French colonial rule, the modern state of Benin became independent in 1960 as Dahomey, the name of the ancient kingdom of which it was once the center. In 1972, General Kerekou put an end to successive coups and counter coups by seizing power. Kerekou renamed the country Benin in 1975, imposed a one-party state under the Benin People's Revolutionary Party, and pursued Marxist-Leninist policies. By 1989, economic hardships had led to rising internal unrest. Kerekou agreed to a transition to a multiparty system that culminated in his defeat by Nicephore Soglo in March 1991 presidential elections. The country's human rights record subsequently improved.

President Kerekou's comeback as a democrat was cemented by his victory in March 1996 presidential polls. The largely peaceful campaign included a broad civic education program conducted by state-owned media and nongovernmental organizations (NGOs).

The coalition of several ethnically based parties formed after the 1995 elections splintered in May when opposition leader and Prime Minister Adrien Houngbedji and his political allies resigned. The defection of some of his own party members has left President Kerekou without a majority in the National Assembly.

Historically, Benin has been divided between northern and southern ethnic groups, which are the main bases of current political parties. Northern ethnic groups enlisted during Kerekou's early years in power still dominate the military.

Political Rights and Civil Liberties: Benin held its first genuine multiparty elections in 1991. Its citizens again exercised their right to elect and change their leaders freely in 1995 legislative and 1996 presidential elections. Legislative polls in March 1995 returned an opposition majority. While marred by some irregularities, the March 1996 presidential contest was generally free and fair. The president may serve two five-year terms, while national assembly members may serve an unlimited number of four-year terms. Adult suffrage is universal, and voting is by secret ballot.

The June replacement of the widely respected president of the Constitutional Court, which has ruled against both the president and the legislature on various issues, has raised questions of its continued impartiality. The judiciary is generally considered to be independent, but inefficient due to lack of staff and training. Pretrial detainees comprise three-fourths of inmates in severely overcrowded prisons, where poor medical care and diet cause many preventable deaths. Harsh police practices to combat a wave of violent crime have raised civil liberties concerns.

Constitutional guarantees of freedom of expression are respected in practice. Most broadcast media are state-owned, but allow opposition and other reports critical of the government. The High Authority for Audiovisual Media and Communications' notification of programming requirement is not enforced. Independent radio and television stations began operating in 1997 under a liberalized broadcasting law, but steep license fees are likely to keep community radio and television stations off the air. An independent and pluralistic print media that include nine party-affiliated and other dailies publish articles highly critical of both government and opposition leaders and policies. Foreign periodicals are readily available. Harsh libel laws, however, have been used against journalists. In August, media workers launched a strike to protest the arrest and beating of a reporter.

Numerous NGOs operate without governmental hindrance. Freedom of assembly and association are respected, and requirements for permits and registration are often ignored. Religious freedom is respected.

Women enjoy fewer educational and employment opportunities than men, particularly in rural areas. In family matters, in which traditional practices prevail, their legal rights are often not respected. Only six women serve in the 83-member National Assembly. Trafficking in children for domestic service is reportedly widespread.

The right to organize and join unions is constitutionally guaranteed. Strikes are legal, and collective bargaining is common. Several labor federations are affiliated with political parties and international labor groups.

Bhutan

Polity: Traditional monarchy
Economy: Pre-industrial
Population: 800,000
PPP: $1,382
Life Expectancy: 66
Ethnic Groups: Bhote (50 percent), Nepali-speaking (35 percent), indigenous or migrant tribes (15 percent)
Capital: Thimphu

Political Rights: 7
Civil Liberties: 6*
Status: Not Free

Ratings change: Bhutan's civil liberties rating changed from 7 to 6 due to a change in Freedom House methodology to reflect an easing in state intrusion into the personal lives of its citizens.

Overview:
Amid pressure for democratic change in this absolute monarchy, in 1998 Bhutanese King Jigme Singye Wangchuk initiated limited political reforms while authorities continued to arrest and detain dozens of dissidents.

Britain began to guide this Himalayan land's affairs in 1865 and installed the ruling Wangchuk dynasty in 1907. Britain's role ended with a 1949 treaty that gave India control over Bhutan's foreign affairs. Since then, New Delhi has supported the Wangchuk family's continued rule as an absolute monarchy. In 1972, Jigme Singye Wangchuk, the current monarch, succeeded his father to the throne. The 150-member National Assembly has little independent power. Every three years, village headmen choose 100 National Assembly members, while the king appoints members to 40 seats. Religious groups appoint members to 10 seats.

By the mid-1980s, the government, dominated by the minority Tibetan-descended Ngalong Drukpa ethnic group, increasingly viewed the country's more populous Nepali-speakers, who are also known as Southern Bhutanese, as a threat to its absolute power. The regime introduced cultural restrictions in 1987, and, in 1988, after a census revealed Southern Bhutanese to be in the majority in five southern districts, authorities began to apply a discriminatory citizenship act arbitrarily to strip thousands of Southern Bhutanese of their citizenship.

Southern Bhutanese carried out pro-democracy demonstrations in southern Bhutan in 1990, accompanied by some arson and violence. Between 1990 and 1992, soldiers raped and beat Southern Bhutanese villagers, and forcibly expelled tens of thousands. There are currently some 94,500 Bhutanese refugees in Nepal.

In 1994, dissidents from the country's third and perhaps largest major ethnic group, the Sarchop community in eastern Bhutan, launched the Druk National Congress (DNC) party in exile. In 1997, the DNC and several Southern Bhutanese-based exile groups formed the United Front for Democracy. By July 1997, authorities had arrested scores of suspected DNC members and sympathizers.

In June 1998, the King dissolved the council of ministers, or cabinet; removed himself as its chairman; gave parliament the power, in theory, to remove the king through a two-thirds vote; and allowed the legislature to elect a majority of the cabinet, although the king will still assign portfolios. In July, diplomat Jigme Thinley became head of the council of ministers. Analysts said the changes were limited in practice and were an attempt to improve the regime's international image and divide the pro-democracy movement.

Political Rights and Civil Liberties:

The Bhutanese people lack the democratic means to change their government. The king wields absolute power, and policymaking is centered around the king and a small group of largely interrelated Ngalong elites. The National Assembly is often a forum for diatribes against the Southern Bhutanese, who hold a disproportionately small number of seats. Political parties are prohibited in practice.

The rule of law is nonexistent. Between 1990 and 1992, the army and police committed grave human rights violations against Southern Bhutanese, including arbitrary arrests, beatings, rape, destruction of homes, and robbery. Few if any of those responsible have been punished, resulting in a climate of impunity. The Royal Bhutan Army maintains a considerable presence in the south and continues to conduct arbitrary searches, harass residents, and intimidate police and local officials. Assamese and Bodo militants from northeast India keep bases in southern Bhutan and contribute to a climate of insecurity.

The rudimentary judiciary is not independent. The King appoints and can dismiss judges, most of whom have little legal training. Several detainees and prisoners have reportedly died in custody in recent years due to poor conditions. Tek Nath Rizal, South Asia's best-known political prisoner, was sentenced in 1993 to life in prison under a broadly drawn national security act that was passed three years after his imprisonment. According to Amnesty International, since July 1997, authorities have reportedly arrested more than 150 suspected DNC members and sympathizers and subjected them to incommunicado detention, torture, and other abuses.

Freedom of speech is restricted, and criticism of the king is not permitted, except indirectly during National Assembly discussions. The state-owned weekly *Kuensel*, Bhutan's only regular publication, is government-controlled. Satellite dishes are banned. Freedom of assembly is nonexistent, and there is no freedom of association for political purposes, although some business and civic organizations are permitted.

The country's sixth Five-Year Plan (1987 to 1992) introduced a "One Nation, One People" program to promote Driglam Namzha, the national dress and customs of the ruling Ngalongs. A 1989 royal decree made Driglam Namzha mandatory for all Bhutanese, although enforcement has been sporadic. The government also banned the Nepali language as a subject of instruction in schools.

Southern Bhutanese are required to obtain official "No Objection Certificates" (NOCs) to enter schools, take government jobs, and sell farm products. In practice, NOCs are frequently denied. Anecdotal data from Bhutanese refugees with relatives in Bhutan suggest that large numbers of Southern Bhutanese children have no local schools to attend.

The Drukpa Kagyu sect of Mahayana Buddhism is the official state religion, and Buddhist priests wield significant political influence. During a 1997 crackdown, authorities reportedly closed 13 monasteries of the Nyingmpa school of Buddhism that is practiced by most Sarchops. Many Southern Bhutanese are Hindus and, due to persecution, cannot worship freely.

Independent trade unions and strikes are not permitted. Villagers are often forced to contribute "voluntary" labor for state projects. Property rights are limited, and in recent years authorities have resettled some northern Bhutanese on land belonging to refugees.

Bolivia

Polity: Presidential-legislative democracy
Economy: Capitalist
Population: 8,000,000
PPP: $2,617
Life Expectancy: 60
Ethnic Groups: Quechua (30 percent), Aymara (25 percent), mestizo (25-30 percent), European (5-15 percent)
Capital: La Paz (administrative), Sucre (judicial)

Political Rights: 1
Civil Liberties: 3
Status: Free

Overview:

Hugo Banzer Suarez, a former dictator turned democrat, spent his first year as an elected president by implementing a series of major institutional reforms passed during his predecessor's administration. These include the creation of an independent council in charge of judicial appointments, a public ombudsman, and a constitutional tribunal chosen by Congress.

After achieving independence from Spain in 1825, the Republic of Bolivia endured recurrent instability and military rule. The armed forces, responsible for more than 180 coups in 157 years, have remained in their barracks since 1982.

As a result of recent reforms, presidential terms are for five years, and Congress consists of a 130-member House of Representatives and a 27-member Senate. The principal parties are Banzer's conservative National Democratic Action (ADN); its governing coalition partner, the social-democratic Movement of the Revolutionary Left (MIR); and the center-right National Revolutionary Movement (MNR). Banzer finished first in elections in 1985, but a parliamentary coalition instead selected octogenarian former President Victor Paz Estenssoro, the founder of the MNR, to lead the country. In 1989. the MIR's Jaime Paz Zamora, who had run third in the polls, became president through an alliance with the ADN. In 1993, the MIR-ADN candidate was retired general Banzer, who finished second to the MNR's Gonzalo Sanchez de Losada, who oversaw the privatization of Bolivia's state-owned enterprises and, under U.S. pressure, increased coca eradication. After a series of strikes and protests in 1995, Sanchez de Losada imposed a six-month state of siege. Throughout 1996, the government privatization program brought regular street protests. As Sanchez de Losada's term ended, a government otherwise hailed for democratic reforms had become mired in increasingly bitter labor disputes. Banzer's government, which came to power in August 1997, has promised to eradicate all illegal coca plantations by the year 2002. It has faced strong opposition from coca growers, as well as protests over economic policies from organized labor.

Political Rights and Civil Liberties: Citizens can change their government through elections. National elections in 1997 were free and fair. The judiciary, headed by the Supreme Court, remains the weakest branch of government. Like Bolivia's mayoral, customs, and revenue offices, it is rife with corruption and manipulated by drug traffickers. The governments of Sanchez de Losada and Banzer have made serious efforts to improve the administration of justice, including making it more accessible.

Government-sponsored and independent human rights organizations operate and frequently report of police brutality, including torture. Activists and their families are subject to intimidation. Prison conditions are poor, and nearly three-quarters of prisoners have not been formally sentenced.

Bolivia is the world's second largest producer of cocaine, after Peru. Evidence abounds that drug money has been used to finance political campaigns and influence police, military, and government officials.

A U.S.-sponsored coca eradication program has angered peasant unions representing Bolivia's 50,000 coca farmers. Critics say that the 1988 law that regulates coca is excessively harsh, restricts suspects' constitutional rights, and violates international norms and standards of due process. In their efforts to eradicate coca in the tropial lowland region of Chapare, government forces, particularly the troops of the Mobile Rural Patrol Unit, continue to commit serious human rights abuses, including murder, arbitrary detentions, and the suppression of peaceful demonstrations.

The constitution guarantees free expression, freedom of religion, and the right to organize political parties, civic groups, and labor unions. Unions have the right to strike. The languages of the indigenous population are officially recognized, but the 40 percent Spanish-speaking minority still dominates the political process. More than 520 indigenous communities have been granted legal recognition under the 1994 popular participation law, which guarantees respect for the integrity of native peoples.

The press, radio, and television are mostly private. Journalists covering corruption stories are occasionally subject to verbal intimidation by government officials, arbitrary detention by police, and violent attacks. In 1997, a Santa Cruz court sentenced an investigative journalist to two-and-a-half years in prison for his exposes on alleged white-collar crime. The procedure moved jurisdiction to common courts from press courts established by law.

In 1998, the Banzer government repeatedly asked Congress to condemn alleged corruption and human rights abuses during the Sanchez de Losada government. Following the detention of former Chilean dictator Capt. Gen. Augusto Pinochet in Britain, Sanchez de Losada's MNR called for former ally Banzer to be tried for alleged crimes against humanity committed during his seven-year reign in the 1970s.

Bosnia-Herzegovina

Polity: Presidential-parliamentary democracy
Economy: Mixed statist
Population: 4,000,000
PPP: na
Life Expectancy: 72
Ethnic Groups: Serb (40 percent), Bosnian/Muslim (38 percent), Croat (22 percent)
Capital: Sarajevo

Political Rights: 5
Civil Liberties: 5
Status: Partly Free

Overview:

In September 1998, Bosnia-Herzegovina saw a second national election since the U.S.-brokered 1995 Dayton Accords, which ended five years of war and divided the country into two fully autonomous entities, the Muslim-Croat Federation and Republika Srpska. Voters cast ballots for the following: a three-member national collective presidency consisting of a representative from each major ethnic group (Muslim, Serb, Croat); a regional president for Republika Srpska; a national parliament consisting of the 42-member House of Representatives elected by proportional representation (28 members from the Muslim-Croat Federation and 14 members from Republika Srpska); a 140-member Muslim-Croat House of Representatives; and the 83-member National Assembly of Republika Srpska.

In the race for the collective presidency, President Alija Izetbegovic of the Muslim-based, nationalist Party of Democratic Action (SDA) won reelection with 86 percent of the vote, while Zivko Radisic of the moderate Sloga coalition, consisting of the Serbian People's Union (SNS), the Socialist Party of Republika Srpksa (SPRS), and the Party of Independent Social Democrats (SNSD), defeated hardline Serb member Momcilo Krajisnik of the Serbian Democratic Party (SDS) by a vote of 51 percent to 45 percent. Incumbent Croatian moderate Kresmir Zubak of the New Croatian Initiative (NHI) came in third behind Ante Jalevic, the Croatia-backed hardliner from the Croatian Democratic Union (HDZ).

In other election highlights, incumbent Republika Srpska President Biljana Plavsic, backed by the West for her support of the Dayton Accords, was defeated by Nikola Poplasen, leader of the ultranationalist Serbian Radical Party (SRS), who nominated hardline nationalist Dragan Kalinic of the SDS and a wartime ally of accused war criminal Radovan Karadzic to replace moderate incumbent Milorad Dodik as prime minister of the Serb entity. But Kalinic's nomination was blocked by the newly elected republican parliament, in which the moderate Serb bloc led by the pro-Plavsic Sloga and the hardliners led by the SDS and the SRS controlled about 30 seats each. The rest belonged to Muslim and Croat deputies representing mainly refugees who fled the Serb entity during the 1992-95 war to areas that became the Mulsim-Croat Federation. By year's end, parliament could not agree on a prime minister, and the international Office of the High Representative and the United States said that a hardline Serb nationalist opposed to the Dayton agreement would not be acceptable.

Of the 140 seats in the federation House of Representatives, the SDA-led Coalition for a Unified and Democratic Bosnia-Herzegovina won 68 seats, followed by the Social Democratic Party of Bosnia-Herzegovina, with 19, and the HDZ with 15.

Bosnia-Herzegovina became one of six constituent republics of Yugoslavia in 1945. After a 1992 referendum boycotted by Serbs favored secession, President Alija Izetbegovic declared independence, leading to the outbreak of war launched by ethnic Serbs with the support of Serbia that was marked by "ethnic cleansing" that killed several hundred thousand and displaced 2 million people. In 1995, after NATO launched air strikes on Serb forces and battlefield gains by Bosnians and Croats, the presidents of Bosnia, Croatia and Serbia initialed the Dayton Accords, formally accepted in December. Key provisions included: a united Sarajevo; internationally supervised elections; a constitution calling for loose federative state with semi-autonomous Muslim-Croatian (51 percent) and Serb (49 percent) entities, a rotating presidency and the assignment of posts by nationality; UN-supervised disarmament; and the introduction of a 32,000-member NATO-led international peace force (IFOR, later renamed the stabilization force, or SFOR) to separate the warring factions and maintain the peace. Indicted war criminals, including Bosnian Serb President Karadzic and Gen. Ratko Mladic, would be barred from public office.

The 1996 national elections and the 1997 local elections for 136 municipal councils saw the dominance of the major nationalist parties, the SDA, HDZ, and SDS. But in mid-1997, tensions between Republika Srpksa President Plavsic, a former Karadzic protégé elected as an SDS stalwart, and hardliners erupted after she dissolved the SDS-dominated parliament, pledged to honor the Dayton Accords, and accused police of corruption and usurping her authority. International troops blocked a coup attempt by Karadzic loyalists, protected pro-Plavsic media facilities from nationalist mobs, and closed transmitters of the nationalist Bosnian Serb radio and television (SRT). After new elections in November, the SDS won 24 of 83 seats, down from 45 it won in 1996.

In January 1998, the stalemate over a prime minister was resolved with the appointment of moderate Milorad Dodik, which led to an influx of foreign aid into Republika Srpksa, including a pledge of $5 million from the U.S. But Plavsic's defeat in September's vote again left the republic without a government by year's end, and the U.S. said $100 million of additional aid pledged to the Bosnian Serbs depended on continued commitment to the peace process and Dayton.

In other issues, the national government continued to function sporadically, and the joint institutions of the Muslim-Croat Federation existed mainly on paper. And while $5.1 billion in reconstruction aid for 1996-99 helped to rebuild roads, bridges, schools, and housing, distrust among ethnic groups and officials and parties forced top Western envoy Carlos Westendrop to push through the design for a common currency, the Kovertiblina Marka, introduced in the summer, and the introduction of a passport and flag. In several key cities, municipal councils elected in 1997 under a system where 90 percent of registered voters signed up to cast absentee ballots in the place where they actually lived before the war, were not allowed to convene, blocked by nationalist parties that stood to lose control of towns captured during the war, though by May some type of power-sharing arrangements were imposed on 131 of 136 municipalities. The city of Mostar remained bitterly divided, and the fate of Brcko, under Serb control, remained undecided.

The return of refugees remained largely unrealized. The United Nations had billed 1998 as "The Year of Return," hoping that as many as 50,000 of the estimated 1.8

million people displaced by the war would return to their homes in areas controlled by members of another ethnic group. By the end of August, however, only 6,063 Bosnians had registered as "minority" returnees, and probably no more than 4,000 had returned without registering. Of these, no more than 1,700 were Croats and Serbs who came back to Sarajevo. And while Republika Srpska officials early in the year promised to orchestrate the return of 70,000 Muslims and Croats to their prewar homes, they reneged as a result of hardline pressure in an election year, and according to the UN, only 859 Muslim and Croat returnees had registered by the end of August.

In economic matters, the Bosnian economy showed double-digit growth, and inflation remained low. But the postwar growth was fueled by a $5.1 billion reconstruction package and on Western aid, and in December U.S. officials urged Bosnian leaders to undertake major economic reforms in order to attract badly needed foreign investment. The U.S. also criticized the country's politicians over widespread corruption, tax evasion, and burdensome regulations.

In 1998, several war criminals were arrested. In December, Gen. Radilsav Krstic, a close military ally of indicted war criminal Radovan Karadzic, was taken into custody by SFOR near Brcko.

Political Rights and Civil Liberties:

Citizens of Bosnia and its constituent entities can change their government democratically under a constitution provided in the Dayton Accords. The September 1997 local elections included irregularities, particularly in voter registration lists. Voters, including refugees who cast ballots for where they used to live, could not endow their representatives with de facto power since sitting authorities refused to implement election results. Hardliners charged irregularities in the November elections for the parliament of Republika Srpska. According to the OSCE and the Council of Europe, the 1998 national elections were conducted in "a more constructively competitive political environment" than previous ones. Several HDZ candidates were barred from running for "serious breaches of campaign and media regulations."

The OSCE-led Media Experts Commission (MEC) was established to assist authorities in promoting free media during election campaigns. Articles 80 and 81 of the criminal code criminalize libel. In January 1998, a municipal court convicted Senda Pecanin of the Sarajevo-based *Dani* magazine of criminal libel against Fahrudin Radoncic, editor of the daily *Dnevni Avaz*, controlled by the SDA. Pecanin had published an investigative article of Radoncic's business practices.

Approximately 25 percent of media outlets are privatized. There are several private or semi-privatized newspapers in Muslim-controlled areas of the federation and in Republika Srpksa in addition to local papers in Bosnian-Croat controlled areas. There are about 50 TV and 150 radio stations in Bosnia, most operating without official approval. In broadcasting, private media in the Muslim-controlled area of the federation include two major television stations—Studio 99 and TV Hayat—as well as several private and semi-private radio stations, including the Sarajevo-based Radio Stari Grad. In the Croat-controlled areas, the HTV Mostar station strongly supports the HDZ. In the Republika Srpska, most stations have links with political parties. There are several foreign-funded media outlets. Most private media are nominally independent, though they can broadly be characterized as pro- or anti-government. In December, MEC said that Bosnian radio and TV stations must apply by February 1999 for an operating license or risk closure. Journalists are still regularly harassed or detained by police and authorities.

Muslims, Catholic Croats and Orthodox Serbs practice their religions in areas they control. Mosques, churches and cemeteries were intentionally targeted in war zones.

While the constitution provides for freedom of assembly, the 1998 campaign occasionally saw restrictions placed on political rallies. The Provisional Election Commission (PEC), established under the Dayton agreement, approved 67 parties to contest the 1998 elections. Some 82 parties registered for the 1997 municipal votes. Security forces have harassed opposition parties in Republika Srpska and in the Muslim-Croat federation.

Trade unions exist, but their functions have been limited by economic and social dislocation. The largest union is the Confederation of Independent Trade Unions, which evolved from the Yugoslav Communist Trade Union Confederation. In November, trade unions in the Muslim-Croat federation protested the government's decision to lower the monthly minimum wage in key industrial sectors. The unions also urged the government to adopt legislation on collective bargaining.

The constitution provides for an independent judiciary, with the administration of justice reserved for the two entities. The judiciary has come under political pressure in the constituent entities such as in Republika Srpksa, where judges were intimidated in the ongoing struggle between moderates and hardliners. Courts remain under the control or influence of ruling parties.

Independent watchdog agencies reported in November that the human rights situation in Bosnia had improved despite ineffective, politically influenced police. Ethnically motivated crimes and the reluctance to investigate them remained a serious problem. Refugees attempting to return, and municipal councils attempting to assume their posts were subject to attacks and harassment throughout the country.

Freedom of movement across entity boundaries remains constricted, though the situation improved somewhat over previous years, and corruption remains a serious issue in both entities. There have been several charges by international officials claiming that aid money had been siphoned off by officials, and that the civil service experienced endemic smuggling and corruption, particularly in the Republika Srpska.

Property rights are tenuous throughout Bosnia. Property laws have generally been used as a tool to consolidate the results of "ethnic cleansing." Displaced owners of property have been unable to reclaim their homes and other assets. Business continues to be constrained by legal, administrative, and bureaucratic obstacles.

Botswana

Polity: Parliamentary
democracy and
traditional chiefs
Economy: Capitalist
Population: 1,500,000
PPP: $5,611
Life Expectancy: 41
Ethnic Groups: Batswana (95 percent), Kalanga, Basarwa
and Kgagaladi (4 percent), white (1 percent)
Capital: Gaborone

Political Rights: 2
Civil Liberties: 2
Status: Free

Overview:

Former central bank chief Festus Mogae succeeded Quett Masire as Botswana's president in April. Mogae's smooth transition to power reflected both the country's entrenched democratic institutions and the dominance of the ruling Botswana Democratic Party (BDP). A referendum on whether the president should be directly elected was withdrawn shortly before a scheduled vote in late 1997, and the majority party in the National Assembly will continue to appoint the country's leader. With the main opposition party increasingly fractured, the BDP is expected to dominate the next legislative elections, which are due by October 1999. In general, Botswana respects human rights, although occasional police misconduct, slow progress in improving women's rights, and the continued relocation of indigenous Baswara, or *N/oakwe* ("red people"), from traditional lands to make way for game parks and cattle ranching lingered as problems.

Elected governments have ruled Botswana for more than three decades since the country gained independence from Britain in 1966. The country is now Africa's longest continuous multiparty democracy. Economic progress has been built on sound fiscal management and low rates of corruption, but most of the country's people remain poor. In the past two years, the government has committed scarce resources to major weapons purchases, including fighter aircraft and tanks. Analysts believe that the escalation is linked to territorial and riparian disputes with neighboring Namibia. Both countries, however, have pledged to resolve these disputes through negotiations. Botswana sent about 400 soldiers to join a South African intervention in Lesotho in September to quell protests against alleged election irregularities.

Political Rights and Civil Liberties:

The legislative elections through which Botswana's 1.5 million citizens choose their government are now considered free and generally fair, despite accusations that the BDP, which has held power since independence, has regularly manipulated the electoral process. Election conduct has steadily improved, and the Independent Election Commission created in 1996 is expected to reduce partisanship in polls administration still further. The National Assembly elects the president to serve a concurrent five-year term. The opposition Botswana National Front won 13 of 35 seats contested in October 1994, but suffered from crippling infighting in 1998. The new United Action Party could draw some support, but a disunited opposition is not expected to defeat the BDP.

Botswana's human rights record is outstanding in Africa and was praised by President Bill Clinton during his March visit to the country. Several laws regarding sedition and allowing detention without trial (under the National Security Act), however, remain on the books. While rarely invoked, they remain a threat to freedom of expression and political activity. Another law bars "uttering words with intent to bring into ridicule the president of Botswana."

The courts are generally considered to be fair and free of direct political interference. Trials are usually public, and those accused of the most serious violent crimes are provided public defenders. The University of Botswana Legal Assistance Center and the Botswana Center for Human Rights offer free legal services, but are limited by a lack of resources.

Political debate is open and lively, and there is a free and vigorous print media in cities and towns. The opposition and government critics, however, receive little access to the government-controlled broadcast media. Issuance of licenses for commercial FM radio stations in late 1998 could help to break this monopoly. The government has not reintroduced the media legislation that was withdrawn after strong local and international protests last year. The law would have demanded stricter registration of newspapers and accreditation of journalists. In May, the government dropped charges of "spreading false rumours likely to cause alarm" against a resident British journalist.

Treatment of Botswana's indigenous Baswara, known as "Bushmen," has drawn local and international concern. Government relocation schemes reportedly include forcible evictions of Baswara from their traditional lands. Baswara are subject to widespread discrimination and abuse. Only a few thousand are still permitted to practice traditional nomadic lifestyles in the central Kalahari desert. Almost 50,000 others have been resettled in villages or as laborers on farms. Baswara demands include restitution of land and the right to hunt on traditional lands, much of which are now wildlife preserves.

Women's rights are not fully respected. Married women may not take a bank loan without their husbands' permission, and women, especially those in rural areas, face traditional discrimination. Only four of 44 National Assembly members are women, and only two women serve in the cabinet. Domestic violence against women is reportedly rampant, with little action to stem it through police action or education.

Concentration of economic power has hindered labor organization. While independent unions are permitted, workers' rights to strike and to bargain for wages are restricted. Botswana's competent financial management and relatively low rates of corruption have attracted both Korean and Swedish automobile manufacturers to build assembly plants in the country, but unemployment remains at approximately 35 percent. A 1996 law requires the president, members of the cabinet, and parliamentarians to declare their assets.

Brazil

Polity: Federal presidential-legislative democracy
Economy: Capitalist-statist
Population: 162,100,000
PPP: $5,928
Life Expectancy: 67
Ethnic Groups: White (55 percent), mixed (38 percent), black (6 percent), other (1 percent)
Capital: Brasilia

Political Rights: 3
Civil Liberties: 4
Status: Partly Free

Overview:

In 1998, Brazilian voters, worried about their country's economic collapse and a lack of public safety, once again opted for modernization and moderation by reelecting President Fernando Henrique Cardoso for a second term. However, allegations of corruption involving two top government officials threatened to undermine Cardoso's plan to stabilize South America's largest economy.

After gaining independence from Portugal in 1822, Brazil retained a monarchical system until a republic was established in 1889. Democratic rule has been interrupted by long periods of authoritarian rule, most recently under military regimes from 1964 to 1985, at which time elected civilian rule was reestablished. A new constitution went into effect in 1988 providing for a president elected for four years, a bicameral Congress consisting of an 81-member Senate elected for eight years, and a 503-member Chamber of Deputies elected for four years.

Civilian rule has been marked by corruption scandals. The scandal having the greatest political impact led to the impeachment by Congress of President Fernando Collor de Mello (1989-92). Collor resigned and was replaced by a weak, ineffectual government led by his vice president, Itamar Franco.

In early 1994, Cardoso, Franco's finance minister and a market-oriented centrist, forged a three-party, center-right coalition around his own Social Democratic Party (PSDB). As his anti-inflation plan appeared to work dramatically, former Marxist Cardoso jumped into the lead, backed by big media and big business. In October 1994, Cardoso won the presidency with 54 percent of the vote, against 27 percent for Luis Ignacio "Lula" de Silva, the leader of the leftist Workers' Party (PT) and an early-form front-runner. The Senate was divided among 11 parties and the Chamber of Deputies among 18. Cardoso's coalition did not have a majority in either house.

Cardoso spent 1995 cajoling and horse-trading for the congressional votes needed to implement his economic liberalization program. That fall his government was rocked by a bribery and phone-tapping scandal. In April 1996, Cardoso indicated that he favored a constitutional amendment to drop the one-term limit, allowing him to run for re-election in 1998, and in 1997, he secured Congressional approval for such a measure.

Land issues were high on the political agenda in 1996. In January, Cardoso announced presidential decree 1775, which allows states, municipalities, and non-Indians to challenge, at the federal level, proposed demarcation of Indian land. Following the decree, miners and loggers increased their encroachments on Indian land. In another development, a radicalized movement representing landless peasants continued to occupy mostly fallow land in rural areas in order to pressure the government to settle rural families. The activism contributed to scores of violent conflicts between peasants and the military, police, and private security forces, which act with virtual impunity.

Cardoso's first-ballot victory (nearly 52 percent of the votes cast) over Lula, his nearest rival, was tempered by a less convincing win at the congressional and gubernatorial levels. His win was also overshadowed when published accounts of secretly recorded conversations seemed to indicate that two top officials appeared to be steering a bid to privatize part of the state-run telephone holding company to a consortium of personal friends, who ended up losing the auction.

Political Rights and Civil Liberties:

Citizens can change governments through elections. The 1998 elections were considered free and fair, with opposition candidates winning the governorships of three of the biggest states: Rio de Janeiro, Minas Gerais and Rio Grande do Sul. Parliament remains dominated by the executive branch. Professional staff capabilities are not used by members of Congress. Concern has been expressed about Cardoso's use of "provisional measures" (decrees) in order to bypass Congress.

The constitution guarantees freedom of religion and expression as well as the right to organize political and civic organizations. Cardoso is credited with initiating a sea-change in attitudes concerning international criticism on rights issues, from aggressive nationalistic rejection to dialogue and openness. He created a ministerial rank secretariat charged with defending human rights. The crime of torture was upgraded from a misdemeanor to a serious crime punishable by up to 16 years in prison. He has also proposed making all violations of rights federal crimes, thus moving their investigation from the jurisdiction of state, civil, and military police forces. In an attempt to roll back the current climate of police impunity, Cardoso has pledged to put federal judges in charge of cases involving allegations of military police brutality, removing them from the jurisdiction of military tribunals. In Sao Paulo state, Cardoso ally Governor Mario Covas has taken the lead in combating police misconduct even as anti-crime hysteria seized the population.

The climate of lawlessness is reinforced by a weak judiciary. Brazil's Supreme Court is granted substantial autonomy by the constitution. However, the judicial system is overwhelmed (with only 7,000 judges for a population of more than 150 million), and vulnerable to the chronic corruption that undermines the entire political system. It has been virtually powerless in the face of organized crime. A national breakdown in police discipline and escalating criminal violence—fueled by a burgeoning drug trade and increasing ties to Italian and other foreign criminal organizations—have intensified a climate of lawlessness and insecurity. Human rights, particularly those of socially marginalized groups, are violated with impunity on a massive scale.

Brazil's police are among the world's most violent and corrupt. Grossly underpaid in the lower ranks, their work conditions are poor. Extra-judicial killings are disguised as shootouts with dangerous criminals. Federal police as well as the state civil and military police routinely practice torture, particularly against poor criminal suspects. Military policemen in Sao Paulo and Rio de Janeiro have secretly been caught on videotape attacking people on the street, extorting money, opening fire upon, and killing motorists during routine operations. Although officers are rarely punished, in October 1998, a former policeman nicknamed "Rambo," captured on videotape beating motorists and fatally shooting one passenger, was sentenced to 65-years imprisonment. In Rio de Janeiro, state civil police sold weapons to drug-trafficking gangs that control many of the city's hillside shantytowns. In many cities, "death squads," often composed of off-duty state police, terrorize shantytown dwellers and intimidate human rights activists attempting to investigate abuses. Opinion polls in Sao Paolo showed 42 percent of those interviewed had either experienced police violence or had a relative who had, and fully 70 percent of city residents were terrified of the military police.

Since 1994, the federal government has deployed the army in order to quell police strikes and bring order to Rio de Janeiro's 400 slums, most of which are ruled by gangs which are in league or in competition with corrupt police and local politicians. Public distrust of the judiciary has resulted in poor citizens taking the law into their own hands, with hundreds of reported lynchings and mob executions. In response to U.S. pressure, the Brazilian military is playing an increasing role in anti-narcotics efforts.

The press is privately owned. There are dozens of daily newspapers and numerous other publications throughout the country, and the print media have played a central role in exposing official corruption. In January, the editor of a weekly newspaper in Bahia was murdered after publishing several articles linking several individuals close to the state's governor and one of its senators with corruption. A photographer who was a key witness in the 1996 massacre by police of 19 landless peasants was murdered in November 1998 shortly before he was scheduled to testify in the government's investigation of the case.

Brazil has one of the most concentrated land distribution patterns in the world. Large landowners control nearly 60 percent of arable land, while the poorest 30 percent share less than two percent. In rural areas, violence linked to land disputes is declining, but courts have supported increasingly backing the eviction of landless farmers. Land disputes have risen sharply in recent years, as innumerable invasions of "unproductive" land have been organized by rural activists in order to draw attention to the plight of an estimated 4.8 million families without land. According to the Catholic Church, in 1997 there was a drop in the number of assaults, torture, death threats and illegal expulsions sponsored by landowners in response to the disputes. Thousands of workers are forced by ranchers in rural areas to work against their will, and have no recourse to cops or courts.

Violence against women and children is a common problem as protective laws are rarely enforced. In 1991, the Supreme Court ruled that a man could no longer kill his wife and win acquittal on the grounds of "legitimate defense of honor," but juries tend to ignore the ruling. Forced prostitution of children is widespread. Child labor is prevalent, and laws against it are rarely enforced. A recent UNICEF study reported that 53 percent of the 17.5 million children and young people forced to work in Latin America are in Brazil, and of these 1,000,000 are under the age of ten. A report from the state juvenile court in Rio de Janeiro claims that, on average, three street children are killed every day in Rio, many by police at the request of local merchants. In July 1998, the Brazilian government announced a major initiative against domestic violence.

Violence against Brazil's 250,000 Indians continues. In May 1998, the coordinator of the Organization of Indigenous Peoples was murdered by unidentified gunmen. The

1988 constitution guarantees indigenous peoples land rights covering some 11 percent of the country, and by law, outsiders can only enter Indian reserves with permission. Decree 1775 has opened Indian land to greater pressure from predatory miners and loggers. A government decision to reduce and fragment the key Raposa-Serra do Sol area in Roraima state was considered a payoff to special interests in Congress for their support for Cardoso's reelection gambit, despite its implications for Indian lands. Cardoso also slashed the budget of the agency responsible for demarcating Indian lands.

Industrial labor unions are well organized and politically connected, and many are corrupt. The right to strike is recognized, and there are special labor courts. Hundreds of strikes have taken place in recent years against attempts to privatize state industries.

Brunei

Polity: Traditional monarchy
Economy: Capitalist-statist
Population: 300,000
PPP: $31,165
Life Expectancy: 71
Ethnic Groups: Malay (64 percent), Chinese (20 percent), others (16 percent)
Capital: Bandar Seri Begawan

Political Rights: 7
Civil Liberties: 5
Status: Not Free

Overview:
Consisting of two noncontiguous enclaves on the northern coast of the Southeast Asian island of Borneo, Brunei became a British protectorate in 1888. The country's first written constitution of 1959 provided for five advisory councils: the Privy Council, the Religious Council, the Council of Succession, the Council of Ministers, and a Legislative Council. In 1962, the leftist Brunei People's Party (PRB) won all ten elected seats in the 21-member Legislative Council. Late in the year, British troops crushed a PRB-backed rebellion seeking an independent state encompassing nearby British territories. The sultan assumed constitutionally authorized emergency powers for a stipulated two-year period. These powers have since been renewed every two years. Elections have not been held since 1965. Sultan Haji Hassanal Bolkiah Mu'izzaddin Waddaulah ascended the throne in October 1967.

Brunei achieved independence from Great Britain in 1984. In 1985, the government recognized the moderate Brunei National Democratic Party (PKDB) and, a year later, the offshoot Brunei National Solidarity Party (PPKB). In 1988, the sultan dissolved the PKDB and detained two of its leaders for two years, reportedly after the party called for elections. In 1995, the authorities permitted a PPKB general assembly that elected Abdul Latif Chuchu, one of the two former PKDB leaders detained from 1988 to 1990, as party president. Chuchu later resigned under government pressure, and since then, the PPKB has been inactive.

Relations between the sultan and his younger brother Prince Jefri deteriorated after the collapse of the nation's largest private company, Amedeo Development Corporation, which was run by Prince Jefri. The sultan subsequently removed Prince Jefri as head of the Brunei Investment Agency (BIA), which manages the royal family's vast worldwide assets, amid charges of financial mismanagement and misappropriation of funds.

Political Rights and Civil Liberties:

Citizens of Brunei, a hereditary sultanate, lack the democratic means to change their government. The sultan serves as prime minister, rules by decree, and, along with an inner circle of relatives, holds absolute power. The Legislative Council has been fully appointed and the constitution partially suspended since 1970. Currently, only the Council of Ministers, composed largely of the sultan's relatives, and the Legislative Council convene. Since 1992, village chiefs have been chosen for life terms through local elections in which all candidates must have a knowledge of Islam (although they may be non-Muslims) and cannot have past or current links with a political party. The chiefs communicate with the government through a village consultative council, although the sultan appoints the council's advisors. Citizens may also petition the sultan. There has been no public political party activity since 1995. Some members of non-Malay ethnic groups, including ethnic Chinese and others born in Brunei, are not automatically accorded citizenship, and Brunei's colonial-era nationalization laws are generally considered to be in need of reform.

The only privately owned newspaper practices self-censorship on political and religious issues. The government-controlled Radio Television Brunei operates the only local broadcast media. A cable network offers international programming. Foreign journals with articles critical of the royal family or government are not allowed into the country. Islam is the official religion, and non-Muslims face bans or restrictions on building or repairing places of worship, importing religious books or educational materials, and providing religious education in non-Muslim schools. Since 1991, the sultan has promoted local culture and the primacy of the monarchy as the defender of Islam through a conservative Malay Muslim Monarchy (MIB) ideology, apparently in an effort to ward off any incipient calls for democratization. Islamic studies and MIB must be taught at all schools.

The government constrains the activities of international service organizations, such as Rotary and Lions clubs. There are three independent, but largely inactive, trade unions, all of which are in the oil sector, but their membership comprises less than five percent of that industry's workforce. Legislation neither explicitly recognizes nor denies the right to strike, and, in practice, strikes do not occur.

The judiciary is independent of the government. A 1996 appellate-level decision formally established the courts' power to discharge and acquit a defendant even if not requested by the prosecution. Defendants enjoy adequate procedural safeguards, and, in civil cases, there is a right of appeal to the Privy Council in London. Although *Shari'a* (Islamic law) supercedes civil law in some areas, it is not applied to non-Muslims. The police force is under civilian control. Police have broad powers of arrest without warrants, although in practice they generally obtain a warrant from a magistrate. The Internal Security Act (ISA) permits the government to detain suspects without a trial for renewable two-year periods. The ISA has occasionally been used to detain political dissidents.

Although the law permits government intrusion into the privacy of individuals, families, or homes, this rarely happens. Citizens can travel freely within the country and abroad. Women face discrimination in divorce, inheritance, and child custody matters, which are handled under Shari'a. Muslim women are encouraged to wear the *tudong*, a traditional head covering, but there is no official pressure on non-Muslim women to do so. Female domestic servants are occasionally beaten or otherwise treated poorly.

Bulgaria

Polity: Parliamentary democracy
Economy: Mixed capitalist (transitional)
Population: 8,300,000
PPP: $4,604
Life Expectancy: 71
Ethnic Groups: Bulgarian (85 percent), Turk (9 percent), Macedonian (3 percent), Gypsy (3 percent)
Capital: Sofia

Political Rights: 2
Civil Liberties: 3
Status: Free

Overview: Fighting corruption and stimulating private business and foreign investment were key priorities for Prime Minister Ivan Kostov and the ruling Union of Democratic Forces (UDF) in 1998. In September, the International Monetary Fund approved an $840 million loan to support reforms and economic growth. The opposition Bulgarian Socialist Party (BSP) criticized the deal, however, by claiming that it would inflict further hardship on an already disadvantaged population by necessitating higher taxes and the closing of industrial enterprises.

Bulgaria was occupied by Ottoman Turks from 1396 to 1878. It did not achieve complete independence until 1908. Communists seized power in conjunction with the "liberation" of Bulgaria by the army of the Soviet Union in 1944. From 1954 until 1989, the country was ruled by Communist Party leader Todor Zhivkov, who resigned after the fall of the Berlin Wall. With the exception of a short-lived democratic government elected in 1991, Bulgaria continued to be governed by former Communists until 1997.

Thirteen candidates competed in the 1996 presidential vote. In the first round in October, the UDF's Petar Stoyanov and running mate Todor Kavaldzhiev received 44 percent of the vote, while the BSP's Ivan Marazov and Deputy Foreign Minister Irina Bokova won 26.9 percent. In the November runoff, Stoyanov won with 59.9 percent of the vote. Immediately prior to the October presidential vote, a group of BSP leaders asked for the resignation of Prime Minister Zhan Videnov, who had been accused of implementing regressive social and economic policies. Some reformers in the BSP then threatened to split the party and support early elections. In December, Videnov resigned.

Mounting street protests and the threat of strikes in 1997 ultimately forced the BSP to agree to early elections. In the April voting, which were labeled free and fair by international observers, the UDF and its allied factions won 52 percent of the vote and 137 of 240 parliamentary seats. The BSP captured 58 seats; the ethnic Turkish-based

Movement for Rights and Freedoms (MRF), 15; the Euroleft, 14; and the Bulgarian Business Bloc, 12. UDF leader Kostov became prime minister.

In 1998, the government faced growing pressure to implement reforms and battle endemic corruption. During an official visit to Washington in February, President Stoyanov sought to increase foreign investment, which totaled only $502 million in 1997. An obstacle to investment continued to be widespread pirating of compact discs and other violations of intellectual property rights. In May, the World Bank reported that Bulgaria's track record in transition had been "very weak" and warned that, without forceful reform, Bulgaria would not be able to attract the financing necessary to maintain macroeconomic stability.

Political Rights and Civil Liberties:

Bulgarians can change their government democratically. The 1997 parliamentary elections and 1996 presidential vote were free and fair.

In 1997, the UDF-led government pledged to pass a new media law that would minimize partisan interference in the state-owned broadcast media. Parliament amended the 1996 law to require that, of the seven members of the supervisory National Council on Radio and Television (NCRT), four would be elected by parliament and three appointed by the president. Under the previous law, all seven were named by parliament. In September 1998, the parliament made further changes, but President Stoyanov vetoed the law and sent it back to parliament. Stoyanov stated that the proposed composition of an 11-member NCRT, with seven members appointed by parliament and two each by the president and prime minister, did not guarantee the entity's political independence. He also rejected an article that stipulated that national radio and television programs should be broadcast only in the Bulgarian language and that restricted programs targeting the 800,000-strong ethnic Turkish minority. In June, the Constitutional Court ruled that three penal code articles proscribing "libel" and "insult" against state authority were not unconstitutional. Virtually all print media are privately owned. There are more than 60 private radio stations and several privately owned regional television stations. The country's economic crisis has caused hardship for the independent press. In July, a journalist in southern Bulgaria was attacked and beaten after a series of articles on the local mafia. Also in July, a regional prosecutor blocked the bank account of *Sedmitza*, a weekly southeastern newspaper, after the paper published articles criticizing her work.

Freedom of worship is generally respected, although the government regulates churches and religious institutions through the Directorate of Religious Beliefs. A 1994 law on registration led to 39 associations, most of which were Protestant, losing their status as "juridical entities," thereby barring them from re-registration.

The constitution provides for the right to peaceful assembly. Permits are required for demonstrations and outdoor rallies, but are routinely granted.

Approximately 200 political parties and associations are registered. The constitution prohibits the formation of political parties along religious, ethnic, or racial lines. Nevertheless, the overwhelmingly ethnic-Turkish MRF operates freely and is represented in parliament.

Bulgaria has two large labor union confederations, the Confederation of Independent Trade Unions, a successor to the Communist-era union, and Podkrepa, an independent federation founded in 1989. The smaller Promyana Trade Union Association was formed by the UDF in 1996. In February 1998, hundreds of miners held a ten-day hunger strike to protest the restructuring of the state-run Gorubso lead and zinc mining complex. In November, the miners struck again after management failed to raise their wages as had been promised eight months earlier.

Under the constitution, the judiciary is guaranteed independence and equal status with the legislature and executive branch. Corruption, inadequate staffing, low salaries, and lack of experienced personnel continue to hamper the system. Police frequently mistreat prisoners and detainees, according to domestic and international monitoring groups.

Free movement within the country and emigration rights are generally respected. Private property is formally protected and, in general, private property rights are respected in practice and enforced by the judiciary.

High rates of corruption, widespread organized crime, and continued government control of significant sectors of the economy impede competition and equality of opportunity.

Women are well represented in administrative and managerial positions and in higher education.

Burkina Faso

Polity: Dominant party
Economy: Mixed statist
Population: 11,300,000
PPP: $784
Life Expectancy: 47
Ethnic Groups: Mossi, Gurunsi, Senufo, Lobi, Bobo, Mande, Fulani
Capital: Ouagadougou

Political Rights: 5
Civil Liberties: 4
Status: Partly Free

Overview:
President Blaise Compaoré was returned to office for a second seven-year term with nearly 88 percent of the vote in November elections. Oppositionists charged that the vote was manipulated by the ruling Congress for Democracy and Progress (CDP). The polls, which were marked by heavy use of state patronage, resources, and media to bolster the incumbent's campaign, further entrenched Compaoré's dominance over Burkina Faso's political life. President Compaoré and the ruling CDP, which is led primarily by members of the military juntas that ruled the country from 1983 to 1991, effectively wield all power in the country. Compaoré's lavish lifestyle and allegations of corruption have nurtured wide mistrust of the CDP government. Burkina Faso's human rights record is mixed. While civil society and the independent media generally operate without official interference, serious abuses by security forces go unpunished. The December 13 death of a leading journalist, Norbert Zongo, reportedly in a road accident, set off violent demonstrations in the capital and several other cities. About 50,000 people attended his funeral amidst widespread disbelief of official accounts of Zongo's demise.

After receiving independence from France in 1960 as Upper Volta, Burkina Faso suffered a succession of army coups. In 1983, Compaoré installed himself as president at gunpoint in a bloody fratricide among members of a junta that had seized power four years earlier. Populist, charismatic President Thomas Sankara and 13 of this closest associates were murdered. More Sankara supporters were executed two years later.

Political Rights and Civil Liberties:

Burkina Faso's 1991 constitution guarantees its people the right to elect their government freely through periodic multiparty elections. In practice, this right has not been realized. Despite a reported turnout of more than 50 percent, President Compaoré's 1998 re-election victory may not reflect a genuine expression of the will of the Burkinabé people. The independent election commission established in May did not have control over important parts of the electoral process, particularly electoral rolls and voter's cards. The preceding presidential polls in December 1991 were marred by widespread violence and an opposition boycott. Only 25 percent of registered voters cast ballots, and Compaoré was declared the victor with a reported 85 percent of the vote. Legislative polls in May 1992 also drew a small turnout. Opposition parties and independent observers charged that 1997 legislative elections for five-year National Assembly terms were marred by fraud. Opposition disunity and electoral rules sharply combined to reduce the opposition's representation in the legislature to well below the 31 percent of the popular vote total opposition parties had received. This further reduced the role of the country's 60 opposition parties in shaping national policy. State patronage boosted ruling party fortunes as the CDP took 101 of 111 national assembly seats.

The Burkinabé judiciary is subject to executive interference in political cases, but is more independent in civil and criminal cases. Training and proper administration of justice are also hampered by a lack of resources. National security laws permit surveillance and arrests without warrants. Police routinely ignore proscribed limits on detention, search, and seizure. Prison conditions are harsh, with overcrowding, poor diets, and minimal medical attention.

Freedom of assembly is constitutionally protected and generally respected, with required permits usually issued routinely. Many nongovernmental organizations operate openly and freely, including human rights groups such as the Burkinabé Movement for Human and Peoples Rights, which has reported detailed accounts of security force abuses. Burkina Faso is a secular state, and religious freedom is respected.

A dozen private radio stations, a private television station, and numerous independent newspapers and magazines function with little governmental interference. The media, which are often highly critical of the government, play an important role in public debate.

Customary law sanctions discrimination against women and is used by traditional courts to resolve civil and family disputes, especially in rural areas, and constitutional and legal protections for women's rights are nonexistent or poorly enforced. Women's educational and employment opportunities are scarce in the countryside. Women hold few parliamentary seats or senior government posts. Female genital mutilation is still widely practiced, even though it is illegal and a government campaign has been mounted against the practice.

Labor unions are a strong force in society. With the exception of individuals employed in essential services, workers enjoy a broad range of legal protections for labor rights, including the right to strike. Several labor confederations and independent unions bargain with employers. Efforts to reform the civil service have been met with marches and strikes, but are considered a vital element of economic progress and improvements in public administration.

Approximately four-fifths of the country's nearly 11 million people are subsistence farmers. As of 1995, 70.5 percent of Burkinabé men and 90.8 percent of the country's women were unable to read or write. A major internationally assisted literacy campaign is underway, but poor educational levels remain a major obstacle to development. Privatization of the state-owned electricity sector is part of an economic liberalization program, but the state retains broad powers to intervene in the country's economic and social life. Reports of widespread official corruption persist, although the government has taken action against some officials, including a district mayor in the capital, Ouagadougou.

Burma (Myanmar)

Polity: Military
Economy: Statist
Population: 47,100,000
PPP: $1,130
Life Expectancy: 61
Ethnic Groups: Burman (68 percent), Shan (9 percent), Karen (7 percent), Rakhine (4 percent), Chinese (3 percent), Mon (2 percent), Indian (2 percent), other (5 percent)
Capital: Rangoon

Political Rights: 7
Civil Liberties: 7
Status: Not Free

Overview: Ten years after crushing pro-democracy demonstrations, in 1998 the military remained firmly in control of Burma behind a younger and more internationally savvy, but equally brutal, generation of officers.

Following the Japanese occupation in World War II, Burma achieved independence from Britain in 1948. The army overthrew an elected government in 1962 amidst an economic crisis and insurgencies by ethnic rebel groups. During the next 26 years, General Ne Win's military rule impoverished what had been one of Southeast Asia's richest countries. In 1988, an estimated 3,000 people were killed in an army crackdown on massive, peaceful pro-democracy demonstrations. Army leaders General Saw Maung and Brigadier General Khin Nyunt created the State Law and Order Restoration Council (SLORC) to rule the country.

In 1990, in the first free elections in three decades, the opposition National League for Democracy (NLD) won 392 of the 485 parliamentary seats. The SLORC refused to cede power and jailed hundreds of NLD members. In 1992, it implemented superficial liberalizations, including the replacement of hardliner Saw Maung with General Than Shwe as prime minister and junta leader. In 1993, however, the limits of the reforms became apparent as a sham constitutional convention drafted guidelines granting the military 25 percent of seats in a future parliament and formalizing its leading role in politics. Since then, the convention has met sporadically. In 1995, the SLORC released Aung San Suu Kyi, the NLD leader and the country's preeminent pro-democracy campaigner, after six years of house arrest. The generals have rejected the 1992 Nobel Laureate's calls for a dialogue on democratic reform. Authorities quelled student demonstrations in 1996 by closing universities and detaining scores of people.

In November 1997, the SLORC reconstituted itself as the 19-member State Peace and Development Council, elevated relatively junior commanders, and sidelined at least 14 of the 21 SLORC members. By early 1998, the junta had also removed numerous corrupt ministers in an apparent effort to improve its international image, attract foreign investment, and promote an end to U.S.-led sanctions. Lieutenant General Khin Nyunt, the intelligence chief and formally one of the junta's top five members, continues to be the regime's strongman. In April, the regime reportedly detained nearly 250 lawyers, Buddhist monks, and student leaders in an intensified crackdown. It also reportedly sentenced six pro-democracy activists to death after claiming that they had been caught with explosives.

In May, the NLD called for the parliament elected in 1990 to be convened by August. The military responded by ordering NLD members of parliament outside of Rangoon to report to local authorities twice a day. In July, the NLD reported that the junta had detained 79 elected representatives for defying the restrictions. In August, riot police reportedly arrested dozens of anti-junta protesters at Rangoon University, although in September, authorities allowed thousands of students to hold rare protests at two other universities in Rangoon.

The ethnic minorities that comprise more than one-third of Burma's population have been fighting for autonomy from the Burman-dominated central government since the late 1940s. Since 1989, the SLORC has co-opted 15 ethnic rebel armies with ceasefire deals that allow them to maintain their weapons and territory. Many warlords have become drug traffickers and have helped to make Burma one of the world's largest heroin exporters while pouring the proceeds into Rangoon real estate and other business ventures. In recent years, the country's dry season has seen intense fighting between the army and the predominantly-Christian Karen National Union (KNU), the largest active insurgency. In 1997 and 1998, regular troops and the Democratic Karen Buddhist Army, a pro-regime militia of KNU defectors, attacked Karen refugee camps inside Thailand and destroyed homes.

Political Rights and Civil Liberties: Burma is effectively a garrison state ruled by one of the most repressive regimes in the world. The junta controls the judiciary, and the rule of law is nonexistent. The SLORC has imprisoned or driven into exile most of its vocal opponents; severely restricted freedoms of speech, press, association and other fundamental rights; and used a tightly controlled mass movement, the Union Solidarity Development Association, to monitor forced labor quotas, report on citizens, and intimidate opponents. The army is responsible for arbitrary beatings and killings of civilians; the forced, unpaid use of civilians as porters, laborers, and human mine sweepers under brutal conditions, with soldiers sometimes killing weakened porters or executing those who resist; summary executions of civilians who refuse to provide food or money to military units; arrests of civilians as alleged insurgents or insurgent sympathizers; and widespread incidents of rape. In April, the UN Special Rapporteur for Burma said that, based on well-documented reports, "extrajudicial, summary, or arbitrary executions, the practice of torture, portering, and forced labor continue to occur in Myanmar, particularly in the context of development programs and of counterinsurgency operations in minority-dominated regions."

Gross human rights violations during counterinsurgency operations against ethnic rebel groups have driven more than 100,000 mainly Karen, Karenni, Shan, and Mon refugees into Thailand. In January, Danish doctors who examined 200 Burmese refugees in Thailand reported that two-thirds were victims of rape and other abuses. Fighting has internally displaced thousands of other ethnic minorities. The Burmese army also forcibly relocates ethnic minority villagers as part of its military strategy, generally without providing food or shelter at the new sites. In April, Amnesty International reported that, since 1996, the army has forcibly relocated at least 300,000 villagers as part of its counterinsurgency operations against the Shan States Army in Shan state. Soldiers have burned homes, killed hundreds of Shan civilians, and subjected others to beatings, rape, and forced porterage and other labor. Amnesty International also reported that armed opposition groups have committed killings and other abuses against ethnic Burmans in Shan state. Ethnic Chin communities on the western border also face forced labor and other abuses.

Since 1994, most of the 250,000 Muslim Rohingyas who fled to Bangladesh in 1991 and 1992 to escape extrajudicial executions, rape, religious persecution, and other abuses in northern Arakan state have returned to Burma. Nevertheless, the Rohingyas have not received increased protection, and, in 1996 and 1997, thousands sought asylum in Bangladesh to escape forced labor, porterage, arbitrary taxation, land confiscation, and other hardships. The Rohingya refugee issue occurs in the context of the xenophobic regime's broader persecution of the Muslim minority. Human Rights Watch/Asia has noted that the 1982 Citizenship Act was designed to deny citizenship to the Rohingyas and make them ineligible for basic social, educational, and health services. In 1997, soldiers fighting the KNU in Karen state also leveled mosques and forcibly expelled Muslims from their homes.

Since the early 1990s, the junta has increasingly used forced labor for building roads, railways, and other infrastructure projects and military facilities. The laborers toil under harsh conditions and receive no compensation. There are credible reports that the army is using civilian porters and forced labor while protecting the construction of a foreign-financed pipeline that will transport offshore natural gas across Burma's southern peninsula to Thailand. The army is also using forced labor for roads and a railway line that will cross the pipeline.

The junta is equally brutal towards dissidents. In April, opposition leader Aung San Suu Kyi estimated that there are between 1,000 and 2,000 political prisoners in Burmese jails. In May, the *Financial Times* published a study that found that 78 NLD parliamentarians elected in 1990 have spent time in prison, with one jailed for three years for illegal possession of foreign currency after a search of his house found his toddler playing with two Singaporean coins. Twenty more are in exile, and 112 have either resigned or have been disqualified. In April, the junta jailed San San, an elderly elected NLD member of parliament, for 25 years under the Official Secrets Act after she criticized the regime in a BBC interview. The junta has used numerous broadly drawn laws to criminalize peaceful pro-democracy activities such as distributing pamphlets and distributing, viewing, or smuggling videotapes of Suu Kyi's public addresses. For example, Decree 5/96 of 1996 authorizes jail terms of five to 25 years for aiding activities that "adversely affect the national interest." Prison conditions are abysmal, torture of both political prisoners and common criminals is routine, and, in recent years, several NLD members have died in prison.

The press is tightly controlled, there are no independent publications or broadcast services, and, according to the Paris-based Reporters Sans Frontieres, since 1988 the regime has incarcerated at least 14 journalists, seven of whom are currently imprisoned and two of whom have died in jail. In 1996, the government subjected unauthorized Internet use to lengthy jail terms. Decree 5/96 also authorizes the Home Ministry to ban any organization that violates a law against public gatherings of five or more people. The Directorate of Defense Services Intelligence arbitrarily searches homes, intercepts mail, and monitors telephone conversations. In 1997, the *Far Eastern Economic Review* reported that the regime had opened a high technology information warfare center capable of intercepting telephone, fax, E-mail, and radio communications. Universities are closely monitored and have largely remained closed since late 1996.

Thousands of Burmese women and girls, many from ethnic minority groups, have been forcibly sent to Thailand by criminal gangs for prostitution. The army forcibly recruits children and routinely uses child porters. Authorities closely monitor monasteries and interfere in Buddhist religious affairs. The regime continues to hold many of the 300 monks arrested during a violent 1990 crackdown on monasteries. Reports in 1997 suggested that 16 monks have died in prison. Trade unions, collective bargaining, and strikes are illegal. The junta's severe economic mismanagement is exacerbated by pervasive official corruption and the army's arbitrary levies on peasants.

Burundi

Polity: Civilian-military   **Political Rights:** 7
Economy: Mixed statist   **Civil Liberties:** 6*
Population: 5,500,000   **Status:** Not Free
PPP: $637
Life Expectancy: 46
Ethnic Groups: Hutu [Bantu] (85 percent), Tutsi (14 percent), Twa [pygmy] (1 percent)
Capital: Bujumbura
Ratings change: Burundi's civil liberties rating changed from 7 to 6 due to a slight easing of repression in the country.

Overview: In June, Burundi's leading Hutu and Tutsi political parties implemented an accord that legitimized the presidency of retired army Major Pierre Buyoya, who seized power for the second time in 1996. A transitional constitution promised reforms to end the country's five years of bloody ethnic war. Nevertheless, human rights abuses by both the government and insurgents continued to wrack the country. Extremist elements of both the majority Hutu and minority Tutsi communities sought to block compromise aimed at ending the civil war, which has claimed nearly 250,000 lives since 1993. Tutsi chauvinists believe that they should never share power with the Hutu, who comprise approximately 85 percent of the country's people, while radical Hutu continue to call for the extermination of all Tutsi. In the countryside, fighting lessened, but still flared with savagery. Almost 500,000 Hutu have been driven from their homes to relocation camps where abysmal conditions include disease and malnutrition, and most Hutus have been driven from the capital, Bujumbura.

Burundi received its independence from Belgium in 1962 under a system that gave political and military power firmly to the 15 percent Tutsi minority. Since then, massacres by and against the country's ethnic Hutu majority have repeatedly torn the country. Major Buyoya mounted his first coup in 1987 by deposing the widely unpopular authoritarian President Jean-Baptiste Bagaza. In 1992, the Tutsi dominated Unity for National Progress (Uprona) party agreed to multiparty elections, which were held one year later. Melchior Ndadaye of the Burundi Front for Democracy (Frodebu) defeated Buyoya with more than 60 percent of the vote and became the country's first Hutu president. Frodebu also scored a large victory in legislative elections.

In 1993, radical Tutsi soldiers ended Burundi's democratic experiment and sparked the ongoing ethnic civil war by assassinating President Ndadaye and several other senior officials. Cyprien Ntaryamira, Ndadaye's successor, was killed along with Rwanda President Juvenal Habyarimana in 1994 when their plane was apparently shot down while approaching Kigali airport. The event provoked intensified killings in Burundi and marked the start of the anti-Tutsi genocide in Rwanda. Under a 1994 power-sharing arrangement between the main political parties, Hutu politician Sylvestre Ntibantunganya served as Burundi's new president until his ouster by Major Buyoya in 1996.

Political Rights and Civil Liberties: In 1993, Burundi's citizens freely elected their president and legislative representatives to five-year terms by secret ballot in the country's first and only open multiparty elections. The subsequent murders of Presidents Ndadaye and Ntaryamira eventually led to the formation of the coalition government overthrown by Major Buyoya in 1996. The national assembly, banned after the coup, was nominally restored through a 1996 Buyoya decree that provided for a resumption of political activities. The June agreements and transitional constitution negotiated between Buyoya, Frodebu, and Uprona expanded the National Assembly to 121 members and established two vice presidencies, with one filled by each party. The new government brings the Hutu majority effectively back into government, but real authority still lies with President Buyoya and his supporters. No date for new elections has been discussed.

Murder, rape, and torture by both government and rebel forces has been reported from the countryside. Efforts to resolve the political impasse are complicated by deep divisions within both communities over the goals for any negotiations. Various Tutsi faction leaders have been arrested, and Hutu guerrillas are split into competing groups that have sometimes turned their guns on each other.

Constitutional guarantees regarding arrest and detention are widely disregarded. Approximately 8,000 people, nearly all of whom are Hutu, are detained without trial. In July, an Amnesty International report described Burundi's justice system as often arbitrary, grossly unfair, and marked by summary trials. According to the report, torture while in detention is commonplace. Judicial reforms to create more ethnic balance were agreed to in June and may help to end the distrust felt by the Hutu majority due to Tutsi control over the courts. Burundi's first official executions since 1981 were carried out in 1997, when six men were hanged after being sentenced for ethnic killings in trials criticized by observers as grossly unfair. More than 250 others have received death sentences. Discrimination against the Hutu minority is systemic in both economic and political life. The small Twa (pygmy) minority of approximately two percent of the population is almost entirely excluded from the modern state.

Official press restrictions were formally lifted in 1996, but journalists practice extensive self-censorship for fear of reprisals. In March, authorities seized copies of the Frodebu-backed *L'Aube de la democratie* and closed the offices of *Net-Press*, a local news agency. With the exception of *Le Renouveau*, the thrice-weekly official government organ, few newspapers are available, and most are little more than extremist propaganda sheets. The government runs the two main radio stations, which reach a larger audience, especially in the countryside. The European Union has operated a radio station that offers nonpartisan programming promoting peace and ethnic tolerance, and similar American-funded programming, including a radio soap opera, is broadcast on national radio. Sporadic clandestine broadcasts by Hutu radicals are filled with crude propaganda and incitements to violence. Foreign journalists have been regularly harassed by soldiers.

Formation of political parties or associations is permitted, although political activists have been detained by the government and attacked by death squads of various factions. Under highly militarized and dangerous conditions, pro-development nongovernmental organizations and human rights groups such as the Burundi Human Rights Association face extreme difficulties. Religious practice is not restricted.

Burundian women face legal and customary discrimination. It is very difficult for women to receive credit, and they may be dispossessed by inheritance laws. Especially in the countryside, women's educational opportunities are far fewer than those of men, and laws providing for equal pay for equal work have resulted in few advances for women in the formal sector. Violence against women has been reported.

Constitutional protections for unionization are in place, and the right to strike is protected by the labor code. The Organization of Free Unions of Burundi is the sole labor confederation and has been independent since the rise of multipartyism in 1992. Most union members are civil servants and have bargained collectively with the government. Approximately 80 percent of Burundi's people are subsistence farmers, often with few links to the modern economy.

Cambodia

Polity: Monarchy, dominant party (insurgency)
Economy: Statist
Population: 10,800,000
PPP: $1,110
Life Expectancy: 52
Ethnic Groups: Khmer (90 percent), Vietnamese (5 percent), Chinese (1 percent), other (4 percent)
Capital: Phnom Penh

Political Rights: 6*
Civil Liberties: 6
Status: Not Free

Ratings change: Cambodia's political rights rating changed from 7 to 6 because the July 1998 elections, although neither free nor fair, permitted some degree of opposition participation.

Overview: Seeking international legitimacy, strongman Hun Sen held deeply flawed elections in July 1998 that are unlikely to weaken Cambodia's deep hatreds and culture of impunity fostered by 30 years of war, mass killings, and political violence.

After achieving independence from France in 1953, Cambodia was ruled in succession by King Norodom Sihanouk, the U.S.-backed Lon Nol regime in the early 1970s, and the Maoist Khmer Rouge between 1975 and 1979. The Khmer Rouge's radical agrarian policies led to the killing of at least 1.7 million of Cambodia's 7 million people through executions, overwork, and starvation. In 1978, Vietnam invaded and installed the Communist Khmer People's Revolutionary Party (KPRP).

A civil war between the KPRP government and the allied armies of Sihanouk, the Khmer Rouge, and former premier Son Sann ended with an internationally brokered 1991 peace accord, although the Khmer Rouge eventually continued its guerrilla insurgency. Contrary to the accord, the KPRP government, headed by Hun Sen, a Khmer Rouge defector, maintained control of 80 percent of the army, most key ministries, and provincial and local authorities. In Cambodia's first free National Assembly elections, organized by the United Nations in 1993, the royalist opposition United Front for an Independent, Neutral, and Free Cambodia (FUNCINPEC), headed by Prince Norodom Ranariddh, a Sihanouk son, won 58 of the 120 seats. The CPP, the successor to the KPRP, won 51.

Hun Sen forced Ranariddh into accepting a coalition government with the two leaders as co-premiers. The new government carried out political violence and legal and physical attacks on the press. In 1994, FUNCINPEC removed reformist Finance Minister Sam Rainsy. By 1996, Hun Sen had used his continuing control of the army and political institutions to grab near total power. In 1997, Hun Sen seized full power in a coup, apparently after Ranariddh had secured the backing of a breakaway Khmer Rouge faction. Pro-CCP security forces summarily executed at least 41 FUNCINPEC officials, activists, and soldiers and arrested hundreds of others.

After the coup, the United Nations refused to allow Hun Sen's government to represent Cambodia, the Association of Southeast Asian nations postponed the country's admission, donor governments and multilateral institutions cut most aid, and foreign investment and tourism dwindled. In an attempt to to hold a controlled election that would meet minimal international standards, Hun Sen agreed to a Japanese-brokered plan under which two show trials in March 1998 convicted Ranariddh in absentia of conspiracy and weapons smuggling, King Sinhanouk issued a royal pardon, and the Prince returned to Cambodia after nine months in exile.

Despite considerable constraints, opposition parties ran vigorous campaigns for the July elections, which drew a turnout of more than 90 percent. The CPP won a reported 41.4 percent of the vote and approximately 59 seats, but, as counting ended, the CCP-controlled National Election Council changed the electoral formula, thereby giving the CCP a majority with 64 seats. FUNCINPEC won 43 seats, while the Sam Rainsy Party won 15. Police forcibly dispersed election-related protests in September. In late November, Hun Sen formed a new government as the head of a coalition of his CPP and FUNCINPEC.

Since 1996, key Khmer Rouge leaders and thousands of guerrillas have formally ended their armed struggle. In April, the Khmer Rouge announced the death of former leader Pol Pot, the architect of the 1970s killings. In late December, Khieu Samphan, former nominal leader of the Khmer Rouge, and Nuon Chea, the movement's chief ideologue, surrendered to the government. Hun Sen rejected calls for an international tribunal to try the men on charges of genocide or crimes against humanity.

Political Rights and Civil Liberties:

Cambodia's 1998 elections were neither free nor fair. The campaign was held in a climate of violence due to the government's failure to investigate dozens of political killings. Hun Sen wielded his near monopoly over the civil service, local administration, military police, and Khmer-language media to a decisive advantage, and the CCP used intimidation and violence to purge numerous political rivals at the national and local levels. Authorities denied opposition parties access to broadcast media, disrupted some opposition rallies, and banned political demonstrations in Phnom Penh during the official election campaign.

Politicians have deliberately kept institutions weak, and the rudimentary judiciary is not independent. Following the 1997 coup, courts reportedly convicted several FUNCINPEC members on false charges in summary trials. Prisons are dangerously overcrowded and unsanitary, and inmates are mistreated.

Numerous FUNCINPEC supporters were reportedly detained and beaten in the months following the coup. In April, UN officials reported evidence of 50 new political killings, in addition to the 41 killings reported following the 1997 coup. They later reported at least 21 political killings, mainly of FUNCINPEC supporters, between late May and election day. The CCP continues to loot FUNCINPEC offices and otherwise target the party's infrastructure. Security forces routinely harass and intimidate non-governmental human rights activists.

Many of the country's private newspapers closed after the coup. While some reopened, the press operates under severe pressure. Journalists are routinely harassed, threatened, and attacked, and there have been no convictions in the cases of at least four journalists murdered since 1993. The 1995 press law subjects the press to criminal statutes and authorizes the government to suspend publication of a newspaper for up to one month without a court order. In January, the Information Ministry temporarily suspended publication of six pro-opposition newspapers after they published articles critical of the government. Hun Sen and his allies control the 10 radio stations and six television stations. In 1996, the government suspended authorization of new broadcast media and newspapers.

The Constitution refers only to the rights of the ethnic Khmer majority, thereby complicating the legal status of the estimated 200,000 to 500,000 Vietnamese residents. The Khmer Rouge has massacred scores of Vietnamese villagers in recent years. In April, it killed at least 21 ethnic Vietnamese villagers in Kompong Chhnang province.

Traditional norms relegate women to an inferior status, and domestic violence is common. In April, police forcibly ended a Phnom Penh demonstration by garment workers protesting poor working conditions at foreign-owned factories. Official corruption is widespread.

In 1996, Khmer Rouge leader Ieng Sary nominally defected to the government with several thousand soldiers, but he has been allowed to maintain control of the area around the western town of Pailin. This Khmer Rouge remnant rules its minuscule territory in a brutal manner, denying basic rights and largely banning Buddhist religious practices. In the spring of 1998, heavy fighting between Cambodian troops and Khmer Rouge guerrillas drove approximately 30,000 villagers to the Thai border. The last remaining active Khmer Rouge fighters no longer hold territory.

Cameroon

Polity: Dominant party
Economy: Capitalist
(highly corrupt)
Population: 14,300,000
PPP: $2,355
Life Expectancy: 55
Ethnic Groups: Cameroon Highlander (31 percent),
Equatorial Bantu (19 percent), Kirdi (11 percent), Fulani (10 percent),
Northwestern Bantu (8 percent), Eastern Nigritic (7 percent), other African (13 percent)
Capital: Yaounde

Political Rights: 7
Civil Liberties: 5
Status: Not Free

Overview: President Paul Biya and the ruling Cameroon People's Democratic Movement (CPDM) continued their autocratic rule and sporadic attacks on media and opposition supporters in a country divided by ethnic and linguistic differences. A new coalition government brought at least the appearance of a broader base for the Biya regime by including groups outside of the CPDM. In 1997, Biya was returned for a seven-year term as Cameroon's president in an election largely boycotted by the opposition and devalued by rampant intimidation, manipulation, and fraud.

Cameroon's people are comprised of nearly 200 ethnic groups. A German colony from 1884 until 1916, Cameroon was seized in World War I and divided between Britain and France. Distinct Anglophone and Francophone areas were reunited as an independent country in 1961. Approximately one-fourth of Cameroonians are Anglophone, and this linguistic distinction constitutes the country's most potent political division.

For more than three decades after independence, Cameroon was ruled under a repressive one-party system. In March 1992, President Biya held fraudulent multiparty elections, which he won after a boycott by the Social Democratic Front (SDF), the main opposition party. The CPDM's October 1992 and 1997 legislative elections wins were even more clearly fraudulent.

In April 1998, tensions with neighboring Nigeria over the disputed and oil-rich Bakassi peninsula remain flared into armed clashes.

Political Rights and Civil Liberties: Cameroon's constitution provides for a multiparty republic, but citizens have not been allowed to choose their government by democratic means. The 1997 legislative and presidential elections were marred by serious irregularities and outright fraud. The ruling CPDM won 116 seats and the SDF won 43 in legislative elections overseen by regime loyalists in the Ministry of Territorial Administration. Demands for creation of an independent election commission were dismissed by the Biya regime, and most election observers were barred.

Institutions of representative government are largely a facade. The National Assembly meets only two months each year; for the other ten months, the president rules by decree. Constitutional amendments in 1995 gave even more power to the presidency and only nominally strengthened a pliant judiciary. Nearly all power is held by President Biya and his cronies, most of whom are senior CPDM figures from the president's own Beti ethnic group.

The Beti ethnic group often receives preference in employment, and Anglophone Cameroonians claim discrimination that amounts to disenfranchisement. Pygmy people indigenous to southeastern Cameroon often toil under conditions tantamount to slave labor. Reports of actual slavery reportedly persist in the country's north. There, powerful traditional chiefs known as *lamibée* run their own private militia, courts, and prisons that are used against the regime's political opponents. In these unofficial prisons and in government prisons, conditions are reportedly extremely harsh and life threatening. Detainees and convicts are said to be routinely subjected to torture and other mistreatment. Legal requirements regarding detention periods and access to detainees and prisoners are often ignored. Indefinite pretrial detention under extremely harsh conditions is permitted after a warrant is issued or to "combat banditry."

The executive branch controls the judiciary and appoints provincial and local administrators. Courts and local administration are often corrupt and subject to heavy political influence. Various intelligence agencies operate with impunity, and opposition activists are often held without charges. In August, police used water cannons to disperse thousands of people protesting against police brutality. Despite occasional arrests, attacks, and intimidation of opposition supporters and other activists, numerous nongovernmental organizations still operated. Freedom of religion is generally respected, but most other civil liberties remain at risk.

Serious restrictions and intimidation of media inhibit open political exchange. The regime retains its tight monopoly on broadcasting. In May, a program offering parliamentary parties free airtime was resumed after a year's suspension. Nevertheless, authorities continue to censor, suspend, seize, and close independent publications, which in any case have little impact outside of urban areas. Pre-publication censorship is permitted, and criminal libel law is regularly used to silence regime critics. Licensing was made more difficult under 1995 legislation that expanded government seizure and banning powers. In April, Pius Njawe, the editor of *Le Messager*, was sentenced to one year in prison for suggesting that President Biya suffered from heart problems.

Violence against women is reportedly widespread. Women are often denied inheritance and land ownership rights even when these are codified, and many other laws contain unequal gender-based provisions and penalties. Female genital mutilation is widely practiced in some parts of the country.

Trade unions formation is permitted under the 1992 labor code, but some of the code's provisions have not been implemented, and many government workers are not covered. The Confederation of Cameroonian Trade Unions is technically independent, but still influenced or intimidated by the ruling party. In 1996, the regime launched the Union of Free Trade Unions of Cameroon to further undermine union autonomy.

Privatization is underway, but graft and the absence of independent courts inhibit business development. Transparency International has ranked Cameroon as the world's most corrupt country.

Canada

Polity: Federal parliamentary democracy
Economy: Capitalist
Population: 30,600,000
PPP: $21,916
Life Expectancy: 78
Ethnic Groups: British (40 percent), French (27 percent), other European (20 percent), Indian and Inuit (1.5 percent), other, mostly Asian (11.5 percent)
Capital: Ottawa

Political Rights: 1
Civil Liberties: 1
Status: Free

Overview: Three years after Canada's divisive 1995 referendum on independence for Quebec, separatism for the province remained a primary and contentious political issue. Quebec premier Lucien Bouchard vowed to hold another referendum in late 1998 or early 1999. In the meantime, Prime Minister Jean Chretien's Liberal government, which was narrowly re-elected in 1997, continued to focus on reviving the country's faltering economy.

Colonized by French and British settlers in the seventeenth and eighteenth centuries, Canada came under the control of the British Crown under the terms of the Treaty of Paris in 1763. After granting home rule in 1867, Britain retained a theoretical right to overrule the Canadian Parliament until 1982, when Canadians established complete control over their own constitution. The country is governed by a prime minister, his cabinet, and the parliament. The parliament includes an elected 301-member House of Commons and an appointed 104-member Senate. The British monarch remains nominal head of state, represented by a ceremonial governor-general appointed by the prime minister.

Political Rights and Civil Liberties: Canadians can change their government democratically, and due to government canvassing, Canada has nearly 100 percent effective voter registration. Prisoners have the right to vote in federal elections, as do citizens who have lived abroad for less than five years. In the 1993 elections, the government held three days of advance voting for people unable to vote on election day.

In 1995, a federal law prohibiting the broadcasting of public opinion poll results two days prior to and during federal elections was upheld. A 1988 act to limit all forms of cigarette advertisement, however, was struck down as a violation of free speech. After passage in the House of Commons, a modified, less comprehensive bill was passed by the Senate in 1997.

The judiciary is independent. Limitations on freedom of expression range from unevenly enforced "hate laws" and restrictions on pornography to rules on reporting. In September, Prime Minister Chretien and his aides came under strong attack for ordering improper arrests and using pepper spray against student demonstrations at a November 1997 international summit in Vancouver. Investigations into these abuses led to reports of other improper attempts by the government to suppress demonstrations. The media are generally free, although they exercise self-censorship in areas such as violence on television.

Civil liberties have been protected since 1982 by the federal Charter of Rights and Freedoms, but have been limited by the constitutional "notwithstanding" clause, which permits provincial governments to exempt themselves by applying individual provisions within their jurisdictions. Quebec has used the clause to retain its provincial language law, which restricts the use of English on signs. The provincial governments, with their own constitutions and legislative assemblies, exercise significant autonomy. Each has its own judicial system as well, with the right of appeal to the Supreme Court of Canada.

Canada's criminal law is based on British common law and is uniform throughout the country. Its civil law is also based on the British system, except in Quebec, where it is based on the French civil code.

In 1996, parliament amended the constitution to outlaw discrimination based on "sexual orientation" by adding this term to a 1977 Human Rights Act list that includes age, sex, race, religion, and disability. At the same time, women's rights issues have grown in prominence. In the June elections, the ruling Liberal Party met a self-imposed target of fielding female candidates in 25 percent of its parliamentary races.

Canada boasts a generous welfare system that supplements the largely open, competitive economy. Property rights for current occupants are generally strong, but increasing Indian land claims have led to litigation and strained relations between the government and Canadian Indians.

Trade unions and business associations enjoy high levels of membership and are free and well-organized.

Religious expression is free and diverse, but religious education has been the subject of controversy in recent years. Many provinces have state-supported religious school systems that do not represent all denominations.

Despite restrictions announced in 1994, the flow of immigrants into the country remains strong. In October, the head of Canada's intelligence service warned that the country's open immigration and refugee policies made it particularly vulnerable to organizational and fund-raising activities by terrorist groups.

Cape Verde

Polity: Presidential-par-
liamentary democracy
Economy: Mixed statist
Population: 400,000
PPP: $2,612
Life Expectancy: 70
Ethnic Groups: Creole [mulatto] (71 percent),
African (28 percent), European (1 percent)
Capital: Praia

Political Rights: 1
Civil Liberties: 2
Status: Free

Overview:

Cape Verde continued to seek improvements to its people's very low living standards by pursuing privatization and seeking international investment from business and from the country's diaspora, which outnumbers the nation's current 400,000 inhabitants. The country appears to have made a firm transition to multiparty democracy, but extreme poverty has so far allowed no party to offer much material incentive for supporting constitutional rule. The government's austerity program is unpopular, but has drawn increased donor assistance. Very low voter turnout marked President Antonio Mascarenhas Monteiro's 1996 re-election to a second five-year term. His free market policies are also supported by Prime Minister Carlos Alberto Wahnon de Carvalho Veiga and the ruling Movement for Democracy (MPD), which holds 50 of 72 seats in the country's parliament. Veiga was injured in a plane crash in late September, but resumed his official duties a few days later.

Cape Verde achieved independence from Portugal in 1975, and, for 16 years, was governed under Marxist, one-party rule by the African Party for the Independence of Cape Verde. The MPD won a landslide 1991 victory in the first democratic elections after Cape Verde became the first former Portuguese colony in Africa to abandon Marxist political and economic systems. In December 1995, the MPD was returned to power with 59 percent of the vote. The country's stagnant economy has been bolstered somewhat by increased exports and tourism, but infrastructure improvements are still needed to assist in private sector development. Located off West Africa's coast, Cape Verde is one of Africa's smallest and poorest lands. It has few exploitable natural resources and relies heavily on imported food. Foreign aid and remittances by Cape Verdean expatriates provide a large portion of national income. Cape Verde has enthusiastically joined Portugal's efforts to create a Lusophone commonwealth, and in 1998 hosted a meeting of representatives from Portuguese-speaking countries.

Political Rights and Civil Liberties:

The president and members of the National People's Assembly, including six representatives chosen by citizens living abroad, are elected through universal suffrage in free and fair elections. Since the country's 1991 transition to multiparty democracy, Cape Verdeans have changed their government twice by democratic means. The 1992 constitution circumscribed the powers of the presidency, which was left with little authority beyond delaying ratification of legislation, proposing amendments, and dissolving parliament after a vote of no confidence. Referenda are permitted in some circumstances, but may not challenge civil liberties or the rights of opposition parties.

Human rights groups, including the National Commission of the Rights of Man and the Organization of Cape Verdean Women, operate freely. There are no reported political prisoners.

Reforms to strengthen an overburdened judiciary were implemented in 1998. Comprised of a Supreme Court and regional courts that generally adjudicate criminal and civil cases fairly, the judiciary is independent, although cases are frequently delayed. Free legal counsel is provided to indigents, defendants are presumed innocent until proven guilty, and trials are public. Judges must lay charges within 24 hours of arrests. The police, which were controlled by the military until 1994, are now separate and answerable to civilian authority.

The freedoms of peaceful assembly and association are guaranteed and respected. The constitution requires the separation of church and state, and religious rights are respected in practice. The vast majority of Cape Verdeans belongs to the Roman Catholic Church.

Freedoms of expression and of the press are guaranteed and generally respected in practice. No authorization is needed to publish newspapers and other publications. The most widely read newspaper and radio and television broadcasts are state-controlled. Criticism of the government is limited by self-censorship resulting from citizens' fear of demotion or dismissal. National Assembly sessions, including sharp attacks by opposition members, are broadcast live via radio in their entirety. In March, however, the government closed *Radio Comercial,* which is partially owned by an opposition politician, on the contested claim of an improperly allocated frequency. In previous years, government officials have unsuccessfully sought to use libel charges to silence opposition newspapers.

Despite legal prohibitions against gender discrimination, as well as provisions for social and economic equality, discrimination against women persists. Many women do not know their rights or do not possess means to seek redress, especially in rural areas. Women receive less pay for equal work and are excluded from traditionally male professions. They are also subject to allegedly common, but seldom reported, domestic violence. Serious concerns about child abuse and the prevalence of child labor persist. Campaigns to promote women's civil and human rights and awareness of child abuse have been mounted by local nongovernmental organizations with international assistance.

The right to unionize is constitutionally protected, and workers may form and join unions without restriction. Two confederations, the Council of Free Labor Unions and the National Union of Cape Verde, include 25 unions with approximately 27,000 members.

Central African Republic

Polity: Presidential-par- **Political Rights:** 3
liamentary democracy **Civil Liberties:** 4*
Economy: Capitalist- **Status:** Partly Free
statist
Population: 3,400,000
PPP: $1,092
Life Expectancy: 46
Ethnic Groups: Baya (34 percent), Banda (27 percent),
Mandjia (21 percent), Sara (10 percent), Mboum (4 percent), M'Baka (4 percent)
Capital: Bangui
Ratings change: Central African Republic's civil liberties rating changed from 5 to 4
due to a slight easing of repression in the country.

Overview:
In December, parliamentary elections in the Central African Republic (CAR) produced a nearly even split between supporters and opponents of President Ange-Félix Patassé and appear unlikely to resolve a three-year political crisis that has repeatedly flared into serious violence. A 1,250-member UN peacekeeping force from Canada, France, and seven African countries maintained a sometimes uneasy but effective truce in Bangui. The UN mission included the August launch of a local radio station that offered civic and voter information regarding the legislative polls and delayed presidential elections now scheduled for early 1999. Army mutinies and political infighting wracked the capital and destabilized the elected government in 1996 and 1997. Order was restored only through a vigorous French military intervention. While the foreign forces have kept the capital quiet, conditions in the countryside have become more difficult. Conflicts in neighboring countries mean that modern weapons are easily available in the CAR's hinterlands. France's withdrawal of its last remaining garrison after a 17-year army presence will leave a vacuum that the national army will be hard-pressed to fill.

President Patassé has been unable to maintain a popular base since his 1993 election victory. His failure to implement reforms agreed at a 1996 national conference remains a source of criticism by soldiers and dissidents.

The CAR, a sparsely populated country with the approximate size of Texas, gained independence from France in 1960 after a period of particularly brutal colonial exploitation. Colonel Jean-Bedel Bokassa seized power in 1967, and, as self-declared emperor, imposed an increasingly bizarre personal dictatorship on the renamed Central African Empire. After Bokassa began to murder schoolchildren, French forces finally ousted him in 1979. A French-installed successor was deposed by General André Kolingba in 1981. Kolingba accepted a transition to multipartyism that led to democratic elections in 1993. Even without a troop presence, Paris will continue to play a potentially powerful role in the country. There are fears that President Patassé's increasing reliance on his own ethnic group as a power base will revive and exacerbate traditional north-south regional and ethnic rivalries.

Political Rights and Civil Liberties: Presidential and legislative elections in 1993 under the 1986 constitution gave the CAR's people their first opportunity to choose their government in an open and democratic manner. The exercise failed to produce stability, however, as President Patassé's triumph was not matched by his party in national assembly elections. Legislative elections in December produced a one-seat opposition majority in the 109-member National Assembly, but, by year's end, there was no agreement on replacing the national unity government. A Mixed National Electoral Commission may help to allay opposition fears over electoral conduct.

Open public discussion is permitted, but constitutionally guaranteed freedom of assembly is not always honored by authorities. Public meetings must be registered 48 hours in advance. Several human rights and other nongovernmental organizations operate unhindered. Broad prohibitions against "fundamentalism" are widely considered to be aimed at Islamist tendencies and could provide scope for official restrictions on worship. Religious groups must register with the government, although religious freedom is respected in practice.

Corruption, political interference, and lack of training hinder the efficiency and impartiality of judicial institutions. Limitations on searches and detention are often ignored. Conditions for prisoners, including many long-term pretrial detainees, are extremely difficult and sometimes life threatening. Police brutality is also a serious problem, and security forces act with impunity. Extrajudicial executions of criminal suspects are reported, and robbery and other abuses by various military factions have become a serious problem in the capital.

The new UN-sponsored "Radio Minurca" provides nonpartisan civic and voter educational programming, as well as rebroadcasts of international news. Other broadcast media are dominated by the state and offer little coverage of opposition activities. The only licensed private radio stations are music- or religion-oriented. Private print media have suffered from little direct governmental interference, but several journalists have been sued for printing accusations of official malfeasance. Approximately one dozen newspapers are published with various regularity, but they have little impact beyond the capital. The non-state print media are often partisan and critical of various political groups, but have no sound financial base.

Societal discrimination in many areas relegates women to second-class citizenship, especially in rural areas, and constitutional guarantees for women's rights are generally not enforced. Female genital mutilation is still practiced, but is reportedly diminishing. Only three women hold seats in the 85-member National Assembly.

The CAR's largest single employer is its government, and government employee trade unions are especially active. Worker rights to form or join unions are legally protected, and five labor federations compete for union affiliates. Before unions may call strikes, a conciliation process is required. Wage guidelines are set by the government in consultation with employers and unions, but unions sometimes reach agreements with employers through collective bargaining. A broad privatization program is underway, but corruption and economic mismanagement have stifled growth. Most of the country's people are subsistence farmers.

Chad

Polity: Presidential-
parliamentary
(military-dominated)
Economy: Capitalist
Population: 7,400,000
PPP: $1,172
Life Expectancy: 48
Ethnic Groups: Sara (28 percent), Sudan and
Arab (12 percent), many others
Capital: N'Djamena

Political Rights: 6
Civil Liberties: 4*
Status: Not Free

Ratings change: Chad's civil liberties rating changed from 5 to 4 due to
a slight easing of repression in the country.

Overview: Lingering rebellions and security force abuses in southern Chad raised doubts over the potential success of oil field exploration and an environmentally sensitive pipeline project that could bring one of the world's very poorest countries billions of dollars in new revenues. President Idriss Déby's continuing reliance on his northern Zaghawa clan as his main power base, despite the formality of multiparty elections, is hindering the country's democratic transition. In September, Chad dispatched an expeditionary force to aid Congo President Laurent Kabila in his struggle against rebels. France, which remains highly influential in Chad, maintains a 1,000-member garrison in the country and serves as Deby's main political and commercial supporter. Brutality by soldiers and rebels marked insurgencies in the vast countryside, but another peace pact with the principal southern rebel group seemed to be holding.

Chad has been in a state of almost constant war since achieving its independence from France in 1960. President Déby gained power by overthrowing Hissein Habré in 1990. Turmoil exacerbated by ethnic and religious differences is also fanned by clan rivalries and external interference. The country is divided by Nilotic and Bantu Christian farmers who inhabit the country's south and Arab and Saharan peoples who occupy arid deserts in the north.

Chad was a militarily dominated one-party state until Déby lifted the ban on political parties in 1993. A national conference that included a broad array of civic and political groups then created a transitional parliament, which was controlled by Déby's Patriotic Salvation Movement (MPS). Scores of political parties are registered. The current coalition government is dominated by the MPS with 65 seats, but also includes the Union for Renewal and Democracy, which won 29 seats. The National Union for Renewal and Democracy, which holds 15 seats, withdrew after a May cabinet shuffle in which its leader, Wadal Abdelkader Kamougué, lost his post. Chad's army and political life are dominated by members of the small Zaghawa and Bideyat groups from President Déby's northeastern region. This is a source of ongoing resentment among the more than 200 other ethnic groups in the country. The formal exercise of deeply flawed elections and democratic processes has produced some opening of Chadian society, but real power remains with President Déby.

Political Rights and Civil Liberties: Chad has never experienced a peaceful and orderly transference of political power, and both presidential and legislative elections have been marred by serious irregularities and indications of outright fraud. President Déby's 1996 victory in Chad's first multiparty election was strongly endorsed by France, despite opposition and independent criticism. It is impossible to ascertain if President Déby's second-round victory with 69 percent of the vote was credible. Déby's most potent challengers were disqualified, opposition activists were intimidated, and the vote count was manipulated. Allegations of fraud also devalued the 1997 legislative elections, in which Déby's MPS took an absolute majority and was awarded with 65 of 125 National Assembly seats by a pliant election commission. Intimidation and harassment by the National Security Agency hinder opposition efforts to organize.

In 1998, killings and torture with impunity by Chadian security forces reportedly continued. The forces also reportedly continued an officially backed anti-crime policy of summary executions of suspected thieves. Déby's elite presidential guard is blamed for some of the worst violations. Tens of thousands of Chadians have fled their country to escape the violence. Several of the 20 or more armed factions have reached peace pacts. Several of these agreements have failed, however, and sporadic abuses by the various factions, rebel groups, and the government continue in southern districts. Chad's long and porous borders are virtually unpoliced. Trade in weapons among nomadic Sahelian peoples is rife, and banditry adds to the pervasive insecurity.

State control of broadcast media allows little exposure for dissenting views. Newspapers critical of the government circulate freely in N'djamena, but have scant impact among the largely rural and illiterate population. Freedom of expression is generally respected, but media freedom was hampered in 1998 when several journalists received suspended sentences for publishing allegations of corruption against senior officials. The rule of law and the judicial system remain weak, with courts heavily influenced by the executive. Security forces routinely ignore constitutional protections regarding search, seizure, and detention. Overcrowding, disease, and malnutrition make prison conditions life threatening, and many inmates spend years in prison without charges.

Despite harassment and occasional physical intimidation, the Chadian Human Rights League, Chad Nonviolence, and several other human rights groups operate openly and publish findings critical of the government. Although religion is a source of division in society, Chad is a secular state, and freedom of religion is generally respected. Women's rights are protected neither by traditional law nor the penal code. Female genital mutilation is commonplace. The literacy rate for women is very low, and few educational opportunities are available, especially in rural areas.

Workers' right to organize and to strike is generally respected, but the formal economy is small. Union membership is low. Most Chadians are subsistence farmers.

Chile

Polity: Presidential-
legislative democracy
Economy: Capitalist
Population: 14,800,000
PPP: $9,930
Life Expectancy: 75
Ethnic Groups: European and European-Indian (95 percent),
Indian (3 percent), other (2 percent)
Capital: Santiago

Political Rights: 3*
Civil Liberties: 2
Status: Free

Ratings change: Chile's political rights rating changed from 2 to 3 due to a worsening of civil-military relations following the detention of former dictator, Capt. Gen. Augusto Pinochet, in London.

Overview:

In 1998, former dictator Augusto Pinochet was expected to retire as head of the army and begin service as senator-for-life, a post that he himself created in order to maintain military influence on Congress. Instead, he was detained in Britain on a Spanish extradition warrant that seeks to hold him accountable for the torture and death of thousands of opponents following his assumption of power in a U.S.-backed coup in 1973. Pinochet's detention produced a strong political polarization in Chile and, according to one top general, has left the country in a "critical situation."

The Republic of Chile was founded after independence from Spain in 1818. Democratic rule predominated in this century until the 1973 overthrow of Salvador Allende by the military under Pinochet. The 1980 constitution provided for a plebiscite in which voters could reject another presidential term for Pinochet. In 1988, 55 percent of voters rejected the prospect of eight more years of military rule, and competitive presidential and legislative elections were scheduled for 1989.

In 1989, Christian Democrat Patricio Aylwin, the candidate of the center-left Concertacion for Democracy, was elected president over two right-wing candidates, and the Concertacion won a majority in the Chamber of Deputies. With eight senators appointed by the outgoing military government, however, it fell short of a Senate majority. Aylwin's government was unsuccessful in its efforts to reform the constitution and was stymied by a right-wing Senate bloc in its efforts to prevent Pinochet and other military chiefs from remaining in their posts until 1997. In 1993 elections, the Concertacion's Eduardo Frei won handily over right-wing candidate Arturo Alessandri. He promised to establish full civilian control over the military, but did not have the necessary votes in Congress.

The Senate has 48 seats, including the senator-for-life position for Pinochet and nine designated senatorial seats mandated by the 1980 constitution. In 1997, Frei chose the army chief of staff as Pinochet's replacement from a list of names submitted by Pinochet himself. Also in 1997, the ruling coalition won a convincing victory in an election for all 120 lower house and 20 senate seats. Nevertheless, the binomial electoral system, which allows a party receiving only 33 percent of the votes to share power in two-seat constituencies with parties receiving as much as 66 percent, resulted in pro-Pinochet forces retaining their veto over constitutional reforms.

Political Rights and Civil Liberties: Citizens can change their government democratically, but the Pinochet extradition crisis has shown that Chile's democratic transition remains incomplete and requires constitutional reforms to ensure civilian control of the military. Frei has appeared to be slowly wresting important levers of power from the armed forces, but the failure to eliminate some of the 1980 constitution's most egregious features, including the nine appointed senatorial seats, has heightened the sense of emergency sparked by the retired general's detention in London.

In 1990, a Truth and Reconciliation Commission was formed to investigate rights violations committed under military rule. Its report implicated the military and secret police leadership in the death or forcible disappearance of 2,279 people between 1973 and 1990. In 1978, however, the Pinochet regime issued an amnesty for all political crimes, and the Supreme Court, packed by Pinochet before he left office, has blocked all government efforts to lift it. The amnesty has not prevented civilian governments from investigating rights cases. Hundreds of cases involving incidents after 1978 have been brought to civilian courts, but have resulted in few convictions.

Military courts can bring charges against civilians for sedition, which is labeled as any comment that may affect the morale of the armed forces or police. In these cases, the military tribunal plays the role of victim, prosecutor, and judge. Physical abuse of prisoners, particularly by the Carabinero uniformed police, remains a problem.

Most laws limiting political expression and civil liberties were eliminated by constitutional reforms in 1989. Nevertheless, a 1958 State Security Law punishes those who "defame, libel, or calumniate" the president, government ministers, parliamentarians, senior judges, and the commanders in chief of the armed forces. In January, two journalists were jailed overnight for saying that a former Supreme Court justice facing allegations of corruption and impeachment motions was "old, ugly, and had a murky past."

Scores of publications present all points of view, although self-censorship regarding Chile's recent political history is widespread. Radio station ownership is both pubic and private. The national television network is state-run, but open to all political voices. Chile has a strong trade union movement. Government corruption is comparatively minor for the region, although military graft has not been investigated. A 1993 indigenous rights law guarantees that Indian lands cannot be embargoed, sold, expropriated, or taxed. New government-promoted development projects continue to threaten Mapuche Indian lands in the south of Chile. The appointment of a non-Native American to head the government's Indian development agency was viewed by Mapuches as emblematic of the agency's failure to protect them.

China

Polity: Communist
one-party
Economy: Mixed statist
Population: 1,242,500,000
PPP: $2,935
Life Expectancy: 71

Political Rights: 7
Civil Liberties: 6*
Status: Not Free

Ethnic Groups: Han Chinese (92 percent), Tibetan, Mongol,
Korean, Manchu, and other (8 percent)
Capital: Beijing
Ratings change: China's civil liberties rating changed from 7 to 6 due to a change
in Freedom House methodology to reflect an easing in state intrusion into the
personal lives of its citizens.

Overview:
In 1998, new Chinese premier Zhu Rongji initiated potentially
significant economic reforms, while authorities continued to
crush political dissent and flout international human rights
standards. Labor unrest over rising joblessness in a country with negligible unemployment benefits and nonexistent worker's rights continued to be one of the regime's key
concerns. Zhu had to modify plans to restructure China's crumbling state-owned enterprises
(SOEs) in the face of slowing economic growth and spreading worker's protests.

Chinese Communist Party (CCP) Chairman Mao Zedong proclaimed the People's
Republic of China in 1949 following victory over the Nationalist Kuomintang. Mao's
death in 1976 largely ended the brutal, mass ideological campaigns that had characterized his rule and resulted in millions of deaths. Deng Xiaoping emerged as paramount
leader and, in 1978, began market reforms that included ending collectivized agriculture. The army's bloody crackdown on pro-democracy demonstrators near Tiananmen
Square in 1989 signaled the government's wholesale rejection of political reform. Deng
selected hardliner Jiang Zemin, the Shanghai mayor and party boss, to replace the relatively moderate Zhao Ziyang as CCP secretary general.

In 1992, Deng, the nation's paramount leader, even though he no longer held formal office, touched off an economic boom by making a highly symbolic visit to two
special economic zones on the southern coast. In 1993, Jiang assumed the presidency.
Since then, the CCP has attempted to maintain its monopoly on power by improving
living standards through economic reform, while stifling dissent. By 1997, Jiang had
consolidated his power to the extent that Deng's death, once seen as a possible prelude
to upheaval in this fractious country, passed unremarkably. At the CCP's quinquennial
party congress in 1997, Jiang ousted several potential rivals from top posts and pushed
several military figures out of politics.

As in past years, the annual meeting of the National People's Congress (NPC) in
1998 served mainly to approve the CCP leadership's closed-door decisions. With
hardliner Li Peng having served the two terms as premier permitted under the constitution, the NPC approved conservative technocrat Zhu Rongji, 69, as premier. Jiang
began a second term as state president, and Hu Jintao, at age 55, became the youngest
member of the politburo's seven-member standing committee. Zhu's reforms included

closing thousands of unprofitable SOEs, cleaning up the technically insolvent banking system, slashing the number of government agencies from 40 to 29, separating the regulatory role of ministries from their business interests, abolishing state-subsidized housing, and encouraging home ownership. The restructuring was predicated on continued strong economic growth that would create jobs for newly unemployed state workers. By the autumn, Zhu was forced to scale back his plans, as slowing domestic demand made it less likely that China would reach the 8.2 percent annual growth that it averaged from 1978 to 1996.

In November, authorities cracked down on the fledgling China Democracy Party, which dissidents launched in the aftermath of United States President Bill Clinton's trip to China in June. In December, courts sentenced the group's three most influential leaders to prison terms of 11 years or more.

In 1998, tensions continued in the vast northwestern Xinjiang "Autonomous Region." The seven-million strong, Turkic-speaking Uighurs and other smaller Muslim groups accuse Beijing of exploiting the region's rich mineral resources, controlling religious affairs, cracking down harshly on separatist movements, and altering the demographic balance by encouraging an influx of Han Chinese.

Political Rights and Civil Liberties: Chinese citizens lack the democratic means to change their government. The CCP holds absolute power, has imprisoned nearly all active dissidents, uses the judiciary as a tool of state control, and severely restricts freedoms of speech, press, association, and religion. In practice there is little separation between party and state. The NPC, constitutionally the highest organ of state authority, has little independent power and has never rejected legislation. Recently, however, delegates have registered protest votes over the government's handling of corruption, rising crime rates, and other issues.

Under the 1987 Village Committees Organic Law, approximately 60 percent of the country's 928,000 village bodies are chosen through local elections. Campaigns generally focus on local corruption and economic matters, but only prescreened CCP and some independent candidates can compete. In many villages, independents have won seats. However, throughout the country balloting is characterized by irregularities and unfair procedures. Moreover, unelected CCP village secretaries and county authorities hold real power.

The CCP controls the judiciary. Corruption is rampant, and local governments intervene in cases. Judges are poorly trained and are generally retired military officers selected on the basis of party loyalty. Suspects are routinely tortured to extract confessions. Judges are often reluctant to handle class action suits or rule against local governments, which provide their salary and appointments. Some local governments have responded to lawsuits by harassing the plaintiffs. Favorable judgments are hard to enforce.

Authorities can arbitrarily detain dissidents and ordinary criminals through several extrajudicial administrative procedures, thereby contributing to a vast network of forced labor camps. Activist Harry Wu has identified 1,100 *laogai*, or "reform through labor," camps holding six to eight million prisoners without trial under brutal conditions. Abuse of prisoners, particularly ordinary workers, is routine and widespread, and authorities often encourage inmates to beat political prisoners. There are persistent reports of authorities selling organs of executed prisoners for transplant purposes. Nearly

70 crimes are punishable by the death penalty, and, in recent years, many people have been executed during crackdowns on corruption and drug trafficking or for nonviolent offenses such as theft of farm animals, often immediately following summary trials.

The government admits that it is holding approximately 2,000 people for political crimes, although the actual figure is probably higher. In 1997, authorities eliminated the category of "counterrevolutionary" crimes, under which courts have imprisoned thousands of dissidents, as part of revisions to the criminal code. The revised code incorporates key elements of the 1993 State Security Law, which authorizes punishment of groups and individuals for working with foreign organizations or individuals, expands the criminal concept of "state secrets," and creates a separate article aimed at pro-independence and autonomy movements in Xinjiang, Inner Mongolia, and Tibet. *(A separate report on Tibet appears in the Related Territories section.)* In 1998, authorities continued to arrest dissidents for contacting foreign human rights groups and reporters, publicizing incidents of labor unrest, and other nonviolent acts. Unrelenting police harassment prevents many dissidents from holding jobs or otherwise leading normal lives. In April, authorities allowed Wang Dan, one of China's few prominent political prisoners, to go into exile in the United States.

The media never directly criticize the CCP's monopoly on power or top leaders. At least a dozen journalists are in prison, some merely for meeting with Western counterparts. Since 1996, Jiang has tightened control over the media and the arts. The government has introduced regulations to control Internet access and content for the country's one million users, closed dozens of Internet web sites, and placed small newspapers run by private organizations under CCP control. In recent years, there has been a proliferation of nonpolitical talk radio shows and tabloid magazines. The market-driven press is allowed to report on inefficient government agencies, environmental damages, official corruption, and other issues that dovetail with Beijing's interests. The government has tolerated the existence of several thousand nongovernmental organizations (NGOs) that focus on areas that the government does not consider to be politically threatening, including the environment and the rights of women and migrant workers. Authorities use a complex process to weed out any groups that could potentially oppose the government. Independent labor organizations or other NGOs cannot serve a function ostensibly served by an existing government-sponsored organization. Each NGO must report to a specific government department and must receive official approval to receive foreign funding.

Freedom of assembly is limited. In recent years, authorities have tolerated some public protests on labor, housing, and local government issues, while forcibly ending others. The government tightly controls organized religious practice. Officials pressure Roman Catholic and Protestant churches to register with either the official Catholic Patriotic Association or its Protestant counterpart. In return for an easing of harassment, churches must accept Beijing's power to appoint clergy; monitor religious membership, funding and activities; and regulate the publication and distribution of religious books and other materials. Official Roman Catholic churches cannot maintain loyalty to the Vatican. While many unregistered Protestant churches and openly pro-Vatican Roman Catholic groups are able to function, scores of churches have been raided, closed, or demolished. Hundreds of bishops, priests, and ordinary worshippers have been detained for months or years. In Xinjiang, authorities have used the pretext of quelling ethnic separatism to place sharp restrictions on the construction of mosques and Islamic religious publishing and education, and have closed dozens of mosques and Koranic schools. Only five religions are officially recognized in China, with all others being *prima facie* illegal.

China's harsh family planning policy limits urban couples to one child, while in rural areas parents of a girl can petition authorities for permission to have a son. Some local officials zealously enforce the policy through sanctions and even forced abortion and sterilization. Couples adhering to the policy receive preferential education, food, and medical benefits, while those failing to comply face a loss of benefits and fines. Failure to pay the fines sometimes results in seizure of livestock and other goods and destruction of homes. Dissidents in Xinjiang report that authorities often force Muslim women to have abortions and sterilizations after their first child. Women face social and economic discrimination and sexual harassment in the workplace. In rural areas, there are high incidences of women being abducted or otherwise sold into prostitution or marriage.

Independent trade unions are illegal. All unions must belong to the CCP-controlled All-China Federation of Trade Unions. Strikes are occasionally permitted in foreign-owned factories to protest dangerous conditions and low wages. In March, the U.S.-based National Labor Committee accused American clothing manufacturers of avoiding direct responsibility for labor rights by subcontracting production to non-American-owned factories in China where workers receive low pay, are forced to work overtime, have no contracts, and are subject to arbitrary dismissal. Most prisoners are required to work and receive little if any compensation.

Urban middle-class Chinese enjoy increased freedom to work, travel, enter into relationships, and buy homes as they choose. The successes of both the Special Economic Zones in the south and the small-scale township and village enterprises in the countryside have also helped remove tens of millions of rural Chinese from dependence on the danwei, or state work unit. However, for many urban dwellers the danwei controls everything from the right to change residence to permission to have a child. The system of hakou, or residence permit, has also been loosened to give workers more flexibility in filling jobs in areas of fast economic growth.

Colombia

Polity: Presidential-
legislative democracy
(insurgencies)
Economy: Capitalist-
statist
Population: 38,600,000
PPP: $6,347
Life Expectancy: 69

Political Rights: 3*
Civil Liberties: 4
Status: Partly Free

Ethnic Groups: Mestizo (58 percent), white (20 percent), mulatto (14 percent),
black (4 percent), mixed black-Indian (3 percent), Indian (1 percent)
Capital: Bogota
Ratings change: Colombia's political rights rating changed from 4 to 3 due to the
selection of a new president, believed not to be beholden to narcotics traffickers,
in largely free and fair elections.

Overview:
With the U.S military predicting that Colombia could fall into
the hands of left-wing guerrillas in as little as five years, newly
elected President Andres Pastrana launched a series of mea-
sures to improve the country's faltering economy and bolster a fledgling peace process. Political violence and growing labor unrest, however, threaten Pastrana's gamble
on negotiations with Latin America's oldest guerrilla insurgency. The peace process is
also imperiled by an increasingly politically assertive military.

After independence from Spain in 1819 and a long period of federal government
with what are now Venezuela, Ecuador, and Panama, the Republic of Colombia was
established in 1886. Politics have since been dominated by the Liberal and Conservative parties, which have been led largely by the country's traditional elite. Under Liberal President Cesar Gaviria from 1990 to 1994, Colombia approved a new constitution that limits presidents to a single four-year term and provides for an elected bicameral Congress, with a 102-member Senate and a 161-member Chamber of Representatives.

Modern Colombia has been marked by the corrupt machine politics of the Liberals
and Conservatives, left-wing guerrilla insurgencies, right-wing paramilitary violence,
the emergence of vicious drug cartels, and gross human rights violations committed by
all sides. In the 1994 elections, the Liberals retained a majority in both houses of Congress and won the presidency. Ernesto Samper, a former economic development minister, won the latter with 50.4 percent of the vote in a runoff election. With strong U.S.
encouragement, Samper presided over the dismantling of the Cali drug cartel, most of
whose leaders were captured in 1995. The arrests, however, netted persuasive evidence
that the cartel had given $6 million to Samper's campaign with his approval. In 1996,
the country's prosecutor general formally charged Samper with illegal enrichment, fraud,
falsification of documents, and a cover-up of his campaign financing. The House, dominated by Samper's Liberals, voted 111 to 43 to clear Samper on grounds of insufficient
evidence. In the June 1998 election, Andres Pastrana, a former mayor of Bogota and
the son of a former Colombian president, who lost to Samper in 1994, won the presi-

dency in an impressive victory over Liberal party candidate and Interior Minister Horacio Serpa.

After more than three decades of fighting primarily in rural areas, guerrillas have pushed their insurgency ever closer to Bogota and other major cities and are now believed to control more than 40 percent of the country's territory. In November, in an effort to consolidate the peace process, Pastrana oversaw the regrouping by guerrillas in, and the withdrawal by a dispirited military from, a demilitarized zone of five southern districts. Skeptics worried, however, that the move would hamper Colombia's anti-drug campaign.

Political Rights and Civil Liberties:

Citizens can change their government through elections. The 1991 constitution provides for broader participation in the system, including two reserved seats in the Congress for the country's small Indian minority. Political violence and a generalized belief that corruption renders elections meaningless have helped to limit voter participation, although 60 percent of the electorate voted in the 1998 presidential contest. In 1998, President Pastrana proposed a broad reform of the political system to combat corruption and promote greater public participation in decision making. He also offered the guerrillas a presidential pardon and guarantees for their post peace participation in legal political activities.

The justice system remains slow and compromised by corruption and extortion. Strong evidence suggests that the Cali cartel, through its lawyers, virtually dictated the 1993 penal code reform to Congress. It allows traffickers who surrender as much as a two-thirds sentence reduction and the dismissal of any pending charges in which they do not plead. The country's national police, once a focal point of official corruption, have been reorganized and are now Colombia's most respected security institution.

Constitutional rights regarding free expression and the freedom to organize political parties, civic groups, and labor unions are severely restricted by political and drug-related violence and by the government's inability to guarantee the security of its citizens. Political violence in Colombia continues to take more lives than in any other country in the hemisphere, and civilians are the primary victims. In the past decade, an estimated 35,000 have died, and approximately one million have been displaced from their homes. More than 90 percent of violent crimes are never solved. Conditions in the country's 168 prisons, which are severely overcrowded, are dire. In 1998, the government announced plans to privatize their expansion and management.

Human rights violations have soared to unprecedented highs, with atrocities being committed by all sides in the conflict. Human rights workers in Colombia are frequently murdered by rightist paramilitary forces or the country's untrained, undisciplined, and inadequately funded military. The paramilitary groups, who are protected by the military and paid by narcotics traffickers and large landowners, have grown exponentially. In May, a military intelligence unit was disbanded after credible reports tied it to support for death squads and a string of political assassinations, including the 1995 murder of Colombia's top opposition leader. In 1998, left-wing guerrillas used as many as 400 villagers in a single town as human shields to protect themselves against aerial bombardment. Perpetrators of political violence operate with a high degree of impunity.

Journalists are frequently the victims of political and revenge violence. More than 120 journalists, including at least seven in 1998, have been murdered in the past decade. Many were killed for reporting on drug trafficking and corruption. Another category of killings is known as "social cleansing," or the elimination of drug addicts, street children, and other marginal citizens by vigilante groups often linked to the police.

After threatening mass suicide, the 5,000-member Uwa Indian tribe has reported that foreign oil companies have retreated from plans to exploit their ancestral lands. In August, however, an Embera Katio community leader was murdered by a right-wing death squad because he was protesting the planned construction of a dam that would flood tribal lands. In a positive development in September, the constitutional court overturned as discriminatory a 1979 law that allowed teachers to be dismissed for homosexuality.

Murders of trade union activists continued as Colombia remained the most dangerous country in the world for organized labor. According to the United Nations, approximately 948,000 children under the age of 14 work in "unacceptable" conditions.

Comoros

Polity: Dominant party   **Political Rights:** 5
Economy: Capitalist   **Civil Liberties:** 4
Population: 500,000   **Status:** Partly Free
PPP: $1,317
Life Expectancy: 59
Ethnic Groups: Antalote, Cafre, Makoa, Oimatsaha, Sakalava
Capital: Moroni

Overview: The Federal Islamic Republic of the Comoros, a tiny Indian Ocean islands nation, was shaken by the November death of President Mohamed Taki Abdoulkarim as it struggled with the continuing secession of Anjouan and Mohéli islands. High Council President Tadjidine Ben Said Massonde will serve as interim president until elections set for 1999. Wracked by coups and rebellions since independence in 1975, the former French colony sought mediation by the Organization of African Unity to end the rebellion, but also warned that it would seek external military intervention against the separatists if the talks fail. Anjouan rebels are split between those who have declared independence and those who seek to be repossessed by their former colonial masters. Both groups cite neglect and discrimination by the central government on Grande Comore island. Separatists on Mohéli have also declared independence, but appear more willing to compromise. Mayotte Island, the fourth island of the Comorian archipelago, voted to remain a French overseas territory in a 1974 referendum and today enjoys a far higher, French-subsidized standard of living. President Mohamed Taki Abdoulkarim has faced mounting internal unrest due to the deteriorating economy and mounting criticism of his handling of the Anjouan crisis. Violence by striking students and protests by teachers have been met by police violence and arrests.

Since independence, two mercenary invasions and 17 other coups and attempted coups have shaken the Comoros. France reestablished its military presence in 1996 at President Taki's invitation. Divisive personal, clan, and inter-island rivalries persist.

Ahmed Abdallah Abderrahman, the Comoros' first president, was overthrown by an army coup shortly after independence. French mercenary Bob Denard aided Abdallah's successful counter-coup in 1978. With Denard's backing as head of the army and presidential guard, Abdallah was returned unopposed in 1978 and 1984 one-party show elections. In 1989, he was allegedly assassinated by his own troops on Denard's orders. Subsequent unrest drew French military intervention, and Denard fled the country.

In 1990, in the country's first contested elections, Supreme Court Justice Said Mohamed Djohara won a six-year term as president. A September 1995 attempted coup by elements of the Comoros security forces, which were aided by foreign mercenaries and again led by Bob Denard, was reversed by French soldiers. President Djohar was flown into exile and not allowed to resume office.

Political Rights and Civil Liberties: March 1996 presidential and November 1996 parliamentary elections allowed Comorians to exercise the constitutional right to change their government democratically in open elections for the first time. Mohamed Taki Abdoulkarim, leader of the National Union for Democracy won the presidency in a runoff election with more than 60 percent of the vote. The polls were viewed as the most fair and efficient in Comoros' history. A new constitution adopted in an October 1996 referendum increased the role of Islamic law and reduced local autonomy, which had helped to spark the Anjouan rebellion. The conservative Islamic main opposition party also holds several seats in the National Assembly. The government's current constitutional status is unclear, however, since President Taki's assumption of emergency powers in 1997 required new elections that have not yet been scheduled. Many constitutionally mandated institutions exist only on paper.

The ruling Rally for Democracy and Renewal has split since President Taki's death. Defeated presidential candidate Abbas Djoussouf heads an opposition alliance. The secessionist movement on Anjouan is led by Abdullah Ibrahim. In July, armed clashes erupted between the competing Anjouan factions.

The Comorian legal system is based on Islamic law and remnants of the French legal code. Islam is the official state religion. Non-Muslims are permitted to practice, but not proselytize. The opposition and the country's few independent newspapers have strongly criticized Taki's use of decree power. The largely independent judiciary is headed by a Supreme Court. Most minor disputes are settled by village elders or a civilian court of first instance. Harsh prison conditions are marked by severe overcrowding and the lack of sanitation, medical attention, and proper diet. The Comoros Human Rights Association operates in a restrained manner reportedly because its civil servant members fear that strong criticism of the government could cost them their jobs.

Freedoms of expression and association are not constitutionally guaranteed. The semiofficial weekly *Al-Watwan* and several private newspapers sharply critical of the government are published in the capital. All, however, are believed to exercise extensive self-censorship. A few private television and radio stations operate without overt governmental interference. Transmissions from French-controlled Mayotte are easily received, and some people have access to satellite and other international broadcasting. Foreign publications are readily available.

Trade unions and strikes are permitted, but collective bargaining is rare in the country's small formal sector. Women possess constitutional protections despite the influence of Islamic law. In practice, however, they enjoy little political or economic power and have far fewer opportunities for education or salaried employment. Comorians are among the world's poorest people, and the ongoing secessionist crisis has further damaged an already tenuous economy. Remittances from the large overseas Comorian community sustain many families. The country relies heavily on foreign aid.

Congo, Republic of (Brazzaville)

Polity: Military-backed dictatorship
Economy: Mixed statist
Population: 2,700,000
PPP: $2,554
Life Expectancy: 47
Ethnic Groups: Kongo (48 percent), Sangha (20 percent), Teke (17 percent), M'Bochi, others
Capital: Brazzaville

Political Rights: 7
Civil Liberties: 5
Status: Not Free

Overview: Former military dictator Denis Sassou-Nguesso sought to consolidate his return to power in the wake of the 1997 civil war in which he ousted the elected government of President Pascal Lissouba. Sassou-Nguesso was backed by Angolan air, armor, and infantry units and political support from France. He also reportedly received financial aid from the French ELF oil company, whose monopoly over Congo oil exports was threatened by President Lissouba's policy of diversifying Congo's trade partners. Sassou-Nguesso, who received only 17 percent of the vote in 1992 presidential elections, has promised to conduct open, multiparty elections in 2001. He is highly unlikely to keep this pledge, however, since sharp ethnic divisions among the country's nearly three million people can be expected to produce electoral results similar to those in 1992, when voting along ethnic lines gave him little support outside his minority ethnic base in the north. In December, fighting flared in Brazzaville after repeated clashes in the southern Pool region.

Serious human rights abuses and occasional fighting continue. Civil wars in the neighboring Democratic Republic of Congo and nearby Angola have made large numbers of weapons and fighters available to all sides in the conflict.

A decade after its independence from France, a 1970 coup established a Marxist state in Congo. In 1979, General Sassou-Nguesso seized power and maintained one-party rule as head of the Congolese Workers' Party. Domestic and international pressure forced his acceptance of a transition to open, multiparty elections in 1992. Pascal Lissouba of the Pan-African Union for Social Democracy won a clear victory over Bernard Kolelas of the Congolese Party for Genuine Democracy and Development in a second round presidential runoff that excluded Sassou-Nguesso, who had run third in the first round. Legislative elections produced no clear majority. After an anti-Lissouba coalition formed, the president dissolved the assembly and called for fresh polls. Legislative polls in 1993 produced a presidential majority, but were marred by numerous irregularities. Several parties boycotted the second round.

The disputed elections led to armed conflict. In late 1993, Brazzaville suffered what proved to be only a foretaste of the far larger violence among ethnic-based militias in 1997. Sassou-Nguesso built his private army in his native northern Congo, and, with foreign aid, forcibly retook the presidency that he had lost in a free election. His ability to maintain stability and promote economic development is uncertain unless he can cultivate new coalitions with ethnic groups from the country's southern regions.

Political Rights and Civil Liberties:

The Congolese constitution has been suspended, and the future of the country's existing political parties is unclear. A 75-member transitional assembly was appointed by Sassou-Nguesso in January, but exercises no real power. The Congolese exercised their constitutional right to elect their president and National Assembly deputies to five-year terms of office through competitive multiparty elections for the first time in 1992 and 1993, respectively. President Lissouba's 1992 polls victory was widely considered to be free and fair, but 1993 legislative election results were disputed by the opposition. Presidential polls set for July 1997 were pre-empted by the civil war that returned Sassou-Nguesso to power.

There have been numerous reports of killings by security forces and militia, which act with apparent impunity. Freedoms of assembly and association are constitutionally guaranteed, but Interior Ministry permission for public gatherings is occasionally denied, and there is a real threat of violence by government security forces or other armed factions. Human rights groups such as Congolese Human Rights Watch continue to operate, but often with great difficulty. Religious freedom is respected in law and practice.

Scarce resources and understaffing create a backlog of court cases and long periods of pre-trial detention in extremely harsh prison conditions. The three-tier formal court system of local courts, courts of appeal, and the Supreme Court was generally considered to be politically independent until the civil war. In rural areas, traditional courts retain broad jurisdiction, especially in civil matters.

Freedom of expression is limited. The government monopoly over electronic media is complete except for a radio station operated by political allies of Sassou-Nguesso. Broadcasts from neighboring countries are widely heard. A July 1996 law imposed registration requirements and severe penalties for slander and defamation. A 1995 law also provides stronger penalties for defamation of senior officials, requires media to "show loyalty to the government," and permits seizure of private printing works during emergencies. There is extensive self-censorship. In September, journalist Fabien Fortune Bitoumbo was murdered by militia fighters. A few days earlier, offices of the magazine *La Rue Meurt* in Brazzaville had been raided by uniformed men who seized the publication's computer equipment.

Women suffer extensive legal and societal discrimination despite constitutional protections. Access to education and employment opportunities, especially in the countryside, are limited, and civil codes regarding family and marriage formalize women's inferior status. Adultery is legal for men, but not for women. Polygyny is legal, while polyandry is not. Violence against women is reportedly widespread, but not formally recorded. Discrimination against pygmy groups is also reported. Many pygmies are effectively held in lifetime servitude through customary ties to Bantu "patrons."

Workers' rights to join trade unions and to strike are legally protected. Six labor confederations operate with various linkages to the government and political parties. Unions are legally required to accept nonbinding arbitration before striking, but many strikes have proceeded without adherence to this process.

Physical reconstruction and restoration of investor confidence will be a post-war priority. In June, a $60 million reconstruction package was awarded by Western donors. In July, the IMF approved a $10 million loan.

⬇ Congo, Democratic Republic of (Kinshasa)

Polity: Military-backed dictatorship
Political Rights: 7
Civil Liberties: 6
Economy: Capitalist- statist
Status: Not Free
Population: 49,000,000
PPP: $355
Life Expectancy: 49
Ethnic Groups: More than 200 ethnicities, mostly Bantu
Capital: Kinshasa
Trend Arrow: Congo (Kinshasa) receives a downward trend arrow due to increased repression in the country.

Overview: Domestic and intra-African strife continued to threaten the survival of the Democratic Republic of Congo. In August, rebels seeking to overthrow the regime of President Laurent Kabila were stopped at the outskirts of Kinshasa only through the intervention of Angolan, Namibian, and Zimbabwean troops. The rebels, who were supported by Rwanda, Uganda, and perhaps other African states, mounted the uprising in response to sporadic clashes in eastern Congo and Kabila's moves to transfer power to inhabitants of his native Katanga region. While failing to conquer Kinshasa, the rebels seized broad areas in eastern Congo. In September, approximately 1,000 Chadian troops and an unknown number of Sudanese forces entered the fray in support of Kabila. Rwandan and Ugandan army units are reportedly fighting in northeastern Congo, where an array of insurgent groups opposed to various governments in the region also operate.

Longtime guerrilla fighter Laurent Kabila came to power in May 1997 after a seven-month campaign that had been sparked by a small rebellion in the northeastern corner of what was then still Zaire. His quick advance was backed by Rwanda, but also revealed a clear lack of support for President Mobutu Sesse Seko, who fled to Morocco and died of cancer shortly after Kabila's takeover. It is estimated that Mobutu systematically looted as much as $10 billion from his country during his 32 years in power.

Kabila today holds all executive and legislative power through the coalition Alliance of Forces for the Liberation of Congo-Zaire. He has grown increasingly reliant, however, on a narrow base of backers who share his Katangan ethnicity. The Rwandan and Zairian Tutsi who helped him to seize power were largely dismissed from their posts by midyear. Their purge helped spark the new rebellion. Parliament has been dissolved. Opposition supporters and journalists are routinely arrested and harassed, and public demonstrations are forbidden. Kabila's declining international image suffered further in June when a U.N. report blamed his regime for the "systematic" killings of thousands of Rwandan Hutu refugees. Kabila has promised presidential and legislative elections in April 1999, but is unlikely to honor his commitment.

As the Belgian Congo, the vast area of central Africa that is today the Democratic Republic of Congo was exploited with a brutality that was notable even by colonial standards. The country was a center for Cold War rivalries from Belgium's withdrawal in 1960 until then-Colonel Joseph Désiré Mobutu's seizure of power in 1964. The pro-Western Mobutu was forgiven for severe repression and kleptocratic excesses that made him one of the world's richest men and his countrymen among the world's poorest people.

Domestic agitation for democratization forced Mobutu to open the political process in 1990. In 1992, Mobutu's Popular Revolutionary Movement, the sole legal party after 1965, and the Sacred Union of the Radical Opposition and Allied Civil Society, a coalition of 200 groups, joined scores of others in a national conference to establish a High Council of the Republic to oversee a democratic transition. Mobutu manipulated and delayed the transition, but civil society grew stronger. Kabila has begun to reverse these advances.

Political Rights and Civil Liberties: The people of the Democratic Republic of Congo have never been permitted to choose or change their government through democratic and peaceful means. The transitional parliament has been dissolved, and President Kabila rules by decree. There are no elected representatives in the entire country. Mobutu's successive unopposed presidential victories and legislative polls were little more than political theater. Infrastructure and institutions to support a free and fair election are almost entirely absent. More than 300 political parties registered since their 1990 legalization are now banned, although many still operate and are likely, if allowed, to join the political process.

Serious human rights abuses, including extrajudicial executions, torture, beatings, and arbitrary detention reportedly continue. Ethnic killings by both government and rebel forces have been reported. Scores of thousands of Rwandan Hutu civilians, militia, and soldiers who fled in 1994 are still missing. Opposition supporters have been detained and some jailed after brief and reportedly unfair trials. In July, more than 50 members of the Union for Democracy and Social Progress party, led by veteran opposition figure Etienne Tshisekedi Wa Mulumba, were arrested. Some remain in detention.

Congo's judiciary is only nominally independent. The president may dismiss magistrates at will. Courts are grossly ineffective in protecting constitutional rights, and security forces and government officials generally act with impunity. Long periods of pretrial detention are common in prisons in which poor diet and medical care can be life threatening.

Freedom of expression and assembly are sharply limited by decree. Newspapers are not widely circulated beyond the country's large cities. Church radio networks are growing, but the state-controlled broadcasting network reaches the largest number of citizens. After the rebellion began in August, some state stations broadcast virulent incitements of listeners to "massacre" Rwandan Tutsis "without mercy" by using "spades, rakes, nails, truncheons, electric irons, barbed wire, stones, and the like." Independent journalists are frequently threatened, thereby prompting self-censorship. Albert Bonsange Yema, the director of the newspaper *L'Alarme,* was detained in February for publishing an opposition statement and was convicted in June of "threatening state security" and sentenced to one year's imprisonment.

Numerous nongovernmental organizations, including human rights groups, operate despite sporadic harassment. Freedom of religion is respected in practice, although religious groups must register with the government to be recognized.

Despite constitutional protections, women face de facto discrimination, especially in rural areas. They also enjoy fewer employment and educational opportunities and often do not receive equal pay for equal work. Married women must receive their husband's permission to enter into many financial transactions.

More than 100 new independent unions have registered since one-party rule ended in 1990. Previously, all unions had to affiliate with a confederation that was part of the ruling party.

Under Mobutu, the country's formal economy nearly ground to a halt. It has been further damaged by the ongoing war. Most of the country's approximately 48 million people live marginal lives as subsistence farmers.

Costa Rica

Polity: Presidential-
legislative democracy
Economy: Capitalist-statist
Population: 3,500,000
PPP: $5,969
Life Expectancy: 76
Ethnic Groups: White and mestizo (96 percent),
black (2 percent), Indian (1 percent), Chinese (1 percent)
Capital: San Jose

Political Rights: 1
Civil Liberties: 2
Status: Free

Overview:

The February 1998 election of conservative opposition leader Miguel Angel Rodriguez strengthened the pattern of alternating power between the two largest parties in Central America's oldest and most stable democracy. In response to the growing use of Costa Rica as a transit country for cocaine shipments from South America, the government has reacted by instituting tough new regulations on money laundering.

The Republic of Costa Rica achieved independence from Spain in 1821 and became a republic in 1848. Democratic government was instituted in 1899 and briefly interrupted in 1917 and 1948, when the country was torn by a brief but brutal civil war. The 1949 Constitution, which bans the formation of a national army, has proved to be the most durable in Latin America.

The social democratic National Liberation Party (PLN) was the dominant party for nearly three decades. In the 1994 presidential elections, Jose Maria Figueres narrowly defeated Rodriguez, a conservative congressman, respected economist, and leader of the Social Christian Party (PUSC), the country's other principal political organization. Figueres, son of the legendary former President Jose "Pepe" Figueres, campaigned against the neo-liberal economic policies of outgoing President Rafael A. Calderon, Jr., of the PUSC. Despite his earlier campaign pledges, Figueres' last two years in office were characterized by some of the free market policies championed by his opponent in the presidential elections.

Jose Miguel Corrales, an anti-corruption crusader and former congressman and soccer star, sought the PLN nomination in the February 1998 presidential contest. He was opposed by Rodriguez, who won with slightly less than 47 percent of the vote. The PUSC, however, failed to win a working majority in the unicameral National Assembly and was forced to make an alliance with smaller parties to sustain its legislative program.

Costa Rica's heavily armed police appear unable to stem the increase in drug-related corruption and money laundering. Public safety has become a primary concern of the residents of San Jose, which had been a safe haven in a region wracked with violence.

Political Rights and Civil Liberties: Costa Ricans can change their government democratically. The February 1998 victory of presidential candidate Rodriguez, while far narrower than expected, reflected the domination of the political landscape by the PLN and PUSC. Allegations regarding drug-tainted campaign contributions continue to plague both major parties. New campaign laws have been instituted to make party financing more transparent. In the 1998 elections, analysts noted that the high rate of abstention and spoilage of ballots reflected popular disillusionment with established parties and a sense of exclusion from the process.

The constitution provides for three independent branches of government. The president and the 57-member legislative assembly are elected for four years and are prohibited from seeking second terms. The assembly has equal power, including the ability to override presidential vetoes.

The judicial branch is independent, with members elected by the legislature. A supreme court with power to rule on the constitutionality of laws is in operation, as are four courts of appeal and a network of district courts. An independent national election commission is elected by the supreme court.

The judicial system is marked by delays that create volatile situations in the country's overcrowded, violence-prone prisons. The problem is linked to budget cuts affecting the judiciary and to the nation's economic difficulties, which have led to a rise in violent crime and clashes in the countryside between squatters and landowners. An estimated 420,000 Nicaraguans, or 15 percent of Costa Rica's total population, live in the country. More than half are there illegally. In the aftermath of Hurricane Mitch, Costa Rica declared a temporary amnesty for these and other Central American illegal immigrants.

Numerous charges are still made of human rights violations by police. Independent Costa Rican human rights monitors report increases in allegations of arbitrary arrests and brutality. An official ombudsman provides recourse for citizens or foreigners with human rights complaints. The ombudsman has the authority to issue recommendations for rectification, including sanctions against government bodies, for failure to respect rights.

The written press, radio, and television are generally free. Several independent dailies serve a society that is 90 percent literate. Television and radio stations are both public and commercial, with at least six private television stations providing an influential forum for public debate. At the same time, restrictive libel laws continue to dampen full exercise of press freedoms.

Constitutional guarantees regarding freedom of religion and the right to organize political parties and civic organizations are respected. In recent years, however, a reluctance to address restrictions on labor rights has been noted.

Solidarity, an employer-employee organization that private businesses use as an instrument to prevent independent unions from organizing, remains strong and has generally been tolerated by successive governments. Solidarity remains entrenched in Costa Rica's free-trade zones, where labor abuses by multinational corporations are rife. Minimum wage and social security laws are often ignored, and fines for noncompliance are minuscule. Female workers are often sexually harassed, made to work overtime without pay, and fired if they become pregnant.

Côte D'Ivoire

Polity: Dominant Party   **Political Rights:** 6
Economy: Capitalist   **Civil Liberties:** 4
Population: 15,600,000   **Status:** Not Free
PPP: $1,731
Life Expectancy: 52
Ethnic Groups: Baoule (23 percent), Bete (18 percent), Senoufou (15 percent), Malinke (11 percent), Agni, foreign Africans, non-Africans
Capital: Yamoussoukro (official); Abidjan (de facto)

Overview: President Henri Konan Bédié initiated constitutional changes to expand presidential powers, reduce judicial independence, and dilute representative government by creating an upper house of parliament, with one-third of its members appointed by the president. With elections in late 2000, the presidential term will be extended to seven years, and Bédié will have new powers to delay or cancel polls entirely. Opposition parties and civic groups have strongly protested the changes. In December, however, the ruling Democratic Party of the Ivory Coast (PDCI) and the principal opposition, Ivorian Popular Front Party (FPI), signed an accord providing for a new national election commission, revised campaign finance rules, and amnesty for opposition supporters imprisoned during the "active boycott" of the 1995 presidential election.

The 2000 elections are likely to be contested by reformist Alassane Dramane Ouattara, a former prime minister and now senior World Bank official, although the Bédié regime is expected to seek his disqualification on the basis that he was not born in Côte d'Ivoire. A major economic aid and debt forgiveness package arranged by international donors in February could boost the country's economy, although alleged endemic corruption by Bédié and the PDCI may hamper equitable growth.

Côte d'Ivoire retains strong political, economic, and military backing from France, its former colonial power and main trading partner. France maintains a military garrison near Abidjan, and its advisors serve with many units of Côte d'Ivoire's 14,000-strong armed forces. American military trainers visited the country this year to train security forces in controlling crowds and conducting humanitarian missions.

Political Rights and Civil Liberties: President Bédié was declared president with 95 percent of the vote in a 1995 presidential election that was neither free nor fair. Alassane Ouattara, the opposition's most formidable candidate, was barred from the contest. Many of the 40 percent of Ivorians who share his Muslim faith viewed his exclusion as an act of religious discrimination.

The presidential poll was boycotted by all of the major opposition parties. Demonstrations were banned, and the media were intimidated. At the same time, the ruling party made profligate use of state resources. At least 23 people were killed in communal clashes during protests against electoral misconduct. The credibility of the November 1995 legislative elections was devalued by dubious voter lists, bans on opposition demonstrations, and harassment of opposition supporters. The National Assembly is overwhelmingly dominated by the ruling PDCI, which holds 149 of the 175 seats. There is no genuinely independent election commission.

Only a few of the more than 40 officially registered political parties are active. Official harassment and lack of unity hamper the opposition FPI and Rally for a Democratic Republic, but there are signs that the parties may align to support Alassane Ouattara's candidacy if the scheduled elections are held in 2000. A requirement for private associations to register with the government may be unconstitutional, but has not generally been used to ban groups. Several human rights organizations, including the Ivorian Human Rights League and the Ivorian Women's Movement, are active in the country. Muslims complain of bias in both governmental and private spheres, although there is no evidence of systematic or official discrimination.

State-owned newspapers and state-run broadcasting are usually unreservedly pro-government. Several private radio stations and a cable television service operate, but only the state broadcasting reaches a national audience. The private print media continued their role of watchdog and advocate, but remained under threat of governmental repression. "Insulting the president," "threatening public order," and "defaming or undermining the reputation of the state" are criminal offenses that authorities interpret broadly to silence unwanted criticism.

Côte d'Ivoire does not have an independent judiciary, and the 1998 constitutional changes give the president increased powers of judicial appointment. Judges are political appointees without tenure and are highly susceptible to external interference. Legal provisions regarding search warrants, rules of evidence, and pretrial detention are often ignored. An August 1996 law denounced by human rights groups gave police sweeping new search powers. The Special Anticrime Police Brigade reportedly follows an officially sanctioned shoot-to-kill policy in confrontations with suspected criminals. In many rural areas, traditional courts still prevail, especially in handling minor matters and family law. Very harsh prison conditions are reportedly ameliorated only for prisoners wealthy enough to pay for special treatment. Many deaths from diseases aggravated by a poor diet and inadequate or nonexistent medical attention have been reported. A large portion of inmates are pretrial detainees who sometimes wait for years for a court date.

Prison conditions for women are especially hazardous and mirror prevailing societal discrimination, despite official encouragement for respect for constitutional rights. Equal pay for equal work is offered in the small formal sector, but women have few chances to obtain or advance in wage employment. In rural areas that rely on subsistence agriculture, education and job opportunities for women are even scarcer. Violence against women is reportedly common. A 1998 study by the Ivorian Association for the Defense of Women's Rights found that more than 80 percent of women in Abidjan had been victims of violence by their partners. Female genital mutilation is still widespread.

The government has sometimes taken harsh action against strikers, although union formation and membership are legally protected. For three decades, the General Union of Workers of Côte d'Ivoire was closely aligned to the sole legal party. The Federation of Autonomous Trade Unions of Côte d'Ivoire represents several independent unions formed since 1991. Notification and conciliation requirements must be met before legal strikes can be conducted. Collective bargaining agreements are often reached with the participation of government negotiators who influence wage settlements.

The privatization of many of the Côte d'Ivoire's state-run corporations continues and is attracting renewed foreign investment. The launching of a West African regional stock market in September could also stimulate growth. The IMF and World Bank announced a three-year $385 million aid package in February. Whether the current regime will apply this aid to genuine economic development and improved social services remains unclear. Charges of pervasive corruption persist, and poverty remains endemic.

⬇ Croatia

Polity: Presidential-parliamentary democracy
Economy: Mixed capitalist (transitional)
Population: 4,200,000
PPP: $3,972
Life Expectancy: 72
Ethnic Groups: Croat (78 percent), Serb (12 percent), Muslim (1 percent), Hungarian (0.5 percent), Slovenian (0.5 percent), other (8 percent)
Capital: Zagreb

Political Rights: 4
Civil Liberties: 4
Status: Partly Free

Trend Arrow: Croatia receives a downward trend arrow due to corruption, harassment of the press, and failure to repatriate refugees.

Overview: In 1998, President Franjo Tudjman faced financial, wiretapping, and corruption scandals amid continuing international pressure for the repatriation of Serb refugees, an end to support for Bosnian Croat separatists, and a decrease in government coercion of the media.

Hungary ruled most of what is now Croatia from the 1100s until World War I. In 1918, Croatia became part of the Kingdom of Serbs, Croats, and Slovenes, which was renamed Yugoslavia in 1929. An independent state was proclaimed in 1941 by the pro-fascist Ustasa movement. In 1945, Croatia joined the People's Republic of Yugoslavia under Communist leader Josip Broz (Tito). After Croatia and Slovenia declared independence in 1991, the Serb-dominated Yugoslav army, backed by Serbian militias, seized parts of Croatia and ultimately controlled one-third of the territory. Beginning in 1993, Croatia supported Bosnian Croat separatist forces, which had opened a separate front in the war in Bosnia. In 1994, President Tudjman endorsed a U.S. peace accord that ended the conflict and created a federated statelet in loose confederation with Croatia. In 1995, Croatian forces recaptured Western Slavonia and Krajina from Serbian control. Late that year, Croatia became a signatory to the Dayton Accords, which ended the Bosnian war.

In 1995 elections to the 127-member House of Representatives, Tudjman's Croatian Democratic Union (HDZ) won 75 seats. International observers criticized the government for allowing 300,000 Bosnian Croats to vote. In the 1997 presidential elections, President Tudjman easily defeated Zdravko Tomac of the Social Democrats with 61 percent of the vote.

In October 1998, the opposition demanded an investigation after it was revealed that President Tudjman's wife, who was understood to have had no appreciable financial holdings of her own, had deposited $130,000 in a Croatian bank. In June, an independent publication had detailed the vast financial holdings acquired by President Tudjman's family after the HDZ came to power. In October, the government was rocked by the resignation of Defense Minister Andrija Hebrang, who had replaced the late hardliner Gojko Susak. Hebrang claimed that he no longer had the president's support to dismiss corrupt officials with links to organized crime and reform the defense ministry. The resignation followed allegations by two senior HDZ moderates that they had been subjected to security service wiretaps and surveillance.

In January, UN administrators withdrew from Eastern Slavonia and returned the region, which had been captured by Serbian forces and purged of ethnic Croats in 1991, to Croatian control. In February, approximately 5,000 ethnic Serbs left Eastern Slavonia, Baranya, and the West Srem region.

Political Rights and Civil Liberties: Citizens can change their government democratically, but the strong presidency and the emergence of the HDZ as an entrenched, dominant party contribute to an authoritarian political environment. Parliamentary elections in 1995 were marked by irregularities. The 1997 presidential elections were "free, but not fair."

The constitution guarantees freedom of thought and expression and freedom of the press and other media. In an attempt to meet Council of Europe standards, parliament passed a law in 1996 to protect journalists from revealing their sources and from criminal charges for publishing false information unintentionally. Current provisions, however, still prescribe fines and imprisonment for reporters who insult top state officials. In April, the editor-in-chief and a journalist from the independent weekly *Globus* received suspended sentences for allegedly libeling the defense ministry. More than 130 libel cases are pending. The government retains controlling interest in two of four daily newspapers, several weeklies, and HINA, the country's only news agency. In October, the publisher of the independent weekly *Nacional* accused the authorities of trying to close his newspaper due to its reporting on splits within the HDZ. The three national television stations are part of the state-owned Croatian Radio and Television Enterprise (HRT). In October, parliament endorsed a bill to create a 23-member HRT Council that would include 10 members of the lower house, in proportion with party representation. Since all members would be appointed by parliament, the opposition protested that the HDZ would exercise political influence on the council. Six local television stations operate with varying degrees of independence. More than 50 local and independent radio stations operate throughout the country, but with limited reception. In June, three local radio stations were registered to broadcast to regional ethnic Serbian populations.

Freedom of religion is nominally assured. Approximately 150,000 ethnic Serbs remain from a pre-1991 population of 580,000, and many face intimidation and violence. Laws from Zagreb have threatened Italian schools and cultural institutions in Istria, which is home to 30,000 ethnic Italians. Roma (Gypsies), who constitute two percent of the population, face discrimination.

Ethnic Serbs who seek to return to Croatia face enormous bureaucratic obstacles. Government policy has been to permit only the return of Serbs who have relatives remaining in Croatia. The family member living in Croatia must apply on behalf of the returnee. Serbs are frequently rejected under a law that allows the government to deny citizenship to applicants who "pose a threat to national interests."

Freedom of assembly and demonstration are generally respected, although demonstrations must be approved by authorities. In February, tens of thousands rallied in Zagreb to protest poor living conditions. More than 60 political parties function legally in Croatia.

All workers except the armed forces, police, government administrators, and public services employees are guaranteed the right to strike. Croatia's labor movement includes five major labor confederations and several large unaffiliated unions. Trade unions have been very active in response to high unemployment, low average wages, and declining living standards. There were several labor actions in 1998.

A High Judicial Council appoints judges and public prosecutors. Members are nominated and approved by parliament for eight-year terms. Through parliamentary nomination and election, the HDZ wields influence over the High Judicial Council and, thus, over the selection of judges. In recent years, the government has purged the judiciary of judges and attorneys who were either non-Croats or whose political views were at odds with the government or HDZ.

Property rights are guaranteed under the constitution, but the law has effectively expropriated the property of many minority Serbs who fled Croatia in 1995. In 1997, the courts revised some of the more discriminatory parts of the law, but Serbs still encounter difficulty in regaining property that has already fallen under the administration of Croatian authorities. While citizens have the right to establishes businesses, the government's privatization program has been criticized for allotting shares in prime enterprises to HDZ loyalists. Government cronyism and corruption are endemic.

Women are guaranteed equal rights under the law and are involved in politics, government, and business.

↑ Cuba

Polity: Communist one-party
Economy: Statist
Population: 11,100,000
PPP: $3,100
Life Expectancy: 75
Ethnic Groups: Mulatto (51 percent), white (37 percent), black (11 percent), Chinese (1 percent)
Capital: Havana

Political Rights: 7
Civil Liberties: 7
Status: Not Free

Trend Arrow: Cuba receives an upward trend arrow due to a slight relaxation of religious freedom and the release of some political prisoners.

Overview: In the wake of Pope John Paul II's historic January visit to Cuba, President Fidel Castro's government has reduced its repression of dissidents, including long-term detentions, to one of the lowest levels in years. At year's end, government approval for the migration of 19 Roman Catholic priests and 21 lay religious workers raised the number of priests on the island to approximately half of the number in 1961. This was viewed as a sign of a carefully nuanced bow to foreign pressure, but the gesture was balanced against signs that four leading political dissidents, already imprisoned for more than a year, were soon to be tried for "sedition." It remains to be seen whether minor efforts to reduce the level of repression have been a carefully calibrated response to foreign pressure to begin to democratize the island or merely recognition that a heavier hand was not needed to preserve the regime and maintain its control of society.

Cuba achieved independence from Spain in 1898 as a result of the Spanish-American War. The Republic of Cuba was established in 1902, but was under U.S. tutelage under the Platt Amendment until 1934. In 1959, Castro's July 26 Movement, which was named after an earlier, failed insurrection, overthrew the dictatorship of Fulgencio Batista, who had ruled for 18 of the previous 25 years. Since then, Castro has dominated the Cuban political system and has transformed it into a one-party police state. Communist structures were institutionalized by the 1976 constitution installed at the first congress of the Cuban Communist Party (PCC). The constitution provides for a National Assembly which, in theory, designates a Council of State. The Council, in turn, appoints a Council of Ministers in consultation with its president, who serves as head of state and chief of government. In reality, Castro is responsible for every appointment. As president of the Council of Ministers, chairman of the Council of State, commander-in-chief of the Revolutionary Armed Forces (FAR) and first secretary of the PCC, Castro controls every lever of power in Cuba. The PCC is the only authorized political party, and it controls all governmental entities from the national to the municipal level.

Since the collapse of the Soviet Union, which subsidized the Cuban economy, Castro has sought Western foreign investment. A U.S. embargo has been in effect since 1960. Most investment has come from Europe and Latin America, but it has not compensated for the lost $5 billion in annual Soviet subsidies. The government claims that the economy has rebounded in the past three years, but the "special period" austerity program, involving drastic cutbacks in energy consumption and tight rationing of food and consumer items, remains in place.

The legalization of the dollar in 1993 has heightened social tensions, as the minority with access to dollars from abroad or the tourist industry has emerged as a new moneyed class and increased the desperation of the majority. State salaries have shrunk to four dollars or less a month, although the economy appears to be slowly improving.

Neither the Fifth Congress of the PCC in 1997, at which one-party rule was reaffirmed, nor the one-party national elections held in 1998, provided any surprises. Castro proudly pointed to the fact of a reported 95 percent turnout at the polls. Meanwhile, critics noted that, in his paranoid paradise, nonparticipation could be construed as dissent and that many people were afraid of the consequences of being so identified. At the Communist Party congress, Castro alluded to his own mortality and bequeathed to the nation his own hand-picked successor: his brother, Vice President Raul Castro.

The number of dissidents confirmed to be imprisoned has dropped from 1,320 in 1996 to 381 in June 1998. Part of the decline was due to the release of 140 of 300 prisoners who were held for political activities or common crimes and whose freedom was sought by the Pontiff. At year's end, however, four top opposition leaders faced sedition charges after being arrested in July 1997. Cuba's efforts to break the isolation imposed by the U.S. embargo increased during the year, with Castro making highly publicized trips to several Caribbean neighbors and offering humanitarian assistance to the countries that faced the most damage from Hurricane Mitch.

Political Rights and Civil Liberties:

Cubans cannot change their government through democratic means. In January, members of the National Assembly were elected in a process with a reported turnout of 98.35 percent of 7.8 million registered voters. Reportedly, there were only 601 candidates for an equal number of seats. Opposition and dissident groups were forbidden from presenting their own candidates. The National Assembly is vested with the right of legislative power, but, when not in session, this faculty is delegated to a 31-member council of state elected by the Assembly and chaired by Castro.

In Cuba, all political and civic organization outside of the PCC is illegal. Political dissent, spoken or written, is a punishable offense, and those so punished frequently receive years of imprisonment for seemingly minor infractions. A person can even go to jail for possession of a fax machine or a photocopier. Although there has been a slight relaxation of strictures on cultural life, the educational and judicial systems, labor unions, professional organizations, and all media remain state controlled. A small, courageous group of human rights activists and dissident journalists, together with a measure of activity by the Catholic Church, provide the only glimmer of an independent civil society.

The executive branch controls the judiciary. The 1976 constitution concentrates power in the hands of one individual: Fidel Castro, president of the Council of State. In practice, the Council serves as a de facto judiciary and controls both the courts and the judicial process as a whole.

There is continued evidence of torture and killings in prison and in psychiatric institutions, where a number of dissidents arrested in recent years are held. Since 1990, the International Committee of the Red Cross has been denied access to prisoners. Local human rights activists report that more than 100 prisons and prison camps hold between 60,000 and 100,000 prisoners of all categories. In 1993, vandalism was decreed to be a form of sabotage, which is punishable by eight years in prison.

Cuba under Castro still has one of the highest per capita rates of imprisonment for political offenses of any country in the world. Most political prisoners are held in cells with common criminals, and many are convicted on vague charges such as "disseminating enemy propaganda" or "dangerousness." Since 1991, the United Nations has voted annually to assign a special investigator on human rights to Cuba, but the Cuban government has refused to cooperate. Groups that exist apart from the state are labeled "counterrevolutionary criminals" and are still subject to systematic repression, including arrests, beatings while in custody, and confiscations and intimidation by uniformed or plainclothes state security forces.

The press in Cuba is the object of a targeted campaign by the government. Independent journalists, particularly those associated with five small news agencies, have fallen victim to endless repression, including jail terms at hard labor and assaults while in prison by state security agents. Foreign news agencies must also hire local reporters only through government offices, thereby limiting employment opportunities for independent journalists. In mid-1998, foreign lifestyle magazines such as *Cosmopolitan* and *Hola* were removed from the state-controlled newsstands open to the general public on the grounds that they were "damaging to our culture and ideology." In July, Castro ordered the expulsion of foreign news correspondents covering the opening of the new National Assembly. They had to leave, he claimed, so that he could "speak with complete freedom." On a more positive note, in November, the government announced that, after 29 years, the Associated Press would reopen its bureau in Havana.

Freedom of movement and the right to choose one's residence, education, or job are severely restricted. Attempting to leave the island without permission is a punishable offense. Cuban authorities have failed to investigate adequately the 1994 sinking of a tugboat carrying at least 66 people, of whom only 31 survived, as it sought to flee Cuba. Several survivors alleged that the craft sank as it was being pursued and assaulted by three other vessels acting under official orders and that the fleeing boat was not allowed to surrender. The government denied any responsibility and claimed that the tragedy was an accident caused by irresponsible actions by those on board. Citing what it calls compelling evidence, including eyewitness testimony, Amnesty International called the deaths an "extrajudicial execution." Those in Cuba who have commemorated the event or who have peacefully protested the sinking have faced harassment and intimidation.

In 1991, Roman Catholics and other believers were granted permission to join the Communist Party. The constitutional reference that mandated official atheism was dropped in 1992. Religious freedom has made small gains. Afro-Cuban religious groups are now carefully courted by Cuban officials. In preparation for the Pope's visit, Roman Catholic pastoral work and religious education activities were allowed to take place relatively unimpeded, and Christmas was celebrated for the first time in 28 years.

In the post-Soviet era, the right of Cubans to own private property and operate joint ventures with foreigners and non-Cuban businesses has been recognized. In practice, there are few rights for those who do not belong to the Cuban Communist Party. Party membership is still required for good jobs,serviceable housing, genuine access to social services such as medical care, and educational opportunities.

Cyprus (Greek)

Polity: Presidential-
legislative democracy
Economy: Capitalist
Population: 700,000
PPP: $13,379
Life Expectancy: 78
Ethnic Groups: Greek (78 percent), Turkish (18 percent),
other (4 percent)
Capital: Nicosia

Political Rights: 1
Civil Liberties: 1
Status: Free

Overview: Reunification of the divided island remained at the center of
Cypriot political life, even as President Glafcos Clerides'
center-right coalition government prepared for European
Union (EU) assession talks scheduled for the end of the year. The talks were approved
over the strong objections of Turkey. In 1997, the Council of Europe had recommended
that the EU offer membership to Cyprus in order to produce "significant economic and
political advantages for the two communities" and a "major factor of stability."

Clerides and the government were also forced to devote inordinate efforts to defend their decision to deploy Russian-made anti-aircraft air defense missiles on Greek
Cypriot territory. By year's end, the missiles, which were purchased in 1996, remain
undeployed due to major opposition by the United States and EU-member countries.
Efforts by the United Nations and the United States to settle the decades-old dispute
over Cyprus have repeatedly stalled in the face of violence, land disputes, and unwill-
ingness on the part of either side to agree on terms for formal talks. U.S. and UN officials attempted to break the impasse during the year with rounds of shuttle talks. Occasional goodwill gestures, such as the UN-sponsored visit of Greek Cypriots to an Orthodox monastery in the Turkish-controlled north, were overshadowed by larger-scale
political tensions and the bellicose rhetoric of the two communities' political leaders.
During the year, parades of massive military hardware in the south and north marked
the anniversaries of Cypriot independence and the 1974 Turkish invasion.

Annexed to Britain in 1914, Cyprus gained independence in 1960 after a ten-year
guerrilla campaign to demand union with Greece. In July 1974, Greek Cypriot national
guard members, backed by the military junta in power in Greece, staged an unsuccessful coup aimed at unification. Five days later, Turkey invaded, seized control of 37
percent of the island, and expelled 200,000 Greeks from the north. Currently, the entire Turkish Cypriot community resides in the north, and property claims arising from
the division and population exchange remain unsettled.

A buffer zone called the "Green Line" has divided Cyprus since 1974. The capital,
Nicosia, is the world's last divided city. The division of Cyprus has been a major point
of contention in the long-standing rivalry between Greece and Turkey in the Aegean.
Tensions and intermittent violence between the two populations have plagued the island since independence.

UN resolutions stipulate that Cyprus is a single country of which the northern third
is illegally occupied. In 1982, Turkish-controlled Cyprus made a unilateral declaration

of independence that was condemned by the UN and that remains unrecognized by every country except Turkey. [See Turkish Cyprus under Related Territories.]

Peace in Cyprus remains fragile. Propaganda in schools and in the media has sustained hostility among Cypriot youth. Blatant economic disparity exists between the prosperous south and the stagnating north. Even before President Clerides launched a $300 million-a-year rearmament program, Cyprus was among the most heavily militarized countries in the world.

Political Rights and Civil Liberties: Greek Cypriots can change their government democratically. Suffrage is universal and compulsory, and elections are free and fair. The 1960 constitution established an ethnically representative system designed to protect the interests of both Greek and Turkish Cypriots.

The independent judiciary operates according to the British tradition, upholding the presumption of innocence and the right to due process. Trial before a judge is standard, although requests for trial by jury are regularly granted.

Freedom of speech is respected, and a vibrant independent press frequently criticizes authorities. Several private television and radio stations in the Greek Cypriot community compete effectively with government-controlled stations. In addition, the government also publishes a Cyprus Internet home page, which features information regarding efforts to resolve the island's protracted dispute as well as regarding current developments and policy statements by Cypriot leaders.

Freedom of assembly and association as well as the right to strike are respected.

Czech Republic

Polity: Parliamentary democracy
Economy: Mixed capitalist
Population: 10,300,000
PPP: 9,775
Life Expectancy: 74
Ethnic Groups: Czech (94 percent), Slovak (3 percent), Polish (1 percent), German (0.5 percent), Gypsy (0.5 percent), other (1 percent)
Capital: Prague

Political Rights: 1
Civil Liberties: 2
Status: Free

Overview: In June parliamentary elections, the Social Democrats (CSSD) led by Milos Zeman won the most seats and formed a minority government with the support of former Prime Minister Vaclav Klaus, who had resigned in late 1997 amid allegations of financial improprieties in his Civic Democratic Union (ODS). In other issues, parliament ratified the Czech Republic's membership in NATO, and an ailing Vaclav Havel was re-elected president by parliament.

The Czech Republic emerged in 1993 after the peaceful dissolution of Czechoslovakia, which had been created in 1918 after the Austro-Hungarian empire's collapse. Czechoslovak President Vaclav Havel, a leading anti-Communist dissident and playwright, was elected Czech President. Premier Klaus and his pro-market ODS led a four-party coalition that had won control of the Czech parliament in 1992. In 1996 parliamentary elections, the ODS and coalition partners from the Christian Democratic Union and the Civic Democratic Alliance won only 99 of 200 seats, with the Zeman-led opposition winning 61 seats, or four times its 1992 returns. The unreconstructed Communist Party of Bohemia and Moravia won 22 seats, and the ultra-nationalist Republican Party won 18. There is one independent.

In 1997, a sluggish economy and allegations of corruption led to a sharp drop in Prime Minister Klaus' popularity. In November, the government collapsed after the Christian Democrats and the Civil Democratic Alliance left the ruling coalition amid the ODS's admission that it had received a substantial donation from a businessman who had recently acquired a large stake in a steel firm privatized by the Klaus government. President Havel asked Josef Tosovsky, the central bank governor, to form a caretaker government. In January 1998, the government announced that new elections would be held in June.

In January, the ODS split when 30 of the party's 69 deputies formed a new party called the Freedom Union (US), which is led by Jan Ruml. Key issues in the campaign were corruption and an economy on the verge of recession. The CSSD won 32 percent of the vote and 74 seats. Klaus's ODS won 63 seats; the Communists, 24; the Christian Democrats, 20; and the US, 19. Weeks of negotiations between the CSSD and the center-right Christian Democrats failed to produce a coalition. In July, the CSSD and the OSD reached a surprise deal to allow Zeman to form a minority left-wing government. In exchange, the ODS won the posts of speaker in both houses of parliament and the chairmanships of several key committees. Prime Minister Zeman was formally appointed by President Havel on July 17. In November elections for 27 seats in the 81-member Senate, candidates for the four-party coalition led by the Christian Democrats and the Freedom Union won in 13 districts. They were followed by Klaus's Civic Democratic Party, which won nine. The ruling Social Democrats took three.

Political Rights and Civil Liberties: Czech citizens can change their government democratically under a multiparty system. The 1998 elections were free and fair.

Freedoms of expression and media are respected. Defamation of the president and slander of government officials and departments are prohibited by law. In January, police in Olomouc detained the owner and director of the private Studio ZZIP television station on charges of criminal libel stemming from a 1997 report that implicated a police investigator for bribery. There are scores of private newspapers and magazines. Of the country's four television stations, two are private. There are 60 private radio stations, in addition to Czech Public Radio. A private news agency, CTA, began to operate in 1994.

Freedom of religion is respected, though there was a series of attacks on Jewish monuments. Issues regarding restitution for church property seized by the Communists remain unresolved. Freedoms of assembly and demonstration are respected, although permits are generally required for rallies.

More than 50 political parties have emerged since 1989, but most are small and have no national structures. In the 1998 election, 13 parties fielded candidates, but only five passed the five percent threshold.

Most unionized workers belong to the Czech-Moravian Chamber of Trade Unions, which was established in 1990 and includes approximately 35 unions. Approximately two-thirds of all workers are members of a union.

The judiciary is independent in law and in practice, but court delays and a lack of experienced judges remain problems. There are few reports of abuses by security forces and police, although Roma (Gypsies) have complained of police and judicial indifference to bias and hate crimes. The Roma, who number between 200,000 and 300,000, suffer disproportionately from poverty, unemployment, interethnic violence, and discrimination.

Czech citizens have freedom to travel and the right to choose residences and employment. Property rights are guaranteed under the constitution and by law. While there are no major restrictions to operating a business, problems persisted during Klaus's five-year tenure. An unregulated stock market allowed for abuses by speculators; privatization vouchers were bought in large quantities by investment funds, most of which were owned by a handful of large banks controlled by the state; and poorly managed banks sustained money-losing industries with loans.

Despite structural economic problems, the country's market system allows for equality of opportunity. Women are guaranteed equal rights and face no overt discrimination in employment, government service, or education.

Denmark

Polity: Parliamentary democracy
Economy: Mixed capitalist
Population: 5,300,000
PPP: $21,983
Life Expectancy: 75
Ethnic Groups: Mostly Danish, some German and Eskimo
Capital: Copenhagen

Political Rights: 1
Civil Liberties: 1
Status: Free

Overview: In March, Denmark's fragile coalition government, which is led by the Social Democratic Party (SDP), won re-election to another four-year term. In a national referendum in May, voters approved the European Union (EU) Amsterdam Treaty, which the government had endorsed, by a 55-to-45 percent margin.

In late September, government officials began to consider an early referendum on membership in the European economic and monetary union. The government had pledged that the issue would not be on the agenda before the next general election in 2002, but severe pressure on Danish currency may lead the government to reverse its decision.

Danish voters approved the Maastricht Treaty in 1993, after voting it down in 1992, but only after securing exemptions from its provisions for a common defense and currency, EU citizenship, and police cooperation.

Denmark is the oldest monarchy in Europe. Queen Margrethe II, whose reign began in 1972, appoints the premier and cabinet ministers in consultation with parliamentary leaders. The 1953 constitution established a unicameral parliament (*Folketing*), in which 135 of 179 members are elected in 17 mainland districts. Two representatives from each of the autonomous regions of the Faeroe Islands and Greenland are also elected. The remaining seats are allocated on a proportional basis to parties receiving over two percent of the vote. An extensive system of local representation includes both regional and local councils.

Political Rights and Civil Liberties:

Danes can change their government democratically. Representatives are elected to the Folketing at least once every four years in a modified system of proportional representation. The independent judiciary includes approximately 100 local courts, two high courts, and a 15-member Supreme Court with judges appointed by the Queen, on recommendation from the government. Danes enjoy freedom of association and assembly, and workers are free to organize and strike. The vast majority of wage earners belong to trade unions and their umbrella organization, the SDP-affiliated Danish Federation of Trade Unions.

Danish media reflect a wide variety of political opinions and are frequently critical of the government. The state finances radio and television broadcasting, but state-owned television companies have independent editorial boards. Independent radio stations are permitted by the state, but are tightly regulated and have occasionally been prohibited from broadcasting. In 1995, the Danish national Socialist Movement was banned from opening a radio station, as its campaign for a "racially clean" country was considered illegal incitement to racial hatred, going beyond Denmark's high threshold of tolerance for speech. In recent years, this high threshold has prompted criticism from human rights groups, which claim that the country is overly tolerant of indigenous and foreign neo-Nazi groups.

While freedom of worship is guaranteed to all, more than 90 percent of the population belongs to the state-supported Evangelical Lutheran Church of Denmark. In 1997, the church became the first to approve a religious ceremony for same-sex marriages. In 1989, Denmark became the first country to allow same-sex civil marriages. Discrimination on the basis of race, language, and sex is illegal, and the media have taken a strong role in educating the public about non-Nordic immigrants and refugees in order to prevent the rise of racism. Women constitute approximately 45 percent of the wage labor force and generally hold 20 to 30 percent of national legislative seats. The civil rights of homosexuals are protected.

Djibouti

Polity: Dominant party
Economy: Capitalist
Population: 700,000
PPP: $1,300
Life Expectancy: 48
Ethnic Groups: Somali (60 percent), Afar (35 percent), other (5 percent)
Capital: Djibouti

Political Rights: 5
Civil Liberties: 6
Status: Not Free

Overview:

Djibouti's people continue to be deeply divided on ethnic and clan bases, and a simmering Afar insurgency festers in the country's northern zones. The main schism is between the majority Issa (Somali) and minority Afar peoples. Competition among the Issa clans has also contributed to rising tensions over the succession to ailing octogenarian President Hassan Gouled Aptidon, whose term expires in 1999. Legislative elections in 1997 in this strategically positioned Horn of Africa country returned the ruling Popular Rally for Progress (RPP) party to power, thereby reinforcing the long dominance of President Aptidon's Mamassan clan of the majority Issa ethnic group.

Before receiving independence from France in 1977, Djibouti was known as the French Territory of the Afar and Issa. Afar rebels of the Front for the Restoration of Unity and Democracy (FRUD) launched a three-year guerrilla war against Issa dominance in 1991. Ethnic violence has receded since the largest FRUD faction agreed in 1994 to end its insurgency in exchange for inclusion in the government and electoral reforms. Despite some concessions, President Gouled's sub-clan retains most power. Approximately 3,500 French troops are among 10,000 French residents of Djibouti. French advisors and technicians effectively run much of the country, and France is highly influential in Djiboutian affairs, although Paris has announced a reduction in its military presence.

President Gouled has ruled since independence with solid French backing. He controlled a one-party system until 1992, when a new constitution adopted by referendum authorized four political parties. In 1993, Gouled was declared winner of a fourth six-year term in Djibouti's first contested presidential elections. Both the opposition and international observers considered the poll fraudulent. The election was boycotted by the ethnic Afar-dominated FRUD, and nearly all of the candidates were of the Issa ethnic group. Today, Gouled's nephew and cabinet chief Ismail Omar Gelleh is widely considered to be the de facto head of government and his uncle's most likely successor in a closely controlled 1999 presidential election.

Djibouti's politics reflect the country's principal ethnic division between the Issa and related Somalian groups, which comprise approximately half of the population and are concentrated in the south, and Afar people who constitute approximately 35 percent of the population and occupy the northern and western regions. Somalis from Somalia and Yemeni Arabs comprise most the remainder of the population. In 1991, FRUD launched its rebellion with demands for an end to "tribal dictatorship" and installation of a democratic, multiparty system.

Political Rights and Civil Liberties: The trappings of representative government and formal administration have little relevance to the real distribution and exercise of power in Djibouti. Djiboutians have never been able to choose their government democratically despite the advent of limited multiparty elections. The 1997 legislative elections were marginally more credible than the plainly fraudulent 1992 polls, but easily reinstalled the RPP, which, in coalition with the legalized arm of FRUD, won all 65 National Assembly seats. President Gouled has sought the appearance of ethnic balance in government by appointing Afars as prime ministers. FRUD leaders joined the cabinet as part of the 1994 peace pact.

Political activities are sharply constrained. Freedoms of assembly and association are nominally protected under the constitution, but the government has effectively banned political protest. The judiciary is not independent due to routine government interference.

Security forces commonly arrest dissidents without proper authority despite constitutional requirements that arrests may not occur without a decree presented by a judicial magistrate. The fate of three FRUD officials arrested in Ethiopia in 1997 and handed to Djibouti authorities remains unknown. Prison conditions are reportedly harsh, although Red Cross delegates have been allowed access.

Despite constitutional protection, freedom of speech is severely curtailed. The government closely controls all electronic media. Independent newspapers and other publications are generally allowed to circulate freely, but pressure on the independent media increased in 1998. Islam is the official state religion, but freedom of worship is respected. In May, the newspapers *Le Populaire* and *Le Renouveau* were suspended for six months and their editors sentenced to three months imprisonment after they published allegations of governmental corruption. Two other journalists were detained for a week in February after criticizing the country's finance minister.

Despite equality under civil law, women suffer serious discrimination under customary practices in inheritance and other property matters, divorce, and the right to travel. Women have few opportunities for education or in the formal economic sector. There are no women in the cabinet or parliament. Female genital mutilation is almost universal among Djibouti's women, and legislation forbidding mutilation of young girls is not enforced.

The formal sector in the largely rural agricultural and nomadic subsistence economy is small. Workers may join unions and strike, but the government routinely obstructs the free operation of unions. Wages are extremely low. The country's economy is heavily dependent on French aid. Efforts to curb rampant corruption have met with little success.

Dominica

Polity: Parliamentary
democracy
Economy: Capitalist
Population: 100,000
PPP: $6,424
Life Expectancy: na
Ethnic Groups: Mostly black and mulatto,
Carib Indian
Capital: Roseau

Political Rights: 1
Civil Liberties: 1
Status: Free

Overview:

In 1998, Prime Minister Edison James, the leader of the United Workers' Party (UWP), remained a regional spokesperson as a dispute with the European Union and the United States over banana imports grew more intense.

Dominica has been an independent republic within the British Commonwealth since 1978. Internally self-governing since 1967, it is a parliamentary democracy headed by a prime minister and a House of Assembly with 21 members elected to five-year terms. Nine senators are appointed, five by the prime minister and four by the opposition leader. The president is elected by the House for a five-year term.

In 1993, Prime Minister Eugenia Charles of the Democratic Freedom Party (DFP) announced her intention to retire in 1995 after 15 years in power. External Affairs Minister Brian Alleyne defeated three other candidates in a vote of DFP delegates to become the new party leader. In parliamentary elections in June 1995, the UWP won 11 of the 21 House seats. The UWP's James, the former head of the Banana Grower's Association, became prime minister. The UWP victory marked a significant power shift from the traditional establishment to a new and younger business class.

The DFP and the Dominica Labor Party (DLP) won five seats each and agreed to share the official opposition post by alternating each year. Alleyne assumed the post first. A High Court, however, ruled that one of the winning DFP candidates was not qualified to sit in parliament since he still held a public service position. The ruling reduced the DFP's representation in parliament to four seats. The UWP won the seat in special elections in 1996. Douglas became the opposition leader. In early 1996, Alleyne resigned as head of the DFP and was replaced by former diplomat Charles Savarin.

Dominica's offshore business sector continued to show strong growth in 1998. Approximately 4,600 international companies, five offshore banks, and five Internet gaming companies are registered.

Political Rights and Civil Liberties:

Citizens are able to change their government through free and fair elections. There are no restrictions on political, civic, or labor organizations. In recent years, several civic groups have emerged to call for more accountability and transparency in government.

There is an independent judiciary, and the rule of law is enhanced by the court's subordination to the inter-island Eastern Caribbean Supreme Court. The judicial system is understaffed, which has led to a large backlog of cases. The only prison on Dominica is marked by overcrowding and sanitation problems.

The Dominican Defense Force was disbanded in 1981 after being implicated in attempts by supporters of former prime minister Patrick John to overthrow the government. John was convicted in 1986 for his involvement and given a 12-year prison sentence. He was released by executive order in 1990, became active in the trade union movement, and lost as a DLP candidate in the 1995 election. The Dominica police, which were the object of a 1997 commission of inquiry into corruption, are the only security force.

The press is free, varied, and critical. Television and radio, both public and private, are open to a variety of views. Since 1990, television has been used as an effective campaign tool by all parties. The government respects academic freedom. Freedom of religion is recognized, but the small Rastafarian community has charged that its religious rights are violated by a policy of removing the "dreadlocks" of those who are imprisoned and by harassment of Rastafarian women by immigration officials who single them out for drug searches.

Since 1990, the 3,000 indigenous Carib Indians, many of whom live on a 3,700-acre reserve on the northeast coast, have been represented in the House of Assembly by an elected Carib parliamentarian. In 1994, Hilary Frederick was elected chief of the Carib people for a five-year term. A policeman was charged with the murder of a young man during the ensuing celebration.

Inheritance laws do not fully recognize women's rights. When a husband dies without a will, the wife cannot inherit the property, although she may continue to inhabit the home. There are no laws mandating equal pay for equal work for private sector workers. In the 1995 elections, two women won parliamentary seats. Government welfare officials have expressed concern over the growing number of cases of child abuse.

Workers have the right to organize, strike, and bargain collectively. Although unions are independent of the government and laws prohibit anti-union discrimination by employers, less than 10 percent of the workforce are union members.

Dominican Republic

Polity: Presidential-
legislative democracy
Economy: Capitalist-
statist
Population: 8,300,000
PPP: $3,923
Life Expectancy: 70
Ethnic Groups: Mixed (73 percent),
white (16 percent), black (11 percent)
Capital: Santo Domingo

Political Rights: 2*
Civil Liberties: 3
Status: Partly Free

Ratings change: The Dominican Republic's political rights rating changed from 3 to 2, and its status changed from Partly Free to Free, due to improvements in the conduct and administration of legislative and municipal elections.

Overview:
In 1998, President Leonel Fernandez found that the price of attacking corruption and inefficiency in his country's state-run industries cost him the support of old-guard bosses of his coalition partner. The result was an electoral front that never gelled into a governing alliance, and a major defeat in congressional elections that robbed him of the chance to run for re-election in the year 2000.

After achieving independence from Spain in 1821 and from Haiti in 1844, the Dominican Republic endured recurrent domestic conflict. The assassination of General Rafael Trujillo in 1961 ended 30 years of dictatorship, but a 1963 military coup led to civil war and U.S. intervention. In 1966, under a new constitution, civilian rule was restored with the election of the conservative Joaquin Balaguer.

The constitution provides for a president and a Congress elected for four years. The Congress consists of a 30-member Senate and, as a result of a recent census, a House that increased in 1998 from 120 members to 149. Balaguer was re-elected in 1970 and 1974, but was defeated in 1978 by Silvestre Antonio Guzman of the social-democratic Dominican Revolutionary Party (PRD). The PRD was triumphant again in 1982 with the election of Salvador Jorge Blanco, but Balaguer, heading the right-wing Social Christian Reformist Party (PRSC), returned to power in 1986 and was re-elected in 1990 in a vote marred by fraud. In the 1994 election, the main contenders were Balaguer, fellow octogenarian Juan Bosch of the Dominican Liberation Party (PLD), and the PRD's Jose Francisco Pena Gomez. Balaguer was declared the winner by a few thousand votes in an election rife with fraud. Amid street protests and international pressure, Balaguer agreed to hold new presidential elections in 18 months. The legislative results stood. The PRD and allies took 57 seats in the House and 15 in the Senate, while the PRSC won 50 in the House and 14 in the Senate. The PLD won 13 House seats and one Senate seat.

When Congress convened, the PLD backed the PRSC's plan to lengthen Balaguer's shortened term from 18 months to two years, with elections in 1996. In exchange, Balaguer named a PLD legislator as president of the Chamber. The PRD protested, but tacitly conceded by announcing that Pena Gomez would again be its candidate in 1996.

Although Vice President Jacinto Peynado won the PRSC primary, the PLD's lavish spending campaign lent credence to the view that the money was coming from Balaguer, who wanted to stop Pena Gomez and thus avoid any future corruption investigation. Pena Gomez won the presidency with 51.3 percent of the vote in a runoff election.

In May 1998, legislative and municipal elections were held for the first time since Balaguer had been forced to reduce his term. The campaign was violent. Fernandez, a U.S.-trained lawyer, won the presidency with 51.3 percent of the vote in a runoff election that was, again, racially charged.

Political Rights and Civil Liberties:

Citizens of the Dominican Republic can change their government through elections. Constitutional guarantees regarding free expression, freedom of religion, and the right to organize political parties and civic groups are generally respected. Nevertheless, violent political campaigns, frequent government-labor clashes, and repressive measures taken by police and the military mean that free expression is somewhat circumscribed. In 1998, legislative and municipal elections, which were marred by a record 48 percent abstention rate as well as violence, were held independently from the presidential contest for the first time. The election results effectively ended any hopes by Fernandez that he would garner the congressional support needed to overturn a constitutional ban on successive presidential terms.

The judiciary, headed by a Supreme Court, is politicized and riddled with corruption. The courts offer little recourse to those without money or influence. Prisons, in which nine out of ten inmates have not been convicted of a crime, are abysmal, and violence is routine. Security forces, which, like the rest of the judiciary, are militarized, reportedly engage in torture and arbitrary arrests.

In 1997, Fernandez moved to reform the country's anti-narcotics forces and to restructure the Supreme Court in an effort to eliminate corruption and reduce growing complaints of human rights abuses by the police. He led the effort in his role as chairman of the National Judicial Council, which oversees judicial appointments. In the past, responsibility for appointing judges was held by the Senate, which tended to increase politicization and de-emphasize professional criteria. The Supreme Court will assume this role. In 1997, Fernandez created a department to prevent administrative corruption within the Attorney General's office and dismissed the head of the National Drug Directorate due to allegations that the anti-narcotics squad routinely tortured suspects. The drug czar's chief accuser, the federal district's chief prosecutor and an outspoken champion of human rights and clean government, was also fired. In 1998, the government closed more than 100 betting offices that were allegedly linked to money laundering.

The media are mostly private. Newspapers are independent and diverse, but subject to government pressure through denial of advertising revenues and taxes on imported newsprint. Dozens of radio stations and at least six commercial television stations broadcast. In 1997, the National Commission on Public Events and Radio Broadcasting closed dozens of programs with religious-magic content.

Labor unions are organized. Although legally permitted to strike, they are often subject to government crackdowns. Peasant unions are occasionally targeted by armed groups working for large landowners.

Haitians, including children, work in appalling conditions on state-run sugar plantations. A 1992 labor code recognizes sugar workers' right to organize, but abuses continue. In 1998, a report by Christian Aid stated that as many as 800,00 stateless Haitians are treated as virtual slaves on the plantations.

Ecuador

Polity: Presidential- **Political Rights:** 2*
legislative democracy **Civil Liberties:** 3
Economy: Capitalist-statist **Status:** Free
Population: 12,200,000
PPP: $4,602
Life Expectancy: 69
Ethnic Groups: Mestizo (55 percent), Indian (25 percent),
Spanish (10 percent), black (10 percent)
Capital: Quito

Ratings change: Ecuador's political rights rating changed from 3 to 2, and its status changed from Partly Free to Free, due to free and fair elections, ending a period of fragile democratic legitimacy dating to early 1997.

Overview:
Hopes for political stability returned to Ecuador in 1998, as the country elected as president the respected mayor of the capital city of Quito, Jamil Mahuad. Mahuad was the candidate of the centrist Democracia Popular Party (DP). Two years earlier, Ecuador's political stability had been in doubt after the election as president of a populist nicknamed "The Crazy Man." The composition of the Harvard graduate's new cabinet, which was heavy on technocrats and short on party regulars, appeared to serve as a first step in his pledge to modernize Ecuador's creaky state apparatus, while cracking down on crime, corruption, and rights abuses.

Established in 1830 after achieving independence from Spain in 1822, the Republic of Ecuador has endured many interrupted presidencies and military governments. The last military regime gave way to civilian rule when a new constitution was approved by referendum in 1978.

The constitution provides for a president elected for four years, with a runoff between two front runners if no candidate wins a majority in the first round. The 77-member unicameral National Chamber of Deputies is composed of 65 members elected on a provincial basis every two years as well as 12 members elected nationally every four years.

The 1992 national elections were won by Sixto Duran Ballen, who won 57 percent of the vote, but whose Republican Union Party garnered only 13 of 77 legislative seats. Duran Ballen's term was marked by general strikes against his economic austerity measures, allegations of corruption, indigenous protests against business-backed land reform, and the impeachment of cabinet ministers by an opposition-controlled congress.

In 1996 elections, Abdala Bucaram Ortiz, a former flamboyant mayor of Guayaquil known as "El Loco," won 54 percent of the vote in runoff elections, carrying 20 of Ecuador's 21 provinces. Once in office, Bucaram, who previously fled the country twice under threat of prosecution for corruption, applied a stringent market-oriented austerity program. The authoritarian flavor and frenetic corruption of his government sparked mass protests.

In February 1997, a 48-hour general strike led by Indians and students prompted Congress to depose Bucaram on grounds of "mental incapacity." Parliamentary Speaker Fabian Alarcon was selected as his replacement after the military high command jettisoned its support for Bucaram's Vice President and constitutionally mandated successor Rosalia Arteaga.

In July 1997, Alarcon, himself accused of employing more than 1,000 "no-show" employees while speaker, dismissed the Supreme Court. He justified this action by citing the referendum's mandate to carry out the "depoliticization" of the justice system. The effect, however, was to remove the chief justice while he was pursuing an investigation of the interim president. Alarcon's feverish efforts to seek permission to complete Bucaram's four-year term was met by strong political and civic opposition.

In May 1998, Mahuad posted a first-place finish in presidential elections in which the runner-up was Alvaro Noboa. Despite being the candidate of Bucaram's Partido Roldosista Ecuadtoriano (PRE), Noboa promised neither that the party nor the ex-president would play any part in his campaign. In the July 12 election, Mahuad bested Noboa, a banana tycoon, 51-49 percent. In late 1998, a new leftist rebel group made its debut with a dynamite attack which it said was in protest of the government's economic austerity program.

Political Rights and Civil Liberties: Citizens can change their government through elections. The 1998 campaign seemed to mark a reversal of a national retreat from electoral means as a way of resolving political differences. Mahuad's victory came after Noboa ran what is believed to be the most expensive national campaign in Ecuadoran history. In 1998, the national Constituent Assembly decided to retain Ecuador's presidential system. It also mandated that in the year 2002, a presidential candidate will need to win 40 percent of valid votes in first round balloting and exceed those received by his nearest rival by ten percent in order to avoid a runoff.

Constitutional guarantees regarding freedom of expression, religion, and the right to organize political parties are generally respected. However, for several years, Ecuador appeared to be virtually ungovernable due to near-constant gridlock among the executive, legislative, and judicial branches, particularly as a result of congressional use of easy and sometimes frivolous votes of censure and impeachment used to block executive initiatives.

The judiciary, which is generally undermined by the corruption afflicting the entire political system, is headed by a Supreme Court. Until 1997, the Court was appointed by the legislature and was thus subject to its political influence. In reforms approved by referendum in May 1997, power to appoint judges was given over to the Supreme Court, with congress having a final chance to choose that 31-member body based upon recommendations made by a special selection commission.

Evidence suggests that drug traffickers have penetrated the political system through campaign financing, and that sectors of the police and military have been corrupted through bribery. Ecuador is a money-laundering haven and a transshipment point for cocaine passing from neighboring Colombia to the U.S.

There are numerous human rights organizations, and, despite occasional acts of intimidation, they report on arbitrary arrests and instances of police brutality. The military is responsible for a significant percentage of abuses, particularly when deployed in states of emergency. Since police and military personnel are tried in military rather than civilian courts, abuses, including torture, are committed with relative impunity. Indians are frequent victims of the military, who work with large landowners during land disputes. A corollary has emerged to the continuing lack of access of Native Americans to effective systems of justice: In 1998, Ecuadoran Indians held several U.S. oil company employees against their will, in support of a demand that the firm pay royalties and contribute to health care, education, and housing. Gays are also often the victims of police brutality and harassment. The media are mostly private and outspoken, and the government controls radio frequencies.

Labor unions are well organized and have the right to strike, although the labor code limits public sector strikes. Workers in the country's booming flower industry are routinely exposed to harmful pesticides.

Egypt

Polity: Dominant party (military-influenced)
Economy: Mixed statist
Population: 65,500,000
PPP: $3,829
Life Expectancy: 67
Ethnic Groups: Eastern Hamitic stock [Egyptian, Bedouin, Berber] (99 percent), other, including Greek, Armenian (1 percent)
Capital: Cairo

Political Rights: 6
Civil Liberties: 6
Status: Not Free

Overview:

In 1998, the Egyptian government moved to increase economic openness even as it continued a full-scale assault on political dissent. Arbitrary arrest, detention, torture, and summary justice against suspected Islamic militants continued unabated despite a sharp decline in terrorist activity. Meanwhile, a renewed commitment to economic reform resulted in the removal of barriers to privatization and investment.

Egypt gained formal independence from Great Britain in 1922, though the latter continued to exercise gradually dwindling control until its surrender of the Suez Canal Zone in 1956. Colonel Gamel Abdel Nasser became head of state in 1954 after leading a coup that overthrew the monarchy, and ruled until his death in 1970. A constitution adopted in 1971 under Nasser's successor, Anwar al-Sadat, grants full executive powers to the president, who is nominated by the 454-member People's Assembly and elected to a six-year term in a national referendum. Sadat was assassinated by Islamic militants in 1981 for making peace with Israel. Under his successor, Hosni Mubarak, the ruling National Democratic Party (NDP) continues to dominate a tightly controlled political system. In 1993, Mubarak won a third presidential term with 96.3 percent approval in a national referendum.

In the spring of 1992, the radical Islamic Group tapped into popular discontent concerning official corruption, high unemployment, and widespread poverty. It escalated its attacks on the police, Coptic Christians, and tourists in a campaign to establish an Islamic republic by force. The authorities responded with harsh crackdowns, and in early 1994 began arresting members of the nonviolent Muslim Brotherhood, a fundamentalist movement dating from the 1920s which is technically outlawed but tolerated by the government.

Years of repression by authorities appear to have neutralized the threat of Islamic terrorism. The leaders of the major militant groups, along with thousands of their followers, remain in jail or in exile. More than 70 political prisoners have been executed since 1992 under special military courts set up to handle terrorist offenses. Popular support for militant Islamists has dwindled as their campaign has focused more on violence than on alternative policy. Ideological rifts and policy disputes within the Islamic Group and the Muslim Brotherhood have left both groups divided. In addition, Egypt's rapidly growing economy has mitigated the discontent that fueled the spread of militant Islam.

Yet the threat of unrest remains. While the economy is currently growing at a rate of 5 percent a year, some 10 to 30 percent of the workforce is unemployed or underemployed. Violent rebellion still appeals to those in poorer areas that have not felt the effects of economic growth. There is widespread frustration with a government that is perceived to be corrupt and unresponsive. And, as indicated by the massacre of 62 people in Luxor in November 1997 and several other incidents of terrorism in 1997 and 1998, isolated gangs and splintering factions remain a viable threat even as militant leaders appear to be rethinking their strategies.

The Egyptian government has quickened the pace of economic reform, prompted by a sharp decline in tourism after the Luxor massacre, declining oil prices, and the Asian financial crisis. It has relaxed its opposition to privatization of public utilities such as telecommunications and electricity, and approved legislation in June which will lead to the privatization of state-owned banks as well as allow foreigners to own majority stakes in insurance companies. In January, parliament voted to scrap highly restrictive regulations of Company Law 159, making it easier to form new joint-stock companies and to gain access to investment capital. Furthermore, new legislation is expected to increase transparency in the public sector's tenders procedure.

Political Rights and Civil Liberties: Egyptians cannot change their government democratically. Parliamentary elections held in 1995 were characterized by widespread fraud and irregularity. Political violence led to the deaths of 51 people and wounded over 850 more. The Muslim Brotherhood could not compete because of a ban on religious-based parties. While its members may run as independents, Muslim Brothers planning to contest the elections were arrested. Just before the vote a military court sentenced 54 members to jail terms of up to five years for non violent activities.

Elections took place in June 1998 for half of the 264-member Shura Council; the president appoints the other half. The upper house of parliament has no legislative authority; its role is restricted to issuing opinions and reports on topics of its choosing. The landslide victory of the ruling NDP (97 percent of the Council seats) came as a surprise to no one; opposition leaders called the elections "fraudulent and corrupt."

Requests to form political parties are routinely denied by the state-controlled Political Parties Committee (PPC), usually because their platforms are "unoriginal." The application of Wasat, a younger generation of Muslim Brotherhood activists trying to break away from the party, was delayed for nearly two years before being rejected in May. The Social Justice Party and its newspaper were suspended by the PPC in April ostensibly because of internal infighting, though Egyptian pro-democracy groups allege that the government will seize any chance to dissolve an opposition party.

The militant Islamist battle against the government, now contained mainly in Assiut and al-Minya provinces, has resulted in over 1,200 deaths since 1992. Security forces have been accused of extrajudicial killings of militants during antiterrorist operations.

The Emergency Law has been in effect since Sadat's assassination in 1981, and is up for renewal every three years. Its provisions allow for detention of suspects without charge for up to 90 days. By some estimates, over 25,000 activists have been jailed or detained since 1992.

International human rights groups regularly condemn arbitrary arrest, abuse, and torture of detainees by police, security personnel, and prison guards. It is not uncommon for security forces to arrest friends or family members of suspects, either as punishment for the suspects' activities or as incentive for a suspect to turn himself in. At least two people died in police custody in 1998. One of these was the visiting father of a detainee.

The Egyptian judiciary enjoys limited independence. The president appoints both the general prosecutor and the head of the Court of Cassation, Egypt's highest court. Under Law 25/1996, the president may refer civilian cases to military courts. Since 1992, suspected Islamic Group and Muslim Brotherhood activists have been tried in military courts where due process rights are severely curtailed. There is no appellate process for verdicts by military courts; instead, verdicts are subject to review by other military judges and confirmed by the president. While convicted members of the Islamic Group are frequently executed, Muslim Brothers have never been sentenced to death, reportedly because of their wide popular support.

The Press Law, the Publications Law, the Penal Code, and libel laws all restrict press freedom. Critics of the president, members of the government, and foreign heads of state may incur heavy fines or imprisonment for violations. Newspapers published outside Egypt can be distributed with government permission. A January 1998 company law includes a provision that requires permission from the prime minister to establish a newspaper. The prime minister's decision is not subject to appeal. The government has used its monopoly on newspaper printing and distribution to control the output of opposition publications. The ministry of information owns and operates all domestic television production.

In order to combat "yellow journalism," a government campaign launched in March 1998 resulted in the banning of at least three newspapers, prison sentences for at least four journalists on charges of libel and slander, and the confiscation of numerous newspapers. On March 31, authorities banned the distribution of 36 newspapers printed in tax-free industrial zones for two months.

The interior ministry may withhold approval for public demonstrations under the Emergency Law. The ministry of social affairs has broad powers to merge and dissolve nongovernmental organizations. Human rights organizations such as the Egyptian Organization for Human Rights (EOHR) and the Arab Program for Human Rights Activists (APHRA) are frequently subject to harassment by the government. In December, the secretary-general of the EOHR was detained for six days on charges of "accepting funds from a foreign country with the aim of carrying out acts harmful to Egypt."

Women face discrimination in many legal and social matters. Foreign husbands and children of Egyptian women are denied Egyptian nationality, and women must have permission from husbands or male relatives to travel abroad. A ban on female genital mutilation took effect in December 1997, though it is not widely enforced.

The government portrays itself as a staunch supporter of Islam, the state religion, while it cracks down on fundamentalist influences in academia, mosques, and other institutions. In addition to the 40,000 already government-controlled mosques in Egypt, the government announced in December that 6,000 others would be placed under control of the ministry of religious endowments by June 30, 1999. The Imams of all newly appropriated mosques are required to attend state-run religious indoctrination courses. Female students who wear the traditional *munaqabat*, a veil covering the entire body, have been ordered to adopt standard school dress or be dismissed.

Muslims have murdered, kidnapped, or raped scores of Coptic Christians in recent years and burned or vandalized Copt houses, shops, and churches. The government has seized Coptic church-owned land, closed churches, and frequently uses an Ottoman Empire-era law to deny permission to build or repair churches. The murder of two Copts in August, allegedly by five Muslims, was followed by the arrest and reported torture of up to 1,200 Copts. Authorities claimed that the arrests were meant to preempt sectarian violence that might result from the two murders.

The 1976 law on labor unions sets numerous restrictions on the formation and operation of unions and the conduct of elections. The government-backed Egyptian Trade Union Federation is the only legal labor union federation. Article 124 of the Penal Code criminalizes labor strikes.

Child labor is a serious problem. By law, children under 14 are not allowed to work, except in agriculture, where they may take seasonal jobs at 12 years old as long as they do not miss school. The law is routinely ignored, however; the Egyptian Center for Social Research finds that nearly one in ten children under the age of 14 works. They comprise over seven percent of the total work force, and nearly all of them work in agriculture for wages no higher than $1.50 per eight-hour day.

El Salvador

Polity: Presidential-leg-
islative democracy
Economy: Capitalist
Population: 5,800,000
PPP: $2,610
Life Expectancy: 69
Ethnic Groups: Mestizo (94 percent), Indian (5 percent),
white (1 percent)
Capital: San Salvador

Political Rights: 2
Civil Liberties: 3
Status: Partly Free

Overview:

The former guerrilla organization that has become El Salvador's second largest political force, *Frente Farabundo Marti para la Liberacion Nacional* (FMLN), has all but ruined its chances to wrest control of the presidency from the long-ruling *Alianza Republicana Nacionalista* (ARENA) in March 1999 elections due to infighting in the opposition. Crime and public safety continue to pose grave challenges in El Salvador, one of the most violent countries in the Americas.

Independence from the Captaincy General of Guatemala was declared in 1841, and the Republic of El Salvador was established in 1859. Over a century of civil strife and military rule followed.

Elected civilian rule was established in 1984. The 1983 constitution provides for a president elected for a five-year term, and an 84-member, unicameral National Assembly elected for three years. Over a decade of civil war, which left more than 70,000 dead, ended with the United Nations-mediated peace accords signed in 1992 by the Farabundo Marti National Liberation Front (FMLN) and the conservative government of President Alfredo Cristiani.

The FMLN participated in the 1994 elections, supporting former ally Ruben Zamora of the Democratic Convergence (CD) for president and running a slate of legislative candidates. The incumbent National Republican Alliance (ARENA) nominated San Salvador Mayor Armando Calderon Sol, and the Christian Democrats (PDC) nominated Fidel Chavez Mena. The PDC had previously held power under President Jose Napoleon Duarte (1984-89).

The well-oiled ARENA political machine sounded populist themes and attacked the PMLN as Communists and terrorists. The FMLN-CD coalition offered a progressive but moderate platform and called for compliance with the peace accords.

In March 1994, Calderon Sol won just under 50 percent of the vote, setting up a runoff against Zamora, who came in second with 25 percent. In the legislature, ARENA won 39 seats, the FMLN 21, the PDC 18, the CD 1, and the Unity Movement (MU), a small evangelical party, won 1. The right-wing National Conciliation Party (PCN) won four seats, giving ARENA an effective right-wing majority. In the runoff, Calderon Sol defeated Zamora, 68 percent to 32 percent.

In the March 16, 1997, elections, ARENA won 28 congressional seats, 11 less than in it did in 1994, and the FMLN won 27, with other parties splitting the difference. The FMLN also dramatically improved its municipal presence, winning two of the three largest cities (in coalition with other parties), six of 14 departmental capitals, and ten of the 19 municipalities in the San Salvador department. At the same time, ARENA's suffered significant reversals, reflected in its 35 percent of the vote, as compared to 45 percent in previous polls.

In 1998, the FMLN's electoral chances in the following year's elections appeared to dim, as the party split into hardline Marxist and reformist camps. The two factions fought bitterly over who was to control the party, as well as whether it should support an ARENA sponsored project for a national development commission. Although Social Democratic leader Facundo Guardado, himself a former guerrilla leader and a leading reformist, emerged as the party's presidential nominee, the party was under renewed scrutiny by business and social sectors that worried that the party was still committed to social revolution. Guardado faces ARENA nominee Francisco Flores, a philosopher and the former president of the legislature.

Political Rights and Civil Liberties:

Citizens can change their government democratically. The 1997 elections were a marked improvement over those held in 1994. However, 250,000 fewer voters turned out in 1997 than in the previous election in which 1.45 million people voted. Political parties have agreed to a set of electoral reforms needed to improve the process, such as updating the voter registry and reforming the registration process.

Political rights improved significantly in 1997, as evidenced by the fact that the left-wing FMLN nearly equaled the vote of the ruling ARENA in the March congressional and municipal elections in contests which were generally considered free and fair. ARENA accepted their losses without threatening extra-legal action; the once-feared army remained neutral as it had since Christiani's election, and the new National Civilian Police (PNC) enforced election laws in a professional manner. Random killings, kidnappings and other crimes—particularly in rural areas—have reinforced the country's reputation as one of the most violent countries in Latin America.

The constitution guarantees free expression, freedom of religion, and the right to organize political parties, civic groups, and labor unions. Although the 1992 peace accord has led to a significant reduction in human rights violations, political expression and civil liberties are still circumscribed by sporadic political violence, repressive police measures, a mounting crime wave and right-wing death squads, including "social cleansing" vigilante groups. The crime wave has also intensified due to the deportation of hundreds of Salvadorans with criminal records from the United States.

The judicial system remains ineffectual and corrupt, and a climate of impunity is pervasive. A first step toward judicial reform came in 1994 with the naming by the new legislature of a more politically representative 15-member Supreme Court, which controls the entire Salvadoran judiciary. Public confidence in the justice system is undermined by poor training and a lack of sustained disciplinary action for judges, in addition to continued corruption, a lack of professionalism, and a painfully slow system of processing cases.

El Salvador is one of the few Latin American countries to restrict military involvement in internal security, and the army's strength has been slashed to 30,000, about half of what it was before the 1992 peace accords were signed. The National Civilian Police (PNC), which incorporated some former FMLN guerrillas, has yet to prove capable of the task of curbing the country's rampant crime while protecting human rights. Police accountability is a problem, although scores of policemen have been imprisoned on rights charges. Some 200 PNC officers have been killed in the five years since the force was created. In 1998, the government called on the FBI to assist in the investigation of three murders in which national police members are suspects.

Prisons are overcrowded, conditions are wretched, and up to three-quarters of the prisoners are waiting to be charged and tried. Dozens of inmates have been killed during prison riots.

The media are privately owned. Election campaigns feature televised interviews and debates among candidates from across the political spectrum. The FMLN's formerly clandestine *Radio Venceremos* operates from San Salvador, and competes with nearly 70 other stations. Left-wing journalists and publications are occasionally targets of intimidation. In 1998, a newspaper publisher was jailed for reporting on alleged police corruption.

Although the country is overwhelmingly Roman Catholic, evangelical Protestantism has made substantial inroads, leading to friction.

Labor, peasant, and university organizations are well organized. The archaic labor code was reformed in 1994, but the new code lacks the approval of most unions because it significantly limits the rights to organize in areas including the export-processing zones known as *maquiladoras*. Unions that strike are subject to intimidation and violent police crackdowns. According to UNICEF, the number of working children between the ages of 10 and 17 increased from 130,000 in 1995 to 311,000 in 1997.

Equatorial Guinea

Polity: Dominant party (military-dominated)
Economy: Capitalist-statist
Population: 400,000
PPP: $1,712
Life Expectancy: 48
Ethnic Groups: Fang (83 percent), Bubi (10 percent)
Capital: Malabo

Political Rights: 7
Civil Liberties: 7
Status: Not Free

Overview:

Equatorial Guinea president Teodoro Obiang Nguema M'basogo reinforced his dominance over his country's political life in November legislative elections that saw his ruling Democratic Party of Equatorial Guinea (PDGE) retain its large parliamentary majority in elections neither free nor fair. Corruption and brutality continue to mark the life of Equatorial Guinea and scar the lives of its roughly 425,000 citizens. A rare but remarkable window into the workings of one of the world's most venal and violent regimes was offered in May when the Obiang regime allowed journalists and other observers to attend a trial in the capital, Malabo, of 117 people charged in connection with a January attack on barracks on the oil-rich island of Bioko. The attack was blamed on the Bioko Island Self-Determination Movement (MAIB), which is based among the Bubi people native to the island. They have long been excluded from national power by the country's Fang majority and are now denied any real share of the new oil wealth from their home area. The trial, dismissed by independent observers as grossly unfair, returned 11 death sentences and 75 long prison sentences. Defendants were apparently tortured, and eight Spanish journalists were expelled before the verdict was returned. One MAIB leader, 58-year-old Martin Puye, died after being jailed under conditions Amnesty International described as tantamount to "slow execution." In September, however, the regime commuted the death sentences under strong international pressure.

The Obiang regime has sought to improve its international image to convince donors to resume international aid largely suspended after security forces' violence against oppositionists during rigged 1993 legislative polls. Nguema and his backers, almost all from his Esangui clan, seem unable to rise above the political gangsterism that has characterized their rule for three decades. New oil wealth could help raise living standards in the desperately poor land, but there is no sign that the new revenues are being treated as much more than a personal windfall for Obiang and his cronies.

Following 190 years of Spanish control, Equatorial Guinea achieved independence in 1968. It has since been one of the world's most tightly closed and violently repressive societies. President Obiang seized power in 1979 by deposing and murdering his uncle, Francisco Macias Nguema. He was declared victor of another seven year presidential term in a February 1996 election contest that resembled a free and fair election in neither form nor conduct. Despite electoral trappings, the country is effectively ruled by a small clique close to President Obiang.

Pressure from donor countries demanding democratic reforms prompted Obiang to proclaim a new "era of pluralism" in January 1992. Political parties were legalized and multiparty elections announced. Three elections since have been mockeries of the democratic process. Opposition parties are continually harassed and intimidated. Unlawful arrests, beatings, and torture remain commonplace.

Political Rights and Civil Liberties: Equatorial Guinea's citizens are unable to change their government through peaceful, democratic means. The November legislative elections for the 85 member House of People's Representatives were manipulated by the regime. The February 1996 presidential election, too, was neither free nor fair, marred by official intimidation, a near-total boycott by the political opposition, and very low voter turnout. Opposition parties were widely believed to have won in September 1995 municipal elections overwhelmingly. The regime's official results, released eleven days after balloting, reported a unconvincing but unsurprising landslide victory by the ruling Democratic Party of Equatorial Guinea (PDGE).

There are persistent reports of torture by soldiers and police to extract confessions. Prisons conditions are extremely harsh for all inmates, and Black Beach prison in Malabo, the capital, is described by survivors as hellish. The judiciary is not independent, and laws on search and seizure as well as detention are routinely ignored by security forces, who act with impunity.

President Obiang's wields broad decree-making powers, and effectively bars public participation in the policymaking process. The November 1991 constitution prohibits the impeachment of the head of state. Opposition parties, while legal, may not be organized on an ethnic, regional or provincial basis. Each recognized party must pay a prohibitive deposit of CFA 30,000,000 (approximately U.S.$60,000). Opposition activists face harassment, arrest, and torture, particularly outside the capital. The Progress Party (PP), whose exiled leader Severo Moto was sentenced to over 100 years imprisonment in absentia for an alleged coup conspiracy, was banned in 1997. Dozens of members of the Convergence for Social Democracy party (CPDS) and the Republican Democratic Force party (FDR) and other parties, who were arrested in mid-1997, were reportedly tortured.

With partial exception for members of legalized political parties, neither freedom of association nor freedom of assembly are allowed. Opposition demonstrations without prior authorization were banned in 1993. Any gathering of ten or more people for purposes the government deems political is illegal. There are no free trade unions. Freedom of movement is also restricted as citizens and residents must obtain permission for travel both within the country and abroad.

Nearly all media are state-run and tightly controlled. A few small independent newspapers publish occasionally but exercise considerable self-censorship, and all journalists must be registered. Criticism of the president is not tolerated. Some underground pamphlets appear irregularly. The regime sponsored an August 1997 conference on the importance of an independent press to democracy in Africa, apparently gleaning that it must continue to repress media to prevent democracy. At the end of May, eight Spanish journalists were expelled, and the country's foreign minister lashed out at international media coverage.

Constitutional and legal protections of equality for women are largely ignored. Traditional practices discriminate against women and few gain educational opportunities or participate in the formal economy of government. Violence against women is reportedly widespread. About 80 percent of the population is Roman Catholic, and freedom of individual religious practice is generally respected, although President Obiang has warned the clergy against interfering in political affairs. In July, the archbishop of Malabo, Father Obama, was reported as stating that local authorities now require priests to obtain permission before conducting mass after the Church denounced "the constant violation of human rights, social injustice, and corruption in Equatorial Guinea."

Unions are permitted by the constitution, but no law enabling their formation has been enacted. Strikes are barred. Membership in the ruling party is a prerequisite for nearly all government jobs and now for positions in the expanding oil industry. Billions of investment dollars by U.S. oil company Mobil, France's Total, and other companies has, as yet, done little to alleviate the grinding poverty of the largely agricultural and rural work force.

Eritrea

Polity: One-party (transitional)
Economy: Mixed statist
Population: 3,800,000
PPP: $983
Life Expectancy: 54

Political Rights: 6
Civil Liberties: 4
Status: Partly Free

Ethnic Groups: Tigrinya (50 percent), Tigre and Kunama (40 percent), Afar (4 percent), Saho (3 percent)
Capital: Asmara

Overview:
Eritrea appeared on the verge of renewed war with its southern neighbor, Ethiopia, as both sides reinforced their military strength after six weeks of midyear territorial clashes which killed hundreds of people, mostly civilians. Mediation efforts from numerous quarters, including African leaders and the United States, have failed. Since 1992, both Eritrea and Ethiopia have been close to the U.S., each led by a new generation of leaders committed to open markets, if not open societies. Eritrean President Isaias Afwerki was a brother-in-arms to his Ethiopian counterpart, Zenawi Meles, in a long war against the Marxist regime which their insurgent movements together defeated.

The fighting between the two poverty-stricken countries over a small patch of barely arable land along their common frontier is fed, at least in part, by the strong nationalism used by each leader as a political tool for mobilizing domestic constituencies. Thousands of Ethiopians resident in Eritrea were expelled, and an unknown number of Ethiopians were detained for unclear reasons. The International Committee of the Red Cross has been allowed access to civilian detainees in both Eritrea and Ethiopia.

War costs are seriously impacting Eritrea's economy. It is one of the world's poorest countries, and its remarkable strides since independence in 1992 are now in jeopardy. Eritreans saw the national goal of sustainable development slip further into the future as the conflict diverted desperately needed resources from economic and social programs. The loss of port fees when Eritrea closed its Red Sea entrepot of Assab to Ethiopian trade was a severe blow to government revenues, which may never be fully recovered if port facilities in neighboring Djibouti are upgraded as planned.

A constitution adopted in May 1997 was to have produced the first national elections this year since Eritrea won independence from Ethiopia in 1992 after nearly three decades of war. This event appears to have been postponed indefinitely, another early victim of the hostilities. The Eritrean government did accept the decision of an international tribunal that awarded sovereignty to Yemen over the Red Sea Hanish islands, where the two countries clashed briefly in 1996, defusing another possible regional conflict.

Ethiopia gained control over Eritrea in 1950 after a half century of Italian occupation. Eritrea's independence struggle began in 1962 as a nationalist and Marxist guerrilla war against the Ethiopian government of Emperor Haile Sailaise. The war's ideological basis faded when a Marxist junta seized power in Ethiopia in 1974, and by the time it finally defeated Ethiopia's northern armies in 1991, the Eritrean Peoples Liberation Front (EPLF) had discarded Marxism. Internationally recognized independence was achieved in May 1993 after a UN-supervised referendum produced a landslide vote for statehood.

The government seeks to balance senior governmental positions between the (roughly equal) Christian and Muslim population. Guerrilla attacks by the Eritrean Islamic Jihad, believed to be backed by Sudan's fundamentalist regime, have hit the country's western lowlands. Eritrea has broken diplomatic ties with Sudan and openly supports the armed Sudanese opposition. The ruling Popular Front for Democracy and Justice (PFDJ) party's austere and single-minded commitment to rebuilding Eritrea has earned international kudos. Its current bellicosity and military spending is seriously tarnishing that hard-won image.

Political Rights and Civil Liberties:

Eritrea has never known democratic rule with open elections. The current 150 transitional national assembly is comprised of the PFDJ's 75 central committee members, 60 members of the constituent assembly which drafted the constitution and 15 representatives of the Eritrean diaspora of over a half million people. It is unsure when presidential and legislative elections required by the new constitution will be held. Independent political parties authorized by the new charter are not yet registered, and those based on ethnicity or religion will be barred. The government's desire to reduce ethnic identification has extended to the renaming of the country's regions on geographical rather than the former ethnic bases.

The PFDJ seems to maintain broad support. Created in February 1994 as a successor to the wartime EPLF, the PFDJ maintains a dominance over the country's political and economic life that even open elections are unlikely to change. The new constitution's guarantees of civil and political liberties are unrealized as pluralistic media and rights to political organization are absent. President Isaias Afwerki often restates his mistrust of multiparty democracy. A number of uncharged political prisoners were reportedly detained, and no free media is allowed. The clashes with Ethiopia, added to Eritrea's near state of war with neighboring Sudan, may reinforce PFDJ's already authoritarian tendencies.

An independent judiciary was formed by decree in 1993 and is apparently operating without executive interference, although the ruling party's dominance over all areas of governance may compromise that autonomy. Lack of training and resources limit the courts' efficiency, and jurists have not been called upon to deliberate difficult cases that might challenge government policies. Constitutional guarantees are often ignored in relation to cases relating to state security. Amnesty International estimates that over 100 political prisoners remain incarcerated, many of them sentenced at secret trials to long jail terms.

Open discussion in public fora is tolerated; disseminating dissenting views is not. Government control over all broadcasting and pressures against the small independent print media has constrained public debate. In late December, Ruth Simon, a former Eritrean guerrilla fighter and correspondent for *Agence France-Presse*, was released and given "amnesty" after 20-months' detention without charge for allegedly misquoting President Afwerki regarding Eritrean incursions into Sudan. A 1997 press law allows only qualified freedom of expression, subject to the official interpretation of "the objective reality of Eritrea." Broadcast media will remain under state control and external funding for independent print media is barred. A small civil society sector is taking hold, although it is hindered by the absence of free media, and there are no independent domestic human rights groups. A new labor code guarantees workers' rights, but it is not clear that these will be respected in practice.

Religious freedom is generally respected, although Islamist activities believed to be sponsored by Sudan and Iran could harm relations among religious communities. Jehovah's Witnesses who refused to serve in the armed forces or to take a national oath of allegiance were stripped of citizenship and had property seized, and the government has denounced what it describes as political activities by the Roman Catholic Church.

Women comprised at least a third of EPLF independence fighters, and the government has strongly supported improvements in the status of women. Equal educational opportunity, equal pay for equal work, and penalties for domestic violence have been codified, yet traditional societal discrimination persists against women in the largely rural and agricultural country. Female genital mutilation is still widely practiced, despite official education campaigns.

A serious lack of infrastructure and the task of post-war reconstruction is complicated by severe environmental problems and the threat of renewed war. Military spending and uneven rainfall that cuts crop yields hurt Eritrea's economy in 1998. A broad privatization program and economic liberalization continued, but with a distinct preference for self-reliance over short term efficiencies.

Estonia

Polity: Presidential-parliamentary democracy
Economy: Mixed capitalist
Population: 1,400,000
PPP: $4,062
Life Expectancy: 68
Ethnic Groups: Estonian (64 percent), Russian (29 percent), Ukrainian (3 percent), other (4 percent)
Capital: Tallinn

Political Rights: 1
Civil Liberties: 2
Status: Free

Overview:
Estonia's parliament voted in 1998 to ease citizenship restrictions for the country's resident stateless children; the banking sector was marked by further consolidation, including several mergers and bankruptcies; and Estonia began formal negotiations for fast-track accession to the European Union (EU).

Dominated by Sweden in the sixteenth and seventeenth centuries and annexed by Russia in 1704, Estonia became independent in 1918. Soviet troops occupied the country during World War II, following a secret protocol in the 1939 Hitler-Stalin pact which forcibly incorporated Estonia, Latvia, and Lithuania into the Soviet Union. Under Soviet rule, approximately one-tenth of the population was deported, executed, or forced to flee to the West. Subsequent Russian immigration substantially changed the country's ethnic composition, with ethnic Estonians comprising 88 percent of the population before the Second World War and just over 61 percent in 1989. Estonia regained its independence with the disintegration of the Soviet Union in 1991.

Estonia's second post-independence election for the 101-member parliament, in March 1995, saw a shift to the center-left Coalition Party/Rural Union (KMU) over conservatives in the Fatherland Party/Estonian National Independence Party coalition. The election results reflected popular dissatisfaction among the elderly and rural electorate, hardest hit by the previous government's market reforms. The KMU subsequently formed a majority coalition government with the leftist Center Party. In October 1995, Prime Minister Tiit Vahi resigned after dismissing from office Interior Minister Edgar Savisaar, who was implicated in secretly taping conversations of leading politicians. Savisaar's Center Party, with 16 seats, left the ruling coalition. At the end of the month, parliament approved a new coalition government, again led by Vahi, in which the right-of-center Reform Party joined with the KMU. The delicate left-right partnership held until February 1997, when Vahi resigned following allegations that he had participated in the illegal procurement of luxury apartments during the 1993-1995 privatization process. In March, President Lennart Meri approved Mart Siiman, the leader of the parliamentary faction of the Coalition Party, as the new prime minister.

In early 1998, the ruling KMU minority government was unable to increase its support in parliament after failing to expand the membership of its coalition. Finding it increasingly difficult to carry out his political programs, including difficult legislative reforms for EU membership, Prime Minister Siiman called for early elections through a no-confidence vote in his government. The ruling coalition ultimately rejected the proposal, and the next national elections will take place as scheduled in March 1999.

After several unsuccessful attempts, parliament voted in November to abolish electoral alliances, just four months before the next legislative ballot. The effectiveness of the ban, which is an attempt to promote the consolidation of the country's numerous political parties and allow for a workable coalition government, remains a source of considerable debate.

In December, parliament adopted controversial legislation requiring all elected officials and candidates for public office, both at the national and local levels, to demonstrate sufficient proficiency in Estonian to participate in debates and understand legal acts. Max van der Stoel, the OSCE's High Commissioner for National Minorities, criticized the new legislation as unfairly limiting the voters' choice of candidates and inhibiting the integration of Russian-speakers into Estonian society. The language requirements, which enter into force in May 1999, will not affect the March elections.

Russia's financial crisis had a strong impact on Estonia's agricultural sector, especially the dairy and fishing industries for which Russia is an important export market, and a more limited effect on the country's banking system, which has greater ties to the West.

Political Rights and Civil Liberties:

Estonians can change their government democratically. However, the country's citizenship law has been criticized for disenfranchising many Russian-speakers who arrived in Estonia during the Soviet era and are regarded as immigrants who must apply for citizenship. Although noncitizens may not participate in national elections, they can vote, but not serve as candidates, in local elections. The 1992 constitution established a 101-member unicameral legislature elected for four-year terms, with a prime minister serving as head of government and a president as head of state. After the first president was chosen by popular vote in 1992, subsequent presidential elections reverted to parliamentary ballot. According to international observers, both the 1995 national and 1996 local elections were conducted freely and fairly. Political parties are allowed to organize freely, although only citizens may be members.

The government respects freedom of speech and the press, and the media routinely conduct critical investigative reports. There are several major independent television and radio stations which broadcast Estonian and Russian-language programs. Dozens of privately-owned national and regional newspapers offer diverse viewpoints. Religious freedom is respected in law and practice in this predominantly Lutheran country. The constitution guarantees freedom of assembly, and there were no reports in 1998 of government interference in political rallies or other mass gatherings. Workers have the right to organize freely and to strike, and unions are independent of the state as well as of political parties. Collective bargaining is permitted, though few agreements have been concluded between management and workers. One-third of the country's labor force belongs to one of the three main trade union organizations.

The judiciary is independent and judges may not hold any other elective or appointive office. There have been reports that some members of the police force use excessive force and verbal abuse during the arrest and questioning of suspects. Despite some recent improvements in the country's prison system, overcrowding and a lack of financial resources and adequately trained staff remain a problem. Parliament voted in March to abolish the death penalty, despite opinion polls indicating that the majority of Estonians favor capital punishment.

Of Estonia's population of just under 1.5 million, over 1 million are Estonian citizens, of which 105,000 have been naturalized since 1992. Almost 330,000 are stateless, but hold Estonian residence permits, and over 100,000 are citizens of other countries, most of Russia. On December 8, parliament amended the Citizenship Law to allow stateless children born in Estonia after February 26, 1992, to legally resident stateless parents to acquire Estonian citizenship at the request of their parents and without having to pass a language test. Both the EU and OSCE supported easing the country's naturalization requirements, which could immediately affect an estimated 6,500 Russian-speaking children.

Women enjoy the same legal rights as men, although they frequently earn lower salaries and are underrepresented in senior level positions and the government.

Ethiopia

Polity: Dominant party   **Political Rights:** 4
Economy: Mixed statist   **Civil Liberties:** 4*
Population: 58,400,000   **Status:** Partly Free
PPP: $455
Life Expectancy: 42
Ethnic Groups: Oromo (40 percent), Amhara and Tigrean
(32 percent), Sidamo (9 percent), Shakella (6 percent),
Somali (6 percent), Afar (4 percent), Gurage (2 percent), other (1 percent)
Capital: Addis Ababa
Ratings change: Ethiopia's civil liberties rating changed from 5 to 4 due to improvements in civil society and greater economic freedom.

Overview:

Ethiopia diverted desperately needed developmental resources to strengthen its armed forces for renewed hostilities against its northern neighbor, Eritrea, with which it fought a brief border war in May and June. Skirmishes over small patches of barely arable land along the countries' ill-defined frontier escalated into air strikes that led to scores of civilian deaths and mass deportations by each country of the other's nationals. The United Nations warned in October that Ethiopia faces a serious food crisis, but national attention remained focused on war preparations. Small-scale insurgencies simmered in the southern Oromo areas and in the vast and ethnic Somali-inhabited Ogaden, with reports of security forces abuses including torture and killings. The government launched decentralization and anti-corruption programs, but made scant progress toward genuine democracy with respect for the rule of law. Attacks on and jailings of journalists and opponents of the ruling Ethiopian People's Revolutionary Democratic Front (EPRDF) government continued through 1998. The government's narrow ethnic base divides Ethiopian politics. Ethnic Tigrayans from the country's north, whose guerrilla forces defeated the Marxist military regime in 1991, still dominate. The EPRDF faces political opposition from the traditionally dominant Amhara people as well as Oromo, Somali, and other ethnic groups that demand self-rule far more substantial than the decentralization proposed by the government.

The EPRDF formed a transitional government after its 1991 victory over the Dergue military junta led by Colonel Mengistu Haile Mariam. The junta had overthrown Emperor Haile Sailaise in 1974. As many as 100,000 people were killed in efforts to crush ethnic rebellions during waves of political terror over 17 years of Dergue rule. Mengistu's downfall saw a sharp decline, but not an end, to extrajudicial executions, torture, and detention without trial.

The ruling EPRDF government was elected in 1995 polls that were generally free, but not fair. Set amidst harassment of the political opposition and independent media, the polls were conducted under a constitution adopted in 1994 by a newly elected constituent assembly. Most opposition parties boycotted both votes, and the EPRDF won 483 of 548 seats in the Council of People's Representatives. Under the new constitution, Meles Zenawi was elected prime minister by the Council and retains much of the power that he held as president of the transitional government from 1991 to 1995. Prime Minster Meles' Tigray Peoples Liberation Front, which led the military drive that toppled the Mengistu regime, is the most important political grouping and at the heart of the EPRDF. A president with only symbolic powers was also appointed.

Political Rights and Civil Liberties: The people of Ethiopia chose their government through a relatively open electoral process for the first time in May 1995 legislative elections. Most international observers judged the election as largely free despite substantial government manipulation and inadequate protection of basic rights, including a crackdown on the independent media in the months before the vote. There are few signs that a more level electoral playing field will exist for scheduled 2000 elections.

The December 1994 constitution provides for significant decentralization, including regional autonomy and, nominally, even secession from the federation. The government has devolved some power to regional and local governments and courts. The EPRDF today controls all of the elected regional councils directly or with coalition partners, and there is little likelihood that any regional government will seek to exercise its right to secede.

The ethnic Somali Islamist-leaning *Al-Ittihad Al-Islam* movement continues the centuries-old conflict between the Somali clans who inhabit the vast Ogaden Desert and Ethiopian rulers who have long maintained at least nominal suzerainty over the area. In 1977, Ethiopia repelled a Somalia invasion aimed at annexing the territory. A rebellion in the south by the banned Oromo Liberation Front (OLF) and the Islamic Front for the Liberation of Oromia is potentially far more dangerous. Oromos, who constitute 40 percent of Ethiopia's population of nearly 60 million, are the country's single largest ethnic group. Sporadic fighting in the countryside has produced numerous casualties and reports of human rights abuses. Many OLF supporters are imprisoned or detained without trial. Oromo grievances include governmental neglect of their region, which is desperately poor even by Ethiopian standards, and migration of other ethnic groups onto traditional Oromo lands. In August, at least 140 people were killed in land clashes between the Gudji and Hadyia ethnic groups.

Nonviolent activists are also intimidated, harassed by security officials, or detained without charges. The Ethiopian Human Rights Council and other human rights groups are active, but the government has closed numerous nongovernmental organizations for failing to comply with new registration requirements. Thirty UN workers were forced to leave in September after being accused of spying. The mass expulsion of Eritreans and the detention of an unknown number without charges have been condemned by local and international rights groups. Ethiopia is one of only two African states that has not ratified the African Charter on Human and Peoples' Rights. The government launched an official Human Rights Commission and an Ombudsman's office in May, but it is unclear whether these will operate autonomously.

Broadcast media remain firmly under government control. Harassment and intimidation of the independent print media have led to significant self-censorship. Prohibitively high bail is set for detained journalists, and severe fines effectively close publications. In January, the offices of the *Tobiya* newspaper were burned soon after the arrests of four employees. In February, Abay Hailu, the editor of the *Wolafen,* died of lung disease soon after he had served a two-year jail sentence for writing about the alleged threat of Islamic fundamentalism. Today, approximately 20 journalists, the most in any African country, remain jailed.

Women traditionally have few land or property rights and, especially in rural areas, have few opportunities for employment beyond agricultural labor. Violence against women and social discrimination are reportedly common despite legal protections. Trade union freedom to bargain and strike has not yet been fully tested. Religious freedom is generally respected. Privatization programs are proceeding, and the government has announced sweeping financial liberalization to attract foreign investment.

Fiji

Polity: Parliamentary democracy and native chieftains
Economy: Capitalist
Population: 800,000
PPP: $6,159
Life Expectancy: 63
Ethnic Groups: Fijian [Melanesian-Polynesian] (49 percent), Indian (46 percent), other (5 percent)
Capital: Suva

Political Rights: 4
Civil Liberties: 3
Status: Partly Free

Overview: In July 1998, a new, more liberal constitution took effect in Fiji, but premier Sitiveni Rabuka's governing coalition undermined the constitution's civil liberties protections by enacting new emergency powers legislation.

Fiji's paramount chiefs ceded sovereignty over these South Pacific islands to the British in 1874 in order to end territorial conquests among rival kingdoms. In 1879, the British started to bring Indian laborers to work on plantations. Upon gaining independence in 1970, the indigenous -Fijian and Indo-Fijian communities were roughly equal in population.

Following 17 years of rule by the indigenous-Fijian Alliance Party, the 1987 elections brought the first Indo-Fijian-dominated government to power, comprised of the National Federation Party (NFP) and the Fijian Labor Party (FLP). In May and September of 1987, then-Lieutenant Colonel Sitiveni Rabuka took power in the Pacific's first coups, backed by hardline indigenous-Fijians who were alarmed at the emerging political influence of the economically successful Indo-Fijian community.

The 1990 constitution, promulgated under an unelected civilian government, guaranteed indigenous-Fijians a perpetual parliamentary majority by reserving for them 37 of the 70 seats in the House of Representatives, and 24 of the 34 seats in the appointed Senate. The constitution also placed voting on communal rolls and required the prime minister to be an indigenous-Fijian.

Elections in 1992 and 1994 led to coalition governments headed by Rabuka's Fijian Political Party (SVT). In the 1994 vote, in the indigenous Fijian voting the SVT won 31 seats; the Fijian Association Party, five, and independents, one. In the Indo-Fijian voting, the NFP took 20 seats and the FLP seven. The General Voters' Party took four of five seats reserved for "other races," with one seat reserved for the island dependency of Rotuma.

In July 1997, parliament unanimously passed constitutional amendments ending the indigenous-Fijians' guaranteed parliamentary majority and permitting an Indo-Fijian premier. Beginning with the elections due in 1999, the 71-seat House will have 25 seats open to all races, 23 for indigenous-Fijians, 19 for Indo-Fijians, three for general electors, and one for Rotuma. The reforms also hope to achieve multiracial government by requiring the largest party in parliament to invite parties crossing a certain threshold into government. The Great Council of Chiefs, a group of unelected, traditional rulers, will still appoint the largely ceremonial president. The Senate also remains appointed.

In July 1998, parliament passed an Emergency Powers Act (see below), which the Fiji Times called a "knee-jerk reaction" to ongoing cane farmer protests and separate landowner protests that threatened the country's hydroelectric supply. With general elections expected in May 1999, political parties began forming multiracial alliances. The ruling SVT was reportedly negotiating with the main opposition NFP, while in August, the opposition FLP and the indigenous-Fijian-based Fijian Association signed a coalition agreement.

Political Rights and Civil Liberties:

Fijians have voted twice under a constitution that was promulgated by an unelected government without a referendum, and that ensures indigenous-Fijians a parliamentary majority. Opposition parties are active and influential within the limits of the system. The opposition FLP has criticized the 1997 constitutional amendments as inadequate for ending race-bound politics. For example, 46 of the 71 seats are still on communal rolls; an independent constitutional review commission had recommended only 25 such seats.

While the electoral changes will take effect with the 1999 vote, other constitutional amendments including a new Bill of Rights took effect in July 1998. However, in July, parliament undermined the Bill by enacting a new Emergency Powers Act. The Act authorizes the president to declare a state of emergency, which would empower parliament to impose broad press and communications censorship, seize private property, conduct searches without warrants, and ban public meetings.

The judiciary is independent. Police abuse of detainees and prisoners is a persistent problem. The June 1997 Pacific Islands Monthly reported allegations of rampant drug dealing and abuse of authority at the capital's Suva Prison.

The press is free and vigorous, but government criticism of the media leads to some self-censorship. In a positive development in January, the government responded to a report by Britain's Thompson Foundation by approving plans for new media laws which would expand the industry's current self-regulatory Fiji News Council into a still-independent Fiji Media Council. The government also scrapped the colonial-era Press Correction Act, which had authorized criminal libel for printing "malicious" material, and rejected licensing of the print media, which had been favored by some politicians in response to media coverage of official corruption and ethical violations. The press created a new Fiji Media Council which apparently conformed to the Thompson Foundation's recommendations. However, in August, the Pacific Islands News Association reported that the government favored a Council with greater regulatory powers.

Two restrictive laws on expression remain on the books. The seldom-used Public Order Act prohibits speech or actions likely to incite racial antagonism. The Parliamentary Privileges and Powers Act (PPPA) authorizes jail terms of up to two years for breaching parliamentary privilege. In April, the Fiji Times mounted a legal challenge after a Senate Privileges Committee held that the newspaper had breached parliamentary privilege by reporting and editorializing on the cost of a brief Senate meeting, and warned it would impose sanctions under the PPPA in any future breaches. The partially private Fiji One Television provides objective news coverage.

Rape and domestic violence are serious problems. In some rape cases, the practice of Bulubulu (traditional reconciliation) allows the offender to apologize to a victim's relatives in order to avoid a felony charge. Cultural norms relegate many women to traditional roles, although women have made inroads in the civil service and professions. In 1997, Rabuka named a woman as deputy premier. Increasing media reports of child sexual exploitation have put pressure on the government to strengthen laws against pedophila. Indo-Fijians occasionally face racially motivated harassment and are underrepresented in the senior civil service. Indigenous Fijians hold 83 percent of the land, and Indo-Fijians, who are primary cash crop farmers with limited land tenure, fear farmers will be evicted as current leases expire between 1997 and 2000.

Indo-Fijians hold leading posts in the vigorous, independent trade union movement. Working conditions, particularly in the garment and canning industries, are often poor, and enforcement of safety standards is weak.

Finland

Polity: Presidential-parliamentary democracy
Economy: Mixed capitalist
Population: 5,200,000
PPP: $18,547
Life Expectancy: 77
Ethnic Groups: Finn (93 percent), Swede (6 percent), other, including Lapp (Saami) and Gypsies (1 percent)
Capital: Helsinki

Political Rights: 1
Civil Liberties: 1
Status: Free

Overview:
Under Prime Minister Paavo Lipponen, Finland's coalition government has sought closer integration into the European Union. Lipponen's Social Democratic Party (SDP) heads a "rainbow" coalition with the country's Conservative, Green, Swedish minority, and ex-Communist parties. In October, Lipponen survived a no-confidence vote that had been prompted by a party cronyism scandal.

Finland declared independence in 1917, following eight centuries of foreign domination. Its current constitution, issued in July 1919, provides for a 200-seat parliament elected for a four-year term by universal suffrage. The directly elected president holds considerable power, particularly because the multiparty, proportional representation system prevents any single party from gaining a parliamentary majority. The president can initiate and veto legislation, dissolve parliament at any time, and call for elections.

He also appoints the prime minister. The president currently holds primary responsibility for national security and foreign affairs, while the prime minister's mandate covers all other areas. Eleven mainland provinces are headed by governors appointed by the president, while the Swedish-speaking island province of Aland enjoys autonomy.

Political Rights and Civil Liberties: Finns can change their government by democratic means. In 1994, the country held its first direct presidential election since independence. Legislation passed in 1992 provides all Finnish citizens with the right to their own culture and equal protection under the law. Nevertheless, Gypsies, who have lived in Finland for nearly 500 years and who outnumber the Saamis (or Lapps), often report being treated as outsiders by the largely homogeneous population. Discrimination on the basis of race, religion, sex, language, or social status is illegal. By law, newspapers cannot identify people by race.

A wide selection of publications is available to the Finnish public. Newspapers are private, and the self-censorship that was traditionally practiced on issues relating to the Soviet Union is no longer in effect. Traditionally, many political parties owned or controlled newspapers, but several dailies have folded in recent years. The Finnish Broadcasting Company controls most radio and television programming, but limited private broadcasting is available.

Finnish workers have the right to organize, bargain, and strike, and an overwhelming majority belong to trade unions. The 1.1-million-member Central Organization of Finnish Trade Unions, which is linked to the SDP, dominates the labor movement.

Only 60,000 people in the country are foreign residents. While a strict refugee quota of 500 persons per year maintains the homogeneity of the population, those refugees who are granted admission receive free housing, medical care, monthly stipends, and language lessons. In an effort to prevent "ethnic ghettoes" from forming, some refugees are placed in small villages in which the residents have never seen foreigners. The government has instituted educational programs to teach children about their new neighbors.

Finns enjoy freedom of religion, and both the predominant Lutheran church and the smaller Orthodox church are financed through a special tax from which citizens may exempt themselves.

France

Polity: Presidential-parliamentary democracy
Economy: Mixed capitalist
Population: 58,800,000
PPP: $21,176
Life Expectancy: 78
Ethnic Groups: French, regional minorities (Corsican, Alsatian, Basque, Breton), various Arab and African immigrant groups
Capital: Paris

Political Rights: 1
Civil Liberties: 2
Status: Free

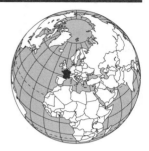

Overview:
In his second year in office, Socialist Prime Minister Lionel Jospin presided over a slight rebound in the French economy. Unemployment rates, however, remained at more than ten percent.

Jospin began a government of "cohabitation" with conservative President Jacques Chirac after winning an upset election in 1997. Although the Socialists won an absolute majority in the National Assembly (parliament), Jospin named some ministers from the Communist and other leftist parties. The Communists have vowed to increase pressure on Jospin to increase taxes and social reforms, halt the privatization of state-owned companies, and end efforts to obtain French membership in the European Monetary Union and assession to the European Union's Amsterdam Treaty.

In recent years, the National Front, a far-right party led by the racist Jean-Marie Le Pen, has exerted strong influence in regional politics. In 1998, however, it suffered a number of setbacks. Le Pen was stripped of his immunity by the European Parliament and may face prosecution for making remarks that trivialized the Holocaust. He also faces a possible ban from French political office for physically attacking a Socialist parliamentary candidate. Another party leader lost in his re-election effort as mayor of Toulon. In September, the party lost its only remaining parliamentary seat.

After World War II, France established a parliamentary Fourth Republic, which was governed by coalitions and ultimately failed due to the Algerian war. The Fifth Republic began in 1958 under Prime Minister (and later president) Charles de Gaulle. Election of the president by popular suffrage began in 1965. In 1992, French citizens narrowly approved European political and economic union under the Maastricht Treaty.

Political Rights and Civil Liberties:
French citizens can change their government democratically by directly electing the president and National Assembly. The constitution grants the president significant emergency powers, including rule by decree under certain circumstances. The president may call referenda and dissolve parliament, but may not veto its acts or routinely issue decrees. Decentralization has given mayors significant power over housing, transportation, schools, culture, welfare, and law enforcement. The judiciary is independent.

France has drawn criticism for its treatment of immigrants and asylum-seekers. Despite legal provisions authorizing refugee seekers to cross the border without visas or identity papers, border guards have occasionally used excessive force to discourage crossings.

The status of foreigners in France is confused by a succession of sometimes contradictory immigration laws. The National Front and other far-right groups have gained popularity by blaming immigrants for high unemployment. In fact, the jobless rate of immigrants is three times higher than that of the native French.

Soon after taking office, Prime Minister Jospin eased the country's residency rules by giving illegal immigrants a one-year period to apply for legal residency. Approximately 150,000 of the country's estimated one million illegal residents applied for papers. Government officials stated that approximately two-thirds of the applicants would be allowed to remain in France.

In August, the government further eased residency requirements by allowing foreigners to remain in France legally if they are seriously ill, if they are joining family members who are legally present, or if they are single, financially self-sufficient long-term residents.

The press in France is free, although the government's financial support of journalism and the registration of journalists has raised concerns about media independence. Publication of opinion polls results is prohibited in the week preceding any election.

Despite open suspicion toward Muslims and prohibitions against wearing religious garb or symbols in state schools, religious freedom is protected. Labor rights are respected in practice, and strikes are widely and effectively used to protest government economic policy. In October, one-fifth of the country's high school students launched street protests against the government's education policies.

Incendiary racist remarks by National Front leader Le Pen led to the introduction of legislation to punish the publication of xenophobic and racist ideas with mandatory jail sentences.

Women enjoy equal rights. In October, conservative members of parliament blocked a government proposal to recognize same-sex partners as legal couples.

Gabon

Polity: Dominant party
Economy: Capitalist
(highly corrupt)
Population: 1,200,000
PPP: $3,766
Life Expectancy: 54
Ethnic Groups: Fang, Eshira, Bapounou, Bateke, other
Bantu, other Africans, Europeans
Capital: Libreville

Political Rights: 5
Civil Liberties: 4
Status: Partly Free

Overview:
In December, President Omar Bongo was returned to office for a seven-year term. The polling, which was partially boycotted by the opposition, was marked by serious irregularities. The nominally independent National Election Commission, which was created under the new constitution approved by referendum in 1995, proved neither autonomous nor competent. Behind a facade of democratic institutions, Bongo used patronage, manipulation, and intimidation to retain power. In Libreville in May, student riots prompted by deteriorating economic conditions were quickly suppressed. At least ten students were seriously hurt. Three decades of autocratic rule have made Bongo among the world's richest men and left the vast majority of oil-rich Gabon's 1.4 million people mired in poverty. Bongo is strongly backed by the army and by France. The highly profitable French ELF oil company plays a dominant role in the country's economic and political life.

Straddling the equator on central Africa's west coast, Gabon gained independence from France in 1960. Bongo, whom France raised from soldier to president in 1967, completed his predecessor's consolidation of power by officially outlawing the opposition. France, which maintains 600 marines in Gabon, has intervened twice to preserve Bongo's regime. In 1990, protests prompted by economic duress forced Bongo to accept a conference that opposition leaders hoped would promote a peaceful democratic transition. Bongo retained power, however, in rigged 1993 elections that sparked violent protests and repression led by his Presidential Guard. The 1994 Paris Accords claimed to institute true democratic reforms. Municipal elections in 1996 saw major opposition gains, including the election of Paul Mba Abbesole, the leader of the largest opposition party, as mayor of Libreville. Legislative polls delayed by decree until December 1996 were again beset by fraud as Bongo's Gabon Democratic Party won an overwhelming, but unconvincing victory.

Political Rights and Civil Liberties:
Despite a gradual political opening since 1990, Gabon's citizens have never been able to exercise their constitutional right to change their government democratically. Bongo's 1998 electoral victory with 61 percent of the vote followed a campaign that made profligate use of state resources and state media to promote his incumbency. Legislative elections have also been seriously flawed.

State institutions are influenced or controlled by Bongo and a small elite around him. The judiciary suffers from political interference. Rights to legal counsel and public criminal trials are generally respected, but the law presumes guilt. Judges may deliver summary verdicts, and torture remains a standard route to produce confessions. Prison conditions are marked by beatings and insufficient food, water, and medical care. The government often detains refugees without charge, and there are reports of forced labor by detainees. Rights of assembly and association are constitutionally guaranteed, but permits required for public gatherings are sometimes refused. Freedom to form and join political parties is generally respected, but civil servants may face harassment based on their associations. Nongovernmental organizations operate openly, although the Gabonese League of Human Rights has reported threats and harassment.

A government daily and approximately one dozen private weeklies, which are primarily controlled by opposition parties, are published. The government overwhelmingly dominates the broadcast media, which reach a far larger audience. Only a few private broadcasters have been licensed, and their viability is tenuous. A 1998 crackdown on private media has raised serious concerns for free expression. In February, *Radio Soleil,* which was associated with the main Bucherons opposition party, was closed. In January, a cartoonist was sentenced to six months imprisonment for lampooning Bongo. Publication of his newspaper was suspended for one month. The president of the journalists' union was jailed for eight months. In August, the opposition newspaper *La Griffe* was closed, and three of its staff received eight-month suspended sentences after publishing allegations of ivory smuggling by the national airline. Soldiers raided *La Griffe* offices and seized equipment. Foreign newspapers, magazines, and broadcasts are usually widely available, but editions criticizing Bongo have been seized.

Most of the small formal sector work force is unionized, although unions must register with the government in order to be officially recognized. Despite legal protections, the government has taken action against numerous strikers and unions and used force to suppress illegal demonstrations. While no legal restrictions on travel exist, harassment on political and ethnic bases has been reported. Religious freedom is constitutionally guaranteed and respected. An official ban on Jehovah's Witnesses is not enforced.

Legal protections for women include equal access laws for education, business, and investment. In addition to owning property and businesses, women constitute more than 50 percent of the salaried workforce in the health and trade sectors. At the same time, there are only six women in the 120-member National Assembly and one woman in the cabinet. Women continue to face legal and cultural discrimination, particularly in rural areas, and are reportedly subject to widespread domestic violence.

Little wealth from Gabon's oil revenues reaches the broad populace, most of which is engaged in subsistence farming. Corruption is endemic.

The Gambia

Polity: Dominant party (military-dominated)
Economy: Capitalist
Population: 1,200,000
PPP: $948
Life Expectancy: 45

Political Rights: 7
Civil Liberties: 5*
Status: Not Free

Ethnic Groups: Mandinka (42 percent), Fula (18 percent), Wolof (16 percent), Jola (10 percent), Serahuli (9 percent), other (5 percent)
Capital: Banjul
Ratings Change: The Gambia's civil liberties rating changed from 6 to 5 due to a slight decrease in government repression.

Overview:
Gambian President Yahya A.J.J. Jammeh made only slow progress in gaining international credibility for his government and convincing Western donors to resume international aid. Governmental oppression, including arrests of opposition supporters and sharp restrictions and attacks on the press, continued throughout the year. Jammeh seized power as an army lieutenant in 1994 and was proclaimed president after a show election in September 1996. Legislative elections in January 1997 produced a sweeping victory for the ruling Alliance for Patriotic Reorientation and Construction party, but were deeply flawed. Several of Jammeh's former comrades-in-arms hold key cabinet posts. Abuses by the military and National Intelligence Agency (NIA) continued, and security forces acted with impunity.

After receiving independence from Britain in 1965, The Gambia functioned as an electoral democracy under President Sir Dawda K. Jawara and his People's Progressive Party for almost 30 years. A 1981 coup by leftist soldiers was reversed by intervention from Senegal, which borders The Gambia on three sides. The two countries formed the Confederation of Senegambia a year later, but the Gambia withdrew in 1989. Senegal declined to rescue the Jawara government again when Jammeh struck in 1994.

The leaders of the 1994 coup denounced the ousted government's alleged corruption and promised transparency, accountability, and early elections. Instead, they quickly imposed draconian decrees curtailing civil and political rights and the free media. A reported November 1994 countercoup was apparently crushed, and several alleged plotters were summarily executed. Several other coup attempts have been reported.

The Gambia is a tiny, poor country of approximately one million people, most of whom are subsistence farmers. It depends upon foreign aid for approximately three-quarters of its national budget. A reported security agreement with Libya has evoked fears of a Gambian and Libyan connection to the guerrilla struggle in Senegal's southern Casamance province by people of President Jammeh's Jola ethnicity. Jammeh has denied involvement in Casamance and in the army mutiny in Guinea-Bissau.

Political Rights and Civil Liberties:
The Gambia's citizens are denied their right to choose or change their government by peaceful means. The country's 1996 presidential and 1997 legislative elections were neither

free nor fair, and President Jammeh and his parliamentary majority cannot be considered as democratically elected. The 1996 presidential contest barred the most formidable opposition candidates and was marked by military intimidation of the opposition and heavy use of state resources and media to promote Jammeh's candidacy. A new constitution adopted by a closely controlled 1996 referendum allowed Jammeh to transform his military dictatorship to a nominally civilian administration.

Occasional state violence marked the broader pattern of human rights abuses. The Jammeh regime has awarded itself extensive repressive powers. A 1995 decree allows the NIA to cite "state security" to "search, arrest, or detain any person, or seize, impound, or search any vessel, equipment, plant, or property without a warrant." The interior minister may arrest without warrant anyone "in the interest of the security, peace, and stability of The Gambia." In such cases, the right to seek a writ of *habeas corpus* is suspended. A number of United Democratic Party leaders and activists were seized in May on the eve of their annual party congress. Several were reportedly tortured during three weeks' detention. The Gambia's legal system exists in form, but with little substance. Arbitrary detention and the denial of due process are common. Extrajudicial killings and torture in jails and barracks have been reported. Except for religious observances, public assembly is severely limited. Human rights groups and other nongovernmental organizations (NGOs) still operate in several areas. Severe and life-threatening conditions prevail in Gambian prisons, and NGO requests for visits have been ignored.

Free expression and the independent press have been constant targets of Jammeh's repression. Three *Daily Observer* journalists, including the chair of the Gambian Press Union, were detained for nearly two weeks in August. The paper's offices were raided and staff detained earlier in the year as part of a campaign of harassment. Self-censorship is widespread. Possession and distribution of documents deemed to be "political literature" is barred by decree. State-run Radio Gambia broadcasts only tightly controlled news that is also relayed by private radio stations. A single government-run television station now operates. In February, the private Citizen FM radio station was closed.

Women suffer de facto discrimination despite legal protections. Education and wage employment opportunities for women are far fewer than those for men, especially in rural areas. *Shari'a* law provisions regarding family law and inheritance restrict women's rights. Female genital mutilation is widely practiced.

All workers except civil servants and security forces may unionize under the 1990 Labor Act, which also provides the right to strike. The country's two labor federations, the Gambian Worker's Confederation and the Gambian Workers' Union, have not been banned, but their activities are limited by broader restrictions on political rights and civil liberties.

Georgia

Polity: Presidential-par-   **Political Rights:** 3
liamentary democracy   **Civil Liberties:** 4
Economy: Mixed   **Status:** Partly Free
capitalist (transitional)
Population: 5,400,000
PPP: $1,389
Life Expectancy: 73

Ethnic Groups: Georgia (70 percent), Armenian (8 percent), Russian (6 percent),
Azeri (6 percent), Ossetian (3 percent), Abkhaz (2 percent), other (5 percent)
Capital: Tbilisi

Overview: In 1998, President Eduard Shevardnadze faced an assassination attempt, a mutiny by troops loyal to a renegade commander in October, violence along the border with the
breakaway republic of Abkhazia, and divisions in his ruling Union of Georgian Citizens
(SMK). Other issues included continued construction on a pipeline that will carry Azeri
oil to the Georgian Black Sea port of Supsa, and continued negotiations for the withdrawal of Russian troops.

Shevardnadze, a former Soviet foreign minister and politburo member, won over
75 percent of the vote in the 1995 elections, and his centrist Union of Georgian Citizens
won 150 of 235 seats in parliament. In an effort to stabilize the country, the president
pushed through a new constitution, disbanded the paramilitary Mkhedrioni, and implemented an economic austerity program that improved the country's economic outlook.

Absorbed by Russia in the early nineteenth century, Georgia proclaimed independence in 1918, gaining Soviet recognition two years later. In 1921, it was overrun by
the Red Army. In 1922, it entered the USSR as a component of the Transcaucasian
Federated Soviet Republic, becoming a separate union republic in 1936. Georgia declared independence from a crumbling Soviet Union after a referendum in April 1991.
Nationalist leader and former dissident Zviad Gamsakhurdia was elected president, but
his authoritarian and erratic behavior led to his violent ousting by opposition units that
included the Mkhedrioni.

In early 1992, Shevardnadze was asked by a temporary State Council to head a
new government, and he was subsequently elected speaker of the parliament, making
him acting head of state. In 1993, Georgia experienced the violent secession of the
long-simmering Abkhazia region and armed insurrection by Gamsakhurdia loyalists. Although
Shevardnadze blamed the Russians for arming and encouraging Abkhazian separatists,
he legalized the presence of 19,000 Russian troops in five Georgian bases in exchange
for Russian support against Gamsakhurdia, who was defeated and reportedly committed suicide. In early 1994, Georgians and Abkhazians signed an agreement in Moscow
that called for a cease-fire, the stationing of CIS troops under Russian command along
the Abkhazian border, and the return of refugees under United Nations supervision.

On February 9, 1998, a presidential motorcade was attacked by a group of assas-
sins. President Shevardnadze was not hurt, but two bodyguards and one assassin were
killed. A week later, Georgian security forces arrested five suspects and seized a large

cache of arms. In a parliamentary speech, Shevardnadnze accused elements in Russia of participating in the assassination attempt.

Throughout the year, there were numerous clashes along the Georgian-Abkhaz border involving Georgian paramilitary groups, Abkhazians, and Russian peacekeepers. In March, Abkhazia held local elections that excluded participation by displaced ethnic Georgian refugees. October signaled a breakthrough of sorts when Abkhaz President Ardzinba, who served under Russian Prime Minister Yevgeny Primakov in the 1980s, announced a reassessment of the republic's pro-Russian position, and made concessions over the conditions under which Georgian displaced persons could return to Abkhazia. On November 2, the U.S. government offered $15 million to help repatriate refugees.

In domestic political issues, the entire Cabinet resigned in July after President Shevardnadze announced that a reshuffle was needed to speed reforms and fight corruption. Among those was State Minister Niko Lekishvili, the top minister in a political hierarchy that does not include a prime minister. The resignations sparked debate about constitutional changes that would broaden presidential power over the bureaucratic government apparatus and reintroduce the post of prime minister.

On October 19, several hundred soldiers in western Georgia, led by Akakiy Eliava, a former Gamsakhurdia commander, revolted and moved on the city of Kutaisi. The insurgency was put down in one day, and 31 rebels were arrested. Many in Georgia blamed Russian intrigue for fostering instability, noting that the revolt took place as a consortium of oil companies was deliberating on a major new pipeline route for Azeri oil considering Georgia as one of the proposed options. In early November, Eliava, who escaped capture, allegedly called on Shevardnadze to resign. Georgian authorities announced that he could be pardoned if he turned himself in.

Contributing to heightened instability were long-simmering issues of greater local autonomy. The Russian-backed leader of the autonomous republic of Adjaria on the Black Sea coast continued to defy central jurisdiction. The ethnic Armenian population of the southern region of Djanakheti lobbied for autonomous status. In South Ossetia, over which Georgia virtually forfeited control in 1992, a new government was confirmed in August, and discussions over the region's status continued throughout the year.

Relations with Russia remained strained. In April, the chairman of Georgia's parliament, Zurab Zhvania, said in Washington that Russian military bases in his country have absolutely no legal basis. In late October, Russian Defense Minister Igor Sergeyev told a press conference in China that Russia had no plans to close the bases.

Political Rights and Civil Liberties: Georgians can change their government democratically. The government's loss of control over Abkhazia and South Ossetia, and its weak hold of Adjaria, affects the scope of the government's power and representation. The November 1995 elections were judged generally free and fair by international observers. However, voting in 10 of 85 districts, in Abkhazia and South Ossetia, was postponed indefinitely.

Article 24 of the constitution allows for free expression and open dissemination of information. Under a 1991 press law, journalists are obliged to "respect the dignity and honor" of the president and not impugn the honor and dignity of citizens or undermine the regime. Publications can face legal action for "malevolently using freedom of the press, [and] spreading facts not corresponding to reality..." State-run radio and television generally reflect official views. Independent newspapers publish discerning and sophisticated political analyses, though electronic media eclipse their importance. There are some dozen local independent television stations which have faced varying degrees of government harassment. Self-censorship occurs, particularly in state-run media. In September 1998, the editor-in-chief of the daily *Asaval-Dasavali* and a prominent correspondent were attacked by a group of armed men in Tblisi.

Freedom of religion is generally respected in this predominantly Christian Orthodox country. There are, however, restrictions on the activities of "nontraditional" religions, aimed at foreign missionaries. The Armenian Orthodox and Catholic churches have sought restitution of churches closed by the Communists which are now held by the Georgian Orthodox Church.

Freedom of assembly is guaranteed under the constitution and under law, and is generally respected, though supporters of the late President Gamsakhurdia have been denied the right to demonstrate.

There are nearly 100 political parties and associations registered, 52 of which contested the 1995 elections. Only three groupings met the five percent threshold for representation in parliament. In September 1998, the Unified Communist Party of Georgia was denied registration for the November 15 local elections. In a June 1998 by-election in eastern Georgia, the Central Election Committee overturned an apparent victory by the Socialist Party candidate, and awarded the parliamentary seat to the ruling SMK. There are over 100 NGO's registered some of which enjoy tax exemptions.

The major trade union confederation is the Amalgamated Trade Unions of Georgia, the renamed successor to the Soviet-era Confederation of Trade Unions of Georgia. The confederation consists of 30 unions, and workers have the right to strike.

The judiciary is not fully independent. Under a June 1997 Law on the Courts, Georgia retained a three-tier court system. Administration of the court system shifted from the Justice Ministry to a new 12-member Council of Justice, with four members from each branch of government. Nevertheless, courts are influenced by pressure from the executive branch. A nine-member Constitutional Court represents the three main branches of government and arbitrates constitutional questions, treaties, referendums, elections, and jurisdictional disputes. Prison conditions are generally abysmal, and domestic and international human rights groups say abuse of detainees is widespread. In March 1998, Russia extradited former Georgian Finance Minister Guram Absandze who was wanted in the February assassination attempt against President Shevardnadze. He was also charged with embezzling $18 million.

The Gali region along the Abkhazia-Georgia border was the scene of violent skirmishes that cost the lives of Russian peacekeepers, civilians, and Georgian paramilitary operatives. While some Georgian refugees have returned to Abkhazia, repatriation plans have been slowed by violence against ethnic Georgians and stalled negotiations. Separatists have blocked the return of Georgians to South Ossetia. These factors have impaired freedom of movement.

Corruption is endemic and reaches all levels of government. Senior officials have been accused of such crimes as embezzlement, smuggling, insider dealing, and conflict of interest. Customs and tax evasion is rampant. The right to property and inheritance is guaranteed by the constitution. Business registration is hampered by bribery and an inefficient, corrupt bureaucracy, and organized crime preys on small business owners.

The informal economy is estimated at 40-45 percent of the GDP. These factors have an adverse impact on equality of opportunity and the ability of Georgians to share in legitimate economic gains.

Official concern about the status of and discrimination against women is minimal, but NGO's dealing with women's issues have proliferated. Women are found mostly in traditional, low-paying occupations.

Germany

Polity: Federal parliamentary democracy
Economy: Mixed capitalist
Population: 82,300,000
PPP: $20,370
Life Expectancy: 77
Ethnic Groups: German (92 percent), Turkish (2 percent), other (6 percent)
Capital: Berlin

Political Rights: 1
Civil Liberties: 2
Status: Free

Overview:

In October, Gerhard Schroeder replaced Helmut Kohl, Europe's longest serving leader, as Chancellor of Germany.

In September elections, Schroeder's Social Democratic Party SPD had defeated Kohl's Christian Democratic Union (CDU), thereby ending Kohl's 16-year rule. The SPD, which received approximately 40 percent of the vote, formed a coalition with the Green Party, which was given the foreign ministry and two other ministerial-level positions in the new government.

In his first year as chancellor, Schroeder is expected to focus on unemployment and other domestic issues.

After World War II, Germany was divided into Soviet, U.S., British, and French occupation zones. Four years later, the Allies helped to establish a democratic Federal Republic of Germany, while the Soviets oversaw the formation of the communist German Democratic Republic (GDR). The division of Berlin was reinforced by the 1961 construction of the Berlin Wall. After the collapse of Erich Honecker's hard-line GDR regime in 1989 and the destruction of the wall in 1990, citizens voted in the country's first free parliamentary election, in which parties supporting rapid re-unification triumphed.

Political Rights and Civil Liberties:

German citizens can change their government democratically. The federal system provides for a considerable amount of self-government among the 16 states. Individuals are free to form political parties and to receive federal funding as long as the parties are democratic in nature. The country's judiciary is independent.

The Basic Law (Constitution) provides for unrestricted citizenship and legal residence immediately upon application for ethnic Germans entering the country. Individuals not of German ethnicity may acquire citizenship if they meet certain requirements, including legal residence for ten years (five if married to a German) and renunciation of all other citizenships. At year's end, the new government pledged to liberalize this citizenship law, which has been strongly criticized by international human rights groups for being nationalistic and outdated. Under the new proposal, citizenship will be granted to children born in Germany to non-German citizens, at least one of whom has lived in Germany since the age of 14. Children born in Germany to one or two German-born parents will automatically acquire German citizenship. Foreign adults will be able to receive citizenship after living in Germany for eight years. In addition, dual citizenship will be allowed for the first time.

Germany has no anti-discrimination law to protect immigrants, and even ethnic German immigrants increasingly face hostility from citizens who attribute the country's economic woes and high unemployment to immigration.

The German press and broadcast media are free and independent, offering pluralistic viewpoints. Nazi propaganda and statements endorsing Nazism are illegal. Germany has exceeded other countries' practices in its attempts to police the Internet by blocking access to obscene, violent, or "dangerous" material. The government has brought charges against service-providers and individual users. During the year, however, the law was modified to exempt service-providers from legal responsibility for material beyond their control. The legislative change resulted in part from criticism of the sentencing in May of the head of a major service-provider to a two-year suspended jail term for spreading pornography.

Nazi-related, anti-foreigner, anti-immigrant, and racist incidents all increased during the year, and xenophobic political policies and pronouncements continued to find support among voters. The country's internal security agency has registered a strong rise in racist and far-right radical tendencies. In April, the far-right German People's Union won 12.9 percent of the vote–the best election result for a far-right party since World War II–in regional elections in Saxony-Anhalt. In October, the leader of another far-right party was sentenced to six months in jail for glorifying violence through CDs in which the party described the brutal murder of its political opponents.

In June, the government drew criticism from human rights groups for tightening the country's liberal asylum law. In a move that critics decried as electioneering, all of the major political parties collaborated in the passage of a provision that dramatically cut government benefits to asylum seekers.

Freedom of religion is established under the Basic Law. State governments subsidize church-affiliated schools and provide religious instruction in schools and universities for those of the Protestant, Roman Catholic, and Jewish faiths.

Scientologists, who claim 30,000 adherents in Germany, have been at the center of a heated debate over the group's legal status. Major political parties, which exclude Scientologists from membership, hold that the group does not constitute a religion, but a for-profit organization based on anti-democratic principles. Officials have stated that the group financially exploits its followers and exerts extreme psychological pressure on those who attempt to leave the group. They have also stated that Germany's unique history necessitates their close scrutiny of extremist groups that could, like the Nazi Party, begin as a small organization and then undergo explosive growth.

Labor, business, and farming groups are free, highly organized, and influential. In recent years, however, trade union federation membership has dropped sharply due to the collapse of industry in the East and layoffs in the West.

Ghana

Polity: Presidential-
parliamentary democracy
Economy: Capitalist-
statist
Population: 18,900,000
PPP: $2,032
Life Expectancy: 56

Political Rights: 3
Civil Liberties: 3
Status: Partly Free

Ethnic Groups: Akan (44 percent), Moshi-Dagomba (16 percent),
Ewe (13 percent), Ga (8 percent), other tribes (19 percent)
Capital: Accra

Overview:

Ghana's political class appeared focused on the 2000 presidential elections set to mark President Jerry Rawlings' departure from office after nearly two decades in power. December 1996 presidential and legislative elections were judged free and fair by international observers, and the country slowly continued to consolidate democratic institutions. Vice President John Atta Mills received Rawlings' endorsement for the candidacy of the ruling National Democratic Congress (NDC). The opposition New Patriotic Party's John Kufuor could mount a serious challenge, although state patronage and resources are expected to bolster the ruling party's choice. A vigorous independent print media criticized both the ruling and opposition parties, but continued to be subject to criminal libel suits by government officials and other harassment.

Once a major slaving center and long known as the Gold Coast, the former British possession became black Africa's first colony to achieve independence. After the 1966 overthrow of its charismatic independence leader, Kwame Nkrumah, the country was wracked by a series of military coups for 15 years. Successive military and civilian governments vied with each other in both incompetence and mendacity. In 1979, then-Flight-Lieutenant Jerry Rawlings led a coup against the ruling military junta and, as promised, returned power to a civilian government after a "housecleaning" of corrupt senior army officers. However, the new civilian administration did not live up to Rawlings' expectations, and he seized power again in December 1981 and set up the Provisional National Defense Council (PNDC). The PNDC junta was radically socialist and populist and brutally repressive, banning political parties and free expression. Facing a crumbling economy, Rawlings in the late 1980's transformed Ghana into an early model for structural adjustment programs urged by international lenders. A new constitution adopted in April 1992 legalized political parties, and Rawlings was declared president after elections held in November 1992 which were neither free nor fair.

Ghana has experienced a slow liberalization since Rawlings' severe repression and failed socialism. Despite real progress, the rule of law is not yet assured and the judiciary is not yet truly independent. Police and other security forces often act with impunity. While the government claims that there are no political prisoners in the country, Amnesty International still lists about a dozen "prisoners of conscience" in Ghana. The transparency and accountability that are the cornerstones of good governance are lacking, and corruption could block economic growth.

Political Rights and Civil Liberties: The December 1996 presidential and parliamentary elections under Ghana's 1992 constitution allowed Ghanaians their first opportunity since independence to elect their representatives in genuine elections. A broad civic education campaign and international assistance with registration and other electoral procedures preceded voting. However, the elections were also marked by the ruling party's extensive use of state media and patronage to support incumbents. Rawlings' five percent re-election victory, which extended his sixteen-year rule, was also assured by opposition disunity. Ghana's 200-member legislature, elected on a single-member district system, is controlled by the NDC, which holds 133 seats.

Freedom of expression is constitutionally guaranteed and generally respected. Ghanaians enjoy open political debate reflected in a robust private print media. Financial problems and government pressure, however, constrain the independent press. The government uses criminal libel laws that make reporting false information a felony in order to intimidate the media. In July, *The Weekend Statesman* editor Haruna Atta and Kweku Baako Jr. of *The Guide*, were jailed for 30 days on charges of criminal libel. In a statement that accompanied a public protest march, the local NGO Friends of Freedom declared, "The courts are now becoming an institution to subvert press freedom," and that heavy fines against journalists and publishers are weakening media freedom. Other obscure and rarely used laws have been invoked to intimidate the media. A 1964 law makes anyone publishing a report "likely to injure the reputation of Ghana or its government and which he knows or has reason to believe is false" subject to felony charges. Another 1960 law provides ten-year prison sentences for defaming or slandering the "Ghanaian State."

Despite the licensing of several independent radio and television stations, the power of state media also creates serious imbalances. The government allows little expression of opposition views over the national radio and television networks as well as in the two daily newspapers it controls.

The right to peaceful assembly and association is constitutionally guaranteed, and permits are not required for meetings or demonstrations. Numerous nongovernmental organizations operate openly and freely, including human rights groups. Religious freedom is respected, but there are occasional tensions between Christians and Muslims and within the Muslim community itself.

Ghanaian courts have acted with increased autonomy under the 1992 constitution but are still subject to considerable governmental influence, especially in media-related cases. Traditional courts often handle minor cases according to local customs that fail to meet constitutional standards. Scarce judicial resources leave many people imprisoned for long periods under harsh conditions without trial.

Ghanaian women suffer societal discrimination that is particularly serious in rural areas, where opportunities for education and wage employment are limited, despite their equal rights under the law. Domestic violence against women is reportedly common, but often remains unreported. NGOs and the national human rights commissioner are campaigning against the *tro-kosi* system which is practiced in parts of northern Ghana, in which of young girls are forced into indefinite servitude to traditional religious priests. In September, the Federation of Women Lawyers (FIDA), announced victory in forcing the closure of a traditional detention center for women deemed by customary courts to be witches.

Trade union registration requirements under the Trades Union Ordinance are not now used to block union formation, but civil servants may not join unions. The Industrial Relations Act demands arbitration before strikes are authorized. The only labor confederation, the Trade Union Congress, is still aligned with the ruling party, although it is has shown signs of autonomy.

Ghana's ambitious privatization program has continued to draw foreign investment into a stock exchange that in 1998 defied global drops in share values. Gold mining profits and increased cocoa exports have contributed to growth, officially recorded at over five per cent for the past 12 years. Other analysts contest this figure, arguing that the growth barely matches a population expanding by three percent annually, and that incentives to boost agricultural production among the country's largely rural 19 million people are necessary. Corruption is reportedly on the rise as the country falls deeper into debt.

Greece

Polity: Parliamentary democracy
Political Rights: 1
Civil Liberties: 3
Economy: Mixed capitalist
Status: Free
Population: 10,500,000
PPP: $11,636
Life Expectancy: 78
Ethnic Groups: Greek (98 percent), other, including Macedonian and Turk (2 percent)
Capital: Athens

Overview:

In their third year in office, Prime Minister Costas Simitis and his Socialist Party continued their moderate domestic political and economic policies, but suffered setbacks in nationwide municipal elections.

Greek-Turkish relations remained tense throughout the year. In a rare meeting, the two countries' prime ministers pledged to work at NATO to cool tensions, but saw no signs of progress on the issues that divide them. During Greek-Cypriot military exercises in October, Greek and Turkish fighter aircraft engaged in what the U.S. Ambassador to Greece termed "mock dogfights." Also in October, the United States and Greece called for the Greek-Turkish dispute over scores of eastern Mediterranean islands to be submitted to the International Court of Justice.

Greece gained independence from the Ottoman Empire in 1830. The ensuing century brought continued struggle between royalist and republican forces. Occupation by the Axis powers in 1941 was followed by civil war between non-Communist and Communist forces until 1949. Following a 1967 coup that brought a military junta to power, a failed countercoup by Naval officers in 1973, aiming to overthrow the colonels' junta and restore the king, led to the formal deposition of the monarch and the proclamation of a republic. The current constitution, adopted in 1975, provides for a parliamentary system with a largely ceremonial presidency.

Political Rights and Civil Liberties: Greeks can change their government democratically. Voting is compulsory for citizens between the ages of 18 and 70, yet change of voting address is not permitted. As a result, nearly 650,000 people are forced to travel to prior residences to participate in elections.

The judiciary is independent. With the exception of politically related restrictions, the media have substantial freedom. The public prosecutor may press charges against publishers and can seize publications deemed offensive to the president or to religious beliefs. A controversial law bans "unwarranted" publicity for terrorists from the media, including terrorists' proclamations following explosions.

Ninety-eight percent of the population are nominal adherents to Greek Orthodoxy, the state religion. Orthodox bishops have the privilege of granting or denying permission to other faiths to build houses of worship in their jurisdictions. The European Court of Human Rights condemned this practice in 1996. Members of non-Orthodox communities have been barred from entering occupations such as primary school teaching, the military, and the police.

The constitution prohibits proselytizing, and Jehovah's Witnesses have been a target of political and legal persecution. Despite objections from Roman Catholics, Jews, Muslims, and other minorities, national identity cards, which have been required since 1992, continue to list the bearer's religious affiliation.

Western Thrace's Turkish Muslim minority, whose religious rights were guaranteed under the 1923 Treaty of Lausanne, objects to its classification as a "Turkish" rather than "Muslim" minority and to the Greek government's ability to choose its mufti, or Muslim community leader. The country's ethnic Slavic minority, which is not recognized by the state, makes similar objections. Gypsies, who may number as many as 300,000, encounter large-scale discrimination in receiving education and other social benefits.

In June, the parliament abolished Article 19, a discriminatory law that stripped non-ethnic Greeks of their citizenship if they left the country for an extended period. The law primarily affected the 120,000 Muslims in the country's Turkish border areas.

Greeks enjoy freedom of association, and all workers except military personnel and the police have the right to form and join unions, which are linked to political parties, but independent of party and government control.

Greece has a long history of jailing conscientious objectors to military service. In 1997, however, the government passed a new law to allow objectors to perform alternative, civilian service. Amnesty International condemned the measure, however, as "punitive" because it requires objectors to serve twice as long as military conscripts.

Women's groups have begun to organize to seek more equitable child custody and divorce laws, including the creation of a family court.

Grenada

Polity: Parliamentary democracy
Economy: Capitalist-statist
Population: 100,000
PPP: $5,425
Life Expectancy: 71
Ethnic Groups: Mostly black
Capital: St. George's

Political Rights: 1
Civil Liberties: 2
Status: Free

Overview:

Paving the way for elections in 90 days, Grenada's parliament was dissolved in December 1998 after the ruling New National Party (NNP) was plunged into crisis over the resignation of its foreign minister, whose loss left the party with only 7 of 15 parliamentary seats.

Grenada, a member of the British Commonwealth, is a parliamentary democracy. The British monarchy is represented by a governor-general. Grenada gained independence in 1974 and includes the islands of Carriacou and Petite Martinique. The bicameral parliament consists of a 15-seat House of Representatives and a 13-seat Senate, to which the prime minister appoints ten senators and the opposition leader appoints three.

Maurice Bishop's Marxist New Jewel Movement seized power in 1979. In 1983, Bishop was murdered by New Jewel hardliners Bernard Coard and Hudson Austin, who took control of the country. A joint U.S.-Caribbean military intervention removed Coard and Austin, and in the 1984 elections, the NNP, now a coalition of three parties, won the majority of seats. Herbert Blaize became prime minister until his death in 1989, when Deputy Prime Minister Ben Jones replaced him.

In the 1990 elections, the NNP coalition had unraveled and there were five principal contenders: The National Party (TNP) headed by Jones; the centrist National Democratic Congress (NDC) led by Nicholas Braithwaite, head of the 1983-1984 interim government; the NNP, headed by Keith Mitchell; the leftist Maurice Bishop Patriotic Movement (MBPM), led by Terry Marryshow; and Eric Gairy's rightist Grenada United Labour Party (GULP).

The NDC won seven seats and took in a defector from the GULP, and Braithwaite became prime minister with a one-seat majority. After implementing unpopular economic reforms, the aging Braithwaite stepped down in early 1995 in favor of agricultural minister George Brizan.

The 1995 campaign was a raucous affair. Brizan sought to retain power by pointing to the improved economy, and other candidates accused the ruling NDC of corruption and harped on high unemployment. The NNP startled local observers by winning eight of 15 seats. The NDC won five seats, the GULP won two, and Mitchell became prime minister. Afterwards, NDC deputy leader Francis Alexis split off to form the Democratic Labour Party (DLP), underscoring the fractious nature of Grenadian politics.

In his first months in office, Mitchell was accused by opposition leader Brizan and others of censoring news unfavorable to the government in state-run television and radio broadcasts, and of purging civil servants appointed during the NDC administration. Mitchell denied the allegations. In 1996, Mitchell's reorganization of the state-owned Grenada Broadcasting Corporation (GBC) was viewed by some as another attempt to fill political positions with NNP supporters and to control the dissemination of information at GBC. In 1997, the NDC charged the government with granting a casino license to a foreign company, which it alleged has gangster connections.

In May 1998, a year after Gairy died, former deputy prime minister Herbert Preudhomme was elected leader of the bitterly divided GULP. The December decision to call parliamentary elections came after Mitchell was threatened with a no-confidence vote on the day in which he was to present the new national budget. The parliament was dissolved after Foreign Minister Raphael Fletcher resigned and accused the governing party of corruption. Mitchell, in turn, accused Fletcher of plotting with Libya to overthrow him.

Political Rights and Civil Liberties:

Citizens are able to change their government through democratic elections. Many political parties exist, and few obstacles face those establishing new parties. But there has been a decline in turnout as young people, in particular, appear to have lost confidence in a system riddled with fragmented politics and allegations of corruption.

The independent, prestigious judiciary has authority generally respected by the 750-member Royal Grenada Police Force. There are no military or political courts. In 1991, Grenada rejoined the Organization of Eastern Caribbean States court system, with the right of appeal to the Privy Council in London. Detainees and defendants are guaranteed a range of legal rights that the government respects in practice. Like many Caribbean island nations, Grenada has suffered from a rise in violent drug-related crime, particularly among increasingly disaffected youth. Prison conditions are poor, though they meet minimum international standards, and the government allows human rights monitors to visit.

Newspapers, including four weeklies, are independent and freely criticize the government. Television is both private and public, and the main radio station is part of the Grenadian Broadcasting Corporation, a statutory body not directly controlled by the government. Since the 1995 elections, a number of new radio and television stations, not one of which is aligned with the NNP, were issued licenses to operate.

Constitutional guarantees regarding the right to organize political, labor or civic groups are respected. The exercise of religion and the right of free expression are generally respected.

Numerous independent labor unions include an estimated 20 to 25 percent of the workforce. A 1993 law gives the government the right to establish tribunals empowered to make "binding and final" rulings when a labor dispute is considered of vital interest to the state. The national trade union federation claimed that the law was an infringement on the right to strike. Workers have the right to organize and to bargain collectively.

Women are represented in the government, though in greater numbers in the ministries than in parliament. No official discrimination takes place, but women generally earn less than men for equal work. Violence against women is common.

↓ Guatemala

Polity: Presidential-leg-
islative democracy
Economy: Capitalist-
statist
Population: 11,600,000
PPP: $3,682
Life Expectancy: 65
Ethnic Groups: Mestizo (56 percent), Indian (44 percent)
Capital: Guatemala City

Political Rights: 3
Civil Liberties: 4
Status: Partly Free

Trend Arrow: Guatemala receives a downward trend arrow due to an increase in personal insecurity.

Overview: President Alvaro Arzu's government's largely successful implementation of peace accords signed in late December 1996 risked being obscured by a continuing high rate of violent crime and the personal insecurity of Guatemalans, much of which was linked to organized crime and drug trafficking. Promises to establish a new civilian police force to replace the thuggish former militarized security corps have been subverted by the wholesale recycling of the veteran cops into the new institution, as well as by corruption and mismanagement at the police training academy. A report issued by the Church cataloguing the military's dominant role in civilian massacres committed during 36 years of internal conflict was followed two days later by the murder of a Catholic bishop which added to the general public's sense of unease.

The Republic of Guatemala was established in 1839, 18 years after gaining independence from Spain. The nation has endured a history of dictatorship, *coups détat,* and guerrilla insurgency, with only intermittent democratic rule. It has experienced elected civilian rule since 1985. Amended in 1994, the 1985 constitution provides for a four-year presidential term and prohibits re-election. An 80-member unicameral Congress is elected for four years.

Right-wing businessman Jorge Serrano became president in 1991 after winning a runoff election. In 1993, he attempted to dissolve the legislature. After initially supporting him, the military changed its mind as a result of mass protests and international pressure, and Serrano was sent into exile. The Congress chose Ramiro de Leon Carpio, the government's human rights ombudsman, as his replacement.

De Leon Carpio was practically powerless to halt human rights violations by the military or to curb the military's power as final arbiter in national affairs. After UN-mediated talks were launched between the government and the URNG left-wing guerrillas, the latter called an unilateral truce for the 1995 election and backed the left-wing New Guatemala Democratic Front (FDNG). The top presidential contenders were former Guatemala City mayor Arzu, of the National Advancement Party (PAN) and Alfonso Portillo Cabrera of the hard-right Guatemalan Republic Front (FRG). FRG founder and military dictator Efrain Rios Montt was constitutionally barred from running.

Arzu won with 36.6 percent of the vote, and Portillo Cabrera won 22 percent. In the January 7, 1996 runoff, Arzu defeated Portillo, 51.2 to 48.8 percent. The PAN won

43 seats in Congress, the FRG 21, the centrist National Alliance nine, and the URNG-backed FDNG six.

Soon after taking office, Arzu reshuffled the military, forcing the early retirement of generals linked to drug-trafficking, car-theft rings, and human rights abuses. The purge had the backing of a small but influential group of reformist officers who dominate the military high command. After a brief suspension of peace talks in October 1996 because of a rebel kidnapping, subsequent agreement on the return of rebel forces to civilian life and a permanent cease-fire led to the December 1996 peace accords.

In 1997, Arzu's government won plaudits for important advances in implementing the peace process. These included the successful demobilization of the URNG guerrillas and their political legalization, the retirement of more than 40 senior military officers on corruption and narcotics charges, and gains in the reduction of the army's strength by on- third by the end of the year. In August 1997, a truth commission mandated by the peace accords began receiving tens of thousands of complaints of rights violations committed during the 36-year internal conflict.

In April 1998, Guatemala was shaken by the murder of Auxiliary Bishop Juan Gerardi, a case that has become a test of the government's willingness to control the armed forces and to hold accountable those who abuse human rights. As head of the Church's human rights office, Mons. Gerardi played a pivotal role in preparing the report, *Guatemala, Nunca Mas*, in which the military were held responsible for 80 percent of some 55,000 documented human rights violations. Official attempts to place responsibility for the outrage initially on a crippled vagrant and then on a spat between the prelate and a priest were met with outrage and claims of defamation and orchestration by the military intelligence services. In June, the URNG presented candidates under its own banner for the first time, and the PAN won 22 of 30 contested municipal governments in a partial election, of which there are a 330 jurisdictions in all.

Political Rights and Civil Liberties:

Citizens can change their governments through elections, but recent voter turnouts suggest that people are increasingly disillusioned with the process. The constitution guarantees religious freedom and the right to organize political parties, civic organizations, and labor unions. However, political and civic expression is severely restricted by a climate of violence, lawlessness, and military repression. Efforts by President Arzu to reduce the armed forces' ability to restrict constitutional powers granted to civilian administrations appeared to have taken hold. However, the rule of law is undermined by the systemic corruption that afflicts all public institutions, particularly the legislature and the courts.

Despite penal code reforms in 1994, the judicial system remains a black hole for most legal or human rights complaints. Drug trafficking is a serious problem, and Guatemala remains a warehousing and transit point for South American drugs entering the U.S. In general, the justice system suffers from chronic problems of corruption, intimidation, insufficient personnel, lack of training opportunities, and a lack of transparency and accountability. Native Americans are largely excluded from the national justice system. Although indigenous languages are now being used in courtrooms around the country, traditional justice systems receive only lip service from Guatemalan authorities. Similarly, cursory recruitment efforts have resulted in only a handful of Native American recruits for the new civilian police.

Guatemala remains one of the most violent countries in Latin America, and ranks fourth in the number of kidnappings in the region. The closing of military barracks throughout the country, in a nation in which the armed forces were the only Guatemalan institution to enjoy a truly national presence, created a noticeable vacuum in which criminal interests are free to operate. One result was an upsurge of lynchings, as communities organized to take the law into their own hands. In Guatemala City, neighborhood patrols, some armed with automatic weapons, have arisen in a desperate attempt to arrest the spiraling crime wave. In a positive development, in 1998, the first convictions on war crimes charges were handed down in November when three pro-government paramilitary force members were sentenced to death for their role in a 1982 massacre of Indian peasants.

The press and most of the broadcast media are privately owned, with several independent newspapers and dozens of radio stations, most of which are commercial. Five of six television stations are commercially operated. However, journalists remain at great risk. In recent years, more than a dozen Guatemalan journalists have been forced into exile. The 1993 murder of newspaper publisher Jorge Carpio Nicolle, a former presidential candidate, remains unsolved.

The Runejel Junam Council of Ethnic Communities (CERJ) represents the interests of the country's Indians, a majority of the population who have faced severe repression and violence by the army and allied paramilitary organizations as well as being manipulated by the URNG guerrillas. In 1996, Indians showed signs of flexing some political muscle. Indian candidates won control of an estimated 40 urban areas, including Guatemala's second largest city, as well as 10 percent of congressional seats. Under a new law, Mayan descendants are allowed to seek office as independents and not as representatives of the national political parties that have ignored their needs.

Workers are frequently denied the right to organize and are subjected to mass firings and blacklisting, particularly in export-processing zones where a majority of workers are women. Existing unions are targets of systematic intimidation, physical attacks, and assassination, particularly in rural areas during land disputes. Guatemala is among the most dangerous countries in the world for trade unionists. Child labor is a growing problem in the agricultural industry, and use of Guatemala as a transit point for illegal aliens, particularly from Asia, frequently leads to abuses, including death.

Guinea

Polity: Dominant party
(military-influenced)
Economy: Capitalist
Population: 7,500,000
PPP: $1,139
Life Expectancy: 45
Ethnic Groups: Peuhl (40 percent), Malinke (30 percent),
Soussou (20 percent), smaller tribes (10 percent)
Capital: Conakry

Political Rights: 6
Civil Liberties: 5
Status: Not Free

Overview:

President Lansana Conté was returned to office in a December presidential election that lacked credible opposition as state patronage and media strongly backed the incumbent. Harassment of political opponents and disregard for the rule of law continued to mark dominance of the long-serving president and his ruling Progress and Unity Party (PUP). A wave of arrests followed the election, including that of the official third place finisher, Alpha Conde. Security forces, including the elite presidential guard, enjoyed impunity for past and ongoing human rights abuses.

Oppositionists, independent media and nongovernmental organizations seeking to expand the limited democratic space faced resistance from a clique of President Conté's cronies, mostly from his own Susu ethnic group, which dominates the country's political and economic life. The lack of a strong electoral challenge to President Conté's grip on power could encourage armed anti-government activity from dissidents who are reportedly based in neighboring Liberia and Sierra Leone. An array of insurgencies opposed to various governments in the region operate along Guinea's frontiers. Guinea dispatched about 500 troops to battle a military mutiny in Guinea-Bissau. President Conté himself seized power in a 1984 coup, and was nearly toppled by a 1996 army mutiny. Amidst general looting in Conakry, the capital, Conté, rallied loyal troops and re-established his rule. Legislative polls in June 1995 were deeply flawed, and Guinea remains far from achieving either a genuine democratic transition or respect for human rights and the rule of law.

Under Ahmed Sékou Touré and his Guinea Democratic Party, Guinea declared independence from France in 1958. Alone among France's many African colonies, it rejected the domination of continued close ties with France. France retaliated quickly, removing or destroying all "colonial property" and enforcing an unofficial but devastating economic boycott. Sékou Touré's one-party rule became highly repressive after an early effort to introduce egalitarian laws. Guinea was increasingly impoverished under his disastrous Soviet-style economic policies, and today the country ranks near last on international social development indicators.

Guinean politics and parties are largely defined on ethnic bases. President Conté's ruling PUP is strongly Susu; the Rally of the Guinean People (RPG) party is mostly Malinké; and both the Party for Renewal and Progress (PRP) and the Union for the New Republic (UNR) party are Fulani-dominated. Ethnicity, patronage, and nepotism provide the subtext to almost every political debate. Ethnic wars in neighboring states raise fears of similar conflict and national disintegration among Guinea's seven million people. Today, the country hosts about over 500,000 refugees, mostly from Sierra Leone, Senegal, and Guinea-Bissau.

Political Rights and Civil Liberties:

The Guinean people's constitutional right to freely elect their government is not yet respected in practice. President Conté's December re-election, with 54.1 percent of about 2.7 million votes reported, was unconvincing, although broad manipulation of the electoral process and opposition disunity likely made more blatant forms of vote rigging unnecessary to ensure another five year presidential term. Union for Progress and Renewal party leader Mamadou Ba placed second with 24.6 percent of the vote. The Higher Council on Electoral Affairs which replaced the Independent Electoral Commission in September was neither autonomous nor powerful enough to level the electoral landscape, although the polls were an improvement over past elections. Electoral manipulation and fraud in the 1993 presidential polls made a mockery of the vote. The June 1995 national assembly elections were more open. A total of eight opposition parties won just enough seats to deny the PUP the two-third's majority required to enact constitutional changes; but the ruling PUP's share of seats in the 114-member assembly was probably fraudulently inflated far above the proportion of votes it received.

The president retains decree power that could eviscerate the parliamentary process. While nominally independent, the judicial system remains infected by corruption, nepotism, ethnic bias, and political interference, and lacks resources and training. Minor civil cases are often handled by traditional ethnic based courts. A new State Security Court, whose proceedings may be secret and whose verdicts cannot be appealed, was established in June 1997. Arbitrary arrests and detention are common, and persistent maltreatment and torture of detainees is reported. Conditions in the country's prisons, which are harsh and sometimes life threatening, were denounced in January by a delegation of the International Observatory of Prisons (OIP).

Several statutes restrict freedom of association and assembly in apparent contravention of constitutional guarantees. The government may ban any gathering that "threatens national unity." Registration requirements seem insignificant obstacles to political party formation, and at least 46 have been recognized. But many opposition politicians have been harassed or arrested; the RPG party is a special target. Several leaders and activists of the UNR were jailed in June after police clashed with protesters. Several human rights groups, such as the Guinean Organization for the Defense of Human Rights (OGDH), and many nongovernmental groups operate openly. Various groups promoted civic education projects, although such efforts seem to have little impact on those in power. Constitutionally protected religious rights are respected in practice, although the main body representing the country's Muslims, who comprise over 80percent of the population, is government controlled. Christian missionaries operate freely.

The government has wide powers to bar any communications that insult the president or, in its opinion, disturb the peace. All broadcasting as well as the country's largest and only daily newspaper are state-controlled, and offer little coverage of the opposition and scant criticism of government policy. The print media has little impact in rural areas where incomes are low and illiteracy high. Several weekly newspapers in the capital, Conakry, offer sharp criticism of the government despite frequent harassment. A restrictive press law allows the government to censor or shutter publications on broad and ill-defined bases. In 1998, several foreign journalists from West African countries working in the independent media were expelled. Parliamentary proposals to open broadcasting were rejected by the president, and a reformist information minister, Michel Kamano, was dismissed in 1997.

Women have far fewer educational and employment opportunities than men, and many societal customs discriminate against women. Constitutionally protected women's rights are often unrealized. Spousal abuse and other violence against women is said to be prevalent. Female genital mutilation as a traditional rite is widely practiced.

The constitution provides the right to form and join unions. However, about 80 percent of Guinea's seven million people are subsistence farmers. Only a very small formal sector exists and about one-twentieth of the work force is unionized. Several labor confederations compete in this small market and have the right to bargain collectively. Labor grievances are regularly heard by a labor court in the capital as well as in civil courts elsewhere.

Privatization efforts affecting the country's bauxite industry —which provides about 90 percent of export earnings—other mining concerns, and various state enterprises continued. New IMF loans and debt rescheduling are opening the way for new, private international lending and investment. However, endemic corruption and the concentration of power around President Conté remain serious obstacles to investment and economic growth.

Guinea-Bissau

Polity: Presidential-
legislative democracy
(military-influenced)
(transitional)
Economy: Mixed statist (transitional)
Population: 1,100,000
PPP: $811
Life Expectancy: 43
Ethnic Groups: Balanta (30 percent), Fula (20 percent), Manjaca (14 percent), Mandinga (13 percent), Papel (7 percent), other (16 percent)
Capital: Bissau
Ratings change: Guinea-Bissau's civil liberties rating changed from 4 to 5 due to an increase of abuses against civilians as a result of the country's civil war.

Political Rights: 3
Civil Liberties: 5*
Status: Partly Free

Overview: A June army mutiny including most of the country's soldiers led to pitched battles against a small loyalist force, which was aided by about 3,000 troops who intervened from neighboring Senegal and Guinea. The army mutiny in Guinea was sparked by the arrest in January of several army officers and the June dismissal of army chief of staff General Ansumane Mané in connection with alleged arms smuggling to rebels in the neighboring Senegalese province of Casamance. The fighting has caused considerable damage in the capital, Bissau, and displaced hundreds of thousands of people. Senegalese troops have been accused of abuses against civilians.

A cease-fire negotiated in late July was repeatedly broken until the establishment of a November agreement for a government of national unity which would rule presidential elections already scheduled for March 1999. Under the auspices of the Economic Community of West African States Military Observer Group (ECOMOG), troops from several West African nations began arriving in the country in late December to oversee the pact. The rebellion underlined dwindling popular support for Guinea-Bissau President Joao Bernardo Vieira, who won office in the country's first open elections in June 1994. Legislative elections scheduled for July were already likely to be delayed before the mutiny, and are now indefinitely postponed. The Senegalese intervention, justified on the basis of a mutual defense pact, is more practically aimed at cutting off the rear bases and supplies to rebels in Senegal's southern Casamance province.

The ruling African Party for the Independence of Guinea-Bissau and Cape Verde (PAIGC) held power for thirteen years under one party after Guinea-Bissau achieved independence from Portugal in 1973 following a fierce twelve-year guerrilla war. 1991 constitutional revisions ended the PAIGC's repressive one-party state and its official status as the "leading force in society." Political parties were legalized, and direct elections for both the president and members of parliament to five year terms were introduced. The PAIGC won a majority in parliament among 13 parties, and President Vieira retained his post in a runoff vote, in elections accepted as free and fair by both the opposition and a UN observer mission. President Vieira's current reliance of foreign forces to prop up his government, and the postponement of elections are diminishing his democratic credentials. Amnesty International stated concern in July over reports of abuses by both rebel and government forces as well as allegations of threats against opposition politicians.

Political Rights and Civil Liberties:

Guinea-Bissau's first open elections took place in 1994, and both direct presidential polls and legislative elections were judged free and fair by international observers. The PAIGC retained the presidency and a parliamentary majority, but five opposition parties are represented in the national assembly. Municipal elections first set for 1996 have been repeatedly delayed, and the ongoing army rebellion will indefinitely delay the July 1998 legislative elections.

The Guinean Human Rights League has raised allegations of numerous instances of torture and other mistreatment by security forces. Freedoms of assembly and expression are constitutionally guaranteed and generally respected. The judiciary enjoys some autonomy, but is largely controlled by the executive branch. Judicial performance is often unpredictable due to political interference, poor training, and scant resources. Traditional law usually prevails in rural areas. Police routinely ignored rights of privacy and protections against search and seizure. Suspected "subversives" may be legally detained, and detention without resort to any statute, and severe mistreatment of detainees, is reported. Outside of conflict areas, citizens may generally travel freely within the country, and there are no legal restrictions on foreign travel. However, all civil liberties have been seriously, even if perhaps temporarily, abridged by the country's civil war.

State media practice broad self-censorship and rarely question or criticize government policies. The mainly rural population is 60 percent illiterate, and radio remains the most important medium for reaching the people. Several private radio stations and community radio stations have begun broadcasting, two of which rebroadcast French and Portuguese programming, offering more balanced coverage than government services. However, one popular private radio state was seized by rebels and much broadcasting was dominated by partisan propaganda. Few private newspapers publish, and the lack of a vibrant independent media may be more due to financial constraints than government interference.

Most people follow traditional religions, but proselytizing is permitted and there is a significant Muslim population, as well as a small Christian minority and foreign missionary activity. While official registration is required, no religious group has been denied registration since 1982, and religious freedom is respected.

Women face some legal and significant traditional and societal discrimination. They generally do not receive equal pay for equal work and have fewer opportunities for education and jobs in the small formal sector. Only eight of 100 national assembly members are women. Domestic violence against women is common, and female genital mutilation is widespread.

The vast majority of Guinea-Bissau's one million citizens survive on subsistence agricultural. Eleven labor unions operate in the formal sector, and workers have the right to organize and to strike with prior notice. Guinea-Bissau's low life expectancy, high infant mortality, and declining living standards are consequences both of Portuguese colonial neglect and misrule since independence. Economic reforms encouraged by international donors include sharp cuts in the civil service and reduction of imports. In July 1997, the country formally joined the Communauté Financière Africaine (African Financial Community) monetary union, adopting the French-backed CFA *franc* as its new currency, a popularly resented move intended to stabilize the country's finances. A broad privatization plan has been slowed by the rebellion, and new grants, credits, and investment will likely await the conflict's resolution.

Guyana

Polity: Parliamentary democracy
Economy: Mixed statist
Population: 700,000
PPP: $3,205
Life Expectancy: 66
Ethnic Groups: East Indian (49 percent), black (32 percent), mixed (12 percent), Indian (6 percent), white and Chinese (1 percent)
Capital: Georgetown

Political Rights: 2
Civil Liberties: 2
Status: Free

Overview: The good offices of the leaders of Caricom, the Caribbean trade group, helped new Guyana President Janet Jagan to reach an accord with the political opposition in order to enact constitutional reform and to combat racial discrimination, in exchange for an end to growing political violence. Jagan, the widow of legendary independence leader Cheddi Jagan, had been elected in December 1997 in a vote bitterly disputed as rigged. Before the June 1998 accord was reached, intervention of the army was necessary to help quell civil disturbances, even after a special Caricom commission found no evidence of election fraud.

Guyana is a member of the British Commonwealth. From its independence in 1966 until 1992, it was ruled by the autocratic, predominantly Afro-Guyanese, People's National Congress (PNC). The 1980 constitution provides for a strong president and a 65-seat National Assembly which is elected every five years. Twelve seats are occupied by elected local officials. The leader of the party which wins the plurality of parliamentary seats becomes president for a five-year term. The president appoints the prime minister and cabinet.

The first free and fair elections were held in 1992, and 80 percent of the eligible population voted. The PNC lost to the predominantly Indo-Guyanese People's Progressive Party (PPP)-Civic alliance. Having moderated his Marxism since the collapse of communism, PPP leader, Cheddi Jagan, became president.

The Indo-Guyanese outnumber Afro-Guyanese, 52 percent to 36 percent, and their leader, Jagan, won 52 percent of the vote; PNC leader Desmond Hoyte took 41 percent. A third candidate from the Working People's Alliance (WPA), the only mixed-race party in the country, won less than two percent. Fear and distrust of the Indo-Guyanese ruling party continues among Afro-Guyanese, despite the PPP's record of governing in a relatively evenhanded manner.

Cheddi Jagan's work was cut short by his death in March 1997. He was replaced by Samuel Hinds, a member of Civic, the PPP's coalition partner. Hinds called elections for December 15, 1997. Janet Jagan, a 77-year-old American-born journalist, beat the PNC's Hoyte by a 5-4 margin, approximately 60,000 votes. In a first for a member of the Caribbean community, the parliament was elected by proportional representation. In 1998, progress was made on constitutional reform as parliament began the process of setting up a broad-based committee to oversee changes in the 1980 Constitution.

Political Rights and Civil Liberties:

Citizens can change their government through direct, multiparty elections. Claims by opposition PNC concerning vote rigging and mismanagement in the 1997 elections were determined by a Caricom-selected investigative commission to be largely without merit, although numerous administrative shortcomings were detected. In 1997, an effort was made to reduce the possibility of the fraud and impersonation that marred previous contests, by requiring voters to have identification cards bearing their photographs when they went to the polls. Under the 1980 constitution, the president has wide powers and immunities. Because it lacks explicit guarantees, political rights and civil liberties rest more on government tolerance that on constitutional guarantees—a situation the PPP/Civic coalition appears ready to change by July 1999, when the constitutional reform process is due to end. The rights of free expression, freedom of religion, and freedom to organize political parties, civic organizations, and labor unions are generally respected. The judicial system is independent; however, due process is undermined by the shortage of staff and funds. Prisons are overcrowded, and conditions are poor. Guyana is the only Caribbean country to have cut all ties to the British Privy Council, the court of last resort for other former colonies in the region. Guyanese officials have complained that U.S. efforts to deport Guyanese from their northern neighbor have caused an upsurge in violent crimes including carjackings and shootouts with police.

The police force is prone to corruption, particularly due to penetration of the hemispheric drug trade. The Guyana Human Rights Association has charged the police with frequent recurrence to excessive force, sometimes causing death. The GHRA is autonomous, effective, and supported by independent civic and religious groups.

Several independent newspapers operate freely, including the *Stabroek News* and the *Catholic Standard*, a church weekly. Only two radio stations operate; both are government owned. The government owns one television station. Fifteen privately-owned television stations freely criticize the government.

The largely PNC opposition complains that the governing alliance discriminates on the basis of race, and gives preferential treatment for jobs and contracts to the East-Asian population to the detriment of the Afro-Guyanese. In November 1998, the government reinstated a custom's chief who had been suspended six years earlier on corruption charges. The comptroller's case had been a rallying point for government workers of African descent who charge that racism is rampant within the PPP/Civic coalition. Guyana's Amerindian Act gives indigenous groups title to their land but without subsoil rights. Native American groups complain that the government sells mining and logging concessions in Guyana's immense rain forest without regard for the land rights of native peoples. In November 1998, the government granted a 5.1-million-acre mining concession on Indian lands.

Domestic violence against women is troubling, as is the government's reluctance to address the issue.

Labor unions are well organized. In 1995, the government sought to dilute the right to strike among some public sector unions. Companies are not obligated to recognize unions in former state enterprises sold off by the government.

Haiti

Polity: Presidential-parliamentary democracy
Economy: Capitalist-statist
Population: 7,500,000
PPP: $917
Life Expectancy: 51
Ethnic Groups: Black (95 percent), mulatto and white (5 percent)
Capital: Port-au-Prince

Political Rights: 5*
Civil Liberties: 5
Status: Partly Free

Ratings change: Haiti's political rights rating changed from 4 to 5 due to a lack of a prime minister for 18 months and an undercount of representatives in both houses of parliament.

Overview: President Rene Preval's inability to reach agreement with the opposition, after more than a year and a half, on the appointment of a new prime minister, is emblematic of a government that seems to exist in name only. The lack of a prime minister and a full Cabinet is exacerbated by a Senate with only 17 serving members of 27, and 78 parliamentary deputies serving in the 83-seat lower chamber. In November, 1998, the Senate extended its term, from January 1999 to October of that year, citing the extended power vacuum as the cause.

Since gaining independence from France in 1804 following a slave revolt, the Republic of Haiti has endured a history of poverty, violence, instability, and dictatorship. A 1986 military coup ended 29 years of rule by the Duvalier family, and the army ruled for most of the next eight years.

Under international pressure, the military permitted the implementation of a French-style constitution in 1987. It provides for a president elected for five years, an elected parliament composed of a 27-member Senate, an 83-member House of Representatives, and a prime minister appointed by the president.

In the 1990 elections, Jean-Bertrand Aristide, a charismatic left-wing priest, won in a landslide over conservative Marc Bazin. Aristide sought to establish civilian authority over the military; he also railed against corruption. Haiti's mostly mulatto elites and the military then conspired to overthrow him. In response, he overstepped the constitution by calling upon supporters to defend the government by violent means.

Aristide was overthrown in September 1991. Haiti came under the ruthless control of the military triumvirate of General Raoul Cedras, General Philippe Biamby, and Colonel Michel Francois. Tens of thousands of paramilitary thugs reigned terror on the populace, and the regime was steeped in narcotics trafficking. The U.S. and the UN imposed a trade and oil embargo.

In September 1994, facing an imminent U.S. invasion, Cedras and Biamby agreed to step down. U.S. troops took control of the country, and Aristide was reinstated. His security, as well as that of average Haitians, now depended upon the U.S. and UN forces.

Aristide dismantled the military before the June 1995 parliamentary elections got underway. International observers questioned the legitimacy of the June election, and Aristide's supporters fell out among themselves. The more militant Lavalas movement remained firmly behind him. But the National Front for Change and Democracy (FNCD), a leftist coalition that had backed him in 1990, claimed fraud and boycotted the runoff elections. In the end, the Lavalas won an overwhelming parliamentary majority.

In the fall, the Lavalas nominated Preval, Aristide's prime minister in 1991, as its presidential candidate. With Aristide backing him and the FNCD and most other major opposition parties boycotting, the result of the December 17 election, which opposition politicians claimed marred by serious irregularities and fraud, was a forgone conclusion. Preval won about 89 percent of a turnout of less than one-third of those eligible.

Preval took office February 7, 1996. The UN had planned to withdraw its troops by the end of the month. The new U.S.-trained Haitian National Police, however, clearly lacked the competence to fill the void. At Preval's urging, the UN extended its stay, but by June it cut its presence to 1,300. The final U.S. combat force had withdrawn two months earlier.

In September 1996, Preval purged much of his security force which, according to American officials, was involved a month earlier with the murders of two politicians from the right-wing Mobilization for National Development (MDN) party, which counted heavily on support from former soldiers.

Senate elections held in April 1997 were fraught with irregularities, and the resulting ongoing election dispute meant that parliament would not approve a new prime minister to replace Rosny Smarth, who resigned in June following growing criticism of the government's economic policies. In September, Aristide announced an alliance with other congressional groups to oppose Preval's economic reform plans.

The continuing impasse of the appointment of a prime minister has prevented passage of two government budgets, scared off foreign investment, and put millions of dollars of desperately needed foreign aid on the shelf. In October 1998, U.S. drug czar Barry McCaffrey said that 50 percent of the Colombian drug trade which was smuggled through the Caribbean passed through Haiti.

Political Rights and Civil Liberties: Overseen by a politicized and incompetent electoral commission, the April 6, 1997 elections for one-third of the Senate and 565 local councils were characterized by fraud, significant violations of law, and a five percent turnout of eligible voters. In July 1998, the Provisional Electoral Council shut its doors after its remaining two members resigned. The virtual government shutdown indefinitely postponed the legislative and municipal elections scheduled for November 1998.

The constitution guarantees a full range of political rights and civil liberties. The protection of such rights in 1998, however, remained precarious, as the rule of law is tenuous at best and is aggravated by a yawning security vacuum. Several people were killed in ongoing subterranean political warfare involving the former military, Aristide supporters, and others.

The judicial system remains corrupt, inefficient, and essentially dysfunctional, particularly in rural areas, and U.S. reform efforts have been tainted by allegations of corruption involving contractors and others. Prison conditions are grim, and a severe backlog of cases means that hundreds suffer lengthy pre-trial detention periods.

The new 5,200-member Haitian National Police is inexperienced and lacking in resources. Human rights groups say the police frequently use excessive force and mistreat detainees, and several unarmed civilians have been murdered. Accusations of corruption have also grown more frequent; in 1998, the United Nations mission in Haiti said that an increasing number of police were involved in drug smuggling. Although efforts by police authorities to sanction misdeeds have met with mixed success, there is no evidence that the grave violations of human rights by the police form part of official policy. The police have been increasingly called upon to put down protests against the government's economic austerity program.

Mob violence and armed gangs posed severe security threats in urban areas. Former soldiers, others linked to the former military regime, and common criminals were responsible for much of the violence, including political assassinations. Haitian officials also say that the rise in crime is due to convicted criminals who have been repatriated from other countries, particularly the U.S. Turf wars between rival drug gangs have resulted in the killing of scores of people, including several policemen. Private security forces that carry out extra-legal search and seizures are illegal but flourishing.

A number of independent newspapers and radio stations exist. Outlets critical of the government remain targets of official intimidation, including mob attacks. Television is state-run and strongly biased toward the government. In October 1998, a former Haitian judge was arrested in connection with the 1982 murder of a well-known journalist.

Labor rights, as with all other legally sanctioned guarantees, remain essentially unenforced. Unions are generally too weak to engage in collective bargaining, and their organization efforts are undermined by the high unemployment rate.

Honduras

Polity: Presidential-leg-
islative democracy
Economy: Capitalist-statist
Population: 5,900,000
PPP: $1,977
Life Expectancy: 68
Ethnic Groups: Mestizo (90 percent), Indian (7 percent),
black (2 percent), white (1 percent)
Capital: Tegucigalpa

Political Rights: 2
Civil Liberties: 3
Status: Free

Overview:

The honeymoon for incoming President Carlos Flores came to a halt in 1998, as Hurricane Mitch devastated the economy of Central America's poorest nation. Flores had promised to continue his predecessor's efforts to reign in an unruly military, but a wave of bank robberies, kidnappings, burglaries, and unsolved murders resulted in army troops patrolling the Honduras' industrial capital and other major cities in an effort to squelch violent crime.

The Republic of Honduras was established in 1839, 18 years after gaining independence from Spain. It has endured decades of military rule and intermittent elected government. The last military regime gave way to elected civilian rule in 1982. The constitution provides for a president and a 130-member, unicameral congress elected for four years.

The two main parties are the center-left Liberal Party (PL) and the conservative National Party (PN). In the 1993, the PN nominated Oswaldo Ramos Soto, an outspoken right-winger. The PL, which held power during most of the 1980's, nominated Roberto Reina, a 67-year-old progressive and former president of the Inter-American Court of Human Rights. Reina won with 52 percent of the vote. The PL won 70 seats in congress, and the PN won 56. Two small left-wing parties took the remaining four.

Reina promised a "moral revolution" and greater civilian control over the military. His administration had a positive though mixed record. The size of the military was reduced greatly, although its spending remained secret, and officers suspected of rights' offenses were protected. The process of separating the police from the military was undertaken following the December 1996 approval by Congress of a constitutional amendment to place the police under civilian control; however, a virulent crime wave believed to be, in part, the work of former and serving military and intelligence officers, continued unabated. Several leaders of Indian and Garifuna minority groups attempting to defend their land from encroachments by non-Indian landowners were murdered.

On November 30, 1997, Liberal presidential candidate Flores, a U.S.-trained engineer and newspaper owner, won a resounding 54 to 41 percent victory over National Party candidate Nora Melgar. The ruling party won 67 congressional seats and retained control over 180 of Honduras' 297 municipal districts. Flores immediately announced that civilian control of the armed forces would be strengthened by the creation of a functional defense ministry, and that the newly civilianized police would enjoy an increased budget. He also appointed five women to high level posts, including as minister of security, the portfolio in charge of the new civilian national police. In September 1998, just weeks before the Hurricane hit, Congress voted to end more than 30 years of military autonomy by suppressing the post of commander-in-chief of the armed forces, a move that created unrest in the barracks. At the end of 1998, however, it was uncertain how much, if any, of Flores' agenda would survive in the aftermath of "Mitch."

Political Rights and Civil Liberties: Citizens are able to change their government through elections, and the 1997 presidential contest was considered to be generally free and fair.

Constitutional guarantees regarding free expression, freedom of religion, and the right to form political parties and civic organizations are generally respected. But repressive measures in the face of peaceful protests and mounting crime have limited political rights and civil liberties.

Headed by the Supreme Court, the judicial system is weak and prone to corruption. In 1998, the new court was packed with lawyers who were close both to the military and to officials accused of corruption. Death threats and violent attacks face judges who assert themselves in human rights cases. Although 90 percent of the 10,000 people incarcerated are awaiting trial, they share deplorable prison conditions with convicted inmates. Drug-related corruption is rampant, and in 1998, a top leader of the Atlantic narcotics cartel escaped through the front gate of the National Penitentiary after bribing prison officials.

In 1997, the government moved to place the police under civilian control, a task made easier by the emergence of a cadre of police professionals at the top reaches of a force controlled by the military since 1963. However, Reina frequently used the military for internal security tasks such as putting down labor unrest, quelling street protests, and seeking to control street crime; the latter action was continued by Flores. Police still practice arbitrary detention and torture. A crime wave throughout Honduras has been fueled by the presence of some 120 youth gangs whose main activities include murder, kidnapping, and robbery. Where crime rings have been effectively dismantled, good police work, rather than troops in the streets, has made the difference.

The military exerts considerable, if waning, influence over the government. By naming a civilian instead of a general to head the armed forces, Flores Facusse said he hoped to strengthen government control over the armed forces. Since 1963, Honduras has had 12 armed forces commanders, five of whom were deposed by their own troops. A constellation of military-owned businesses makes the armed forces one of Honduras' ten largest corporations. Most criminal cases against the military remain in military court jurisdiction, and the charges are usually dismissed. In 1999, however, military personnel will no longer be immune from prosecution in civilian courts, and elected officials will oversee the armed forces' budget and be able to investigate military business ventures, which are the sources of much high-level corruption.

In 1998, army officers were implicated in drug trafficking, including taking sides in cartel turf wars and protecting drug shipments in transit through Honduras. The military remains the country's principal human rights violator, and the institution protects members linked to both political repression and to street crime, often linked to narcotics. In February 1998, human rights leader Ernesto Sandoval was murdered in a "death squad"-style assassination. The death squads are now also reportedly involved in the "social cleansing" murders of youth gang members in San Pedro Sula, the country's second largest city.

Labor unions are well organized and can strike, although labor actions often result in clashes with security forces. Labor leaders, religious groups and indigenous-based peasant unions pressing for land rights remain vulnerable to repression. Some 85,000 workers, mostly women, are employed in the low-wage maquiladora export sector.

Hungary

Polity: Parliamentary democracy
Economy: Mixed capitalist
Population: 10,100,000
PPP: $6,793
Life Expectancy: 70
Ethnic Groups: Hungarian (90 percent), Gypsy (4 percent), German (3 percent), Serb (2 percent), other (1 percent)
Capital: Budapest

Political Rights: 1
Civil Liberties: 2
Status: Free

Overview: Led by the Federation of Young Democrats-Civic Party (Fidesz), center-right parties won May's parliamentary elections, ousting the ruling coalition of the Hungarian Socialist Party (MSzP) and the Alliance of Free Democrats (SzDSz) led by Prime Minister Gyula Horn. Thirty-five-year-old Fidesz leader Viktor Orban, whose party won 148 of 386 seats, formed a government with the populist Independent Smallholder's Party (FKGP), which took 48 seats, and the Hungarian Democratic Forum (MDF), Fidesz's electoral ally, which won 17 seats.

With the collapse of the Austro-Hungarian empire after World War I, Hungary lost two-thirds of its territory under the 1920 Trianon Treaty, leaving 3.5 million Hungarians as minorities in neighboring Romania, Slovakia, Serbia, Croatia, and Ukraine. After World War II, Soviet forces helped install a Communist regime. In 1956, Soviet tanks quashed an armed uprising by Hungarians, and by the late 1980s, with the economy deteriorating, the ruling Hungarian Socialist Worker's Party (MSzMP) lost its legitimacy. The ouster of Janos Kadar in 1988 led the way to political reform and the eventual introduction of a multiparty system in 1989.

The run-up to the 1998 parliamentary elections saw decreasing popularity for the Horn government. In 1994, the Socialists had defeated the conservative-populist MDF with promises to ease the transition to a market economy. But in 1995, it adopted an unpopular reform package that saw radical spending cuts, a devaluation of the forint, and stepped up privatization. In 1996, the government was rocked by a privatization scandal, the so-called "Tocsik affair," which centered around a record consulting fee paid to an independent expert.

Despite macroeconomic gains attributed to its austerity program, which gave Hungary the fastest growing economy in East-Central Europe, Hungarians were disillusioned with corruption, crime, and an unequal distribution of wealth. Under Orban, Fidesz, which began a decade before as a youth party, positioned itself as a conservative, pro-market, and anti-socialist alternative. Fidesz also pledged to attack corruption, tax evasion, and organized crime. Its foreign policy plank supported membership in NATO and the EU.

In the May vote, Fidesz captured 148 seats (up from 20 in 1994); the Socialists won 134 (down from 209); the Smallholders, 48 (up from 26); and the Democratic Forum, 17 (down from 37). The extreme right Justice and Life Party, led by anti-Semitic demagogue Ivan Csurka, won 14 seats. The Christian Democrats, who won 22 seats in 1994, did not win a seat.

Local elections for 38,440 local councilors, almost 3,200 mayors, and national minorities' self-governing bodies were held on October 18. In Budapest, Gabor Demszky of the SzDSz was re-elected to another four-year term. Independent candidates fared the best, winning 2,600 mayoralties and more than 60 percent of councilor seats.

Political Rights and Civil Liberties: Hungarians can change their government democratically under a multiparty system enshrined in an amended Communist-era constitution. The 1998 elections were free and fair.

A 1995 media law was meant to end years of political wrangling over control of the electronic media. It provided for the privatization of TV-2 and Radio Danubis, and the operation of public service television and radio as joint-stock companies run by public foundations. There are three national public television channels, around 26 private commercial television stations, over 200 regional cable outlets, and over 30 radio stations. In 1997, the Radio and Television Regulatory Body (ORTT) offered concessions for television channels to foreign broadcasting companies. In October, the chairman of parliament's cultural committee, a SzDSz deputy, said the government was dragging its feet in nominating members of the ORTT. There are a wide variety of independent newspapers and publications that offers diverse opinions. In early October, the French media group, Reporters Without Borders, expressed concern over the suspension of *Kurir*, a leading opposition newspaper, by the government-controlled Postabank. The bank stopped funding the paper on the grounds that it wanted to streamline its media portfolio, but Reporters Without Borders said that bank continued to publish five other pro-Orban newspapers. On October 7, *Kurir* launched an Internet web site.

Freedoms of conscience and religion are viewed as fundamental liberties not granted by the state. On October 1, the government and the Federation of Jewish Communities signed an agreement on land and property reclaimed by the Jewish community in the form of an annuity. Under law, churches in Hungary may retrieve from 1998 to 2001 an annual 4.5 percent of their one-time property in the form of annuities, and 5 percent subsequently.

Freedoms of assembly and association are respected. There were several farmer protests in 1998. Some 200 political parties, movements, and associations have been registered since 1989, though the number of viable parties is about 20.

The two largest trade unions are the Democratic Confederation of Free Trade Unions (LIGA), and the Hungarian Workers Council. The National Federation of Hungarian Trade Unions (MSzOSz) is a successor to the Communist-era union. A national Interest Coordination Council was established in 1992 to provide a forum for consultations between the government, employers, and employees on wage policy and other labor matters.

The judiciary is independent and the Constitutional Court has ruled against the government on several occasions, notably nullifying aspects of the 1995 austerity economic program and the 1997 referendum issues. In 1997, the country's three-tier judicial system was replaced by a four-tier model that includes regional courts. Criteria for would-be judges were made more rigorous, calling for four rather than two years of preparatory practice as a lawyer. Court procedures are often slow. An ombudsman monitors civil complaints and reports to parliament. In September 1998, parliament began discussions on a package of amendments aimed at putting the prosecutor's offices, which are now answerable to parliament, under government control. Such a change would ultimately entail amending the constitution.

Hungary's half-million Roma (Gypsies) continue to suffer discrimination in employment, housing, and education. Major ethnic groups such as Roma, Bulgarians, Germans, Slovaks, Poles, Armenians, Greeks, and Serbs have special units of self-government which receive funds from the central budget proportional to the size of their respective minorities.

There is freedom of movement, and the state does not control choice of residence or employment. Property rights are formally guaranteed by the constitution and are upheld de facto by contract and property laws. Foreigners are not allowed to acquire land. Transition to a market economy has provided much greater equality of opportunity, though many Hungarians, particularly outside the large cities, are employed in the so-called "black economy" which accounts for about 30 percent of the GDP.

Women are represented in government, business and education, and several organizations represent women's issues.

Iceland

Polity: Parliamentary democracy
Economy: Capitalist
Population: 300,000
PPP: $21,064
Life Expectancy: 78
Ethnic Groups: Icelander
Capital: Reykjavik

Political Rights: 1
Civil Liberties: 1
Status: Free

Overview:

Since 1995, Iceland has been governed by a center-right coalition led by Prime Minister David Oddsson. In 1996, former leftist party chairman and finance minister Olafur Ragnar Grimsson was elected president with 41 percent of the vote. Reykjavik has established European Union (EU) links through membership in the European Economic Area (EEA). In 1996, Iceland, along with four other Nordic countries, joined Europe's Schengen Convention as observer states. The convention provides for the abolition of systematic internal border controls, a common visa policy, and close cooperation in police matters. These steps, taken to preserve the Nordic countries' "passport union," suggest that, despite Iceland's reluctance to join the EU, Iceland cannot avoid participation in EU policies. Although their country has strong historical, cultural and economic ties with Europe, Icelanders are hesitant to agree to the EU common fisheries policy, which they believe would threaten their marine industry. This industry accounts for 80 percent of Iceland's exported goods and half of its export revenues.

In November, Prime Minister Oddsson stated explicitly that, due to its reliance on this industry, Iceland had no interest in joining the EU. He also stated that the country's trade interests in Europe were already covered through membership in the EEA.

Iceland achieved full independence in 1944. Multiparty governments have been in power since then. In 1995, after attempting to appeal to younger voters and nonmarine industry interests by advocating EU membership, the Social Democratic Party (SDP) lost three seats and more than four percent of the popular vote. The Independence Party joined forces with the anti-EU Progressive Party and pledged to continue economic stabilization efforts and to eliminate the country's budget deficit. In late 1998, opinion polls revealed that 69.5 percent of voters support the governing coalition.

Political Rights and Civil Liberties:

Icelanders can change their government democratically. The constitution, adopted by referendum in 1944, provides for a popularly-elected, primarily ceremonial president, who is responsible for appointing a prime minister from the largest party in the 63-member Althing (parliament). The parliament is elected on the basis of a mixed system of proportional and direct representation. Elections are held every four years.

There are six major political parties. The Awakening of the Nation party broke away from the SDP shortly before the 1995 elections and won four Althing seats.

The country's judiciary is independent. The law does not provide for trial by jury, but many trials, especially during the appeals process, use panels comprised of several judges. All judges serve for life. The Ministry of Justice administers the lower courts, and the Supreme Court ensures that the judicial process is fair. Defendants are presumed innocent and are entitled to legal counsel. Two special courts handle cases of impeachment of government officials and labor disputes.

The constitution provides for freedom of speech, freedom of peaceful assembly and association, and freedom of the press. These freedoms are respected in practice. Constitutional bans on censorship are respected. A wide range of publications includes both independent and party-affiliated newspapers. An autonomous board of directors oversees the Icelandic State Broadcasting Service, which operates a number of transmitting and relay stations. There are both public and private television broadcast companies. In 1997, the country's two private television companies merged. There are six major radio stations.

Most eligible workers belong to free labor unions, and all enjoy the right to strike. Citizens have the right to hold private property. Disabled persons enjoy extensive rights in employment and education.

Virtually everyone in the country holds at least nominal membership in the state-supported Lutheran Church. Legal protections against discrimination are respected. Freedom of worship is allowed, and discrimination on the basis of race, language, social class, and gender is outlawed.

No legal barriers oppose women's participation in the political process. An active women's party, the Women's List, holds three of the 63 seats in the Althing. Women are paid 20 to 40 percent less than their male counterparts for comparable work, and labor union membership is predominantly male.

India

Polity: Parliamentary democracy (insurgencies)
Economy: Capitalist-statist
Population: 988,700,000
PPP: $1,422
Life Expectancy: 59

Political Rights: 2
Civil Liberties: 3*
Status: Free

Ethnic Groups: Indo-Aryan (72 percent), Dravidian (25 percent), other (3 percent)
Capital: New Delhi
Ratings change: India's civil liberties rating changed from 4 to 3, and its status changed from Partly Free to Free, due to the continued growth of civic organizations that are actively working to strengthen human rights protections, and for methodological reasons.

Overview:

The right-wing Indian People's Party (BJP) formed a coalition government following the winter 1998 elections, capping a decade's-old drive for political power and legitimacy by India's Hindu nationalist movement. The balloting, however, gave no party an outright majority and suggested no clear policy direction. Voters indicated disillusionment with India's corrupt, criminalized political system by rejecting incumbents.

India achieved independence from Britain in 1947 with the partition of the sub-continent into a predominantly Hindu India, under premier Jawaharlal Nehru, and a Muslim Pakistan. The 1950 constitution provides for a lower Lok Sabha (House of the People), with 543 seats elected for a five-year term (plus two appointed Anglo-Indian seats), and an upper Rajya Sabha (Council of States) with executive power vested in a prime minister, who is the leader of the party commanding the most support in the lower house.

The centrist, secular Congress party ruled continuously except for periods in opposition in 1977-80 and 1989-91. In the late 1980s, a non-Congress administration introduced government job quotas for "backward" castes, triggering violent protests. In the aftermath, lower-caste-based parties increasingly championed caste causes, and angry upper-caste voters increasingly supported the BJP. During the campaign for the 1991 elections, a suspected Sri Lankan Tamil separatist assassinated the former premier Rajiv Gandhi, heir to the political dynasty of Congress standard bearers Nehru and Indira Gandhi. With India facing a balance of payments crisis, new Congress premier P.V. Narasimha Rao introduced reforms aimed at transforming an autarkic, control-bound economy into a market-based system partially open to foreign investment.

In December 1992, Hindu fundamentalists, incited by the BJP and militant Hindu organizations, destroyed the sixteenth century Babri mosque in the northern town of Ayodhya, setting off weeks of deadly communal violence. In the mid-1990s, Congress lost eleven state elections due to a string of corruption scandals, a backlash against economic reforms by poor and lower-caste voters, and Muslim anger over the government's failure to prevent communal violence. Regional parties in southern India, and lower-caste-based parties and the BJP in the northern Hindi-speaking belt, made large gains.

In the April-May 1996 elections, the BJP surged to 161 seats, mainly in five northern and western states. Congress had its worst showing ever with 140 seats, as low-caste Hindus and Muslims deserted the party in droves. In May, a BJP-led minority government resigned after 13 days after failing to attract secular allies. The United Front (UF), a 13-party minority coalition of regional and leftist parties, took power in June backed by Congress.

UF governments led by H.D. Deve Gowda and I.K. Gujral proved fractious and ineffective. In November 1997, a commission investigating Rajiv Gandhi's death linked a tiny, Tamil Nadu-based UF constituent party to Sri Lankan guerrillas implicated in the assassination. Congress withdrew its support from the UF, leading President K.R. Narayanan to call for fresh elections.

With Congress suffering splits and defections and apparently headed for a worse defeat than in 1996, Sonia Gandhi, Rajiv Gandhi's widow, broke a long political silence and galvanized the party with more than 140 campaign speeches nationwide in January and February 1998. Gandhi, 51, apologized for past Congressional mistakes and attacked the BJP as divisive and inimical to India's secular traditions. The BJP campaigned as the only party that could deliver strong, stable government and fight corruption. The party also promised to introduce protectionist economic policies, eliminate the separate Shari'a (Islamic law) code for marriage, divorce and inheritance followed by the country's 120 million Muslims, build a Hindu temple at the site of the Babri mosque, and consider "inducting" nuclear weapons into the country's arsenal.

However, for many Indians the primary concern appeared to be rising food and fuel prices, unemployment, and the need for better housing and services. In voting staggered over three weeks between February 16 and March 7, the BJP (178 seats) and its allies won 245 seats; Congress (140 seats) and its allies, 166; the UF, 95; minor parties and vacant, 39. Throughout India, voters rejected parties in power at the state level. The BJP made inroads in southern Andhra Pradesh and Tamil Nadu states, but lost seats in two former strongholds, Maharashtra and Rajasthan. Commentators said the "Sonia effect" had prevented Congress from being routed.

In the aftermath, Gandhi consolidated her control of the Congress party by becoming president and parliamentary leader, even though she did not stand in the elections. In late March, the BJP and more than a dozen allies won a vote of confidence with 274 votes, and formed a government under Atal Bihari Vajpayee.

The BJP gave up most of its sectarian agenda in order to attract secular parties into its coalition. But in May, India carried out a series of underground nuclear tests, which the government said were in response to a growing Chinese military threat. The opposition accused the government of isolating India diplomatically, of incurring trade, banking, and aid sanctions imposed by the United States and other countries, and of betraying the 350 million Indians living in absolute poverty. Many urban Hindus initially supported the tests as an assertion of the country's geopolitical aspirations, although anti-nuclear activists later sharply criticized the government's decision. Significantly, the June budget raised military spending by 14 percent.

By the fall, the coalition government's internal instability contributed to policy drift. With inflation rising and the federal deficit at nearly five percent of GDP, the government offered few solutions to the country's slowing economic growth. In November, the soaring price of onions and other staples helped Congress oust BJP governments in elections in Delhi and Rajasthan. Congress also fought off a BJP challenge in populous Madhya Pradesh.

Many observers believe Home Minister Lal Krishna Advani, the hardline BJP leader, is the real power behind the Vajpayee government. More broadly, observers suggest that the government is ultimately controlled by the National Volunteer Service (RSS), a far-right Hindu group modeled after 1930's European fascist parties. Vajpayee and other BJP leaders are RSS members, and the RSS reportedly vetted key cabinet appointments. The Vajpayee government reportedly replaced the governors of several key states with RSS supporters, and placed pro-RSS bureaucrats into top posts.

Political Rights and Civil Liberties:

Indian citizens can change their government democratically; however, widespread official corruption and the criminalization of politics perpetuate poverty, disease and illiteracy, and contribute to civil liberties violations.

The 1996 and 1998 elections were the fairest in India's history. Authorities monitored compliance with campaign spending limits and restricted the use of state resources for campaigning. Photo identity cards helped prevent fraud. Nevertheless, in the 1998 elections, the independent election commission ordered repolling in 1,420 of the 350,000 stations involved in the first stage of balloting. In Bihar, left-wing militants attacked polling stations, while in Assam and other northeastern states separatist militants exploded landmines and killed several election officials and candidates. On February 14, a series of bomb explosions in the southern city of Coimbatore killed 56 people shortly before a rally headed by L.K. Advani, the BJP president. Police blamed the explosions on two underground Islamic militant organizations. Overall, election violence killed more than 150 people.

In 1998, the election commission tightened the restrictions against participation by convicted criminals. Nevertheless, since the 1970's the criminalization of politics has accelerated. In February, the *New York Times* cited studies showing that more than a third of state legislators in Uttar Pradesh, India's most populous state, have criminal records. The London-based *Financial Times* reported that Indian newspapers claimed it took three kidnappings to pay for a poll campaign in the state. Nationwide, in 1997, the Election Commission estimated that 40 MP's and 700 state assembly representatives faced charges or had been convicted of offenses ranging from murder to extortion. In the 1996 vote, one study found that more than 1,500 of the 13,886 candidates had criminal records, including murder, kidnapping, rape, and extortion.

The situation is worst in the impoverished northern state of Bihar. Many legislators reportedly lead criminal gangs and buy their way into politics; gang warfare often pits upper-caste landowners against lower-caste tenant farmers; political killings are routine; and in 1997 the chief minister resigned after allegations that he and his associates stole nearly $300 million in state funds.

The constitution allows the central government to dissolve state governments following a breakdown in normal administration. Successive governments have misused this power to gain control of states under opposition administration, although in 1997 and 1998 President Narayanan persuaded central governments not to impose central rule on Uttar Pradesh despite political turmoil there. Overall, economic reforms are steadily devolving power to the states.

The judiciary is independent and in recent years has exercised unprecedented activism in response to public interest litigation over official corruption, environmental issues, and other matters. However, the judicial system has a backlog of more than 30 million cases, is widely considered to be subject to corruption and manipulation at the lower levels, and is largely inaccessible to the poor.

Police, army, and paramilitary forces are responsible for rape, torture, arbitrary detentions, "disappearances," and staged "encounter killings," and occasionally destroy homes, particularly in Kashmir, Punjab, and the northeastern states. (A separate report on Kashmir appears in the Related Territories section.) The 1983 Armed Forces (Punjab and Chandigarh) Special Powers Act grants security forces wide latitude to use lethal force in Punjab, where a brutal army crackdown in the early 1990s largely ended a Sikh insurgency that began in the early 1980s.

The broadly drawn 1980 National Security Act allows police to detain suspects for up to one year (two years in Punjab) without charges. Police torture of suspects and abuse of ordinary prisoners, particularly low-caste members, is routine, and rape of female convicts remains a problem. Since its establishment in 1993, the National Human Rights Commission has monitored custodial deaths and other incidences of torture, although it cannot investigate complaints of human rights violations committed by security forces. The Criminal Procedure Code requires central or state government approval for prosecutions of armed forces members, and in practice, this generally protects security forces from prosecution.

The seven states of northeast India, a resource-rich, strategic region awash in arms and drugs from Burma, continued to be swept by anti-government militancy and inter-tribal, internecine conflict among its 200 ethnic groups. In recent decades, hundreds of thousands of migrants from other parts of India and Bangladesh have settled in the region, generating local unrest over land tenure and underdevelopment. More than 40 mainly indigenous-based rebel armies are seeking either greater autonomy or independence. The 1958 Armed Forces (Special Powers) Act grants security forces broad powers to use lethal force and detention in Assam and four nearby states, and provides near immunity from prosecution for security forces acting under it. The army has committed atrocities with impunity during counterinsurgency operations in Assam, Manipur, and other states. Guerrillas commit hundreds of killings, abductions, and rapes each year, and extort millions of dollars annually from tea gardens and merchants. In May, Amnesty International reported that security forces are increasingly subjecting children in Manipur to torture, "disappearance," and extrajudicial executions, and occasionally rape mothers in front of their children.

Maoist Naxalite guerrillas control large areas and kill dozens of police, politicians, landlords and villagers each year in Andhra Pradesh, Madhya Pradesh, Bihar and Orissa. Guerrillas run parallel courts in parts of Bihar.

The private press is vigorous. The Official Secrets Act empowers authorities to censor security-related articles; in practice, authorities occasionally use the Act to limit criticism of the government. Journalists are occasionally harassed and attacked by government officials, party activists, militant Hindu groups and others. In 1998, police and soldiers increasingly arrested and attacked journalists in Assam and other northeastern states. Radio is both public and private, although the state-owned All India Radio is dominant, and its news coverage favors the government. The government maintains a monopoly on domestic television broadcasting. In recent years, foreign-backed satellite television channels have proliferated, although only about one-third of Indians have access to television, and only about one-eighth have access to any satellite channel. BJP leaders have proposed setting foreign equity limits on satellite channels.

Section 144 of the Criminal Procedure Code empowers state authorities to declare a state of emergency, restrict free assembly, and impose curfews. Authorities occasionally use Section 144 to prevent demonstrations. In recent years, authorities have forcibly suppressed protests against foreign-sponsored power projects. In April, Human Rights Watch reported that in recent months police and hired thugs had beaten and arbitrarily detained villagers who were protesting their forced relocation from the sites of two World Bank-supported power projects in central India. Police occasionally react to demonstrations that turn violent by opening fire on protesters.

Nongovernmental human rights organizations generally operate freely, but face harassment in rural areas from landlords and other powerful interests. In June, a court released on bail Rongthong Kuenley Dorji, the exile-based Bhutanese opposition leader. Authorities had arrested Kuenley in 1997 in response to a Bhutanese government extradition request.

Each year, dowry disputes cause several thousand women to be burnt to death, driven to suicide, or otherwise killed, and cause countless others to be harassed, beaten, or deserted by husbands. Although dowry is illegal, convictions in dowry deaths are rare. Rape and other violence against women is prevalent, and authorities take little action. Many of the hundreds of thousands of women and children in Indian brothels, including tens of thousands of Nepalese trafficking victims, are held in debt servitude and subjected to rape, beatings, and other torture in a system that thrives with the complicity of local officials. Hindu women are often denied inheritances, and under Shari'a (Islamic law), Muslim daughters generally receive half the inheritance a son receives. Tribal land systems, particularly in Bihar, deny tribal women the right to own land.

The constitution bars discrimination based on caste, but in practice members of so-called scheduled castes and scheduled tribes, as well as religious and ethnic minorities, routinely face discrimination. Scores of people are killed each year in caste-related violence. Freedom of religion is respected. However, the United Christian Forum for Human Rights, a lay Christian NGO, recorded more than 90 cases of rape, assault, Bible burning, and other violence against Christians in 1998, more violence than in any other year since independence. Most of the attacks took place in the BJP-controlled western state of Gujarat, where mobs also attacked several churches late in the year. Christian activists blamed several militant Hindu organizations linked to the BJP. The militant Hindu organizations denied responsibility but suggested the attacks were in retaliation for conversions by Christian missionaries.

Numerous religious traditions that place children in positions of servitude contribute to child sexual exploitation in rural India. Major cities have tens of thousands of street children, many of whom work as porters, vendors, and in other informal sector jobs. A 1996 Human Rights Watch/Asia report detailed illegal detentions, beatings, and torture of street children by police.

UNICEF estimates that up to 60 million children, mostly from lower castes and ethnic minorities, work in fireworks, carpet, and glass factories, as well as in agriculture and other sectors. Several million are bonded laborers. In 1996, the Supreme Court ordered states to enforce the 1986 Child Labor Act, which bans child labor in 16 industries but excludes agriculture and the informal sector, and directed employers to provide compensation to children in nine major industries. Notoriously corrupt inspectors compromise implementation. Trade unions are powerful and independent, and workers exercise their rights to bargain collectively and strike.

Most of the 70,000 Bangladeshi Chakma refugees in northeast India returned home in 1998.

Indonesia

Polity: Dominant party (military-influenced)
Economy: Capitalist-statist
Population: 207,400,000
PPP: $3,971
Life Expectancy: 62
Ethnic Groups: Javanese (45 percent), Sundanese (14 percent), Madurese (8 percent), Malay (8 percent), other (25 percent)
Capital: Jakarta

Political Rights: 6*
Civil Liberties: 4*
Status: Partly Free

Ratings change: Indonesia's political rights rating changed from 7 to 6, its civil liberties rating changed from 5 to 4, and its status canged from Not Free to Partly Free, following an easing of restrictions on freedoms of association and expression in the wake of President Suharto's May 1998 ouster.

Overview:

Peaceful student protests, mounting anger over the cronyism and corruption that brought Indonesia's economy to its knees, and a final explosion of rioting and mayhem in Jakarta and other cities swept President Suharto out of office in May 1998 after 32 years of often brutal authoritarian rule. Suharto's failure to plan for the inevitable transition left the world's fourth most populous country, once cynically hailed by some as a paragon of political stability, tottering at an historical crossroads. His successor, Vice President B.J. Habibie, inherited Indonesia's most severe economic crisis in a generation, including soaring unemployment and severe food shortages. By year's end, the Suharto-era power structure remained largely intact while students, trade unionists, human rights activists, and journalists continued to push Habibie into legalizing many once-banned activities, and the new president outlined plans for elections in 1999.

President Sukarno proclaimed Indonesia's independence from the Dutch in 1945. Following a left-wing coup attempt in 1965, the Army Strategic Reserve, headed by then-General Suharto, led a slaughter of an estimated 500,000 suspected Indonesian Communist Party members. In 1968, two years after assuming key political and military powers, Suharto formally became president.

Under Suharto's highly-centralized regime, economic development lifted millions of Indonesians out of poverty. But the president's family and cronies held interests in some 1,200 companies and controlled key trading monopolies. Rampant corruption drained state resources. In addition, authorities heavily restricted political and social freedoms. Suharto allowed only three political parties: the ruling Golkar; the Christian, nationalist Indonesian Democratic Party (PDI); and the Muslim-oriented United Development Party (PPP). However, neither the PDI nor the PPP functioned as a true opposition, and the 500-seat parliament had little independent power. In theory, the 1,000-member People's Consultative Assembly (MPR), consisting of the parliament plus 500 appointed members, elected the president and vice president every five years. In reality, the MPR merely rubber-stamped Suharto's decision to hold another term.

In 1996, a government-backed, rebel PDI faction ousted Megawati Sukarnoputri—the daughter of the first president and the leading opposition figure—as PDI leader, touching off the worst rioting in the capital since the mid-1970's. The May 1997 parliamentary elections followed a violent campaign. With the government having banned Megawati and several other PDI figures from running, the PPP became the party of protest. Official results gave Golkar 74 percent of the vote; the PPP, 22 percent; and the PDI, 3 percent.

By early August, the growing Asian financial crisis had forced the government to float the rupiah. Years of profligate borrowing and poor investment decisions had left Indonesian companies with some $80 billion in debt owed to foreign banks. As money began fleeing the economy, Indonesian companies began selling rupiah to cover their dollar-denominated debts. This triggered a vicious circle, as the rupiah's slide brought companies even closer to default. In late October, the government agreed to a $43 billion International Monetary Fund-led stabilization package conditioned on banking sector reforms and a reduction in trading monopolies owned by Suharto's relatives and cronies.

By January 1998, the rupiah's 70 percent tumble from its July level had caused food prices to skyrocket. Attacks against the ethnic Chinese minority, which had been accelerating in number since 1996, continued across Java, Sulawesi, Sumatra, and other parts of the archipelago. Because Suharto had allowed a handful of ethnic-Chinese to become prominent tycoons, many Indonesians accused ordinary ethnic Chinese traders of having gained their wealth through government connections. Many of the attacks appeared to be orchestrated, leading to speculation that the government was instigating the riots to deflect attention from the economy.

By February, students began demonstrating across the country over soaring prices and unemployment. These protests later made unprecedented demands for Suharto's resignation. Suharto repeated his pledges to reform the economy but took little action.

On March 11, Suharto had the MPR re-elect him for a seventh term. As protests intensified, police often violently attacked students who tried to take campus demonstrations into the streets.

In early May, Suharto raised prices for fuel, public transportation, and electricity by as much as 70 percent, provoking rioting in Medan and Ujung Padang. On May 12, security forces shot and killed six students during a demonstration at Jakarta's Trisakti University—the first students killed in several months of demonstrations—setting off three days of devastating riots across the country. Organized groups, believed by some to be soldiers, instigated deadly arson attacks on ethnic-Chinese businesses, raping and killing ethnic-Chinese women. The official National Commission on Human Rights later reported the rioting killed at least 1,188 people in Jakarta, mainly looters trapped in burning stores, and faulted security forces for failing to curb the mayhem.

The deaths of the Trisakti students caused unprecedented calls for Suharto's resignation from within the establishment, and soldiers allowed students to stage a sit-in at the parliament building. With his support among rank-and-file soldiers clearly crumbling, Suharto resigned on May 21. He was immediately succeeded by Vice President

B. J. Habibie, a long-time crony with little support in the political and military establishments. General Wiranto, the defense minister, consolidated his position over the armed forces by demoting General Prabowo Subianto, a Suharto son-in-law and the commander of the strategic reserves.

During the summer and fall, students continued demonstrating to demand Habibie's resignation, early elections, an end to the military's formal role in politics, and an investigation into Suharto's wealth. Habibie released some political prisoners, scrapped the ban on political parties, and ended numerous bans on freedom of expression and association. In November, a special session of the MPR scheduled fresh elections for June 1999, to be followed by an MPR session in August that will elect a new president. In December, prosecutors questioned Suharto on corruption allegations and indicated that charges could be forthcoming. Forbes magazine has estimated Suharto's personal wealth at $16 billion, and his family's overall wealth at $40 billion.

The country's political outlook is unclear. After three decades during which Suharto forcibly depoliticized society opposition figures have few grassroots connections to draw upon. Not surprisingly, many of the new political parties have formed around existing Muslim organizations. Some fear that this could introduce religion into politics for the first time in decades. Perhaps the best-positioned presidential candidate is Amien Rais, a Suharto critic and the leader of the urban Muslim-based, 28-million strong Muhammadiyah organization. Megawati Sukarnoputri is also expected to compete as the PDI's candidate on a secular, nationalist platform.

Indonesia also experienced a severe social crisis. Poverty had returned to mid-1970s levels; inflation leveled off but only after reaching an annualized rate of 82 percent in the first three quarters; and food prices were still punishingly high. With the banking system paralyzed by bad loans and corporate bankruptcies mounting, the economy was expected to contract 13.7 percent for the year, with tens of millions of people facing severe poverty and hunger. The hardship was blamed for the sporadic rioting, arson, and looting against ethnic-Chinese businesses that continued throughout the archipelago.

Political Rights and Civil Liberties:

Indonesians lack the democratic means to change their government. While many of the tight restrictions on political activity and free expression that characterized the Suharto era have been lifted, the existing power structure will remain in place at least until the June 1999 parliamentary elections. Even then, the presidency will continue to be indirectly elected. Under the doctrine of dwifungsi (dual function), the armed forces are responsible for territorial defense and for maintaining internal cohesion. The military currently holds 15 percent of seats in national, provincial, and district legislatures, and it is not yet clear whether they will be forced to relinquish this perogative. Moreover, the overarching consensus-oriented Pancasila philosophy, which Suharto had used to justify restrictions on human rights, is still considered to be the guiding state ideology. While the 1999 elections will undoubtedly be freer than the tightly controlled exercises that took place under Suharto, the government has yet to articulate fully the electoral laws and rules.

The most severe rights' violations occur in Aceh, East Timor, and Irian Jaya (separate reports on East Timor and Irian Jaya appear in the Related Territories section). In the resource-rich Aceh province on the tip of Sumatra, the military's counterinsurgency operation against Aceh Merdeka (Free Aceh) separatists peaked between 1989-92, although there have been continuing reports of killings, incommunicado detentions, and other abuses. In April, the New York-based Human Rights Watch estimated that hundreds of Acehnese are being detained without charge or trial. In early August, Defense Minister Wiranto offered an unprecedented apology for past army abuses in Aceh, and pledged to withdraw combat troops fully from the province. Several weeks later, rioting flared as the last contingent of soldiers pulled out. Soldiers fired on rioters and the army postponed the withdrawal. Some observers accused the military of instigating the unrest as a pretext for maintaining troops in Aceh. Also in August, the Legal Aid Foundation, a nongovernmental organization (NGO) with branches throughout the country, said that ten mass graves had been found in the province, believed to contain the remains of hundreds of people killed by soldiers during counterinsurgency operations in the early 1990s.

The judiciary is not independent and is rife with corruption. The executive branch appoints and can dismiss or reassign judges at will. Police frequently torture suspects and prisoners.

Human rights groups have documented an apparently organized campaign of attacks, public gang rapes, and killings of ethnic-Chinese women in several cities during the mid-May riots, with at least 100 women and girls attacked in Jakarta alone. Numerous human rights groups have accused soldiers of instigating and participating in the attacks. In the ensuing months, activists investigating the attacks received death threats, and in October unknown assailants brutally murdered an ethnic-Chinese woman in Jakarta who had counseled the rape victims.

The Agency for Coordination of Assistance for the Consolidation of National Security (BAKORSTANAS) has wide latitude in curbing alleged security threats. The Habibie government has maintained the 1963 Anti-Subversion Law, which Suharto had used to imprison hundreds of political prisoners for peaceful dissent. In April, the International Commission of Jurists (ICJ) released a report on six anti-subversion trials that it observed in 1997, which it said were characterized by improper procedures, witness tampering, and other irregularities. The ICJ criticized the Anti-Subversion Law for allowing authorities to detain suspects for up to one year without charge, which it said contributed to torture and ill treatment of detainees. The Suharto government had also jailed hundreds of people, many of them political dissidents, under sedition or hate-sowing statutes, and had frequently cited alleged Communist threats to chill free expression and justify crackdowns on political and social activists.

In the months after taking office, Habibie released several political prisoners, including labor leader Muchtar Pakpahan. However, several dozen political prisoners are still jailed, including Dita Indah Sari, a labor activist who in 1997 received a six-year term for organizing a 1996 strike.

Under Suharto, security forces violated human rights with impunity. While it is too early to detect any real improvement, the new government has taken the positive measure of acknowledging that abuses have occurred. In December, authorities opened the court martial of 11 members of Kopassus, an elite security force, on charges of kidnapping more than 20 anti-Suharto activists earlier in the year. Survivors had reported being tortured, and by year's end, at least 13 kidnap victims were still missing. However, critics charged that the soldiers were used as scapegoats to protect former Kopassus leader and Suharto son-in-law Prabawo Subianto, who had been sacked from the armed forces in August after a military inquiry found that troops under his command were responsible for abductions and torture.

Under Suharto, authorities frequently denied the permits required for public assemblies and demonstrations, and police often forcibly broke up peaceful, unsanctioned demonstrations. In 1998, student demonstrations that began in February played a pivotal role in Suharto's downfall. Police and soldiers generally tolerated campus demonstrations, but violently repelled students who tried to take their protests to the streets. As protests continued after Suharto's ouster, police opened fire on demonstrators at times, either with rubber bullets or with live ammunition. More than 15 people were killed in clashes in mid-November as students protested during a special meeting of the MPR. Earlier, in October, parliament adopted a law allowing demonstrations and guaranteeing freedom of speech. However, the law made organizers of demonstrations responsible for the conduct of participants, which could make organizers legally liable if demonstrations get out of control.

During Suharto's rule, the approximately 286 private newspapers and magazines operated under frequent threats from authorities to kill sensitive stories, and they practiced considerable self-censorship. Political coverage on TVRI and other state-owned media heavily favored Golkar. Suharto supporters own all five private television stations, and until recently, coverage favored the ex-president. However, in the weeks following Suharto's mid-March re-election, the print media began openly criticizing the president, and private television stations reported on student demonstrations and revelations of torture by the armed forces. By August, the Habibie government had issued 60 new publishing licenses, including licenses for magazines that had been banned by Suharto. However, the rupiah's slide in value sent the cost of imported newsprint soaring, forcing some provincial papers to close. In recent years, authorities had arrested several journalists associated with the independent Alliance of Independent Journalists or with underground political publications. The Alliance and other press groups now operate legally.

Under Suharto, authorities frequently imprisoned NGO activists, restricted them from public speaking, and raided their offices. The Habibie government scrapped a permit requirement for gatherings of more than ten people, and NGOs now operate more freely. However, as the October murder of a Jakarta NGO activist (see above) indicates, human rights protections in post-Suharto Indonesia are still fragile. Meanwhile, the official National Commission on Human Rights continued to gain credibility by investigating the violence that surrounded Suharto's final days in office.

In addition to being targeted for violent attacks in recent years, ethnic Chinese face severe cultural, educational, and business restrictions. Islam is the official religion, and 90 percent of the population is Muslim. In recent years, numerous churches have been razed during attacks against ethnic Chinese, many of whom are Christian. Christians often have difficulty obtaining permits to build churches. Women face discrimination in education and employment opportunities. Female genital mutilation is widely practiced. Thousands of street children live in Jakarta and other cities.

In the fall, there were at least 182 murders of Koranic teachers and alleged black magicians on Java. Observers said the killings appeared to be organized, and some suspected the army's involvement.

The Habibie government ended the de facto monopoly of the government-controlled All Indonesian Workers Union. It also signed an International Labor Organization covenant on freedom of association and recognized the dissident Indonesian Welfare Labor Organization, headed by Muchtar Pakpahan. In a country where the military frequently intervened on behalf of factory owners in labor disputes, workers are now holding their largest strikes in decades. Yet actual guarantees for labor rights remain poor, and factory owners routinely ignore minimum wages, dismiss labor activists and strike leaders, and physically abuse workers.

In addition to the wholesale graft and influence peddling carried out by the Suharto family, corruption is pervasive at all levels of government. Ordinary citizens reportedly must pay bribes to receive routine services, and security forces frequently take bribes to ignore labor abuses and other civil liberties violations.

Iran

Polity: Presidential-
parliamentary
(clergy-dominated)
Economy: Capitalist-statist
Population: 64,100,000
PPP: $5,480
Life Expectancy: 67

Political Rights: 6
Civil Liberties: 6*
Status: Not Free

Ethnic Groups: Persian (51 percent), Azerbaijani (24 percent),
Gilaki and Mazandarani (8 percent), Kurd (7 percent), Arab (3 percent),
Lur (2 percent), Baloch (2 percent), Turkmen (2 percent), other (1 percent)
Capital: Teheran
Ratings change: Iran's civil liberties rating changed from 7 to 6 because of increased tolerance of political expression and association.

Overview:
Nineteen ninety-eight saw an escalation of tensions between Iran's hardline ruling establishment, led by Ayatollah Ali Khamenei, and its relatively moderate president, Mohammed Khatami. Khatami's vocal support for economic reform, rule of law, civil society, and improved foreign relations has put him at odds with hardliners who see him as a threat to Iran's theocratic state. Whenever possible, conservatives have used their legal and moral authority to undermine him and to block any efforts at reform.

In January 1979, Shah Mohammad Reza Pahlavi, the hereditary monarch whose decades-long authoritarian rule was marked by widespread corruption, fled Iran amid mounting religious and political unrest. A month later, the exiled Ayatollah Ruhollah Khomeini returned to lead the formation of the world's first Islamic republic. The 1979 constitution provides for a directly elected president and a 12-member Council of Guardians, which certifies that all bills passed by the directly elected, 270-member *majlis* accord with Islamic law. The Council must approve all presidential and parliamentary candidates, and thus maintains the political dominance of a few Shi'ite Muslim clerics and their allies. Khomeini was named supreme religious leader for life and invested with control over the security and intelligence services, armed forces, and the judiciary. He was also invested with the power to dismiss the president following a legislative request or a ruling by the Supreme Court and given the final word in all areas of national and foreign policy.

Following Khomeini's death in June 1989, Ayatollah Ali Khamenei assumed the role of supreme religious leader and chief of state. That August, Ali Akbar Hashemi Rafsanjani, a cleric, became president after running unopposed and winning nearly 95 percent of the vote. During his first term, Rafsanjani introduced limited free-market reforms, overcoming opposition from hardliners favoring statist economic policies. Again unopposed, he won a second term in 1993. But this time, he won only 63 percent of the vote, reflecting popular discontent with declining living standards due largely to the economic devastation resulting from the 1980-88 war with Iraq.

Popular disaffection has grown in recent years because of the rising cost of living, a huge foreign debt, and 25 percent inflation. Since the revolution, per-capita income has decreased while prices of basic items such as food and fuel have soared. Furthermore, two-thirds of Iranians are under age 25, and do not identify closely with the ideals of the revolution. They are increasingly resentful of a government that restricts personal freedom while offering little in the way of education and employment opportunities.

In March 1997, the Council of Guardians selected four of 238 hopefuls for the race to succeed Rafsanjani, who was constitutionally barred from seeking a third term. Speaker of parliament Ali Akbar Nateq-Nouri, the favorite of Khamenei and the majority conservatives in the *majlis*, was expected to claim an easy victory over Khatami, a former culture minister who was forced to resign in 1992 because he was considered too tolerant. But Khatami's liberal reputation won him the support of intellectuals, women, youths, and business groups who seek greater social openness as well as an end to state interference in the economy. Ninety percent of the electorate turned out to vote, and 70 percent voted for Khatami.

Under the constraints of a highly restrictive political system, Khatami holds very little real power. He is accountable to the conservative-dominated *majlis* and bound by the absolute authority of the supreme leader. Thus, in his first year and a half in office, he has been unable to implement the kind of institutional reforms reportedly favored by most Iranians. He cannot realistically challenge the religious basis of the government, and therefore cannot legislate political pluralism. In response to his efforts, his supporters have been harassed, jailed, and in some cases murdered by hardline elements. Notably, Teheran mayor and close Khatami ally Gholamhossein Karbaschi was tried and convicted in July on charges of graft. He was sentenced to five years in prison and 60 lashes, fined $333,000, and banned from public office for 20 years.

Yet Khatami's popularity has afforded him room to maneuver politically, and he has successfully asserted his authority on a number of issues. Domestically, he won approval for his choice of Minister of Culture and Islamic Guidance, Ataollah Mohajerani, a controversial figure who has been criticized by hardliners for advocating dialogue with the U.S. Since then, restrictions on publishing, filmmaking, and the news media have been loosened. In an unusual turn of events, Karbaschi's trial was televised live. Women are taking liberties in their dress and are increasingly allowed to attend sporting events, and even to participate in recreational activities alongside men. And Iranians have turned out on a number of occasions to protest vociferously against the arrests of dissident clerics and politicians.

Khatami also achieved success with his foreign policy. When foreign minister Kamal

Kharazzi declared in September that the government would not carry out the nine-year-old fatwa against Salman Rushdie, Britain agreed to an exchange of ambassadors and discussed opening "a new chapter" in relations between Iran and the European Union. Khatami sparked a thaw in U.S.-Iran relations with a televised CNN interview in January and an address to the UN General Assembly in September. He expressed regret over the 1979 seizure of American hostages in Teheran and invited Americans to participate in "a dialogue of civilizations." In response, the Clinton administration defied Congress to waive sanctions against three foreign companies that invest in the Iranian oil industry. Arab-Iranian relations have improved under Khatami as well. An agreement with Saudi Arabia in May provides for cooperation in economic, scientific, and cultural affairs. And agreements with Iraq have led to the exchange of thousands of prisoners of war this year.

Political Rights and Civil Liberties:

Iranians cannot change their government democratically. As all legislative and presidential candidates must support the ruling theocracy, meaningful opposition is effectively barred. Political parties are strongly discouraged, and the few that exist are not allowed to participate in elections. As the power struggle between reformists and hardliners intensified in 1998, supporters of Khatami have formed their own political groupings and have won legal recognition by the interior ministry. Over 100 political and cultural figures founded the Islamic Iran Participation Front in November with the objective of promoting civil participation, social justice, and the rule of law.

The March 1997 presidential election was marred by violations of free expression and low-level harassment of Khatami's campaign. No international observers were permitted to oversee polling or ballot counting.

The state continues to maintain control through terror: arbitrary detention, torture, disappearance, summary trial, and execution are commonplace. A penal code adopted in 1996 is based on *shari'a* (Islamic) law and provides for the death penalty for a range of social and political misconduct. Human Rights Watch reported that hundreds of people were executed in 1998 after trials that failed to comply with minimum international standards of fairness. The intelligence and interior ministries operate vast informant networks. Security forces enter homes and offices, open mail, and monitor telephone conversations without court authorization.

Extrajudicial killings have been used by hardline factions to silence political criticism, apparently with the encouragement of the supreme leader. Ayatollah Khamenei made statements urging that conspirators against the *velayat-e faqih*, or absolute power of the preeminent religious jurist, be dealt with "firmly." The statements have been interpreted as a green light for a campaign against dissent. Dariush Forouhar, the former labor minister and head of the Iran Nation Party, and his wife Parvaneh, who were outspoken critics of human and political rights violations, were murdered in November. Four writers were also killed at the end of the year, evidently for criticizing the Islamic regime.

The judiciary is not independent. Judges, like all officials, must meet strict political and religious qualifications. Bribery is common. Civil courts provide some procedural safeguards, though judges may serve simultaneously as prosecutors during trials. Revolutionary courts try political and religious cases, but are often arbitrarily assigned cases that normally fall under civil court jurisdiction. Charges are often vague, detainees are often denied access to legal counsel, and revolutionary courts do not uphold due process. There is no right of appeal.

Press freedom improved slightly in 1998, though tolerance remains arbitrary and crackdowns occurred. At least 11 journalists were arrested and charged with offenses such as "publishing insults and lies" and "propagating anti-Islamic attitudes." One journalist was found guilty of slandering the armed forces and banned from the profession for a year. Several newspapers and journals which criticized the Iranian leadership were closed down. Besides official repression, hardline vigilantism emerged as a new threat to the press, apparently in response to the greater freedom exercised by journalists. Two outspoken journalists and two writers/translators were abducted and murdered in November and December.

The broadcast media remain closely controlled by conservatives, although there were some bright spots. The Karbaschi trial, which was televised live, exposed misconduct in the judicial system as Karbaschi accused authorities of torturing senior municipality officials to extract false confessions against him. Also, the Farsi-language service of Radio Free Europe/Radio Liberty began broadcasting to Iran in October. The print media are enjoying considerable new freedom, and it has been reported that some 1,000 new newspapers and journals have been licensed since Khatami became president. One notable paper, *Jameah*, published interviews with the head of the outlawed Freedom Movement and with a former government spokesman convicted of spying for the U.S. *Jameah* has been shut down and has reopened twice under different names.

The constitution permits public assembly as long as it does not "violate the principles of Islam." Thousands of protesters against the prosecution of Karbaschi were dispersed, at times violently, by riot police in April. Hardline militants attacked some 2,000 mourners of slain dissidents Dariush and Parvaneh Forouhar in December. As police restored order, they arrested a number of the mourners, but no militants.

Women face discrimination in legal, educational, and employment matters. Women's rights provided yet another arena in the battle between hardliners and moderates, and the issue has gained increasing prominence since Khatami's election. In a positive development, the *majlis* passed a law in November allowing judges to award custody of minor children to the mother in divorce cases. In a break with taboo, women attended celebrations of the national soccer team's advancement to the World Cup alongside men, and openly flouted the dress code without penalty. Women may be fined, imprisoned, or lashed for violating Islamic dress codes, though enforcement of these provisions slackened somewhat this year. Unlike women in Saudi Arabia and the Gulf states, Iranian women may vote, stand for public office, and drive. However, a woman must have permission from a male relative to obtain a passport.

Religious freedom is limited. The 1979 constitution recognizes Zoroastrians, Jews, and Christians as religious minorities. Authorities rarely grant approval for publication of Christian texts, and church services are routinely monitored. Christians and Jews are restricted in opening schools, and in areas such as employment, education, and property ownership. Demonstrable knowledge of Islam is required for university admission and civil service employment. Jewish families may not travel abroad together.

The Baha'i faith is not recognized. Some 300,000 Iranian Baha'is face official discrimination, a complete lack of property rights, arbitrary detention, a ban on university admission, heavy employment restrictions, and prohibitions on teaching their faith and practicing their religion communally. According to the National Spiritual Assembly of the Baha'is of the United States, over 200 Baha'is have been executed since 1979. In July 1998, a Baha'i convicted of converting a Muslim to the Baha'i faith was executed by stoning. The Iranian Kurdish community also faces state-sanctioned discrimination.

There are no independent labor unions. The government-controlled Worker's House is the only legal federation. Collective bargaining is nonexistent. Private sector strikes are infrequent and risk being disbanded by the militant Revolutionary Guards. Over 100 people were detained in Najafabad when merchants repeatedly closed their shops in protest over the house arrest of Ayatollah Hossein Ali Montazeri, the 75-year-old former heir apparent to Khomeini. Montazeri fell out of favor for questioning Khamenei's legitimacy as supreme leader.

Iraq

Polity: One-party
Economy: Statist
Population: 21,800,000
PPP: $3,170
Life Expectancy: 59
Ethnic Groups: Arab (75-80 percent), Kurd (15-20 percent), other, including Turkoman and Assyrian (5 percent)
Capital: Baghdad

Political Rights: 7
Civil Liberties: 7
Status: Not Free

Overview:

The Iraqi government began and ended 1998 in confrontation with the international community over UN-mandated weapons inspections and trade sanctions. Throughout the year, President Saddam Hussein exploited divisions among the states that were allied against him in the 1990 Persian Gulf War and reached out for support from his Arab neighbors. He also maintained domestic control by executing political prisoners and opponents while easing some restrictions on the Iraqi people, who suffered through their eighth year of sanctions.

Iraq gained formal independence in 1932, though the British maintained influence over the Hashemite monarchy. In 1958, the monarchy was overthrown in a military coup. A 1968 coup established a government under the Arab Ba'ath (Renaissance) Socialist Party, which has kept power since. The frequently amended 1968 provisional constitution designated the Revolutionary Command Council (RCC) as the country's highest power, and granted it virtually unlimited and unchecked authority. In 1979, Saddam Hussein, long considered the strongman of the regime, formally assumed the titles of state president and RCC chairman.

In 1980, Iraq attacked Iran, touching off an eight-year war of attrition during which the economy suffered extensively and at least 150,000 Iraqis died. In August 1990, Iraq invaded Kuwait. At least 100,000 Iraqi troops were killed in the Persian Gulf War before a 22-nation coalition liberated Kuwait in February 1991. In April, the UN Security Council passed Resolution 687, which called on Iraq to destroy its weapons of mass destruction, to accept long-term monitoring of its weapons facilities, and to recognize Kuwait's sovereignty. The UN also imposed an oil embargo on Iraq, which may be lifted when the government complies with the terms of Resolution 687.

Iraq barred United Nations Special Commision (UNSCOM) weapons inspectors from dozens of presidential palaces in January 1998. Inspectors suspected that the palaces were used as storage sites for weapons and military materials. Iraq denied this and claimed that inspection teams were spying for the U.S.; the U.S. responded by preparing to take military action. Other UN Security Council members such as France, Russia, and China, increasingly eager to renew economic ties with Iraq, called for diplomacy and expressed concern about the ineffectiveness of and suffering caused by sanctions.

As Iraq gained sympathy from some Security Council members, it also improved relations with Arab neighbors by releasing Egyptians, Jordanians, and Palestinians from its jails. Diplomatic ties with Iran, severed since 1988, were renewed in January when the two countries held discussions that led to prisoner exchanges and the opening of holy sites in Iraq to Iranian religious pilgrims and tourists.

Military strikes by the U.S. and Britain were averted in February when UN General Secretary Kofi Annan negotiated an agreement that allowed for inspections of some palaces. It also subjected inspection teams to greater international oversight and provided Iraq with assurances that the easing or complete lifting of sanctions would be reviewed every six months.

Chief weapons inspector Richard Butler's April progress report to the Security Council recommended that sanctions remain in place. According to Butler, Iraq had provided much information about its nuclear and chemical weapons programs, but was less forthcoming about biological weapons. Iraq maintained that it was in compliance with Resolution 687 and demanded an end to sanctions.

Iraq's claims of compliance were undercut in June when traces of a nerve agent were found on missile fragments in an Iraqi weapons dump. The discovery prompted a protracted standoff. In September, the Security Council voted 15-0 to suspend sanction reviews, and thus guaranteed no chance of relief for Iraq until it fully complied with UN resolutions. By October, Iraq had ended all cooperation with UNSCOM, and the U.S. began building up its forces in the Gulf. Britain and the U.S. launched air strikes against military and potential weapons production sites in December. Other Gulf War coalition partners had advocated a diplomatic solution and did not participate in the strikes. Although Iraq's regional neighbors had warned Saddam to cooperate with the UN, only Kuwait fully supported the use of force against Iraq.

Iraqi citizens continued to suffer in 1998. A population that was considered overweight before 1991 was barely receiving the UN's recommended minimum daily calorie intake in 1998. One-quarter of all Iraqi children under five years old suffered from malnutrition. In February, the UN increased the amount of oil that Iraq could sell for food from $2 to $5.2 billion every six months. Yet Iraq could only sell $1.6 billion from May to November because of falling oil prices, deteriorating production facilities, and delays in receiving replacement parts. The UN also allowed Iraq to increase medical imports from $220 million in 1997 to $770 million in 1998, but shortages of basic medicines continued. Meanwhile, black markets thrived, and, according to one high-level defector, officials used revenues from oil smuggling to build up Iraq's security forces. In January 1998, rival Kurdish factions continued talks which started in November 1997 over re-establishing joint governance of the territory they control in northern Iraq. The Kurdistan Democratic Party (KDP) and the Patriotic Union of Kurdistan (PUK) have been at odds since 1994 over the administration of territory and revenues from cross-border trade with Turkey. In September, the two sides signed a formal peace agreement brokered by the U.S. Throughout 1998, Kurdish leaders expressed hopes for negotiation with Saddam and emphasized that they sought autonomy within a united Iraq, not full independence.

Political Rights and Civil Liberties:

Iraqis cannot change their government democratically. Saddam holds supreme power in one of the world's most repressive regimes. Relatives and close friends from Saddam's hometown of Tikrit hold most key positions. A 1991 law outlaws opposition parties, and the 250-seat national assembly has no power.

The regime eased some restrictions on the press in 1998. In March, non-Ba'ath papers were allowed to publish for the first time since 1968. Criticism of local officials and investigation into corruption was occasionally tolerated as long as it did not extend to Saddam or major policy issues. The government made little effort to block the signal of the newly launched Radio Free Iraq in October, and several analysts concluded that Iraq was trying to improve its international image through a more open media. Nonetheless, the government carefully controls most information available to Iraqis, and one journalist was detained in August over a series of articles on corruption. Satellite dishes have been banned since 1994, and penalties for ownership include confiscation of all household furniture, fines, and imprisonment.

Citizens are denied freedom of speech, assembly, and religion. The rule of law is nonexistent. Saddam's son, a newspaper publisher, is allowed to make arbitrary decisions in criminal cases. State control is maintained by the extensive use of intimidation through arrest, torture, and summary execution.

Although some safeguards for defendants exist in civil cases, political and "economic" cases are tried in separate security courts, where confessions extracted through torture are admissible as evidence, and no procedural safeguards are apparent. Punishments are often disproportionate to the crimes committed. Theft, corruption, desertion from the army, and currency speculation are punishable by amputation, branding, and execution. Doctors have been executed for refusing to carry out these punishments and for attempting reconstructive surgery. The UN and exiled opposition groups reported that at least 1,500 political prisoners had been executed in 1997. By October 1998, continued reports of political executions and torture prompted Human Rights Commissioner Max Von Stoel to conclude that no human rights improvements had been made in Iraq.

The Shi'ite Muslim majority, comprising over 60 percent of the population, faces severe persecution. The army has arrested thousands of Shi'ites and executed an undetermined number of these detainees. Security forces have desecrated Shi'ite mosques and holy sites. The army has indiscriminately targeted civilian Shi'ite Marsh Arab villagers, razed homes, and drained southern Amara and Hammar marshes in order to flush out Shi'ite guerillas. By 1998, analysts concluded that the regime had made Shi'ites in the south submissive and dependent through its overwhelming military presence and the administration of food and housing.

A 1981 law gives the government control over mosques, the appointment of clergy, and the publication of religious literature. The government harasses the small Turcomen and Christian Assyrian communities, and Jewish citizens face restrictions on travelling abroad and on communications with Jews outside Iraq. In 1998, displays of Shi'ite religious symbols were allowed and clerics could preach publicly. Yet two outspoken clerics were murdered in mysterious circumstances in June.

The state-backed General Federation of Trade Unions is the only legal labor federation. Independent unions do not exist. The right to collective bargaining is not recognized by law and is not practiced. The right to strike is limited by law, and strikes do not occur.

Human rights monitors and other observers are restricted from investigating abuses. The government and security forces have harassed, intimidated, and reportedly offered rewards for killing international relief personnel.

Men are granted immunity for killing daughters or wives caught committing "immoral deeds." Women are not permitted to travel abroad unescorted by a male relative. Numerous areas are off-limits for travel inside the country. Foreign travel for all citizens is tightly restricted. In 1998, the government imposed extremely high exit fees on Iraqis leaving the country and, in an attempt to staunch "brain drain," banned the emigration of well-educated citizens. These measures led to increases of illegal migration to Greece, Turkey, and Jordan. Within Iraq, the regime continued relocation policies of "Arabization" in 1998. At least 1,600 Kurds were removed from the oil-rich Kirkuk area and sent to Kurdish enclaves in the North.

Ireland

Polity: Parliamentary democracy
Economy: Capitalist
Population: 3,700,000
PPP: $17,590
Life Expectancy: 75
Ethnic Groups: Celtic, English minority
Capital: Dublin

Political Rights: 1
Civil Liberties: 1
Status: Free

Overview:

Despite concerns that his minority ruling coalition would fray, Fianna Fail's Bertie Ahern and his Progressive Democrat partners worked together successfully in 1998 and presided over unprecedented economic prosperity, a Northern Ireland peace settlement, and preparations for the January 1999 launch of the Euro. In fact, the only threat to the government's stability appears to be the outcome of investigations into two payments-to-politicians scandals that have tainted political figures close to the prime minister.

Ireland's 26 counties held Dominion status within the British Commonwealth from 1921 until 1948, when Ireland became a fully independent state. The six counties of Northern Ireland remained part of the United Kingdom at the insistence of their Protestant majority (See *Northern Ireland* under United Kingdom, Related Territories). Despite Articles 2 and 3 of the Irish constitution, which claim Irish sovereignty over the entire island, the republic has played only a consultative role in Northern affairs, as defined by the 1985 Anglo-Irish accord. As part of the 1998 peace agreement, the Irish voted in May to amend the articles so that a united Ireland may not be established without the consent of a majority of people in both jurisdictions. The government has until April 1999 to implement the amendments, based on its satisfaction that other parts of the agreement are in place.

After June 1997 elections, Ahern assembled a coalition of his populist Fianna Fail, the right-of-center Progressive Democrats, and a handful of independents to unseat John Bruton's Fine Gael-led "Rainbow Coalition" with Labor and the Democratic Left. Although Bruton's two-and-a-half year-old government presided over the largest economic boom in Irish history—7 percent growth per year since 1994—and led a major effort to reduce drug-related crime, he came under attack over a stalemate in the Northern Ireland peace process and was denounced for being "soft" on Sinn Fein. His integrity was also called into doubt by a questionable donation made to Fine Gael by a department store magnate.

As expected, Ahern brought no major policy changes to the new government; economic policy is largely determined by Maastricht Treaty provisions for European Monetary Union (EMU), and Ireland is set to join the single currency in January 1999. The current wave of economic prosperity is expected to last well into the next decade. In a referendum on May 22, 62 percent of Irish voters approved the Amsterdam treaty on closer ties with the European Union. The treaty, a successor to the Maastricht treaty of 1992, provides for greater cooperation on health, crime, unemployment, and the environment among EU states.

The prime minister's popularity was boosted by his success in helping to bring about a peace settlement in Northern Ireland. Described by the *Financial Times* as a renowned conciliator, Ahern quickly established good relations with British Prime Minister Tony Blair as well as the head of the Ulster Unionist Party in Northern Ireland, David Trimble. With concessions to Gerry Adams' republican Sinn Fein, including Irish Republican Army (IRA) prisoner releases, he helped win an IRA ceasefire in 1997 and bolstered Sinn Fein's participation in the final agreement on April 10, 1998. The "Good Friday Agreement" recognizes the "principle of consent" in the status of Northern Ireland, creates a 108-member assembly to be elected by proportional representation, establishes a north-south ministerial council to consult on matters of mutual concern to Ireland and Northern Ireland, and establishes a British-Irish council of British, Irish, Northern Irish, Scottish, and Welsh representatives to discuss particular policy issues. In a May referendum, 94 percent of Irish voted in favor of the agreement.

The government's stability may suffer as a result of the Moriarty and Flood tribunals, two government-appointed high court investigations into questionable political donations and possible abuse of planning rules. Former Fianna Fail leader and Ahern ally Charles Haughey faces the threat of prison if convicted of misleading an investigation into payments made to him by a prominent businessman while he was prime minister in the early 1980s. Ray Burke resigned as Ahern's foreign minister in late 1997 and remains under investigation for alleged undeclared payments from a North Dublin builder. Although Ahern has emerged virtually unscathed from the current scandals, there is concern that the investigations may unearth new allegations, prompting Mary Harney's Progressive Democrats to withdraw support for the government.

Political Rights and Civil Liberties: Irish citizens can change their government democratically. Northern Irish are considered citizens and may run for office in the republic. Currently, only diplomatic families and security forces living abroad may vote by absentee ballot.

Civil liberties activists have denounced Ireland's refusal to incorporate the European Convention on Human Rights into domestic law. Currently, Irish citizens who believe that particular laws or court decisions violate their rights under the Convention cannot bring grievances to the Irish courts, since the Convention is not part of Irish law. But they may not go to the European Commission or the Court of Human Rights in Strasbourg unless they have "exhausted domestic remedies," namely the Irish courts. Great Britain recently incorporated the Convention into its law, thereby giving Northern Irish citizens access to the Convention through the Northern courts.

A 56-year-old state of emergency was lifted in 1995, though the government stopped short of revoking all special powers associated with emergency law. These include special search, arrest, and detention powers of the police, and the juryless Special Criminal Court (SCC) for suspected terrorists. The SCC involves a three-judge panel instead of a jury, and the sworn statement of a police chief identifying the accused as a member of an illegal organization is accepted as prima facie evidence. The Irish Council for Civil Liberties expressed concern that high-profile drug and crime cases would be heard increasingly in the SCC as the number of cases linked to the Northern conflict declines. Such fears were confirmed when it was decided last year that the case of Paul Ward, charged with the 1996 murder of journalist Veronica Guerin, would be tried in the SCC.

The Irish government announced "draconian" measures to combat terrorism after a bombing in Omagh, Northern Ireland, by a radical Republican group in August killed 28 people. These measures include curtailing the right to silence so that a court may infer guilt from the silence of a suspected terrorist or member of an outlawed organization, and extending the maximum period of detention without trial from 48 to 72 hours under the Offences Against the State Act. The measures were implemented less than a month after the bombing, and one suspect was detained under the revised law in early September.

The Irish media are free, though they may not publish or broadcast anything likely to undermine state authority or promote violence. In addition to international cable broadcasts, international newspapers, particularly from Britain, are gaining a growing share of the Irish market. The government has been accused of placing Irish newspapers at a disadvantage by levying on them the highest value-added tax in the EU. Concentrated ownership and harsh libel laws also restrict information.

The Supreme Court in March lifted an injunction against Radio Telefis Eireann (RTE), whose journalists were investigating an alleged tax evasion scheme by the National Irish Bank (NIB). The NIB had tried to prevent RTE from disclosing information relating to the case. However, the court warned RTE that innocent bank customers could sue the station if they were defamed.

A Freedom of Information Act came into effect in April. It allows citizens access to personal information as well as official records held by government departments or other public bodies. Exempted records will include cabinet meetings, law enforcement and public safety, security, defense, international relations, and commercially sensitive information. Critics point out that information brochures about the law may scare civil servants into withholding information by narrowly defining the scope of information covered by the law. Also, the brochure carefully reminds civil servants that only "designated officers" may distribute information. Furthermore, a fee of about $25 per hour for the provision of nonpersonal data may deter citizens and journalists from seeking information.

Gender discrimination in the workplace is unlawful, though inequality of treatment regarding pay and promotion generally favors men in both public and private sectors. According to the Employment Equality Agency, weekly earnings of women in 1997 amounted to approximately 69 percent of the weekly earnings of men. An August 1998 Labor court ruling found that a Dublin corporation discriminated against a woman seeking promotion, and recommended that she be appointed to the position she had sought with back pay. A government task force on violence against women reported in 1997 that domestic violence is a widespread problem, and that many women believe that existing services are inadequate to address the issue.

Labor unions are free to organize and to bargain collectively. About 55 percent of workers in the public and private sectors are union members. Police and military personnel are prohibited from striking, but they may form associations to represent themselves in matters of pay and working conditions. The Gardai Representative Association (police association) held two 24-hour work stoppages in June 1998 by calling in sick in large numbers. Their demand was a 15 percent pay increase.

Israel

Polity: Parliamentary democracy
Economy: Mixed capitalist
Population: 6,000,000
PPP: $16,699
Life Expectancy: 78
Ethnic Groups: Jewish (82 percent), non-Jewish [mostly Arab] (18 percent)
Capital: Jerusalem

Political Rights: 1
Civil Liberties: 3
Status: Free

Overview: Internal infighting, largely over the continued stagnation of the Middle East peace process, kept Benjamin Netanyahu's fragile governing coalition in crisis throughout 1998. The Israeli prime minister scrambled to appease coalition hardliners who are opposed to any concessions to Palestinians, while fellow Likud members, coalition moderates, and Labor party opponents grew increasingly frustrated with what they perceived as government intransigence. Foreign Minister David Levy resigned in January over the peace issue as well as allocations for social welfare in the 1998 budget, leaving Netanyahu with a 61-59 majority in the *Knesset* (parliament). By year's end, an interim agreement with Palestinian leader Yassir Arafat to revive the 1993 Oslo accords went unimplemented, prompting a Likud rebellion and a sweeping Knesset vote for early elections.

Israel was formed in 1948 from less than one-fifth of the original British Palestine Mandate. Its neighbors, rejecting a United Nations partition plan that would have also created a Palestinian state, attacked immediately following independence in the first of several Arab-Israeli conflicts. Israel has functioned as a parliamentary democracy since independence. Since 1977, the conservative Likud and the center-left Labor party have shared or alternated power.

Following June 1992 Knesset elections, Yitzhak Rabin's Labor-led coalition government secured a breakthrough agreement with the Palestinian Liberation Organization (PLO) in 1993. The Declaration of Principles, negotiated secretly between Israeli and Palestinian delegations in Oslo, Norway, provides for a phased Israeli withdrawal from the Israeli-occupied West Bank and Gaza strip, and for limited Palestinian autonomy in those areas. Negotiations on the status of Jerusalem, Jewish settlements, refugees, and Israel's borders were to follow the final Israeli redeployment.

On November 4, 1995, a right-wing Jewish extremist, opposed to the peace process on the grounds that it would lead to a Palestinian state in the West Bank, assassinated Rabin in Tel Aviv. Foreign Minister Shimon Peres became acting prime minister and served until 1996 elections.

The peace process, strained since Netanyahu's election, stalled in March 1997, when Israel began constructing a Jewish housing settlement at Har Homa in disputed East Jerusalem. Since then, efforts by the U.S., Britain, and Egypt to bring the two sides to the negotiating table have produced little progress. With Netanyahu's coalition dependent on the votes of extreme right-wing religious parties, he avoided conceding land to Palestinians for as long as possible, citing the need to preserve Israeli security.

On October 23, 1998, after nearly a year of intense pressure from the U.S., Netanyahu signed an interim peace accord with Arafat following nine days of talks at Wye River Plantation, Maryland. The agreement calls for Israeli withdrawal from 13.1 percent of the West Bank in exchange for security guarantees from the Palestinians, including a provision for CIA monitoring of Palestinian action to combat terrorism. The Knesset ratified the agreement in November, though a majority of the governing coalition voted against it.

Faced with a backlash from right-wing cabinet members, Netanyahu continued to expand Jewish settlements in the West Bank despite an agreement under Wye not to change the status of the territory. Following the beating of an Israeli soldier in December by a Palestinian mob in the West Bank, Netanyahu formally suspended implementation of the accord, provoking a rebellion within Likud as well as criticism from the opposition. Finance minister Yaakov Neeman resigned, declaring that the government had "ceased to function." Recognizing that Netanyahu would not win majority support for his suspension of the peace agreement, the governing Likud faction announced its intention to vote for early elections. On December 21, the Knesset voted 81-30 in favor.

By year's end, at least six contenders had emerged to challenge Netanyahu, and at least four Likud members had either defected or threatened to do so. Foreign Minister and renowned political hawk Ariel Sharon suggested that he might oppose Netanyahu for the Likud leadership. In late December, opinion polls showed Ehud Barak of Labor leading in popularity. Elections are scheduled for May 17, 1999.

Beset by the crisis in the peace process, the government turned its attention in March to its increasingly costly military involvement in southern Lebanon. Following the deaths of four Israeli soldiers early in the year, the Israeli cabinet in April adopted UN Security Council Resolution 425, which calls for withdrawal from the region. Netanyahu announced that he would condition a pullback on guarantees that Lebanon would position its army to prevent cross-border guerrilla attacks. Lebanon and Syria rejected the initiative, pointing out that Resolution 425 calls for an unconditional withdrawal.

Political Rights and Civil Liberties:

Israeli citizens can change their government democratically. Although Israel has no formal constitution, a series of Basic Laws has the force of constitutional principles.

In July 1998, Israel belatedly presented its initial report to the UN Human Rights Committee, which monitors implementation of the International Covenant on Civil and Political Rights. The Committee's concluding remarks on the report expressed concern about the state of emergency, which has been in effect in Israel since independence. The Committee also denounced Israeli interrogation practices regarding suspected terrorists as well as administrative detention without trial and discriminatory attitudes and practices toward Arabs, women, and other ethnic minorities.

The judiciary is independent, and procedural safeguards are generally respected. Security trials, however, may be closed to the public on limited grounds. The Emergency Powers (Detention) Law of 1979 provides for indefinite administrative detention without trial. Most administrative detainees are Palestinian, but there are currently 21 Lebanese detainees being held as "bargaining chips" to be used in prisoner exchanges to secure the release of Israeli servicemen. In March 1998, the Supreme Court unveiled a four-month-old ruling sanctioning these detentions despite acknowledging that the Lebanese pose no threat to Israeli security.

The Shin Bet (General Security Service) has been accused by Human Rights Watch of "widespread and systematic" torture of Palestinian detainees. The Supreme Court in May heard a major case contesting the use of "moderate physical pressure" during the interrogation of prisoners, and the Knesset debated legislation that would legalize such treatment. Practices in question include violent shaking, binding, gagging, forcing suspects to wear vomit- or urine-soaked hoods, and sleep deprivation. Neither the court nor the Knesset came to a conclusion on the issue.

Freedoms of assembly and association are respected. Newspaper and magazine articles on security matters are subject to a military censor, though the scope of permissible reporting is expanding. Editors may appeal a censorship decision to a three-member tribunal that includes two civilians. Arabic-language publications are censored more frequently than are Hebrew-language ones. Newspapers are privately owned and freely criticize government policy. In March, an Israeli journalist received death threats from Jewish extremists for her part in producing a television series marking the 50th anniversary of the Israeli state. She was accused of treating Palestinian guerrillas as freedom fighters rather than terrorists. In January, an ultra-nationalist Jewish woman was sentenced to two years in jail for publicly displaying posters depicting the Islamic prophet Mohammed as a pig.

Freedom of religion is respected. Each community has jurisdiction over its own members in matters of marriage, burial, and divorce. In the Jewish community, the Orthodox establishment handles these matters. A heated debate has erupted in recent years over the Orthodox monopoly on conversions, which denies certain rights such as citizenship and marriage to Reform or Conservative converts. A court decision in late December ordered the Israeli government to recognize conversions performed by non-Orthodox rabbis, but the government, which is largely dependent on religious parties, is expected to obtain a restraining order on the ruling pending appeal in early 1999. In a similar debate, taxpayer-financed religious councils, formerly the domain of the ultra-Orthodox, were ordered by the Supreme Court to admit Reform and Conservative members by the end of December. In May, a bill that would impose heavy fines on individuals who preach "with the intention of causing another person to change his religion" passed its first reading.

Women are underrepresented in public affairs; only nine women were elected to the 120-seat Knesset in 1996. They continue to face discrimination in many areas, including military service, where they are barred from combat units, and religious institutions.

Some 900,000 Arab citizens receive inferior education, housing, and social services relative to the Jewish population. Israeli Arabs are not subject to the military draft, though they may serve voluntarily. Those who do not join the army do not enjoy the financial benefits available to Israelis who have served, including scholarships and housing loans. Bedouin housing settlements are not recognized by the government and are not provided with basic infrastructure and essential services. In April, Arabs staged a general strike to protest the destruction of Bedouin homes in the Negev.

Workers may join unions of their choice and enjoy the right to strike and to bargain collectively. Three-quarters of the workforce either belong to unions affiliated with Histadrut (General Federation of Labor) or are covered under its social programs and collective bargaining agreements.

Italy

Polity: Parliamentary democracy
Economy: Capitalist-statist
Population: 57,700,000
PPP: $20,174
Life Expectancy: 78
Ethnic Groups: Italian, small minorities of German, French, Slovene, and Albanian
Capital: Rome

Political Rights: 1
Civil Liberties: 2
Status: Free

Overview:

After securing Italian participation in the first round of European Monetary Union (EMU), Prime Minister Romano Prodi fell victim to the political infighting that has characterized Italian coalition governments since World War II. He succumbed in October, when Fausto Bertinotti's Communist Renewal (RC) voted against the government's draft 1999 budget. Meanwhile, constitutional reform, seen as the most important item on the political agenda after EMU, died at the hands of opposition leader Silvio Berlusconi in May.

Modern Italian history dates from the nineteenth-century movement for national unification. Most of Italy had merged into one kingdom by 1870. Italy allied with Germany and Austria-Hungary at the outset of World War I, but switched to side with the

Allied Powers. From 1922-43, the country was a fascist dictatorship under Benito Mussolini. A referendum in 1946 replaced the monarchy with a republican constitution.

Ongoing tensions between Prodi's center-left government, led by Massimo D'Alema's Democrats of the Left (DS) and the far left, on whom it depended for parliamentary support, largely centered around government efforts to bring the economy into line with Maastricht Treaty criteria for EMU. While economic austerity had been Prodi's top priority since he took office in 1996, Bertinotti consistently opposed measures that would cut into Italy's bloated welfare state. After the European Commission declared Italy eligible for the first round of EMU in late March, hardline leftists increased pressure on Prodi to reward their cooperation with his economic policies. Demands included aid to the underdeveloped south, where unemployment reaches 25 percent, and implementation of a 35-hour work week.

Relations fell into crisis in late June, when the RC voted against the government on NATO expansion. A new center-right grouping led by Francesco Cossiga helped pass the measure, but the viability of the coalition was thrown into doubt. On October 4, the RC voted against the 1999 draft budget, sparking a vote of confidence in the government as well as a rebellion within the RC. Opposed to splitting with the government, RC chairman Armando Cossutta resigned, taking 21 of the RC's 34 members with him. Despite their support, Prodi lost the vote of confidence and resigned on October 9.

After nearly two weeks of political wrangling, Massimo D'Alema formed a new center-left government and took office on October 21 as the first former Communist to lead a major Western European country. D'Alema's government, which comprises his DS along with Cossiga's centrists and Cossutta's Party of Italian Communists, declared its commitment to stay Prodi's economic course, develop and boost jobs in the south, and continue to participate in NATO. D'Alema also announced his intention to cooperate with the conservative opposition on electoral reform.

The *bicamerale*, which was set up in 1997 to tackle constitutional reform, collapsed in early June when center-right leader Berlusconi withdrew his support. Berlusconi, beset by corruption allegations and handed two jail sentences in July for bribery and illegal political donations, had demanded a complete overhaul of the judiciary. Analysts expressed concern that the failure of the bicamerale would jeopardize a range of economic and structural reforms necessary for Italy's effective participation in EMU. And only electoral reform will do away with the system of proportional representation which allows the influence of numerous small parties to destabilize coalitions.

D'Alema faced his first test of foreign policy in November, when Abdullah Ocalan, leader of the Kurdistan Workers' Party (PKK) was arrested at Rome's Fiumicino airport on an outstanding Turkish warrant. Italy's leftist politicians campaigned for asylum, while Turkey demanded extradition. Because of a policy prohibiting extradition to countries which practice capital punishment, Italy refused to send Ocalan to Turkey. Despite Turkish threats of retaliation, a Rome court in December declared Ocalan free to leave the country.

Political Rights and Civil Liberties:

Italians can change their government democratically. The president, whose role is largely ceremonial, is elected to a seven-year term by an assembly of parliamentarians and delegates from the Regional Councils. The president chooses the prime minister, who is often, but not always, a member of the largest party in the Chamber of Deputies, the lower house of parliament. Members of the upper house, the Senate, represent the regions.

Italian citizens are free to form political organizations, with the exception of the constitutionally forbidden prewar fascist party. The postwar constitution, designed to prevent another Mussolini-style dictatorship, sharply restricts the powers of the executive in favor of the legislative and judicial branches. The result has been unstable governing coalitions, political deadlock, and heavy reliance on the referendum as a political tool.

Italy's judiciary is independent but notoriously slow. A 1995 law allows for preventive detention as a last resort or in cases in which there is convincing evidence of a serious offense, such as a crime involving the Mafia or related to drugs, arms, or subversion. A maximum of two years' preliminary investigation is permitted. The average waiting period for a trial is about 18 months, but can exceed two years. In Italy, a defendant is given two chances to appeal a guilty verdict, during which he is presumed innocent and not jailed. Some 93 percent of people convicted in a first trial never go to jail. The average civil trial lasts between three and five years.

The Italian press is free and competitive, with restrictions on obscenity and defamation. Most of the 80 daily newspapers are independently owned. The main state-owned network and the three main channels of Radio Audizioni Italiane (RAI) provide Italians with most of their news. Their boards of directors are entirely parliament-appointed.

In June 1997, the government instituted an 18-month trial period during which bars, petrol stations, supermarkets, and other businesses were granted licenses to sell newspapers and magazines. Traditionally, these items are sold only at kiosks or shops with exclusive licenses, and the newspaper vendors' association has lobbied to protect its monopoly. The result has been poor availability of print news outside major town centers.

An authority created in 1997 to monitor privacy issues may censure the media for violating citizens' right to privacy, and may impose fines for repeat offenses. A privacy law also introduced in 1997 requires that information be published in a "lawful and correct" manner and carries penalties of up to three years in jail.

In November 1998, Reporters Sans Frontiers reported that at least five Turkish journalists were beaten and arrested by police on their way to cover the arrest of Abdullah Ocalan.

Freedom of assembly and association are guaranteed by the constitution, though fascist and racist groups are excepted. Unions are active, and labor groups have been bolstered recently by the increasing influence of leftist hardliners in government. However, unions were weakened by a 1995 voter referendum and government legislation aimed at restricting their power.

Religious freedom is guaranteed in this overwhelmingly Roman Catholic country. Italy's first grand mosque opened in 1995. North African migrants comprise many of the estimated 650,000 Muslims residing in Italy.

Under pressure from EU partners, the Italian parliament approved a new immigration law in February 1998 which would allow police to detain people who enter the country without applying for asylum. Until now, those denied asylum were given 15 days to leave Italy, a period used by many to travel north to countries such as Germany and France. Others have found jobs in the black economy.

Jamaica

Polity: Parliamentary democracy
Economy: Capitalist
Population: 2,600,000
PPP: $3,801
Life Expectancy: 71
Ethnic Groups: Black (76 percent), Creole (15 percent), European, Chinese
Capital: Kingston

Political Rights: 2
Civil Liberties: 2*
Status: Free

Ratings change: Jamaica's civil liberties rating changed from 3 to 2 due to a reduction in violence associated with political campaigns.

Overview: Confidence in Prime Minister Percival Patterson's unprecedented second full term was reaffirmed in local elections held in September 1998, as the ruling People's National Party (PNP) garnered 75 percent of the vote and took possession of the capital and all 13 rural parishes. Patterson's pet project, a proposed referendum on constitutional reform, was postponed until 1999, after he agreed that election reforms must first be completed.

Jamaica, a member of the British Commonwealth, achieved independence from Great Britain in 1962. It is a parliamentary democracy, with the British monarchy represented by a governor general. The bicameral parliament consists of a 60-member House of Representatives elected for five years and a 21-member Senate, with 13 senators appointed by the prime minister and eight by the leader of the parliamentary opposition. Executive authority is vested in the prime minister, who leads the political party commanding a majority in the House.

Since independence, power has alternated between the social-democratic PNP and the conservative Jamaica Labor Party (JLP). The PNP's Michael Manley, who died in 1997, was prime minister from 1972 to 1980, and again from 1989 until his resignation for health reasons in 1992. JLP leader Edward Seaga held the post from 1980 until 1989.

In 1992, the PNP elected P.J. Patterson to replace Manley as party leader and prime minister. In the 1993 elections, the PNP won 52 parliamentary seats, and the JLP eight. The parties differed little on continuing the structural adjustment begun in the 1980's, but the JLP was hurt by long-standing internal rifts.

Irregularities and violence marred the vote. The PNP agreed to address subsequent JLP demands for electoral reform. Meanwhile, the Patterson government continued to confront labor unrest and an unrelenting crime wave.

In October 1995, Bruce Golding, a well-respected economist and businessman and former chairman of the JLP, left the party to launch the National Democratic Movement (NDM), one of the most significant political developments since independence. Golding brought with him a number of key JLP figures, including one other member of parliament, cutting the JLP's seats to six.

Politically motivated fighting between supporters of the JLP and the NDM claimed at least ten lives during 1996. On December 1997, the PNP won a third successive victory in parliamentary elections, winning 50 seats in the lower house to the JLP's 10. The 1997 vote and that in 1998 were characterized by unusually low levels of political violence and were judged generally free and fair, despite a creaky electoral administration.

Political Rights and Civil Liberties: Citizens are able to change their government through elections. However, voter apathy in the 1998 local elections resulted in one of the lowest turnout rates—31 percent—in Jamaican history. Although the violence associated with the 1997 pre-electoral period was significantly less than in previous years, they were nonetheless marked by thuggery on both sides, police intimidation, and large-scale confusion. Progress on electoral reform has been slow, and the municipal elections had been postponed for five years in order for electoral rolls to be updated and the voting system reformed. International concern has been expressed about candidate access to so-called "garrison communities"—armed political fiefdoms in nine of the 60 parliamentary districts. Seaga's JLP controls only one—Tivoli Gardens—while the PNP controls seven and the NDM one.

Constitutional guarantees regarding the right to free expression, freedom of religion, and the right to organize political parties, civic organizations, and labor unions are generally respected.

The judicial system is headed by a Supreme Court and includes several magistrate courts and a Court of Appeal, with final recourse to the Privy Council in London. The system is slow and inefficient, particularly in addressing police abuses and the deplorable, violent conditions of prisons. Despite government efforts to improve penal conditions, a mounting backlog of cases and a shortage of court staff at all levels continue to undermine the judicial system. In February 1997, Jamaica signed on to the hemispheric anti-drug strategy formulated by the Organization of American States (OAS).

Violence is now the major cause of death in Jamaica, and the murder rate is one of the highest in the world. In 1997 alone, there were 1,038 murders. Much of the violence is the result of warfare between drug gangs known as posses. Criminal deportees from the United States and a growing illegal weapons trade are major causes of the violence. Mobs have been responsible for numerous vigilante killings of suspected criminals. Inmates frequently die as a result of prison riots.

In October 1997, Amnesty International issued a report in which it expressed concern about the imposition of death sentences following proceedings that fall short of international standards for fair trials. It also expressed concern regarding killings by law enforcement officials in disputed circumstances and deaths in custody (some 110 deaths in the first nine months of 1997) in addition to infliction of corporal punishment, alleged ill-treatment by police and prison wardens, appalling conditions in places of detention and prisons, and laws punishing consensual sexual acts in private between adult men.

A mounting crime rate led the government to take the controversial steps of restoring capital punishment and flogging. Rights groups protested both measures. Critics charge that flogging is unconstitutional because it can be characterized as "inhuman or degrading punishment," which the Constitution prohibits. In 1998, a six-month limit on death row appeals to international bodies was adopted. Jamaica has also announced its intention to withdraw from an agreement with the Inter-American Human Rights Commission of the OAS that gives prisoners the right to appeal to the commission, in order to remove barriers to executions. There are 600 prisoners on death row.

Newspapers are independent and free of government control. Journalists are occasionally intimidated during election campaigns. Broadcast media are largely public but are open to pluralistic points of view. Public opinion polls play a key role in the political process, and election campaigns feature debates on state-run television.

In 1998, a woman was elected for the first time as Speaker of Parliament.

Labor unions are politically influential and have the right to strike. An Industrial Disputes Tribunal mediates labor conflicts.

Japan

Polity: Parliamentary democracy
Economy: Capitalist
Population: 126,400,000
PPP: $21,930
Life Expectancy: 80
Ethnic Groups: Japanese (99 percent), other, mostly Korean (1 percent)
Capital: Tokyo

Political Rights: 1
Civil Liberties: 2
Status: Free

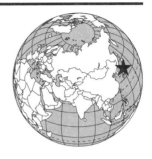

Overview:

Japan's national malaise continued in 1998 as an economy that had been troubled since the early 1990s tumbled into its worst recession since World War II. The two main institutions that oversaw the country's strong post-War growth—the ruling Liberal Democratic Party (LDP) and the Finance Ministry—looked increasingly paralyzed. In July, the LDP's Keizo Obuchi became premier after voters signaled a desire for leadership and economic reform by punishing the party in upper house elections.

Following its defeat in World War II, Japan adopted an American-drafted constitution in 1947 that vested legislative authority in the two-house Diet (parliament) and ended the emperor's divine status. In 1955, the two wings of the opposition Japan Socialist Party (JSP) united, and the two main conservative parties merged to form the LDP. This "1955 system" remained in place throughout the Cold War, as the LDP won successive elections, presided over what became the world's second largest economy, and maintained close security ties to the United States. The leftist JSP became an institutional opposition.

By the early 1990s, the LDP's factionalism and corruption, combined with an easing of Cold War security tensions, had led ordinary Japanese to question the "iron triangle" of politics, business, and the bureaucracy that favored corporations, farmers, and other special interests and allowed the powerful bureaucracy to control policy and impose costly regulations. The party lost power for the first time in the 1993 elections, but returned to power in 1994 in a coalition government. In December 1994, LDP defector Ichiro Ozawa helped organize nine conservative opposition parties into the center-right New Frontier Party (NFP), which promised economic deregulation, a more assertive foreign policy, and a competitive two-party system.

In 1995, the LDP named Ryutaro Hashimoto as premier in a bid for fresh leadership. In early elections in October 1996, held with a 59.6 percent turnout, voters opted for the stability and conservatism of the LDP, which won 239 seats and formed a minority government under Hashimoto. The NFP won 156; the new, reformist Democratic Party, 52; the Communist Party, 26; the Socialist Democratic Party (SDP), the successor to the JSP, 15; and minor parties and independents, 12.

By late 1997, financial crises in Southeast Asia and South Korea threatened Japan's already overburdened banking system. Ever since the collapse of the "bubble economy" and its inflated asset prices in the early 1990s, the Japanese economy had been dragged down by a banking system staggering under some $600 billion of bad debt. Ending a decades-old practice of forcing solvent banks to bail out weak ones, the Hashimoto government allowed three major financial institutions to fail in November. Meanwhile, in December 1997, Ozawa dissolved the NFP and formed a new Liberal Party with the hope of merging it with the more conservative wing of the LDP.

In January 1998, a months-long investigation into financial sector corruption shifted from the corporate sector to the bureaucracy with the first of several arrests at the Ministry of Finance, arguably Japan's most powerful institution. While the Japanese have known for decades that bureaucrats accept bribes and favors from the banks they regulate, reports of bureaucrats being entertained in sex clubs damaged public confidence in a ministry which had already been questioned for its inability to boost the economy.

By the end of the first quarter of 1998, the economy had sunk into its first recession in 23 years. Record-high unemployment of 4.1 percent, negligible wage growth, anxiety that future governments will be unable to provide for the country's aging population, and the effects of an April 1997 increase in the national sales tax had led to anemic consumer demand. The government's spiraling spending on Japan's aging population, and its desire to reduce its budget deficit to less than 3 percent of the GDP by 2003, largely prevented it from using Keynesian stimulus measures.

In the July 12 elections for 126 upper house seats, turnout surged from 44 percent in the 1995 upper house vote to 59 percent. The LDP lost 17 of the 61 contested seats it held, and the party's support came mainly from Japan's shrinking rural population. The Democratic Party solidified itself as the main opposition by gaining 9 seats, although voters seemed primarily attracted to the party as a protest vote, or for its popular leader, Naoto Kan, rather than on policy grounds. Although the LDP still controlled the more important lower house, Hashimoto resigned and Obuchi, the foreign minister, became premier. In November, parliament announced a $195 billion stimulus plan, the largest of several announced during the year. But many analysts argued that only structural reforms will deliver long-term growth, including greater economic deregulation and an end to the bureaucracy's control of policy making.

Political Rights and Civil Liberties:
Japanese citizens can change their government democratically. The lower house has 500 seats with 300 single-seat districts and 200 seats chosen by proportional representation. The upper house has 152 single-seat districts and 100 seats chosen by proportional representation. While recent corruption scandals in the Ministry of Finance may shift some power to the politicians, the Ministry's strength and expertise mean that it still sets financial policy. Moreover, in the spring, the government cut the size of the prosecution team investigating financial sector corruption, and transferred its head to a remote district.

A continuing civil liberties concern involves the 700,000 Korean permanent residents, many of whom trace their ancestry in Japan for two or three generations. Ethnic Koreans regularly face discrimination in housing, education, and employment opportunities; they are not automatically deemed Japanese citizens at birth, and must submit to an official background check and adopt Japanese names to become naturalized. Both the Burakumin, who are descendants of feudal-era outcasts, and the indigenous Ainu minority also face unofficial discrimination and social ostracism.

The judiciary is independent. The Criminal Procedure Code allows authorities to restrict a suspect's right to counsel during an investigation, and bars counsel during interrogations. The common practice of using police cells to hold the accused between arrest and sentencing reportedly encourages physical abuse to extract confessions. Human rights groups criticize the penal system's extreme emphasis on regimentation and dehumanizing punishments. Immigration officers are accused of regularly beating detained illegal aliens.

Civic institutions are strong and freedoms of expression, assembly and association are generally respected in practice. Exclusive private press clubs provide journalists with access to top politicians and major ministries, and in return, journalists often practice self-censorship with sensitive stories. The Education Ministry routinely censors passages in history textbooks describing Japan's World War II atrocities. In 1997, the Supreme Court affirmed the government's right of censorship, but for the first time ruled that the Education Ministry had broken the law by censoring references to well-documented Japanese germ warfare experiments in China in the 1940s.

Women face significant employment discrimination and are frequently tracked into clerical careers. A 1997 law banned workplace discrimination against women, and lifted restrictions on women's working hours, which unions say had been used to keep women out of management positions. However, sanctions for corporate violators are weak. In April, police announced a crackdown on gangsters who traffic Filipino and Thai women to Japan with the promise of regular jobs, and then force them to work as prostitutes. There is full freedom of religion; Buddhism and Shintoism have the most adherents. Trade unions are independent and active.

Jordan

Polity: Monarchy and elected parliament
Economy: Mixed capitalist
Population: 4,600,000
PPP: $4,187
Life Expectancy: 68
Ethnic Groups: Arab (98 percent), Armenian (1 percent), Circassian (1 percent)
Capital: Amman

Political Rights: 4
Civil Liberties: 5*
Status: Partly Free

Ratings change: Jordan's civil liberties rating changed from 4 to 5 due to increased restrictions on freedom of expression.

Overview:
Restriction of democratic freedoms, political scandal, economic stagnation, and the failing health of King Hussein fueled public anxiety about Jordan's future in 1998.

Great Britain installed the Hashemite monarchy in 1921 and granted it full independence in 1946. The current monarch, 62-year-old King Hussein, ascended the throne in 1952. Under the 1952 constitution, executive power rests with the king, who appoints the prime minister and can dissolve the national assembly. The assembly currently consists of a 40-member Senate appointed by the king and an 80-member, directly elected Chamber of Deputies.

In 1989, after rioting erupted over fuel price increases, Hussein eased tensions by lifting restrictions on freedom of expression and ending a 32-year ban on party activity. In November of that year, the kingdom held its first elections since 1956 with the participation of the political wing of the Muslim Brotherhood, the Islamic Action Front (IAF). The Islamists took 22 seats. The electoral law was soon amended to allow "one man, one vote" instead of votes for parties. The changes were meant to prevent an even stronger showing by the IAF in the 1993 elections in which Islamists won 16 seats.

Jordan and Israel signed a peace treaty in October 1994, formally ending a 46-year state of war. In part, the treaty was an attempt by the king to improve his international standing after the Gulf War, in which Jordan supported Iraq. In July 1995, municipal elections, progovernment candidates won significant victories over IAF candidates opposed to the peace accord.

In 1997, nine opposition and Islamist parties, led by the IAF, boycotted the November parliamentary elections. The parties objected to normalization of relations with Israel, government restrictions on public freedom, ineffective economic policies, and the 1993 amendments to the electoral law, which leaves Islamists at a disadvantage vis-a-vis tribal leaders who support the king. The boycott was partly to blame for the 54 percent voter turnout—the lowest since 1989.

By August 1998, Prime Minister Abdul Salaam al-Majali's government was engulfed by a scandal over contaminated drinking water and inaccurate economic statistics. King Hussein, who acknowledged his long illness to the Jordanian people for the first time in August, allowed his brother and designated successor, 51-year-old Prince Hassan, to remove Majali. Hassan appointed Fayez al-Tarawnah as the new prime minister. Tarawnah then reshuffled the cabinet and prioritized the economy as well as the elimination of public and private corruption.

Although Jordan has been cited as a model country in following IMF policies, this resource-starved nation still faces significant economic challenges. In 1998, independent sources estimated that 27 percent of Jordanian families lived in poverty. Unemployment continues to hover at 25 percent. Privatization of Jordan's telecom, utilities, transport, and construction sectors has slowed. Although it provoked Jordan's population, half of whom are of Palestinian origin, normalization with Israel has led to greater economic cooperation. However, it has not created the rapid, widespread prosperity that the government had expected. Jordan has also become increasingly dependent upon Iraq. Because of its support for Iraq during the Gulf war, Jordan lost favor with oil-rich Gulf states. Now, much of Jordan's oil comes from Iraq through barter agreements that are exempt from the UN trade embargo.

Many observers are skeptical about whether an ailing King Hussein can maintain good relations with Israel and the U.S. as well as preserve the trust of his people and Arab neighbors. In February, the Jordanian government cracked down on pro-Iraqi demonstrations in the southern city of Ma'an. The conflict resulted in Jordan's worst riots since 1989. Scores of citizens were detained and the military conducted house-to-house searches for weapons. A prominent former assemblyman and opposition member was charged with inciting the riots and spent several months in prison. In September, Prime Minister Tarawnah, in an attempt at reconciliation, appointed two critics of the Israeli peace accord to the upper house of the assembly. Yet many Jordanians still perceive the government as hostile to their interests.

Political Rights and Civil Liberties:

Jordanians cannot change their government democratically. King Hussein holds broad executive powers, can dissolve parliament, and must approve all laws. The electoral districts favor the king's rural stronghold. Constitutional changes are unlikely, since they require a two-thirds majority of the 120 parliamentary seats, and the king approves the entire 40-member Senate.

Authorities frequently arrest Islamic fundamentalists arbitrarily, and police abuse detainees to extract confessions. The judiciary is not independent in sensitive cases. Defendants in state security courts often lack sufficient pre-trial access to lawyers.

Amendments that severely limited press freedoms and were enacted in 1997 by the government without public or parliamentary debate were ruled illegal on technical grounds by the Supreme Court in January 1998. The government proceeded to devise a new set of amendments that triggered a long period of conflict between authorities and the Jordanian press. At least a dozen journalists were detained and intimidated by the government, and both domestic and foreign publications were censored. In April, the Committee to Protect Journalists (CPJ) named Prime Minister Majali as one of the world's top ten enemies of the press. Journalists and lawmakers were allowed to read and comment on the drafts of the new press amendments. Their objections and alternative proposals, however, were ignored. By September, the new amendments had been approved by Prime Minister Tarawnah's government and signed by Prince Hassan. The amendments require publications to have many times their current capitalization in order to operate and to give the government unchecked power in issuing and denying licenses. They also prohibit the publishing of material that is critical of the king, "corrupts morals," or represents the ideas, opinions, or stands of Jordan's professional associations, which are the government's traditional opponents. In November, the government closed a satellite TV station for reporting "intentional assaults against the Jordanian people and political regime."

The government grants permits for demonstrations. In the interest of not offending allies such as the U.S., Jordan has had a long-standing ban against pro-Iraqi demonstrations. During 1998, however, students and women were allowed to hold limited demonstrations supporting Iraq and opposing U.S. policies. Women's groups have also been allowed to protest against "honor killings."

Some 30 to 60 women are victims of "honor killings" by their male relatives each year for alleged moral offenses. Greater newspaper coverage of these killings and activism by Jordanian women and international agencies is prompting change. In October, the government began to consider tougher penalties for "honor killings." Women must receive permission from a male guardian to travel abroad and are discriminated against in inheritance and divorce settlements.

Islam is the state religion. The government does not permit the Baha'i faith to run schools, and Baha'i family legal matters are handled in the Islamic Shari'a courts. As of 1997, Christian students in public schools have been allowed to study their religion, using a curriculum from Syria since. Islamists have criticized the decision to teach Christianity, asserting that it will breed sectarianism that will lead to disputes.

Private sector workers may join independent trade unions. The government can prohibit private sector strikes by referring a dispute to an arbitration committee. Some government employees can form unions but none may strike. The International Confederation of Trade Unions has called for greater protection against anti-union discrimination.

⬇ Kazakhstan

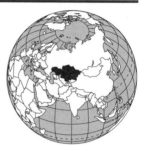

Polity: Presidential (dominant party)
Economy: Mixed statist (transitional)
Population: 15,600,000
PPP: $3,037
Life Expectancy: 65
Ethnic Groups: Kazakh (46 percent), Russian (35 percent), Ukrainian (5 percent), German (3 percent), Uzbek (2 percent), Tatar (2 percent), other (7 percent)
Capital: Astana

Political Rights: 6
Civil Liberties: 5
Status: Not Free

Trend arrow: Kazakhstan receives a downward trend arrow due to an unfair presidential campaign and persecution of the opposition.

Overview:

In October 1998, parliament unexpectedly approved holding presidential elections in January 1999, a year before they were scheduled. This allowed President Nursultan Nazarbayev to get a jump on the opposition which had little more than a month to register a candidate. On November 4, in another move to assure Nazarbayev's re-election, the Central Election, which was stacked with government loyalists, banned the key challenger, former Prime Minister Akezhan Kazhegeldin, because he participated in a meeting of the unsanctioned Movement for Fair Elections.

In all, parliament adopted 19 amendments to the constitution, 13 of which were proposed by President Nazarbayev. One prolonged the presidential term from five to seven years, allowing him to run for more than two terms, and also removed the age restriction of 65.

This sparsely populated, multi-ethnic land, which is the size of India and stretches from the Caspian Sea east to the Chinese border, was controlled by Russia from 1730 to 1840. After a brief period of independence in 1917, it became an autonomous Soviet republic in 1929 and a union republic in 1936. Kazakhstan formally declared independence from a crumbling Soviet Union in December 1991. President Nazarbayev, former first-secretary of the Kazakhstan Communist Party and head of the Kazakhstan National Unity Party (PNEK), was directly elected in 1991. In March 1995, Nazarbayev dissolved parliament and ruled by decree. Nazarbayev ordered a referendum extending his rule to the year 2000 (his term expired in 1996), and on April 29, a reported 95 percent supported the measure. Four months later, voters overwhelmingly approved a new constitution, which gave the president the right to dissolve parliament if it approves a no-confidence vote in the government or twice rejects his nominee for prime minister. It also codified periods of presidential rule by decree. The December Senate elections were largely uncontested, with Nazarbayev supporters taking all the seats. The PNEK dominated the vote for the *Majilis*, or lower house.

In 1998, despite some macroeconomic improvement, there were signs that the economy was in trouble. In February, the government suspended privatization in the oil sector. In July, the prime minister reported that the oil sector faced a "very serious crisis" because of the international financial crisis and low prices. The prospect of economic crisis, according to analysts, was the basis for President Nazarbayev to call for early elections and extend his term.

In July, the government implemented a package of austerity measures aimed at staving off an economic crisis. The plan pledged to cut 10,000 state employees, along with spending by state organizations. The government also pledged to review contracts with foreign companies which have not met government obligations.

Key parts of the economy and government positions continued to be dominated by clans loyal to President Nazarbayev and members of his family. His daughter, Dariga, controls the national television network, while her husband, Rakhat Aliyev, is head of the tax police. Another son-in-law, Timur Kulidayev, is the financial director and vice president of Kazakhoil. The company is believed to have provided funds for President Nazarbayev's pet projects, such as the construction of the new capital of Astana (the name was changed from Akmola in May 1998).

Political Rights and Civil Liberties:

Citizens can participate in multiparty elections, but under the constitution, power is centered in the hands of President Nazarbayev, whose regime has cracked down on the opposition and the media. Parliament is largely powerless, and in 1997, President Nazarbayev restructured the government to broaden and safeguard his authority. In 1998, parliament passed amendments that lengthened the president's term to seven years and extended the terms of both houses of parliament.

There are several independent newspapers, including those that reflect oppositionist views. The most popular, *Karavan*, reports on corruption and is critical of the government. Newspaper distribution system is controlled by the state. In December 1996, the government announced that it would hold a tender for broadcast frequencies. The cost of licenses and annual fees are extremely high. Several independent broadcasters were forced out of business, including the popular Radio Max and TV-M, which aired "Open Zone," a popular political program that provided a platform for the opposition. As a result of the tender, there are now only four nominally non-state television channels and three independent radio stations in Almaty. In 1997, three popular channels in Akloma (Atana) were arbitrarily disconnected from state transmitters. Libel laws are used by authorities to discourage free speech. After he publicly criticized Nazarbayev during a rally in April 1998, Madel Isamailov, a leader of Almaty's Workers Movement, was sentenced to one year in prison for "using the mass media for insulting the president."

The constitution guarantees freedom of religion, but religious associations may not pursue political goals. Christians, Muslims, and Jews can worship freely. In Septemeber, six Wahhabi missionaries from Pakistan were expelled from the country.

Freedom of assembly is restricted. Several unsanctioned rallies by workers, pensioners, and the political opposition to protest deteriorating social and economic conditions were broken up by police who detained demonstrators. In April, police beat a group of demonstrators who rallied in front of the prosecutors office in Almaty to protest the trial of a leading Workers Movement activist.

Opposition parties include the Azamat, Socialists (former Communists), the nationalist Azat (Freedom) Party, the ethnic-Russian Unity Party, and the rightist Respublika Party, as well as smaller groups. Opposition parties have complained of harassment, surveillance, denial of access to the state-run media, and arbitrary banning from registering candidates. In late October, Azamat leader Pyotr Svoik was detained in Almaty and charged with slander, inciting national conflict, and insulting an official.

The largest trade union remains the successor to the Soviet-era General Council of Trade Unions, a government organ in practice. The Independent Trade Union Center, with twelve unions, includes the important coal miners' union in Karaganda. A new labor law places restrictions on the right to strike. Workers who join independent unions are subject to threats and harassment by enterprise management, and have no legal recourse.

The judiciary is not free of government interference and remains under the control of the president and the executive branch. Judges are subject to bribery and political bias. Judges are appointed by the Ministry of Justice with little or no parliamentary oversight. Supreme Court and lower court judges are now required to take exams attesting to their professional qualifications. The Constitutional Court was replaced in 1995 by a seven-member Constitutional Council; three of its members, including the chairman, are appointed by the president. Rights to an attorney and open trial have been denied political detainees. Corruption is evident at every level of the judicial system.

Russians, Germans, and other non-Kazakhs have charged discrimination in favor of ethnic Kazakhs in state-run businesses, government, housing and education. Ethnic Germans and Russians have left in droves, particularly from the northern industrial cities, such as Karaganda. Uighurs who have ethnic ties to their restive kin in China's Xinjiang province have been banned from demonstrating and holding political meetings.

Freedom of movement and the free right to chose a residence are guaranteed under the constitution, and the "propiska" system of residence permits has been abolished. In practice, citizens are still required to register in order to prove legal residence and to obtain city services.

Under the 1995 constitution, private property is an inviolable right. Basic rights of entrepreneurship are codified, but bureaucratic hurdles and the control of large segments of the economy by clan elites and government officials who are loyal to President Nazarbayev impede equal opportunity and fair competition.

Kenya

Polity: Dominant party
Economy: Capitalist
(highly corrupt)
Population: 28,300,000
PPP: $1,438
Life Expectancy: 49

Political Rights: 6
Civil Liberties: 5*
Status: Not Free

Ethnic Groups: Kikuyu (22 percent), Luhya (14 percent), Luo
(13 percent), Kalenjin (12 percent), Kamba (11 percent), Kisii (6 percent), Meru
(6 percent), other African (15 percent), Asian, European, and Arab (1 percent)
Capital: Nairobi
Ratings change: Kenya's civil liberties rating changed from 6 to 5 due to a slight
loosening of state repression of civil society, media, and opposition politicians.

Overview:
In October, President Daniel arap Moi marked two decades in power as his country faced a grave economic crisis and increasing ethnic polarization. Moi's December 1997 re-election was ensured by massive use of state patronage and the official media to promote his candidacy and by harassment of the divided opposition. Throughout 1998, Moi strove to tighten his tenuous hold over the ruling Kenya African National Union (KANU) and to create ties between his small Kalenjin ethnic groups and other minority groups in a de facto alliance. Ethnic violence that took thousands of lives in the Rift Valley in 1993 flared again in 1998, with hundreds of casualties and renewed suspicions of governmental complicity in the attacks. Kenya's multiparty system is today largely a reflection of the country's ethnic divisions. Harassment of Moi's critics in the government, media, and nongovernmental organizations (NGOs) continued. Corruption remained a severe problem.

Kenya also suffered more than 250 deaths and at least $500 million in damage in the August car bombing of the U.S. Embassy in Nairobi, which was apparently carried out by Islamist terrorists and unrelated to U.S.-Kenya ties. Beyond the casualties and immediate material damage, the bombing has also curbed foreign tourism, a major foreign exchange earner for the country.

Britain conquered Kenya in the late eighteenth century in order to open a route to control the River Nile headwaters in Uganda. President Jomo Kenyatta, a leader of the Mau-Mau rebellion dominated by people of his Kikuyu ethnicity, led the country to independence in 1963 under the KANU party. Kikuyu remained preeminent in Kenyan politics until Kenyatta's death in 1978. Vice President Moi's succession kept KANU in power, but gradually diminished Kikuyu influence.

Opposition parties proscribed in 1982 were allowed to operate almost ten years later as a result of domestic unrest and pressure from international aid donors. In elections in 1992, Moi was proclaimed the victor with 36 percent of the vote. The multiparty polls, however, were marked by opposition discord and highly suspect electoral conduct. Today, there is no clear successor to Moi, who has promised not to seek reelection after his current presidential term expires in 2003.

Political Rights and Civil Liberties: Kenyans are unable to exercise their right to choose their leaders in genuinely open and competitive elections. Moi's election victories have been achieved through political repression, media control, and dubious electoral procedures. Moi's rejection of an independent election commission has provided additional insurance against his ouster. Physical violence, a usually docile judiciary, police powers, and executive decrees have been used against political opponents and in efforts to undermine the wider civil society. Power is heavily concentrated in the executive branch of government.

Many laws directly limit freedom of association and political organization, including the Public Order Act, the Public Security Act, and the Chief's Authority Act. The security forces regularly violate constitutional guarantees regarding detention, privacy, search, and seizure. Groups such as Release Political Prisoners, which was founded in 1992 by former detainees, and the Kenyan Human Rights Commission, an NGO, have publicized abuses and demanded respect for human rights, but leaders of the organizations have occasionally been the victims of deadly assaults. Attacks by police on ethnic minority Somali people, who must carry special identification, are reportedly common and regularly go unpunished. A series of judicial reforms was announced in 1998, but courts are still heavily influenced by the executive and cannot be relied on to protect constitutional rights or offer fair trials. Local chiefs still exercise sometimes arbitrary and violent power. Mob attacks against suspected criminals increased sharply as commentators decried a lack of public confidence in the justice system. Prison conditions are harsh and often life threatening. Interpol has identified Kenya as a major center for the transit of drugs from Asia to Western Europe.

Freedom of expression is severely limited by lack of access to the dominant state broadcast media and continued repression of the private press. The country's few private radio and television stations are either pro-Moi or carefully apolitical, although new licenses issued in 1998 may gradually open the airwaves. Private print media remain vibrant, but under serious threat. In October, a government minister urged ruling party activists to attack journalists "in self-defense." Journalists have been charged with criminal libel, and independent publications are subject to harassment in their business operations. President Moi has decreed that it is a crime to "insult" him, and sedition laws are used in efforts to silence any criticism. Numerous books are banned. The Network for the Defence of Independent Media in Africa, which monitors press freedom, was denied NGO registration in March, but continues to operate.

Kenyan Asians, who are heavily represented in the country's commercial class, were targeted with racist propaganda during last year's election campaign and may again become scapegoats if the economic situation continues to deteriorate. In September, the indigenous Muslim minority protested the banning of five Islamic NGOs that allegedly had ties to extremist activity.

Women face legal discrimination, including restrictions on obtaining credit and passports, and societal inequalities in inheritance and property rights. They are also afforded fewer educational opportunities, especially at higher levels. Domestic violence against women is reportedly widespread, and female genital mutilation is still common. Women's groups such as the International Federation of Women Lawyers-Kenya and the Legal Advice Center offer legal aid and advocate on behalf of victims of domestic violence. There are an estimated 50,000 street children in Nairobi and other cities.

Unions are active and have occasionally defied a 1993 Ministry of Labor decree that forbids all strikes, despite constitutional guarantees to the contrary. A teachers' strike in October met was met with violence by security forces. Civil servants and university academic staff may join only government-designated unions. Approximately one-fifth of the country's 1.5 million industrial work force is unionized.

Most of Kenya's 29 million people are poor and survive through subsistence agriculture. Donor demands for better governance, which led to suspension of a major IMF loan in 1997, have not been met. An anti-corruption commission produced few results in 1998, and the fate of a new ombudsman's office created by parliament in October is likely to be similarly unsuccessful as long as Moi is in power. Nepotism and fraud inhibit economic opportunity and discourage greater foreign investment.

Kiribati

Polity: Parliamentary democracy
Economy: Capitalist-statist
Population: 80,000
PPP: na
Life Expectancy: na
Ethnic Groups: Micronesian (84 percent), Polynesian (14 percent), others
Capital: Tarawa

Political Rights: 1
Civil Liberties: 1
Status: Free

Overview:

Following September parliamentary elections, incumbent President Teburoro Tito was reelected in November over Amberoti Nikora of the opposition Boutokan Te Koaua party and veteran politician Dr. Harry Tong.

The Republic of Kiribati consists of 33 inhabited islands of the Gilbert, Line, and Phoenix groups scattered over two million square miles of the central Pacific Ocean, as well as Banaba Island in the west. The country, with a Micronesian majority and a Polynesian minority, achieved independence from Great Britain in 1979.

The first post-independence legislative elections were held in March 1982. In July 1991, President Ieremia Tabai, who came to office at independence, served out his third and final term and then threw his support in the presidential election behind Tetao Teannaki, who defeated his main competitor, Roniti Teiwaki. In May 1994, however, Teannaki was forced to resign after his government lost a vote of no-confidence introduced by the parliamentary opposition, which accused his administration of financial irregularities. In accordance with the constitution, government authority passed to a three-member caretaker Council of State, consisting of the speaker of parliament, the chief justice, and the chairman of the Public Service Commission (PSC), pending new elections. A brief constitutional crisis ensued after acting head of state Tekire Tameura was removed forcibly on the grounds that his tenure as chairman of the PSC had expired three days earlier.

In early parliamentary elections in July 1994, the Protestant-based Christian Democratic Party (MTM) won 13 seats; the incumbent Gilbertese National Progressive Party

(GNPP), 7; and independents, 19. The MTM and the GNPP later merged to form the Christian Democratic Unity Party. In September, Teburoro Tito won the presidential election, in which all four candidates represented the MTM, with 51 percent of the votes.

A record 191 candidates competed in the September 1998 general elections, in which the opposition and the government each lost seven seats. Among the main issues of the campaign were economic and constitutional reform, the sale of Kiribati passports to foreigners, and the foreign establishment of a rocket launch facility in international waters just east of Kiribati. In the subsequent presidential election in November, Teburoro Tito was reelected with 52 percent of the vote.

A five-member committee, established in late 1994, continues to review the 1979 constitution. The 1994 constitutional crisis, although minor, highlighted the fact that many clauses relating to key issues are vague and ill defined.

In recent years, Kiribati has sought economic benefits due to its location along the equator, which is ideal for monitoring satellite launches and operations. In October 1997, China completed construction of an aerospace tracking station in Tarawa, the capital city. Because of the low elevation of most of its islands, Kiribati has also become increasingly concerned about the impact of the global greenhouse effect on surrounding sea levels.

Political Rights and Civil Liberties:

Citizens of Kiribati can change their government democratically. The 1979 constitution established a unicameral legislature, the *Maneaba ni Maungatabu*, with 40 members directly elected for a four-year term, one appointed member, and one ex-officio member. The president, who serves as both head of state and head of government and is limited to three terms, is chosen in a nationwide ballot from among three or four candidates selected by parliament. Local island councils serve all inhabited islands. Several parties exist, although most lack true platforms and are organized around specific issues or in support of particular individuals.

Freedom of speech and of the press is respected. The government-run radio station and newspaper offer diverse views, and Protestant and Catholic churches publish newsletters and other periodicals. Christianity is the predominant religion, but there is no state religion and freedom of worship is respected.

The constitution provides for freedom of assembly and association, and the government respects these rights in practice. Although more than 90 percent of the workforce is involved in fishing or subsistence farming, the small wage sector is represented by the well-organized and independent Kiribati Trade Union Congress, with approximately 2,500 members. The law provides for the right to strike, though the last strike occurred in 1980.

The judiciary is independent and free of government interference. The judicial system is modeled on English common law and provides adequate due process rights. The police force of about 250 is under civilian control. Traditional customs permit corporal punishment, and island councils on some outer islands occasionally order such punishment for petty theft and other minor offenses.

Citizens are free to travel domestically and abroad. The law prohibits interference in personal or family matters, and the government respects these provisions in practice. Employment opportunities for women in this traditionally male-dominated society are slowly improving, and women enjoy full rights to own and inherit property.

Korea, North

Polity: Communist
one-party
Economy: Statist
Population: 22,200,000
PPP: $4,058
Life Expectancy: 66
Ethnic Groups: Korean
Capital: Pyongyang

Political Rights: 7
Civil Liberties: 7
Status: Not Free

Overview:

On September 9, 1998, North Korea celebrated its fiftieth anniversary against a backdrop of economic collapse, mass starvation, and increasing international concern over its suspected nuclear weapons program. The country's deterioration, together with the election of a more conciliatory government in South Korea, had led to speculation that the year would yield new openness from the reclusive government in Pyongyang. However, as 1998 drew to a close, North Korea remained one of the world's most closed and secretive societies and showed little sign of change.

The Democratic People's Republic of Korea (DPRK) was established on September 9, 1948, following the end of World War II, and the division of the Korean peninsula. With assistance from Moscow, Kim Il-sung, a former Soviet army officer, became head of the North Korean government. In June 1950, Kim, with Soviet military support, invaded South Korea in an attempt to reunify the peninsula under Communist rule. The three-year Korean War ended in a truce after intervention by U.S. and Chinese troops, which left the two Koreas bitterly divided.

Throughout the cold war, Kim solidified his power base in the north through an extensive personality cult and the development of *Juche* (self-reliance), a home-grown ideology said to be an application of Marxism-Leninism specific to North Korea. In practice, it became an ideological justification for Communist leadership under Kim's rule and for the pervasive Stalinist control of the economy and all aspects of public and private life.

By the 1990s, the North Korean economy was achieving negative growth rates every year. The disintegration of the Soviet Union in 1991 meant the loss of Pyongyang's Cold War patrons in Moscow and increasing isolation for North Korea. As a result, North Korea has been periodically forced into negotiations over its nuclear weapons programs in return for food aid to support its malnourished population.

Kim Il-sung died suddenly of a heart attack in 1994, paving the way for his son and appointed successor, Kim Jong-il, to assume power, marking the first-ever Communist dynastic succession. While the younger Kim was regarded as the ruler of North Korea after his father's death, he delayed formally assuming positions of power for several years, not becoming general secretary of the Korean Workers' Party until October 1997.

1998 was marked by midyear elections for representatives of the Supreme People's Assembly (SPA), North Korea's rubber-stamp legislature, and by Kim Jong-il's ascension as head-of-state. On July 26, 687 deputies were chosen for the Tenth SPA in the first elections held in eight years. Although the constitution calls for elections every five years, North Korea had failed to form a new parliament following the end of the ninth SPA's five-year term in April 1995. The balloting was a mere formality. Only one candidate was registered in each of the country's 687 districts. Sixty-seven percent of the deputies were replaced by new figures (compared with 31 percent in the previous election), indicating a possible generational and ideological shift in the North Korean ruling elite.

The formation of the tenth SPA was viewed as the opening of the Kim Jong-il era. The SPA convened in Pyongyang on September 5 and, in a surprise move, revised the Socialist Constitution (renaming it the "Kim Il-sung Constitution") and abolished the post of president, which Kim Jong-il had been expected to assume. Kim was reelected chairman of the National Defense Commission (NDC), the nation's highest military supervisory body. With the post of president abolished, the NDC became the highest organ of power in the nation and its chairman the de facto head of state. Kim also holds the country's two other power offices: head of the ruling party and supreme military commander.

On August 31, North Korea launched a three-stage missile that flew over the Japanese island of Hokkaido and crashed into the Pacific, raising new concerns over the North's ability to threaten its neighbors. Pyongyang claimed that the launch was part of an effort to put a satellite into space. International concern also mounted in 1998 over North Korea's ambitions to develop nuclear weapons. The concern surrounded a number of underground complexes at a site north of Pyongyang where weapons construction was suspected. American demands to inspect the site were countered with North Korean demands for $300 million in cash and food aid in return for inspection rights. The demands were rejected and the deteriorating situation threatened to undermine the 1994 Agreed Framework, under which North Korea agreed to abandon its nuclear program in exchange for light-water nuclear reactors which could not easily be used to make weapons.

There were some indications in 1998 that North Korea may be considering modest openings in the economic sphere. An agreement was reached between the North Korean government and Hyundai, South Korea's largest conglomerate, to develop a tourist facility in the Diamond Mountains in North Korea and to organize tours for South Koreans. For this, Hyundai agreed to pay North Korea $906 million over the next six years. The first group of South Koreans visited the North late in the year—under heavily restricted conditions. There were also signs that Pyongyang would experiment with more free economic zones, in addition to the existing Rajin-Sonbong area and the Nampo-Wonson area south of the capital. The government has come to view such zones as a means to revive the economy without undertaking serious reform. The SPA decided in September that business and trade activities within these zones would be extended to so-called "socialist cooperative groups."

A combination of floods and droughts in recent years, combined with a legacy of agricultural mismanagement and the end of food subsidies from former Communist states, has produced severe food shortages in North Korea. Details regarding the full impact and extent of the resulting famine are difficult to come by, but first-hand accounts, particularly from the border region near China, have told of widespread hunger and even cannibalism. The government has rejected requests by human rights and aid organizations to evaluate fully the extent of the humanitarian crisis. In September, the French-based Médecins Sans Frontières, which had been running the largest interna-

tional aid operation in North Korea, removed its workers from the country, citing government interference in the distribution of aid. UN workers also reported being denied access to famine-affected counties for "security reasons." There were also reports that food aid was being diverted to the military and government officials.

The governments of North and South Korea resumed efforts in 1998 to end their long-standing hostilities, though little substantive progress was noted. In April, the two sides met in Beijing for direct government-to-government talks for the first time in four years. The talks were part of a continuing series of negotiations aimed at bringing a formal end to the Korean War, which was ended by a truce but without a formal treaty, leaving the two Koreas technically at a state of war. The border between the two Koreas is the world's most heavily-armed, with some 2 million troops deployed on both sides.

Political Rights and Civil Liberties:

North Korea is arguably the most tightly-controlled country in the world. Its citizens cannot change their government democratically. Elections are held regularly, but all candidates are state-sponsored and belong to either the ruling Workers' Party or smaller, state-organized parties. The Supreme People's Assembly, nominally the highest organ of state power, provides little more than a veneer of legitimacy to government decisions. Opposition parties are illegal, and there appears to be little organized dissent due to the regime's repression, widespread internal surveillance, and isolationist policies. Even the most basic elements of a civil society do not exist in North Korea.

The judicial system consists of the Central Court, under which there are various municipal courts, and it is merely another extension of state authority. The SPA has the power to elect and recall the president of the Central Court. The criminal law subjects citizens to arbitrary arrest, detention, and execution for "counterrevolutionary crimes" and other broadly defined political offenses. In practice, these can include non-violent acts such as attempted defection, criticism of the leadership, and listening to foreign broadcasts. Defense lawyers persuade defendants to plead guilty rather than advocate for them. The rule of law is nonexistent.

Prison conditions are characterized by severe mistreatment of prisoners and, by some accounts, frequent summary executions. The regime operates "re-education through labor" camps that reportedly hold tens of thousands of political prisoners and their families. Defectors say some political prisoners are "re-educated" and released after a few years, while others are held indefinitely.

Authorities implement arbitrary checks of residences, use electronic surveillance, and maintain a network of informants to monitor the population. At school, children are encouraged to report on their parents. The government assigns a security rating to each individual that, to a somewhat lesser extent than in the past, still determines access to education, employment, and health services. North Koreans face a steady onslaught of propaganda from radios and televisions that are pre-tuned to government stations.

Travel within the country generally requires a permit which is normally granted only for state business, weddings, or funerals, although some reports suggest that internal travel restrictions have been slightly eased. Travel into the capital is heavily restricted, with permission usually granted only for government business. The government reportedly forcibly resettles politically suspect citizens. Chinese authorities return some refugees and defectors at the border, many of whom are reportedly summarily executed. Chinese sources say many North Koreans are in fact returned by North Korean agents operating across the border. Only a handful of foreign journalists are accredited in North Korea and entry for foreign visitors is highly restricted.

The General Federation of Trade Unions is the sole legal trade union federation, and its affiliates are used to monitor workers. The regime does not permit strikes, collective bargaining, or other core labor activity. Religious practice is restricted to state-sponsored Buddhist and Christian services. Private property ownership is banned.

Korea, South

Polity: Presidential-parliamentary democracy
Economy: Capitalist-statist
Population: 46,400,000
PPP: $11,594
Life Expectancy: 74
Ethnic Groups: Korean
Capital: Seoul

Political Rights: 2
Civil Liberties: 2
Status: Free

Overview:

As South Korea struggled through its deepest economic crisis in decades, veteran pro-democracy campaigner Kim Dae Jung took office as president in February 1998 in the country's first transfer of power to the opposition. Kim, who won presidential elections two months earlier, began tackling the crony capitalism and staggering corporate debt problems that had wracked this advanced industrial economy.

The Republic of Korea was established in August 1948 with the division of the Korean Peninsula. In the next four decades, authoritarian rulers suppressed civil liberties while undertaking a state-directed industrialization drive that transformed a poor, agrarian country into the eleventh largest economy in the world. South Korea's democratic transition began in 1987, when violent student-led protests rocked the country after Chun Doo Hwan, a former general who had seized power in a 1980 coup, picked another army general, Roh Tae Woo, as his successor. Roh called for direct presidential elections in December 1987, and beat the country's best-known dissidents, Kim Young Sam and Kim Dae Jung.

The 1988 constitution limits the president to a single five-year term and ended his power to dissolve the 299-seat National Assembly. Kim Young Sam merged his party with the ruling party to form the governing Democratic Liberal Party (DLP) in 1990, and won the 1992 presidential election to become the first civilian president since 1961.

Kim curbed the internal surveillance powers of the security services, shook up the military hierarchy, and launched an anti-corruption campaign. But his popularity waned as the reforms slowed. At the April 1996 legislative elections, the DLP, re-named the New Korea Party, won only a 139-seat plurality, with the opposition divided between Kim Dae Jung's center-left National Congress for New Politics (NCNP) and the conservative United Liberal Democrats (ULD). In an unprecedented development in the fall, a court sentenced former presidents Chun and Roh to death and 22-years' imprisonment, respectively, on charges of corruption and treason during the military era. Kim Young Sam reduced both sentences, and as president-elect, Kim Dae Jung pardoned both men as a goodwill gesture toward political conservatives.

In 1997, an economic slowdown caused eight highly leveraged chaebol, or conglomerates, to collapse under heavy debts and triggered a banking crisis. For decades the government had directed bank lending to chaebols in order to develop strategic industries, and the chaebols funneled cash back to the ruling party. But this politicized lending ultimately encouraged the chaebols to diversify haphazardly and pursue market share rather than profit. In November, as corporations bought dollars in anticipation of higher overseas borrowing costs, the value of the won plummeted, and the country came within weeks of a private-sector debt default.

With Kim constitutionally barred from a second term, the 1997 presidential election turned into a wide-open race. Kim Dae Jung ran a strong campaign that sought to refute his portrayal by past military governments as a radical who would be soft on Communist North Korea. He formed an alliance with conservative ULD leader Kim Jong Pil, whom he promised to name as prime minister, and pledged to transform the polity into a parliamentary system. As the campaign continued, on December 3, the government agreed to a $57 billion dollar International Monetary Fund-led bailout conditioned on corporate reform and an end to lifetime labor guarantees. As popular anger mounted over the country's worst economic crisis in decades, Kim won the December 18 election with 40.4 percent of the vote, as Lee Hoi Chang, the ruling party's candidate, and Rhee In Je, a ruling party defector, split the conservative vote.

Kim took office on February 25, 1998. His challenges included dealing with an opposition-dominated National Assembly, making his alliance with Kim Jong Pil's ULD work, reforming the chaebols, breaking the entrenched alliance between government and big business, and convincing his labor allies to accept layoffs. In negotiations that began while he was president-elect, Kim opened financial markets to foreigners, ordered the chaebols to adopt international accounting standards, and persuaded trade unions to accept new labor laws that ended a tradition of lifetime employment in return for improved social benefits and further corporate reforms. The government also restructured some $150 billion in private-sector foreign debt.

As the financial crisis appeared to bottom out, labor leaders charged that even though huge numbers of workers were being laid off, corporations were still largely resisting reform. In December, the five largest chaebols announced that they would sell more than half of their subsidiaries, but many observers greeted the news with skepticism.

Political Rights and Civil Liberties:

South Koreans can change their government democratically. The judiciary is independent. In 1997, a court sentenced then-president Kim Young Sam's youngest son to a three-year prison term for bribery and tax evasion (currently on appeal). Along with other recent high-profile corruption cases, this is an unprecedented development in a country in which rulers and their corporate patrons and families had been considered above the law. Anecdotal reports suggest that corruption in politics, business, and daily life has decreased in recent years but is still pervasive.

Despite its democratic status, South Korea holds hundreds of political prisoners, a legacy of its authoritarian past and of the omnipresent security threat from North Korea. Most are either labor activists convicted of holding illegal strikes, or supporters of North Korea who refuse to renounce communism. Authorities continue to apply the broadly-drawn National Security Law (NSL), under which hundreds of people are arrested each year for allegedly pro-North Korean statements, for unauthorized ownership of North Korean publications or contact with North Koreans, and for other nonviolent activities. In March, Kim freed 74 political prisoners. Minkahyup, a human rights organization, said it had submitted a list of 478 political prisoners it felt should be pardoned. Both political prisoners and ordinary detainees are often beaten to extract confessions, and generally do not have access to an attorney during interrogation.

In 1996, parliament restored the National Security Planning Agency's authority to investigate and interrogate people accused of pro-North Korean sympathies, powers that had largely been rescinded in 1994. The government says legislative oversight has made the Agency more accountable than under the military rule. In March, Kim fired 24 top officials at the agency and ordered further reforms.

In recent years, courts have convicted and jailed several journalists under criminal defamation laws for articles critical of officials or corporations. Courts convicted at least one journalist of criminal defamation in 1998. Authorities reportedly pressure editors to kill critical articles, and the largely private media practice some self-censorship. The broadcast media are subsidized by the state but offer varied viewpoints. Television featured significantly for the first time in the 1997 presidential election campaign, although citizens complained of an emphasis on frivolity and personality rather than policies.

Civic institutions are strong and local human rights groups operate openly. Student protests have become a ritual occurrence and frequently turn violent. Women face social and professional discrimination, and domestic violence is reportedly fairly widespread. Religious freedom is respected.

Labor relations are frequently characterized by union militancy and forceful responses by authorities. In 1997, parliament lifted a ban on multiple trade unions in each industry that had maintained the dominance of the military-rule-era Federation of Korean Trade Unions. The independent Korean Confederation of Trade Unions had been technically illegal despite representing 550,000 workers. However, union monopolies at the company level will continue until 2002.

New labor laws in February ended the tradition of lifetime employment by allowing job dismissals, but also allowed unions to engage in political activity and granted state-employed teachers the right to organize. Other civil servants received the right to form "consultative" groups. Foreign workers are frequently forced to work longer hours and for less pay than initially promised, and are occasionally beaten and otherwise abused.

Kuwait

Polity: Traditional monarchy and limited parliament
Economy: Capitalist-statist
Population: 1,900,000
PPP: $23,848
Life Expectancy: 72
Ethnic Groups: Kuwaiti (45 percent), other Arab (35 percent), South Asian (9 percent), Iranian (4 percent), other (7 percent)
Capital: Kuwait City

Political Rights: 5
Civil Liberties: 5
Status: Partly Free

Overview:

Kuwait was buffeted by political and economic uncertainty throughout 1998. Hostilities between the government and the parliament led to conflict in June, while slumping oil prices underscored the need for economic reform. Although the government made progress on human rights through prisoner releases, it delivered a blow to the political rights of Kuwaiti women and also considered increased restrictions on access to information for all Kuwaitis.

The al-Sabah family has ruled Kuwait since 1756. Under a special treaty, Kuwait ceded control of its foreign affairs and defense to Britain in 1899. The sheikdom was granted full independence in 1961, and the 1962 constitution provides for an *emir* with broad executive powers who rules through an appointed prime minister and Council of Ministers. The emir shares power with an elected 50-member National Assembly, which is subject to dissolution or suspension by decree.

In March 1998, the government resigned after its Information Minister allowed a book deemed inappropriate by Islamists to be displayed at an exhibition. The emir appointed Crown Prince Sheikh Saad al-Abdulla al-Sabah as prime minister and charged him with forming a new government. In June, the new government and parliament were locked in a standoff over the government's refusal to allow several ministers to be questioned by legislators regarding drug enforcement and human rights issues. The government claimed that some ministries are not accountable to parliament, while legislators maintained that the constitution allows them to question whomever they like. Discussions between the two sides eased tensions but did not result in a formal resolution to the problem.

Economists routinely express concerns that Kuwait's cradle-to-grave welfare state cannot be maintained indefinitely. Ninety-three percent of working Kuwaitis draw monthly tax-free salaries from the state, while an estimated 55 percent of the workforce is "underemployed"—that is, placed in menial state jobs for the sake of employment statistics. Oil revenues that support this system dropped by 26 percent in 1998, and Kuwait began dipping into its $50 billion foreign investment fund. Tensions emerged in October as the government contemplated cuts to the welfare state, while the public saw corruption as the source of Kuwait's economic ills.

Political Rights and Civil Liberties:

Kuwaitis cannot change their government democratically. According to the constitution, the hereditary emir holds executive power and can declare martial law and suspend both the parliament as well as specific articles of the constitution. The parliament may not overrule the emir.

Kuwait is the only Gulf state to hold legislative elections. Eligible voters in Kuwait include men who can trace their Kuwaiti ancestry back to 1920 as well as men who have been citizens for over 20 years. Women may not vote or stand for office. Political parties are banned under a 1986 decree but operate informally.

During a period of martial law following Kuwait's liberation in 1991, suspected Iraqi collaborators—primarily Palestinians, Iraqis, Jordanians, and *bidoon* (stateless Arabs)—were subject to extra-judicial killings, arbitrary arrest, torture, and "disappearance." Hundreds of alleged collaborators were tried in court proceedings that did not meet international standards of fairness. Throughout 1998, Kuwait and Iraq disputed the numbers of prisoners that each side holds. Relations with Jordan, on the other hand, continued to improve as Kuwait began releasing Jordanian prisoners and closed its Gulf War prison in June.

No military court trials have taken place since 1991. The State Security Courts were dissolved in 1995. One court system tries both civil and criminal cases. Defendants have the right to appeal and, in felony cases, must legally be represented by legal counsel. Women may testify, and a woman's testimony is accorded equal weight to that of a man, except in the *Shari'a* (Islamic law) courts which handle family law cases.

Police reportedly abuse detainees during interrogation. Though the government claims to investigate allegations of abuse, findings of such investigations and information about punishments are not made public. Under the penal code, suspects may not be detained for over four days without charges. In July, Kuwait demonstrated its tough stance against drugs by executing two Iranian smugglers.

Citizens may freely criticize the government, but not the al-Sabah family. The press law prohibits publication of articles critical of the royal family, as well as those deemed likely to provoke hatred or dissent. Seven privately owned newspapers exist. Foreign periodicals are sold freely and rarely censored. The information minister, however, does have arbitrary authority over print content, and at least two journalists were sent to jail for "blasphemous" or "insulting" articles in 1998. Broadcast media are state owned and favor the government. It has been possible to access international media through satellite dishes and radio, yet in September a committee on Islamic law proposed the establishment of a cable system that would allow officials to censor satellite broadcasts.

The government restricts freedom of assembly, though informal political groupings, some of which may be characterized as oppositionist, exist without government interference. Prior government approval is required for public gatherings. Some 150,000 bidoon are considered illegal residents. As many as 160,000 fled Kuwait during the 1990 Iraqi invasion, and were not allowed to return despite claims that their families remain in Kuwait. In June, the government took steps to clarify the bidoons' status by granting work and residency rights to those with families in Kuwait and by considering all others on a case-by-case basis.

Women are restricted from working in certain professions, although they receive equal pay for equal work. They must receive permission from husbands or male relatives to travel abroad. Draft legislation that would have given Kuwaiti women the right to vote was rejected by parliament in March.

Islam is the state religion; both Sunnis and Shi'ites worship freely. Christians may worship and build churches. Proselytizing Muslims is forbidden, and only Muslims may become citizens. People of religions which are not recognized by the Shari'a may gather publicly. Thus, Hindus, Sikhs, and Buddhists may not build places of worship but may practice at home.

The government maintains financial control over unions through subsidies that account for 90 percent of union budgets. Only one union is permitted per industry or profession, and only one labor federation, the progovernment Kuwaiti trade Union Federation, exists. Strikes are legal and do occur, although foreign labor organizers have been arrested and deported.

Foreign workers face discrimination in legal proceedings. They must have five-years' residence in Kuwait before joining labor unions. Roughly 100,000 foreign domestic servants are not covered by the labor law and are subject to abuses including rape and beatings.

Kyrgyz Republic

Polity: Presidential-parliamentary democracy
Economy: Mixed statist (transitional)
Population: 4,700,000
PPP: $1,927
Life Expectancy: 67
Ethnic Groups: Kyrgyz (52 percent), Russian (18 percent), Uzbek (13 percent), Ukrainian (3 percent), German (2 percent), other (12 percent)
Capital: Bishkek

Political Rights: 5*
Civil Liberties: 5*
Status: Partly Free

Ratings change: The Kyrgyz Republic's political rights and civil liberties ratings changed from 4 to 5 due to increased authoritarianism of the executive and corruption.

Overview: In 1998, President Askar Akayev successfully advocated constitutional amendments that would enlarge parliament, provide for private ownership of land, and limit parliamentary immunity to activities connected with parliamentary duties. The revisions were adopted by public referendum in October.

Kubanychbek Dzumaliev, head of the presidential administration, was appointed to the largely ceremonial post of prime minister in March. He replaced Apas Dzumagulov, who resigned allegedly for health reasons. There was wide speculation, however, that he was forced to step down to prevent a possible scandal over gold sales. In April, President Akayev carried out the largest government reshuffle since 1991.

The Kyrgyz Republic declared independence from the Soviet Union in 1991. In what was called the "Silk Revolution," President Akayev, a respected physicist, introduced multiparty democracy and market reforms. But resistance from a Communist-dominated, 350-member parliament elected in 1990 led Akayev to dissolve the legislature in 1994 and decree a national referendum for changes in the constitution as well as the creation of a bicameral, 105-member body (*Jogorku Kenesh*), with a 35-seat lower chamber as a permanent legislature and a 70-member upper chamber to meet only occasionally to approve the budget and confirm presidential appointees. Nearly 75 percent of voters approved the proposal for a new parliament. In 1995 parliamentary elections, 82 seats went to a mix of governing officials, businessmen, intellectuals, and clan leaders, with the Communists gaining only a handful of seats. Akayev then won the presidency with over 60 percent of the vote.

In February 1996, voters approved a referendum that changed more than half of the constitution to enhance presidential power. The new document gave the president the power to appoint all top officials, although the prime minister requires parliamentary approval. If parliament rejects three of the president's nominees, he can dissolve the body.

The April 1998 government reshuffle came amid growing economic difficulties. The country was mired with a $1 billion foreign debt, a substantial budget deficit, plunging exports, and little foreign investment. The shakeup also came amid allegations of corruption involving cost overruns at the Kumtor gold mining operation, owned jointly with the Canadian company Cameco. Corruption in government and business continued to be a problem. Prime Minister Dzumagulov resigned after it was reported that he helped an Austrian firm charged with selling Kyrgyz gold abroad and controlled the country's oil and alcohol industries. The privatization process was widely considered to have been manipulated by officials in order to benefit friends and associates.

In October, the public approved constitutional amendments which expanded the Legislative Assembly (lower chamber) from 35 to 60, and decreased the Assembly of People's Representatives (upper chamber) from 70 to 45. The revisions were proposed by a September presidential decree.

Political Rights and Civil Liberties:

Citizens can elect their government under a multiparty system. The 1996 constitution, approved by referendum, codifies strong presidential rule and a weak parliament. Parliamentary and presidential elections in 1995 included such violations as ballot stuffing, inflation of voter turnout, media restrictions, and intimidation. Constitutional amendments in 1998 increased the number of deputies in the lower house as well as the upper house.

The new criminal code and press law adopted in 1997 placed restrictions on the publication of state secrets, materials that advocate war, violence or intolerance of ethnic groups, and libeling public officials. No private local radio or television stations exist. Only one private radio station, Radio Almaz, and one private television station operate nationally. In February 1998, Radio Almaz was shutdown for a month, but resumed broadcasting a month later on a provisional basis. Independent VOSST tele-radio station in Bishkek was also shut down for 36 hours in February. Licenses were held up for several regional TV and radio stations. There are several independent papers, among them *Res Publica*, *Asaba*, *Delo No*, and *Vecherniy Bishkek*.

Freedom of religion is guaranteed in this predominantly Islamic country, where Christians and Jews can worship freely and openly, though religious groups must register with the State Commission on Religious Affairs. The Commission has refused to register some Protestant denominations. The government was concerned about the spread of Wahhabi Islam in the Osh region.

Freedoms of assembly and movement are respected inconsistently. In September, local authorities in southern Kyrgyzstan banned an opposition rally. Two men were later held for organizing an unsanctioned rally and "circulating materials and rumors aimed against public order and the security of citizens." The rally was held to demand that the referendum on constitution amendments not be held.

Major political parties include the Communists on the left, the nationalist Asaba, and the Social Democrats, the Republican Party, the Agrarians, and Erkin (Freedom). The largest political movement is the progovernment Democratic Movement of Kyrgyzstan. Most parties are small and weak, with vague platforms and little financial support.

A 1992 law permits the formation of independent unions; most workers belong to the Federation of Independent Trade Unions of Kyrgyzstan (FITUK), the successor to the Soviet-era labor federation. Over 450 nongovernmental organizations are registered, ranging from business groups to sports and charitable associations.

The judiciary is not independent and remains influenced by the executive branch. The procurator, not the judge, is in charge of criminal proceedings, and courts of elders still operate in remote regions. A new system of court administration has improved judicial professionalism.

Although the constitution guarantees minority rights, there has been an exodus of educated and skilled Russians and Germans. The Uigur organization Ittipak (Unity) has faced sporadic suspension for "separatist activities." In the south, tensions have eased somewhat between Kyrgyz and Uzbeks, but southern politicians continue to complain about underrepresentation in parliament.

Restrictions remain on freedom of movement. Under a Soviet-era law, citizens need official government permission (a "propiska") to work and settle in a particular area of the country.

The 1990 property law allows foreign and Kyrgyz citizens to own homes, vehicles, means of production, enterprises, and buildings. A 1998 constitutional amendment permitted the private ownership of land. The legal and regulatory environment for business operations is widely regarded as superior to those in neighboring countries. Nevertheless, personal connections, corruption, and insider privatization have put limits on competition and equal opportunity.

Women are well represented in the workforce, business, higher education, and NGOs. Domestic violence against women has reportedly increased since 1991.

Laos

Polity: Communist one-party
Economy: Statist
Population: 5,300,000
PPP: $2,571
Life Expectancy: 54
Ethnic Groups: Lao Loum (68 percent), Lao Theung (22 percent), Lao Soung [includes Hmong and Yao] (9 percent), ethnic Vietnamese/Chinese (1 percent)
Capital: Vientiane

Political Rights: 7
Civil Liberties: 6
Status: Not Free

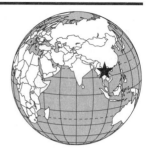

Overview:
In 1998, Laos was marked by changes in leadership, a downturn in its struggling economy, the death of an imprisoned political activist, and increased repression of religious freedoms.

This landlocked, mountainous Southeast Asian country became a French protectorate in 1893. In October 1953, following the Japanese occupation during World War II, the Communist Pathet Lao (Land of Lao) won independence from the French. Royalist, Communist, and conservative factions turned on each other in 1964. In May 1975, the Pathet Lao took the capital, Vientiane, from a royalist government and seven months later established a one-party state under Prime Minister Kaysone Phomvihane's Lao People's Revolutionary Party (LPRP).

In theory, the 85 member National Assembly is elected for a five-year term and names the president. In reality, the parliamentary elections are tightly controlled, and the presidential election is decided by the LPRP leadership. The 1991 constitution codified the leading political role of the LPRP and transition to a limited market economy. Kaysone subsequently took over as president, while veteran revolutionary Khamtay Siphandone succeeded him as prime minister. The constitution also expanded the powers of the president, who heads the armed forces and can remove the prime minister.

Kaysone died in 1992. Assembly Speaker Nouhak Phoumsavan and Prime Minister Khamtay became state president and LPRP chairman, respectively. The government permitted pre-approved independents to compete for the first time in the December 1992 parliamentary elections. Four independents have won seats.

In March 1996, the sixth LPRP congress carried out personnel changes that continued a generational shift in leadership. But the congress also strengthened the military's political role and promoted several hardliners who feared that privatization and other economic reforms could erode the LPRP's authority. At the December 21, 1997 parliamentary elections, the party's pre-approved roster of candidates supported old-guard conservatives over technocrats favoring market reforms.

In February 1998, the national assembly chose Khatmay to replace Nouhak as president. Former minister of agriculture and Vice President Sisvath Keobounphanh filled the vacated prime minister's seat. These changes continued the trend towards more conservative leadership in Laos.

The LPRP introduced market reforms in 1986 to revive an economy that had been decimated by a decade of central planning. The authorities have privatized farms and some state-owned enterprises, removed price controls, and encouraged foreign investment. By 1998, Thailand was the biggest source of foreign direct investment in Laos, pouring $3 billion into the country over the last ten years. Nonetheless, annual per capita income in Laos for 1998 was $400. Fears of Thai economic hegemony along with continued poverty and international isolation led to the government's successful push for membership in the Association of Southeast Nations (ASEAN) in 1997. Since then, however, the government has been concerned that ASEAN may pressure Laos to abide by international legal and human rights standards. And ASEAN membership has done little to protect Laos from the Asian economic crisis. By June 1998, Laos's national currency, the *kip*, had depreciated 70 per cent to the dollar and inflation was 60 percent annually. The economy's poor performance has increased government skepticism towards market reforms.

Political Rights and Civil Liberties:

Laos is a one-party state controlled by the Lao People's Revolutionary Party, and citizens cannot change their government democratically. Opposition parties are not expressly banned, but in practice are not tolerated by the government.

Some elements of state control, including the widespread monitoring of civilians by police, have been relaxed in recent years. Domestic and international travel restrictions were eased in 1994. However, the security services still search homes without warrants, monitor some personal communications, and maintain neighborhood and workplace committees that inform on the population.

The rule of law is nonexistent. The judiciary is not independent of the government, and trials lack adequate procedural safeguards. Prison conditions are harsh.

In February 1998, one of three former government officials imprisoned in 1990 for advocating peaceful political reform died because he was denied medical treatment for diabetes. The two other men remain in prison. Most of the tens of thousands of people who were sent to "re-education" camps following the Communist victory in 1975 have been released. Unconfirmed reports, however, suggest that the regime may be holding several hundred political prisoners.

Although the constitution allows for freedom of speech and expression, they are extremely limited in practice. The government owns all newspapers and electronic media and uses them to spread state propaganda. The LPRP controls all associations, and the government does not permit independent elements of civil society. Political assemblies, except for those organized by the government, are usually prohibited. In February, however, 350 Hmong tribespeople protested in front of the U.S. embassy in Vientiane over land policy and did eventually win some concessions from the Laotian government.

The government's record on religious freedom took a turn for the worse in 1998. According to Open Doors International, Laos went from twenty-third to seventh among the world's least tolerant countries for religious expression. Buddhists can generally worship freely, but the Catholic Church is unable to operate in the north. In January, a group of 44 Christians, including five citizens from France, the United States, and Thailand, was arrested for holding bible study classes. They were charged with carrying out unauthorized activities and using Christianity to slander government officials. The foreigners were deported. Ten Laotians were sentenced to one to three year prison terms. Three others received one-year suspended sentences. The appeal of a former military officer who was charged with sedition for his work as a Christian activist in 1996 was rejected in January. He was then sent back to prison and has not been heard from since. Amnesty International estimated that at least two dozen people had been imprisoned in 1998 for either practicing their religious beliefs or associating with foreign religious organizations.

Women and members of minority groups are represented in the national assembly, although not proportionate to their overall presence in the population. There are no women and only a few minorities in the Politburo and Council of Ministers.

The Hmong, the largest of several hill tribes, have conducted a small-scale insurgency since the Communist takeover, although they have become less active in recent years. Both the Hmong guerrillas and the armed forces have previously been accused of occasional human rights violations in the context of the insurgency, including extrajudicial killings. The United Nations High Commissioner for Refugees (UNHCR) is still investigating reports in July that the Laotian government had harassed Hmong tribespeople returning from Thailand. Voluntary repatriation of Laotians from Thailand has been implemented with few problems since international accords closed Southeast Asian refugee camps in 1989.

A ministerial decree from 1990 allows for independent trade unions at private companies. These unions, however, are only permitted if they operate within the framework of the party-controlled Federation of Lao Trade Unions. There is no legal right to bargain collectively. The right to strike does exist, but sweeping bans on "subversive or destabilizing activities" prevent strikes from occurring.

⬆ Latvia

Polity: Presidential-parliamentary democracy
Economy: Mixed capitalist
Population: 2,400,000
PPP: $3,273
Life Expectancy: 70

Political Rights: 1
Civil Liberties: 2
Status: Free

Ethnic Groups: Latvian (57 percent), Russian (30 percent), Byelorussian (4 percent), Ukrainian (3 percent), Polish (3 percent), other (3 percent)
Capital: Riga
Trend Arrow: Latvia received an upward trend arrow due to further liberalization of the country's citizenship law.

Overview:

In an October 3 referendum, Latvian voters approved amendments to the country's citizenship law which eased restrictions on naturalization for the country's large noncitizen population. Following concurrent parliamentary elections, the formation of a new government was stalled for almost two months by negotiations in which personal animosities and political feuds outweighed ideological similarities.

After centuries of foreign domination by Germany, Poland, Sweden, and Russia,

Latvia gained its independence in 1918. The country was forcibly incorporated into the Soviet Union during World War II under the provisions of a secret protocol of the 1939 Hitler-Stalin pact. More than 50 years of Soviet occupation saw a massive influx of Russians and the deportation, execution and emigration of tens of thousands of ethnic Latvians. The proportion of Latvians decreased from 77 percent in 1940 to 52 percent in 1991, the year the country regained its independence in the wake of the USSR's disintegration.

Following the October 1995 parliamentary elections, nonparty businessman and former agricultural minister Andris Skele formed a center-right coalition that included Democratic Party Saimnieks, the Latvian Way Union, the Latvian Farmers' Union, and other moderate conservative parties. Subsequently, President Guntis Ulmanis was elected to a second term on June 18, 1996. The year 1997 was marked by continual government instability, with Skele finally turning over the premiership to Guntars Krasts of the nationalist Fatherland and Freedom party in July-August.

On April 8, 1998, Democratic Party Saimnieks (DPS) withdrew from the governing coalition following growing tensions with Krast's Fatherland and Freedom party. With the departure of the DPS, Krasts was left to head a minority government holding only 45 of the legislature's 100 seats.

In the October national legislative elections, six parties secured enough votes to enter parliament. Former Prime Minister Andris Skele's newly created People's Party (PP) won 24 seats; Latvia's Way (LW), 21; Fatherland and Freedom/LNNK (FF/LNNK), 17; the National Harmony Party (NHP), 16; the Alliance of Social Democrats (SDU), 14; and the New Party (NP), 8. After nearly two months of negotiations, parliament finally approved a new minority government on November 26 led by Latvia's Way leader Vilis Kristopans and consisting of the center-right LW, FF/LNNK and NP. The People's Party of Skele, who is widely disliked for his authoritarian and abrasive style, was effectively excluded from the new administration despite its election win and its political similarities with the three coalition parties. With only 46 of 100 seats in parliament, and at best limited cooperation with the SDU, the current government's future stability and effectiveness remains a question.

Russia's economic crisis had a considerable impact on Latvia's economy in late 1998, with the country's significant Russian-oriented trade and banking sectors most strongly affected. In November, Latvia was stung by its exclusion from fast-track membership talks to the European Union, although it may be invited to pre-accession discussions sometime in 1999.

Political Rights and Civil Liberties:

Latvians can change their government democratically. However, Latvia's citizenship laws have been criticized for disenfranchising almost one-third of the country's population which immigrated to Latvia during the Soviet period and must apply for citizenship. The constitution provides for a 100-member parliament (*Saeima*), elected for four-year terms by proportional representation, which in turn selects the country's president. International observers determined that the most recent legislative elections in 1998 were free and fair. More than 40 political parties are officially registered, although Communist, Nazi, and other organizations whose activities would contravene the constitution are banned.

The government respects freedom of the press, and both Latvian- and Russian-language newspapers publish a wide range of political viewpoints. There are a large number of private television and radio stations broadcasting programs in Latvian and Russian. Religious tolerance is widespread and freedom of worship is generally respected in practice.

Freedom of assembly and association are protected by law, and numerous public gatherings and demonstrations occurred in 1998 without government interference. However, two events in the spring of 1998 attracted considerable attention in the Russian media and further soured already tense relations between Latvia and Russia. On March 3, police used rubber truncheons to disperse an illegal demonstration of mostly Russian pensioners who were blocking a road in front of the Riga City Council building where they were protesting low living standards. Although no injuries were reported, Moscow responded by accusing Latvia of violating the rights of ethnic Russians and threatening to impose economic sanctions. Two weeks later, a commemorative march of the controversial Latvian Legion, formed by German occupation forces during World War II, was denounced by Russia and the international community. The head of the National Armed Forces subsequently resigned over criticism that, contrary to a government warning, he had participated in the event dressed in military uniform.

Workers have the right to form trade unions, strike, and engage in collective bargaining. However, some workers in the private sector fear dismissal if they strike, and the government has a limited ability to protect their rights.

The judicial system is weak and inefficient, and corruption is reportedly widespread. Most judges are not adequately trained, and many judges' posts remain vacant. There have been reports of police using excessive force against prisoners and asylum seekers. While prison facilities remain overcrowded and conditions poor, new construction efforts and foreign assistance have facilitated some recent improvements.

In 1998, the country's Law on Citizenship was amended to ease and accelerate the naturalization process. The amendments eliminated the so-called "naturalization windows," or specific periods during which noncitizens may apply for citizenship. They also offer citizenship to noncitizens' children born after August 21, 1991 (the date of Latvia's independence from the USSR) at their parents' request and without a Latvian language test. Although the amendments passed their first two readings in parliament in May and June, their adoption was postponed when a group of MPs, at the initiative of the Fatherland and Freedom Party, requested that a referendum be held on the issue. On October 3, the electorate ratified the amendments with a slim 52.5 percent of the vote. The result was welcomed by international organizations, including the European Union and the Organization for Security and Cooperation in Europe (OSCE). Currently, approximately 650,000 of Latvia's 2.5 million inhabitants are noncitizens. According to estimates of the country's naturalization department, 20,000-25,000 people could be expected to become citizens each year under the new legislation.

On October 15, parliament amended the constitution with a new chapter outlining 27 generally recognized human rights, which until then had been protected by provisions contained in an interim Constitutional Law. Despite objections from Latvia's ethnic Russian population, parliament passed a constitutional amendment declaring Latvian as the official state language and adopted an education law requiring all state schools to teach in Latvian by 2004.

Women possess the same legal rights as men, although they frequently face hiring and pay discrimination and sexual harassment in the workplace.

Lebanon

Polity: Presidential-
parliamentary (military-
and foreign-influenced,
partly foreign-occupied)
Economy: Mixed statist
Population: 4,100,000
PPP: $4,977
Life Expectancy: 70
Ethnic Groups: Arab (95 percent), Armenian (4 percent), other (1 percent)
Capital: Beirut

Political Rights: 6
Civil Liberties: 5
Status: Not Free

Overview:
Lebanon saw significant changes in government in 1998. At the local level, Lebanese voted in their first municipal elections in 35 years. At the national level, parliament voted unanimously to install General Emile Lahoud, the widely popular former Army chief, in the position of president. Refusing to serve under Lahoud, Prime Minister Rafiq Hariri stepped down in December, making way for Salim al-Hoss. It is yet unclear whether Lebanon's new leaders will undertake the badly needed economic reform and rural development advocated by opposition activists.

Lebanon gained full sovereignty from France in 1946. An unwritten National Pact in 1943 gave Christians political dominance over the Muslim population through a mandatory six to five ratio of parliamentary seats. After three decades during which non-Christians tried to end this system, a civil war erupted between Muslim, Christian, and Druze militias in 1975, claiming over 150,000 lives before it ended in 1990. Complicating the situation was the presence of the Palestine Liberation Organization (PLO), which, after having been expelled from Jordan in 1971, used Lebanon as a base for attacks against Israel and constituted an occupying force. Syria sent troops into Lebanon to support the government in 1976. Syrians, who consider Lebanon part of Greater Syria, continue to occupy the country today.

A peace plan put forward by the Arab League was ratified by the Lebanese assembly on November 5, 1989 in Taif, Saudi Arabia. The Taif Accord maintained the tradition of a Maronite Christian president indirectly elected to a six-year term, but it transferred most executive power to the prime minister, a Sunni Muslim, by agreement. A Shi'ite Muslim serves as speaker of parliament, which is now evenly split between Muslims and Christians.

The Lebanese government is not sovereign in its own country. With some 35,000-40,000 troops in Lebanon, Syria dominates the country politically and militarily. The 128-member parliament, elected in September 1996, follows the Syrian line on internal and regional affairs. Israel's South Lebanon Army (SLA) controls a 440-square-mile security zone in the south; the Shi'ite, pro-Iranian Hezbollah militia is still active in many southern towns; and Palestinian groups operate autonomously in refugee camps throughout the country.

Municipal elections held in May and June 1998 were not subject to sectarian quotas, as are legislative elections. After boycotting two legislative elections since 1991 to protest Syrian occupation, Maronite Christians took part in the polls to contest 646 municipal councils and 2,000 mayoral seats. A "Beirut Accord List" representing Hezbollah, Maronites, and others won 23 of 24 seats in Beirut, bringing a balance of Christians and Muslims to the capital's municipal council. The government and the Muslim, pro-Syria Amal movement fared poorly in Mount Lebanon, while Hezbollah and Christians made notable gains. Voter turnout ranged from 32 to 80 percent.

The balance of power enshrined in the Taif Accord resulted in overlapping authority among the speaker, prime minister, and president. Sectarian tensions and conflicting priorities among the three have often led to political infighting and stalled political and economic progress. Syria, meanwhile, has worked to manipulate these tensions in order to keep its position as mediator. But by choosing Emile Lahoud as Lebanon's president, Syria brought in a popular politician who is respected across sectarian lines. As head of the armed forces, he turned fragmented civil war militias into a unified army and gained wide public support in the process. It is thought that Syria, recognizing that political stability is vital to its economic interest, has decided to try to foster internal cooperation rather than incite hostilities.

In late November, Prime Minister Rafiq Hariri sparked a crisis by turning down Lahoud's invitation to form a new government. Though Hariri claimed that Lahoud had conducted unconstitutional dealings with parliament, analysts believe that Hariri was angry over Lahoud's attempts to influence his choice of ministers. In December, Lahoud appointed Salim al-Hoss, a former prime minister and widely respected economist. Al-Hoss scrapped Hariri's agenda of restoring Lebanon to its pre-war glory as a regional trade and financial center, citing the need to be "realistic." Instead, he stressed administrative reform and increased transparency in public departments as priorities. As a first move, the new prime minister cut the number of cabinet ministers from 30 to 16, largely ignoring religious quotas and including 11 first-time members.

Political Rights and Civil Liberties:

Shortcomings in the electoral system limit the right of Lebanese citizens to change their government. Parliamentary elections held in 1996 were neither prepared nor carried out impartially. According to the constitution, a president is to be elected by parliament every six years. In fact, Syria's choice of president is simply ratified by parliament. At the last election in 1995, the Syrian government extended incumbent Elias Hrawi's term for an extra three years. Just prior to the election of Lahoud in October, parliament amended a constitutional requirement that senior government officials resign their posts at least two years before running for office.

Municipal elections held in May and June were considered reasonably free and fair by the U.S. State Department. Opposition activists routinely complain that villages and towns in more remote areas have gone neglected while postwar reconstruction efforts have focused on Beirut. It is hoped that the new municipal councils will address this issue, though their powers are severely limited.

The judiciary is influenced by Syrian political pressure, which affects the appointments of key prosecutors and investigating magistrates. The judicial system comprises civilian courts, a military court, and a judicial council. International standards of criminal procedure are not observed in the military court, which consists largely of military officers with no legal training. The average case is tried in minutes. Extra-governmental groups, such as the Israeli South Lebanese Army (SLA), Palestinian factions, and

Hezbollah, detain suspects and administer justice in areas under their control, generally without due process safeguards.

Arbitrary arrest and detention are commonplace. Security forces detained dozens and searched homes without warrants after a car bombing in Dora in mid-June. Security forces use torture to extract confessions. Prison conditions do not meet international standards. Inmates of the Roumieh prison, Lebanon's largest, rioted in April to protest alleged mistreatment and to demand better conditions.

The government continues its crackdown on independent broadcasting, which flourished during the civil war. In January, a government decree banned two of the country's four satellite television stations from broadcasting news or political programming. Since the crackdown began in 1996, the government has licensed only five television stations, three of which are owned by government figures; it has also licensed six radio stations that may carry news and 20 stations that may carry only entertainment. Fifty-two television stations and 124 radio stations have been closed. The appropriation of frequencies is a slow and highly politicized process.

Print media are independent of government, though their content often reflects the opinions of the various local and foreign groups that finance them. Insulting the dignity of the head of state or foreign leaders is prohibited. All foreign print media are subject to government approval. In 1998, three journalists were charged with defamation for criticizing the judiciary, and one was sentenced to three-years' imprisonment and fined for contempt of authority.

In December 1998, the new government lifted a five-year-old ban on public demonstrations. Protests were banned in 1993 after a demonstration against the Oslo Middle East peace accords turned violent. Public assemblies require government approval, which is frequently denied to Christian groups.

Freedom of religion is generally respected. Citizens may travel abroad freely, though internal travel is restricted in certain areas under Israeli or Hezbollah control. Syrian troops maintain checkpoints in areas under their control. The government does not extend legal rights to some 180,000 stateless persons who live mainly in disputed border areas. Some 350,000–500,000 Palestinian refugees live without adequate electricity and water, and face restrictions on travel, work, building, and purchasing property.

In March 1998, President Elias Hrawi introduced a bill to permit marriages regulated by civil rather than religious authorities, making it easier for interfaith couples to marry. Seen as the first step in abolishing Lebanon's confessional political system, the bill did not make it past the cabinet.

Women suffer legal and social discrimination. Although women commonly work in fields such as medicine, law, journalism, and banking, they are severely underrepresented in politics. Women council members constituted only one percent of the newly elected municipal councils.

All workers except those in government may establish unions, strike, and bargain collectively. Foreign domestic workers are routinely abused by employers who treat them like slaves, pay them little or nothing, and confiscate their passports to prevent them from leaving. Women are most vulnerable to brutality or sexual abuse. Lebanon has no written code to arbitrate domestic worker disputes.

Lesotho

Polity: Parliamentary
(transitional)
(post-conflict)
Economy: Capitalist
Population: 2,100,000
PPP: $1,290
Life Expectancy: 56

Political Rights: 4
Civil Liberties: 4
Status: Partly Free

Ethnic Groups: Sotho (99.7 percent), other, including European and Asian (0.3 percent)
Capital: Maseru

Overview:
Lesotho ended a year of political violence and tumult with the creation of a miltiparty committee to oversee preparations for elections by mid-2000. The 24-member Interim Political Authority (IPA) was formed in December with two representatives from each of the country's 12 main political parties. The agreement allows the elected, but highly unpopular, government, which was nearly toppled by a widely supported army mutiny, to retain power, but sets early elections that are to be strictly supervised by an independent election commission.

In September, South African troops entered Lesotho at the government's request to quell army-backed protests against May election results. The poorly planned intervention was resisted by some of Lesotho's soldiers, and, while fighting raged, mobs looted and burned much of the business district of the capital, Maseru. At least 60 people were reportedly killed before order was restored several days later.

The South African forces, supported by troops from Botswana and operating under the mandate of the 14-country Southern Africa Development Community, intervened to preserve the government led by Prime Minster Pakalitha Mosisili and the ruling Lesotho Congress for Democracy (LCD), which won 60 percent of the vote and 79 of 80 National Assembly seats in the May vote. Street protests against the results, which were described by various international observes groups as largely free and fair, began in August and were marked by sporadic violence involving army and police units. An independent report by a South African constitutional expert in September found various irregularities, but nothing to negate the LCD's overall victory. Junior army officers then mutinied and forced the army commander and senior officers to resign, but soon returned to their barracks. By the time South African troops had entered Lesotho, Maseru was on the brink of anarchy, and a military coup, perhaps with support from King Letsie III, appeared imminent. South Africa's intervention has ensured an at least temporary peace.

Entirely surrounded by South Africa, Lesotho is highly dependent on its powerful neighbor. Its economy is sustained by remittances from its many citizens who work in South Africa. Lesotho's status as a British protectorate saved it from incorporation into South Africa. King Moshoeshoe II reigned from independence in 1966 until the installation of his son as King Letsie III in a 1990 military coup. Democratic elections in 1993 did not lead to stability. After bloody military infighting, assassinations, and a suspension of constitutional rule in 1994, King Letsie III abdicated to allow his father's reinstatement. He resumed the throne following the accidental death of his father in January 1996.

Political Rights and Civil Liberties:

The IPA is preparing for new general elections by mid-2000. Legislative elections in May 1998 were determined to be generally free and fair, but the LCD's 60 percent vote translated into an almost total exclusion of opposition representation from the National Assembly. The appearance of irregularities and the virtual elimination of opposition voices from government fueled protests against the results. The Senate, the upper house of the bicameral legislature, includes royal appointees and Lesotho's 22 principal traditional chiefs, who still wield considerable authority in rural areas. Any elected government's exercise of its constitutional authority remains limited by the autonomy of the military, the royal family, and traditional clan structures.

Courts are nominally independent, but higher courts are especially subject to outside influence. The 1984 Internal Security Act, which provides for up to 42 days of detention without charges in political cases, is among a number of laws that contradict the constitution. Freedoms of assembly, expression, and religion are generally respected. Arbitrary detention and mistreatment of civilians by security forces reportedly continue. Several nongovernmental organizations, including the Lesotho Human Rights Alert Group, operate openly.

Journalists have suffered occasional harassment and attacks. *MoAfrika* newspaper editor Candi Ramainoana has been a particular target. The independent print media suffered badly during South Africa's intervention in September, when nearly all of their offices were pillaged by rioting looters. The government maintains a monopoly over broadcasting, but extensive South African radio and television broadcasts reach Lesotho. In October, the information minister demanded the resignations of all state broadcasting employees who had participated in anti-government demonstrations.

Labor rights are constitutionally guaranteed. Approximately ten percent of the country's labor force, which is mostly engaged in subsistence agriculture or employment in South Africa, is unionized. Collective bargaining and the right to strike are recognized by law, but are sometimes denied by government negotiators. Legal requirements for union registration have not been enforced.

The 1993 constitution bars gender-based discrimination, but customary practice and law still restrict women's rights in several areas, including contracts, property rights, and inheritance. A woman is considered a legal minor while her husband is alive. Domestic violence is reportedly widespread.

The 1995 Privatization Act calls for extensive divestiture of state-run enterprises, which constitute almost all of the modern economic sector. Land is the property of the kingdom, and its distribution is generally controlled by local chiefs.

⬇ Liberia

Polity: Presidential-
parliamentary democracy
Economy: Capitalist
Population: 2,800,000
PPP: na
Life Expectancy: 59
Ethnic Groups: Indigenous tribes (95 percent),
Americo-Liberians (5 percent)
Capital: Monrovia

Political Rights: 4
Civil Liberties: 5
Status: Partly Free

Trend arrow: Liberia receives a downward trend arrow due to increasingly authoritarian tendencies demonstrated by President Taylor, including human rights abuses by state security services.

Overview:

In September, Liberia's tenuous calm was shattered by an outbreak of fighting that killed at least 50 people. More generally, long-term peace was threatened by President Charles Taylor's effort to consolidate his own power rather than reconcile the factions that fought a bloody civil war from 1990 to 1996. Taylor and his National Patriotic Party won convincing victories in July 1997 elections that independent observers judged generally free and fair. Taylor's partisan tactics, however, could again enflame the ethnic divisions that helped to make the civil war so intractable. In December, Roman Catholic Archbishop Michael Francis warned that human rights violations, including killings and arbitrary arrests, were continuing with impunity. Harassment of former faction leaders, journalists, and human rights activists increased in 1998. While relative peace now prevails throughout the country, banditry continues in some areas, and a lack of discipline prevails among security forces.

The recent civil war was marked by a savagery unusual even for the ethnic conflict into which it degenerated. It was sparked on the last day of 1989, when Charles Taylor led a small guerrilla force into Liberia in an effort to overthrow the country's military-dominated dictatorship. Ultimately, the war became a multisided ethnic conflict that claimed more than 150,000 lives and forced approximately half of Liberia's nearly three million people to flee their homes. Several peace plans brokered by West African leaders failed. The war's fourteenth and final peace accord, reached in May 1996, provided for the demobilization of more than 20,000 fighters from nine rival ethnic militias under the supervision of Nigerian and other West African peacekeepers, approximately 12,000 of which remain in Liberia.

Liberia was established as an independent republic in 1847 after its settlement by freed American slaves in 1821. For more than a century the country was dominated by the slaves' "Americo-Liberian" descendants. In 1980, army Sergeant Samuel Doe led a bloody coup and murdered President William Tolbert. His regime concentrated power among members of his Kranh ethnic group and suppressed others. Forces led by Charles Taylor, a former government minister, and backed by Gia and Mano ethnic groups that had been subject to severe repression, launched a guerrilla war against the Doe regime at the end of 1989. In 1990, Nigeria, under the aegis of the Economic Community of

West African States, led an armed intervention force, established an interim government, and twice blocked Taylor's victory against the government's Armed Forces of Liberia. In 1991, fighting ravaged Monrovia, and President Doe was captured and tortured to death.

Political Rights and Civil Liberties:

Charles Taylor and his National Patriotic Party assumed power after 1997 elections that were generally free and fair and that constituted Liberia's most genuine electoral exercise in decades. The votes for the presidency and a national assembly on the basis of proportional representation were held under provisions of the 1986 constitution. Veteran UN official and Unity Party leader Ellen Johnson-Sirleaf, who campaigned on a platform of clean governance, was Taylor's closest challenger and remains the voice of the official opposition. Taylor's victory transcended bitter ethnic divisions and reflected a popular consensus for peace.

Liberia's independent media have survived despite years of war, assaults, and harassment at the cost of extensive self-censorship. The pillaging of Monrovia in 1996 destroyed news offices, presses, and broadcasting stations. Like the rest of the country, the media are continuing to rebuild. Several private radio stations have been used as mouthpieces for various political factions. Charles Taylor owns Kiss-FM, the only countrywide FM radio station. The Roman Catholic Church also operates a radio station. With U.S. funding, the Swiss Hirondelle foundation's Star Radio broadcasts civic education programming. It was closed for a month early in the year, however, and remains the target of official harassment. State television and one private station broadcast only irregularly. In October, the government engaged in cyber-censorship by ordering all local media to stop posting any information on the Internet, thus eliminating a major source of international news on developments in Liberia. A highly restrictive Media Law enacted under the Doe regime gives the Ministry of Information broad power to control the media.

Numerous civil society groups, including human rights organizations such as the Catholic Peace and Justice Commission, operate in Monrovia and in the countryside. Rehabilitation of the more than 10,000 child-soldiers recruited as fighters by various factions remains an important priority. Treatment of women varies by ethnic group, religion, and social status. Many women continue to suffer from physical abuse and traditional societal discrimination, despite constitutionally guaranteed equality. Several women's organizations have sought to assist the estimated 25,000 women raped during the civil war. Union activity is permitted by law, but was greatly curtailed during the war. Efforts to reestablish union activity at the Firestone rubber plantations are underway.

Liberians refugees continued to return home through 1998, but face dismal economic prospects as well as insecurity in the countryside. Attacks on mosques in several areas of the country have raised tensions among Mandingoe Muslims and other groups.

Liberia's economic recovery was burdened by its $3 billion external debt. Arrears on loan repayments disqualify the country from IMF assistance and deter private lending. Corruption is a major obstacle to economic growth, and much of the output of Liberia's diamond mines is smuggled untaxed from the country.

Libya

Polity: Military
Economy: Mixed statist
Population: 5,700,000
PPP: $6,309
Life Expectancy: 65
Ethnic Groups: Arab-Berber (97 percent), other, including Greek, Italian, Maltese, Eyptian, Pakistani, Turkish, Indian, Tunisian (3 percent)
Capital: Tripoli

Political Rights: 7
Civil Liberties: 7
Status: Not Free

Overview:
Colonel Mu'ammar al-Qadhafi survived an alleged assassination attempt and jousted with the United States and Britain over the potential International Court of Justice trial of two Libyan suspects in the deadly 1988 bombing of Pan Am flight 103. UN sanctions against Libya eroded during the year as European countries launched major new investments and African and Arab leaders flouted the UN air embargo. In Tripoli, Libya opened its own international trial to charge senior American officials and navy personnel with "barbaric aggression" in a 1986 air raid that failed to kill Colonel Qadhafi, but left one of his children and many civilians dead. The U.S. attack was in retaliation for alleged Libyan involvement in a Berlin terrorist bombing aimed at American servicemen. The Pan Am bombing may have been Libya's revenge for the raid on Tripoli.

The reported ambush of Qadhafi's motorcade in May near the eastern city of Benghazi was said to have killed several bodyguards, but only lightly wounded the Libyan leader. The mountains around Benghazi are home to several armed dissident movements, some of which are radical Islamists. The Islamic Fighting Group, the Islamic Martyrs Movement, and the Libyan Patriots Movement each claim credit for armed actions. Qadhafi denied news of the attack, but, soon afterward, at least 100 people were reportedly arrested in and around Benghazi on suspicions of links to opposition groups. Amnesty International stated that scores of other people escaped the country. The fate of the detainees, who may have been tortured, remains unclear. A 1997 law allows collective punishment, including the elimination of public services and food subsidies, for communities alleged to support insurgents. Qadhafi sought to co-opt fundamentalist sentiments by broadening *Shari'a* law provisions in 1994, while his expanding cooperation with neighboring Maghreb states to fight Islamist groups has been viewed favorably in Europe.

Qadhafi has sought to decrease Libya's isolation through vigorous international diplomacy focused on sub-Saharan Africa. As head of the newly established Community of Sahel and Saharan States, Qadhafi has undertaken several peacemaking missions. New evidence has emerged, however, of Libyan support for the brutal rebel movement in Sierra Leone. In another exhibition of the idiosyncrasy that has marked his rule since the 1969 overthrow of the Western-oriented King Idriss, Qadhafi has expressed his desire to see Libya become a "black" country and has urged all Libyans to marry black Africans. In August, Libya announced that Fidel Castro would receive the country's $250,000 "Mu'ammar al-Qadhafi Human Rights Award" for 1998.

After 33 years as an Italian colony and seven years of joint Anglo-French administration after World War II, Libya became independent in 1952. Until Qadhafi seized power in a 1969 coup, the country was staunchly pro-Western and hosted a large American military presence. Qadhafi's rule has led Libya to costly failures in regional clashes with Egypt in 1977, Chad in the 1980s, and in adventures such as the 1979 attempt by a Libyan expeditionary force to bolster Idi Amin's crumbling Ugandan army.

Qadhafi, who relies upon close family members as advisors, has become increasingly isolated domestically, even in his own Qadhadhifa clan. Ethnic rivalries among senior junta officials have been reported. High unemployment and perceptions of corruption have also eroded support for the regime. Sanctions have gravely affected Libya's nearly six million people, but their impact has been somewhat ameliorated by the exemption of oil exports that, in 1997, earned Libya nearly $9 billion, or 90 percent of its foreign exchange.

Political Rights and Civil Liberties:

Qadhafi rules Libya by decree, with an almost total absence of accountability and transparency. Libya today has no formal constitution. In the country's 85 years as an organized state under colonial, royal, and military dictatorships, Libyans have never been permitted to choose their representatives through democratic means. A mixture of Islamic belief and socialist theory in Qadhafi's *Green Book* provides principles and structures of governance, but the document lacks legal status. Libya is officially known as a *jamahiriya* (state of the masses), as described in the *Green Book's* "Third Universal Theory." An elaborate structure of Revolutionary Committees and People's Committees could provide for popular participation in government, but instead serves more as a tool of repression. Formal elections include mandatory voting, but real power rests with Qadhafi and a small clique that appoints civil and military officials at every level.

Very limited public debate occurs within the nominally elected bodies, but free expression and free media do not exist in Libya. Rare criticisms of the government or its actions usually indicate policy changes or purges. Reporting on events both in Libya and the wider world are tightly controlled by the monopoly state media. The official iron grip on all media makes formal censorship superfluous, except against foreign programming rebroadcast in Libya and foreign publications allowed into the country.

Political parties and civil society associations are illegal without official sanction. Garnering accurate information regarding events within Libya is problematic. Contacts with foreigners and the outside world are closely monitored, and the regime's multilayered security apparatus is pervasive. Anti-Qadhafi activists outside of Libya are also targeted. The 1996 murder of Mohammad ben Ghali in Los Angeles remains unsolved, but is believed to have been an assassination by Libyan agents. Mansur Kikhiya, one of Libya's most prominent dissidents and a former diplomat and secretary general of the exile opposition National Libyan Alliance, disappeared in Cairo in 1993. He is believed to have been abducted, returned to Libya, and executed.

"Arabization" policies discriminate against Berber and Tuareg peoples outside of Libya's ethnic mainstream and threaten their cultures. Women's access to education and employment has improved under the regime, yet cultural norms that relegate women to an inferior role may regain strength as Qadhafi seeks to placate fundamentalist opinion by stricter imposition of shari'a law, which, among other matters, affects marriage, divorce, and inheritance rights.

Like every other aspect of life in Libya, religion is subject to state control. Mosques are closely monitored for incipient political opposition, and Islamic practice is tailored to Qadhafi's brand of Koranic scholarship. A small Christian community is permitted to worship quietly in two churches. Expatriate Christians may also worship.

There is no freedom to form or join unions, nor are there rights to strike or bargain collectively. All unions are state-run. The economy is statist, although foreign investment in extractive industries, such as a large new Italian-backed gas pipeline project across the Mediterranean Sea to Sicily, has been sought.

Liechtenstein

Polity: Principality and parliamentary democracy
Economy: Capitalist-statist
Population: 30,000
PPP: na
Life Expectancy: 72
Ethnic Groups: Alemannic (88 percent), other, including Italian and Turkish (12 percent)
Capital: Vaduz

Political Rights: 1
Civil Liberties: 1
Status: Free

Overview:　The Principality of Liechtenstein is governed by Prime Minister Mario Frick's Fatherland Union (VU), which won an absolute majority of 13 seats in the 25-member *Landtag* (parliament) in January 1997. The Free List environmentalist party won two parliamentary seats. Soon after the election, the Progressive Citizens' Party (FBP) voted to end its long-standing coalition with the VU.

Since 1995, Liechtenstein has been a member of the European Economic Area (EEA). The country's economy is closely entwined with that of Switzerland, which is not a part of the EEA. Prince Hans Adam, who enjoys substantial political power, has decreased the principality's economic dependence on Switzerland by leading it into membership not only in the EEA, but also in the United Nations, European Free Trade Association, and the General Agreement on Tariffs and Trade.

Liechtenstein was established in its present form in 1719 after being purchased by Austria's Liechtenstein family. The royal family lived mainly in Moravia (formerly part of the Austro-Hungarian empire and now a Czech territory) until 1938, when Nazism forced it to flee to Liechtenstein. Native residents of the state are primarily descended from the Germanic Alemanni tribe, and the official language is a German dialect.

In 1923, Liechtenstein entered into a customs union with Switzerland, which continues to administer the principality's customs and provide for its defense and diplomatic representation. From 1938 until 1997, the principality was governed by an FBP-VU coalition. The FBP was the senior partner for most of this period.

The prince exercises legislative powers jointly with the Landtag. He appoints the prime minister from the Landtag's majority party or coalition, and the deputy chief of the five-member government from the minority. Prince Hans Adam has effectively ruled Liechtenstein since 1984, although he did not assume his father's title until the elder sovereign's death in 1989.

Political Rights and Civil Liberties: Liechtensteiners can change their government democratically. Parties with at least eight percent of the vote receive representation in the Landtag, which is directly elected every four years. The sovereign possesses the power to veto legislation and to dissolve the Landtag. The independent judiciary is headed by a Supreme Court and includes civil and criminal courts, as well as an administrative Court of Appeal and a state court to address questions of constitutionality. Due to the small size of the state, regional disparities are minimal, and modern social problems are few. A strict policy prevents significant numbers of second- and third-generation residents from acquiring citizenship. The native population decides by local vote whether to grant citizenship to those who have five years' residence. Prime Minister Frick has advocated reforms in order to reduce the "immigrant" population to approximately half of its current size.

Liechtenstein has one state-owned television station, as well as one state-owned and one privately owned radio station. Residents receive radio and television broadcasts from neighboring countries. Both major parties publish newspapers five times per week.

Although Roman Catholicism is the state religion, other faiths practice freely. Roman Catholic or Protestant religious education is compulsory in all schools, but exemptions are routinely granted.

Liechtensteiners enjoy freedom of association. The principality has one small trade union. Workers have the right to strike, but have not done so for more than 25 years. The prosperous economy includes private and state enterprises. An ongoing labor shortage coupled with high wage rates has begun to drive some companies to open factories in Switzerland and Austria where labor costs are lower.

Although only narrowly endorsed by male voters, the electoral enfranchisement of women at the national level was unanimously approved in the legislature in 1984 after defeats in referenda in 1971 and 1973. By 1986, universal adult suffrage at the local level had passed in all 11 communes. In the 1989 general elections, a woman won a Landtag seat for the first time. Three years later, a constitutional amendment guaranteed legal equality.

Lithuania

Polity: Presidential-parliamentary democracy
Economy: Mixed capitalist
Population: 3,700,000
PPP: $3,843
Life Expectancy: 71
Ethnic Groups: Lithuanian (80 percent), Russian (9 percent), Polish (7 percent), Byelorussian (2 percent), other (2 percent)
Capital: Vilnius

Political Rights: 1
Civil Liberties: 2
Status: Free

Overview: In a second round of presidential balloting held on January 4, Lithuanian-American Valdas Adamkus narrowly defeated former prosecutor general Arturas Paulauskas. Incumbent Prime Minister Gediminas Vagnorius was chosen in March to serve a second term.

One of the leading states of Europe during the middle ages, Lithuania merged with Poland in the sixteenth century and was subsequently absorbed by Russia in the eighteenth century. After becoming independent at the end of World War I, Lithuania was annexed by the Soviet Union in 1940 under a secret protocol of the 1939 Hitler-Stalin pact. The country regained its independence with the collapse of the USSR in 1991.

In 1992 parliamentary elections, the Lithuanian Democratic Labor Party (LDDP), the renamed ex-Communist Party, won 79 of 141 seats. Algirdas Brazauskas, a former head of the Communist Party, became the country's first directly elected president in 1993. In 1996, with two LDDP-led governments tainted by financial scandal in the wake of a banking crisis, the LDDP was routed in parliamentary elections. Gediminas Vagnorius of the Homeland Union-Conservative Party (HU/LC) was named prime minister, replacing Laurynas Mindaugas Stankevicius. Vytautas Landsbergis, leader of the HU/LC, was made parliamentary chairman.

On January 4, retired Lithuanian-American and independent candidate Valdas Adamkus was elected president in a second round of balloting with 50.4 percent of the vote over former prosecutor general Arturas Paulauskas. The first round of elections on December 21 failed to produce a winner, as none of the seven presidential candidates received more than 50 percent of the vote. Subsequently, Adamkus and Paulauskas, the two front-runners after the first round, continued to a second round of balloting. Although formally independent, Paulauskas was strongly supported by the LDDP, and received most of his backing from those dissatisfied with the effects of post-Communist reforms. On January 6, Adamkus proposed that incumbent Prime Minister Vagnorius of the HU/LC, with which Adamkus agrees on many issues, serve a second term. Parliament approved his nomination on March 10 by a wide margin.

As part of a subsequent government reorganization plan, the ministries of European affairs, communications, and construction were eliminated. These changes, as well as the replacement of some pro-Landsbergis cabinet members, were seen by many as the result of a power struggle between Vagnorius and Landsbergis for control over the HU/LC.

On May 23, the Lithuanian daily *Lieutuvos Rytas* published an article alleging that Landsbergis and former Interior Minister Vidmantas Ziemelis had ordered secret surveillance of high-ranking officials and political rivals. Both Landsbergis and Ziemelis denied the charges. The newspaper quoted the allegations of three cabinet members, all of whom were loyal to Vagnorius. Arturas Paulauskas and former president Algirdas Brazauskas also claimed to have been illegally wiretapped or followed. However, a parliamentary commission found no proof of wrongdoing, and the prosecutor general decided not to press charges due to a lack of evidence.

After previous delays which had provoked criticism from the Israeli government, the U.S. State Department, and Jewish organizations, the trial of accused war criminal Aleksandras Lileikis was postponed again in late 1998 due to the 91-year-old defendant's poor health. The trial would mark the first proceeding against an alleged Nazi war criminal in Lithuania. In the country's first conviction under its broad genocide law, three former employees of the NKVD (the predecessor to the KGB) were found guilty in early December of killing a family of four in 1945.

The European Union failed to invite Lithuania to start formal membership negotiations, a process which is tied partly to the setting of a closure date for the Soviet-designed Ignalina nuclear power plant, the country's principle energy source.

Political Rights and Civil Liberties: Lithuanians can change their government democratically. The 1992 constitution established a 141-member parliament *(Seimas)*, in which 71 seats are directly elected, and 70 seats are chosen by proportional representation, all for four-year terms. The president is directly elected for a five-year term. The 1996 legislative elections and the 1997-1998 presidential vote were declared free and fair by international observers.

The government generally respects freedom of speech and the press. There is a wide variety of privately owned newspapers, including Russian- and Polish-language publications. Several independent, as well as state-run television and radio stations broadcast nationwide. Freedom of religion is guaranteed by law and enjoyed in practice in this largely Roman Catholic country.

Freedom of assembly and association are respected, although the Communist Party of Lithuania continues to be banned. Workers have the right to form and join trade unions, to strike, and to engage in collective bargaining. However, ongoing problems include inadequate or employer-biased legislation, management discrimination against union members, and a lack of expertise on the part of the court system in labor-related issues.

There have been credible reports of police brutality, and prisons remain overcrowded and poorly maintained. A lack of qualified lawyers has resulted in inadequate protection of the rights of detainees, many of whom are held in pre-trial detention without clear legal grounds for their incarceration. In late December, parliament voted to abolish the death penalty, despite recent polls indicating widespread public support for capital punishment.

The rights of the country's ethnic minorities are protected. In 1992, Lithuania extended citizenship to all those born within its borders, and over 90 percent of nonethnic Lithuanians, mostly Russians and Poles, became citizens.

In July, parliament adopted legislation proposed by parliamentary chairman Vytautas Landsbergis banning former KGB officers from holding government office and a variety of private sector jobs for ten years. After President Adamkus vetoed the legislation questioning its constitutionality, parliament agreed to postpone its enactment until January 1, 1999. In October, 31 MPs asked the constitutional court to rule on the law's constitutionality, a decision which was still pending at year's end.

Women face discrimination in education and the workplace, and they are underrepresented in certain professions and in upper level positions in general.

Luxembourg

Polity: Parliamentary democracy
Economy: Capitalist
Population: 400,000
PPP: $34,004
Life Expectancy: 76
Ethnic Groups: Luxembourger (70 percent), other European (30 percent)
Capital: Luxembourg

Political Rights: 1
Civil Liberties: 1
Status: Free

Overview:

Luxembourg, one of the first countries to meet the 1992 Maastricht Treaty's criteria for participation, remains on course for membership in the European Monetary Union. A positive GDP growth rate and the lowest rate of unemployment in the European Union have enabled Luxembourg to fare significantly better economically than its neighbors.

Luxembourg's multiparty electoral system is based on proportional representation. In recent years, it has been ruled by coalition governments led by the Christian Social Party (PCS) or the Democratic Party in alliance either with each other or with the Socialist Workers' Party. The current coalition government is headed by Prime Minister Jean-Claude Juncker of the PCS. Executive authority is exercised by the prime minister and the cabinet on behalf of the Grand Duke. The government is appointed by the sovereign, but is responsible to the legislature. In March, Grand Duke Jean appointed his eldest son Henri as *Lieutenant Representant*. Henri gradually will assume the Duke's constitutional duties.

After centuries of domination and occupation by foreign powers, the small landlocked Grand Duchy of Luxembourg was recognized as an autonomous, neutral state in 1867. It came under the current ruling house of Nassau-Weilbourg in 1890 and formed an economic union with Belgium in 1922, but retains independent political institutions through its 1868 constitution. After occupation by Germany during both world wars, Luxembourg abandoned its neutrality and became a vocal proponent of European integration.

Political Rights and Civil Liberties:

Luxembourgers can change their government democratically. Voting is compulsory for citizens, and foreigners may register to vote after five years of residence. The prime minister is the leader of the dominant party in the Chamber of Deputies, for which popular elections are held every five years. The Grand Duke appoints the 21 members of the Council of State, which serves as an advisory body to the Chamber.

The independent judiciary is headed by the Superior Court of Justice and includes a Court of Assizes for serious criminal offenses as well as two district courts and three justices of the peace. Judges are appointed for life by the Grand Duke. In response to a 1995 decision by the European Court of Human Rights, the government passed legislation establishing an administrative court system contending that Luxembourg's Council of State could no longer serve as both a legislative advisory body and as an administrative court. This dual role was seen as a violation of the right to a fair trial. The new administrative courts began operations in 1997.

Luxembourg enjoys a vibrant free press. All news media are privately owned and free of censorship. While there is no domestic news agency, a number of foreign bureaus operate. Radio and television broadcasts from neighboring countries are available.

Religious freedom is respected in this predominantly Roman Catholic country. There is no state religion, but the state pays the salaries of Roman Catholic, Protestant, and Jewish clergy, and several local governments subsidize sectarian religious facilities.

Although foreigners constitute more than 30 percent of the population, anti-foreigner incidents are infrequent. European Union (EU) citizens who reside in Luxembourg enjoy the right to vote and to run in municipal elections. Minimum residency requirements are six years for voters and 12 years for candidates. Freedom of association is respected, and unions operate without governmental interference. Approximately 65 percent of the labor force is unionized. Workers are organized into two competing labor federations which are affiliated with the Socialist and Christian Social parties. The right to strike is constitutionally guaranteed. In July, public sector workers exercised this right in a one-day strike.

Macedonia

Polity: Parliamentary democracy
Economy: Mixed statist (transitional)
Population: 2,000,000
PPP: $4,058
Life Expectancy: 71
Ethnic Groups: Macedonian (65 percent), Albanian (22 percent), Turkish (4 percent), Gypsies (3 percent), Serb (2 percent), other (4 percent)
Capital: Skopje

Political Rights: 3*
Civil Liberties: 3
Status: Partly Free

Ratings change: Macedonia's political rights rating changed from 4 to 3 due to a free and fair election and the inclusion of Albanian parties in the government.

Overview: In 1998, a center-right coalition led by the Internal Macedonian Revolutionary Organization-Democratic Party for Macedonian Unity (VMRO-DPMNE), which had boycotted elections four years earlier, won parliamentary elections in October; VMRO-DPMNE leader Ljubco Georgievski was named prime minister in late November and formed a government that included members from ethnic Albanian parties.

The VMRO-DPMNE and its coalition partner, the centrist, multi-ethnic Democratic Alternative, won 62 of 120 seats, ousting the ruling Socialist Democratic Alliance for Macedonia (SDSM, former Communists), which took 27 seats, down from 61. The Albanian-based Party for Democratic Prosperity (PDP), which was allied with the SDSM, took 14 seats, while the Democratic Party of Albania won 10. Prime Minister

Georgievski said his government would continue to work toward membership in NATO and the European Union and strive for better relations with neighboring Balkan countries. He pledged to reform the economy by working to end corruption, reduce taxes, eliminate regulations on investments, and attract foreign investment.

In other issues, relations between Macedonians and ethnic Albanians, which in 1997 were marred by a series of violent clashes between Albanians and security forces in Gostivar and Tetovo, improved despite sporadic flare-ups.

Kiro Gligorov, a former Communist leader and head of the SDSM, was appointed interim president in 1992 and directly elected in 1994. The country's first parliamentary elections since independence from Yugoslavia, held in October 1994, were marked by fraud and irregularities; runoffs were boycotted by the VMRO-DPMNE, the free-market nationalist Democratic Party, and others. The Alliance, composed of the SDSM, the Liberals, the Socialists, and the PDPA won 95 of 120 seats, and formed the government from which the liberals resigned in 1996.

Prior to the parliamentary elections, early 1998 saw a series of shifts in alliances and maneuvers. A new party, the Democratic Alternative (DA), was launched in March by well-know Yugoslav-era political figure Vasil Tupurkovski, drawing prominent intellectuals and political figures, some from the Liberal Party and SDSM. The two leading Albanian parties formed an electoral alliance, and the Liberal and Democratic parties merged. The SDSM, led by incumbent Prime Minister Branko Crvenkovski, tried to paint the opposition as pro-Bulgarian and sympathetic to Albanians. For its part, the VMRO-DPMNE under Georgievksi dropped its traditional nationalist orientation and rhetoric. The Crvenkovski government was hurt by charges of corruption and the collapse of the TAT saving institution in 1997 that effected thousands of investors. Bribery was rife in public administration, the customs department, and among civil servants at all levels.

A key issue in the 1998 campaign was the state of an economy crippled by the 1994-95 trade embargo by Greece as well as the United Nations' ban on trade with the states of former Yugoslavia, which was lifted after the signing of the 1995 Dayton Accords on Bosnia. Unemployment remained high, privatization of large-scale enterprises lagged, taxes went uncollected, and living standards dropped.

In March, with the eruption of fighting in Kosovo, the 750-strong United Nations Preventive Deployment Force (UNPREDEP), which was due to withdraw in August, announced plans to stay. Some 350 members of the force are Americans. In July, a prominent Macedonian newspaper reported that 20,000 displaced Kosovo Albanians had sought refuge in Macedonia.

Political Rights and Civil Liberties: Macedonians can change their government democratically. The 1998 parliamentary elections were free and fair. Voting was repeated for six seats due to procedural irregularities.

The constitution enshrines free speech and access to information, and prohibits censorship. Slander and libel laws have led to self-censorship. In October, VMRO-DPMNE leader Georgievski said he was suing the paper *Vecer* for slander because of an article that said his party and Albanian parties had agreed to the division of Macedonia. Most major newspapers and electronic media are government controlled or receive some subsidies. The pro-SDSM NIP Nova Makedonija, which is employee-owned and subsidized by the state, publishes four major dailies. Private, independent newspapers include *Dnevnik*, and the weekly *Fokus*, which covers sensational stories about scandal and crime. Party newspapers include the SDSM's *Demokratija*; the Liberal Party's *Liberal*, and the VMRO-DPMNE's *Glas*. The MIP Nova Makedonija has a virtual monopoly on distribution, controlling a network of more than 500 *kiosks* throughout the country. The 1997 Law on Broadcasting Activity guarantees the independence of the Broadcasting Council, whose members are chosen by parliament and which is empowered to recommend who should be given broadcast licenses. Because recommendations have to be approved by the government, critics have argued that the issuance of licenses has been politicized. Some 30 state-owned radio stations and five state television stations operate in the country. In all, 24 private TV stations and 91 combined radio and television stations share the airwaves, most of which focus on music and entertainment programming. In February, controversy arose when the VMRO-DPMNE local authorities in Stip moved to take over Radio Stip, changing the name to Radio Glas. In October, the government, with aid from the World Bank, launched MIA, a state news agency.

Freedom of religion is respected, and the dominant faiths are Macedonian Orthodox, Roman Catholic, and Islam (Albanians and Turks). Under a 1997 religion law, anyone carrying out religious work or religious rites must register with the Commission on Interreligious Affairs; Protestant groups continue to complain that they cannot register their churches.

There are no significant restrictions on freedom of assembly. In September, ethnic Albanians in the village of Kolari marched to protest the death of man killed by police, allegedly when he resisted arrest.

Macedonia has a multiparty system, and some 50 parties are registered. No parties are explicitly illegal or outlawed. The Union of Independent and Autonomous Trade Unions confederation was formed in 1992. The Council of Trade Unions of Macedonia is the successor to the Communist labor federation. There are some 3,000 NGOs registered, including the autonomous units of national organizations as well as professional groups.

The judiciary is not free of political or governmental interference. Macedonia has a three-tiered system consisting of regular (municipal) and appellate (district) courts and a Supreme Court. The constitution mandates a seven-member Republican Judicial Council, elected by parliament, which proposes the names of judges in consultation with the Justice Ministry and other bodies. The president of the council acknowledged in 1997 that political parties, particularly the ruling coalition, play a critical role in the election of judges and that "efforts should be made to eliminate the political influence in the selection of judges." Since 1996, several judges were removed for bribery. A nine-member Constitutional Court decides if laws conform with the constitution. In March, the Court ruled that the police would no longer be able to detain suspects without first taking them before an executive judge, though police often ignore the ruling as well as proper search warrant procedures.

National minorities, particularly Albanians, have complained about abuses at the hands of police and discrimination. Rufi Osmani, the former mayor of Gostivar, is serving a seven-year sentence for his part in the 1997 ethnic violence. Other minority groups include Turks, Serbs, Vlachs, and Roma (Gypsies). Ethnic Serbs maintain that they cannot worship freely in the Serbian Orthodox Church.

Freedom of movement is unimpaired by government regulation. The constitution and laws enshrine property rights. In February 1998, a citizens' group in Krivolak, whose property was taken away under the denationalization law, threatened to seek redress with the World Bank and international courts. An unreliable legal framework exacerbates bureaucratic delays, which are common in registering a business. While commercial laws are meant to enshrine fair competition, the development of the private sector and privatization has been characterized by the advantageous position of enterprise managers with links to the government and political parties. Several SDSM leaders were implicated in the 1997 TAT financial scandal, a savings scheme that bilked 30,000 savers of some $90 million. Smuggling, drug dealing, and a large gray economy remain serious problems.

Cultural norms discourage women from reporting domestic violence, and women are underrepresented in government and the private sector. There are a number of women's advocacy groups.

Madagascar

Polity: Presidential-parliamentary democracy
Economy: Mixed statist
Population: 14,000,000
PPP: $673
Life Expectancy: 52
Ethnic Groups: Malayo-Indonesian tribes
[Merina (26 percent)], Arab, African, Indian, French
Capital: Antananarivo

Political Rights: 2
Civil Liberties: 4
Status: Partly Free

Overview:

In May, legislative elections returned a majority for President Didier Ratsiraka's forces, but opposition leaders and local church groups claimed that the polls were marred by serious irregularities. The election date was delayed beyond the scheduled August 1997 termination of the sitting parliament in defiance of constitutional requirements. Madagascar's democratic transition appeared more fragile during the year. A number of institutions mandated by the 1995 constitution have still not been established, and political influence appears to have undermined the independence of the judiciary. A decentralization plan was narrowly approved in a March referendum that was boycotted by the country's increasingly fractious opposition. A long history of irregular financial dealings continued as the IMF refused to release scheduled aid. Locust swarms of biblical proportions added to the distress of many of the rural farmers who constitute the vast majority of the country's people.

Ratsiraka won a narrow victory in a December 1996 presidential runoff election that was deemed mostly free and fair by international observers. His campaign pledges of commitment to the democratic rule of law have been honored indifferently. A member of a military junta that seized power in 1972, then-Admiral Ratsiraka emerged as leader in 1975 and maintained power until his increasingly authoritarian regime bowed to social unrest and nonviolent mass demonstrations in 1991. A party led by former

President Albert Zafy, who failed to win re-election after being impeached by the Supreme Court in 1996, fared poorly in the legislative elections except in Zafy's native region in the far north. Independents won a large portion of the vote.

Madagascar, the world's fourth largest island, lies 220 miles off of Africa's southeastern coast. After 70 years of French colonial rule and episodes of severe repression, Madagascar gained independence in 1960. A leftist military junta seized power from President Philbert Tsiranana in 1972. In 1991, mass demonstrations forced Admiral Ratsiraka to cede power to a unity government that included opposition political parties legalized by a High Constitutional Court decree in 1990. Under a new 1992 constitution, Zafy won the presidency with more than 65 percent of the vote in a February 1993 runoff election. Race and ethnicity are important factors in Madagascar's politics. Its mostly very poor population is divided between highland Merina people of Malay origin and coastal peoples mostly of black African origin.

Political Rights and Civil Liberties:

Legislative elections in May 1998 were viewed as less free and fair than polls conducted since Madagascar's transition to multiparty politics in 1992. The Association for Madagascar's Renaissance (Arema) won 63 of 150 parliamentary seats and formed a solid majority with the support of the Leader-Fanilo party's 16 seats. Diverse opposition parties and independents shared the remaining seats. A new party led by Norbert Ratsirahonana, a former prime minister, fared well in and around Antananarivo. The Christian Churches Council and several political groups denounced the elections as marred by fraud and other abuses.

The judiciary is, in general, demonstrating increasing autonomy, despite the Supreme Court's clearly unconstitutional decision to allow the postponement of elections in 1997. Lack of training, resources, and personnel hampers the courts' effectiveness. Case backlogs are prodigious. Most of the 20,000 people held in the county's prison are pretrial detainees who suffer extremely harsh conditions. In many rural areas, customary *dina* courts that follow neither due process nor standardized judicial procedure often issue summary and severe punishments.

Several daily and weekly newspapers publish material sharply critical of the government and other parties and politicians. Television is state-controlled and relatively autonomous. At least ten private radio stations are now broadcasting, and rebroadcasts of Radio France International are available throughout the country.

Women account for more than 40 percent of the small formal labor force and hold significantly more government and managerial positions than their counterparts in continental African countries. At the same time, they still face societal discrimination and enjoy fewer opportunities than men for higher education and official employment.

The right to free association is respected, and hundreds of nongovernmental organizations, including lawyers' and human rights groups, are active. The government does not interfere with religious rights. More than half of the population adheres to traditional Malagasy religions and coexists with Christians and Muslims. In 1997, the Rally for Madagascar's Muslim Democrats was registered as the country's first Islamic political party. Approximately 150 parties are registered amid a welter of shifting political alliances.

Workers' rights to join unions and to strike are exercised frequently. Some of the country's free labor organizations are affiliated with political groups. More than four-fifths of the labor force is employed in agriculture, fishing, and forestry at subsistence wages.

⬇ Malawi

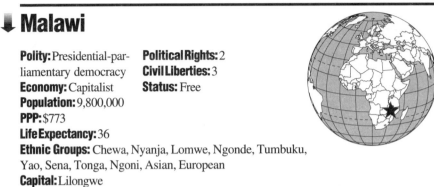

Polity: Presidential-parliamentary democracy
Economy: Capitalist
Population: 9,800,000
PPP: $773
Life Expectancy: 36
Ethnic Groups: Chewa, Nyanja, Lomwe, Ngonde, Tumbuku, Yao, Sena, Tonga, Ngoni, Asian, European
Capital: Lilongwe

Political Rights: 2
Civil Liberties: 3
Status: Free

Trend arrow: Malawi receives a downward trend arrow due to increased state harassment of oppositionists and the media.

Overview: Presidential and legislative elections scheduled for June 1999 will be contested vigorously, but in an uncertain environment of civil unrest, increasing attacks on the media, dubious electoral preparations, rising criminality, and a deteriorating economy. President Bakili Muluzi and his ruling United Democratic Front (UDF) are expected to take full advantage of their incumbency against a divided opposition.

The three main parties contesting power mostly represent narrow regional and ethnic bases. Muluzi's southern-based UDF, however, has found some new support through patronage. The former ruling Malawi Congress Party (MCP), with its strong base in central Malawi, is the principle opposition party. The third-largest party, the Alliance for Democracy (AFORD), is almost entirely confined to northern Malawi. Complicating the ethnic mix are apparently politically motivated efforts to raise tensions between the country's 75 percent Christian majority and the approximately 12 percent of Malawians who are Muslim.

President (later, "President for Life") Hastings Kamuzu Banda ruled Malawi for nearly three decades after the country gained independence from Britain in 1963. Banda exercised dictatorial and often eccentric rule through the Malawi Congress Party (MCP) and its paramilitary youth wing, the Malawi Young Pioneers. Facing a domestic economic crisis and strong international pressure, he accepted a referendum approving multiparty rule in 1993.

In 1994, Muluzi won the presidency in an election beset by irregularities, but seen as largely free and fair. The army's violent December 1993 dispersal of the Young Pioneers helped clear the way for the polls. As many as 2,000 Banda loyalists fled to neighboring Mozambique. In July, Malawi's army chief claimed that former Pioneers were receiving guerrilla training there by the Mozambican Renamo opposition. Allegations of governmental corruption persist.

Political Rights and Civil Liberties: In May 1994, the president and members of the National Assembly won five-year terms in Malawi's first generally free and fair multiparty elections. The MCP and AFORD hold 54 and 33 seats, respectively, in the 177-seat parliament. Suffrage is universal except for serving members of the military. Vote buying and other abuses in elections since 1994 have prompted concerns that the 1999 polls will be less than free and fair. Significant problems in voter registration and electoral rolls and increased media repression have been reported.

The May 1995 constitution provides strong protection for fundamental freedoms, but critics argue that it allows excessive presidential power and does not sufficiently safeguard women's and children's rights. If enabled, a new human rights commission could reverse the slow deterioration of the human rights situation. Rights of free expression and free assembly are generally respected, but police continue to use unprovoked violence to disperse strikers. Many human rights and other nongovernmental organizations operate openly and without interference. Religious freedom is respected.

The judiciary has demonstrated broad independence in its decisions, but due process is not always respected by an overburdened court system that lacks resources and training. There are no reported political prisoners in Malawi, but arrests or suits on apparently political grounds have increased. Police brutality is still said to be common. Appalling prison conditions lead to many deaths, including among pretrial detainees.

Malawi's broadcast media remains largely under state control and government influence. The independent print media suffered a rash of violent attacks and official repression during the year. The state-owned Malawi Broadcasting Corporation controls television and most radio service, which reaches a larger audience. The few licensed private radio stations are owned by allies of the government or restricted to religious broadcasting, although a few development-oriented community radio stations have been authorized. The government has used libel and other laws to harass journalists. In January, soldiers raided the offices of the *Daily Times* after it published news of AIDS in the military. The government withdrew all official advertising from the newspaper and its sister weekly, *Malawi News*, thereby driving them toward bankruptcy. In August, an editor and reporter from the *National Agenda* were badly assaulted. In September, the editor of the weekly *New Vision* was hospitalized after being beaten by police for refusing to reveal sources.

Despite equal protection of the law under the 1995 constitution, customary practices maintain de facto discrimination against women in education, employment, and business. Traditional rural structures deny women inheritance and property rights, and violence against women is reportedly routine.

The right to form unions is constitutionally guaranteed. The right to strike is legally protected, with notice and mediation requirements for workers in essential services. Unions are active, but face harassment and occasional violence during strikes. Collective bargaining is widely practiced, but not specifically protected by law.

Although the country's economy took a sharp plunge in 1998, privatization programs continued, and the IMF and World Bank provided new funding. A reduced crop due to drought will hurt many Malawians, the vast majority of whom rely on subsistence farming.

Malaysia

Polity: Dominant party   **Political Rights:** 5*
Economy: Capitalist   **Civil Liberties:** 5
Population: 22,200,000   **Status:** Partly Free
PPP: $9,572
Life Expectancy: 72
Ethnic Groups: Malay and other indigenous (58 percent),
Chinese (26 percent), Indian (7 percent), other (9 percent)
Capital: Kuala Lumpur
Ratings change: Malaysia's political rights rating changed from 4 to 5 due to the jailing of two leading political opponents and increased restrictions on freedom of expression.

Overview: In 1998, as Malaysia's economic crisis worsened, Premier Mahathir Mohamad tightened his grip over society by arresting his deputy premier, which was viewed as politically motivated, as well as by jailing an opposition leader and applying new pressures on the media and nongovernmental organizations.

Malaysia was established in 1963 through a merger of independent, ex-British Malaya with the then-British colonies of Sarawak, Sabah, and Singapore (Singapore withdrew in 1965). The constitution provides for a 192-seat House of Representatives, which is directly elected for a five-year term, and a 58-member Senate. Executive power is vested in the prime minister and the cabinet. As head of state, the King can delay legislation for thirty days.

The 14-party, ruling National Front coalition has captured at least a two-thirds majority in the lower house in nine straight general elections since 1957. The Front is dominated by the conservative, Malay-based United Malays National Organization (UMNO). Although the government has gained considerable legitimacy by presiding over a rapidly expanding economy, it continues to use security laws to limit peaceful dissent.

Mounting Malay frustration over the economic success of the ethnic Chinese minority exploded into anti-Chinese rioting in 1969. In 1971, the government responded with still-existing quotas for Malays in education, the civil service, and business affairs.

The current premier and UMNO leader, Mahathir Mohamad, took office in 1981 and has since consolidated executive authority and rejected the notion of a loyal opposition. In 1988, following internal UMNO disputes, dissidents formed Semangat '46 (Spirit of '46, the year UMNO was founded in Malaya). In 1989, Semangat '46 joined the country's first Malay-led opposition coalition, but it failed to unseat the Front in the 1990 national elections.

In the 1995 parliamentary elections, the National Front took 162 seats; the remainder went to four opposition parties, including Semangat '46. In 1996, Semangat '46 members, frustrated with being in opposition, folded the party into UMNO.

By 1997, the effects of a decade of excessive corporate borrowing, financial distortions caused by crony capitalism, a high current account deficit, and the government's spending on prestige infrastructure projects drove the ringgit down 40 percent in the second half of the year. Mahathir responded with anti-foreigner and anti-Semitic harangues and threats to restrict currency dealing.

In spring 1998, long-simmering leadership tensions between Mahathir, 72, and Anwar Ibrahim, 51, the deputy premier and Mahathir's presumed successor, flared openly over economic policy. Anwar supported an International Monetary Fund-style program of raising interest rates and cutting spending, while Mahathir favored expansionary policies.

In August, GDP figures confirmed that the Malaysian economy had entered into its first recession in 13 years. On September 2, Mahathir sacked Anwar on charges of sexual misconduct after the deputy premier refused to resign. Anwar then held a series of public rallies calling for political reform and Mahathir's resignation. On September 20, police arrested Anwar under the Internal Security Act on charges of treason. Days later, Anwar appeared in court with bruises. In the ensuing weeks, police used tear gas and water cannons to break up pro-Anwar demonstrations in Kuala Lumpur and smaller towns. On November 2, a court began trying Anwar on 10 charges of corruption and illegal homosexual acts.

Malaysia's political outlook is unclear, and Mahathir faces critical UMNO leadership elections in fall 1999. Meanwhile, the Islamic opposition party PAS and other groups have formed the Malaysian People's Justice Movement in order to demand an end to Mahathir's rule.

Political Rights and Civil Liberties:

Malaysians have a limited ability to change their government through elections. The government exercises significant control over the media, uses numerous security laws to restrict freedoms of expression and association, and reportedly punishes opposition-held states by dissuading foreign investment and reducing development funds. Nevertheless, PAS, an Islamic opposition party, has controlled Kelantan state since 1990. The Mahathir government has made legitimate efforts to curb corruption and money politics.

The judiciary is subject to government influence in sensitive political and commercial cases. Mahathir, as home affairs minister, controls all important judicial appointments. Shari'a (Islamic law) courts have authority over family and property matters in the Muslim community. Nine states in Malaysia have traditional sultans, and the sultans are at the apex of the Islamic religious establishment in each of these states. The king, who is elected by and from among the nine sultans, supervises Islamic affairs in the four remaining states. Mahathir's advocacy of a progressive practice of Islam, his criticism of the ulama (religious scholars), who head the Shari'a courts, for discriminating against women, and his support for unifying the state Islamic laws under a federal system has angered many conservative Malays.

Successive governments have used a series of security laws over the years to detain alleged Communists, religious extremists, Vietnamese boat people, and opposition figures. The exact number of people presently detained is not known. The 1960 Internal Security Act and the 1969 Emergency Ordinance both permit detention of suspects for up to two years. The 1970 Sedition Act Amendments prohibit discussion of the privileges granted to Malays and other sensitive issues. A 1987 amendment to the 1984 Printing Presses and Publications Act (PPPA) bars the publication of "malicious" news, expands the government's power to ban or restrict publications, and prohibits publications from challenging such actions in court.

In July, Lim Guan Eng, the deputy leader of the opposition Democratic Action Party, began serving a three-year sentence on apparently politically motivated charges under the Sedition Act and the PPPA for having publicly criticized the government's handling of statutory rape allegations against a former state chief minister in 1994. The High Court had originally fined Lim, but during his appeal, the government sought and won a jail term. Separately, a court finished the first stage of the trial of Irene Fernandez, who was arrested in 1996 and charged under the PPPA after her organization, Tenaganita, reported on abuses against migrant workers at immigrant detention centers.

Journalists practice considerable self-censorship. The broadcast media and the major newspapers are all owned by individuals and companies close to the ruling National Front, and the opposition receives little coverage. In July and August, Mahathir pressured two top newspaper editors and the head of a leading private television station to resign. All were considered close to Anwar. In September, courts charged four people with spreading rumors of rioting in Kuala Lumpur over the Internet, Malaysia's first such cases.

The 1967 Police Act requires permits for all public assemblies. In September and October, police forcibly broke up numerous peaceful rallies in support of ousted Deputy Premier Anwar, mainly in Kuala Lumpur but also in rural towns. Police also arrested more than 125 people. Since 1969, political rallies have been banned, although indoor "discussion sessions" are permitted. Under the 1966 Societies Act, any association (including political parties) of more than six members must register with the government, and the authorities have deregistered some opposition organizations. Nongovernmental organizations (NGO) operate openly but face some harassment. In the spring, the government banned several scheduled NGO conferences, including one on water shortages.

Conditions in detention centers for political asylum seekers and alleged illegal immigrants are grim. In 1996, authorities admitted that 70 detainees had died in the camps over a four-year period. In 1998, authorities responded to Malaysia's worsening economic crisis by rounding up and deporting thousands of alleged illegal immigrants to Indonesia. On March 26, rioting at one camp and the subsequent police response killed eight detainees and a police officer as police prepared to forcibly repatriate hundreds of Indonesians from Aceh province. Human rights activists warned that some of the Acehnese had valid political asylum claims.

Official policy discriminates against Chinese, Indians, and other minorities in the areas of education, employment, and business affairs. Some 60 percent of Malaysians are Muslim, and Islam is the official religion, although non-Muslims worship freely in this secular country. Observers say the regional economic crisis has contributed to inter-religious tensions. In March 1998, Muslims in Penang attacked a Hindu temple after its bell ringing allegedly disturbed their prayers nearby, leading to riots between Hindus and Muslims.

There are considerable restrictions on trade union association and the right to strike. Each union and labor federation can only represent one trade. In the export-oriented electronics industry, the government permits only "in-house" unions rather than a nationwide union. The government must certify all unions and can deregister them.

Maldives

Polity: Nonparty, presidential-legislative (elite-clan dominated)
Economy: Capitalist
Population: 300,000
PPP: $3,540
Life Expectancy: 62
Ethnic Groups: Sinhalese, Dravidian, Arab, African
Capital: Male

Political Rights: 6
Civil Liberties: 5*
Status: Not Free

Ratings change: The Maldives' civil liberties rating changed from 6 to 5 due to methodological reasons.

Overview:
The Maldives, a 500-mile string of 26 atolls in the Indian Ocean, achieved independence in 1965 after 78 years as a British protectorate. A 1968 referendum ended the ad-Din sultanate's 815-year rule and established a republic. The 1968 constitution provides for a president with broad, largely unchecked executive powers who must be a male Sunni Muslim. The majlis (parliament) has 40 seats directly elected for a five-year term, along with eight members appointed by the president. Every five years the majlis chooses a sole presidential candidate who is elected by citizens in a yes-or-no referendum. Until 1998, the constitution barred individuals from nominating themselves for the presidency.

There have been several coup attempts since independence. Most recently, in 1988, President Maumoon Abdul Gayoom called in Indian commandos to crush a coup attempt by a disgruntled businessman reportedly backed by Sri Lankan mercenaries. In the aftermath, the autocratic Gayoom strengthened the National Security Service and named several relatives to top government posts. In early 1990, authorities permitted a brief period of press freedom as the Maldives prepared to host the South Asian Association for Regional Cooperation summit. Later in the year, authorities banned outspoken publications and arrested several journalists.

Gayoom won the August 1993 parliamentary nomination for the presidential referendum, despite considerable support for Iliyas Ibrahim, a government minister. Iliyas fled the country after the government investigated him for corruption, and Gayoom won a fourth term in October.

Gayoom allowed 229 candidates, all independents, to contest the December 1994 majlis elections. The government heavily restricted campaigning and detained five candidates. In 1996, Gayoom allowed Iliyas to return to the country under house arrest, and in 1997 the president freed his adversary.

In early 1998, Gayoom approved changes to the constitution allowing citizens to nominate themselves for president, after which the election commissioner decides whether candidates meet the necessary criteria and forwards names to the majlis. As before, the majlis selects the final candidate, whose name is then put to a national referendum. In September, the majlis announced that Gayoom was the only candidate it had approved from five who had submitted nominations. On October 18, Gayoom won a fifth term in a referendum, reportedly winning the approval of more than 80 percent of participating voters.

Political Rights and Civil Liberties: Maldivians cannot change their government democratically. President Gayoom heads a small hereditary elite that holds power. Political parties are not expressly banned, but the government discourages their formation and none exist. The government restricts political gatherings during campaigns to small meetings on private premises. On September 25, the day the majlis declared Gayoom to be the sole candidate for the October presidential election, Amnesty International reported that "election preparations are taking place in an atmosphere of fear and intimidation." The organization noted that authorities have kept Ismail Saadiq, a businessman and political dissident, in detention or under house arrest since July 1996 in a possible attempt to prevent him from participating in the presidential elections. In February, authorities transferred him from house arrest to a detention center for allegedly having talked to a foreign journalist, and they canceled his officially accepted nomination to stand in a parliamentary by-election. Gayoom heavily influences the majlis, although in recent years, it has rejected some government legislation and has become a forum for critical debate.

The president influences the judiciary, which is not independent. He appoints and can remove judges, although this latter power is rarely used, and he can review High Court decisions. The legal system is based on both Shari'a (Islamic law) and civil law. Trials fall far short of international standards. The strict 1990 Prevention of Terrorism Act (PTA) permits authorities to detain suspects indefinitely without trial. According to Amnesty International, in recent years, authorities have held dozens of dissidents under house arrest or in detention centers for prolonged periods without trial. Prison conditions are dismal.

Freedom of expression is restricted. The broadly drawn Penal Code prohibits speech or actions that could "arouse people against the government," although a 1990 amendment decriminalized factual newspaper reports about government errors. A 1968 law prohibits speech considered inimical to Islam, a threat to national security, or libelous. In 1994, a court sentenced a Maldivian under this law to six months in prison for making allegedly false statements about the government. Authorities used the PTA to imprison several journalists in 1990, the last of whom was released in 1993. Journalist Mohamed Nasheed spent nearly nine months in prison and house arrest in 1996-97 on defamation charges over a 1994 article criticizing election procedures.

The government can shut newspapers and sanction journalists for articles allegedly containing unfounded criticism. Two outspoken publications, which had their licenses revoked in 1990, remain closed. Regulations make editors responsible for the content of published material. Journalists practice self-censorship, although the mainly private press carries some criticism of the government. The state-run Voice of the Maldives radio and a small state-run television service carry some pluralistic views.

Nongovernmental organizations are legal, although there are no human rights groups and civil society is underdeveloped. Traditional norms generally relegate women to subservient roles, although many women find government employment. Unlike many Islamic countries, women have the same divorce rights as men, although inheritance laws favor men. Islam is the state religion, and all citizens must be Muslim. The government is concerned that the puritanical Wahhabi sect of Islam is gaining adherents on the outer atolls. Practice of other religions is prohibited, although private worship by non-Muslims is tolerated. There are no legal rights to form trade unions, stage strikes, and bargain collectively, and in practice, there is no organized labor activity. The country's high-end tourism industry is the main foreign exchange earner.

Mali

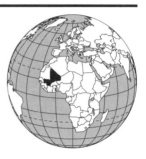

Polity: Presidential-par-   **Political Rights:** 3
liamentary democracy   **Civil Liberties:** 3
Economy: Mixed statist   **Status:** Free
Population: 10,100,000
PPP: $565
Life Expectancy: 46
Ethnic Groups: Mande [Bambara, Malinke, Sarakole]
(50 percent), Peul (17 percent), Voltaic (12 percent),
Tuareg and Moor (10 percent), Songhai (6 percent), other (5 percent)
Capital: Bamako

Overview: Municipal election results solidified the 1997 presidential and legislative victories of President Alpha Oumar Konaré and his ruling Alliance for Democracy in Mali (ADEMA) party. As in 1997, however, the 1998 municipal polls were largely boycotted by opposition parties and marked by very low voter turnout. The umbrella Collective of Opposition Political Parties still refuses to accept the results of the 1997 elections, which, in its view, were rigged and poorly administered. Many foreign donors, however, agree with President Konaré that opposition failures are more the result of their own shortcomings than presidential manipulation. Mali's generally good human rights record was again marred by instances of police brutality and reports of systematic torture by security forces against labor activists and opposition supporters. With nearly full control of the country's political institutions, President Konaré and ADEMA may feel sufficiently secure to allow further openings in the country's civil society.

After achieving independence from France in 1960, Mali was ruled by military or one-party dictators for more than 30 years. After soldiers killed more than 100 demonstrators demanding a multiparty system in 1991, President Moussa Traoré was overthrown by his own military. Traoré and several of his close associates are now on trial in Bamako for "economic crimes." After the 1991 coup, a national conference organized open elections that most observers judged as free and fair. Alpha Oumar Konaré won the presidency in April 1992.

Political Rights   After a transition from more than three decades of authori-
and Civil Liberties: tarian rule, Mali's people first chose their government freely and fairly in presidential and legislative elections in 1992. In 1997, little more than a quarter of registered voters participated as President Konaré was overwhelmingly re-elected against a weak candidate who alone broke an opposi-

tion boycott of the presidential contest. The first round of legislative elections in April 1998 was voided by the Constitutional Court, although international observers saw incompetence rather than fraud as the principal problem. Opposition supporters claimed that the Independent National Election Commission was independent in name only, while many analysts held that President Konaré and ADEMA, running on a record of tolerance, peacemaking, and economic growth, would have easily won against a fractious opposition even in fully competitive polls. ADEMA took 127 of 147 national assembly seats, and five opposition parties shared the remaining 18 seats. President Konaré's 22-member cabinet includes opposition members and four civic society representatives.

Since the end of military rule, Mali's domestic political debate has been open and extensive. Its highlight is a nationally broadcast annual "open forum" with top leaders each December. Nearly 50 political parties are officially registered, and many offer scathing criticism of government policies. The judiciary is not independent of the executive, but has shown considerable autonomy in rendering anti-administration decisions, which President Konaré has in turn respected.

Nearly all of the 150,00 Tuareg people who had fled Mali at the height of the country's civil war have returned. A 1995 agreement ended the brutal multisided conflict among Tuareg guerrillas, black ethnic militias, and government troops. Former guerrilla fighters have been integrated into the national army, but fuller accommodation of the Arab Tuareg people in any political system dominated by the country's black African majority will require genuine commitment to local autonomy and cultural rights. The peace pact provides for development assistance, and three languages spoken by Tuareg people are now national languages that are taught in schools in Tuareg areas.

Mali's media are among Africa's most open. Approximately forty independent newspapers and fifty private radio and television stations operate freely. State-run television, radio, and print media allow a diversity of views. There are approximately 60 independent radio stations throughout Mali, including community stations broadcasting in regional languages. Legislation that provides harsh penalties for slander or "public injury" to public officials may threaten press freedom, but has been rarely invoked. In May, Cheick Oumar Konaré, director of publishing of the private daily *Sud-Info*, was kidnapped and beaten by unidentified men, apparently in response to his newspaper's criticisms of the government.

Labor unions played a leading role in the pro-democracy movement and remain politically active. Mali is a predominantly Muslim, but secular state, and minority and religious rights are protected by law. Most formal legal advances in protection of women's rights have not been implemented, especially in rural areas. Female genital mutilation remains legal, although the government has conducted educational campaigns against the practice. Women hold 18 seats in the 147-member National Assembly.

Despite steady economic growth, Mali remains desperately poor. Hundreds of thousands of Malians are economic migrants across Africa and Europe. In 1998, privatization of major state enterprises continued, and increasing cotton and gold production raised export earnings.

Malta

Polity: Parliamentary democracy
Economy: Mixed capitalist-statist
Population: 400,000
PPP: $13,316
Life Expectancy: 77
Ethnic Groups: Maltese (mixed Arab, Sicilian, Norman, Spanish, Italian, and English)
Capital: Valletta

Political Rights: 1
Civil Liberties: 1
Status: Free

Overview:
In September, the Nationalist Party assumed power in Malta after winning 52 percent of the vote in a snap election. Prime Minister Alfred Sant had called the vote after his Labor Party lost its one-seat majority in a key parliamentary vote.

Upon taking office, new Prime Minister Edward Fenech Adami, who governed from 1987 to 1996, immediately reinstated Malta's application for European Union (EU) membership, which Sant had frozen in 1996. At year's end, the EU pledged to reassess the country's membership suitability in early 1999. Adami also vowed to institute a new indirect taxation system, which is likely to include a value-added tax.

Historically, the strategically located island of Malta was occupied by a long succession of foreign powers. It became independent within the British Commonwealth in 1964. In 1974, it became a republic within the Commonwealth. Under its constitution, Malta is a neutral and nonaligned nation.

When the Labor Party government ended Malta's defense agreement with Britain in 1979, the country lost its British military installations as well as accompanying expenditures. The government then turned to Libyan leader Mu'ammar al-Qadhafi, who promised financial support. Italy later pledged to protect Malta's neutrality and to provide loans and subsidies. Both agreements had lapsed by 1987, but political and economic cooperation with Libya was reaffirmed in 1988. Parliamentary leadership has alternated between the two main parties, the Malta Labor Party and the Nationalist Party. The constitution was amended in 1987 to allow the award of extra seats so that the party with a majority of the popular vote could secure a legislative majority in the House of Representatives.

Political Rights and Civil Liberties:
Citizens of Malta can change their government democratically. Members of the House of Representatives, the country's unicameral legislature, are elected on the basis of proportional representation every five years. Parliament elects the country's president to a five-year term. Although the post is largely ceremonial, the president is charged with appointing a prime minister and the cabinet from the parliament.

The judiciary is independent of the executive and legislative branches. The Chief Justice and nine judges are appointed by the president on the advice of the prime minister. The constitution requires a fair public trial, and defendants have the right to counsel of their choice. If they cannot pay, they are provided with court-appointed counsel at public expense.

Since 1992, the government has sponsored programs to diversify the media. In addition to several Maltese newspapers, two English-language weeklies are published. Television and radio include both public and private domestic broadcasts. Italian television and international radio broadcasts are also popular. The only limit upon freedom of speech and the press is a 1987 law prohibiting foreign involvement in Maltese election campaigns.

Roman Catholicism is the state religion, and an estimated 67 percent of the population attends mass at least once a week. Freedom of worship for religious minorities is respected, and all groups enjoy freedom of association. There are independent labor unions as well as a federation, the General Union of Workers.

A constitutional amendment banning gender discrimination took effect in 1993.

Marshall Islands

Polity: Parliamentary democracy
Economy: Capitalist-statist
Population: 100,000
PPP: na
Life Expectancy: 62
Ethnic Groups: Micronesian
Capital: Majuro

Political Rights: 1
Civil Liberties: 1
Status: Free

Overview: A no-confidence motion against President Imata Kabua, the first such action in the country's history, was narrowly defeated in October following a six-week legislative boycott.

The Marshall Islands, consisting of the Ralik and Ratak chains of coral atolls in the central Pacific Ocean, were purchased by Germany from Spain in 1899. Japan seized the islands in 1914, governing them under a League of Nations mandate until the United States Navy occupied them in 1945. In 1947, they became part of the U.S. Trust Territory of the Pacific Islands under United Nations trusteeship. The Marshall Islands district drafted a constitution, which came into effect on May 1, 1979. On the same date, parliament elected Amata Kabua as the country's first president. He was subsequently reelected to four successive four-year terms, the last in January 1996.

In 1983, the Marshall Islands signed a Compact of Free Association with the United States, which entered into force in 1986. Under the Compact, the country is fully sovereign, but defense remains the responsibility of the United States until at least 2001. In the early years of the Compact, the country enjoyed a steady supply of American-led foreign aid, and the government spent beyond its means. Although the service sector expanded, many government institutions failed, and there was little development in productive industry; the country was left saddled with foreign debt.

As the Compact's expiration in 2001 drew closer, the government focused on securing future development aid and improving the country's private sector. In 1995, the government initiated an austerity program designed by the Asian Development Bank that included budget cuts and civil service layoffs. Renegotiations of the Compact, which is unlikely to provide the same level of funding as in the past, are scheduled to begin in 1999.

Kabua's death in December 1996 left the country bereft of leadership. The president had owed his political longevity to personal loyalties within parliament and a limited pool of viable alternative candidates. On January 14, 1997, parliament elected Imata Kabua, a long-time senator and cousin of the late president, to fulfill the remainder of the term. The Fiji-based *Pacific Islands Monthly* noted that under the constitution, the speaker of the senate should have become acting president.

In October 1998, a six-week legislative deadlock over a no-confidence vote against Kabua ended when opposition senators came one vote short of removing the president. Among the reasons provided by the opposition for wanting to oust Kabua were misuse of government funds and a lack of accountability and transparency in government operations. Parliament had been unable to meet since September 7 when Kabua and his followers staged a walkout to dispute a move by the opposition to conduct the vote by secret ballot. The High Court subsequently ruled that a boycott of parliament could not be used to evade the no-confidence motion, and a vote by secret ballot was finally held on October 16.

The previous government had proposed to rent remote, uninhabited islands to foreign countries as nuclear waste dumps. The proposal attracted strong criticism, particularly after data released in 1994 which indicated that the extent of the radioactive fallout from the U.S. atomic testing program over the islands in the 1940s and 1950s was greater than previously disclosed. The proposal is on hold pending an environmental impact study. In June 1998, a scientific panel convened by the International Atomic Energy Agency agreed with U.S. claims that the former nuclear test site on Bikini Atoll, whose inhabitants were evacuated in the 1940s, can be made safe for habitation if certain cleanup measures are taken to reduce radiation contamination.

Political Rights and Civil Liberties:

Citizens of the Marshall Islands can change their government democratically. The 1979 constitution provides for a bicameral parliament with a 33-seat house of representatives (*Nitijela*) that is directly elected for a four-year term. The lower house chooses a president, who holds executive powers as head of state and head of government, from among its members. The Council of Chiefs, or upper *Iroji*, has twelve traditional leaders who offer advice on customary law. Although two ad-hoc parties took part in the 1991 legislative elections, they soon dissolved and did not play a role in the 1996 elections. Currently, though there are no legal restrictions on the formation of political parties, no formal parties exist.

The government generally respects freedom of speech and of the press. However, journalists occasionally practice self-censorship on sensitive political issues. There is a privately owned weekly paper with articles in both English and the Marshallese language. The government's *Marshall Islands Gazette* monthly contains official news and avoids political coverage. There are two radio stations, one of which is state owned, and both offer pluralistic views. A cable television company shows U.S. programs and occasionally covers local events. There are no restrictions on religious observance in this predominantly Christian country.

Freedom of assembly is respected in practice. The government broadly interprets constitutional guarantees of freedom of association to extend to trade unions, but none have been formed. There is no formal right to strike or engage in collective bargaining, although in practice there are no restraints on such activity.

The judiciary is generally independent, and the rule of law is well established. However, the government has attempted to influence certain judicial matters. Parliament recently amended the Judiciary Act to resolve inconsistencies between the rule of the court and a legislative act in favor of the latter. In general, the government respects the right to a fair trial. Both the national and local police honor legal civil rights protections in performing their duties.

Freedom of internal movement is unrestricted, except on Kwajalein Atoll, the site of a major U.S. military installation. Inheritance of property and traditional rank is matrilineal, and in most matters, women hold a social status equal to men. However, most women working in the private sector hold low wage jobs, and women are underrepresented in politics and government. Spousal abuse is increasingly common, with many victims of domestic violence reluctant to report the crime or to prosecute spouses in the court system.

Mauritania

Polity: Dominant party   **Political Rights:** 6
Economy: Capitalist-   **Civil Liberties:** 5*
statist   **Status:** Not Free
Population: 2,500,000
PPP: $1,622
Life Expectancy: 52
Ethnic Groups: Mixed Maur/black (40 percent),
Maur (30 percent), black (30 percent)
Capital: Nouakchott
Ratings change: Mauritania's civil liberties rating changed from 6 to 5 due
to greater freedom of association.

Overview:

Mauritania's human rights record, which includes racial discrimination marked by vestiges of slavery and attacks on freedom of expression, remains mixed. In December, Ahmed Ould Daddah, a major opposition leader and 1992 presidential candidate, was detained along with three other activists. While human rights groups now operate more openly, several leading activists were jailed early in the year. More newspapers are being published, but some have been repeatedly censored. Black Mauritanians who were expelled or fled during race-based attacks from 1990 to 1991 continue to return, but their reception and treatment have been uneven. Mauritania's narrowly based authoritarian regime has gradually liberalized since 1992, but most power remains in the hands of President Maaouya Ould Sid Ahmed Taya and a very small elite around him. Political activity, open discussion, and criticism of the government are increasingly tolerated, but harassment of opposition supporters and media and reports of abuses by security forces continue. Mauritania's basic political divisions are sharply defined along racial and ethnic lines.

After nearly six decades of French colonial rule, Mauritania's borders as an independent state were formalized in 1960. Its people include the dominant "white Maurs" of Arab extraction and Arabic-speaking Muslim black Africans known as "black Maurs." Other non-Muslim black Africans inhabiting the country's southern frontiers along the Senegal River valley constitute approximately one-third of the population. For centuries, black Africans were subjugated and taken as slaves by both white and black Maurs. Slavery has been repeatedly outlawed, but remnants of servitude and credible allegations of chattel slavery persist.

A 1978 military coup ended a civilian one-party state. A 1984 internal purge installed Colonel Maaouya Ould Sid Ahmed Taya as junta chairman. In 1992, Maaouya won a six-year presidential term in the country's first and deeply flawed multiparty election. Maaouya's Social Democratic Republican Party ruled the country as a de facto one-party state after the main opposition parties boycotted National Assembly elections in 1992. The incumbents maintained their grip on power through victories in 1996 legislative and 1997 presidential elections.

Political Rights and Civil Liberties:

Mauritanians have never been permitted to choose their representatives or change their government in open, competitive elections. Electoral provisions in the country's 1991 French-style constitution have not been respected in practice. Neither the 1997 presidential election nor the 1996 parliamentary vote was free or fair. The absence of an independent election commission, state control of broadcasts, harassment of independent print media, and the incumbent's use of state resources to promote his candidacy devalued Ould Taya's presidential victory. In deeply flawed 1996 legislative elections, the military-backed ruling PRDS won all but one of the 79 National Assembly seats against a divided opposition. The lone opposition seat was awarded in what appears to have been a cosmetic concession by the ruling party. The Front of Opposition Parties, an umbrella coalition, dismissed the polls as fraudulent and boycotted the second round of the 1996 legislative polls and the 1997 presidential vote.

Mauritania's judicial system is heavily influenced by the government. Many decisions are shaped by *Shari'a* law, especially in family and civil matters. In February, several human rights activists were convicted for operating or associating with "non-authorized" organizations. Their arrests followed broadcast of a French television program in which they criticized the Mauritanian government's actions toward reducing slavery. Security forces violently dispersed and seized people protesting the arrests. After a presidential pardon in March, most of the detainees were released, but several people identified as prisoners of conscience by Amnesty International remain incarcerated.

More than 20 political parties and numerous nongovernmental organizations operate, but government registration requirements may now be used to block human rights and anti-slavery groups. A handful of black African activist groups and Islamist parties are banned. There are reports that black Africans are barred from holding meetings and are harassed when they attempt to do so without permission. The banned *El Hor* (Free Man) Movement promotes black rights and is attempting to transform itself into a political party. Widespread discrimination against blacks continues. As many as

100,000 blacks still live in conditions of servitude. In 1996, the U.S. Congress voted to suspend all nonhumanitarian aid to Mauritania until anti-slavery laws are properly enforced. Black resistance movements, including the Mauritanian Forces of African Liberation and the United Front for Armed Resistance in Mauritania, continue to call for armed struggle against discrimination and enforced Arabization.

Pre-publication censorship, arrests of journalists, and seizures and bans of newspapers devalue constitutional guarantees of free expression. Pressure on the independent print media, which are often critical of the government, continued in 1998. All publications must be officially registered. The state owns the only two daily newspapers and monopolizes nearly all broadcast media. A community radio station focusing on women's issues was launched in July. State media forbid dissemination of allegations of continued slavery and criticism of Islam. Punishable offenses include "insulting the president" and "promoting national disharmony."

Mauritania is an Islamic state in which, by statute, all citizens are Sunni Muslims who may not possess other religious texts or enter non-Muslim households. The right to worship, however, is generally tolerated. Non-Mauritanian Shi'a Muslims and Christians are permitted to worship privately, and some churches operate openly.

Under Shari'a law, a woman's testimony is only given half of the weight of a man's. Legal protections regarding property and equality of pay are usually respected only in urban areas among the educated elite. Female genital mutilation is widely practiced. Only three women hold National Assembly seats.

Approximately one-fourth of Mauritania's workers serve in the small formal sector. The government-allied Union of Mauritanian Workers lost its monopoly on trade union activities under the 1993 Labor Code, but remains the dominant labor organization. The government has forcibly ended strikes and detained or banned union activists from the capital. Mauritania is one of the world's poorest countries and faces a virtually unpayable foreign debt. Its vast and mostly arid territory has few resources.

Mauritius

Polity: Parliamentary democracy
Economy: Capitalist
Population: 1,200,000
PPP: $13,294
Life Expectancy: 70
Ethnic Groups: Indo-Mauritian (68 percent), Creole (27 percent), Sino-Mauritian (3 percent), Franco-Mauritian (2 percent)
Capital: Port Louis

Political Rights: 1
Civil Liberties: 2
Status: Free

Overview:

The ruling Labour Party (LP) won a crucial by-election in April, but was riven by internal dissent and criticism of Prime Minister Navin Ramgoola's performance. Allegations of corruption and the introduction of a value-added tax were among the most contentious issues in the country's political debate. The current government's failure to adopt economic reforms that could disadvantage its supporters in the short term has raised new concerns about the future vitality of the Mauritian economy. An opposition alliance aimed at toppling the LP in scheduled December 2000 general elections began to form during the year. Any alliance between the Mauritian Militant Movement (MMM) and the Mauritian Socialist Movement (MSM), however, may prove tenuous. Both MMM leader Paul Bérenger and MSM chief Sir Anerood Jugnauth, a former prime minister, can be expected to fight vigorously for overall leadership.

Prime Minister Ramgoola has suggested revamping the country's election laws to provide proportional representation. The current "first-past-the-post" system has led to sharp swings in power and the exclusion from government of parties that have received substantial popular support.

Mauritius has achieved a stable democratic and constitutional order, and its focus on political competition rather than violent conflict demonstrates a level of political development enjoyed by few other African states. The political process is used to maintain ethnic balance and economic growth rather than dominance for any single group. In addition, political parties are not divided along the lines of the country's diverse ethnicities and religions. At the same time, while Mauritius is often cited as one of post-colonial Africa's few success stories, its Indian Ocean location and largely nonethnic African population mark its experience as quite different from Africa's contiguous continental states.

The country's political stability is underpinned by steady economic growth and improvements in the island's infrastructure and standard of living. Unemployment is rising, but the country's integrated multinational population has provided a capable and reliable work force that, along with preferential European and U.S. market access for sugar and garment exports, is attracting foreign investment. Economic development has been achieved, however, at the cost of the country's native forests and fauna, nearly all of which has been destroyed. In addition, the country's Creole culture is fading.

Mauritius had no indigenous people and was seized and settled as a way station for European trade to the East Indies and India. Its ethnically mixed population is primarily descended from Indian subcontinental immigrants who were brought to the island as laborers during 360 years of Dutch, French, and British colonial administration. Since gaining independence from Britain in 1968, Mauritius has maintained one of the developing world's most successful democracies. In 1993, the island became a republic within the British Commonwealth, with a largely ceremonial president as head of state.

Political Rights and Civil Liberties:

Since independence, Mauritius has regularly chosen its representatives in free, fair, and competitive elections. The unicameral National Assembly includes 62 directly elected members and the attorney general, if he is not already an elected member. Only four of eight "best loser" seats that may be awarded to redress inadequacies in party or ethnic representation are currently assigned. Decentralized structures govern the country's island dependencies. The largest of these is Rodrigues Island, which has its own government, local councils, and two seats in the National Assembly. The generally independent judiciary is headed by a Supreme Court. The legal system is an amalgam of French and British traditions.

Civil rights are generally well respected, although cases of police brutality have been reported. Freedom of religion is respected. Both domestic and international travel are unrestricted, and there are no known political prisoners or reports of political or extrajudicial killings.

The constitution guarantees freedom of expression and the press, but all broadcast media are state owned and usually reflect government views. Several private daily and weekly publications, however, are often highly critical of both government and opposition politicians and their policies. Freedoms of assembly and association are respected, although police occasionally refuse to issue permits for demonstrations. Numerous nongovernmental organizations operate. Nine labor federations include 300 unions.

Women constitute approximately 20 percent of the paid labor force and generally occupy a subordinate role in society. The law does not require equal pay for equal work or prohibit sexual harassment in the workplace. Women are underrepresented at the national university. Government campaigns have sought to improve the status of women by removing some legal barriers to advancement. Official and nongovernmental agencies have mounted educational campaigns to reduce widespread domestic violence and have launched programs to assist abuse victims.

Tensions between the Hindu majority and Muslim and Creole minorities persist despite the general respect for constitutional prohibitions against discrimination and constitute one of the country's few potential political flashpoints.

Mexico

Polity: Dominant party (transitional)
Economy: Capitalist-statist
Population: 97,500,000
PPP: $6,769
Life Expectancy: 72
Ethnic Groups: Mestizo (60 percent), Indian (30 percent), European (9 percent), other (1 percent)
Capital: Mexico City

Political Rights: 3
Civil Liberties: 4
Status: Partly Free

Overview:　President Ernesto Zedillo's once-absolute authority dwindles at a time of unparalleled political and security challenges while he strives to provide Mexico and the political party that has ruled the country for eight decades with greater democracy, which has often proved at cross-purposes with the imperatives of good government. Dramatic upsurges in narcotics-related and common crime come at a time when Mexico's criminal justice system is in shambles, and its military more involved in internal security than at any time in recent memory. At the same time, Zedillo's efforts to reform the long-ruling Institutional Revolutionary Party (PRI) are threatened by powerful conservative party leaders, while attempts to accommodate other political parties are hampered by his own limitations, which are, in some respects, self-created though well intentioned.

Mexico achieved independence from Spain in 1810 and established itself as a republic in 1822. Seven years after the Revolution of 1910, a new constitution was promulgated under which the United Mexican States became a federal republic consisting of 31 states and a Federal District (Mexico City). Each state has elected governors and legislatures. The president is elected to a six-year term. A bicameral Congress consists of a 128-member Senate elected for six years with at least one minority senator from each state, and a 500-member Chamber of Deputies elected for three years, 300 of whom are directly elected and 200 of whom are elected through proportional representation.

Since its founding in 1929, the PRI has historically dominated the country by means of its corporatist, authoritarian structure which is maintained through co-optation, patronage, corruption, and repression. The formal business of government has taken place mostly in secret and with little legal foundation.

Salinas de Gortari won the 1988 presidential elections through massive and systematic fraud. Most Mexicans believe Salinas actually lost to Cuauhtemoc Cardenas, who headed a coalition of leftist parties that later became the Party of the Democratic Revolution (PRD).

Under Salinas, corruption reached unparalleled proportions. In 1998, Swiss officials presented a strong case of complicity by his brother Raul in murder and corruption, as well as his consorting with some of the country's most notorious narcotics kingpins. If true, experts say it is unlikely Carlos Salinas was ignorant of his brother's deeds.

Salinas conceded a few gubernatorial election victories to the right-wing National Action Party (PAN), which had supported his economic policies. In return, PAN dropped its demands for political reform and abandoned plans to establish a pro-democracy coalition with the PRD.

Until the outbreak of the Marxist-led Zapatista rebellion in the southern state of Chiapas on New Year's Day 1994, it was assumed that Salinas' handpicked successor, Luis Donaldo Colosio, would defeat Cardenas and PAN congressman Diego Fernandez de Cevallos in the 1994 presidential election. The Zapatistas' demands for democracy and clean elections resonated throughout Mexico, and Colosio was assassinated on March 23, 1994. As the PRI stand-in, Salinas substituted Zedillo, a 42-year-old U.S.-trained economist with little political experience. Despite PRI hardliners' animosity towards the party's technocrats, they placed the government machinery—the enormous resources of the state as well as the broadcast media—firmly behind Zedillo.

On August 21, 1994, Zedillo won with nearly 50 percent of the valid vote. The PRI won 95 Senate seats, the PAN 25, and the PRD 8. In the Chamber, the PRI won 300 seats, the PAN 118, and the PRD 70. Both opposition parties disputed the elections' legitimacy. Only PRI legislators in the Chamber voted to affirm the results. The next month, the reform-minded PRI secretary general was assassinated, his murder evidently ordered from somewhere within the PRI.

Weeks after Zedillo took office on December 1, 1994, the Mexican *peso* collapsed, and the economy fell into a deep, year-long recession. Under Zedillo, a trend that had started with Salinas accelerated, and Mexico became the leading supplier of illegal drugs to the U.S., accounting for two-thirds of the cocaine and 20 to 30 percent of the heroin entering the country. Many state-owned companies privatized by Salinas were bought by drug traffickers, further exacerbating the well-entrenched corruption.

In 1996, opposition parties of the left and right won important municipal elections in three states. Post-electoral conflicts took place in several regions. In the southern states of Guerrero, Oaxaca, Tabasco, and Chiapas—where many of Mexico's indigenous people live—political violence continued to be a fact of life. But the elections left the PRI governing just two of Mexico's 12 largest cities.

In April 1996, the main political parties, with the exception of the PAN, agreed on reforms aimed at bringing about more fair elections. The reforms introduced direct elections for the mayorality of Mexico City and abolished government control of the Federal Electoral Commission. The government pledged to increase public financing of political parties and to guarantee them fairer access to television during elections. But unilateral changes by the president and PRI limited the scope of the law, and the main opposition parties voted against it in November 1996.

The climate in which Mexicans went to the polls several times in 1997 and 1998 was substantially improved from past elections. For the first time, in 1997, voters chose the mayor of Mexico City and elected PRD opposition leader Cardenas rather than having the municipal chief appointed by the president. That year, an opposition coalition composed of the PRD, PAN, and two other parties not only took control over the lower house of Congress following July elections, but also reached a consensus whereby the presidency of 61 house committees were allocated on an equitable basis. By year-end, the PAN held six governorships.

Elections held in 1998 in several states for gubernatorial, legislative, and municipal posts indicated the uneven ability of the opposition to build upon its successes in the state and federal elections. One of the most important lessons learned, observers say, was that PRI candidates were able to win in contests that were not fixed, as the party won seven of ten gubernatorial contests. In May, a three-year undercover U.S.-sting operation, code named "Casablanca," linked several leading Mexican banks to drug money laundering and seriously angered Mexican officials who were kept in the dark about the probe.

Political Rights and Civil Liberties: Elections in Mexico held in 1997-1998 were the fairest in the country's history. The electoral playing field was substantially improved, although the PRI sustained important advantages. In 1998, the PRI wrested one governorship away from the PAN, lost one to the PAN, and lost another to the PRD. Zedillo ceded a significant quota of power in pursuit of democratization of the PRI when he announced he was giving up the *dedazo*—in which the outgoing president handpicks his party's presidential nominee. Instead, a primary election will decide who will lead the party into the general election slated for the year 2,000.

Supreme Court judges are appointed by the executive and rubber-stamped by the Senate. The judicial system is weak, politicized, and riddled with the corruption infecting all official bodies. In most rural areas, respect for laws by official agencies is nearly nonexistent, and in general, lower courts and law enforcement are undermined by widespread bribery.

Constitutional guarantees regarding political and civic organizations are generally respected in the urban north and central parts of the country. However, political and civic expression is restricted throughout rural Mexico, in poor urban areas, and in poor southern states where the government frequently takes repressive measures against the left-wing PRD as well as peasant and indigenous groups.

Civil society has grown in recent years: human rights, pro-democracy, women's, and environmental groups are active. However, government critics remain subject to forms of sophisticated intimidation that range from gentle warnings by government officials and anonymous death threats, to unwarranted detention and jailings on dubious charges. In 1998, dozens of international human right activists were expelled from Mexico after being accused by the government of meddling in politics. According to Amnesty International, Mexican government attempts to curtail the visits by international activists and to limit their movement inside Mexico were an attempt to "kill the truth."

An official human rights commission was created in 1990. However, it is barred from examining political and labor rights violations, and cannot enforce its recommendations. For more than four years, the human rights situation has seriously deteriorated, with hundreds of arbitrary detentions, widespread torture, scores of extra-judicial executions, and a number of forced disappearances reported by nongovernmental organizations.

Torture and ill-treatment by law enforcement agents continue despite government promises to reform the police agencies, even as Mexico's soaring crime rate and lack of effective law enforcement have begun to be viewed as serious barriers to economic development. An estimated ten percent of all extortive kidnappings carried out in Mexico, which ranks second only to Colombia in the greatest number of attacks in Latin America, were carried out by police officers. In November 1998, Mexico City authorities, stung by repeated scandals including the arrest of 15 officers charged with raping three teenage girls, tried a new crime-fighting tactic: They jailed 35 police officers on charges ranging from armed robbery to murder. In a much-touted effort to restore public confidence in law enforcement, the federal capital's police chief announced plans to decentralize the 94,000-person force and place it under greater civilian control.

During the outbreak of the still-simmering Chiapas rebellion, the military was responsible for widespread human rights violations. Army counter-insurgency efforts continue to cause numerous rights violations in Chiapas and in the state of Guerrero, where a shadowy Popular Revolutionary Army (EPR), thought by some to be infiltrated by agents provocateurs, has provided a pretext for military action against local PRD leaders. Credible reports say that nearly a dozen guerrillas attempting to surrender were murdered by army troops in June.

The growing role of the military in internal security—ostensibly to combat domestic terrorism, drug trafficking and street crime—has contributed to grave human rights problems, particularly in rural areas. The official human rights commission refuses to investigate some nearly 2,000 cases of reported human rights violations by the military.

Published reports offered continuing evidence of close links between drug traffickers and the armed forces, contradicting official versions which have sought to portray the military as less prone to corruption and drug cartel influence than civilian law enforcement. At least six serving generals have been arrested on drug charges in the last two years. Meanwhile, Brigadier Jose Francisco Gallardo Rodriguez, under military arrest since 1993 for advocating strict armed forces compliance with human rights standards, was sentenced by a military court to 15 years in prison. (In contrast, former anti-narcotics czar Gen. Juan Jesus Gutierrez Rebollo was sentenced to 13 years and 9 months for being in the pay of the country's largest drug cartel.) Many observers say the charges of embezzlement, insubordination and destruction of army property were trumped up and fly in the face of a 1996 finding by the Inter-American Commission on Human Rights that said he had been imprisoned "without reason and legal justification" and called for his immediate release.

The media, while mostly private and nominally independent, depend on the government for advertising revenue. A handful of daily newspapers and weeklies are the exceptions. The ruling party dominates television, by far the country's most influential medium. Violent attacks against journalists are common, with reporters investigating police issues, narcotics trafficking, and public corruption at particular risk.

In 1992, the constitution was amended to restore the legal status of the Catholic Church and other religious institutions. Priests and nuns were allowed to vote for the first time in nearly 80 years. Nonetheless, activist priests promoting the rights of Indians and the poor, particularly in southern states, remain subject to threats and intimidation by conservative landowners and local PRI bosses.

Officially-recognized labor unions operate as political instruments of the PRI, and most are grouped under the Confederation of Mexican Workers, whose leadership in recent years has been increasingly challenged by trade union dissidents. The government does not recognize independent unions, denying them collective-bargaining rights and the right to strike. The *maquiladora* regime of export-only production facilities has created substantial abuse of worker rights. Most maquiladora workers are young, uneducated women who accept lower pay more readily, with annual labor turnover averaging between 200 percent and 300 percent. They have no medical insurance, holidays, or profit sharing, and female employees are frequently the targets of sexual harassment and abuse. The companies also discriminate against pregnant women, in order to avoid providing them with maternity leave. Violence against women is rampant and the government consistently fails to enforce child labor laws.

Independent unions and peasant organizations are subject to intimidation, blacklisting, and violent crackdowns. Dozens of labor and peasant leaders have been killed in recent years in ongoing land disputes, particularly in the southern states where Indians comprise close to half the population.

Micronesia

Polity: Federal parliamentary democracy
Economy: Capitalist
Population: 100,000
PPP: na
Life Expectancy: 66
Ethnic Groups: Micronesian , Polynesian
Capital: Palikir

Political Rights: 1
Civil Liberties: 2
Status: Free

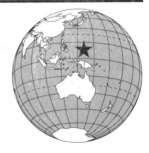

Overview: The Federated States of Micronesia consists of 607 islands in the archipelago of the Caroline Islands located in the north Pacific Ocean. In 1899, Germany purchased the Carolines from Spain, and in 1914, Japan seized the islands, ruling them from 1920 under a League of Nations mandate. During World War II, the United States occupied the islands, which became part of the U.S. Trust Territory of the Pacific in 1947.

In 1978, four districts of the Trust Territory–Yap, Chuuk, Pohnpei, and Kosrae–approved a constitution creating the Federated States of Micronesia. The constitution became effective the following year, and the country elected its first president, Tosiwo Nakayama. In 1982, the territory concluded a Compact of Free Association with the United States, which entered into force in 1986. Under the terms of the Compact, the country is fully sovereign, although the U.S. is responsible for defense until at least 2001. In 1990, the United Nations formally dissolved the trusteeship.

In 1991, congress elected Bailey Olter of Pohnpei state, a former vice president under Nakayama, as the country's third president. Olter was subsequently elected to a second term in 1995 over Kosrae state's Senator Jacob Nena. In July 1996, Olter suffered a stroke, and in November, congress ruled him unable to fulfill his responsibilities and installed Nena as acting president.

The economy is dependent on fishing, subsistence agriculture, tourism, and U.S. aid. In anticipation of the expiration of the current Compact of Free Association in 2001, when the country is likely to lose substantial U.S. funding, the government has begun paying greater attention to improving the country's foreign investment environment and increasing the size of the private sector.

Political Rights and Civil Liberties:

Citizens of the Federated States of Micronesia can change their government democratically. The constitution provides for a unicameral, 14-senator congress. One senator is elected at-large from each of the four states for a four-year term, with the remaining ten senators elected for two-year terms from single-member districts based on population. The president and vice president are selected by congress from among its four at-large members. Politics are based on state, clan, and individual loyalties. Political parties are permitted, although none has been formed. Although in practice there is an informal rotation system for the top elected offices of the country, the alleged political dominance of Chuuk state, which holds nearly half the population and a proportionate number of congressional seats, has created tensions with the three smaller states. The country held its last elections for the single-member congressional districts on March 4, 1997. The next full elections are scheduled for 1999.

The state of press freedom showed some signs of improvement in 1998. A new independent weekly newspaper, *The Island Tribune*, which was launched in December 1997, explores controversial and politically sensitive issues. This positive development contrasts the events of 1997, when congress adopted a resolution calling for the deportation of Sherry O'Sullivan, a Canadian citizen who was the editor of the now defunct *FSM News*, then the country's only independent newspaper. O'Sullivan charged that the action was the result of her exposes of alleged government corruption. After she left Micronesia when her employment contract ended, the government refused to grant her permission to return on the pretext that she had broken immigration and labor laws.

Each of the four state governments and a religious organization operate radio stations, and the residents of Pohnpei have access to satellite television. The federal government publishes a twice-monthly information bulletin, *The National Union*, and the state governments produce their own newsletters. Other papers which generally avoid sensitive topics include the *Pohnpei Business News* and *Micronesia Weekly*. Religious freedom is respected in this predominantly Roman Catholic country.

Freedom of assembly and association are respected, although there are few non-governmental organizations other than churches and student organizations. Workers have the legal right to form or join associations. However, no unions have been formed because of the small size of the wage economy. There are no laws specifically addressing collective bargaining.

The judiciary is independent, and trials are conducted fairly. The local police are under the control of the civil authorities. However, in several cases, police were found guilty of mistreating citizens and were subsequently dismissed from the force. Prison conditions meet minimum international standards.

Domestic abuse is common, but effective prosecution of such offenses is rare in what is often regarded as a private, family matter. There have also been a growing number of physical and sexual assault cases against women outside of the family context. Although women are increasingly active in the private sector and in lower and midlevel government positions, they remain underrepresented at the highest levels of government.

Moldova

Polity: Parliamentary democracy
Economy: Mixed capitalist (transitional)
Population: 4,200,000
PPP: $1,547
Life Expectancy: 66
Ethnic Groups: Moldovan/Romanian (64.5 percent), Ukrainian (14 percent), Russian (13 percent), Gagauz (3.5 percent), Bulgarian (2 percent), Jewish (1.5 percent), other (1.5 percent)
Capital: Chisinau

Political Rights:2*
Civil Liberties:4
Status: Partly Free

Ratings change: Moldova's political rights rating changed from 3 to 2 due to freer parliamentary elections.

Overview:

In March 1998 parliamentary elections, the Communists, who were banned from running in the 1994 vote, won 40 out of 101 seats and 30 percent of the vote. But a center-right coalition led by Prime Minister Ion Ciubuc formed a new government in April, leaving Communists out of the cabinet.

Key issues during the year were ongoing negotiations about the status of the breakaway Transdniester Republic and the withdrawal of an estimated 3,500 Russian troops still in the region.

Moldova, a predominately Romanian-speaking former Soviet republic bordering Ukraine and Romania, declared independence from the Soviet Union in 1991 when Mircea Snegur, who ran unopposed with the backing of the nationalist Moldovan Popular Front (MPF), was elected president. In 1990, Slavs in the Transdniester region proclaimed the Dniester Moldovan Republic (DMR). The 150,000-member Gagauz, a Turkic Christian people, did the same. The fighting in the Transdniester, where local Slavs were supported by elements of Russia's Fourteenth Army, ended with a cease-fire in mid-1992. In 1994 parliamentary elections, the PDAM—a coalition of former Communists and moderate supporters of Moldovan statehood, won 56 of 104 seats.

In 1996, strained relations between President Snegur, who had resigned from the PDAM and formed the Party of Revival and Accord Of Moldova (PRCM), and then-Prime Minister Andrei Sangheli of the PDAM paved the way for Petru Lucinschi who ran as an independent to be elected president. Ciubuc was approved as prime minister by parliament in January 1997. To consolidate their activities, pro-Lucinschi forces formed the Movement for a Democratic and Prosperous Moldova. Pro-Snegur forces established the Democratic Convention, which included the PRCM, the Christian Democratic-Popular Front group, and several smaller parties.

In March 1998, capitalizing on growing popular discontent with continued economic problems, the Communists won that parliamentary elections, gaining 30 percent of the vote and 40 seats. The nationalist Democratic Convention won 19 percent and 26 seats; the Bloc for a Democratic and Prosperous Moldova, 18 percent and 24 seats; and the center-right Party of Democratic Forces won 8 percent and 11 seats. Eleven other political groups, including the PDAM, and 60 independent candidates failed to pass the four percent threshold necessary to win seats. Turnout was 69 percent. After difficult negotiations, the new government was formally approved by parliament on May 22. The 16-member cabinet consisted of leaders from the Movement for Democratic and Prosperous Moldova, the Democratic Convention, and the Party of Democratic Forces.

On September 9, the country was rocked by the collapse of the lei. The International Monetary Fund took steps to shore up the currency, but the agency, which had suspended aid in July 1997, continued to press Moldova to cut its large budget deficit by cutting expenditures, mainly in social programs.

In other issues, the Organization for Security and Cooperation in Europe (OSCE) told Russia in July to honor its promise to withdraw all troops and ammunition from Transdniester. In October, with Transdniester leaders insisting that Russian troops stay until a final political settlement is reached, Russian Prime Minister Yevgeny Primakov and Prime Minister Ciubuc held what were called "constructive talks" in Moscow, but no resolution was reached.

Political Rights and Civil Liberties:

Moldovans can change their government democratically under a multiparty system enshrined in the 1994 constitution. International monitoring groups, including OSCE, characterized the November 1996 presidential elections as "free and fair." The March 1998 parliamentary vote was also free and fair.

The constitution and law provide for freedom of speech and press. However, defamation of the "state and people" is proscribed. Most political parties publish their own newspapers, which frequently criticize government policies. Most electronic media are controlled by the state-owned Teleradio-Moldova. The main private station, Catalan TV-based in Chisinau, generally avoids political issues. There are several independent radio stations; press agencies include Basa-Press, Flux, and Interlic.

Freedom of religion is generally respected, though a 1992 law on religion contains restrictions that could inhibit the activities of some religious groups as it prohibits proselytizing. In 1997, a Court of Appeal ruled that the government must recognize the Bessarabian Metropoly, which has ties to the Russian Orthodox hierachy in Moscow and had sued the government after it failed to register the church in 1992. The government took the case to the Supreme Court, and the decision was overturned on a technicality. The issue remained unresolved in 1998.

There are some restrictions on freedom of assembly. Under law, rallies that slander the state or subvert the constitution are banned. There are some 50 political parties and groupings spanning the political spectrum. In November, President Lucinschi signed amendments to the law on political parties and public movements that stipulated that such organizations had to have no less than 5,000 members representing at least half of Moldova's territories. Only about 10 to 12 parties meet the criteria.

The Federation of Independent Trade Unions of Moldova (UFSM), which replaced the Soviet-era confederation, is the largest labor organization. In January 1998, the Federation filed an inquiry with the Constitutional Court requesting to amend the constitution and to grant the right to legislative initiatives to trade unions. In June, teachers went on a hunger strike in Ungheni to protest salary arrears. In October, employees of state radio threatened to strike over unpaid wages. There are several hundred NGOs registered in Moldova, among them women's groups, student organizations, policy institutes, and environmental groups.

The judiciary is still is not fully independent, with the prosecutor's office having undue influence which undermines the presumption of innocence. Trials are generally open to the public. The Constitutional Court exercises judicial review, and has overturned actions of parliament and the president.

Moldova has ratified the Council of Europe's Convention on the Protection of Ethnic Minorities. In 1998, discrimination against Romanian-Moldovan speakers continued in the Transdniester.

Freedom of movement is not restricted, though Transdniester authorities have searched incoming and outbound vehicles. The government may also deny emigration to anyone with access to "state secrets."

Corruption in government, the civil service, and organized crime hinder fair competition and equal opportunity. In February, the Department for Combating Corruption and Organized Crime initiated proceedings against administrators in the state energy company accused of embezzling funds meant for oil purchases. In April, unidentified gunmen shot at the chief of the anti-corruption department.

Women are well represented in government, education, and the private sector, though they are disproportionately represented among the unemployed.

Monaco

Polity: Principality and
legislative democracy
Economy: Capitalist-statist
Population: 30,000
PPP: na
Life Expectancy: na
Ethnic Groups: French (47 percent), Italian (16 percent),
Monegasque (16 percent), other (21 percent)
Capital: Monaco

Political Rights: 2
Civil Liberties: 1
Status: Free

Overview:

Since assuming power in 1949, Prince Rainier III has been responsible for Monaco's impressive economic growth. Under his direction, the economy has ended its exclusive dependence on gambling revenue. Rainier has also implemented urban redevelopment programs and built major sports and cultural facilities. At the same time, the municipality has been strongly criticized for lax banking regulations that, in the words of *Le Monde*, make it a "fiscal paradise" for criminals. In November, 1998, the principality rendered its first conviction of an individual on charges of money laundering.

The Principality of Monaco is an independent and sovereign state and a full member of the United Nations. In 1997, the royal Grimaldi family celebrated its 700th anniversary of rule over the principality. During the first six centuries of Grimaldi rule, Monaco was intermittently controlled by European powers. It achieved independence from France in 1861. Under a treaty ratified in 1919, France pledged to protect the territorial integrity, sovereignty, and independence of the principality in return for a guarantee that Monegasque policy would conform to French interests.

Of 32,000 residents, Monaco is home to only 5,000 Monegasques. Only they may participate in the election of the 18-member National Council. As head of state, Prince Rainier holds executive authority, formally appoints the four-member cabinet, and proposes all legislation on which the Council votes. Laws initiated by the prince are drafted in his name by the cabinet and then debated for passage in the National Council. The prince holds veto power over the Council.

Political Rights and Civil Liberties:

Citizens of Monaco may change the National Council and their municipal Councils democratically. The Council is elected every five years by universal adult suffrage. The prince delegates judicial authority to the courts and tribunals, which adjudicate independently in his name. Although Monaco does not have a Minister of Justice, it does have a Supreme Court that deals with constitutional claims and jurisdictional conflicts.

Freedom of expression and association is guaranteed by the 1962 constitution. Denunciations of the Grimaldi family are prohibited by an official Monegasque penal code. Press freedom is respected. Two monthly magazines and a weekly government journal are published in the principality, and French daily newspapers are widely available. Radio and television are government operated and sell time to commercial sponsors, and all French broadcasts are freely transmitted to the principality. France maintains a controlling interest in Radio Monte Carlo, which broadcasts in several languages.

Although Monaco experiences chronic labor shortages and relies heavily on migrant and cross-border labor, nationals are given legal preference in employment. Since Monegasques constitute only 16 percent of the population, strict citizenship laws and cultural preservation are considered of vital importance. A 1992 law stipulates that foreign women marrying male Monegasque citizens are no longer accorded automatic citizenship. Instead, a provision was introduced to require women to remain with their spouses for five years to acquire eligibility for citizenship. Also in 1992, women citizens were granted the right to pass their nationality to their children.

Freedom of association, including the right of workers to organize in unions, is respected, and trade unions are independent of the government. Religious freedom is constitutionally guaranteed. The state religion is Roman Catholic, but adherents of other faiths may practice freely.

Mongolia

Polity: Presidential-parliamentary democracy
Economy: Mixed capitalist (transitional)
Population: 2,400,000
PPP: $3,916
Life Expectancy: 57
Ethnic Groups: Mongol (90 percent), Kazakh (4 percent), Chinese (2 percent), Russian (2 percent), other (2 percent)
Capital: Ulaanbaatar

Political Rights: 2
Civil Liberties: 3
Status: Free

Overview:

Mongolia's young democracy showed resilience in 1998 as it weathered a political crisis that left the country without a government for seven months, the unsolved murder of the hero of the 1990 pro-democracy movement, and continued disillusionment over the punishing social cost of economic reform in this fast-changing society.

China controlled this vast Central Asian region for two centuries until 1911 and again from 1919 until a Marxist revolt in 1921. The Soviet-backed Mongolian People's Revolutionary Party (MPRP) formed a Communist state in 1924 following three years of nominal rule by aging Buddhist lamas. For the next 65 years, Mongolia was a virtual republic of the Soviet Union.

Pro-democracy demonstrations forced the government to resign in March 1990, and in July, Mongolia held its first multiparty parliamentary elections. The MPRP easily defeated an unprepared opposition. In September, the Hural (parliament) named the MPRP's Punsalmaagiyn Orchirbat as president.

The 1992 constitution provides for a president with executive powers who is directly elected for a four-year term. The president must approve candidates for premier and can veto legislation, subject to a two-thirds parliamentary override. The constitution also created a directly elected, 76-seat Great Hural and provided for private land ownership.

The MPRP easily retained control of parliament in the 1992 elections, as many voters associated the opposition with free market reforms that had caused higher prices and thrown thousands of people out of work. In 1993, President Orchirbat, having been forced off the MPRP ticket by party hardliners, won re-election as the candidate of the two main opposition parties, the National Democratic Party (NDP) and the Social Democratic Party (SDP).

In 1994, the economy grew after four years of contraction. But the economic restructuring continued to take its toll. The NDP and the SDP formed the opposition Democratic Union Coalition (DUC), which ran an issues-oriented campaign for the June 1996 parliamentary elections. Under a 91 percent turnout, the DUC won 50 seats to sweep the MPRP out of parliamentary power after 72 years. The MPRP won 25 seats and a minor party, one.

New prime minister Mendsaihan Enksaikhan froze spending, lifted price controls, cut pension rolls, and stripped tariff protection from domestic industries. But Enksaikhan's radical reforms coincided with a sharp fall in world prices for Mongolia's two biggest foreign revenue earners, copper and cashmere.

The painful economic reforms became a key issue in the May 1997 presidential elections. Under a turnout of around 85 percent, the MPRP's Nachagyn Bagabandy, a former parliamentary chairman who had stressed social issues and the need to conduct privatization fairly, won with 60.8 percent of the vote against Orchirbat's 29.8 percent.

As Mongolians continued to feel abandoned by the state in the face of rising prices, sharp cutbacks in state benefits and industrial jobs, and other social costs of restructuring, the Asian financial crisis added to their woes by curbing foreign direct investment in Mongolia and slowing exports of copper and other raw materials. In April 1998, the NDP, the larger of the two main coalition partners and an advocate of slower reforms, forced Premier Enksaikhan's government to resign en masse.

In July, the country plunged into political uncertainty after parliament voted to oust a three-month-old government headed by the NDP's Tsakhiagiin Elbegdorj, a 35-year-old former journalist, over the controversial merger of a bankrupt state bank and a private bank. In the ensuing months, president Bagabandy used his constitutional power to reject several replacement candidates.

On October 2, the fractious DUC coalition nominated as premier Sanjaasuren Zorig, the 36-year-old founder of the pro-democracy movement, which Bagabandy accepted. The same day, unknown assailants murdered Zorig in his Ulaanbaatar apartment. Conspiracy theories abounded: it was because he had refused to take bribes for construction contracts while Minister of Infrastructure; it was because as premier he would have exposed cronyism in the privatization process; it was a private deal gone bad; it was the Russian mafia. Finally, on December 9, parliament approved as premier Janlavin Narantsatsralt, the Ulaanbaatar mayor.

Political Rights and Civil Liberties:

Mongolians can change their government democratically. The judiciary is independent. Police and prison officials occasionally beat detainees and prisoners, and prisons are severely overcrowded. In recent years, dozens of prisoners have died from neglect, starvation and illness.

There are scores of private newspapers representing diverse viewpoints. The state broadcast media, which includes a television station and several radio stations, generally offer pluralistic views. A private television station reaches parts of the country, and foreign satellite and cable broadcasts are available.

Freedom of assembly is respected. Nongovernmental organizations (NGO) promote human rights, child welfare, and other causes. The Women's Federation, a coalition of 45 NGOs, has branches in all of Mongolia's provincial centers and helped place microcredit schemes and other women's development programs on the national poverty alleviation agenda.

The hardship associated with the economic restructuring has frayed traditional social support systems and, along with high rates of alcohol abuse, has apparently contributed to domestic violence. Women are often better educated than men, but generally receive lower wages and are underrepresented in parliament, top government and judicial positions, and the upper professional ranks. Freedom of religion is respected in practice, and since the 1990 revolution, Buddhist activity has blossomed throughout the country.

Trade unions are independent, although union membership is declining as large enterprises are shut down or broken up. Due to high unemployment, employers have considerable leverage in collective bargaining. The government lacks the resources to enforce effectively laws on child labor and working conditions. While inflation slowed to 17.5 percent in 1997 from 53.1 percent in 1996, and the economy grew 3.3 percent in 1997, growing income inequalities are a source of social friction. The World Bank estimates that 36 percent of the population lives in poverty in this largely pastoral economy. Major cities have thousands of street children. Corruption, while not as rampant as in some ex-Communist countries, nevertheless remains a problem.

Morocco

Polity: Monarchy and limited parliament
Economy: Capitalist-statist
Population: 27,700,000
PPP: $3,477
Life Expectancy: 72
Ethnic Groups: Arab and Berber (99 percent), other (1 percent)
Capital: Rabat

Political Rights: 5
Civil Liberties: 4*
Status: Partly Free

Ratings change: Morocco's civil liberties rating changed from 5 to 4 due to greater respect for freedom of expression and association and improvements in the electoral system.

Overview:

Political liberalization in Morocco gained pace in February with the election of opposition leader and former political prisoner Abderrahmane Youssouffi as prime minister.

Youssouffi has pursued a reformist program that emphasizes social spending and greater respect for human rights. He heads a center-left government that commands broad support in the 325-member House of Representatives, which was elected directly for the first time in 1997. Most power, however, still resides with King Hassan II and the royal palace. The new cabinet retains royal loyalists, most notably Driss Basri, the hardline security minister. In June, an official delegation of Amnesty International was welcomed amid pledges to end abuses. Approximately 60 political prisoners remain incarcerated, however, and a violent October police assault against jobless protesters demonstrated that respect for many fundamental freedoms is still lacking.

Morocco's people have escaped both the extreme Islamist violence and severe authoritarian repression that have gripped their neighbors in the Maghreb. Islamist parties are largely proscribed, but still find fertile ground for clandestine recruitment among the growing ranks of the unemployed. Economic expansion, especially outside of the agricultural sector, has not kept pace with rapid population growth.

An oft-delayed UN-supervised referendum on independence in the former colony of Spanish Sahara, which was occupied by Morocco in 1976, was postponed from December 1998 until February 1999 or later. The Popular Front for the Liberation of Saguia el-Hamra and Rio de Oro (Polisario) had agreed to hold the vote, but Morocco has continually obstructed the process. The territory was ravaged by a 15-year guerrilla war until a 1991 peace pact. Its people have suffered severe human rights violations by Moroccan security forces.

Morocco regained independence in 1956 after 44 years of French rule. Upon the death of his father Mohammed V in 1961, Hassan II assumed the throne and began a gradual and limited evolution of democratic institutions. Nevertheless, the king retains most power in the country. He appoints the prime minister and dissolves the legislature at his discretion. While the new bicameral legislature has greater legitimacy, it will not be permitted to challenge Hassan II's core conservative policies.

Hassan II carries the title of "Commander of the Faithful" and claims direct lineage from the prophet Mohammed. Islamist radicals reject his religious credentials and have substantial backing among poor and unemployed Moroccans. Morocco has close ties with Western nations and is considered a bulwark against the spread of Islamist influence in the Maghreb.

Political Rights and Civil Liberties:

Morocco's electoral process is more open today than at any time in its history. The 325 members of the House of Representatives were elected in largely free balloting in November 1997. The lower chamber's power is balanced by an 270-member Chamber of Advisors indirectly selected by an electoral college of trade union, employer, professional group, and local council representatives. It is also seriously limited by the legal and de facto power of the royal palace. Any constitutional changes must be approved by the king, who is head of state and, through his ministers, rules as well as reigns. Provincial and local officials are appointed, while the less powerful municipal councils are elected. Despite greater openness, governance remains neither transparent nor accountable.

Judicial reform has been identified as a high priority for the new government. Courts at all levels, however, are subject to political control, especially by interior ministry officials who are loyal to the palace. Pretrial detention of one year or less is legal. Decrees demanding Interior Ministry permits for public gatherings negate constitutional protections of freedom of assembly. The government appears to tolerate small and quiet protests, but not public marches, as reflected in the October attack on jobless protesters. The government uses registration requirements to deny Islamist and other groups legal status and the right to meet. Religious practice is limited to Islam, Christianity, and Judaism. Non-Islamic proselytizing is prohibited. Ninety-nine percent of Morocco's population is Sunni Muslim, and the government closely monitors mosque activities. Meetings by the Baha'i community are barred.

Officially recognized human rights groups are among the numerous nongovernmental organizations that operate openly, but under official scrutiny. Most prominent is the Moroccan League for the Defense of Human Rights. Its reports have denounced deaths and torture in police custody, harsh prison conditions, harassment of former political prisoners, and failures to investigate the disappearance of at least 300 Western Saharan activists during the last decade. Official impunity for past abuses appears intact, even for those admitted by the government.

Constitutional guarantees of free expression are sometimes ignored in law and practice. Broadcast media are mostly government-controlled. Independent and pluralistic print media operate, but are subject to official pressures and exercise self-censorship. Publication licensing requirements allow political influence over the media, and the Interior Ministry may seize or censor publications under the press code. Criticizing the King or his family or the monarchy is punishable by 5 to 20 years' imprisonment. Criticisms of the validity of Morocco's claim to Western Sahara and the sanctity of Islam are also prohibited. Since 1986, numerous issues of foreign publications have been seized, and at least 16 books, magazines, and newspapers have been banned.

Women face serious legal and societal discrimination and have no rights to receive property or support after a divorce. Many family law cases are handled by special judges under the *Moudouwana*, or "Code of Personal Status." The code is based on *Shari'a* law, which treats women as inferior to men. Much domestic violence is said to be unreported and unpunished, and women receive fewer opportunities for education and formal sector employment. In July, the government announced proposals to preserve and promote Berber culture. Berber activists claim that 60 percent of Morocco's population is of Berber descent and demand that their native *Amzaghi* be recognized as an official language and be taught in schools.

Morocco's strongly unionized formal labor sector includes 17 umbrella federations, some of which are aligned with political parties, and all of which are subject to heavy governmental pressure. The government generally respects labor rights, however, including the rights to bargain collectively and strike.

Mozambique

Polity: Presidential-
legislative democracy
Economy: Mixed statist
Population: 18,600,000
PPP: $959
Life Expectancy: 44
Ethnic Groups: Indigenous tribal groups, including
Shangaan, Chokwe, Manyika, Sena, Makua (> 99 percent)
Capital: Maputo

Political Rights: 3
Civil Liberties: 4
Status: Partly Free

Overview:

National elections due by October 1999 will likely return President Joaquim Alberto Chissano and his ruling National Front for the Liberation of Mozambique (Frelimo) to renewed five-year terms. Frelimo will seek to encourage a far greater voter turnout than the roughly 15 per cent of registered voters who participated in the country's first municipal elections in June. The campaign and voting were seen as largely free and fair. Frelimo's sweeping victory in all 33 contests was tainted, however, by a boycott by the main opposition party, the Mozambique National Resistance (Renamo), and the Democratic Union, the only other party represented in the parliament. In December, the parliament adopted two constitutional amendments that will create an independent electoral commission.

Political divisions and apathy characterize the country six years after negotiations ended 20 years of anti-colonial and civil war. Frelimo continues to dominate government institutions. Renamo, its former guerrilla foe and now primary parliamentary opponent, maintains a small military force in its northern stronghold and complains bitterly of official manipulation of elections and international aid to secure the ruling party's position. Abuses by myriad security forces and banditry are endemic. While economic growth has continued with extensive foreign aid, widespread corruption has damaged the government's standing.

Mozambique won its independence from Portugal in 1975 after a protracted and costly guerrilla war led by Frelimo leader Samora Machel. A one-party state was established under the then-Marxist Frelimo party. Renamo rebels were organized and armed for the ensuing bush war by the white-minority Rhodesian regime and, after Zimbabwe's independence, by covert South African forces.

After the 1992 Rome Accords, both sides accepted multiparty elections and largely disarmed. Under President Joaquim Chissano, Frelimo abandoned its socialist economic policies and one-party rule. Chissano, who succeeded Machel after his death in a mysterious plane crash ascribed to South Africa's apartheid regime, won a clear victory in internationally supervised and generally free and fair 1994 elections that also gave Frelimo 129 seats in the 250-seat parliament. Renamo and the smaller Democratic Union party won the remaining seats.

Renamo leader Afonso Dhlakama has repeatedly expressed his commitment to the democratic process, although Frelimo's adamant refusal to share power and its exploitation of state resources for patronage has made reconciliation more difficult.

Political Rights and Civil Liberties: In 1994, Mozambicans freely chose their government in the country's first genuinely open elections. U.N. and other civic and voter education efforts led to a massive turnout and renewed confidence in the electoral process. Democratic consolidation, however, remains tenuous. Fifteen political parties are registered under a statute that bars those based on ethnicity or religion.

Rule of law remains problematic. The judiciary is inadequately funded, understaffed, and subject to Frelimo influence. Mozambique's legal structures are relics of Portuguese colonialism and often conflict with new statutes or the constitution. In many parts of the country, customary courts settle local grievances and occasionally order executions for alleged witchcraft. Brutality by the police and other security forces, including the presidential State Information and Security Service, has been reported. There is apparent impunity for official misconduct and broad disregard of constitutional protections. Persons under investigation for vaguely defined "security crimes" may be legally detained for months without charges. Many prison inmates are pretrial detainees who suffer under sometimes fatally appalling conditions. Freedom of assembly is broadly guaranteed, but limited by notification and timing restrictions.

The constitution protects media freedom, but the state controls nearly all broadcast media and owns or influences all of the largest newspapers. Licenses were issued in July for more than a dozen private radio and television stations, which are nevertheless likely to join the private print media in exercising self-censorship. The opposition receives inadequate coverage in government media, especially national radio and television, which remain largely a Frelimo propaganda tool. The independent media have enjoyed moderate growth, but publications in Maputo have scant influence among the largely illiterate rural population. Criminal libel laws are another important deterrent to open expression.

Nongovernmental organizations, including the Mozambican Human Rights League, operate openly and issue critical reports. International human rights and humanitarian groups are also allowed to operate in the country. There is no reported interference with free religious practice. Women suffer from both legal and societal discrimination. Domestic violence is reportedly common, and the government has joined campaigns by women's groups such as Women, Law, and Development to reduce wife beating.

During the period of one-party rule, Frelimo tightly controlled Mozambique's labor movement. The Organization of Mozambican Workers, the country's major trade confederation, is now nominally independent. The Organization of Free and Independent Unions, a more independent group, was formed in 1994. All workers in nonessential services have the right to strike. The right to bargain collectively is legally protected.

A strong agricultural performance has aided Mozambique's economy, but the country remains among the world's poorest and suffers from one of the world's highest infant mortality rates.

Namibia

Polity: Presidential-
legislative democracy
Economy: Capitalist-statist
Population: 1,600,000
PPP: $4,054
Life Expectancy: 42

Political Rights: 2
Civil Liberties: 3
Status: Free

Ethnic Groups: Ovambo (50 percent), Kavangos (9 percent),
Herero (7 percent), Damara (7 percent), Nama (5 percent), Caprivian (4 percent),
Bushmen (3 percent), Baster (2 percent), white (6 percent), mixed (7 percent)
Capital: Windhoek

Overview:

The ruling South West Africa People's Organization (SWAPO) succeeded in passing a bitterly contested constitutional amendment to allow President Sam Nujoma to seek a third five-year term in elections set for December 1999. Nujoma, the leader of the country's struggle against apartheid and Namibia's only president since independence in 1990, appears certain to win re-election against a divided and weak opposition. A revamped electoral commission will have greater autonomy and could increase confidence in the electoral process.

SWAPO, which commands two-thirds majorities in both houses of the country's bicameral legislature, has become increasingly centralized. Namibia's democratic credentials remain largely intact, but restrictions on media and the apparent impunity of security force members who commit abuses remain causes for concern.

In October, an alleged secessionist plot in the country's far northeastern Caprivi strip was reportedly foiled as more than 700 people sought refuge in neighboring Botswana. Former guerrilla fighters of the People's Liberation Army of Namibia continued to demand jobs, land, and other benefits that they had been promised.

Namibia was seized by German imperial forces in the late 1800s. Thousands of people were massacred by German troops in efforts to crush all resistance to colonial settlement and administration. The territory became a South African protectorate after German forces were expelled during World War I and was ruled under the apartheid system for 42 years after 1948. A UN-supervised democratic transition with free and fair elections followed 13 years of bloody guerrilla war, and Namibia achieved independence in 1990. SWAPO scored a sweeping victory, and President Nujoma was re-elected in the country's first post-independence elections in November 1994. SWAPO still enjoys wide support, but has demonstrated sometimes flagrant disrespect for the rule of law. President Nujoma has adopted an increasingly authoritarian governing style.

Political Rights and Civil Liberties:

Namibia's 1994 elections were free and fair and allowed Namibians to exercise their constitutional right to choose their representatives for the second time. SWAPO matched President Sam Nujoma's landslide re-election victory by capturing 53 of 72 National Assembly seats. In 1998, the electoral commission was removed from the prime minister's office and reorganized as an independent agency. While the president will still appoint commission members, he will do so on the advice of a board that includes representatives of civil society. The new commission may increase the credibility of the electoral process. The ruling party's main base is among the country's largest ethnic group, the Ovambo, whose prominence within SWAPO has evoked allegations of ethnic discrimination. Herero and Damara people are among minority ethnic groups demanding larger government allocations for development in their home areas.

Respect for human rights in Namibia has been among the best in Africa, although reported large-scale killings on the country's northern border remain unresolved. Political discussion is generally open and vigorous. Political parties can organize and operate freely. Scant funding is the greatest impediment to political party growth. In November, the government announced plans for legislation to ban homosexuality, which President Nujoma has denounced as "foreign and corrupt."

Public statements by senior officials against the independent press and several direct actions against journalists have raised fears of a diminution of press freedoms. The Media Institute of Southern Africa and other press watchdog groups have warned against proposed laws that would require journalists and others to reveal sources of information. A reporter was jailed in February for contempt after refusing to surrender documents to the court. Private radio stations and critical independent newspapers usually operate without official interference. The electronic media are mostly controlled by the state, but the state-run Namibia Broadcasting Corporation has regularly presented views critical of the government.

Security forces still commit abuses with impunity, and allegations of abuses by Namibian soldiers have emerged both from the Caprivi Strip and from the Democratic Republic of Congo, where Namibian forces have helped preserve President Laurent Kabila's government. In rural areas, local chiefs use traditional courts that often ignore constitutional procedures. Despite constitutional guarantees, women continue to face serious discrimination in customary law and other traditional societal practices. Violence against women is allegedly widespread.

Constitutionally guaranteed union rights are respected. The two main union federations are the National Union of Namibian Workers and the Namibia People's Social Movement. Essential public sector workers do not have the right to strike. Domestic and farm laborers remain the country's most heavily exploited workers, in part because many are illiterate and do not know their rights.

Capital-intensive extractive industries such as diamond and uranium mining have drawn significant foreign investment and are the centerpiece of Namibia's economic growth. Most Namibians, however, continue to live as subsistence farmers, and many lack basic services.

Nauru

Polity: Parliamentary democracy
Economy: Mixed capitalist-statist
Population: 10,000
PPP: na
Life Expectancy: na

Political Rights: 1
Civil Liberties: 3
Status: Free

Ethnic Groups: Nauruan (58 percent), other Pacific islander (26 percent), Chinese (8 percent), European (8 percent)
Capital: Yaren

Overview:

In June, President Kinza Clodumar was defeated in a no-confidence vote and was replaced by Bernard Dowiyogo, a former president of Nauru and the country's longest-serving member of parliament.

Nauru, a small isolated island located 1,600 miles northeast of New Zealand in the west-central Pacific, became a German protectorate in the 1880s. Following World War I, Australia administered the island under a League of Nations mandate. The Japanese occupied Nauru during World War II, shipping 1,200 Nauruans to the island of Truk to work as forced laborers. In 1947, Nauru was made a United Nations Trust Territory under Australian administration. In a move toward greater autonomy, elections were held in 1966 for members of a Legislative Council, which was responsible for all matters except defense, foreign affairs, and the local phosphate industry.

The country achieved full independence in January 1968. Hammer DeRoburt, who had been head chief of Nauru since 1956, became the country's first president in May 1968.

Following the November 1995 general elections, parliament elected former president Lagumot Harris as president over three-term incumbent Bernard Dowiyogo in a nine to eight vote. However, the intense personal rivalries in the tiny, faction-ridden parliament, where a single vote can break a presidency, led to a period of political instability a year later, when three governments fell between November 1996 and February 1997. Following early elections on February 8, 1997, parliament named Kinza Clodumar, a former finance minister, as president. In June 1998, after 16 months in office, Clodumar was deposed in a no-confidence vote and replaced by Dowiyogo, who is serving his fifth term as president.

Phosphate mining gave Nauru a per capita income that peaked at $17,000 in 1975, but has since fallen by more than half. Decades of mining have left 80 percent of the land uninhabitable. In 1989, Nauru sued Australia in the International Court of Justice for additional royalties for mining done during the trusteeship period, claiming that Australia had sold the phosphates domestically at below world prices, and for compensation for the physical damages done to the eight-square-mile island. In an out of court settlement reached in 1993, Australia agreed to pay $70.4 million in compensation over 20 years.

With the phosphate deposits nearly depleted, future generations will draw income from the government's Nauru Phosphate Royalties Trust. However, the trust has lost millions of dollars through failed investments, speculation in the Tokyo stock market, and international financial scams. As part of the government's fiscal austerity program, parliament adopted a dramatically reduced annual budget in October 1998.

Political Rights and Civil Liberties:

Citizens of Nauru can change their government democratically. The 1968 republican constitution provides for an 18-member parliament, representing 14 constituencies, directly elected for a three-year term. Parliament elects the president, who serves as head of state and head of government, from among its members. An elected Nauru Island Council serves as the local government and provides public services. Although there have been several changes of government during the last two years, all have occurred peacefully and in accordance with the constitution. Since independence, there have been ad hoc parties, but in general, politics are based on personal loyalties and occasional issue-based coalitions. There have been multiple candidates for all parliamentary seats in recent elections.

The government respects freedom of speech and of the press. There is no regular independent news publication, though the government produces an information bulletin. The state owns Radio Nauru, which carries Radio Australia and BBC broadcasts, and the local Nauru TV. All religious faiths worship freely.

Freedoms of assembly and association are respected. The constitution guarantees workers the right to form independent unions, although successive governments have generally discouraged labor organizing and no trade unions have formed. There is no legal basis for collective bargaining or holding strikes, and these activities rarely occur in practice. The private sector employs only about one percent of all salaried workers. The judiciary is independent, and the right to a fair public trial is respected. Many cases are settled out of court through traditional mediation procedures. The country's small police force of less than 100 members is under civilian control. However, some foreign workers have alleged that they receive inferior police protection compared with Nauruan citizens.

Although citizens enjoy freedom of domestic and foreign travel, foreign workers must apply to their employers for permission to leave the country during the period of their employment contracts. If they choose to leave without permission, they are likely to lose their jobs. A law requiring foreign workers who are fired to leave the country within 60 days has created serious hardship for many guest workers. Women legally possess the same rights as men, but they continue to face discrimination in education and employment opportunities.

⬇ Nepal

Polity: Parliamentary democracy
Economy: Capitalist
Population: 23,700,000
PPP: $1,145
Life Expectancy: 55
Ethnic Groups: Newards, Indians, Tibetans, Gunings, Sherpas, Magars, Tamangs, Bhotias, Rais, Limbus, Bhotia, others
Capital: Kathmandu

Political Rights: 3
Civil Liberties: 4
Status: Partly Free

Trend arrow: Nepal receives a downward trend arrow due to increased civil liberties violations by Maoist guerillas and corresponding abuses by security forces.

Overview:
Veteran Nepali Congress (NC) politician G.P. Koirala became Nepal's fifth prime minister in four years in April 1998. The country's corrupt political class continued to battle over the survival of governments while ignoring pressing issues of poverty and illiteracy.

King Prithvi Narayan Shah unified this Himalayan land in 1769. In 1959, following two centuries of palace rule, the center-left NC won the country's first elections and began initiating land reforms. In 1960, King Mahendra dissolved parliament and banned political parties. Pro-democracy demonstrations beginning in early 1990 climaxed violently in April when police fired on demonstrators in Kathmandu. King Birendra agreed to a constitution, promulgated in November, that vested executive power in the prime minister and cabinet. The two-tier parliament consists of a 205-seat House of Representatives that is directly elected for a five-year term, and a 60-member National Council.

Nepal's first multiparty elections in 32 years in 1991 brought the NC to power under premier Giraja Prasid Koirala. The Koirala government began liberalizing the economy and privatizing state enterprises. Opposition protests over a 1991 hydroelectric agreement with India and NC infighting forced mid-term elections in November 1994 that were dominated by the electorate's concern with rising prices and the NC's factionalism and corruption. The Communist Party of Nepal (United Marxist-Leninist) (CPN-UML) won 88 seats; the NC, 83; the pro-monarchist National Democratic Party (RPP), 20; minor parties and independents, 14. The hung parliament contributed to political instability. Between 1994 and 1998, the CPN-UML, NC, and two RPP factions headed opportunistic coalition governments that lacked ideological coherence.

In February 1996, the underground Communist Party of Nepal (Maoist) (CPN (Maoist)) launched a "People's War" in the midwestern hills, where officially, 62.4 percent of villagers live in absolute poverty. CPN (Maoist) guerrillas have targeted government offices, landowners, and local party officials, killing more than 100 people.

In March 1998, the CPN-UML split into two parties following a power struggle between general secretary Madhav Kumar Nepal and former deputy premier Bam Dev Gautam, with Gautam forming the Communist Party of Nepal (Marxist-Leninist) (CPN-ML). This left the NC as the largest party in parliament with 87 seats. In April, Koirala returned as premier as head of an NC minority government. In December, Koirala formed a new government with the CPN-UML and pledged to hold elections in spring 1999, several months early.

With the four parties that won seats in the 1994 elections now totaling six after splits within the RPP and the CPN-UML, the outlook for the 1999 elections is for another hung parliament. Some legitimate policy differences exist. The Communists have criticized the NC over the continued presence of a decades-old Indian security post in Kalapani in far western Nepal, and over the 1996 Mahakali River Treaty with India, which critics say affords greater electricity and irrigation benefits to New Delhi. Within the NC, many members accuse Koirala of running the party autocratically. However, Nepal's political instability has mainly been caused by opportunistic politicians who are constantly maneuvering for greater advantage in influence peddling, bribery, or outright theft.

Political Rights and Civil Liberties:

Nepalese can change their government democratically. Widespread violence and other irregularities marred the 1997 local elections. CPN (Maoist) guerrillas threatened, kidnapped, and killed several NC candidates, and CPN-UML activists attacked NC workers. The government reported 24 election-related deaths; observers say the true figure is at least twice as high. Following the vote the foreign minister, a member of the RPP, quit, accusing the then ruling coalition's dominant CPN-UML of "widespread rigging and intimidation."

Low-caste Hindus and ethnic minority groups are politically marginalized. Overall, the political system is hugely corrupt and ineffective. During the spring 1998 parliamentary session, there were allegations of ministers and senior officers being involved in gold smuggling and violations of foreign currency regulations. Because institutions are viewed as weak and corrupt, political parties often resort to mobilizing supporters in the streets. Demonstrations and strikes frequently turn violent. In April, at least two people were killed and more than a dozen injured in remote parts of the country as the Maoists' political wing enforced a general strike. In a common practice, police arrested more than 1,000 people before the strike on the grounds of trying to prevent violence.

The Supreme Court is independent but politicians reportedly manipulate lower courts. The judiciary is reportedly rife with corruption. Many courts lack funds for legal texts and other basic resources. Prison conditions are life-threatening.

Human rights practices have improved considerably since the end of the absolute monarchy, but the rule of law is weak and serious problems remain. Since CPN (Maoist) guerrillas declared a "People's War" in February 1996, more than 350 civilians, guerrillas, and police have been killed. Armed guerrillas have killed and tortured civilians, and security forces have responded with extrajudicial executions, arbitrary arrests and detentions, and torture of suspected members or sympathizers of the CPN (Maoist) or its political wing. In July, Amnesty International accused the government of murder, torture, "disappearances," and arbitrary detention of suspected members of the CPN (Maoist) in a crackdown that began in May. Amnesty reported that police often carried out extrajudicial killings as an alternative to arrest, and that many civilians had been killed. The organization also accused CPN (Maoist) members of extrajudicial killings of NC activists and other mainstream political party members.

As amended in 1991, the Public Security Act (PSA) allows authorities to detain suspects for up to 12 months without charge. The 1970 Public Offenses and Penalties

Act grants the 75 chief district officers powers to detain suspects for 25 days pending investigation. Police act largely with impunity, using excessive force in routine situations, beating suspects to extract confessions (leading to several custodial deaths in recent years), and abusing prisoners. In February, police shot dead three men in the Salyan district for contesting orders to disperse a public event.

The Constitution restricts expression that could jeopardize national security, promote communal discord, or do harm in other broadly defined areas. The Press and Publications Act restricts reporting on the monarchy, national security, and other sensitive issues. Nevertheless, private newspapers and magazines represent views ranging from Maoist to monarchist and vigorously criticize government policies. In 1998, conditions worsened for journalists. In January, police arrested two editors on charges of participating in Maoist activities, and authorities jailed a correspondent after he reported on official corruption in the Janakpur area. The Paris-based Reporters Sans Frontieres reported that in June, police in several districts seized copies of newspapers that had reported allegations of police abuses during crackdowns on Maoist rebels. In August, a judge sentenced a journalist to five days in prison over an article recounting the details of a report on judicial corruption prepared by the Parliament Economic Committee for the auditor general's office.

The government owns the sole television station and the influential Radio Nepal. Political coverage on the state broadcast media favors the party in power, which is a key issue in a largely illiterate society where people depend on radio for their news. The first private FM radio station, Radio Sagarmartha, began broadcasting in March. Successive governments have restricted public criticism of China's occupation of Tibet and Indian abuses in Kashmir. Nongovernmental organizations are active and operate freely. However, both police and CPN (Maoist) guerrillas have reportedly harassed human rights activists over disclosures of abuses.

Although the constitution describes Nepal as a Hindu kingdom, the true religious breakdown is unknown. Low-caste Hindus and ethnic minorities face discrimination in the civil service, courts, and government institutions.

Property and divorce laws discriminate against women. In addition, women rarely receive the same educational opportunities as men due to early ages of marriage and entry into the workforce. Although the incoming Koirala government in April included the country's first female deputy premier, women are generally underrepresented in government and the civil service. According to the International Labor Organization, organized gangs traffic some 5,000 to 7,000 women and girls to India to work in brothels each year. Trafficking is facilitated by the complicity of corrupt local officials and by traditional norms that relegate women to an inferior status. Most victims are from the Tamang and other minority communities. Nepalese jails hold many women who were convicted of murder for abortions and infanticide as well as for acts of self-defense against men.

Nepal hosts some 90,000 Bhutanese refugees (see Bhutan report). Police occasionally use excessive force against Tibetans crossing the border, and in recent years, authorities have forcibly deported, turned back, or handed over scores of asylum seekers to Chinese authorities.

Nepal has upwards of five million child laborers working in carpet factories, mines, and construction sites which have been spawned by rapid urbanization, or in agriculture and other traditional areas. The Labor Act and the Children's Act are rife with vague, inadequate, and inconsistent language, which compounds the problem of non-enforcement. Kathmandu and other cities have hundreds of street children working as ragpickers or in other informal jobs. Child marriage continues despite being outlawed. In 1997, the London-based Anti-Slavery International said that illegal, forced bonded labor takes two main forms: a feudal-based system enslaving 100,000 people in the lowland terai; and caste-based servitude in the western hills. Bonded labor also exists in agriculture and in manufacturing in the Kathmandu Valley. Laborers are often bought and sold, and debts are passed on to children. Activists allege that numerous politicians in western districts hold bonded laborers.

Trade unions are independent but are politicized and often militant. More than 80 percent of the population is engaged in agriculture, and 45 percent live in absolute poverty.

Netherlands

Polity: Parliamentary democracy
Economy: Mixed capitalist
Population: 15,700,000
PPP: $19,876
Life Expectancy: 78
Ethnic Groups: Dutch (96 percent), other (4 percent)
Capital: Amsterdam

Political Rights: 1
Civil Liberties: 1
Status: Free

Overview: Since 1994, the Netherlands has been governed by a three-party coalition that includes Prime Minister Wim Kok's Labor Party, the Liberal Party, and the Democrats-66 party. Throughout its term, the coalition has concentrated on economic issues, such as decreasing budget deficits and unemployment and reforming the country's extensive social welfare system. For his second term, which began in May, Kok has vowed to continue to deregulate and to revamp the country's tax system, while giving his new government a more socially conscious face. The Netherlands is on track to join the European Monetary Union in 1999.

After the Dutch won independence from Spain in the sixteenth century, the governors of the House of Orange assumed rule over the United Provinces of the Netherlands. A constitutional monarchy based on representative government emerged in the early 1800s. Queen Beatrix appoints the arbiters of executive authority, the Council of Ministers, and the governor of each province on the recommendation of the majority in parliament. The bicameral States General (parliament) consists of an indirectly elected First Chamber and a larger, more powerful and directly elected Second Chamber.

From the end of World War II until December 1958, the Netherlands was governed by coalitions in which the Labor and Catholic parties predominated. From 1958 to 1994, governments were formed from center-right coalitions of Christian Democrats and Liberals, with the social-democratic-oriented Labor party usually in opposition.

The Netherlands' tolerant drug policy has met with growing opposition in the EU, most notably from France. Drugs are not legal in the Netherlands, but they are commonly bought and sold in urban coffee shops. Dutch policy stresses prevention and treatment, and treats drug use as a health, rather than a legal issue. In 1997, the government announced plans for an experimental program to issue free heroin to 50 long-term users.

Political Rights and Civil Liberties: The Dutch can change their government democratically. A series of amendments to the original constitution has provided for welfare and democratic reform. Local voting rights are accorded to foreigners after five years in residence.

A 24-member Supreme Court heads the country's independent judiciary, which also includes 5 courts of appeal, 19 district courts, and 62 lower courts. All judicial appointments are made by the crown on the basis of nominations by the parliament. Judges are nominally appointed for life, but retire at age 70.

The press is free and independent, although journalists practice self-censorship when reporting on the royal family. All Dutch newspapers cooperate in the administration of the independent Netherlands News Agency. Radio and television broadcasters operate autonomously under the supervision and regulation of the state and offer pluralistic views. Free speech is guaranteed, with the exceptions of promulgation of racism and incitement to racism.

Integration of racial and ethnic minorities into the social and cultural mainstream remains a difficult domestic issue. Discrimination on the basis of race or nationality is prohibited by law, and those who believe that they have been victims of discrimination may take the offender to court under civil law. According to the Criminal Investigation Service, the number of incidents of violence against foreigners and ethnic minorities has increased in recent years.

Immigrant groups face some de facto discrimination in housing and employment. Concentrated in the larger cities, immigrants suffer from a high rate of unemployment. The government has been working for several years with employers' groups and unions to reduce minority unemployment levels to the national average. As a result of these efforts in recent years, the rate of job creation among ethnic minorities has been higher than among the general population.

A new law to tighten criteria for acceptance of refugees was implemented in 1997; nevertheless, the country's asylum policies remain generous. Refugees whose applications for asylum are denied are allowed to remain temporarily.

Membership in labor unions is open to all workers, including military, police, and civil service employees. Workers are entitled to form or join unions of their own choosing without previous government authorization, and unions are free to affiliate with national trade union federations.

Freedom of religion is respected. More than half of the population is Protestant. Approximately 35 percent is Roman Catholic. The state subsidizes church-affiliated schools. The subsidies are based on the number of registered students.

Gender-based discrimination is prohibited. Women are well represented in government, education, and other fields. Same-sex marriages—with the same pension, social security, and inheritance rights as married heterosexual couples–were legalized in January. In November, the government approved a plan to allow homosexuals to adopt children. The plan is expected to be submitted to parliament in early 1999.

New Zealand

Polity: Parliamentary democracy
Economy: Capitalist
Population: 3,800,000
PPP: $17,267
Life Expectancy: 72
Ethnic Groups: New Zealand European (74.5 percent), Maori (10 percent), other European (4.5 percent), Pacific islander (4 percent), Asian and other (7 percent)
Capital: Wellington

Political Rights: 1
Civil Liberties: 1
Status: Free

Overview:

Prime Minister Jenny Shipley's center-right coalition unraveled in mid-1998 following a split between leaders of the National Party and its coalition partner, New Zealand First (NZF). New Zealand was left with a minority government to face the damaging effects of the Asian economic crisis.

New Zealand achieved full self-government prior to World War II, and gained formal independence from Great Britain in 1947. Since 1935, political power in this parliamentary democracy has alternated between the mildly conservative National Party and the center-left Labor Party, both of which helped develop one of the world's most progressive welfare states. In response to an increasingly competitive global trade regime, the incoming Labor government began restructuring the economy in 1984 by cutting farm subsidies, trimming tariffs, and privatizing many industries.

The harsh effects of the economic reforms and a deep recession contributed to a National Party landslide at the 1990 parliamentary elections. However, new Prime Minister Jim Bolger's government pushed the reforms even further by slashing welfare payments, reworking the labor law to discourage collective bargaining, and ending universal free hospital care.

With the economy showing signs of an upswing, the National Party narrowly won the 1993 elections with 50 seats. In a concurrent referendum, voters chose to replace the current first-past-the-post electoral system with a mixed member proportional system (MMP). The MMP is designed to increase the representation of smaller parties by combining geographic constituencies with proportional representation balloting.

In the October 12, 1996 elections for an expanded 120-seat parliament, the NZF joined in a coalition with the National Party. In 1997, the strains of merging the National Party's fiscal conservatism with NZF's populism led to a policy drift. In October 1997, Transport Minister Jenny Shipley led an intra-party coup that forced Bolger to resign. As Prime Minister, Shipley announced a cabinet dominated by conservatives favoring further economic deregulation.

A dispute broke out in August 1998 between members of NZF and the National Party ostensibly over plans to sell government-owned shares of Wellington International Airport. On August 13, NZF leader Winston Peters organized an NZF walkout from a cabinet meeting. Shipley, in turn, removed him from his posts as deputy prime minister and treasurer, and the coalition collapsed. Shipley held on to power and won a narrow confidence vote in September. Elections are scheduled for 1999.

In 1998, the Asian economic crisis sent New Zealand into a recession. Asia is the destination for 40 percent of New Zealand's exports and the source of 30 percent of its tourists. New Zealand's current-account deficit soared to 8 percent of GDP by September amid falling exports. GDP was expected to contract by 9 percent in the year to March 1999. The economy also suffered from a serious drought that hit agricultural production in the 1997-98 summer season. There were signs of recovery at the end of the year, but analysts predicted it would be several years before the country fully recovered.

Political Rights and Civil Liberties:

New Zealanders can change their government democratically. New Zealand has no written constitution, although fundamental freedoms are respected in practice. The judiciary is independent. The private press is varied and vigorous. The broadcast media are both privately and publicly held and express pluralistic views. Civil society is advanced and nongovernmental organizations, trade unions, and religious groups are outspoken. Religious freedom is respected. The authorities are responsive to complaints of rape and domestic violence, and a Domestic Violence Act came into effect in July 1997.

Trade unions are independent and engage in collective bargaining. The 1991 Employment Contracts Act (ECA) has weakened unions by banning compulsory membership and other practices that had made trade unions the sole, mandatory negotiators on behalf of employees. Contracts are now generally drawn up at the factory or even individual level, and wages and union membership rolls have fallen. In 1994, the ILO criticized a provision of the ECA prohibiting strikes designed to force an employer to sign on to a multicompany contract.

The Maori minority and the tiny Pacific Islander population face unofficial discrimination in employment and education opportunities. The 1983 Equal Employment Opportunities Policy, designed to bring more minorities into the public sector, has been only marginally successful. An agreement reached in the nineteenth century and codified in 1955 leases Maori land in perpetuity to the "settlers." Today, the rents received by the Maori on some 2,500 leases average far lower than those received by commercial landowners. Four parliamentary seats are reserved for Maori representatives. In the 1996 elections, 15 Maori politicians won seats, proportionate to the 13 percent Maori population. Maori activists say that the state-run TVNZ television network's Maori-language programming is insufficient.

Nicaragua

Polity: Presidential-leg-islative democracy
Economy: Capitalist-statist
Population: 4,800,000
PPP: $1,837
Life Expectancy: 66

Political Rights: 2*
Civil Liberties: 3
Status: Free

Ethnic Groups: Mestizo (69 percent), European (17 percent), black (9 percent), Indian (5 percent)
Capital: Managua
Ratings change: Nicaragua's political rights rating changed from 3 to 2, and its status changed from Partly Free to Free, due to increasing civilian control of the military, significant efforts by the government to decentralize political power through regional elections, and a groundbreaking proposal for the titling of communal lands of eastern Nicaragua's Native American peoples.

Overview:

In 1998, Conservative President Arnoldo Aleman seemed to slip the noose of Sandinista blackmail, successfully ignoring threats of massive disruptions in protest of his policies on land reform and economics. Nicaragua was one of the countries hardest hit by Hurricane Mitch, but at year's end, a long-awaited reconciliation by Nicaragua's frequently war-ring political factions appeared to be measurably closer.

The Republic of Nicaragua was established in 1838, 17 years after gaining independence from Spain. Its history has been marked by internal strife and dictatorship. The authoritarian rule of the Somoza regime was overthrown in 1979 by the Sandinistas. Subsequently, the Sandinista National Liberation Front (FSLN) attempted to impose a Marxist dictatorship, which led to a civil war and indirect U.S. intervention on behalf on the Contras. In 1987, the FSLN finally conceded to a new constitution that provides for a president and a 96-member National Assembly elected every six years. Shortly before the 1990 elections, hundreds of thousands of acres of farmland were turned over to peasant cooperatives under a land reform program, while Sandinista leaders confiscated the best luxury properties and businesses for themselves.

In 1990, newspaper publisher Violeta Chamorro easily defeated incumbent President Ortega. Her 14-party National Opposition Union (UNO) won a legislative majority in the National Assembly. Chamorro gave substantial authority to her son-in-law and presidency minister Antonio Lacayo, who reached an agreement with Ortega's brother Humberto, allowing him to remain head of the military.

In 1994, the MRS and the anti-Lacayo UNO factions proposed constitutional reforms to limit the powers of the president and end nepotism in presidential succession. Lacayo and Daniel Ortega opposed the measure. In February 1995, after passage of a law ensuring the military's autonomy, Humberto Ortega turned over command of the military to General Joaquin Cuadra. The army was reduced from 90,000 to 15,000 troops. Despite the apparent "depoliticization" of the army, including the integration of former Contras, the leadership remained essentially the same. The armed forces continued to own a profitable network of businesses and property amassed under the Sandinistas. Mrs. Chamorro was forbidden by law to seek a second term. The 1996 elections were held under the auspices of the five-member Supreme Election Council (CSE), an independent branch of government. During the campaign, Ortega tried to portray himself as a moderate committed to national unity and reconciliation. Aleman ran on a platform that promised economic reforms, dismantling of the Sandinista-era bureaucracy, cleaning up the army, and returning property confiscated by the Sandinistas to its original owners. He defeated Ortega 51 to 38 percent, avoiding a runoff.

President-elect Aleman's top priority was to reform the army and the police. President Chamorro had served as nominal Minister of Defense, with real power exercised by General Humberto Ortega as military commander. President-elect Aleman named civilian Jaime Cuadra Somarriba as head of a civilian-led Defense Ministry, with a new military code reinforcing his position. The size of the national police was reduced from 16,000 to 6,800, but its leadership is still composed of old Sandinista cadres. In 1998, the Sandinista leadership was in turmoil over Ortega's adopted daughter's charging him of sexual abuse, which he denies, and complaints that he rules the party through strongman tactics and political inflexibility. More than two dozen armed gangs terrorized nine central and northern departments, some of which are composed of former ex-Contras and former Sandinistas. In February, a political crisis in the National Assembly was overcome when the ruling party and the Sandinistas agreed to a reorganization of six legislative committees. In July, Aleman reduced the number of cabinet ministries from 16 to 12. In mid-August, tension with neighboring Costa Rica rose to a near-boil when Nicaragua cancelled a month-old accord allowing armed Costa Rican police to use Nicaragua's San Juan river for patrols. The spat was ended only after Costa Rica agreed that Nicaraguan army craft will accompany their patrol boats on duty. In the wake of Hurricane Mitch, Aleman and Ortega appeared to join forces in an effort to rebuild much of a country devastated by the storm.

Political Rights and Civil Liberties:

Nicaraguans can change their government democratically. Regional elections held in March on the Atlantic coast were generally free and fair, although independent watchdog organizations questioned the government's use of public funds to support its candidates. The military remains a political force, although increasingly less so, through substantial property and monetary holdings. Political parties are allowed to organize; more than 20 candidates ran for president and nine parties or blocs are represented in the National Assembly. But political and civic activities continue to be conditioned on occasional political violence, corruption, and drug-related crime.

The judiciary is independent but continues to be susceptible to political influence and corruption. Large case backlogs, long delays in trials, and lengthy pretrial detention have caused the Supreme Court and National Assembly to initiate comprehensive structural reforms of the judicial system. The Ministry of Government oversees the National Police, which is formally charged with internal security; in practice, the police share this responsibility with the army in rural areas. Reflecting enhanced civilian control, the security forces' conduct continues to improve, although abuses of human rights still occur. Abuses are particularly pronounced among members of the army implementing rural law enforcement duties, as they occasionally kill criminal suspects instead of arresting them. Forced confessions to the police remain a problem, as do cases in which security forces arbitrarily arrest and detain citizens. Prison and police holding cell conditions are poor.

The print media are varied and partisan, representing hardline and moderate Sandinista, as well as pro- and anti-government positions. Before leaving office, the Sandinistas "privatized" the national radio system, mostly to Sandinista loyalists. There are five television stations, three of which carry news programming with partisan political content. A September 1996 law established a professional journalists' guild requiring journalists in the Managua area to have a bachelors' degree in journalism or five years of journalistic experience; opposition forces claimed the law was a blow to freedom of expression. In 1998, the pro-Sandinista newspaper, *Barricada*, ceased publication.

Discrimination against women and indigenous people is a problem, although significant progress was recorded in 1998 in Native American rights. Violence against women, including rape and domestic abuse, remained a serious problem. Indigenous peoples, about six percent of the population, live in two autonomous regions, the Northern Autonomous Atlantic Region (RAAN) and the Southern Autonomous Atlantic Region (RAAS). These are primarily the Miskito, Sumo, Rama, and Garifuna peoples. In 1998, the Aleman government proposed a law that would give title to communal lands traditionally settled by Native Americans in the Atlantic region. Indian parties also showed significant political strength in the March regional elections, in which 45 autonomous councils were chosen.

Labor rights are complicated by the Sandinistas' use of unions as violent instruments to influence government economic policy. By means of the public sector unions, the Sandinistas have managed to gain ownership of more than three dozen privatized state enterprises. The legal rights of non-Sandinista unions are not fully guaranteed. Citizens have no effective recourse when labor laws are violated either by the government or by violent Sandinista actions. Child labor is also a problem.

Niger

Polity: Dominant party (military-controlled)
Economy: Capitalist
Population: 10,100,000
PPP: $765
Life Expectancy: 47
Ethnic Groups: Hausa (56 percent), Djerma (22 percent), Fula (9 percent), Tuareg (8 percent), Beri Beri (4 percent), other (1 percent)
Capital: Niamey

Political Rights: 7
Civil Liberties: 5
Status: Not Free

Overview: Niger experienced a turbulent year that included mass demonstrations against the repressive military-dominated regime of President General Ibrahim Baré Maïnassara, who overthrew a democratically elected government and won fraudulent elections in 1996. Maïnassara's rule was shaken during the year by brief army mutinies, strikes by unpaid teachers and civil servants, and defections of his own supporters. International financial inflows, however, have at least temporarily bolstered Maïnassara's position. Opposition parties have boycotted elections since Maïnassara's coup, but have decided to participate in 1999 local elections, provided that a revision of voter rolls and other demands are met. Maïnassara's nominally civilian administration remains a military dictatorship barely disguised by the trappings of representative rule.

Intimidation aimed at opposition politicians, labor activists, and the independent media continued in 1998. The regime made progress, however, in defusing ethnic armed conflict. A peace pact with the Democratic Revolutionary Front, which is comprised mostly of minority ethnic Tobou people in southeastern Niger, was reached in August and could end the country's last serious insurgency.

After receiving independence from France in 1960, Niger was governed for 30 years by one-party and military regimes dominated by leaders of Hausa and Djerma ethnicity. Thirteen years of direct military rule were transformed into a nominally civilian one-party state in 1987 under General Ali Seibou.

International pressure and pro-democracy demonstrations led by the umbrella Niger Union of Trade Union Workers forced Niger's rulers to accede to the Africa-wide trend towards democratization in 1990. An all-party national conference drafted a new constitution that was adopted in a national referendum in 1992. The Alliance of Forces for Change (AFC) party led by Mahamane Ousmane took the majority of seats in 1993 legislative elections that were deemed free and fair by international observers. Ousmane then won a five-year term as the country's first democratically elected president. New elections were called for 1995 after defections cost the AFC its parliamentary majority. The victorious former sole legal party named its leader as prime minister. The ensuing rivalry between president and prime minister paralyzed the government and was cited by Maïnassara as a justification for his coup.

Political Rights and Civil Liberties: The people of Niger are not allowed to exercise their right to choose their representatives. The July 1996 presidential election that followed the January 1996 military coup was held under a revised constitution and was not deemed free or fair by independent observers. Parliamentary elections in November 1996 were held in an atmosphere of intense intimidation and were boycotted by most opposition parties. The pro-Maïnassara Rally for Democracy and Progress party now holds 69 of 83 seats in the National Assembly and is the core of the Convergence for the Republic coalition formed in August.

The revised 1996 constitution guarantees many basic rights and gives more power to the presidency. Human rights safeguards and the formal allocation of constitutional authority are largely ignored, however, and President Maïnassara holds power closely. The judicial system is theoretically independent, but retains little autonomy. Courts are subject to external influences and limited by scant training and resources. Thousands of pretrial detainees are imprisoned under very difficult and sometimes deadly conditions.

Constitutionally guaranteed freedoms of assembly and association are often not respected. Authorities can prohibit gatherings and have banned or dispersed numerous opposition demonstrations. Freedom of religion is respected, although political parties formed on religious, ethnic, or regional bases are barred. Human rights and other nongovernmental organizations face increasing pressure.

Constitutional protections for free expression are often ignored by security forces. Several newspapers have been closed for various offenses and periods. Professional training requirements that were announced in October for editors may force many senior independent journalists from their jobs. These requirements add to severe restrictions imposed on the independent media by a 1997 press law, including licensing of journalists and harsh penalties for offenses such as "insulting" the president. The government has also barred local stations from broadcasting foreign news programs. The popular and internationally respected independent *Anfani* radio station was forced off the air briefly and threatened with permanent closure.

Islamic conservatives have squelched moves to amend portions of the legal code most discriminatory against women. A number of laws and the practice of "proxy voting" by husbands for their wives appear to contradict constitutional guarantees. Women also suffer extensive societal discrimination. Family law gives women inferior status in property, inheritance rights, and divorce. Domestic violence against women is reportedly widespread. Only one woman sits in the National Assembly.

Notice of intent must be given and negotiations attempted before a strike is legal, and workers can be required to provide essential services. Collective bargaining agreements are negotiated under the framework of a tripartite agreement among the government, employers, and unions.

Nigeria

Polity: Transitional military rule   **Political Rights:** 6*
Economy: Capitalist   **Civil Liberties:** 4*
Population: 121,800,000   **Status:** Partly Free
PPP: $1,270
Life Expectancy: 50
Ethnic Groups: Hausa (21 percent), Yoruba (21 percent), Ibo (18 percent), Fulani (11 percent), other (29 percent)
Capital: Abuja
Ratings change: Nigeria's political rights rating changed from 7 to 6, its civil liberties rating changed from 6 to 4, and its status changed from Not Free to Partly Free, due to the beginnings of an uncertain democratic transition at year's end, the release of a number of political prisoners, and the cessation of many human rights abuses.

Overview: Nigeria's tumultuous year ended with hopes for a peaceful transition to a genuine representative government, an event transition virtually unthinkable less than six months earlier when army dictator Sani Abacha was preparing mock elections that would have left him in power and thrust the country toward ethnic strife and economic collapse. Abacha's mysterious death on June 8 was met with street celebrations throughout the country. The death in detention just five weeks later of Moshood K.O. Abiola, winner of the army-annulled 1993 presidential election, sparked rioting that left scores dead. An international forensic team declared there was no foul play in Abiola's demise, although lack of proper medical care and the stress of confinement surely contributed to his sudden death.

The sudden departure of the two most significant figures on Nigeria's political landscape opened possibilities for a new page in the country's often bloody post-colonial history. Army Chief of Staff General Abdulsalami Abubakar emerged as the consensus choice of the military's Provisional Ruling Council (PRC) as the country's next leader and immediately pledged that he would remain in office only long enough to oversee a transition to real civilian rule. Abubakar's promises were met with considerable cynicism, but the second half of 1998 saw the lifting of most of the repression that had grown steadily worse under Abacha. Numerous political prisoners were freed, and harassment, intimidation, arrests, and assaults on journalists, trade unionists, human rights workers, and political activists nearly ceased. Political parties were registered for peaceful and largely well-run local elections that took place in December as part of an electoral schedule set to culminate in national polls in February and a full to transfer full to civilian rule on May 29, 1999. A national debate on a draft constitution began in December, and courts began to reassert their autonomy.

These developments are cause for considerable optimism. Yet a democratic transition has just begun and faces considerable perils. The State Security (Detention of Persons) Decree of 1984, popularly known as "decree two," which allows unchallenged detention by military authorities of anyone deemed harmful to state security or the economy, is still in effect. Restrictive media statutes remain in force, and proposed constitutional provisions would create an official media court. Scores of people convicted of treason or other politically connected charges are still incarcerated. The stability of the military, which has ruled Nigeria for all but ten years since its independence from Britain in 1960, is far from certain. The country's deep ethnic divides, between and among northern and southern groups, worsened under Abacha's rule, and may be exacerbated if politicians emphasize ethnicity as a campaign issue. Nigeria's 106 million people include more than 250 ethnic groups. The Hausa-Fulani groups from northern Nigeria have dominated the military and the country since independence. The Yoruba and Ibo people and smaller groups of the south deeply resent this domination, and what many see as exploitation of their far richer lands. Civil conflict risks degenerating into a replay of the horrific Biafra civil war of 1967-70 that suppressed Ibo secession efforts and killed millions in famine and fighting. Sporadic religious and ethnic strife continued through 1998. Shiite fundamentalists in northern Nigeria have launched attacks on the region's Christian minority. Clashes among ethnic groups in the country's southeastern delta region took hundreds of lives and disrupted oil production.

The country's economic distress, rising from years of gross mismanagement and rampant corruption, is being compounded by a sharp drop in international oil prices. Oil exports are Nigeria's main source of foreign exchange and government revenues, but the country has recently suffered a chronic gasoline shortage that limits economic activity. There is rising militancy among impoverished minority Ogoni, Ijaw and other peoples which could interfere with oil production; much oil is pumped from their lands, but they have been almost entirely excluded from a share of its revenues.

As Africa's most populous state, and potentially one of its wealthiest, events in Nigeria affect all of West Africa and are a bellwether for the rest of the continent. The nature of Nigeria's government will affect resolution of a simmering dispute with neighboring Cameroon over the oil-rich Bokassi peninsula and will shape the many regional interventions that affect events in nearby countries. The country's democratic transition in 1999 will severely test the willingness of all Nigeria's political actors to achieve compromise beyond personal ambition and group interests. Failure to do so will court disaster.

Political Rights and Civil Liberties: The democratic transition program underway in Nigeria began with local council elections in December. The election schedule will culminate in February national elections on May 29, 1999. PRC head Abubakar has promised open elections, but many details of the new constitution, electoral code, and voter registration were still unclear as 1998 ended. Nigerians were denied the right to choose their representatives when Chief Moshood K.O. Abiola's 1993 election victory was quickly annulled by the military regime of General Ibrahim Babangida. General Abacha, a principal architect of previous coups, moved in November 1993 to take power himself after the high court declared an army-installed interim government illegal. A predominantly military PRC was appointed, and all democratic structures were dissolved and political parties banned. Chief Abiola was arrested in June 1994 after declaring himself Nigeria's rightful president.

While the first half of 1998 witnessed severe repression of civil society and increasing security force abuses, many political prisoners were freed after Abacha's death, including ex-general Olusegun Obasanjo. Obasanjo, who led a military regime from 1976-79, but relinquished power to a civilian government, is now a leading candidate for president. As a Yoruba, he claims strong southern support, and as an ex-general may be palatable to military conservatives. Treason charges against exiled democracy activist and Nobel prize wining author Wole Soyinka were dropped, and he visited the country to encourage quick reform. The writings of Ken Saro-Wiwa, executed in November 1995 after a show trial on murder charges, are again available after being banned under the Abacha regime. Saro-Wiwa's exposés detailed military brutality against southeastern Nigeria's Ogoni people whose traditional land has been usurped and despoiled by oil drilling. Seven other Ogoni activists were hanged with Saro-Wiwa, but several others have been freed from prison. However, the June 1996 daylight assassination of Moshood Abiola's wife Kurdiat remains officially unsolved. Leaders of the Islamist Brotherhood remain jailed on sedition charges, and while officials have announced plans to improve conditions, incarceration remains harsh and often life threatening. Nearly 10,000 prisoners are reported to have died of disease or other causes from 1990-95. Almost 36,000 prisoners were detained awaiting trial, some for several years.

Media freedom improved markedly since June. Restrictive decrees remain in force, however, and press groups are opposed to new constitutional provisions that would entrench government control over media. The heightened tensions of the coming election season raise fears of pressure and attacks on journalists by competing political groups as well as security forces. Free trade union activities are resuming after being suppressed for several years.

Bold but unimplemented proposals for liberalization and privatization remaining from the Abacha regime could help revive Nigeria's sagging economy. The severe corruption and endemic mismanagement fostered by the nepotism and unnaccountability of successive military regimes, pervasive government involvement in the economy through parastatals, and a plethora of other regulatory disincentives must be addressed before strong economic development is possible. Depressed oil prices and election costs could hurt growth in 1998, but revenues from foreign companies including Shell (Anglo-Dutch), Elf (French), Agip (Italian), and America's Chevron will continue to provide a large amount of foreign exchange.

Norway

Polity: Parliamentary democracy
Economy: Mixed capitalist
Population: 4,400,000
PPP: $22,427
Life Expectancy: 78
Ethnic Groups: Norwegian, Finnish, Lapp (Saami) minority
Capital: Oslo

Political Rights: 1
Civil Liberties: 1
Status: Free

Overview:

In 1997, a centrist government took power in Norway for the first time in 25 years.

Prime Minister Kjell Magne Bondevik leads a coalition of the Center Party, Liberal Party, and his own Christian People's Party. In September elections, the three parties had won a total of 42 seats in the 165-member *Storting* (parliament).

In August, Bondevik took more than three weeks' leave due to a "depressive reaction" caused by the stress of his job. The stress was induced at least in part by plunges in the price of oil, surges in interest rates, and decreases in the value of the country's currency. During the year, these crises led to an increase in support for the opposition Labor Party, which recorded its highest popularity rating since 1995.

European Union (EU) membership, which the traditionally dominant Labor Party supports, remains a contentious political issue. In 1994, Norwegians voted against membership. Thereafter, the Labor government sought to delay reconsideration until after the 2001 parliamentary elections. In the current coalition, the Liberal Party supports membership, while the Center Party strongly opposes any form of EU association.

In 1996, Norway became an observer in the Schengen Convention, an accord that ends border controls, establishes a common visa policy, and mandates close cooperation in police matters. Norway enjoys nearly full access to the EU's single market through membership in the European Economic Area.

The Eisvold Convention, Norway's current constitution, was adopted during a period of de facto independence immediately prior to the acceptance of the Swedish monarch as king of Norway in 1814. After the peaceful dissolution of its relationship with the Swedish crown, Norway chose a sovereign from the Danish royal house and began to function as a constitutional monarchy with a multiparty parliamentary structure.

Political Rights and Civil Liberties:

Norwegians can change their government democratically. The Storting is directly elected for a four-year term by universal suffrage and proportional representation. It then selects one quarter of its own members to serve as the upper chamber (*Lagting*). Neither body is subject to dissolution. A vote of no-confidence in the Storting results in the resignation of the cabinet, and the leader of the party that holds the most seats is then asked to form a new government.

Since 1989, the approximately 20,000-strong Lappic (Saamic) minority has elected an autonomous, 39-member assembly that functions as an advisory body on issues such as regional control of natural resources and preservation of Saami culture. In 1997, King Harald V apologized to the Saami for the historic repression and "policies of Norwegianization" by the state.

The constitution guarantees freedom of peaceful assembly and association and the right to strike. Sixty percent of the work force belong to unions, which are free from government control, and collective bargaining is customary for the purpose of work constraints. In June, the government used emergency laws to impose a mandatory settlement in a strike by 20,000 nurses.

The independent judicial system is headed by a Supreme Court and operates at the local and national levels. Judges are appointed by the king under advisement from the ministry of justice. A special labor relations court handles disputes between both public and private sector employers and workers.

Human rights are widely respected. In 1997, however, the government released a European Council commission report that recommended that Norway review its legislation against discrimination and take local preventive action against xenophobia and anti-Semitism. The Labor government had initially suppressed the report, which also criticized Norwegian police and prosecutors for failing to act upon claims of racial harassment and discrimination against immigrants. Anti-immigrant sentiment has continued to grow in the country, even though strict laws prevent more than a few thousand refugees from settling in Norway each year.

Women's rights are protected under a law that provides for equal wages for men and women engaged in the same work activity. Women constitute approximately 45 percent of the labor force, half of whom are employed part-time. They are concentrated in sales, clerical, and social service jobs. In the Storting, women hold approximately 40 percent of the seats—more than in any other national assembly. Nine of the country's 19 cabinet ministers are women. By law, fathers must take at least four weeks' leave from their jobs after a baby is born.

The state finances the Evangelical Lutheran Church, in which more than 90 percent of the population hold at least nominal membership. While other churches receive public funding if they register with the government, there are some restrictions on religious freedom. The law requires that the sovereign and at least half of the cabinet be Lutheran. Potential employers are permitted to inquire about applicants' religious convictions and practices for certain teaching positions. The state religion is taught in schools, and religious groups are required to register with the government only if they seek state support. Discrimination on the basis of race, gender, language, and class are prohibited by law.

Freedom of the press is constitutionally guaranteed, and many newspapers are subsidized by the state in order to promote political pluralism. The country enjoys an especially strong regional press. A majority of newspapers are privately owned and openly partisan. Although radio and television broadcasting is also funded by the state, the government does not interfere with editorial content. Private radio stations were authorized in 1982, and the first commercial television channel was licensed in 1991. The Film Control Board has the right to censor blasphemous, overly violent, and pornographic films. The power to censor alleged blasphemy has not been exercised in more than 20 years.

Oman

Polity: Traditional
monarchy
Economy: Capitalist-
statist
Population: 2,500,000
PPP: $9,383
Life Expectancy: 70
Ethnic Groups: Arab, Baluchi, South Asian, African
Capital: Muscat

Political Rights: 6
Civil Liberties: 6
Status: Not Free

Overview:

Political advances made by Omani women in 1997 continued into 1998. In 1997, women were allowed to cast ballots
and to run as candidates for Oman's lower advisory cham-
ber, the *majlis al shura* (consultative council). Two women were eventually selected
for seats in the majlis. By January 1998, the sultan had selected four women for his
newly created upper advisory chamber, the *majlis addawla* (council of state). The presence of women in both of Oman's upper and lower advisory chambers does not, however, diminish the fact that political rights and civil liberties in Oman are tightly controlled.

Oman, an absolute sultanate, gained independence from Great Britain in 1951. The
current sultan, Qabus ibn Sa'id al Sa'id, overthrew his father in a palace coup to take
power in 1970. A five-year rebellion by left-wing guerillas opposed to the sultan's regime was crushed in 1975 with military assistance from Saudi Arabia, Jordan, Iran, and
Pakistan. Since a formal cease-fire in 1976, the sultan, who rules by decree with the
advice of the Council of Ministers, has faced little opposition.

In 1991, the sultan organized caucuses of prominent citizens in each of the country's
59 provinces to nominate three citizens per province for the new majlis. The majlis
comments on legislation and voices citizens' concerns but has no legislative power. In
1994, the sultan named an expanded, 80-seat majlis to sit through 1997. Two more
members were appointed with the 1997 October elections. In these elections, 51,000
selected Omanis voted for their choice of majlis delegates whose terms will end in 2000.
This was the first time since the creation of the majlis in 1991 that women, as voters
and candidates, could participate in delegate elections. Two women were among the
nominees chosen by the sultan to fill the council's 82 seats. In December, the sultan
created the majlis addlawa. He appointed 41 members to this chamber, including four
women. By the beginning of 1998, the majlis addlawa and the majlis al shura were
functioning as the sultan's bicameral advisory body, the *majlis Oman* (council of Oman).

Falling oil prices and decreasing demand for petroleum products by Asian economies slowed Oman's economic reform and diversification programs in 1998. Government spending, crucial to Oman's plans for creating a diverse private sector, has been
held to 38 percent of GDP, one of the lowest ratios in the Gulf. The year also saw a
doubling of Oman's budget deficit, and despite prudent planning for diversification,
Oman is still dependent on oil for 80 percent of government revenues.

Social services, public utilities, health, and education are on par with industrialized nations, and infant mortality rates compare well with Western Europe. Although the government was faced with tough economic challenges in 1998, officials pledged to avoid cuts which would erode living standards or affect low income groups. The government cut oil production levels and future exploration projects and is considering introducing value-added tax on luxury items.

Political Rights and Civil Liberties:

Omanis cannot change their government democratically. The sultan has absolute power and rules by decree. The sultan picks citizens who will vote for members of the councils that advise him. Citizens have access to senior officials and can file grievances through the traditional practice of petitioning their patrons, usually the sultan-appointed local governor. Citizens may also appeal to the sultan directly during his annual three-week tour of the country.

The Basic Law, Oman's first de facto written constitution, was promulgated by the sultan in 1996. The Basic Law was intended to take effect in 1998, but many of its provisions will be phased in gradually by the year 2000. It does not provide for political parties or direct elections. In theory, the Basic Law provides rights for citizens such as an independent judiciary, freedom of the press and assembly, and prohibitions against discrimination on the basis of sex, ethnicity, race, religion, and social class. In reality, many of the Basic Law's provisions have yet to be consistently enforced and adopted as normative practices for the maintenance of political rights and civil liberties.

Oman's rudimentary judicial system operates largely according to tradition. There are no jury trials; a single judge tries misdemeanors, and a panel of three judges tries felonies and national security offenses. Arbitrary arrest, mistreatment of prisoners, detention without charge beyond the legal 24-hour limit, and denial of access to legal counsel have been reported. The Criminal Code does not specify the rights of the accused. In practice, defendants are presumed innocent and do enjoy some procedural rights.

Criticism of the sultan is prohibited, although citizens do criticize government policies. Criticism from government agencies and officials is tolerated, but it does not receive media attention. All publications are censored, and distribution of foreign publications critical of Oman is rarely allowed. Journalists practice self-censorship. Two of the four daily newspapers are government owned, while the other two rely heavily on government subsidies. All four papers support government policy. Some criticism of foreign affairs issues, however, is permitted

State-controlled television and radio carry only official views. Private broadcast media are not permitted. Yet this control is being eroded by the increased availability of satellite dishes which provide Omanis with foreign broadcasting and unofficial views. The national telecommunications system also provides Internet service to citizens and foreigners with minimal restriction; however, the government has taken steps to restrict information products in the interest of protecting property rights. In August, the government warned resellers to clear out their stocks of pirated computer software, audio, and videotapes by the beginning of the year or face prosecution. According to the Business Software Alliance, 93 percent of the software products sold in Oman are counterfeit. In addition to reducing black market activity, the government hopes that increased enforcement of copyright laws will attract more foreign investment.

The new Basic Law provides for limited freedom of assembly. All public gatherings must be approved by the government, though this is not always strictly enforced. The Ministry of Social Affairs and Labor must register all associations, and political groups and human rights organizations are prohibited.

Islam is the state religion; the majority of Omanis are Sunni Muslim. Mosque sermons are monitored for content by the authorities. Christians and Hindus may worship freely at churches and temples built on land donated by the sultan. These groups are allowed to bring in printed material from abroad, but only Muslims may publish religious books.

Despite noticeable gains in education and career opportunities, particularly for younger women, Omani women as a group face discrimination in public and private life. Women comprise 54 percent of the students at Sultan Qabus University and nearly 20 percent of civil servants, yet scholarships abroad are limited almost exclusively to men. Women must receive permission from their husbands or nearest male relatives to travel outside of Oman, and face discrimination in inheritance claims under Islamic law. Female genital mutilation is practiced in some rural areas.

Calls for autonomy sporadically come from Shihayeen tribesmen in Rous al-Jibal province in the Musandam Peninsula. Administered by Oman since 1970, the province is geographically separate from the rest of the country.

There are no trade unions and no provisions for them under law. Employers of more than 50 workers must form a body of labor and management representatives to discuss working conditions. However, these committees may not negotiate wages. Strikes are illegal, though worker actions occasionally occur. Foreign workers must obtain letters of release from employers before they may change jobs.

⬇ Pakistan

Polity: Presidential-par-
liamentary democracy
(military-influenced)
Economy: Capitalist-statist
Population: 141,900,000
PPP: $2,209
Life Expectancy: 58
Ethnic Groups: Punjabi, Sindhi, Pashtun [Pathan], Baloch
Capital: Islamabad

Political Rights: 4
Civil Liberties: 5
Status: Partly Free

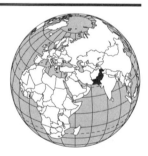

Trend arrow: Pakistan receives a downward trend arrow due to increased anarchy and lawlessness in several areas and the government's corresponding curbs on civil liberties.

Overview: In 1998, Pakistan's slide into bankruptcy and lawlessness continued. Rather than use his huge parliamentary majority to enact painful but necessary economic reforms, Premier Nawaz Sharif's foundering government restricted political rights and civil liberties, attempted to introduce Islamic law, and incurred economic sanctions by detonating nuclear tests.

Pakistan was founded in 1947 as a Muslim homeland with the partition of the former British India. In 1971, Bangladesh (ex-East Pakistan) achieved independence after a nine-month civil war. The 1973 constitution provides for a lower National Assembly, which currently has 217 members (including ten seats reserved for non-Muslims) elected for a five-year term, and an 87-seat Senate appointed by the four provincial assemblies. An electoral college chooses the president for a five-year term.

Pakistan has been under military rule for 25 of its 51 years of independence. Military governments have suspended political rights and civil liberties, crushed democratic institutions, and fostered a culture of violence. In 1985, the last military ruler, General Zia ul-Haq, amended the constitution to allow the president to dismiss elected governments. Successive presidents sacked three elected premiers between 1990 and 1996, and none has served a full term. Since Zia's death in 1988, the president, premier, and army chief of staff have informally shared power. There is widespread disillusionment with a corrupt political elite, dominated by rural landowners and industrialists, that has failed to address poverty and illiteracy.

The 1993 elections, held after the president dismissed a government headed by Sharif, returned Benazir Bhutto to a second term in power. During her term, political and sectarian violence killed at least 3,000 people in Karachi, the commercial capital. In 1996, President Farooq Ahmed Leghari ordered fresh elections after dismissing Bhutto's government on charges of corruption, undermining the judiciary, and sanctioning extrajudicial killings during an army crackdown in Karachi.

Barely 35 percent of voters turned out for the February 1997 elections. Sharif's Pakistan Muslim League (PML) and its allies won more than 160 seats, and Bhutto's Pakistan People's Party (PPP) won 18. Regional parties and independents won the remainder. Sharif has used his parliamentary majority to consolidate his power. In April 1997, parliament repealed the president's constitutional power to sack unilaterally national and provincial governments, and made the premier's advice on top military appointments binding. In the fall, a political battle between Sharif and the judiciary over Supreme Court appointments climaxed in December when a judicial panel ousted the chief justice and President Leghari resigned. In late December, parliament and the provincial legislatures elected Sharif's candidate, Rafiq Tarar, an Islamic fundamentalist and former Supreme Court justice, as president.

Following nuclear tests by archrival India in early May 1998, Sharif responded to mounting political pressure and ordered Pakistan to conduct tests on May 28. The same day, Sharif declared a state of emergency, preventing citizens from going to court to enforce fundamental rights. Sharif claimed the move was necessary to deal with external threats, curb violence, and introduce economic reforms. The Supreme Court restored constitutional rights in July, but the move underscored the fragility of Pakistan's institutions.

On October 9, the national assembly approved a constitutional amendment making the Koran and the Sunnah, the sayings of the prophet Mohammad, the country's supreme law. Opponents claimed Sharif was trying to divert attention from an economic crisis that only worsened after the nuclear tests prompted United States-led sanctions, and to placate fundamentalist groups enraged over U.S. missile attacks on Afghanistan and Sudan in August. Although the amendment is unlikely to receive the two-thirds majority in the Senate it needs to become law, critics said by pandering to Islamists, Sharif was eroding Pakistan's secular foundations and endangering women and minorities. On October 30, Sharif imposed direct federal rule in the Sindh province amidst escalating violence. In November, the government suspended human rights guarantees in areas of Sindh where the army is deployed, and ordered new military courts in Karachi to try "terrorists and criminals."

With the country facing an impending default on $42 billion in foreign debt, Sharif attempted to resurrect an International Monetary Fund (IMF) loan program which was suspended after the nuclear tests. By year's end, the government had not accepted the IMF's conditions of raising tariffs charged by state utilities and improving revenue collection.

Adding to Sharif's woes, three of Pakistan's provinces stepped up pressure on the federal government for more autonomy and economic benefits, and denounced the fact that Sharif, Tarar, and the military brass come from the Punjab province, home to 60 percent of the population. The tensions underscored a national identity dilemma in a society fractured by regional, ethnic, linguistic, and religious differences and where Islam has failed to serve as the anticipated unifying force.

Political Rights and Civil Liberties:

Pakistanis can change their government through elections. The electoral system concentrates political power in a rural landowning elite that dominates both main parties and defeats efforts at political and economic reform. Some 70-80 percent of parliamentary seats represent rural areas, but this is based on a 1981 census. The rural urban split is now believed to be about 50-50. In 1998, the government held its first census in 17 years, but the feudal political elite is unlikely to permit a drastic redrawing of the electoral boundaries. Widespread official corruption severely undermines democratic institutions, stunts economic development, and contributes to often severe civil liberties violations. Civilian governments and the country's crumbling institutions have been unable to implement economic reforms or provide law and order. Consequently, the relatively disciplined army is arguably the country's most respected institution and continues to influence politics from the sidelines.

Pakistan has not formally annexed its Northern Areas, which form part of the disputed territory of Kashmir, in order to avoid legitimizing Kashmir's de facto separation. Therefore, the million plus residents of the Northern Areas are not represented in parliament. In the 1997 elections, tribal leaders in the Federally Administered Tribal Areas (FATA) of the North West Frontier Province (NWFP) threatened to fine families and burn houses for allowing women to vote, and consequently, few women voted. In other parts of the NWFP, political parties reportedly mutually agree not to let women vote. According to the independent Human Rights Commission of Pakistan (HRCP), some 20 million bonded laborers cannot vote. Christians and other minorities must vote on separate electoral rolls.

The Supreme Court is independent. Lower courts are corrupt and subject to manipulation, and government officials frequently ignore court orders. The central government has little influence in the FATA, where tribal law prevails. In November, Sharif established military courts in the Sindh province. By year's end, military courts had sentenced several persons to death in trials that lasted just days. The government also invoked article 245 of the constitution in Sindh, which allows authorities to ban political meetings as well as strikes, suspends the High Court's jurisdiction to enforce basic human rights in areas where the army is deployed, and prevents defendants from appealing military court rulings in civilian courts.

The police are ill disciplined, frequently involved in crime, and subject to political manipulation. Police routinely torture detainees in order to extract confessions or bribes, use excessive force in routine situations, and rape female detainees and prisoners. Police are also responsible for scores of deaths in custody and, each year, commit dozens of extrajudicial executions of criminals and opposition politicians. Successive governments have used a 1960 public order law as well as complaints registered with the police or outright false criminal charges to arrest or detain political opponents.

By November 1998, ethnic and sectarian violence in Karachi had killed more than 1,000 people. Most of the violence had occurred between three rival factions of the Mohajir Quami Movement, which represents Urdu-speaking migrants from India. Sectarian violence in Punjab between the Sunni-based Sipah-e-Sahaba and the minority Shiite Sipah-e-Mohammed extremist groups kills scores of people each year. In some of the worst violence, in January Sunni extremists killed 28 Shiites praying in a Lahore cemetery.

In 1997, parliament passed an anti-terrorism law giving police broad powers to conduct searches, make arrests, and use lethal force. The law created special courts that must conclude trials within seven days under limited safeguards and must provide limited rights of appeal. Critics fear the law is encouraging police brutality. Authorities have arrested hundreds of people under the law but few have been charged or tried. The law also authorized the government to ban groups and associations.

Freedom of expression is restricted by laws and constitutional provisions that cover broad subjects including the army and Islam. Authorities occasionally detain, file false charges against, threaten, and assault journalists. Police occasionally attack newspaper offices and interfere with newspaper distribution. Islamic fundamentalists also frequently target journalists. Nevertheless, Pakistan's press is among the most outspoken in South Asia. The government owns nearly all electronic media, and news coverage favors the ruling party. Freedom of assembly is generally respected, but police forcibly break up many demonstrations.

Section 295-C of the penal code, imposed in 1986, mandates the death sentence for defiling the Prophet Mohammed. Thus far, appeals courts have overturned all blasphemy convictions. Magistrates are now required to conduct investigations before accepting charges. Nevertheless, Muslims have filed spurious blasphemy charges against Ahmadis, Christians, and Hindus in order to extort land and money. Human rights groups say that more than 200 Christians are jailed after being sentenced to death for blasphemy. In May, the bishop of Faisalabad, John Joseph, committed suicide after a court sentenced a Christian to death for alleged blasphemy. Although there were some doubts over the circumstances of his death, Joseph reportedly killed himself to protest the death sentence and the blasphemy law.

A 1984 ordinance prohibits Ahmadis, who are legally considered non-Muslims, from worshipping as Muslims. In 1997, Amnesty International reported that in recent years courts had charged 152 Ahmadis with blasphemy. Many have spent lengthy periods in pre-trial detention or prison. Christians, Ahmadis, and Hindus face economic and social discrimination, and are occasionally violently attacked by Islamists.

The 1979 Zina Ordinance introduced Shari'a (Islamic law) into the penal code regarding sexual offenses. Courts have imprisoned many women for alleged extramarital sexual intercourse, often following false allegations by their husbands, or following rape when a victim cannot meet the strict legal requirement to prove the crime and then is charged with adultery. Although the most severe penalties, including death for adultery, have never been carried out, the ordinance deters many women from reporting rape and may even encourage rape by police. The Karachi-based Lawyers for Human Rights and Legal Aid estimates that criminal gangs have trafficked some 200,000 Bangladeshi women to Pakistan, often with the complicity of corrupt local officials. Many are sold into prostitution and are subjected to physical abuse. Some 2,000 trafficking victims are detained under criminal charges, mainly for illegal entry or under the Zina ordinances for extramarital sex. Violence against women remains a serious problem. Women continue to be underrepresented in politics. The North West Frontier Province and Baluchistan have no women in their provincial assemblies.

The HRCP estimates there are 11 to 12 million child laborers, including many bonded laborers, working in brick kilns, carpet factories, farms, and elsewhere. Politicians and landlords reportedly forcibly hold thousands of bonded laborers, despite 1992 legislation outlawing bonded labor and canceling enslaving debts. In October, the International Labor Organization and Pakistan's manufacturers and exporters association signed an agreement requiring that at least 8,000 child laborers be sent to school and that their carpet work be monitored. However, the agreement covered fewer than 40 of the estimated 450 towns and villages where carpets are handwoven. Trade unions are independent, but several sectors cannot organize, and unions are prohibited in export processing zones.

Palau

Polity: Presidential-legislative democracy
Economy: Capitalist
Population: 20,000
PPP: na
Life Expectancy: 67
Ethnic Groups: Polynesian, Malayan, Melanesian
Capital: Koror

Political Rights: 1
Civil Liberties: 2
Status: Free

Overview: The Republic of Palau is an archipelago of more than 300 islands and islets at the western end of the Caroline Islands in the Pacific Ocean. Purchased by Germany from Spain in 1889, Palau was seized in 1914 by Japan, which administered the islands under a League of Nations mandate from 1920. In 1944, the United States occupied the islands, which became part of the U.S.-administered United Nations Trust Territory of the Pacific in 1947.

In 1979, Palau adopted a constitution requiring 75 percent approval at a referendum before nuclear-related activities could occur on its territory. In 1981, Palau became self-governing, though still under U.S. control as part of the Trust Territory, and Haruo Remelik was inaugurated as the country's first president. Following his election in November 1984 to a second four-year term, Remelik was assassinated the following year. At a special election held in August, Lazarus Salii defeated Acting President

Alfonso Oiterong to become Remelik's successor. In August 1988, President Salii was found dead in his office from an apparent suicide, and Ngiratkel Etpison was elected as his successor in November.

Between 1983 and 1990, Palau held seven plebiscites on approving a Compact of Free Association with the United States. None managed to cross the three-fourths threshold required for approval. Among the factors which prevented the Compact's early adoption were disagreements over the amount of the U.S. aid commitment, concerns about the requisition of land for U.S. military purposes, and incompatibilities between provisions providing facilities for U.S. nuclear forces and Palau's nuclear-free constitution. In 1992, Vice President Kuniwo Nakamura defeated challenger Johnson Toribiong in the presidential race (Etpison had been defeated in the primaries). In concurrent balloting, voters amended the constitution to require a simple majority for the passage of the Compact, which voters finally approved in 1993 with a 64 percent majority. Under the terms of the Compact, Palau is a sovereign country, although the U.S. remains responsible for defense. The U.S. is providing financial aid over a 15-year period in return for the right to maintain military facilities. In October 1994, Palau proclaimed its independence.

Modest economic gains supported by American aid and East Asian investment helped President Nakamura win reelection on November 6, 1996, over the mayor of Koror, Paramount Chief Ibedul Yutaka Gibbons. Considerable uncertainty exists regarding the prospect of continued U.S. funding at the end of the Compact period and over the likelihood that the government will use the compact money for projects fostering long-term economic development.

Political Rights and Civil Liberties: Citizens of Palau can change their government democratically. The constitution vests executive powers in a president who is directly elected for a four-year term. A vice president is elected on a separate ticket. The bicameral parliament consists of a Senate, currently comprised of 14 members who are elected on a geographical basis, and a 16-seat House of Representatives with one member elected from each of the 16 states. Elections are competitive and tend to revolve around personalities and issues rather than party affiliations. A 16-member Council of Chiefs advises the government on issues involving tribal laws and customs. The chiefs wield considerable traditional authority, and there are often tensions between the chiefs and political leaders.

The government respects freedom of speech and of the press. There are both government and private newspapers, although the state-run radio and television broadcast services are the primary source of news and information. There is also a private cable television system with widespread coverage. Freedom of religion exists in this predominantly Roman Catholic country.

Freedom of association is respected, although no active employee organizations currently exist. There are no laws regarding the right to strike or collective bargaining in this largely non-wage-earning society.

The judiciary, which is free from government interference, enforces the right to a fair trial in practice. There is an independent special prosecutor and independent public defender system. In late 1998, the Ministry of Justice reported that a shortage of government prosecutors has resulted in a large backlog of civil and criminal cases awaiting action. Local police are under direct civilian control. However, foreign residents have reported that law enforcement officials do not investigate crimes against non-Palauans as thoroughly as crimes against citizens.

Foreign nationals comprise nearly half the labor force and face discrimination in employment and education, as well as random violence. Employers occasionally coerce foreign workers, particularly domestic or unskilled laborers, into remaining at their jobs by withholding their passports. A controversial minimum wage law effective January 1, 1999, applies only to Palauan citizens. Opponents of the law have predicted that the new legislation will result in foreign workers gaining an advantage in the local labor market.

Inheritance of property and traditional rank is matrilineal, giving women a high status in society. Nevertheless, domestic violence, often linked to alcohol or drug abuse, remains a problem, and many women are reluctant to report their spouses to law enforcement authorities.

↑ Panama

Polity: Presidential-legislative democracy
Economy: Capitalist-statist
Population: 2,800,000
PPP: $6,258
Life Expectancy: 74
Ethnic Groups: Mestizo (70 percent), West Indian (14 percent), European (10 percent), Indian (6 percent)
Capital: Panama City

Political Rights: 2
Civil Liberties: 3
Status: Free

Trend arrow: Panama receives an upward trend arrow due to the voters' rejection of a constitutional reform which would have allowed President Balladares, whose government was mired in corruption and censorship, to stand for reelection.

Overview:

In 1998, voters rebuffed President Ernesto Perez Balladares, whose government has been mired in a record of censorship, corruption, and an increasingly tenuous claim to fidelity to the rule of law as they overwhelmingly rejected a constitutional reform that would have allowed him to stand for reelection. When the Canal reverts to Panamanian sovereignty, it will be a new president emerging from May 1999 elections, not the incumbent, "El Toro" (The Bull) Perez Balladares, who will be at the helm of the ship of state as it enters into a new century.

Panama was part of Colombia until 1903, when a U.S.-supported revolt resulted in the proclamation of an independent Republic of Panama. A period of weak civilian rule ended with a military coup that brought General Omar Torrijos to power.

After the signing of the 1977 canal treaties with the U.S., Torrijos promised democratization. The 1972 constitution was revised, providing for the direct elections of a president and a legislative assembly for five years. After Torrijos' death in 1981, Gen. Manuel Noriega emerged as Panamanian Defense Force (PDF) chief and rigged the 1984 election that brought to power the PRD, then the political arm of the PDF.

The Democratic Alliance of Civic Opposition (ADOC) won the 1989 election, but Noriega annulled the vote and declared himself head of state. He was removed during a U.S. military invasion, and ADOC's Guillermo Endara became president.

In 1994, the PRD capitalized on the Endara government's record of ineptness, and Perez Balladares, a 47-year-old millionaire and former banker, won the presidency with 33.3 percent of the vote. The PRD won 32 of 71 seats in the Legislative Assembly and achieved an effective majority with the support of allied parties that won six seats.

Perez Balladares kept a campaign promise by choosing for his cabinet technocrats and politicians from across the ideological spectrum. But his orthodox free market economic policies led to widespread protests in 1995 by labor unions and students. The president's popularity declined when the government met protests with harsh crackdowns.

During the 1994 campaign, Perez Balladares pledged to rid the country of drug influence. However, the PRD was accused of involvement in drug trafficking in the aftermath of the collapse of the Agro-Industrial and Commercial Bank of Panama (BANAICO) in January 1996. An investigation by the Banking Commission found accounts empty and $50 million unaccounted for, as well as evidence that the bank was a central money-laundering facility. BANAICO was named in several American drug investigations, including one investigation into Jose Castrillon Henao, a Colombian who was arrested in April 1996 as the reputed organizer of the Cali cartel's seagoing cocaine shipments to the U.S. Mayor Alfredo Aleman, a board member of BANAICO, is also a friend and top advisor to Perez Balladares, and was a major contributor to the party's 1994 campaign. Perez Balladares himself was forced to admit that his campaign unknowingly accepted a contribution from Castrillon Henao, who was extradited to Florida in May 1998 to stand trial for money laundering.

The Perez Balladares administration further damaged its popularity when it restored government jobs and awarded a reported $35 million in back pay to former members of the Dignity Battalions, who had been Noriega's paramilitary enforcers.

In 1997, the son of a prominent PRD politician and two other Panamanians were found innocent of killing an unarmed U.S. soldier in 1992 in a trial plagued by political pressure and irregularities. In August 1998, voters rejected by an almost two-to-one margin a referendum on a proposed constitutional amendment that would have enabled Perez Balladares' reelection. Mireya Moscoso, who narrowly lost the 1994 contest to El Toro, was selected again as the presidential standard-bearer of the Partido Arnulfista.

Political Rights and Civil Liberties: Panama's citizens can change their government democratically. The constitution guarantees freedom of political and civic organization, and more than a dozen parties from across the political system participated in the 1994 elections. In 1998, twelve parties signed an "ethical pact" sponsored by the Roman Catholic Church in which they promised to adhere to standards of decency during the May 1999 national elections.

The judicial system, headed by a Supreme Court, was revamped in 1990. It remains overworked, however, and its administration is inefficient, politicized, and prone to corruption. An unwieldy criminal code and a surge in cases, many against former soldiers and officials of the military period, complicate the panorama. In February 1998, the Supreme Court declared unconstitutional the provisions that authorize the Ombudsman's Office to investigate the administration of justice, claiming that the watchdog agency's role violates the principle of judicial independence.

The PDF were dismantled after 1989, and the military was formally abolished in 1994. But the civilian-run Public Force (National Police) that replaced the PDF is poorly disciplined, corrupt and, like the country's prison guards, frequently uses "excessive force." It has been ineffectual against the drug trade, as Panama remains a money-laundering hub as well as a major transshipment point for both cocaine and illicit arms.

The penal system is marked by violent disturbances in decrepit facilities packed with up to eight times their intended capacity. About two-thirds of prisoners face delays of about 18 months in having their cases heard.

Panama also continues to be a major transshipment point for illegal aliens seeking to enter into the United States, including large numbers from Ecuador.

Panama's media are a raucous assortment of radio and television stations, daily newspapers, and weekly publications. Restrictive media laws dating back to the Noriega regime remain on the books, however. The law permits officials to jail without trial anyone who defames the government. Legal codes establish government control of work permits for journalists, strict defamation and libel rules, and a clause that permits reporters to be punished for "damaging the nation's economy" or national security. In 1995, Perez Balladares began to apply the laws against media critical of his government. In 1998, the Inter-American Press Association protested a decision by the elections tribunal to vet all polls through a process of pre-publication approval.

In January 1998, the government charged Gustavo Gorriti, a Peruvian national who worked as an associate editor of the daily *La Prena*, and another reporter with slandering the Attorney General. The action came only four months after it dropped its two-month effort to deport Gorriti, who headed the newspaper's investigative unit and led the probe of the BANAICO bankruptcy, which linked Perez Balladares to Castrillon Henao. The 1998 case stemmed from the publication of an article which revealed that the chief law enforcement officer had received a check from Castrillon Henao for his reelection campaign.

Labor unions are well organized. However, labor rights were diluted in 1995 when Perez Balladares pushed labor code revisions through Congress. When 49 unions initiated peaceful protests, the government cracked down in a series of violent clashes that resulted in four deaths and hundreds of arrests.

Since 1993, indigenous groups have protested the encroachment of illegal settlers on Indian lands as well as delays by the government in formally demarcating the boundaries of those lands. Indian communities do enjoy, however, a large degree of autonomy and self-government.

Papua New Guinea

Polity: Parliamentary democracy
Economy: Capitalist
Population: 4,300,000
PPP: $2,500
Life Expectancy: 56
Ethnic Groups: Papuan, Melanesian, Negrito, Micronesian, Polynesian
Capital: Port Moresby

Political Rights: 2
Civil Liberties: 3*
Status: Free

Ratings change: Papua New Guinea's civil liberties rating changed from 4 to 3, and its status changed from Partly Free to Free, due to the onset of a peace process in the Bougainville conflict.

Overview:

An April 1998 cease-fire ended the ten-year secessionist rebellion on Papua New Guinea's Bougainville Island that had killed thousands of combatants and civilians. Yet crime and corruption continued to undermine the economy of this young, resource-rich democracy.

This South Pacific country, consisting of the eastern half of New Guinea and some 600 smaller islands, achieved independence from Australia in 1975 under Premier Michael Somare. The 1975 constitution vests executive power in a prime minister and cabinet. As a member of the British Commonwealth, the head of state is a largely ceremonial governor-general who represents the Queen of England. Parliament has 89 at-large members and 20 members representing the 19 provinces and Port Moresby, all elected for a five-year term. Parties are centered around personalities, and since independence, the country has been governed by unstable and shifting coalitions.

In late 1988, miners and landowners on Bougainville Island, 560 miles northeast of the capital, began guerrilla attacks against an Australian-owned mine to demand compensation and profit-sharing. Within months, the rebels transformed their long-standing grievances into a secessionist struggle under the newly-formed Bougainville Revolutionary Army (BRA).

In 1995, Premier Julius Chan's government took advantage of a cease-fire to swear in a Bougainville Transitional Government (BTG) on the island as an outlet for local grievances. The cease-fire broke down in 1996, and in October, gunmen assassinated Bougainville Premier Theodore Miriung.

The February 1997 revelation that the government had signed a $27 million contract with London-based Sandline International to provide mercenaries on Bougainville attracted widespread anger. In March, Chan sacked Brigadier General Jerry Singirok after the armed forces chiefcalled for the premier's resignation. Ordinary citizens and soldiers rallied around Singirok, and Chan resigned after several days of anti-government demonstrations.

At the June 1997 elections, an anti-incumbent mood swept Chan and several other senior politicians out of parliament. Disillusioned voters complained that official corruption and rising crime were keeping the country impoverished despite considerable mineral wealth. In July, parliament elected Bill Skate, a former opposition leader, as prime minister in a surprising coalition government that included his PNG First Party and the incumbent coalition.

In October, with Bougainville's population suffering from years of low-intensity conflict and deprivation, Sydney and Wellington arranged a truce between the government and the BRA. In April 1998, a formal cease-fire took effect, buttressed by a multinational Peace Monitoring Group. By year's end parliament had failed to pass legislation enabling the establishment of a Bougainville Reconciliation Government (BRG). Undaunted, leaders of all factions on Bougainville decided to establish the BRG anyway, calling it the Bougainville People's Congress.

Like its predecessors, Skate's government has been dogged by widespread allegations of corruption, bribery, sex scandals, mismanagement, and nepotism. In November, Skate re-instated Singirok as armed forces chief even though a commission of inquiry into the Sandline affair had accused Singirok of accepting bribes from a military contractor. The government's 1999 budget abolished 15 government agencies, cut more than 7,000 public service jobs, and directed 30 percent of spending towards debt servicing. While these measures may be necessary after years of official corruption and mismanagement, the social cost will be painful.

Political Rights and Civil Liberties:

Citizens of Papua New Guinea can change their government democratically, though elections are generally marred by some irregularities and sporadic violence.

Democratic institutions are faced with fiscal pressures, official corruption, violent crime, and the challenge of nation-building in a country with extreme cultural differences between the cities and isolated highlands, where some 700 tribes speak hundreds of languages. The judiciary is independent. However, the boundaries between tribal law and the formal legal system are still being defined.

The army, army-backed paramilitary groups and the BRA committed torture, "disappearances," arbitrary detentions, and extrajudicial executions against civilians and combatants during the Bougainville conflict. By some estimates, the war killed at least 20,000 combatants and civilians on Bougainville and the nearby Buka Island, many who died due to a lack of medical treatment and supplies. The government faces the challenge of re-integrating an estimated 30-40,000 former combatants into society, many of them teenagers.

An October survey by the Australian National University reported that Papua New Guinea's crime problem is as severe as anywhere in the world. The report said that crime ranks as the country's biggest economic problem, scaring off investment and tourism and constraining the growth of cash crops in rural areas. In urban areas, violent gangs known as "Rascals" have caused a severe law and order crisis. The 1993 Internal Security Act gave police expanded powers to conduct searches without warrants. Police frequently use excessive force against suspects, causing several deaths in recent years, and abuse detainees and prisoners. In the highlands, police occasionally burn homes to punish crimes committed by individuals, or to punish communities suspected of harboring criminals or participating in tribal warfare, which has killed dozens of people in recent years.

The country's two private daily newspapers report freely on official corruption and the Bougainville crisis. The state-run radio's news coverage is generally balanced. There is a private television station. Nongovernmental organizations are active and outspoken. In rural areas, foreign logging companies frequently swindle villagers and often renege on promises to build schools and hospitals. Violence and social discrimination against women are serious problems. A report released in December by the Australian aid agency AusAID said the incidence of rape had risen dramatically in recent years, particularly in the highlands where it frequently occurs during tribal fighting. Since the mid-1980s, some 4,000 refugees from West Papua (Irian Jaya) have lived in a camp at East Awin. The government has offered them permanent residency, and by October, about 1,000 had accepted the offer.

Unions are independent, and workers bargain collectively and stage strikes. The International Labor Organization has criticized a law allowing the government to invalidate arbitration agreements or wage awards not considered in the national interest. Labor leaders criticized the 1999 budget for abolishing several labor-related agencies.

Paraguay

Polity: Presidential-legislative democracy
Economy: Capitalist-statist
Population: 5,200,000
PPP: $3,583
Life Expectancy: 69
Ethnic Groups: Mestizo (95 percent), Indian and European (5 percent)
Capital: Asuncion

Political Rights: 4
Civil Liberties: 3
Status: Partly Free

Overview: The fate of General Lino Oviedo, putative presidential candidate and former head of the army who led a 1996 coup attempt, held Paraguay in its thrall for all of 1998. Newly elected President (and Oviedo stand-in) Raul Cubas ignored a Supreme Court ruling that would force the military man to serve out his ten-year sentence for insurrection. The long-ruling (51 years) Colorado Party expelled Oviedo from its ranks after Cubas' act of defiance. However, Cubas escaped congressional censure for ignoring the constitution when the vote was suspended in December for fear that Oviedo's supporters would threaten the lives of the elected representatives.

In 1989, a coup ended the 35-year dictatorship of General Alfredo Stroessner. Oviedo himself stormed into the bunker of Latin America's oldest surviving dictator with a pistol in one hand and a grenade in the other and demanded that he surrender. General Andres Rodriguez took over Stroessner's Colorado Party and engineered his own election to finish Stroessner's last presidential term.

The Colorados won a majority in a vote for a constituent assembly, which produced the 1992 constitution. It provides for a president, a vice president, and a bicameral Congress consisting of a 45-member Senate and an 80-member Chamber of Deputies elected for five years. The president is elected by a simple majority and reelection is prohibited. The constitution bans the active military from engaging in politics.

In the 1992 Colorado primary election, Luis Maria Argana, an old-style machine politician, defeated construction tycoon Juan Carlos Wasmosy. Rodriguez and Oviedo engineered a highly dubious re-count that made Wasmosy the winner.

The 1993 candidates were Wasmosy, Domingo Laino of the center-left Authentic Radical Liberal Party (PLRA), and Guillermo Caballero Vargas, a wealthy business-man. Wasmosy promised to modernize the economy. Laino played on his decades of resistence to Stroessner, and Caballero Vargas campaigned as a centrist, free of the politics of the past.

Every poll showed Wasmosy trailing until three weeks before the election, when Oviedo threatened a coup if the Colorado Party lost. Fear of a coup proved decisive, as Wasmosy won with 40.3 percent of the vote. Laino took 32 percent and Caballero Vargas 23.5 percent.

Oviedo was then appointed army commander, and Wasmosy allowed him to elimi-nate rivals in the military through forced retirement. The partnership came to a bitter end when Wasmosy moved to reduce the influence of the drug- tainted military in gov-ernment, and it became increasingly obvious that Oviedo and a hardline Colorado fac-tion planned to use Wasmosy as a stepping-stone for the general's own accession to the presidency.

Wasmosy ordered Oviedo's resignation on April 22, 1996. The general in turn threat-ened a coup and mobilized the troops. Wasmosy took refuge in the U.S. embassy and prepared his resignation. International pressure and mass protests in Paraguay allowed Wasmosy to outmaneuver his rival, who then vowed to return as a presidential candi-date in 1998.

Wasmosy's government was shaken by a number of corruption scandals, mostly involving money laundering in the banking system by financial racketeers from neigh-boring countries and by drug traffickers. In 1997, Oviedo won the Colorado party presi-dential nomination by besting Argana by 10,000 votes, or less than one percent of those cast. Argana's supporters claimed fraud and demanded that 50,000 of the votes cast be reviewed. Oviedo warned that if the courts refused to recognize his victory in the 1998 elections, he would head a popular insurrection.

Cubas, a civil engineer and originally Oviedo's vice presidential choice, was elected in May 1998, after Oviedo was jailed in March by a military tribunal for his 1996 at-tempted putsch and banned from standing for election. Despite the deep divisions within the Colorado Party, Cubas not only bested the opposition Democratic Alliance and Laino 54-42 percent, but also led the party to majority status in both chambers of con-gress for the first time since 1989. One of Cubas' first acts was to free Oviedo, in a maneuver widely described as a "constitutional coup." Throughout 1998, rumors of a possible coup circulated throughout Asuncion, as Wasmosy sought to find support for postponing the elections and as a result of the presumed fears of a largely anti-Oviedo military officers' corps.

Political Rights and Civil Liberties:

The 1992 constitution provides for regular elections. More than 80 percent of eligible voters participated in the 1998 elec-tions. Although the presidential campaign was marred by political proscription (of Oviedo) and threats against the national electoral tribunal, voter fraud was held to a minimum by the work of the tribunal, coverage by the media, and willingness of the military to stand firm in favor of the process.

The constitution guarantees free political and civic organization as well as religious expression. However, political rights and civil liberties are undermined by the government's tolerance of threats of intimidation and use of force by its supporters.

The judiciary remains under the influence of the ruling party, and the military remains susceptible to the corruption pervading all public and governmental institutions. Corruption cases languish for years in the courts, and most end without resolution. In the last three years, a lack of legal action concerning a series of fraudulent bankruptcies within the financial sector left potential investors worried about their own juridical security. The courts are generally unresponsive to human rights groups that present cases of rights violations committed either before or after the overthrow of Stroessner. Allegations include illegal detention by police and torture during incarceration, particularly in rural areas. Colombian drug traffickers continue to expand operations in Paraguay, and accusations of high official involvement in drug trafficking date back to the 1980s. In 1997, the commander of the national police was dismissed following a newspaper expose about his force's involvement in car theft, corruption, and bribery.

Overcrowding, unsanitary living conditions, and mistreatment are serious problems in Paraguayan prisons. More than 95 percent of the prisoners held are pending trial, many for months or years after arrest. The constitution permits detention without trial until the accused completes the minimum sentence for the alleged crime.

The media are both public and private. State-run broadcast media present pluralistic points of view and a number of independent newspapers publish. However, journalists investigating corruption or covering strikes and protests are often the victims of intimidation and violent attacks by security forces. Free expression is also threatened by vague, potentially restrictive laws that mandate "responsible" behavior by journalists and media owners.

Peasant and Indian organizations demanding land often meet with police crackdowns, death threats, detentions, and forced evictions by vigilante groups in the employ of landowners. Peasants have been killed in the ongoing disputes. Activist priests who support land reform are frequent targets of intimidation. The government's promise of land reform remains largely unfilled, as nearly 90 percent of agricultural land remains in the hands of foreign companies and a few hundred Paraguayan families. A program financed by the European Union to restore traditional lands to Native Americans in the eastern Chaco region has been wracked with fraud.

There are numerous trade unions and two major union federations. Strikes are often broken up violently by the police and the military, and labor activists are frequently detained. The 1992 constitution gives public-sector workers the rights to organize, bargain collectively, and strike, but these rights are often not respected in practice. A new labor code designed to protect worker rights was passed in October 1993, but enforcement has been weak.

Peru

Polity: Presidential-
authoritarian
Economy: Capitalist-
statist
Population: 26,100,000
PPP: $3,940
Life Expectancy: 69

Political Rights: 5
Civil Liberties: 4
Status: Partly Free

Ethnic Groups: Indian (45 percent), mestizo (37 percent),
European (15 percent), other (3 percent)
Capital: Lima

Overview: President Alberto Fujimori's authoritarian shadow grew even
longer in 1998, as he sought a means to engineer his reelection to a third term, notwithstanding a two-term limit set by
the constitution. His assault on the few remaining independent sources of state power
intensified as his rubber-stamp Congress tampered with the powers of the National
Magistrates Council and, in December of the previous year, the membership of the
National Electoral Board.

Since gaining independence in 1821, Peru has seen alternating periods of civilian
and military rule. Civilian rule was restored in 1980 after 12 years of dictatorship. That
same year, the Maoist Shining Path terrorist group launched a guerrilla war that killed
30,000 people over the next 13 years.

Fujimori, a university rector and engineer, defeated novelist Mario Vargas Llosa in
the 1990 election. In 1992, backed by the military, Fujimori suspended the constitution
and dissolved Congress in a move that was popular due to the people's disdain for Peru's
corrupt, elitist political establishment and their fear of the Shining Path.

Fujimori held a state-controlled election for an 80-member constituent assembly
to replace the Congress. The assembly drafted a constitution that established a unicameral Congress under closer presidential control. The constitution was approved in
a state-controlled referendum following Shining Path leader Abimael Guzman's capture.

Fujimori's principal opponent in the 1995 election was former UN Secretary General Javier Perez de Cuellar, who vowed to end Fujimori's "dictatorship." Fujimori
crushed his opponent with a massive public spending and propaganda campaign that
utilized state resources. Under de facto head Vladimiro Montesinos, who is a Fujimori
ally and one-time legal counsel to drug kingpins, the National Intelligence Service (SIN)
was employed to spy on and discredit Perez de Cuellar and other opposition candidates. On April 9, Fujimori won an easy victory, outpolling Perez de Cuellar by about
three to one, while his loose coalition of allies won a majority in the new 120-seat
Congress.

In August 1996 Congress passed a law allowing Fujimori to run for a third term,
despite a constitutional provision limiting the president to two terms. The law evaded
this by defining Fujimori's current term as his first under the 1993 constitution.

On April 22, 1997, the seizure of the Japanese ambassador's residence came to a violent end when a commando raid liberated all but one of the 72 hostages and killed all 14 of the outgunned insurgents. That May, the president of the seven-person Tribunal of Constitutional Guarantees—the body that assesses the constitutional legality of national legislation—resigned with the words, "the rule of law has broken down in Peru." His action came after Congress dismissed three other tribunal members after they had ruled at the end of 1996 that legislation designed to enable Fujimori to stand for reelection in 2000 was not applicable.

The en masse resignation in March 1998 of the magistrates council came just four months after Fujimori's Congress altered the national elections commission so as to give the president increased influence. In response to an upsurge in common crime, Fujimori received decree-making authority from Congress that allowed him to erase due process protections, including habeas corpus protections, and to use draconian courts reminiscent of the faceless tribunals used against the once-strong guerrillas. In October, the hands-down reelection of the popular mayor of Lima, an outspoken Fujimori critic, led to opposition hopes that they might field a strong challenger to the incumbent in presidential elections scheduled two years later. However, most of the provincial elections were won by non-allied regional movements.

Political Rights and Civil Liberties:

In the past, the Fujimori government has been termed a presidential-military regime with the trappings of a formal democracy. In 1998, however, he was able to turn the tables on a restless army high command and reestablish his primacy over the generals, forcing the commander of the armed forces, Gen. Nicolas de Bari Hermoza, into retirement. Although Fujimori had considerable popular support, the 1995 election was not fair by international standards due to the massive use of state resources and military and state intelligence during the campaign. Electoral laws require any party that failed to obtain five percent of the popular vote in 1995 to obtain 400,000 signatures to re-register; few parties have managed to do so. Given the marginalization of political parties, the lack of an independent judiciary, and the relative weakness of trade unions and other elements of civil society, few independent power centers exist outside of the president and his allies in the military high command.

Under the December 1993 constitution, the president can rule virtually by decree. Fujimori can dissolve Congress in the event of a "grave conflict" between the executive and legislature, as he did in 1992. The constitution overturned Peru's tradition of no re-election.

In 1994, there were judicial reforms and a new Supreme Court was named. However, judicial independence is increasingly circumscribed. In August 1996, Congress installed a Tribunal of Constitutional Guarantees, as called for under the 1993 constitution, with powers of judicial review. However parliament also passed a law requiring the votes of six of the seven members of the Tribunal to declare a law or government action unconstitutional. The first real test of the Tribunal's mandate—the ruling on Fujimori's eligibility for re-election to a third consecutive term—also proved to be the institution's undoing. In August 1998, a vote by Congress appeared to clear the way for Fujimori to run again in the year 2000.

Public safety, particularly in Lima, is threatened by out-of-control violent crime and vicious warfare by opposing gangs, some of which use body armor and high-powered weapons. Police estimate that there are more than 1,000 criminal gangs in the capital alone. Torture remains routine in police detention centers, and conditions remain deplorable in prisons for common criminals. Following the 1996 seizure of hostages by the guerrillas, the government suspended an agreement that had allowed the International Commission of the Red Cross to visit some 4,000 accused or convicted terrorists.

The press is largely privately owned. Radio and television are both privately and publicly-owned. State-owned media are blatantly pro-government. Since 1992, many media, especially television and print journalists, have been pressured into self-censorship or exile by a broad government campaign of intimidation, abductions, death threats, libel suits, withholding advertising, police harassment, arbitrary detention, physical mistreatment, and imprisonment on charges of "apology for terrorism." In 1998, the military intelligence services have been particularly active against opposition media, including printing defamatory articles against them in the sensationalist pro-government press.

In September 1997, a government-controlled court stripped Baruch Ivcher, an Israeli émigré and the owner of the Channel 2 television station, of control of his media business and his Peruvian citizenship after the station aired reports linking the military to torture and corruption, and ran an expose of a telephone espionage ring run by intelligence agents to spy on opposition politicians and journalists. Ivcher, considered a former ally of the intelligence services, fled to Miami after being summoned to appear before a military tribunal on charges of trying to bring the armed forces into disrepute. In September 1998, Ivcher was prosecuted in an openly hostile civilian court using faceless witnesses on charges of customs fraud, tax evasion and falsifying documents. In December, a Lima court ordered Ivcher's arrest.

Racism against Peru's large Indian population is prevalent among the middle and upper classes, although Fujimori's government has made some effort to combat it.

The labor code authorizes the government to disband any strike it deems to be endangering a company, an industry, or the public sector. In 1996, the International Labor Organization criticized the labor code for failing to protect workers from anti-union discrimination, and for restricting collective bargaining rights. Forced labor, including child labor, is prevalent in the gold mining region of the Amazon.

Philippines

Polity: Presidential-legislative democracy
Economy: Capitalist-statist
Population: 75,300,000
PPP: $2,762
Life Expectancy: 66
Ethnic Groups: Christian Malay (91.5 percent), Muslim Malay (4 percent), Chinese (1.5 percent), other (3 percent)
Capital: Manila

Political Rights: 2
Civil Liberties: 3
Status: Free

Overview:

Former movie actor and Vice President Joseph Estrada easily won the Philippines' May 1998 presidential elections after running on a pro-poor platform. Estrada's ties to tycoons and a series of controversial appointments raised fears of economic cronyism.

The Philippines achieved independence in 1946 after 43 years of United States rule and occupation by the Japanese during World War II. Ferdinand Marcos, first elected as president in 1965, declared martial law in 1972 to circumvent a constitutional two-term limit. The 1986 "People Power" revolution, which saw massive street protests over a blatantly rigged election, ended Marcos's dictatorial rule. His opponent, Corazon Aquino, took office. The 1987 constitution vests executive power in a president who is directly elected for a six-year term. The president's power is checked by a strong judiciary and a single-term limit. The Congress consists of a Senate with 24 directly elected members, and a House of Representatives with 201 directly elected members and up to 50 more appointed by the president.

Aquino drew praise for her support for democracy, but right-wing elements in the military and other opponents carried out at least six coup attempts, and she had limited success in reforming a feudal-oriented society and crony-capitalist economy. In the 1992 elections, Aquino backed former army chief-of-staff Fidel Ramos, who won with just 23.5 percent of the vote. Ramos's administration ended power shortages, boosted GDP growth, and weakened some of the family-owned business monopolies that had accumulated substantial political power. However, Ramos's economic reforms widened income disparities and brought only marginal benefits to poorer Filipinos.

In 1996, Ramos's supporters mounted a signature campaign for a referendum on amending the constitution to allow the president to run for re-election. Opponents argued against subordinating the constitution to politics, and said a so-called "charter change" could set a precedent allowing a future strongman to abuse power.

In September 1997, Aquino and Roman Catholic Cardinal Jaime Sin led church groups, business representatives, students, and ordinary Filipinos in a huge rally in Manila that forced Ramos to declare he would not run. In December, Ramos endorsed House speaker Jose de Venecia for president, even though the insider from the president's National Union of Christian Democrats party enjoyed limited popular support. In the campaign for the May 11, 1998 elections, Estrada portrayed himself as an ally of the poor against the feudalistic landlords who control the countryside, pledging to invest heavily in rural infrastructure to boost agriculture. His opponents slammed him as a uneducated, hard-drinking philanderer with close ties to Marcos-era tycoons. Final results gave Estrada 46.4 percent of the vote; de Venecia, 17.1 percent; with the remainder split among 6 candidates. Gloria Macapagal-Arroyo, a high-profile opposition senator and economist, won the separate balloting for vice president. In the House race, the conservative Struggle for Democratic Philippines party maintained its status as the largest party in parliament by winning 110 seats, with the LAKAS-National Union of Christian Democrats coming in second with 50 seats.

Estrada tried to ease fears that his administration would bring a return to crony capitalism and undercut economic reforms by assembling a credible team of ministers and advisors. Yet by the fall, allegations of cronyism had already surfaced over controversial appointments to sensitive posts and a shortening of the mandate for a commission investigating the wealth of the late Marcos and his wife, Imelda. With the Philippines buffeted by the regional economic crisis, opponents also criticized a lack of coherence in economic policy.

Estrada must also build upon improvements to the security situation made under

Ramos. In 1993, right-wing military hardliners agreed to a peace pact. Since 1992, the government has held peace negotiations with the exile-based leaders of a Communist insurgency that began in the late 1960s. In March, the government reached a human rights pact with communist leaders, but a final solution remains elusive. In 1996, the government signed a peace agreement with the separatist Moro National Liberation Front (MNLF), which had waged a 24-year insurgency on southern Mindanao Island. The deal established Nur Misuari, the MNLF leader, as head of a transitional body overseeing development projects in 14 Mindanao provinces, and called for a local plebiscite in 1999 on expanding an existing autonomous region. But two smaller groups, the Moro Islamic Liberation Front (MILF) and Abu Sayyaf, continue to wage a low-grade insurgency for an independent Islamic state.

Political Rights and Civil Liberties:

Filipinos can change their government democratically, although outside of Manila, much of the country is still largely run along feudal lines, with dominant local clans and landowners holding real power. Elections revolve around personalities rather than issues. While the presidential election appeared to be free and fair, some 17,200 other elections for parliamentary and local seats were marred by vote buying and intimidation, and by violence that killed at least 20 people by election day.

Official corruption is widespread. Although the country's strengthened institutions, vigorous media, and a more outspoken public are probably sufficient to prevent a return to Marcos-era crony capitalism, influence peddling and close government-business connections are pervasive.

Complaints of economic and social discrimination by the country's Christian majority against the Moros, or Muslims who live primarily in Mindanao, have been the underlying cause of insurgencies since the 1970s. In recent years, skirmishes between the army and the MILF in Mindanao and nearby Basilan Island regularly displaced tens of thousands of civilians. The army reportedly indiscriminately bombs and shells villages during counterinsurgency operations, and soldiers loot and burn homes. The MILF and other groups often force villagers to evacuate homes, and operate protection rackets and kidnapping syndicates that mainly target ethnic Chinese businessmen and their families.

Members of the army and the Philippine National Police (PNP) are also involved in kidnappings. The judiciary is independent; however, courts are heavily backlogged and are reportedly rife with corruption all the way up to the Supreme Court. In 1997, Amnesty International accused the police of torture and ill treatment of criminal suspects. Private armies kept by politicians, wealthy landowners, and logging operations are allegedly responsible for abductions and extrajudicial killings.

The private press is vigorous, although outside Manila illegal logging outfits, drug traffickers, and other criminal groups harass and intimidate journalists. In the spring, gunmen killed two journalists in separate incidents in the city of Zamboanga and in the town of Sultan Kudarat, both in Mindanao. Both journalists had denounced official corruption and abuses of power. The government sometimes restricts meetings and demonstrations on issues that might antagonize fellow Association of Southeast Asian Nations countries. Nongovernmental human rights organizations are highly active.

Security forces often falsely link human rights activists to Communist groups, which encourage abuses against activists by private armies and other non-state groups. Freedom of religion is respected. Trafficking of Filipino women abroad is a serious problem, and domestic prostitution, including child prostitution, is rampant. These and other abuses flourish with the complicity of corrupt local officials. Cities have large numbers of street children. To clear land for development projects, the government has forcibly resettled thousands of tenant farmers and urban squatters, often to areas with few services and job opportunities. Unions are independent and active. The International Labor Organization has criticized labor code provisions restricting the right to strike, including a 1989 law providing for compulsory arbitration of disputes in "essential" industries. Police often harass striking workers. Anti-union discrimination has prevented workers from organizing in most export processing zones (EPZ). The Rosario EPZ south of Manila is particularly notorious for anti-union discrimination and minimum wage violations.

Poland

Polity: Presidential-
parliamentary democracy
Economy: Mixed
capitalist
Population: 38,700,000
PPP: $5,442
Life Expectancy: 72
Ethnic Groups: Polish (98 percent), German (1 percent), Ukrainian and Byelorussian (1 percent)
Capital: Warsaw

Political Rights: 1
Civil Liberties: 2
Status: Free

Overview: In 1998, negotiations with the European Union (EU) over conditions for membership and the attendant issues of political, social, and economic reforms were key issues for the first-year government of Prime Minister Jerzy Buzek.

In 1997, the Solidarity Electoral Action (AWS) coalition won September's parliamentary elections, ousting President Alexander Kwasniewski's ruling reformed communist Democratic Left Alliance (SLD), which came in second with 164 seats. Buzek, a veteran Solidarity activist, was named to lead a coalition government with the pro-market Freedom Union (UW), which won 60 seats.

Another key issue in 1998 was local elections for a new three-tier administrative structure that reduced the number of provinces (*voivodships*) from 49 to 16, created 300 districts (*powiats*) and retained the *gminas* (townships).

Poland was partitioned by Prussia, Russia, and Austria in the eighteenth century, reemerging as an independent republic after World War I. In 1939, it was invaded and divided by Nazi Germany and Stalinist Russia, coming under full German control after the Nazi invasion of the Soviet Union in 1941. After the war, its eastern territories remained part of the Ukraine but acquired large tracts of eastern Prussia. The Communists gained control after fraudulent elections in 1947.

Roundtable discussions between the opposition and the ruling communists ended post-War Communist dominance in 1989, nine years after the Solidarity trade union first challenged Communist legitimacy and eight years after authorities declared martial law. In 1992, a so-called "Little Constitution" gave considerable power to President Lech Walesa, the former Solidarity leader who had been directly elected president in 1990. A highly fragmented parliament, with some 30 parties, and a powerful president led to a series of failed governments while so-called "shock therapy" market reforms steadily improved economic conditions.

In 1993, voters swept former Communists back into power, and the SLD governed with the support of the Peasant Party (PSL). In March 1995, Prime Minister Waldemar Pawlak of the PSL was replaced by Jozef Oleksy after a three-month crisis during which opposition groups called for a caretaker nonparty government of national unity. Later that year, Kwasniewski defeated President Walesa in a runoff. Oleksy stepped down in January 1996 after charges that he had once worked with Soviet intelligence and was replaced by Wlodzimierz Cimoszewicz. The new government was made up chiefly of SLD and PSL members. In June, AWS, a Solidarity-led coalition of over 30 centrist and right-center parties was created, headed by Solidarity leader Marian Krzaklewski. In the 1997 parliamentary elections, AWS won 33.83 percent of the vote; the SLD, 27.13 percent; the UW, 13.37 percent; the Peasant Party 7.31 percent; and the Movement for the Reconstruction of Poland (ROP), 5.56 percent. Negotiations on forming a government between the AWS and the pro-business UW were often contentious. Leszek Balcerowicz, architect of Poland's post-1990 radical market reforms, was named finance minister.

In November 1998, Poland and the EU, which had in 1997 recommended Poland for eventual membership, held the inaugural meeting on the specific conditions of Poland's membership. The key issues revolved around adapting Poland's legal and administrative system to conform with the formidable body of EU laws and regulations. The EU demanded industrial reforms that would lead to the closure of unprofitable coal mines, the loss of 60,000 to 80,000 jobs, the reduction of steel capacity to sustainable levels, and the full opening of Poland's markets to West European competition. The Buzek government reiterated its support for accelerating privatization to include telecommunications, banking, and the national airlines. The government also was committed to a plan to introduce compulsory private pensions to reduce the burden on the state budget and to radically reform social welfare systems. The government program met with some resistance, with pro-union AWS factions, suspicious of UW influence and concerned about job losses and security. Conservative elements were leery of sacrificing too much national sovereignty for the sake of European integration. While tensions and political infighting flared within the AWS and between the AWS and the UW throughout the year, there was consensus on the need to continue market reforms as well as Poland's commitment to the EU and NATO.

A controversial issue was the restructuring of local government. The government proposed reducing the number of provinces from 49 to 12 under a three-tiered system aimed at giving citizens greater input over the management of public finances, health care, schools, social welfare assistance, and police. The newly created powiats would take over most of the prerogatives of provinces in determining and managing local issues. The restructuring was opposed by the PSL, which objected to the reduction of regions. AWS critics argued that the new system would weaken the unity of the state. After months of debate, the number of provinces was decided at 16, and local elections were held in September. In the vote, AWS and the SLD won most of the provincial assembly seats. One half of the voivodship assemblies would be governed or co-governed by the AWS, and the other half by the SLD. The Social Covenant (PS), which won 89 of the total of 855 assembly seats, was a coalition partner in nine new provinces. The UW won a disappointing 76 seats.

Political Rights and Civil Liberties:

Poles have the means to change their government democratically under a multiparty system. On May 25, 1997, Polish citizens approved a new constitution by referendum. Though 53 percent supported the document, turnout was only 43 percent. The 243-article document, which replaced the 1992 "Little Constitution," confirmed civil and political rights, largely retaining the existing system while weakening some of the appointive powers of the president. It also allowed a presidential veto to be overruled by a vote of three-fifths of the members of parliament rather than two-thirds.

The restructuring of the local government necessitates the need for a new election law, which promises to test the ruling coalition's strength and cohesiveness in 1999, with the AWS proposing a mixed system that would favor large parties.

The constitution guarantees freedom of the press and expression, though there are laws proscribing publicly insulting or deriding the nation and its political system. A 1992 media law transformed state radio and television into joint-stock companies, and led to the growth of private commercial television and radio stations. Over 85 percent of the media has been privatized. There are over 300 newspapers, 119 commercial radio stations (six national stations, five of which are state-owned), as well as ten commercial TV stations. Major private dailies include *Gazeta Wyborcza* (formerly linked to Solidarity) with a circulation of 540,000 daily and 770,000 on weekends; *Rzeczpospolita*, with a circulation of 300,000 daily, and 240,000 on weekends; and *Express Wieczorny*, with a circulation of 140,000 daily, and 400,000 on weekends. State-run television stations, TVP-1 and TVP-2, dominate the market. *Polsat* remains the most popular commercial television network. In 1997, a license for central Poland was granted to TVN, which is owned by the Polish company ITI and the Central European Media Enterprise Group. Private broadcasters face stiff competition from state media, but most are partly owned by well-financed foreign media companies. Major newspapers also have foreign investors, and the print media is restricted to no more than 33 percent of foreign ownership. In November, a new magazine, *Armia* (Army) was launched as the first privately owned publication concerned with the armed forces. The National TV and Radio Council (KRRiTV) is ostensibly independent of the government, but since its nine members are nominated by parliament, the Senate, and the president's office, politics plays a role in its composition. In October, SLD leader Leszek Miller wrote a letter to the prime minister accusing government structures of undermining the independence of the public media by changing the composition of the KRRiTV. He also charged that AWS politicians were meddling in an initiative to sell public television stations. The government flatly denied the charges as politically motivated. RUCH, the national network of newspaper kiosks, remains in state hands, but there is no evidence that the government has used its control over distribution to suppress any publications. Plans to privatize the company were delayed by a civil law suit. PAP, the national wire service, was partially privatized in 1997.

Religious freedom is guaranteed in this overwhelmingly Roman Catholic country. Instances of vandalism against Jewish religious and cultural centers were reported in

1998. In November, the first Jewish book fair in Poland since World War II drew a steady stream of visitors. Tensions exist between the Roman Catholic majority and the Ukrainian Catholic minority in parts of the country with a sizable Ukrainian population. The Roman Catholic Church's most vocal outlet is Radio Maryja, a national station owned by the Redemptorist fathers, who are not directly under the jurisdiction of the Polish church. The station has propelled more than 20 of its own candidates into parliament's lower chamber, elected under a proportional voting system, simply by dictating their names over the air. The popular station has aired thinly veiled anti-Semitic views by its listeners; news broadcasts have criticized EU membership and foreign investment as threatening Poland's sovereignty.

The law provides for freedom of assembly and the government generally respects this right in practice.

Poland has a wide range of political parties estimated to total over 200, but most are small or exist mainly on paper. The existing election law reduced the number of parties in parliament. Poland has about 25,000 NGOs, including professional, environmental, youth, sports, political, religious, cultural, women's, and democracy-building groups, as well as public policy think tanks, educational and academic associations, and charitable organizations.

The constitution (Articles 12 and 57) and laws allow for the formation of independent trade unions. Under law, ten persons may form a local union, and 30 may establish a national union. Unions must be registered with the courts. In 1997, the number of unions rose from 318 to 350. The principal union federations are the National Alliance of Trade Unions (OPZZ), the successor of its Communist-era namesake, and the Independent Self-governing Trade Union Solidarity (NSZZ). In March 1998, the OPZZ claimed it had 2.5 million members, more than 14,000 workplace organizations, and more than 100 industrial federations. The NSZZ has a verified, dues-paying membership of 1.4 million. The country's two million private farmers and agricultural workers are organized in local and regional associations, unions, cooperatives, and marketing groups. Agrarian interests are represented by Rural Solidarity. In March 1998, Solidarity's mining union attacked government plans to close unprofitable coal mines and cut tens of thousands of jobs. The OPZZ also opposed job cuts and reductions in social welfare and health care. In June, railway workers went on strike over wages. In November, employees at an aeronautics plant in Mielec went on strike over back wages. Rural Solidarity staged a series of protests against a planned ten-year transition period for Poland's agriculture following the country's entry into the EU. Under the plan, Poland's farmers would be ineligible for Common Agricultural Policy subsidies, which leaders said would make Poland's farm products less competitive in EU markets.

A new Criminal Code and Code of Criminal Procedure went into effect on September 1, 1998, culminating an eight-year effort to restructure the criminal justice system. The law parallels provisions of the constitution that extend the 48-hour "initial arrest" phase permitted under the old law to 72 hours. Judges rule fairly in criminal and civil case, but the courts are plagued by poor administration, lack of trained personnel, bureaucratic delays, and financial problems. In November, the government established a nationwide police unit modeled on the FBI to combat mounting organized crime.

In June, a bill was introduced in parliament that would ban ex-Communists for five to ten years from a range of public posts, ranging from cabinet ministers to judges and managers of publicly owned companies as well as bosses of state-owned radio and television stations. The ban would not apply to directly elected positions, which would contravene the constitution. But the Constitutional Court had earlier rejected a bill that would dismiss judges who cooperated with the Communist regime. In September, legislators approved a bill allowing Poles to view files on them gathered by the security police in the pre-1989 Communist era. The legislation would create an Institute of National Memory, to be begin work in January 1999, that would take control of all archives of the Communist security service as well as those of courts, prosecutors' offices, the Communist Party, and other institutions. President Kwasniewski, who has opposed lustration measures, is empowered to veto both bills, and it would be difficult to muster the three-fifths majority needed to override his veto.

Freedom of movement is not restricted, and Poles can chose their place of residence and employment. Property rights are secure under law, though registries in land, companies, and property liens are not fully developed. In general, laws regarding the creation of new businesses are fairly liberal and transparent. While there was a measure of "insider" privatization by the *nomenklatura* and Communist-era managers in the early phase of privatization in the early to mid-1990s, the government has encouraged competition and the development of medium- and small-scale businesses and has promoted equality of opportunity.

The constitution guarantees equality of the sexes. Women are represented in government, business, and educational institutions. There are scores of women's organizations and advocacy groups concerned with issues ranging from domestic violence to women's rights.

Portugal

Polity: Presidential-parliamentary democracy
Economy: Mixed capitalist
Population: 10,000,000
PPP: $12,674
Life Expectancy: 75
Ethnic Groups: Portuguese, African minority
Capital: Lisbon

Political Rights: 1
Civil Liberties: 1
Status: Free

Overview:

Portugal has been ruled by Prime Minister Antonio Guterres' minority Socialist government since 1995. Despite opposition from small left- and right-wing groups, the ruling Socialists and opposition Social Democrats both support the country's entry into the European Monetary Union in 1999.

In October, Guterres announced new programs to combat corruption and tighten controls on campaign financing. In November, however, he suffered a major setback when his plan to divide Portugal into eight regions with some degree of autonomy was defeated in a national referendum.

Formerly a great maritime and colonial empire, Portugal ended its monarchy in a bloodless revolution in 1910. The republic, plagued by chronic instability and violence, ended in a military revolt in 1926. A fascist dictatorship under Antonio Salazar lasted from 1932 to 1968. In 1968, the dying Salazar was replaced by his lieutenant, Marcello Caetano. During what is now termed the "Marcello Spring," repression and censorship were relaxed somewhat, and a liberal wing developed inside the one-party National Assembly. In 1974, Caetano was overthrown in a bloodless coup by the Armed Forces Movement, which opposed the ongoing colonial war in Mozambique and Angola. A transition to democracy then began with the election of a constitutional assembly that adopted a democratic constitution in 1976. The constitution was revised in 1982 to bring the military under civilian control, curb the president's powers, and abolish an unelected "Revolutionary Council." In 1989, a second revision of the constitution provided for further privatization of nationalized industries and state-owned media.

The election of the Socialist Party's Jorge Sampaio as president in 1996 marked the end of a conservative era in which Portugal benefited economically, but failed to satisfy its voters' eagerness for social change. In his ten years as prime minister, Social Democrat Anibal Cavaco Silva led the country into the European Union, launched an ambitious privatization program, and channeled massive funding into the country's infrastructure. Sampaio has vowed to continue economic reforms, but he won popularity by adding a social dimension to his agenda. In the minds of constituents, issues such as education, health, housing, and the environment have assumed greater importance.

Political Rights and Civil Liberties:

The Portuguese can change their government democratically. In direct, competitive elections, voters, including a large number of Portuguese living abroad, select both the president and members of parliament. The president, who also commands the country's armed forces, is elected to a five-year term. The president receives advice from the Council of State, which includes six senior civilian officials, former presidents, five members chosen by the legislature, and five chosen by the president. The country's unicameral legislature includes up to 235 deputies.

With the exception of fascist organizations, political association is unrestricted. Members of small, extreme right groups, however, have run candidates for public office without interference. In 1997, the constitution was amended to allow immigrants to vote in presidential elections.

Portuguese courts are autonomous and operate only under the restraints of established law and the constitution. They include a Constitutional Court, a Supreme Court of Justice, and judicial courts of the first and second instance. Separate administrative courts address administrative and tax disputes. They are generally noted for their adherence to traditional principles of independent jurisprudence, but inefficient bureaucratic organization has created an enormous backlog of cases in the system.

Freedoms of speech and assembly are respected with few exceptions. Although the law forbids insults directed at the government or the armed forces and those intended to undermine the rule of law, the state has never prosecuted cases under this provision. Human rights organizations have repeatedly criticized Portugal for the occasional beating of prisoners and other detainees. In general, prison conditions are poor.

The print media, which are owned by political parties and private publishers, are free and competitive. Until 1990, all television and radio media, with the exception of the Roman Catholic radio station, were state-owned. Although television broadcasting is dominated by the state-owned Radioteleivisao Portuguesa, two independent stations have operated in recent years.

Workers have the right to strike and are represented by competing Communist and non-Communist organizations. In recent years, the two principal labor federations, the General Union of Workers and the General Confederation of Portuguese Workers Intersindical, have charged "clandestine" companies with exploiting child labor in the impoverished north.

The status of women has improved with economic modernization. Concentrated in agriculture and domestic service, women workers now comprise 37 percent of the official labor force. Despite a few prominent exceptions, female representation in government and politics averages less than ten percent. Sexual harassment is only illegal if committed by a superior in the workplace.

⬆ Qatar

Polity: Traditional monarchy
Economy: Capitalist-statist
Population: 500,000
PPP: $19,772
Life Expectancy: 71
Ethnic Groups: Arab (40 percent), Pakistani (18 percent), Indian (18 percent), Iranian (10 percent), other (14 percent)
Capital: Doha

Political Rights: 7
Civil Liberties: 6
Status: Not Free

Trend arrow: Qatar receives an upward trend arrow due to a growing effort by the country's ruling family to introduce limited democratic reforms.

Overview:

In a growing effort by the ruling al-Thani family to introduce limited democratic reforms, Qatar began preparing in 1998 for municipal council elections to be held in early 1999. Although the exact functions and powers of the proposed council have not yet been clarified, it is regarded as a significant development in a region where rulers traditionally oppose sharing power with their constituents.

Qatar became a British protectorate in 1919, and gained independence when Great Britain withdrew from the Persian Gulf in 1971. Under the 1970 Basic Law, an *emir* is chosen from adult males of the al-Thani family. The Basic Law also provides for a council of ministers and a partially elected *majlis al shura*, or advisory council. In practice, the 35-member majlis is appointed, and no elections have ever been held.

In 1995, Crown Prince Hamad, long recognized as the real power in the country, deposed his father in a palace coup while the emir vacationed in Switzerland. Since then, the new emir has called for greater political openness, and some small steps have been taken toward that end. Press censorship was formally lifted in 1995, and Sheik Hamad has announced plans to increase popular participation in government. In early 1998, the emirate held direct elections to the board of the powerful chamber of commerce and industry. By the end of 1998, the government had raised the possibility of a directly elected parliament.

The emir introduced a draft law in the December 1997 opening session of the majlis providing for direct election of a 29-member municipal council. In July 1998, the emir introduced a law providing for the organization of the municipal council and enacted an electoral law by decree. Under the new law, the council will be elected by secret ballot on the basis of universal suffrage. In a radical departure from the practices of traditional Arab governments, all citizens over age 18, including women, will be allowed to vote. Furthermore, all citizens over age 25, including women, will be allowed to stand as candidates. The elections are scheduled for March 1999.

Since public pressure to reform is virtually nonexistent in Qatar, many have speculated about the emir's motives for promoting political openness. One explanation is that Sheikh Hamad sees gradual democratization as conducive to long-term economic development. Another is that by boosting the legitimacy of government, Qatar might prevent the type of violent civil unrest occurring in other Arab states, like neighboring Bahrain.

Qatar announced in late 1998 that it would accept international arbitration in a long-standing dispute with Bahrain. The 200-year-old dispute involves a group of tiny islands along Qatar's west coast which are claimed by both countries but controlled by Bahrain. The case has been submitted to the International Court of Justice in The Hague.

Political Rights and Civil Liberties:

Qataris cannot change their government democratically. Political parties are illegal, and elections have never been held. The emir holds absolute power and appoints his cabinet. While the emir consults with leading members of society on policy issues and works to reach a consensus with the appointed Majlis, the only recourse for ordinary citizens is to submit appeals to the emir.

The security apparatus includes the Interior Ministry's *Mubahathat* (Investigatory Police), which handles sedition and espionage cases, and the military's *Mukhabarat* (Intelligence Service), which monitors political dissidents. Both services can detain suspects indefinitely without charge while conducting investigations, though long-term detention occurs infrequently.

The judiciary is not independent. Most judges are foreign nationals whose residence permits may be revoked at any time. Civil courts have jurisdiction in civil and commercial disputes, while Islamic *Shari'a* courts handle criminal and family cases. Shari'a court trials are closed to the general public, although family members are permitted. Lawyers help participants prepare cases but are not permitted in the courtroom. Non-Muslims may not bring suits to the Shari'a courts. In 1998, the Qatari Higher Criminal court continued to hear the case of 132 defendants charged with plotting to overthrow the Qatari regime in a failed coup attempt in 1996. Forty of the defendants are being tried in absentia, having fled the country.

Freedoms of speech, expression, and press are severely restricted. Public criticism of the ruling family or of Islam is forbidden. The emir ended formal censorship in 1995, though newspapers have been shut down twice since then for publishing articles deemed contrary to Qatar's interests. Self-censorship is pervasive. The Ministry of Endowments and Islamic Affairs censors cable television and imported print material.

In a move expected to reduce the incidence of censorship, Qatar dismantled its information ministry in March 1998 and delegated some of its functions to other ministries. The electronic media are state-owned and promote only official views, with the exception of al-Jazeera, a Qatari-based, all-news satellite television channel. Presenting interviews with dissidents and exiles from throughout the region as well as lively debates which include opposition views, al-Jazeera has captivated Middle Eastern viewers and prompted furious protests from regional leaders.

Freedom of association is limited to private social, sports, trade, professional, and cultural societies which must be registered with the government. Political parties do not exist, and participation in international professional organizations critical of the government is prohibited, as are political demonstrations.

Foreign nationals employed as domestic workers face sexual harassment and physical abuse. Although the authorities have investigated and punished several employers, most women apparently do not report abuse for fear of losing their residence permits. Some 25,000 Egyptian nationals live in Qatar, but hiring Egyptians was banned in 1996 when Egypt was accused by Qatari authorities of involvement in the failed coup that year. Some 500 Egyptians have been fired from government jobs since November 1997, when Egypt boycotted an economic conference attended by Israel in Doha.

Women face social and legal discrimination in divorce and inheritance matters. A woman needs permission from a male relative to obtain a driver's license. A woman's right to refuse a marriage proposal is becoming widely accepted, whereas just five years ago it was not. Women enjoy greater opportunity in employment and education than they did under the former emir. In what has been termed a "giant step forward," women were allowed to watch as well as compete in an international track meet in Doha in May 1998, though they were required to abide by conservative dress regulations.

The Wahabbi branch of Sunni Islam is the state religion. Non-Muslims may not worship publicly and face discrimination in employment.

Workers may not form unions or bargain collectively. They may belong to "joint consultative committees" of worker and management representatives that discuss such issues as working conditions and work schedules, but not wages. The government's Labor Conciliation Board mediates disputes. Workers, excepting those in government or domestic employment, may strike if mediation fails. Strikes rarely occur in practice, however, because employers may dismiss workers after the Board has heard a case. Employers sometimes exercise leverage over foreign workers by refusing to grant mandatory exit permits.

Romania

Polity: Presidential-par- **Political Rights:** 2
liamentary democracy **Civil Liberties:** 2
Economy: Mixed statist **Status:** Free
(transitional)
Population: 22,500,000
PPP: $4,431
Life Expectancy: 69
Ethnic Groups: Romanian (89 percent), Hungarian (9 percent), other,
including German, Ukrainian, Serb, Croat, Russian, Turkish, Gypsy (2 percent)
Capital: Bucharest

Overview:

On March 31, 1998, after months of political wrangling which had brought economic reform to a virtual standstill, Prime Minister Victor Ciorbea resigned when the Liberals and Democrats, members of the ruling coalition led by his Democratic Convention (CDR), withdrew their support. In January, the Democrats, the coalition's second-biggest party led by Petre Roman, triggered the crisis by claiming that Ciorbea was incapable of implementing the government's tough reform program launched in 1997 and by withdrawing their ministers from the cabinet. After the leader of Ciorbea's own National Peasant Party publicly withdrew his backing, he was compelled to step down.

In November 1996, the center-right coalition had swept to power, ousting President Ion Iliescu, who had ruled the country since the 1989 revolution that toppled Communist strongman Nicolae Ceausescu. Reformer Emil Constantinescu defeated Iliescu in a runoff, and the CDR won 122 seats in the Chamber of Deputies (lower house), and 53 in the Senate. Iliescu's Party of Social Democracy of Romania (PSDR) took 91 and 41; the Social Democratic Union (USD, of which Roman's Democratic Party was the largest element), 53 and 23; the Hungarian-based Hungarian Democratic Union (UDMR) 25 and 12; the ultra-nationalist Greater Romanian Party (PRM), 19 and 8; and the far-right Romanian National Unity Party (PUNR), 18 and 7. Ciorbea, a lawyer, lead a CDR-USD-UDMR coalition government.

Romania became independent following the 1878 Berlin Congress. It gained territory after World War I, but lost some to the Soviet Union and Bulgaria in 1940. Soviet troops entered the country in 1944, whereupon King Michael dismissed the pro-German regime and backed the Allies. In 1945, he was forced to accept a Communist-led coalition government. Ceausescu's autarkic economics and repressive governance devastated Romania during his rule from 1965-1988. A popular uprising and palace coup by disgruntled Communists toppled Ceausescu, who was tried and executed on Christmas 1989. A provisional government was formed under President Iliescu, a high-ranking Communist and leader of the National Salvation Front (NSF). The 1992 parliamentary elections saw the NSF split between neo-Communist and more reformist members.

On April 1, 1998, President Constantinescu asked Radu Vasile, a proreform economist, senator, and general-secretary of the National Peasant Party, to form a government. The new government faced economic stagnation. Late payments by unreformed state enterprises climbed to $7 billion, about a fifth of GDP. The economy, which shrank seven percent in 1997, shrank by some four percent in 1998. Petre Roman's Democrats, with links to businessmen who would be hurt by reforms that would increase competition and make firms more answerable to private owners, showed little interest in helping the government succeed before the general election due in 2000.

The ruling coalition was also plagued by infighting within the Peasants Party, between paternalistic, conservative, and nationalist elements and more pragmatic politicians aligned with the prime minister. The conservative wing, nicknamed the *Taliban* (after Afghanistan's ruling Islamic fundamentalists), exacerbated relations with the other governing parties, particularly the Hungarian UDMR. In September, Finance Minister Daniel Daianu was dismissed after the Liberals threatened to leave the coalition.

In another important issue, U.S. Senator William Roth, head of the North Atlantic Assembly, said in mid-November that Romania would not be ready for NATO membership in 1999.

Political Rights and Civil Liberties: Romanians can change their government democratically under a multiparty system enshrined in a 1991 post-Communist constitution. The OSCE judged the 1996 presidential and parliamentary elections as "free and generally fair," citing such problems as incomplete voter registration rolls and irregularities in registering candidates.

The 1991 constitution enshrines freedom of expression and the press. Under Law No. 40 of the 1996 Penal Code, journalists face penalties of up to two years' imprisonment for libel and up to five years for disseminating false information that affects Romania's international relations and national security. Most of the print media are private, while electronic media is dominated by state television and radio. Romania has 15 national dailies, three national sports dailies, and many local dailies, most of which are privately owned. There are more than 50 private television stations and over 100 private radio stations. State broadcasters reach the largest rural audience, while private broadcasters do not reach beyond major urban areas. Both public and private broadcasters are regulated by the National Audiovisual Council (NAC). The national broadcaster, Television Romania (TVR), remains the topmost news provider and has the largest audience share in the country. The NAC is subject to political influence, with its top officials appointed by parliament. The chairmen and board of management of both state TV and radio, as well as its 12 members, are not appointed by the NAC but by parliament.

Religious freedom is generally respected, though some Protestant denominations have complained of harassment by local-level officials. The Greek Catholic Church of the Byzantine Rite has had difficulties in regaining property seized under the Communists.

The constitution provides for freedom of assembly, and this right is respected by the government. There were several mass demonstrations and strikes in 1998. In May 1996, Law 27 "On Political Parties" required a political party to have at least 10,000 members before it could be registered, reducing the number of parties from 200 to about 50.

Workers have the right to form unions and strike. The Fratia National Trade Union Confederation claims 3.7 million members. The Alfa Workers Confederation claims one million members. The National Trade Union Block (BNS) is another major confederation. There were several major strikes and job actions in 1998. In March, thousands in Bucharest protested the government's painful economic reforms in demonstrations led by the BNS. Miners in the Jiu Valley, electrical workers, university students, and teachers held strikes.

Under a 1992 law, Romania has a four-tiered legal system: the Supreme Court of Justice; courts of appeals; country courts and the Court of the Municipality of Bucharest; and courts of first instance. Under the law, judges are appointed, promoted, and transferred by the 15-member Higher Council of the Judiciary elected for four-year terms by the two chambers of parliament. To diminish the politicization of the process, a 1997 revision of the law called for the Minister of Justice—not parliament—to appoint the members of the Higher Council. Judges are underpaid and generally under-qualified, and are subject to political pressure and bribery. The Communist-era Criminal Code was replaced by the 1996 Penal Code, which widened the scope of penal law by adding statutes dealing with felonies such as money laundering. Controversial components included Article 200, which punished public homosexual relations, libel statutes, and articles dealing with offense to public authorities. The Helsinki Committee's Association for Human Rights in Romania alleged that police routinely use cruel and abusive tactics. Relations with the Hungarian minority remain strained over amendments to the education law and parliament's reluctance to allow for the creation of a German-Hungarian state university. In March, President Constantinescu made an unprecedented gesture of conciliation by congratulating ethnic Hungarians on their national day—previously a cause of tension and disputes between Romanians and Hungarians, who are concentrated in Transylvania.

Corruption is endemic in the government bureaucracy, civil service, and business. Property rights are secure, though the ability for citizens to start businesses is encumbered by red tape, corruption, bribery, and organized crime.

There are no restrictions on travel within the country, and citizens who want to change their place of residence do not face any official barriers. Women have equal rights with men, and several women's organizations address such issues and job discrimination, domestic violence, and rape.

Russia

Polity: Presidential-parliamentary democracy
Economy: Mixed statist (transitional)
Population: 146,900,000
PPP: $4,531
Life Expectancy: 67

Political Rights: 4*
Civil Liberties: 4
Status: Partly Free

Ethnic Groups: Russian (82 percent), Tatar (4 percent), Ukrainian (3 percent), Chuvash (1 percent), Bashkir (1 percent), Byelorussian (1 percent), other (8 percent)
Capital: Moscow
Ratings change: Russia's political rights rating changed from 3 to 4 due to corruption, the assassination of a leading opposition parliamentarian, and the weakening of the government.

Overview:

In 1998, Russia was plagued by political and economic uncertainty highlighted by three different prime ministers, numerous government reshuffles, President Boris Yeltsin's recurrent health problems, and the collapse of financial markets and the ruble. In addition, Russia experienced the assassination of a leading opposition member of parliament and increased restiveness among its regions, in addition to growing reluctance by the International Monetary Fund (IMF) and other Western lenders to bail out a weakened and demoralized state which was incapable or unwilling to implement true market and fiscal reforms, collect taxes, fight endemic corruption, and weed out cronyism and inefficiency.

Meanwhile, diminished central authority and the lack of civil society and democratic institutions left large segments of the economy and media in the control of a handful of financial-industrial oligarchs; their power, however, was attenuated by the summer's financial crisis that saw the collapse of the ruble, the stock market, and several banks.

With the USSR's collapse in December 1991, Russia—the only constituent republic not to declare sovereignty—gained de facto independence under President Yeltsin, directly elected in June 1991. In 1993, Yeltsin put down a putsch led by hard-line elements in parliament, and Russians approved a constitution which established a bicameral Federal Assembly: a Federation Council (Upper House) consisting of two representatives from the country's eighty-nine regions and territories, and a 450-member State Duma.

In December 1995 parliamentary elections, the Communist Party took 157 seats; Our Home is Russia, 55; the Liberal Democrats, 51; Yabloko, 45; the Agrarians, 20; Democratic Choice, 9; Power to the People, 9; the Russian Communities, 5; and Women of Russia, 3. Independents accounted for 77 seats, and the rest went to smaller parties. In the 1996 presidential vote, Yeltsin edged out Communist Party leader Gennady Zyuganov 35 to 32 percent, with Alexander Lebed getting 14 percent. Yeltsin handily won July's runoff, 53.85 percent to 40.31 percent. His bid was supported and financed by powerful financial-industrial interests, who controlled important media outlets.

In March 1998, an embattled President Yeltsin fired Prime Minister Viktor Chernomyrdin and his entire cabinet that included economic reformers such as Anatoly Chubais. The move sparked a political crisis, as the Communist and hardline dominated parliament initially refused to confirm Sergei Kiriyenko, the little-known minister of fuel and energy, as prime minister. After rejecting Kiriyenko twice, parliament approved the nomination in April rather than risk dissolution and new elections as required by the constitution.

The new prime minister faced Russia's most serious financial crisis since the collapse of the Soviet Union, sparked partly by the fall of oil prices and the Asian economic downturn. In June, the government announced a sweeping fiscal package to stabilize markets, including spending cuts and an emergency tax-collection program to close a large budget deficit. Reformer Chubais was brought back as a deputy prime minister and placed in charge of relations with international lending institutions. The government stated it would need $15 billion in assistance from international lenders as stocks, bonds, and the ruble continued to plummet and interest rates soared. In July, parliament rejected the government's tax-and-spending reforms, forcing President Yeltsin to adopt the anti-crisis program by decree.

In August, the ruble collapsed, forcing devaluation, and the stock market nosedivided, setting off a further crisis as the country faced near default on foreign and domestic debt and the possible collapse of the banking system. In response, President Yeltsin replaced Prime Minister Kiriyenko with Chernomyrdin, the man he had fired in

March. Boris Nemtsov, a prominent reformer, resigned as deputy prime minister. With runs on banks, oligarchs in charge of larger banks cast off old rivalries, as Uneximbank, MOST Bank, and Mentap announced a merger. After the government announced terms of a restructuring of $40 billion of debt, which was expected to drive away foreign investors, the Central Bank canceled sales of U.S. dollars to banks and institutions and suspended all foreign exchange trade in the ruble. There were increased calls in parliament for Yeltsin's resignation, as Communists and other opposition members threatened to block Chernomyrdin's nomination. The political deadlock was broken in September with the appointment of former foreign minister and ex-head of Russian intelligence Yevgeny Primakov as prime minister. Yuri Maslyukov, a former head of the Soviet central planning agency Gosplan, was named first deputy prime minister overseeing the economy. Viktor Gerashchenko, who headed the Central Bank from 1992 to 1994 but was fired when the ruble lost three-quarters of its value, was re-appointed to the post. The new government, which did not include any well-known reformers, signaled a return to greater spending and state control, to printing more money in order to pay off state debts, and to less emphasis on tax collection as demanded by foreign creditors.

At the end of October, the government approved an economic crisis program that included price controls and support to industries, as well as an overhaul of the banking system. Negotiations with the IMF on resuming a $22.6 billion bailout, frozen after the August crisis, continued in December as the ruble continue to slide and inflation crept up. In November, President Yeltsin was hospitalized with pneumonia. In a move that raised concerns among reformers and democrats regarding a concentration of power, Yeltsin announced the appointment of a new chief of staff, Nikolai Bordyuzha, a veteran of the KGB, who also became secretary of the president's Security Council.

In other issues, on November 20, Galina Stratovoitova, a leader of the reformist party Democratic Russia in parliament, was gunned down in St. Petersburg by unknown gunmen. Her murder dramatically underscored the state of lawlessness in Russia, where several bankers, political figures, and businessmen had been murdered during the year.

Several regions and localities in Russia took advantage of the turmoil in Moscow to press for greater autonomy. In November, Kalmykia threatened to secede, and several regions in Siberia used their hold over federal income to press for more control of resources. In October, Prime Minister Primakov flew to the breakaway republic of Chechnya and promised funds to restore the war-shattered economy.

In foreign affairs, Russia and Japan signed an agreement over the disputed Kuril Islands. Russia and China settled a border dispute during a visit to Moscow by Chinese President Jiang Zamin in November, and the Russian parliament ratified a long-delayed friendship treaty with Ukraine. In December, Russia and Belarus announced plans to merge into a single state under a union agreement. U.S.-Russian relations were strained over Russian technology sales to Iran.

Political Rights and Civil Liberties:

Russians have the means to change their government democratically. The 1993 constitution established a strong presidency, but decentralization and institutional checks limit executive authority. The 1995 parliamentary elections were generally free and fair, though over one million votes were invalidated, and the presidential race in 1996 was also free and fair, though several regional governor's races were marred by ballot stuffing, incomplete voter lists and other irregularities.

The 1993 constitution guarantees the freedom of mass media (Article 29) and prohibits censorship. Libel laws have become a common form of intimidation by public officials. While some 80 percent of Russia's 6,000 newspapers and 4,000 magazines have been technically privatized, all but a few receive some form of government subsidies. Russian Television (RTR) and Russian Public Television (ORT), of which the government owns 51 percent of the shares, transmit nationwide and to most of the former Soviet Union. Other nationwide TV stations are NTV and TV-6. Increasingly, Russia's powerful financial groups have acquired control of or fund most major media assets. Because many major media outlets receive some measure of government subsidy and/ or have outside sponsors or private owners with connections to the government, editorial independence has been compromised, particularly over the last several years. *Oblast* or local-level officials exert political pressure, particularly in regions and *krais* where there is competition between local elites. Local authorities and criminal groups routinely threaten and harass journalists. In 1998, the upcoming presidential elections in 2000 and the economic crisis impacted the media. In November, court officials threatened to seize equipment and furniture from ORT for nonpayment of debts to various creditors. On the same day, firemen demanded that the influential *Ekho Moskvy* radio station be shut down for failing to meet safety standards. In March, parliament discussed amendments to the mass media law that could force publishers of electronic information on the Internet to register and obtain a license.

Freedom of religion is generally respected in this primarily Russian Orthodox country. However, in September 1997, President Yeltsin signed a controversial law on religion which favors established religions with national organizations and 15 years of existence. The law aroused international condemnation and protests by Russia's Catholics, Baptists, Pentecostals, and Seventh-Day Adventists. Under a new regulation, foreign religious workers are allowed to stay in Russia for only three months at a time. In September, a group calling itself the Committee for the Rescue of Youth sought to have the Jehovah's Witnesses registration revoked. A Moscow judge delayed court proceedings in the case until February 1999. In October, the issue of anti-Semitism came to the fore when Communist lawmaker Albert Makashov blamed the country's problems on *zhidy*, a derogatory term for Jews.

Freedoms of assembly are generally respected. Through the year, there were many political rallies, anti-government demonstrations, and worker protests. Political parties are allowed to organize. In December 1996, the State Duma passed a law to limit so-called "divan parties," in which all members could fit on a single sofa. The law stipulates that only a group of at least 100 people can found a political party. Parties that seek to violently change the constitutional order or to violate the territorial integrity of the Russian Federation would be prohibited, as would the creation of armed groups or parties that promote racial, ethnic, and religious hatred. In 1998, many new parties and blocs were formed in anticipation of presidential and parliamentary elections in 1999 and 2000. In November, Moscow Mayor Yuri Luzhkov, a potential presidential candidate, announced the formation of a centrist Fatherland Party. Former Prime Minister Kiriyenko set up a party that would run in parliamentary elections.

The Federation of Independent Unions of Russia, a successor to the Soviet-era federation, claims 60 million members (estimates put the figure at 39 million). Newer, independent unions represent between 500,000 and one million workers, including seafarers, dock workers, air traffic controllers, pilots, and some coal miners. In March and April, there were several wage protests staged by unions around the country. Coal miners went on strike in May, and teachers in several Siberian towns went on strike in December to protest wage arrears. Some 3,000 nuclear workers held a one-day strike in November in Snezhinsk, a closed city in the Urals, to demand unpaid wages.

The judiciary is not fully independent and is subject to political interference and corruption. Independence is also threatened by chromic under-funding and by its subordinate position in relation to the executive and the legislature. The Federal Security Service (FSB), which replaced the KGB, has faced persistent allegations that its members moonlight as bodyguards, contract killers, and kidnappers. Pretrial detention centers are generally deplorable, and prisoners who are presumed innocent often languish in overcrowded cells and are subject to violence and abuse.

Corruption in the civil service, government, and business is pervasive. Members of the old Soviet-Communist elite used insider information, contacts, and extra-legal means to obtain control of key industrial and business sectors. Transparency International has ranked Russia among the more corrupt countries it rates.

While the constitution explicitly protects private property, the checkered protection of these rights by parliament and the judicial system limits the protections afforded by the constitution. Enforcement of intellectual property rights is lagging. Corruption, regulations, vague commercial laws, and bureaucratic obstacles impede private business, and organized crime, which includes murder and extortion, is rampant.

In 1997, a new internal passport system dropped a "nationality listing." The *propiska* system that controls residency and movement is still widely in force. Citizens must register to live and work in a specific area within seven days of moving there.

Women enjoy equal protection under law and are well represented in education and government. But domestic violence, discrimination, and societal norms remain serious problems.

Rwanda

Polity: Dominant party (military-dominated)
Economy: Mixed statist
Population: 8,00,000
PPP:na
Life Expectancy: 43
Ethnic Groups: Hutu (80 percent), Tutsi (19 percent), Twa [Pygmy] (1 percent)
Capital: Kigali

Political Rights: 7
Civil Liberties: 6
Status: Not Free

Overview: Killings and disappearances ascribed to government security forces and Hutu rebels continued unabated in the Rwandan countryside as the conflict between Rwanda's two principal ethnic groups continued. The Tutsi-controlled government's Rwanda Patriotic Army (RPA) pursued a ruthless campaign to suppress Hutu insurgents in northwestern Rwanda. Several thousand civilians are believed to have been killed. Many people were also murdered by Hutu militias seeking to overthrow the government. Local officials and Tutsi survivors of the genocide were particular targets of the Hutu militias. The 1994 genocide, in which more than 500,000 Tutsis were slaughtered before an RPA guerrilla force defeated the Hutu-controlled regime, sparked massive dislocations and eventually war in neighboring Zaire, now the Democratic Republic of Congo, where Rwanda has supported two rebellions against the authorities in Kinshasa. Approximately 130,000 suspects in the genocidal killings are now detained in massively overcrowded Rwandan jails. In November, Rwandan authorities announced that it would release more than 30,000 of these due to lack of evidence. Trials of alleged perpetrators continued in Rwanda and at an international tribunal in the northern Tanzanian city of Arusha. In April, 24 people convicted of participation in the genocide were publicly shot after what independent observers described as grossly unfair trials. The RPA has dismissed strong evidence that its soldiers massacred Rwandan Hutu refugees during its 1997 military campaign with rebels in the former Zaire.

Rwanda's ethnic divide is deeply rooted. National boundaries demarcated by Belgian colonists obliged competition for power within the fixed borders of a modern state. Traditional and Belgian-abetted Tutsi dominance ended with a Hutu rebellion in 1959 and independence in 1962. Hundreds of thousands of Tutsi were killed or fled the country in recurring violence during the next decades. In 1990, the Tutsi-led Rwanda Patriotic Front (RPF) launched a guerrilla war to force the Hutu regime led by General Juvenal Habyarimana to accept power-sharing and the return of Tutsi refugees. Hutu chauvinists' solution to claims to land and power by Rwanda's Tutsi minority, which constituted approximately 15 percent of the pre-genocide population, was to pursue their elimination as a people.

The 1994 genocide was launched after the suspicious deaths of President Habyarimana and Burundian President Cyprien Ntaryamira in a plane crash in Kigali. The ensuing massacres had been well plotted. Piles of imported machetes were distributed, and death lists were broadcast by radio. A small UN force in Rwanda fled as the killings spread and Tutsi rebels advanced. French troops intervened in late 1994 not to halt the genocide, but in a futile effort to preserve some territory for the crumbling genocidal regime that was a close client of France.

International relief efforts that eased the suffering among more than two million Hutu refugees along Rwanda's frontiers also allowed retraining and rearming of large numbers of former government troops. The United Nations, which had earlier ignored specific warnings of the 1994 genocide, failed to prevent such activities. The Rwandan war has become inextricably bound in the Congo's conflict, and former Hutu soldiers are now reportedly joining the Congolese government, which is also supported by Chadian, Namibian, and Zimbabwean forces. Rwandan and Ugandan troops supporting the rebels hope to keep their frontiers clear of insurgent activity, and the fighting could spread into a wider war. This climate of unrest makes early improvements in the exercise of human rights and fundamental freedoms very unlikely.

Political Rights and Civil Liberties: Rwandans have never enjoyed their right to choose their representatives in open elections. The last elections were closely-managed 1988 contests under a one-party state. The current self-appointed government is dominated by the RPF, but also includes several other political parties. A 70-member multiparty national assembly was appointed in November 1994. No schedule for elections has been set, and polls are not possible under current security conditions.

Rwanda's basic charter is the Fundamental Law, an amalgam of the 1991 constitution, two agreements among various parties and groups, and the RPF's own 1994 declaration of governance. Two political parties closely identified with the 1994 massacres are banned, and parties based on ethnicity or religion barred. Several other political parties operate and participate in government. The RPF has continued its high-profile efforts to include Hutu representatives in government, including the appointment of President Pasteur Bizimungu.

Constitutional and legal safeguards regarding arrest procedures and detention are widely ignored. The near destruction of Rwanda's legal system and the death or exile of most of the judiciary are severely limiting criminal adjudication.

Rwandan media are officially censored and constrained by fears of reprisals. Several journalists accused of abetting or participating in genocide are in detention. The state controls broadcast media, and the few independent newspapers publishing in Kigali reportedly exercise considerable self-censorship. The role of the media in Rwanda has become a contentious test case for media freedom and responsibility. During the genocide, 50 journalists were murdered, while others broadcast incitements to the slaughter.

Local nongovernmental organizations such as the Collective Rwandan Leagues and Associations for the Defense of Human Rights operate openly. International human rights groups and relief organizations are also active. While numerous clerics were among both the victims and perpetrators of the genocide, religious freedom is generally respected.

There is serious de facto discrimination against women despite legal protection for equal rights. Rape by Hutu soldiers and militias was widespread in 1994. Women are being forced to take on many new roles, especially in the countryside where the dearth of males necessitates their performance of many traditionally male tasks. Constitutional provisions for labor rights include the right to form trade unions, engage in collective bargaining, and strike. The Central Union of Rwandan Workers, which was closely controlled by the previous regime, is now independent.

St. Kitts-Nevis

Polity: Parliamentary
democracy
Economy: Capitalist
Population: 40,000
PPP: $10,150
Life Expectancy: 67
Ethnic Groups: Black (95 percent), mulatto
Capital: Basseterre

Political Rights: 1
Civil Liberties: 2
Status: Free

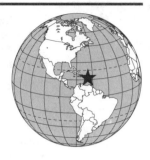

Overview:

In 1998, St. Kitts and Nevis survived a political gale—a decision by the Nevis parliament a year earlier to end its federation with St. Kitts which was defeated in a referendum, only to be hit full force in September by Hurricane Georges. Some 85 percent of St. Kitt's housing was damaged to varying degrees, with extensive damage to the air and seaport, schools, hotels, the sugar industry, the power station, and other economic infrastructure. St. Kitts suffered an estimated $440 million in damage, and Nevis $39 million.

The national government is comprised of the prime minister, the cabinet, and the bicameral legislative assembly. Elected assembly members, eight from St. Kitts and three from Nevis, serve five-year terms. Senators, who are not to exceed two-thirds of the elected members, are appointed—one by the leader of the parliamentary opposition for every two by the prime minister. The British monarch is represented by a governor-general who appoints as prime minister the leader of the party or coalition with at least a plurality of seats in the legislature. Nevis has a local assembly comprised of five elected and three appointed members and pays for all its own services except police and foreign relations. St. Kitts has no similar body. Nevis is accorded the constitutional right to secede if two-thirds of the elected legislators approve and two-thirds of voters endorse it through a referendum.

The center-right People's Action Movement (PAM) gained power in 1980 with Nevis Restoration Party (NRP) support. In 1983, the country achieved independence, and the PAM-NRP coalition won majorities in the 1984 and 1989 elections.

In the 1993 elections, the St. Kitts Labour Party (SKLP) and the PAM each won four seats, though the former won the popular vote. The Concerned Citizens Movement (CCM) took two Nevis seats and the NRP one. The CCM opted not to join the coalition, leaving a PAM-NRP to rule with a five-seat plurality.

SKLP leader Denzil Douglas protested the new government, and violence erupted, leading to a two-week state of emergency. The SKLP boycotted parliament in 1994. The PAM government was shaken by a drugs-and-murder scandal that same year, and the weakened government agreed to hold early elections.

In the July 1995 elections, the SKLP won seven of eight St. Kitts seats and 60 percent of the popular vote. The PAM took the eighth St. Kitts seat and 40 percent of the popular vote. On Nevis, the CCM retained its two seats and the NRP held on to the third. Following the vote, the PAM alleged that the SKLP dismissed or demoted PAM supporters and filled their positions with SKLP supporters.

In July 1996, Nevis premier Vance Armory, reacting to St. Kitts' unwelcome move to open a government office in Nevis, announced his intention to break the 100-year political link between the two islands. On October 13, 1997, Nevis' five-person parliament unanimously voted for succession. However, in an August 10 referendum, successionists won a simple majority of the vote, falling short of the two-thirds margin required by the constitution.

The amount of cocaine passing through the Caribbean en route to the U.S. has reportedly doubled in recent years. St. Kitts is one of more than 10 Caribbean islands to sign drug enforcement pacts with the United States. Nevis has more than 10,000 offshore businesses, operating under strict secrecy laws, and CCM successionists argued these were the bedrock of island strength in a global economy. However, a principal argument used against succession was that Nevis alone could not withstand the wiles of drug traffickers and money launderers. Nevis has resisted central government efforts to impose stiffer regulations on the crime-prone industry.

Political Rights and Civil Liberties:

Citizens are able to change their government democratically. In the run-up to the succession referendum, Douglas promised to give Nevis a bigger role in federation affairs. Constitutional guarantees regarding free expression, the free exercise of religion, and the right to organize political parties, labor unions, and civic organizations are generally respected.

Drugs and money laundering have corrupted the political system. Apart from the 1995 drug-and-murder scandal, whose three hung juries suggest jury tampering and intimidation, there are also questions regarding business relations between SKLP leaders and known drug trafficker Noel "Zambo" Heath, one of three alleged traffickers with government ties whose extradition has been sought unsuccessfully by the United States. In June 1997, despite concerns of its cost to a country of 42,000 people, parliament passed a bill designed to create a 50-member army to wage war on heavily armed drug traffickers.

The judiciary is generally independent. However, in March 1996, when the drug-and-murder scandal came to trial, the Public Prosecutions Office failed to send a representative to present the case. The charges were dropped, raising suspicions of a government conspiracy. The highest court is the West Indies Supreme Court in St. Lucia, which includes a Court of Appeal and a High Court. Under certain circumstances there is a right of appeal to the Privy Council in London.

The traditionally strong rule of law has been tested by the increase in drug-related crime and corruption. In 1995, it appeared that the police had become divided along political lines between the two main political parties. The national prison is overcrowded and conditions are abysmal. In July of 1998, a convicted murderer was hanged, ending a 13-year hiatus in executions and defying pressure from Britain and human rights groups to end the death penalty.

Television and radio on St. Kitts are government owned, and opposition parties habitually claim the ruling party takes unfair advantage; Prime Minister Douglas has pledged to privatize St. Kitts television and radio. Each major political party publishes a weekly or fortnightly newspaper. Opposition publications freely criticize the government and international media are available.

The main labor union, the St. Kitts Trades and Labour Union, is associated with the ruling SKLP. The right to strike, while not specified by law, is recognized and generally respected in practice.

St. Lucia

Polity: Parliamentary democracy
Economy: Capitalist
Population: 100,000
PPP: $6,530
Life Expectancy: 71
Ethnic Groups: Black (90 percent), mulatto (6 percent), East Indian (3 percent), white (1 percent)
Capital: Castries

Political Rights: 1
Civil Liberties: 2
Status: Free

Overview:

In 1998, the new prime minister, Kenny Anthony, head of the St. Lucia Labor Party (SLP), began to address reports of official corruption and the concerns of an electorate weary of economic distress. The long-ruling United Workers Party (UWP), swept out of power the previous year, made an attempt to reform itself in a June party convention.

St. Lucia, a member of the British Commonwealth, achieved independence in 1979. The British monarchy is represented through a governor-general. Under the 1979 constitution, a bicameral parliament consists of a 17-member House of Assembly, elected for five years, and an 11-member Senate. Six members of the upper body are appointed by the prime minister, three by the leader of the parliamentary opposition, and two by consultation with civic and religious organizations. The island is divided into eight regions, each with its own elected council and administrative services.

The UWP government was long headed by John Compton, whose decision to retire in March 1996 was apparently linked to a number of scandals which included an alleged affair with a teenager. He had also been accused of knowing about the misappropriation of UN funds. Soon after his announcement, his deputy, 72-year-old George Mallet, who served as both prime minister and party leader, announced his decision to retire, clearing the way for Compton's handpicked successor, former director-general of the Organization of Eastern Caribbean States (OECS), Vaughan Lewis. Lewis won Mallet's vacated seat in February's by-elections and assumed the party leadership. In April, since his party won the most seats, he automatically became the prime minister.

Upon the retirement of Governor-General Sir Stanislaus James, Mallet was sworn in as the country's fourth governor-general in June 1996 over protests that the post be reserved for those outside the sphere of party politics. Opposition leader Julian Hunte also stepped down after taking third place in the February 1996 by-elections. Former Education Minister Anthony replaced him as leader of the SLP. By the end of 1996, the SLP had merged with smaller opposition parties, and Anthony led the coalition to victory in the May 23, 1997 elections. The biggest electoral landslide in the country's history resulted in the SLP, out of power since 1982, winning 16 of 17 seats in parliament, and unseating Prime Minister Lewis with a 26-year-old political newcomer.

In 1998, Compton, prime minister for 29 years and a member of parliament for 40 years, returned to lead the UWP. Unemployment, which is estimated at 20 percent, remains a potential source of instability.

Political Rights and Civil Liberties: Citizens are able to change their government through democratic elections. Constitutional guarantees regarding the right to organize political parties, labor unions, and civic groups are generally respected, as is the free exercise of religion.

The competition among political parties and allied civic organizations is heated, particularly during election campaigns when one side invariably accuses the other of occasional violence and harassment.

The judicial system is independent and includes a High Court under the West Indies Supreme Court (based in St. Lucia), with ultimate appeal under certain circumstances to the Privy Council in London. The Constitution requires public trials before an independent and impartial court. Traditionally, citizens have enjoyed a high degree of personal security, although there are episodic reports of police misuse of force. In recent years, an escalating crime wave, much of which is drug related, in addition to violent clashes during banana farmers' strikes and increased violence in schools sparked concern among citizens. The island's nineteenth century prison, built to house a maximum of 101 inmates, in fact houses more than 400.

The media carry a wide spectrum of views and are largely independent of the government. There are five privately owned newspapers, two privately held radio stations, and one partially government funded radio station, as well as two privately owned television stations. In November 1995, the government refused to reissue a license for Radyo Koulibwi, a small FM station critical of the then ruling UWP party.

Civic groups are well organized and politically active, as are labor unions, which represent a majority of wage earners. Legislation passed in 1995 restricts the right to strike. The measure provides for a fine of about $2,000 (U.S.) or two years in prison for inciting any person to cease performing any lawful activity on his property or on the property of another person. The government said the measure was aimed at curtailing strikes in the banana industry, which employs more than 30 percent of the workforce. Nonetheless, in October 1996, a 14-day strike took place in which banana industry workers demanded a greater role in management decisions. The strike resulted in violence, and the police used tear gas and rubber bullets to disperse crowds, seriously injuring several people.

Though there are no official barriers to women and minorities participating in government, these groups are underrepresented. A growing awareness of the seriousness of violence against women has led the government and advocacy groups to take steps to offer better protection for victims of domestic violence.

↓ St. Vincent and the Grenadines

Polity: Parliamentary democracy
Economy: Capitalist
Population: 100,000
PPP: $5,969
Life Expectancy: 73
Ethnic Groups: Black (82 percent), white, East Indian, Caribbean Indian
Capital: Kingstown

Political Rights: 2
Civil Liberties: 1
Status: Free

Trend arrow: St. Vincent and the Grenadines receives a downward trend arrow due to controversy over the fairness of the 1998 general election.

Overview:

Sir James F. Mitchell led his New Democratic Party (NDP) to a narrow victory in the June 1998 general elections which were marked by opposition accusations of fraud, bribery, and intimidation. Mitchell's efforts to diversify the islands' banana- and tourism-based economy has met with limited success, and narcotics smuggling remains a major concern.

St. Vincent and the Grenadines is a member of the British Commonwealth, with the British monarchy represented by a governor-general. St. Vincent achieved independence in 1979, with jurisdiction over the northern Grenadine islets of Bequia, Canouan, Mayreau, Mustique, Prune Island, Petit St. Vincent, and Union Island.

The constitution provides for a 15-member unicameral House of Assembly elected for five years. Six senators are appointed, four by the government and two by the opposition. The prime minister is the leader of the party or coalition and commands a majority in the House. In 1994, Mitchell won a third term as prime minister when his center-right NDP won 12 seats. The center-left alliance comprising the St. Vincent Labour Party (SVLP), which had held power in 1979-84, and the Movement for National Unity (MNU) won the remaining three seats. The opposition contested the results, charging that there were irregularities in voter registration.

In 1995, Deputy Prime Minister Parnel Campbell faced charges of financial impropriety when, disregarding government regulations, he took a loan from an offshore bank. With the opposition parties now united into the Unity Labour Party (ULP) pressing for a parliamentary vote of no-confidence, Campbell resigned. In 1998, Mitchell took advantage of internal divisions within the opposition to announce elections a year earlier than expected. Irregularities in the June 15 election for 15 assembly seats caused the ULP to delay its recognition of the NDP's fourth successive win.

Political Rights and Civil Liberties:

Citizens can change their government through elections. Following the June 1998 elections, the government and the opposition began discussing constitutional reforms centering around electoral reform. The ULP claimed it would have won the contest, rather than see the NDP gallop to victory, if a proportional representation system had been used instead of the first-past-the-post framework copied from Britain. The judicial system is independent. The West Indies Supreme Court based in St. Lucia is the highest court and includes a Court of Appeal and a High Court. Under certain circumstances, a right of ultimate appeal reports to the Privy Council in London. Murder convictions carry a mandatory death sentence.

Penetration by the hemispheric drug trade is increasingly causing concern. Allegations have been made of drug-related corruption within the government and police force, and of money laundering in St. Vincent banks. The drug trade has also caused an increase in street crime. In 1995, the U.S. government described St. Vincent as becoming a drug-trafficking center, and alleged that high-level government officials are involved in narcotics-related corruption. Since then, St. Vincent has taken steps to cooperate with U.S. anti-drug trade efforts, in part by signing an extradition treaty in 1996 with the U.S..

Human rights are generally respected. However, a local human rights organization has accused police of using excessive force and illegal search and seizure, and of improperly informing detainees of their rights in order to extract confessions. The regional human rights organization, Caribbean Rights, estimates that 90 percent of convictions in St. Vincent are based on confessions. In 1996, a 12-year-old boy was the victim of police brutality which resulted in the dismissal of two officers and the demotion of a third.

The independent St. Vincent Human Rights Association has criticized long judicial delays and the large backlog of cases which are caused by personnel shortages in the local judiciary. It has also charged that, at times, the executive exerts inordinate influence over the courts. Prison conditions remain poor—one prison designed for 75 prisoners houses more than 400—and there are allegations of mistreatment.

The 1997 trial of James and Penny Fletcher, tourists visiting from West Virginia, resulted in a personal appeal by President Clinton to Mitchell to ensure they received "due process." The appeal came after U.S. media questioned whether the two could receive a fair trial, pointing to weak evidence against them and a reported $100,000 bribe request from the friend of a top police official. A U.S. diplomat was quoted as saying that evidence in the case was so weak that the judge had "taken lint and created a rope with which to hang the Fletchers."

The press is independent, with two privately owned independent weeklies, the *Vincentian* and the *News*, and several smaller, partisan papers. The opposition has charged the *Vincentian* with government favoritism. The only television station is privately owned and free from government interference. Satellite dishes and cable are available to those who can afford them. The radio station is government-owned, and call-in programs are prohibited. Equal access to radio is mandated during electoral campaigns, but the ruling party takes inordinate advantage of state control over programming. Constitutional guarantees regarding free expression, freedom of religion, and the right to organize political parties, labor unions, and civic organizations are generally respected. Violence against women, particularly domestic violence, is a major problem. Labor unions are active and permitted to strike.

Samoa

Polity: Parliamentary de-
mocracy and family heads
Economy: Capitalist
Population: 200,000
PPP: $2,948
Life Expectancy: 65
Ethnic Groups: Polynesian (93 percent), Euronesian
[mixed] (7 percent)
Capital: Apia

Political Rights: 2
Civil Liberties: 3*
Status: Free

Ratings change: Samoa's civil liberties changed from 2 to 3 due to increased government attacks on the media.

Overview:　Government attacks on the country's news media and efforts to restrict freedom of information and expression increased during 1998.

Samoa (formerly Western Samoa) consists of two volcanic islands and several minor islets located west of American Samoa in the south-central Pacific. In 1899, the United States annexed Eastern (American) Samoa, while the Western Samoan islands became a German protectorate. New Zealand occupied Western Samoa during World War I and acquired subsequent control of the territory under first a League of Nations and later a United Nations mandate. A new constitution was adopted in 1960, and on January 1, 1962, Western Samoa became the first Pacific state to achieve independence.

The ruling Human Rights Protection Party (HRPP) has won a plurality in each of the five elections since 1982. At the first direct elections in 1991, Prime Minister Tofilau Eti Alesana won a third term after the HRPP secured 30 of the 47 parliamentary seats. At the April 26, 1996, legislative elections, the HRPP won just 22 seats, the Samoan National Development Party (SNDP) 13, and independents, 14. Several independents joined the HRPP, and in May, parliament reelected Tofilau as premier over the SNDP's Tuiatua Tupua Tamasese Efi.

In July 1998, the country officially changed its name from Western Samoa to Samoa. On November 23, Tofilau, who was ill with cancer, resigned after 16 years as prime minister, and he was replaced by Tuilaepa Sailele Malielegaoi, who had served as deputy prime minister and finance minister.

**Political Rights
and Civil Liberties:**　Samoans can change their government democratically. The 1960 constitution combines parliamentary democracy with traditional authority. Only the 25,000 *matai*, or chiefs of extended families, can sit in the unicameral parliament, *Fono Aoao Faitulafono*, except for two seats which are reserved for citizens of non-Samoan descent. Village high chiefs generally approve candidates. In a 1990 referendum, voters narrowly approved universal suffrage for parliament; previously, only matai could vote. In 1991, parliament increased its term from three to five years. The head of state, who is traditionally drawn from the four paramount chiefs, appoints the premier and must approve legislation. Susuga Malietoa Tanumafili II is head of state for life, although his successors will be

elected by parliament for five-year terms. In rural areas, the government has limited influence, and the 360 village councils, or *fonos*, are the main authority. Although several formal parties exist, the political process is defined more by individual personalities than strict party affiliation.

During the past year, the government sought to impose increasingly greater restrictions on press freedom. In April 1998, Samoan journalists were ordered not to report on the proceedings of a Commission of Inquiry into the disappearance of a police file indicating that Prime Minister Tofilau Eti Alesana was convicted in 1996 and fined on two counts of theft. On May 15, the government ruled to make public funds available to finance defamation suits by high-ranking public officials.

The independent newspaper the *Samoa Observer* has faced several lawsuits brought by government officials and business leaders over stories it has published of growing corruption and abuse of public office in Samoa. According to the Pacific Islands News Association (PINA), in recent years, the paper's printing plant was burned down under suspicious circumstances, the editor was assaulted by relatives of a government minister, state advertising was withdrawn, and the prime minister threatened to pass a law canceling the paper's business license. In July, the *Samoa Observer's* editor Savea Sano Malifa lost a civil defamation suit brought against him and the paper by Prime Minister Tofilau after a story appeared in the paper alleging that funds were used to upgrade a hotel owned by the prime minister's children. The paper warned that the court's decision would effectively deter the media from investigating future allegations of corruption. In a separate case, Tofilau brought a criminal libel charge against Malifa and the paper's Samoan language editor over a letter to the editor which strongly criticized Tofilau. As of year's end, the case was still pending. In October, Malifa received the Commonwealth's most prestigious press freedom honor, the Astor Award.

The state-owned broadcast media, consisting of the country's only television station and Radio 2AP, are heavily government controlled and restrict air time to opposition leaders. There are two private radio stations, and satellite television is available in parts of the capital city, Apia. Several Samoan-language newspapers and two English-language papers are published on a regular basis. The matai often choose the religious denomination of their extended family in this predominantly Christian country, and there is strong societal pressure to support church leaders and projects financially.

The government generally respects the right of assembly. There are two independent trade unions, plus the Public Service Association which represents government workers. Strikes are legal, but occur infrequently. Collective bargaining is practiced mainly in the public sector.

The judiciary is independent, and defendants receive fair trials. However, many civil and criminal matters are handled by village *fonos* according to traditional law. The 1990 Village Fono Law provides some right of appeal in such cases to the Lands and Titles Courts and to the Supreme Court. Village fonos occasionally order houses burned, persons banned from villages, and other harsh punishments. In October 1998, five men reportedly were hogtied, their homes were destroyed, and they were banished from their villages for conducting a non-Methodist service in their village. According to village chiefs involved in the incident, they were following traditional customs which permit only Methodist worship in their village. Although the police force is under civilian control, its impact is limited mostly to the capital city, while fonos generally enforce security measures in the rest of the country. In July 1998, Amnesty International expressed concern that police had been slow to respond to local media reports that a group of men had been assaulted in custody and prohibited from obtaining legal advice following their arrest on gang-related charges.

Traditional norms tolerate domestic violence and discourage women from reporting abuse to the police. Although the long-standing subordinate role of women is slowly changing, women continue to face discrimination and are underrepresented in politics.

San Marino

Polity: Parliamentary democracy
Economy: Capitalist
Population: 30,000
PPP: na
Life Expectancy: 76
Ethnic Groups: Sanmarinese (78 percent), Italian (21 percent)
Capital: San Marino

Political Rights: 1
Civil Liberties: 1
Status: Free

Overview: San Marino, the world's oldest and second smallest republic, has been governed by a centrist Christian Democratic-Socialist party coalition since 1993.

The coalition returned to power after May 1998 elections. Economic issues and efforts to increase governmental transparency and efficiency dominated the government's agenda throughout 1998.

San Marino has the lowest unemployment rate in Europe, a budget surplus, and no national debt. In addition to agriculture, the country's vibrant, primarily private enterprise economy includes production of livestock, light manufacturing, and tourism, which constitutes 60 percent of government revenue. Eighty-five percent of the country's external trade is with Italy.

Although the Sanmarinese are ethnically and culturally Italian, their long history of independence dates from Papal recognition in 1631. An 1862 customs union with Italy began an enduring relationship of political, economic, and security cooperation. Despite substantial reliance on Italian assistance ranging from budget subsidies to news media, San Marino maintains its own political institutions and became a full member of the United Nations in 1992. It joined the International Monetary Fund in the same year.

The Grand and General Council has served as the legislature since 1600. Its 60 members are directly elected by proportional representation every five years. The Secretary of State for Foreign Affairs has come to assume many of the prerogatives of a prime minister. Directly elected Auxiliary Councils serve as arbiters of local government in each of the country's nine "castles." They are led by an elected captain and serve two-year terms. The legislature appoints two captains-regent, representing the city and the countryside respectively, to exercise executive authority for six-month terms.

The government extends official recognition to 17 communities of the more than

13,000 Sanmarinese living abroad. The state funds summer education and travel programs to bring Sanmarinese students living abroad to the republic.

Political Rights and Civil Liberties:

San Marino's citizens can change their government democratically. The country has a long tradition of multiparty politics, with six parties represented in the current Council. Although the ruling center-left coalition maintained a substantial majority in the 1993 elections, three smaller parties emerged, including a hardline splinter group from the recently reconstituted Communist Party. Women were permitted to stand as candidates for seats in the Grand and General Council for the first time in 1974.

The country's independent judiciary is based on the Italian legal system and includes justices of the peace, a law commissioner and assistant commissioner, a criminal judge of the Primary Court of Claims, and two Appeals Court judges. A Supreme Court of Appeal acts as a final court of appeal in civil cases. The judicial system delegates some of its authority to Italian magistrates in both criminal and civil cases.

Workers (including police, but not the military) are free to form and join unions under a 1961 law. Collective bargaining agreements carry the force of law. Unions may freely form domestic federations or join international labor federations. Union members constitute approximately one-half of the country's workforce, which includes approximately 10,000 Sanmarinese and 2,000 Italians. Trade unions are independent of the government and political parties, but they have close informal ties with the parties, which exercise strong influence on them. The right to strike is guaranteed, but no strikes have occurred in the past nine years. Freedom of association is respected.

San Marino enjoys a free press. Italian newspapers and radio and television broadcasts are readily available. The government, some political parties, and the trade unions publish periodicals, bulletins, and newspapers. There are no daily newspapers. The privately operated Radio Titano is the country's only broadcast service. An information bulletin entitled *Notizie di San Marino* is broadcast daily over Radio Televisione Italiano.

San Marino has no formal asylum policy. Instead, it has allowed a small number of refugees to reside and work in the country. Immigrants and refugees are eligible for citizenship only after 30 years' residence.

Another citizenship law grants automatic citizenship to the foreign spouses and children of male Sanmarinese, but not to those of their female counterparts. In 1997, the country legalized homosexuality. Earlier statutes had provided for up to one year's imprisonment for the commission of "libidinous acts with persons of the same sex."

São Tomé and Príncipe

Polity: Presidential-
parliamentary democracy
Economy: Mixed statist
(transitional)
Population: 200,000
PPP: $1,744
Life Expectancy: 64
Ethnic Groups: Mestico (Portuguese-African), African minority
(Angola, Mozambique, immigrants)
Capital: São Tomé

Political Rights: 1
Civil Liberties: 2
Status: Free

Overview:

The Movement for the Liberation of São Tomé and Principe-Social Democratic Party (MLSTP-PSD) won an absolute majority in November parliamentary elections. The balloting, which was conducted by an autonomous electoral commission with technical support from Taiwan, enabled the party to regain democratically the power that it had exercised for 16 years as the sole legal party before the country's democratic transition in 1992. MLSTP-PSD Vice President Guilherme Posser became the new prime minister. In presidential elections scheduled for July 2001, MLSTP-PSD party leader Manuel Pinto da Costa, who served as president during the period of one-party rule, will likely run against incumbent Miguel dos Anjos Trovoada.

A small-island nation lying off the coast of Central Africa, São Tomé and Principe is extremely poor and has few local resources. Unemployment is endemic. Since achieving independence from Portugal in 1975, the country has mostly relied on external assistance to develop its economy. In 1997, the government established diplomatic ties with Taiwan in exchange for promises of assistance reportedly valued at more than $30 million. Beijing suspended relations and demanded immediate repayment of $11 million in bilateral debt. The maneuvering reflects the desperate poverty of most of the country's people. Corruption, including the sale of diplomatic passports, is deeply entrenched.

São Tomé and Principe are two islands approximately 125 miles off of the coast of Gabon in the Gulf of Guinea. Seized by Portugal in 1522 and 1523, they became a Portuguese Overseas Province in 1951. Portugal granted local autonomy in 1973 and independence in 1975. Upon independence, the Movement for the Liberation of São Tomé and Principe (MLSTP), formed in 1960 as the Committee for the Liberation of São Tomé and Principe, took power and functioned as the only legal party until a 1990 referendum established multiparty democracy. In 1991, Trovoada, an independent candidate backed by the opposition Democratic Convergence Party, became the first democratically elected president.

In June, a group of demobilized army officers threatened to take up arms against the government if promises of financial assistance and jobs for former soldiers were not met. A report to negotiators revealed charges of political influence over military advancement and embezzlement of international aid meant for demobilized officers. The government then pledged to hasten restructuring of the armed forces and to seek greater assistance for the retired soldiers, many of whom had participated in an abortive and bloodless coup in 1995.

Political Rights and Civil Liberties: São Tomé and Principe's 1991 presidential and legislative elections gave the country's citizens their first chance to elect their leader in an open, free, and fair contest. Legislative elections in 1994 were generally free and fair, but the November 1998 contest, in which the MLSTP-PSD won 31 of the 55 seats in the unicameral National Assembly, was apparently the country's most democratic election to date. The Independent Democratic Alliance Party, which supports President Trovoada, won 16 seats.

President Trovoada won a second five-year term in July 1996 after receiving 52.74 percent of the approximately 40,000 votes cast in a runoff election. Despite numerous allegations of vote buying and other irregularities, international observers declared the results free and fair.

An independent judiciary, including a Supreme Court with members designated by and responsible to the National Assembly, was established by the August 1990 referendum on multiparty rule. The court system is overburdened, understaffed, inadequately funded, and plagued by long delays in hearing cases. Prison conditions are reportedly harsh.

Constitutionally protected freedom of expression is respected in practice. Newspapers appear only sporadically due to economic constraints. While the state controls a local press agency and the only radio and television stations, no law forbids independent broadcasting. Opposition parties receive free air time, and newsletters and pamphlets criticizing the government circulate freely.

Freedom of assembly is respected. Citizens have the constitutional right to assemble and demonstrate with advance notice of two days. They may also travel freely within the country and abroad. Freedom of religion is respected within the predominantly Roman Catholic country. Women hold few leadership positions. Most occupy domestic roles and have less opportunity than men for education or formal sector employment. Domestic violence against women is reportedly common.

A long decline in production of cocoa, the island's main export, on inefficient state plantations has hurt an economy that has been unable to keep pace with population growth. While successive governments have sought flagship projects, little effort has been made to improve agricultural output among the country's small farmers. The country is saddled with a $600 million foreign debt that it cannot pay. To qualify for debt relief, the government must implement by 2001 economic reforms urged by the IMF and World Bank, and lack of progress has blocked some international loans.

Saudi Arabia

Polity: Traditional monarchy
Economy: Capitalist-statist
Population: 20,200,000
PPP: $8,516
Life Expectancy: 70
Ethnic Groups: Arab (90 percent), Afro-Asian (10 percent)
Capital: Riyadh

Political Rights: 7
Civil Liberties: 7
Status: Not Free

Overview:
Saudi Arabia struggled in 1998 to cope with falling world oil prices. The world's largest oil producer, it depends on oil revenues for one-third of its annual income. Economic difficulties have brought increasing pressure on the Saudi government to speed the restructuring of the economy and to privatize state assets. Although privatization of the state telephone company moved forward in 1998, the Saudi leadership has continued to resist more thorough economic reform.

King Abd al-Aziz Al Saud consolidated the Nejd and Hejaz regions of the Arabian peninsula into the Kingdom of Saudi Arabia in 1932. His son, King Fahd Bin Abd Al-Aziz Al Saud, ascended the throne in 1982 after a number of successions within the family. The king rules by decree and serves as prime minister, appointing all other ministers. In 1992, King Fahd appointed a 60-member consultative council, or *majlis ash-Shura*. The majlis is strictly advisory and is not regarded as a significant political force in the country. The king expanded the majlis in 1997 to 90 members, including three Shi'ite Muslims. The overwhelming majority of Saudis belong to the Wahhabi sect of Sunni Islam.

King Fahd's poor health in recent years has raised concerns about an orderly transfer of power, deemed crucial to the stability of Saudi Arabia's internal and foreign affairs. A power struggle between the two top commanders, deputy prime minister Crown Prince Abdullah and defense minister Prince Sultan, was settled when the king, having suffered a stroke, appointed Abdullah temporary ruler for several months in 1995. Abdullah's success in handling diplomatic and budgetary matters secured his position as future king. In the meantime, he takes on increasing government responsibility as the king's health deteriorates.

Recent terrorist attacks and harsh government crackdowns result from growing internal dissent over widespread official corruption, fiscal mismanagement, denial of basic political rights, and the continuing security alliance with the United States. In 1994, the government arrested some 150 militants and fundamentalist clerics on sedition charges. Bomb attacks against American military facilities in 1995 and 1996 provoked scores of arrests of suspected Shi'ite subversives in a crackdown that pushed much of the opposition underground.

As king, Abdullah is expected to move toward greater economic diversification, less state interference in the economy, and a regional system of alliances designed to reduce dependence on the U.S. for security. With unemployment close to 20 percent and corruption consuming up to a third of government revenue, many question whether Saudi Arabia possesses the political stability to take the steps needed to move from a heavily subsidized welfare state to a market-oriented economy without sparking political unrest; such steps could include increasing political participation and enhancing government accountability for public funds.

A border clash broke out in July 1998 between Saudi Arabia and neighboring Yemen. Territorial disputes over a potentially oil-rich border area led the two countries to war in the 1960s and have caused repeated skirmishes since. Negotiations over disputed territory began in 1995 but are not expected to be resolved in the near future.

In May, King Fahd commuted the sentences of two British nurses who were jailed in 1996 and convicted in September 1997 for the murder of an Australian colleague. One was sentenced to eight years in prison and 500 lashes; the other reportedly received a death sentence. Both have denied any part in the killing. Following their release, one of the nurses accused the Saudi authorities of obtaining her confession through torture.

Political Rights and Civil Liberties:

Saudi citizens cannot change their government democratically. Political parties are illegal, the king rules by decree, and there are no elections at any level. Majlis membership is not representative of the population.

The judiciary is not independent of the monarchy. Under the legal system, which is based on *Shari'a* (Islamic law), persons convicted of rape, murder, armed robbery, adultery, apostasy, and drug trafficking face death by beheading. According to Human Rights Watch, at least 22 executions and three amputations of the hand were carried out between January and October 1998. Police routinely torture detainees, particularly Islamic fundamentalists and non-Western foreigners, in order to extract confessions. Defense lawyers are not permitted in the courtroom, and trials are generally closed and conducted without procedural safeguards. Suspects arrested by the Interior Ministry's general Directorate of Intelligence may be held incommunicado for months without charge. Since 1993, hundreds of Islamic activists, Shi'ites, and Christians have been arbitrarily detained or forced into exile.

Freedom of expression is severely restricted. Criticism of the government, Islam, or the ruling family is forbidden. A 1965 national security law and a 1982 media policy statement prohibit the dissemination of any literature critical of the government. The Interior Minister must approve and can remove all editors-in-chief. Journalists for private papers censor themselves, while the government-owned radio and television report only official views. The government tightly restricts the entry of foreign journalists into the country, and foreign media are heavily censored. In 1994, the government outlawed private ownership of satellite dishes.

Internet usage in Saudi Arabia is growing. Fearing an influx of undesirable material, particularly pornography, the Saudi government has taken steps to restrict access through state-approved service providers which prevent users from viewing prohibited web sites. In practice, it is proving difficult for the government to regulate Internet usage.

Government permission is required to form professional groups and associations, which must be nonpolitical. Islam is the official religion, and all citizens must be Muslims. The government prohibits the public practice of other religions, and conversion is punishable by death. The Shi'ite minority, concentrated in the eastern province, is subjected to officially sanctioned political and economic discrimination. Christians are arrested, flogged, or otherwise harassed.

Women are segregated in workplaces, schools, restaurants and on public transportation; they may not drive and must wear the *abaya*, a black garment covering the head, face, and body. *Mutawwai'in*, or officers with the Committee for the Promotion of Virtue and the Prevention of Vice, harass women for violating conservative dress codes and for appearing in public with unrelated males. A woman may not travel domestically or abroad without being accompanied by a male. African nationals practice female genital mutilation in some areas.

Foreign-born domestic workers are subject to abuse, work long hours, and are sometimes denied wages. The court system discriminates against African and Asian workers, and employers generally hold the passports of foreign employees as leverage in resolving business disputes or as a means of forcing employees to do extra work. Foreign workers constitute two-thirds of those executed in the kingdom.

The government prohibits trade unions, collective bargaining, and strikes. There are no publicly active human rights groups, and the government prohibits visits by international human rights groups and independent monitors.

Senegal

Polity: Dominant party
Economy: Mixed capitalist
Population: 9,000,000
PPP: $1,815
Life Expectancy: 49
Ethnic Groups: Wolof (36 percent), Fulani (17 percent),
Serer (17 percent), Diola (9 percent), Toucouleur (9 percent),
Mandingo (9 percent), European and Lebanese (1 percent),
other (2 percent)
Capital: Dakar

Political Rights: 4
Civil Liberties: 4
Status: Partly Free

Overview: Legislative elections in May 1998 returned President Abdou Diouf's ruling Socialist Party (PS) with a comfortable majority of seats in the National Assembly, but also reflected a continuing slide in the party's share of the popular vote. Ruling party candidates won 93 of 140 parliamentary seats and slightly more than half of the votes. The opposition Senegal Democratic Party (PDS) won 23 seats, while the new Union for Democratic Renewal (URD), which was formed recently by a PS defector, won 11 seats.

The election was overseen by an autonomous electoral body formed in 1997 and was judged by most observers to be the fairest in Senegal's history. The opposition, however, complained of fraud, which has historically helped to ensure successive, robust PS victories. The national unity government that had included the main opposition parties for most of this decade was not revived, and both the ruling party and opposition leaders are now focused on presidential elections scheduled for February 2000. The appointment of Mamadou Lamine Loum as the new prime minister reflects the government's desire to improve economic conditions in order to promote President Diouf's re-election bid.

Open warfare between secessionist rebels and government troops continued in the southern Casamance region. Serious abuses by both government forces and rebels of the Movement of Democratic Forces of Casamance (MFDC) have been reported. Casamance is almost entirely separated from the rest of Senegal by the Gambia, but is vital to Senegal's economy. It produces most of the country's rice and is popular with foreign tourists, but shares little in the revenue from these resources. The MFDC separatist campaign, which is led by Diamacoune Senghor, a former Roman Catholic priest, was launched in 1982. Senghor still officially heads the MFDC from Ziguinchor, Casamance's regional capital, where he is closely monitored by authorities. The intense violence in Casamance has deterred tourism, disrupted rice production, and thereby harmed Senegal's economic growth. It has also tested the capacity and discipline of the country's professional and largely apolitical military, which has recently received U.S. military training in peacekeeping duties.

Senegalese forces in Guinea-Bissau have also reportedly committed abuses. More than 2,000 Senegalese troops fought rebel troops there for several months, ostensibly to support Guinea-Bissau's government, but also to cut supply lines and destroy the rear bases of the MFDC guerrillas.

Since its independence from France in 1960, Senegal has escaped military or harshly authoritarian rule. President Léopold Senghor exercised de facto one-party rule under the PS for more than a decade after independence. Three additional parties were permitted between 1974 and 1981, after which most restrictions were lifted. The PS has dominated the nation's political life through patronage and electoral manipulation. Diouf succeeded President Senghor in 1981 and won large victories in unfair elections in 1988 and 1993. Rising unemployment and prices could strengthen opposition parties or Islamist groups in the country, which is approximately 90 percent Muslim.

Political Rights and Civil Liberties:

The Senegalese people's right to choose presidents and legislative representatives in multiparty elections is constitutionally guaranteed, but has been realized only partially in practice. For decades, the Socialist Party's overwhelming dominance has blocked opposition chances to gain power, even in regular elections. Voting regulations blatantly favored the ruling party for the first three decades after independence. Changes to the 1992 Electoral Code lowered the voting age to 18, introduced secret balloting, and created a nominally fairer electoral framework. The PS-controlled government, however, has used state patronage and state media to protect its position. The new National Elections Monitoring Committee, which was created in 1997, fell short of opposition demands for a fully independent election commission, but performed credibly in overseeing the May legislative polls. Its neutrality in the 2000 presidential poll is still uncertain.

Poor pay and lack of tenure protections create windows for external influence on a judiciary that is, by statute, independent. In high profile cases, there is often considerable interference from political and economic elites. The administration of justice is hindered by scarce resources. Uncharged detainees are incarcerated without legal counsel far beyond the lengthy periods already permitted by law. With the exception of activities by Islamist groups, freedoms of association and assembly are broadly respected.

Religious freedom is honored. Human rights groups working on local and regional issues are among many nongovernmental organizations that operate freely.

Freedom of expression is generally respected. Required registration of publications is today only a formality, and foreign periodicals are circulated without restriction. Independent media are often highly critical of the government and political parties. The government's resort to libel and defamation suits, however, is a worrying trend. The government does not practice formal censorship, but a strong element of self-censorship is instilled through fear of laws against "discrediting the state" and disseminating "false news."

Constitutional rights afforded women are often not honored, especially in the countryside, and women have fewer chances than men for education and formal sector employment. Despite government campaigns, spousal abuse and other domestic violence against women are reportedly common. Many elements of Islamic and local customary law are discriminatory to women, particularly regarding inheritance and marital relations. Female genital mutilation is common among some groups, but is not practiced by the Wolof, the country's largest ethnic group.

Union rights to organize and strike are legally protected, but include notification requirements. Nearly all of the country's small industrialized work force is unionized, and workers are a potent political force. The National Confederation of Senegalese Workers is linked to and provides an important political base for the ruling party. The National Union of Autonomous Labor Unions of Senegal, a smaller rival confederation, is more independent. In July, more than two dozen union activists were arrested after an electrical workers' slowdown.

Senegal's population is mostly engaged in subsistence agriculture. There has been steady growth in the industrial sector, but lack of open competition obstructs independent business development. Major business opportunities in Senegal still require important political connections.

Seychelles

Polity: Presidential-legislative democracy
Economy: Mixed statist
Population: 100,000
PPP: $7,697
Life Expectancy: 70
Ethnic Groups: Seychellois (mixture of Asian, Africans and French)
Capital: Victoria

Political Rights: 3
Civil Liberties: 3
Status: Partly Free

Overview:

President France Albert René and his ruling Seychelles People's Progressive Front (SPPF) party were returned to power in elections in March. René took power in a 1977 coup, but won a legitimate electoral mandate in the country's first multiparty elections in 1993. The March polls were accepted as generally free and fair by opposition parties, which had waged a vigorous campaign. Sir James Mancham's Democratic Party, long the country's primary opposition, fared badly in the polling. The Seychelles National Party of the Reverend Wavel Ramkalawan emerged as the strongest opposition group by espousing economic liberalization, which René has long sought to avoid. However, the ruling party has now begun to privatize state enterprises and is likely to pursue more open policies.

The Seychelles functioned as a multiparty democracy for only one year after receiving independence from Britain in 1976. Prime Minister René seized power the following year by ousting President James Mancham. Mancham and other opposition leaders operated parties and human rights groups in exile after René made his SPPF the sole legal party. President René won one-party show elections in 1979, 1984, and 1989. By 1992, the SPPF had passed a constitutional amendment to legalize opposition parties, and many exiled leaders returned to participate in a constitutional commission and multiparty elections.

President René, who also heads the country's defense and interior ministries, is reportedly in failing health. Vice President James Michel, who also heads the ministries for finance, economic planning, communications, and the environment, has assumed a more prominent role in daily government affairs and is viewed as René's likely successor.

Political Rights and Civil Liberties:

In free and largely fair presidential and legislative elections in March, the Seychellois people were able to exercise their right to choose their representatives. As in 1993, SPPF control over state resources and most media gave ruling party candidates significant advantages in the polls. The president and the National Assembly are elected by universal adult suffrage. As amended in 1996, the 1993 constitution provides for a 34-member National Assembly, with 25 members directly elected and nine allocated on a proportional basis to parties with at least ten percent of the vote. Other amendments have strengthened presidential powers. Local governments comprised of district councils were reconstituted in 1991 after their abolition two decades earlier.

The judiciary includes a supreme court, constitutional court, a court of appeal, an industrial court, and magistrates' courts. Judges generally decide cases fairly, but still face interference in cases involving major economic or political actors.

Freedom of speech has improved since one-party rule ended in 1993, but self-censorship persists. The government monopolizes nearly all media outlets, including the only daily newspaper, which rarely criticizes official policies. At least two other newspapers support or are published by the SPPF. Independent newspapers are sharply critical of the government, but government dominance and the threat of libel suits restrict media freedom. Opposition parties publish several newsletters and other publications. The opposition weekly *Regar* has been sued repeatedly for libel under broad constitutional restrictions on free expression "for protecting the reputation, rights, and freedoms of private lives of persons" and "in the interest of defense, public safety, public order, public morality, or public health." The government-controlled Seychelles Broadcasting Corporation, however, provided substantial coverage to opposition as well as government candidates during the last elections. Academic advancement is reportedly contingent on loyalty to the ruling party.

Women are less likely than men to be literate and have fewer educational opportunities. While almost all adult females are classified as "economically active," most are engaged in subsistence agriculture. Three women serve as ministers in the new cabinet. Domestic violence against women is reportedly widespread, but is rarely prosecuted and only lightly punished. Islanders of Creole extraction face de facto discrimination. Nearly all of the Seychelles' political and economic life is dominated by people of European and Asian origin.

The right to strike is formally protected by the 1993 Industrial Relations Act, but is limited by several regulations. The SPPF-associated National Workers' Union no longer monopolizes union activity. Two independent unions are now active. The government does not restrict domestic travel, but may deny passports for reasons of "national interest." Religious freedom is respected in this overwhelmingly Roman Catholic country.

The country's economy remains weak, but a sharp devaluation in November and revamped tariffs could encourage greater trade and tourism. Reports of official corruption and economic mismanagement persist. There are few natural resources and little industry. Nearly one-third of the Seychelles' population has emigrated, and there is little formal development.

Sierra Leone

Polity: Presidential-legislative democracy (rebel insurgency)
Economy: Mixed capitalist
Population: 4,600,000
PPP: $625
Life Expectancy: 34
Ethnic Groups: Temne (30 percent), Mende (30 percent), other tribes (30 percent), Creole (10 percent)
Capital: Freetown

Political Rights: 3*
Civil Liberties: 5*
Status: Partly Free

Ratings change: Sierra Leone's political rights rating changed from 7 to 3, its civil liberties rating changed from 6 to 5, and its status changed from Not Free to Partly Free, due to the restoration of an elected government and an improvement in security in the capital city and parts of the countryside.

Overview: Sierra Leone's democratically elected government was restored by Nigerian-led West African troops in February, but the country continued to be wracked by a brutal bush war. Hunger and malnutrition afflict displaced people who cannot tend their farms, and rebels regularly punish civilians deemed unfriendly to their cause by chopping off their hands or other mutilations. Thousands of civilians were killed during the year. Many girls and women were raped or seized as sexual slaves for rebel forces.

The restored government of President Ahmed Tejan Kabbah and the Sierra Leone People's Party (SLPP), which had been elected in 1996 and overthrown in a 1997 army coup, faces enormous challenges in bringing security to the countryside and reviving the country's shattered economy. It has adopted a hard line toward captured Armed Forces Revolutionary Council (AFRC) coup leaders, 24 of whom were publicly shot by firing squad in October. It has also resumed the media harassment that began before its 1997 overthrow. Court-martials and trials of AFRC members and supporters continued at year's end, although coup leader Major Johnny Paul Koroma, whose brother was among those executed, remains in exile.

Proceedings against rebel Revolutionary United Front (RUF) leader Foday Sankoh began in November. RUF guerrillas, who had fought against previous governments in Freetown for five years and allied with the AFRC junta, escalated atrocities in the countryside in response to Sankoh's trial. The rebels' philosophy is captured in "Operation No Living Thing," the code name that they assigned for their mid-year guerrilla attacks. Offensives by Guinean and Nigerian troops, who have been backed by loyalist army units and local militia civil defense fighters, including traditional hunters known as *kamajors*, have secured much of the country. Nevertheless, the RUF's experienced and brutal bush fighters can still inflict serious damage to civilians and the country's economy, especially if reports of continued support from neighboring Liberia and Burkina Faso are true. The RUF received assistance from Libya during the civil war and is reportedly influenced by the amalgam of socialist and Islamic philosophies in Libyan leader Colonel Mu'ammar al-Qadhafi's "Green Book." During a visit by Qadhafi to Sierra Leone, however, President Kabbah won offers of economic assistance and a pledge that Libya would end all aid to the rebels.

Plans have been developed to reconstitute the national army to reflect the ethnic diversity of Sierra Leone's people. For the near term, however, foreign forces of the Economic Community of West Africa must maintain security and conduct the brunt of the fighting against remaining rebels. After a conference in New York in July, the United Nations established a 70-member UN Observer Mission in Sierra Leone to oversee the disarmament and demobilization of amnestied rebels.

Founded by Britain in 1787 as a haven for liberated slaves, Sierra Leone became independent in 1961. The RUF launched a guerrilla campaign from neighboring Liberia in 1992 to end 23 years of increasingly corrupt one-party rule by the All Peoples Congress party. Junior army officers led by Captain Valentine Strasser seized power in 1992 in protest against poor pay and working conditions. Political parties were banned. Sporadic harassment of the media and other independent voices followed. In January 1996, Brigadier Julius Maa Bio quietly deposed Strasser as head of the National Provisional Ruling Council amid fears that Strasser intended to clothe his military dictatorship in civilian guise by running for president. Elections proceeded despite military and rebel intimidation, and 60 percent of Sierra Leone's 1.6 million eligible voters cast ballots. In a second round runoff vote in March 1996, Ahmed Tejan Kabbah defeated John Karefa-Smart of United National People's Party.

Since 1992, combat, disease, and starvation have claimed tens of thousands of lives amid massive human rights violations. The country's civil administration and infrastructure have been all but destroyed in paroxysms of looting.

Political Rights and Civil Liberties: Presidential and legislative elections in February and March 1996 were imperfect, but the most legitimate since independence. President Kabbah's February return to office reestablished representative government, although the legislative system, like most of the country's other institutions, is in disarray. Critics claim that President Kabbah is using unfounded charges of collaboration with the army junta against political opponents to undermine opposition parties and any legitimate challenge to his rule.

The judiciary, which was largely inactive under the AFRC junta, has resumed operations, but general dislocation and limited training and resources have sharply decreased the courts' effectiveness. Highly publicized court-martials and trials of AFRC members and supporters on treason charges have proceeded quickly. The highly political and emotional nature of these cases will make fair trials very difficult, but at least 300 other soldiers and policemen have been released for lack of evidence.

Pressure on the media was increased at midyear. In August, five journalists were sentenced to death after being convicted of treason for collaborating with the AFRC junta. Their cases are under appeal. Jonathan Leigh of the *Independent Observer,* Joseph Mboka of the *Democrat,* and four other journalists were arrested in July as the government sought to restrict coverage of security issues.

Despite constitutionally guaranteed equal rights, women face extensive legal and de facto discrimination and limited access to education and formal sector jobs. Married women have fewer property rights, especially in rural areas where customary law prevails. Female genital mutilation is widespread, and the practice was publicly supported by the ousted army junta. Some animist cults allegedly carry out ritual killings of children.

Sierra Leone is ranked by the United Nations as one of the world's poorest countries. Efforts to renew food production have faltered, and deliveries of food imports and humanitarian aid have been disrupted by rebel attacks and widespread banditry.

Singapore

Polity: Dominant party
Economy: Mixed capitalist
Population: 3,900,000
PPP: $22,604
Life Expectancy: 77
Ethnic Groups: Chinese (76 percent), Malay (15 percent), Indian (6 percent), other (3 percent)
Capital: Singapore

Political Rights: 5
Civil Liberties: 5
Status: Partly Free

Overview: In 1998, Singapore's leaders continued to use the law to chill political opposition, even as a recession highlighted the need to foster a freer society more conducive to the city-state's increasingly information-driven economy.

Singapore became a British colony in 1867. Occupied by the Japanese during World War II, the city-state became self-governing in 1959, entered the Malaysian Federation in 1963, and became fully independent under Prime Minister Lee Kuan Yew in 1965. The 1959 constitution provides for a unicameral parliament that is directly elected for a five-year term. Two amendments authorize the appointment of additional MPs to ensure that the opposition has at least three seats. Executive power is vested in the prime minister and cabinet. Since 1993, the president has been directly elected for a six-year term, with limited veto powers over certain budgetary and financial matters and political appointments.

The People's Action Party (PAP) won every seat in every contest from 1968 to 1980 before losing a 1981 by-election. Lee stepped down in 1990 in favor of his hand-picked successor, Goh Chok Tong, although he still exerts considerable influence as senior minister. Prior to Singapore's first presidential elections in 1993, a three-member committee rejected two opposition candidates for lacking proper character and the requisite financial experience. Deputy Premier Ong Teng Cheong managed "only" 58 percent of the vote against a weak candidate. Analysts viewed the results as a protest against the PAP's authoritarian, paternalistic governing style.

The nine-day campaign for the January 2, 1997 parliamentary elections provided rare moments of outspoken politics, even though the opposition contested only 36 seats in an expanded 83-seat parliament. The opposition's calls for greater freedom of expression and criticism of rising costs of living resonated among young professionals. Goh responded by warning that neighborhoods voting against the PAP would be the lowest priority for government-sponsored upgrades of public housing estates, where some 85 percent of the population lives. The PAP won 65 percent of the vote and 81 seats, with the left-leaning Workers' Party (WP) and the centrist Singapore People's Party each winning one.

Following the election, Goh and ten other PAP leaders filed defamation suits against two defeated WP candidates, Tang Liang Hong and party secretary general and veteran dissident J.B. Jayaretnam. The PAP leaders accused Jayaretnam of announcing during a campaign rally that Tang had filed police reports against PAP leaders for calling Tang "anti-Christian" and a "Chinese chauvinist." Tang fled Singapore and courts subsequently ruled against both men. Surprisingly, the judge in Jayaretnam's case awarded Goh only one-tenth of the $118,343 he had requested. In November, a landmark Appeal's Court ruling reduced what it called a "hugely disproportionate" $4.78 million award against Tang. In July 1998, however, the Appeal's Court increased the award against Jayaretnam to $59,172 plus full costs. In October, Goh agreed to allow Jayaretnam to pay the damages and costs in installments in order to avoid bankruptcy, which would force him to relinquish his parliamentary seat. Jayaretnam still faces seven other suits by PAP members. On December 29, opposition politician Chee Soon Juan held a rare public rally in the financial district without a permit, telling reporters that the authorities had delayed or refused his requests. Police said they would charge Chee with providing entertainment without a license, which could result in a fine that would disqualify him from contesting elections.

The financial crises that hit Indonesia and Malaysia, two of Singapore's largest trading partners, slowed exports and retail sales, and in the third quarter Singapore entered into its first recession since 1985. Singapore also faces the broader question of how long its increasingly information-driven, high-tech economy can thrive in an authoritarian environment that stifles free thought and creativity.

Political Rights and Civil Liberties:

Constitutionally, Singaporeans can change their government through elections. In practice, the PAP government has chilled free expression and political dissent through ruinous civil defamation suits, its tight control over the press, its deft use of patronage, and the use of security laws and other harassment against political opponents. Nevertheless, the PAP has considerable popular support as the architect of the country's transformation from a low-wage economy to an industrial and financial power and welfare state.

Opposition parties say they have trouble fielding viable slates for Group Representation Constituencies (GRC), or multimember electoral districts in which at least one candidate must be an ethnic minority. In 1996, parliament increased the number of GRCs to 15, leaving only nine single-member districts, and it increased the maximum number of seats in a GRC from four to six. There are strict regulations on the constitutions and financial affairs of political parties.

The government nearly bankrupted the WP's Jayaretnam through a series of controversial court cases, including a 1986 fraud conviction that the Privy Council in London criticized. In 1993, the National University dismissed Chee Soon Juan, an opposition Social Democratic Party official, for alleged petty financial irregularities. Courts have since fined Chee in two other cases. In 1997, the WP agreed to pay damages to five current and former PAP politicians to settle a 1995 libel case. The judiciary is not independent, although courts have acquitted or reduced monetary damages in some cases brought by the government or PAP figures against political opponents. Amnesty International criticized the 1997 defamation ruling against Jayaretnam (see Overview) for being based not on his actual words but on alleged "innuendo." Amnesty also criticized the 1998 Court of Appeal ruling against Jayaretnam for setting dangerous precedents, including, in part, aggressive questioning by Jayaretnam's lawyer. The Legal Services Commission has discretion over the term and assignments of judicial appointments. Judges, especially Supreme Court judges, have close ties to PAP leaders.

Police reportedly abuse detainees to extract confessions. Caning is used to punish approximately 30 offenses, including certain immigration violations. The Internal Security Act (ISA) permits detention without charge or trial for an unlimited number of two-year periods. Since 1990, there have been no ISA detentions. The ISA also permits the government to restrict the political and civil rights of former detainees. In November, the government lifted such restrictions on Chia Thye Poh, a former MP from the Socialist Front, a one-time breakaway PAP faction. The government had detained Chia without trial from 1966-1989 under the ISA, and upon release restricted his rights. The government actively uses two other acts that permit detention without trial—one to detain people for alleged narcotics offenses or involvement in secret societies, the other to commit drug abusers to rehabilitation centers. A 1989 constitutional amendment prohibits judicial review of the substantive grounds of detentions under the ISA and anti-subversion laws, and bars the judiciary from reviewing the constitutionality of such laws. There is no right to a public trial under the ISA.

Freedom of expression is restricted by broadly drawn provisions of the constitution and the ISA, and by the government's control of the media and its use of civil defamation suits against political opponents and journalists. In 1995, courts ruled against the *International Herald Tribune* for contempt of court and libel, and assessed fines totaling $892,000. The broadly drawn Official Secrets Act bars the unauthorized release of government data to the media. In 1994, a court fined two journalists and three economists under the Act for publishing advance GDP figures.

By law, key "management shares" in the Singapore Press Holdings (SPH) must be held by government approved persons. SPH has close ties to the PAP and owns all general circulation newspapers. Journalists practice self-censorship, and editorials and domestic news coverage strongly favor the ruling party.

The government can legally ban the circulation of newspapers, although it has not done so in recent years. A 1986 amendment to the Newspaper and Printing Presses

Act allows the government to "gazette," or restrict circulation, of any foreign publication that it feels has published articles which interfere in domestic politics. *Time, Far Eastern Economic Review, The Economist*, and other publications have been gazetted. The government-affiliated Singapore International Media PTE, Ltd. operates all four free television stations and at least ten of Singapore's nearly 20 radio stations. Foreign broadcasts are available, although movies, television, videos, music, and the Internet are subject to censorship.

The Societies Act requires most organizations of more than ten people to be registered and restricts political activity to political parties. However, the PAP has close ties with ostensibly nonpolitical associations such as neighborhood groups, while the opposition is not permitted to form similar groups. There are no nongovernmental human rights organizations. Authorities must approve speakers at public functions, and approval is occasionally denied to opposition politicians. The police must approve any public assembly of more than five people.

Freedom of religion is generally respected, although the Jehovah's Witnesses and the Unification Church are banned under the Societies Act. Race riots between Malays and the majority Chinese killed scores of people in the 1960s, and the government takes measures to ensure racial harmony and equity. Minorities are well represented in government, but Malays reportedly face unofficial discrimination and have been disproportionately affected by the recession. Most unions are affiliated with the progovernment National Trade Unions Congress. There have been no strikes since 1986, in part because labor shortages fuel wage increases. A 1997 United States Embassy report found that the government and state-controlled companies account for 60 percent of GDP. The government also plays a dominant role in the economy through land and pension policies.

Slovakia

Polity: Parliamentary democracy
Economy: Mixed capitalist (transitional)
Population: 5,400,000
PPP: $7,320
Life Expectancy: 73
Ethnic Groups: Slovak (86 percent), Hungarian (11 percent), Gypsy (2 percent), Czech (1 percent)
Capital: Bratislava

Political Rights: 2
Civil Liberties: 2*
Status: Free

Ratings change: Slovakia's civil liberties rating changed from 4 to 2, and its status changed from Partly Free to Free, due to a more free media environment and anti-corruption efforts.

Overview: The governing coalition led by controversial Prime Minister Vladmir Meciar was voted out of office in parliamentary elections on September 26, 1998. The center-right Slovak Democratic Coalition (SDK) and its allies, the Party of the Democratic Left (SDL), the Hungarian Coalition Party (SMK), and the Party of Understanding (SOP), took 93 of 150 seats, with Meciar's Movement for a Democratic Slovakia (HZDS) winning 42 (down from 61 seats). The ultra-right Slovak National Party (SNS) won 14 seats, up from 9. SDK leader Milukas Dzurinda became prime minister at the end of October. The ruling coalition won more than the three-fifths majority needed to change the constitution.

Meciar, the dominant political figure is Slovakia since the fall of communism in 1989 and the peaceful dissolution of Czechoslovakia in 1993, had isolated the international community with his increasingly authoritarian rule, and Slovakia was bypassed in the first wave of expansion by NATO and the European Union (EU).

In 1994 parliamentary elections, Meciar's HZDS won 61 seats, and formed a ruling coalition with the left-wing Workers Association (ZRS) and the right-wing SNS. In 1995, Meciar moved to reduce the authority of President Michal Kovac, whom he blamed for the resignation of the previous HZDS government in early 1994. In 1997, political tensions escalated when the government removed a question about direct presidential elections from a referendum initiated by President Kovac. That summer, five opposition parties—the Christian Democrats, the Democratic Union, the Democratic Party, the Social Democrats, and the Green Party—formed the SDK.

Nineteen-ninety-eight opened with a looming constitutional crisis. With President Kovac's term due to expire on March 2, neither the government nor the opposition had the necessary three-fifths majority to push through a candidate. After several failed votes in January, and February, Meciar assumed the largely ceremonial role of president the day after Kovac stepped down, and immediately canceled an April referendum on NATO as well as direct presidential elections. He also recalled 28 ambassadors and halted an investigation of the interior minister into the bizarre 1995 kidnapping of President Kovac's son, allegedly taken by intelligence forces. On July 14, Slovak deputies defused the potential constitutional crisis by unanimously supporting a bill transferring power to appoint a government to the speaker of the parliament.

In September, Slovak voters overwhelmingly backed the SDK and its allies. On October 30, the parliamentary chairman appointed SDK leader Dzurinda prime minister. The government also included members of the Hungarian Coalition Party, which represented the country's estimated 500,000-strong Hungarian minority. On November 4, the ruling coalition agreed to change the constitution and implement direct presidential elections.

The new government's program included pledges to privatize banks, stabilize the economy, to make human and minority rights top priorities, and to push harder for membership in NATO and the EU.

On December 8, Prime Minister Dzurinda scrapped controversial amnesties which barred investigations into alleged abuses of power as well as those which blocked legal probes of the 1995 kidnapping of then President Kovac's son and an investigation of the former interior minister for removing the question of direct presidential elections from a 1997 referendum.

Political Rights and Civil Liberties: Citizens can change the government democratically, and the 1998 parliamentary elections were free and fair. Direct presidential elections are expected in 1999 after constitutional amendments are made.

Article 26 of the Slovak constitution guarantees freedom of expression and the press. Since 1990, sixteen drafts of a new media law have been prepared, but none were debated by parliament. In May 1998, the government adopted a measure aimed at limiting election-related coverage by the private electronic media. Disputes erupted over state-owned TV and radio's monopoly on campaign party broadcasts, the ownership of the pro-opposition, privately-owned TV Markiza, and broadcasts during the 48-hour "quiet period" before the polls opened. A report by an Italian media which monitors groups found that state TV "gave clear preference to the ruling party and government officials," and that TV Markiza devoted 73 percent of its campaign coverage to the opposition. In April 1998, the government charged the editor-in-chief of the independent newspaper *Sme* with "disclosing state secrets" after the paper printed a record of a discussion between the foreign minister and the British ambassador. Article 103 of the Penal Code penalizes defamation of the president, though no action was taken against progovernment papers attacking then President Kovac. All major dailies are private. There are some 20 private radio stations, among them Radio Twist and Fun. State-owned Slovak Television, which reaches the whole country, broadcasts on two channels, STV-1 and STV-2. Private stations include TV Markiza and VTV, which broadcast via cable and satellite. In 1997, a private information agency, SITA, was established.

Freedom of religion is respected in this overwhelmingly Roman Catholic country. Only registered churches and religious organizations have the explicit right to conduct public worship services. There are no significant restrictions on freedom of assembly.

Slovakia is a multiparty state, and there are some 90 political parties and movements. No party has been banned.

Article 37 of the constitution allows for independent trade unions, and almost all are represented in the Confederation of Trade Unions (KOZ), which has 1.1 million members and 42 branches.

The court system consists of local and regional courts with the Supreme Court as the highest court of appeals except for constitutional questions, which are considered by the Constitutional Court. Most judges rule fairly and impartially, though the judicial system is overburdened. From 1993 to early 1998, the Constitutional Court disqualified 13 acts adopted by parliament and two government regulations. The judiciary is constitutionally "independent of other branches of government at all levels." There have been reports of corruption at lower courts and among prosecutors.

The Hungarian and Roma minorities have faced discrimination, leading to criticism by the EU and international organizations. The new government has vowed to improve minority rights.

Corruption was a major problem in the early stages of privatization, which saw high-ranking government and party officials using "insider" knowledge and connections to their advantage.

There are no significant restrictions on freedom of movement, or choice of residence and employment. Article 20 of the constitution guarantees the protection of property rights. There are no serious impediments to operating a business, though growing tax and insurance burdens, increased administrative difficulties, and a shortage of loans and capital have had an impact on small- and medium-sized enterprises. While "insider" privatization and corruption have effected equality of opportunity, Slovaks generally do have the means to share in legitimate economic gains.

Women are equal under the law, and enjoy the same property, inheritance, and other legal rights as men; they are represented in the professions, government, and higher education although wage discrepancies tend to favor men.

Slovenia

Polity: Presidential-par-
liamentary democracy
Economy: Mixed capitalist
Population: 2,000,000
PPP: $10,594
Life Expectancy: 75
Ethnic Groups: Slovene (91 percent), Croat (3 percent),
Serb (2 percent), Muslim (1 percent), other (3 percent)
Capital: Ljubljana

Political Rights: 1
Civil Liberties: 2
Status: Free

Overview:

In 1998, Prime Minister Janez Drnovsek's ruling center-left Liberal Democratic Party (LDS) made a strong showing in local elections. This bolstered the often fragile coalition with the center-right Slovenian People's Party (SLS), which lost seats from the previous vote. The third coalition partner, the small Democratic Party of Pensioners (DeSus), slightly improved its standing.

Before the November 23 vote, the SLS, led by Deputy Prime Minister Marjian Podobnik, had threatened to leave the coalition after the parties sparred over a new general procurator and the best through which to revive slumping state firms. The same month, the European Union, which in 1997 voted to accept Slovenia as a member, issued a report criticizing the failure of the government to make necessary reforms, including restructuring the pension system, opening the economy to foreign investment, modernizing the tax structure, and harmonizing its laws with the EU.

Slovenia was controlled for centuries by the Hapsburg empire before being incorporated into the newly created Yugoslavia after World War I. After it declared independence from a fraying Yugoslavia in June 1991, Slovenia's territorial defense forces secured the nation's sovereignty by overcoming an invasion by the Yugoslav People's Army.

In the November 1996 elections for the 90-member National Assembly, the LDS won 25 seats, five fewer than before. The Slovenian Christian Democrats (SKD) won 10 seats, five fewer than in 1992. The rightist SLS won 19 seats, and the ultraconservative Social Democrats (SDS) led by controversial former defense minister Janez Jansa took 16 seats. The former Communist United List of Social Democrats, won nine; the Democratic Party of Pensioners, five; and the National Party, four. In February 1997, Prime Minister Drvovsek ended a three-month stalemate by forging a coalition with the SLS and DeSus. Incumbent President Milan Kucan was easily re-elected in November 1997.

The central issue in 1998 was implementing the necessary reforms for accession to the EU. The government drew up a "Strategy of the Republic of Slovenia for Accession to the European Union," and one of its main authors, Janez Potocnik, was appointed Slovenia's chief EU negotiator. The study laid out a timetable to institute ambitious changes in the coming years to the existing taxation and pension systems, and for the reform of the financial sector, including the privatization of the state-owned banks and insurance companies. It called for the deregulation of prices, reform of the public utilities and competitive public procurement, as well as reform of the enterprise sector and the replacement of distorting subsidies to ailing industries.

Slovenia was the last of the EU applicant countries from the former Communist bloc to launch a value-added tax (VAT), which was scheduled to start on July 1, 1999. Pension reform was also a contentious issue. Demographic trends have put pressure on the world's most generous pay-as-you-go systems, but planned reforms met with stiff opposition from the trade unions, which considered them a divisive attack on social welfare. Years of foreign domination have also made the government wary of foreign investment.

Keeping the fragile coalition in tact also led to a logjam of laws in parliament and an often laborious decision-making process that stalled reform in 1998. In November, the LDS and SLS agreed to a two-month transitional period to maintain coalition consensus and focus on moving forward on programs and legislation related to EU accession.

In other issues, in November, the foreign minister announced that Slovenia and Croatia would resort to international arbitration to resolve the issue of Croatian money deposited in Slovenia's Ljubljamska Banka in 1991. He said that other problems between the two countries concerning their common border, the operation and funding of the jointly owned Krsko nuclear power plant, and assets owned by each in the neighboring state, would be solved without external help.

In November, President Bill Clinton assured Prime Minister Drnovsek that the United States considered Slovenia a top candidate for the next wave of countries to join NATO.

Political Rights and Civil Liberties: Slovenes can change their government democratically. The 1996 parliamentary elections were contested by many parties and candidates, and were judged "free and fair," as were the 1997 presidential elections.

The constitution guarantees freedom of expression and the press. Article 139 of the Slovenian Civil code prohibits "insulting" officials. Most Slovenian media have been privatized. The major daily newspapers *Delo*, *Vecer*, and *Dnevik*, are supported with private investment and advertising. Slovenia Radio-Television broadcasts over three radio stations and two television stations. There are four independent TV stations , among them Pop TV and Kanal A, and nine major commercial radio stations. The media offer a wide variety of opinion and commentary.

There are no restrictions on freedom of religion in this overwhelmingly Roman Catholic country, and freedom of assembly is guaranteed and respected. Slovenia is a multiparty democracy, and there are at last 30 political parties from the far-left to the far-right, with over a dozen represented in parliament. The main opposition parties are the Social Democrats, the Christian Democrats, and the United List of Social Democrats. There are hundreds of nongovernmental organizations, though most rely on foreign funding.

Trade unions are protected under Article 76 of the constitution, and Article 77 guarantees the right to strike. The Association of Free Trade Unions is an independent federation. The Association of Trade Unions is the de facto successor to the Communist-era trade union. A third, much smaller, regional union operates on the Adriatic coast. Unions are formally and actually independent of the government and political parties, but individual union members hold positions in the legislature. The United List party has wide trade union support.

The judiciary is independent, and the judicial system comprises district courts, regional courts, a court of appeals, and the Supreme Court. Judges are elected by the National Assembly upon recommendation of an eleven-member Judicial Council, five of whose members are selected by parliament on the nomination of the president, and six of whom are sitting judges selected by their peers. In 1997, the government announced changes to the Penal Code to comply with the EU and conform with the requirements of a market economy. New commercial laws, as well as statutes dealing with corruption, money laundering, organized crime, and computer hacking were enacted. Journalists will no longer be punished for betraying state or military secrets if they are guided to reveal illegal or corrupt practices by government officials. In late 1998, the government finalized a Law on the Conditions for the Right of Foreigners to Acquire Real Estate Ownership. In November, an EU report noted that legal proceedings are slow, enforcement legislation must be improved, and procedural law must be revised so that it contains the right to summary procedure.

There are no significant government restrictions on movement, residence or employment. Property rights for citizens are guaranteed under Articles 66-69 of the constitution. A new law presented in late 1998 would allow foreigners to own real estate. Private enterprise and ownership are promoted and protected in Slovenia, both by the constitution and laws. Bureaucratic procedures for starting a business are generally transparent, though commercial legislation is incomplete.

According to a February 1998 report by the European Commission, there is no significant corruption in the civil service. Initiatives to combat corruption have been included as part of the government's efforts to ensure compliance with EU requirements.

Women and men are equal under the law, and women are represented in government, business, and education.

Solomon Islands

Polity: Parliamentary democracy
Economy: Capitalist
Population: 400,000
PPP: $2,230
Life Expectancy: 70
Political Rights: 1
Civil Liberties: 2
Status: Free

Ethnic Groups: Melanesian (93 percent), Polynesian (4 percent), Micronesian (1.5 percent), other (1.5 percent)
Capital: Honiara

Overview:
Two months of political turmoil ended in September when Prime Minister Bartholomew Ulufa'alu's government narrowly survived a no-confidence vote.

In response to the country's ongoing economic crisis caused by years of mismanagement and corruption under previous governments, Ulufa'alu pledged to implement public service and finance reforms. The restructuring program, which includes cutting more than 500 jobs from the country's substantial civil service, has attracted critical support from foreign banks and aid donors.

The Solomon Islands, comprised of a twin chain of islands stretching nearly 900 miles in the western Pacific, became a British protectorate in the late 1800s and an independent member of the British Commonwealth in 1978.

Politics in this parliamentary democracy are characterized by frequently shifting partisan loyalties. In 1990, Solomon Mamaloni, a fixture in politics since 1970 who was then serving his second term as premier, quit his ruling party and formed a "national unity" government that included opposition politicians. Mamaloni later formalized this as the Group for National Unity and Reconciliation (GNUR), which led the field with 21 of 47 seats in the May 1993 elections. However, in June, an opposition alliance formed in parliament to elect Francis Billy Hilly, a businessman who ran as an independent, as prime minister.

In October 1994, Governor General Moses Pitakaka sacked Hilly after the premier lost his majority support in parliament over his declaration of a moratorium on the profitable logging industry and his handling of relations with neighboring Papua New Guinea. In November, parliament elected Mamaloni as premier, who immediately ended the logging moratorium, partially in response to a financial crisis that, by 1995, had the economy near bankruptcy.

Heading into the August 6, 1997, elections, Bartholomew Ulufa'alu, a former labor leader who headed the Alliance for Change and its dominant Solomon Islands Liberal Party, pledged to end years of corruption and mismanagement. The GNUR won 25 seats in an expanded 50-seat parliament, and the Alliance won 24, with one seat vacant. Mamaloni unexpectedly decided not to seek a fourth term. On August 27, parliament elected Ulufa'alu as prime minister over the GNUR's Danny Philip.

Ulufa'alu's government was shaken in mid-1998 with the defection of six MPs to the opposition following the dismissal of the minister of finance in July. For the next two months, the opposition, which now claimed to have a majority of members in parliament, pushed for the convening of a special legislative session in order to introduce a vote of no confidence in Ulufa'alu's government. The September 18 vote resulted in a tie, which, under parliamentary standing orders, meant that the motion was defeated and Ulufa'alu narrowly survived.

The defection of several former opposition MPs, as well as the win of a government-backed candidate in a by-election in mid-October, increased the government's majority in parliament to 28 of 50 seats. On October 8, former prime minister Solomon Mamaloni was sworn in as leader of the opposition to replace the ailing Job Duddley Tausinga.

Parliament adopted an environmental protection bill in October to regulate the country's major export timber industry, which saw half of its workers lose their jobs in 1998 as a result of a large decrease in the demand for tropical timber. The law would help to ensure the sustainable management of forest resources and encourage local participation in the forest industry. Critics have charged that large-scale logging operations by foreign companies have resulted in considerable deforestation and environmental damage.

Political Rights and Civil Liberties: Citizens of the Solomon Islands can change their government democratically. Under the 1977 constitution, the 50-member unicameral parliament is directly elected for a four-year term. Executive power is vested in a prime minister and cabinet, and the British monarchy is represented by a governor-general. Traditional chiefs wield formal authority in local government. Party affiliations are weak and based largely on personal loyalties.

The country's three private newspapers vigorously critique government policies, but have limited circulation outside the towns, and there is a private FM station. The state-owned Solomon Islands Broadcasting Corporation's (SIBC) radio service is the most important source of information and generally offers diverse viewpoints. Under the new reformist government, a prominent local journalist was appointed general manager of the SIBC in 1998; in the past, the SIBC had been subject to government pressure and interference. In mid-1998, an Australian television channel began broadcasting to the Solomon Islands. On May 3, the home of *Solomon Voice* newspaper editor Carol Colville was raided by men claiming traditional "custom" payments as compensation for reports about government land allocations, which the newspaper had allegedly linked incorrectly to Ulufa'alu instead of the previous government. Religious freedom is respected in this predominantly Christian country.

Freedom of assembly is subject to the procurement of a permit, which is not known to have been denied for political reasons. The law recognizes the right of workers to form and join unions and to strike. Although only 10-15 percent of the population is employed in the wage economy, approximately 60-70 percent of them are organized in trade unions. Disputes are usually referred to the independent Trade Disputes Panel for arbitration. Unions frequently exercise their right to bargain collectively, a practice which is used to determine wages and conditions of employment. In July, the Public Employees Union initiated a strike following the government's refusal to negotiate plans for downsizing the country's large public sector, including employee layoff packages. The action followed a High Court decision dismissing the government's request for an injunction against the strike, which it had claimed was illegal.

The judiciary is independent, and procedural safeguards are adequate, with a right of ultimate appeal in certain circumstances to the Privy Council in London. The constitution provides for an ombudsman's office to investigate claims of unfair treatment by the authorities, but its effectiveness is limited in practice by a lack of adequate resources. There have been occasional reports of police abusing suspects, although no reports of excessive force were recorded during the year.

Citizens are free to travel domestically and abroad. Women face discrimination in education and employment opportunities, and authorities generally do not protect victims of domestic violence or enforce relevant laws.

Somalia

Polity: Rival ethnic-based militias; unrecognized de facto state in the north
Economy: Mixed statist
Population: 10,700,000
PPP: na
Life Expectancy: 47
Ethnic Groups: Somali (85 percent), Bantu, Arab
Capital: Mogadishu

Political Rights: 7
Civil Liberties: 7
Status: Not Free

Overview:

The December 1997 Cairo Agreement, the thirteenth peace pact among Somalia's armed ethnic factions since central administration collapsed in 1991, has proved to be no more successful than previous accords. Warring clan leaders have been largely unable to agree on the division of the few spoils resulting from resumed trade and aid, and sporadic fighting has continued in Mogadishu and southern parts of the country. Hundreds of thousands of Somalis have again faced famine as insecurity and unusual flooding made both farming and relief food delivery difficult. In June, the United Nations announced a new policy, backed by the Organization of African Unity, to bolster autonomous regional administrations that have been able to impose effective control over their territory, thereby nominally allowing both economic and democratic development. These administrations could form the basis of a new federal Somalia state, but for now will mainly benefit the self-declared and internationally unrecognized Somaliland Republic, which covers northern territories once held as British Somaliland and the autonomous Puntland. Both have elected their own governments and brought relative peace to their areas.

Somalia has been wracked for over a decade by civil war, clan fighting, and natural disasters ranging from drought to flood to famine. Ali Madhi Mohamed of the Somalia Salvation Alliance (SSA) and Hussein Aideed of the Somali National Alliance (SNA), the main faction leaders in the country's south, are still struggling for control over Mogadishu and other areas.

Extensive television coverage of famine and civil strife that took approximately 300,000 lives in 1991 and 1992 prompted an American-led international intervention in Somalia. The armed humanitarian mission in late 1992 quelled clan combat long enough to stop the famine, but ended in urban guerrilla warfare against Somali militias.

The last international forces withdrew in March 1995 after the casualty count reached the thousands. Approximately 100 peacekeepers, including 20 American soldiers, were killed. The $4 billion United Nations intervention had little lasting impact. Today, neighboring countries and others as far afield as Libya and Egypt are reportedly backing competing warlords. International relief agencies operate only intermittently and have repeatedly suspended assistance for security reasons. In 1998, kidnapping for ransom of relief workers continued, and a Portuguese doctor was murdered. In

October, the last Roman Catholic nuns in Somalia closed their children's clinic and left the country after one nun was briefly abducted.

Somalia, a Horn of Africa nation, gained independence in July 1960 with the union of British Somaliland and territories to the south that had been an Italian colony. Other ethnic Somali-inhabited lands are now part of Djibouti, Ethiopia, and Kenya. General Mohammed Siad Barre seized power in 1969 and increasingly employed divisive clan politics to maintain power. Civil war, starvation, banditry, and brutality have wracked Somalia since the struggle to topple Barre began in the late 1980s. When Barre was deposed in January 1991, power was claimed and contested by heavily armed guerrilla movements and militias based on traditional ethnic and clan loyalties. Savage struggles for economic assets by the various factions led to anarchy and famine. Rebuilding the country will be an enormous task. Somalia can be described as a "failed state." Central authority has disappeared, and local traditional clan authorities have reclaimed state powers, including administration of justice and control of external commerce. The country is unlikely to be reconstituted in its previous form.

Political Rights and Civil Liberties: Somalis have had no opportunity to choose their government on a national basis since 1969. The local administrations in Somaliland and Puntland have conducted some form of elections and installed apparently stable governments with functioning legislative arms and courts. Elsewhere, rival clan warlords rule by force of arms. One faction of the United Somali Congress/Somalia National Alliance (USC/SNA) is now led by its late leader's son, Hussein Mohamed Aideed. His main rivals for "national" power are SSA leader Ali Madhi Mohamed and Osman Hassan Ali "Ato," the leader of another USC/SNA faction. Several smaller armed factions, including the Rahawyayn Resistance Army, also control various parts of southern Somalia.

During the year, Ethiopian troops were reportedly deployed again on Somali territory to deter ethnic Somali rebels who contest Ethiopian rule over that country's Somali-inhabited Ogaden region.

Clan loyalties are the basis for most civil organization in the vacuum left by the disappearance of central authority. Harsh Islamic law has returned a semblance of order to some areas, including parts of Mogadishu long plagued by lawlessness. Islamic courts are imposing sentences that include executions and amputations in accordance with *Shari'a* law. Rights to free expression and association are ignored. Few autonomous civic or political groups can organize or operate safely. Several small newspapers and newsletters are published in Mogadishu, but the few independent journalists are under constant threat. International correspondents visit only at great risk. Radio stations are mainly operated by various factions, although the United Nations now sponsors new "peace programming." During the year, several journalists were arrested in Somaliland for criticizing the local government and suggesting that full press freedom does not exist.

Under customary practices and variants of Koranic law, women experience intense societal discrimination. Infibulation, the most severe form of female genital mutilation, is routine. Various armed factions have recruited children into their militias.

The Republic of Somaliland has exercised de facto independence since May 1991. It is headed by President Mohammed Ibrahim Egal and based in Hargeisa, where resistance to the Siad Barre dictatorship in the 1980s was most intense. Egal has said that a referendum on independence will not take place until a peace agreement covering the rest of the country has been reached. Somaliland is far more cohesive than the rest of the country, although reports of some human rights abuses persist. Aid agencies are able to operate more effectively and safely in the Somaliland Republic and nearby Puntland than elsewhere in Somalia. Somaliland government revenues are derived mostly through duties levied on traffic through the port at Berbera, where large amounts of livestock are exported to the Gulf states.

South Africa

Polity: Presidential-legis-
lative democracy
Economy: Capitalist-statist
Population: 38,900,000
PPP: $4,334
Life Expectancy: 58
Ethnic Groups: Black (75 percent), white (14 percent), mixed race (9 percent), Indian (2 percent)
Capital: Pretoria (administrative), Cape Town (legislative)

Political Rights: 1
Civil Liberties: 2
Status: Free

Overview:
South Africa has begun to prepare for a future without Nelson Mandela, who will retire as president after national elections in mid-1999. He will leave his country with a democratic order, but facing myriad and intractable problems of economic development and group relations. Deputy President Thabo Mbeki, Mandela's designated successor, is expected to be easily elected president by a new National Assembly that the ruling African National Congress (ANC) will again dominate. The ANC's record on fighting common crime and governmental corruption will be a campaign issue for critics on the left and right. The party will also find it difficult to retain full support of its Communist and trade union allies, especially as it pursues conservative economic policies necessary to secure international aid. Some analysts have suggested that Mandela's retirement will deprive South Africa of the moral leadership that has been a cohesive force for South African society and that Mbeki's respect for fundamental freedoms is far from firm.

Consolidation of South Africa's democratic transition continued under the new constitution that took effect in February 1997. The country's independent judiciary and other institutions that protect and promote basic rights are growing stronger. The durability of these democratic structures, however, is uncertain in a country deeply divided by ethnicity and class and plagued by rising crime and corruption. Political violence again flared in the Zulu areas of KwaZulu/Natal Province, and the election campaign could evoke more bloody clashes.

The 1999 polls will be South Africa's first full post-apartheid national elections. The current government of national unity (GNU) was formed by the Zulu-based Inkatha Freedom Party (IFP) and the Afrikaner-dominated National Party (NP) after the April 1994 transitional election. The NP withdrew from the GNU in July 1996 and has diminished sharply as a political force. The Democratic Party, mostly supported by white liberal voters, may overtake the NP as the official opposition. The 1999 polls are likely to be contested by at least a dozen other parties, including the United Democratic Movement, which is led by expelled senior ANC leader Bantu Holomisa and former top NP figure Roelf Meyer. Few white South Africans appear to support far-right parties or the armed resistance that is still being promoted by a few extremist groups. IFP leader Mangosuthu Buthelezi remains in the national cabinet despite disputes with the ANC and may be a contender for the post of deputy president. The NP and the IFP represent the most dangerous schisms in South African politics.

In October, the final report of the Truth and Reconciliation Commission (TRC), which is headed by retired Archbishop and Nobel Peace Laureate Desmond Tutu, was released. Killings by government agents of numerous anti-apartheid activists were admitted and sometimes described in ghastly detail by perpetrators seeking amnesty. The commission condemned the involvement of Winnie Madzhikela Mandela, President Mandela's former wife, in the murder of several people in the black township of Soweto near Johannesburg. It also condemned murders and other violent acts committed by Buthelezi's IFP. The TRC has granted amnesty for many of the people who admitted to crimes, but there is unlikely to be any general amnesty for people who did not apply. The TRC also suggested that special taxes be enacted to provide compensation for victims of apartheid crimes.

The international crisis in emerging markets has hit South Africa hard, as prices of gold and other commodities that South Africa exports tumbled along with the value of the national currency. Economic liberalization is encouraging new investment, but unemployment among blacks is nearly 60 percent. Addressing issues of social and economic development will be crucial to maintaining popular support for the next ANC administration and democratic governance. The country's announcement in November of more than $5 billion in new international arms purchases will divert resources desperately needed for development.

Political Rights and Civil Liberties: South Africans elected their government through nonracial universal suffrage for the first time in parliamentary elections in April 1994. Elections for the 400-seat National Assembly and 90-seat National Council of Provinces are by proportional representation based on party lists. The National Assembly elects the president to serve concurrently with its five-year term. Local council elections in 1995 and 1996 brought nonracial local governance for the first time. In general, the electoral process, including extensive civic and voter education, balanced state media coverage, and reliable balloting and vote-counting, has worked properly. The notable exception is in KwaZulu/Natal, where political violence and credible allegations of vote rigging have devalued the process. New voter registration procedures in 1998 caused concern that some people would be unable to register in time for the 1999 polls, when 13 million citizens will be eligible to vote.

A constitutionally mandated Human Rights Commission is appointed by parliament to "promote the observance of, respect for, and the protection of fundamental rights" and "develop an awareness of fundamental rights among all people of the republic." The commission's judgment was questioned in November, when it ordered an investigation into racism in the media. The eleven-member Constitutional Court has been beyond reproach and has demonstrated its strong independence. Lower courts generally respect legal provisions regarding arrest and detention, although courts remains understaffed. Efforts to end torture and other abuses by the national police force have been implemented. An estimated four million illegal firearms circulate in South Africa, thereby contributing to increased and more violent common crime. A similar number of licensed weapons also increases chances of gun violence. White farmers on isolated homesteads have been particular targets in what some people claim is an organized campaign to drive whites from the land.

Free expression in media and public discourse is respected, and new freedom of information statutes are expected to improve governmental transparency. South Africa's media have suffered little overt interference from government or politicians since the end of apartheid. An array of newspapers and magazines publish reportage, analysis, and opinion sharply critical of the government, political parties, and other societal actors. Concentration of media ownership is a concern, however, especially by conglomerates with other business interests that may conflict with open reporting. Radio broadcasting has been dramatically liberalized, with scores of small community radio stations now operating. The state-owned South African Broadcasting Corporation is today far more independent than during apartheid, but still suffers from self-censorship.

Equal rights for women are guaranteed by the constitution and promoted by a constitutionally mandated Commission on Gender Equality, but discriminatory practices in customary law remain prevalent. Almost one-third of National Assembly members are women, but only three serve in the 28-member cabinet. Women occupy less than five percent of judgeships. High incidence of rape and other violence against women have been reported in both townships and rural areas. Violence against children is also reportedly widespread.

Labor rights codified under the 1995 Labor Relations Act (LRA) are respected, and there are more than 250 trade unions. The right to strike can be exercised after reconciliation efforts. The LRA allows employers to hire replacement workers. The Congress of South African Trade Unions, the country's largest union federation, is formally linked to both the ANC and the South African Communist Party and was among the leaders of the anti-apartheid struggle. It maintained its ties to the government in 1998, despite growing unease with the ANC's economic direction. More radical unions are demanding quick redistribution of the national wealth. More than three-quarters of South Africa's people are black, but they share less than a third of the country's total income. The white minority retains most economic power.

The government's Reconstruction and Development Plan (RDP) envisions major improvements for rural areas and townships where South Africa's poorest people reside. The RDP now coexists uncomfortably with the government's conservative Growth, Employment, and Redistribution macroeconomic strategy. Many large international corporations that left South Africa in the 1980s have now returned, and South African exports are developing new markets in the region and across Africa.

Spain

Polity: Parliamentary democracy
Economy: Mixed capitalist
Population: 39,400,000
PPP: $14,789
Life Expectancy: 77
Ethnic Groups: Spanish (72 percent), Catalan (16 percent), Galician (8 percent), Basque (2 percent)
Capital: Madrid

Political Rights: 1
Civil Liberties: 2
Status: Free

Overview:
At year's end, the Spanish government and leaders of the Basque Fatherland and Liberty (ETA) separatist guerrilla movement, Europe's largest terrorist group, took major steps toward ending the violence that has claimed approximately 800 lives since 1970. In September, the ETA announced a ceasefire. In November, it pledged to consider a "definitive" end to its violent campaign for independence. Also in November, the government agreed to hold direct talks with ETA leaders. The two sides were emboldened to take these steps after witnessing the positive results of the signing of the Northern Ireland peace accords. They were further encouraged by the victory of moderate forces in Basque regional elections in October.

Spain's current government came to power after winning a plurality in 1996 elections that ended 14 years of socialist rule. Prime Minister Jose Maria Aznar's Partido Popular and its parliamentary partners share a commitment to enter into the European Monetary Union in its first stage in 1999.

Spain's Basques were the first group known to have occupied the Iberian Peninsula. The country's current language, religion, and laws are based on those of the Romans, who arrived several centuries later. The unification of present-day Spain dates to 1512. After a period of colonial influence and wealth, the country declined as a European power and was occupied by France in the early 1800s. Subsequent wars and revolts led to Spain's loss of its colonies in the Americas by century's end.

Francisco Franco began a long period of nationalist rule after the victory of his forces in the 1936-39 civil war. In spite of the country's official neutrality, Franco followed Axis policies during World War II. Even with its closed economy, the country was transformed into a modern industrial nation in the post-war years. After a transitional period upon Franco's death in 1975, the country emerged as a parliamentary democracy. It joined the European Union in 1986.

Political Rights and Civil Liberties:
Spanish citizens can change their government democratically. Spain has been governed democratically since 1977, following nearly 40 years of dictatorship under Franco and a brief transitional government under Adolfo Suarez.

The country is divided into 17 autonomous regions with limited powers, including control over such areas as health, tourism, local police agencies, and instruction in regional languages. The bicameral federal legislature includes a territorially-elected Senate and a Congress of Deputies elected on the basis of proportional representation and universal suffrage. Although the Socialist party has ruled that women must occupy 25 percent of senior party posts and a feminist party has been officially registered since 1981, female participation in government remains minimal.

A Supreme Tribunal heads the judiciary, which includes territorial, provincial, regional, and municipal courts. The post-Franco constitution and 1996 parliamentary legislation established the right to trial by jury.

Freedom of speech and a free press are guaranteed. The press has been particularly influential in setting the political agenda in recent years, with national daily newspapers such as *El Mundo, ABC,* and *El Pais* covering corruption and other issues. A new conservative daily, *La Razon*, was launched in November. In addition to the state-controlled television station, which has been accused of progovernment bias, there are three independent commercial television stations.

The rights to freedom of association and collective bargaining are constitutionally guaranteed. The country has one of the lowest levels of trade union membership in the EU, and unions have failed to prevent passage of new labor laws facilitating dismissals and encouraging short-term contracting.

In 1978, the constitution disestablished Roman Catholicism as the state religion, but directed Spanish authorities to "keep in mind the religious beliefs of Spanish society." Freedom of worship and the separation of church and state are respected in practice. Spain is home to many cultural and linguistic groups, some—such as the Basques—with strong regional identities.

Spain lacks anti-discrimination laws, and ethnic minorities, particularly immigrants, continue to report bias and mistreatment. In particular, North African immigrants report physical abuse and discrimination by authorities.

Sri Lanka

Polity: Presidential-parliamentary democracy (insurgency)
Economy: Mixed capitalist-statist
Population: 18,900,000
PPP: $3,408
Life Expectancy: 72

Political Rights: 3
Civil Liberties: 4
Status: Partly Free

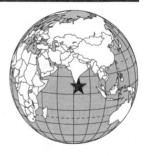

Ethnic Groups: Sinhalese (74 percent), Tamil (18 percent), Moor (7 percent), Burgher, Malay, Vedda (1 percent)
Capital: Colombo

Overview: In 1998, the year marking the fiftieth anniversary of Sri Lanka's independence, opposition parties continued to reject President Chandrika Kumaratunga's proposal to end a 15-year civil conflict that has claimed some 60,000 lives, diverted resources from social welfare to the war effort, and taken a psychological toll on this island nation through ceaseless deaths, detentions, road blocks, and identification checks.

Sri Lanka achieved independence from Britain in 1948. Political power has alternated between the conservative United National Party (UNP) and the leftist Sri Lanka Freedom Party (SLFP). Colonial-era language policies favoring Tamils and other minorities over the Sinhala-speaking majority contributed to communal tensions that continued after independence.

The 1978 constitution provides for a president who is directly elected for a six-year term, has broad executive powers, and can dissolve parliament. The 225-member parliament is directly elected for a six year term.

Tamil's claims of discrimination in education and employment, and the country's overall high unemployment rate continued to inflame communal tensions in the early 1980s. In 1983, a Tamil guerrilla attack on an army patrol and subsequent anti-Tamil riots led to civil war. By 1986, the Liberation Tigers of Tamil Eelam (LTTE), which called for an independent Tamil homeland in the north and east, controlled much of Jaffna Peninsula in the north. The UNP government established an Indian peacekeeping force between 1987-90 that only temporarily halted the fighting. Its presence fomented an anti-government insurgency in the south by the Marxist, Sinhalese-based People's Liberation Front (JVP). The army and military-backed death squads crushed the JVP by 1990, with total deaths estimated at 60,000.

In 1993, a suspected LTTE suicide bomber assassinated President Ranasinghe Premadasa of the UNP. In the August 1994 parliamentary elections, held with a 76 percent turnout, the People's Alliance, an SLFP-dominated coalition led by Kumaratunga that promised to end the war, won 105 seats to oust the UNP (94 seats) after 17 years. In the November presidential elections, Kumaratunga won 62 percent of the vote against the widow of the UNP's original candidate, whom the LTTE had assassinated in October.

Having failed to negotiate a peace agreement with the LTTE early in her term, Kumaratunga turned to a military solution while introducing political reforms aimed at satisfying Tamil aspirations. In 1996, the army recaptured the Jaffna Peninsula, sending the LTTE into the northern jungle. Since 1997, the army has lost thousands of soldiers trying to secure a land route to Jaffna through the rebel-held Vanni region.

In 1998, Kumaratunga failed to gain political support for proposed constitutional amendments that would devolve power to new regional councils and grant greater autonomy to Tamils and other minorities. The UNP and the influential Buddhist clergy rejected the plan, saying it would lead to a Tamil state. Kumaratunga needs opposition support since her PA is short of the two-thirds parliamentary majority required for constitutional amendments. In August, Kumaratunga declared a state of emergency on security grounds and postponed provincial polls. The opposition accused Kumaratunga of trying to avoid the elections.

Political Rights and Civil Liberties:

Sri Lankans can change their government democratically. Institutions have been severely tested by civil war, communal tensions, and partisan violence. The 1997 local elections were marred by the shooting death of a PA MP, by partisan violence, and by intimidation of voters and UNP poll monitors. In January 1998, only 28 percent of voters turned out for the first local elections in Jaffna in 15 years. The LTTE rejected the elections and later killed two mayors of Jaffna; it apparently committed these and other assassinations to eliminate moderate Tamils who could erode the LTTE's support.

The judiciary is independent. Courts in Jaffna have been severely disrupted due to LTTE threats against judges. Conditions in prisons and remand homes are extremely poor.

In August, Kumaratunga reimposed an island-wide state of emergency. The Emergency Regulations allow authorities to detain suspects for up to one year without charge and ban political meetings. The Prevention of Terrorism Act permits authorities to detain suspects for 18 months without charge, and provides broad immunity for security forces. These detention laws and the poor implementation of safeguards for detainees are blamed, in part, for the continuing problem of "disappearances."

Government security forces, the LTTE, and state-backed Sinhalese, Muslim, and anti-LTTE Tamil "home guards" are responsible for considerable human rights abuses related to the civil war. In 1994, Kumaratunga authorized three presidential commissions to investigate past human rights violations, including thousands of disappearances. In 1997, the government announced that the three commissions had found evidence of 16,742 disappearances, and prosecutions would be initiated in cases where there was prima facie evidence.

According to Amnesty International, in 1996, there were an estimated 600 disappearances in Jaffna, often by security forces in reprisal for LTTE attacks. The number of disappearances fell in 1997 and 1998, in part because of charges brought in 1997 against nine soldiers accused in the 1996 murders of schoolgirl Krishanthy Kumarasamy and three others on Jaffna. In a landmark judgment in July, the Colombo High Court sentenced to death five members of the security forces in the Kumarasamy case; it marked the first time members of the security forces had been given a heavy sentence for severe abuses. Authorities also began investigating the site at Chemmani, Jaffna, where one of the defendants in the Kumarasamy case said the army had buried scores of bodies of people who had disappeared in 1996.

Nevertheless, few security personnel have been convicted for rights abuses. In 1998, a presidential commission made slow progress in investigating complaints left over from the previous commissions. An official Human Rights Commission established in 1997 continued to operate, but its effectiveness is unclear. Security forces continued to be implicated in the torture and rape of civilians and the abuse of ordinary criminal detainees.

The LTTE, now reduced to jungle strongholds, continued to be responsible for summary executions of civilians, arbitrary abductions and detentions, denial of basic rights, and forcible conscription of children. The LTTE is responsible for major urban terrorism attacks that have killed hundreds of people, including bombings in Colombo and Kandy in 1998, and the 1996 Central Bank bombing. In response, authorities arbitrarily detained and sometimes tortured thousands of young Tamils in security sweeps. Some 500,000 Tamils have returned to areas formerly held by the LTTE, although food shortages continued in some areas and thousands remained internally displaced.

Kumaratunga came to office promising to respect freedom of expression, but her government has filed criminal defamation charges against several editors. Authorities continued to occasionally harass, threaten, and assault journalists, particularly Tamils. The government continued to limit journalists' access to the civil war, and in June reimposed censorship on war coverage. Restrictive legislation further chills press freedom, and the government controls Lake House group, the largest newspaper chain. Print media are both public and private. Radio and television are predominantly state-owned, and political coverage favors the party in power.

Women's groups report that sexual and physical abuse against women is increasing, with the number of rapes rising sharply. Laws protecting women from violence are weakly enforced. Many of the thousands of child domestic servants are physically abused. In April, the chairman of a presidential task force told Reuters that a study had found that 20 percent of boys in one area had been sexually abused. Enforcement of laws against child prostitution is weak, and Sri Lanka has become a destination for foreign pedophiles. Conditions in asylums are often inhumane.

Human rights and social welfare nongovernmental organizations (NGO) are active. NGOs criticized a March amendment to a law that allows authorities to take control of welfare-oriented NGOs suspected of fraud. Partisan violence on campuses periodically leads to university closings. Religious freedom is respected. However, private disputes occasionally turn into religious and ethnic confrontations, with attacks on Tamils, Muslims, and Christians.

Trade unions are independent, and collective bargaining is practiced. State workers cannot strike. In April, Kumaratunga used the 1989 Essential Services Act to end a strike by postal workers; the act allows the president to declare as illegal a strike in any industry. Labor violations are reported on the tea plantations, where many of the workers are descendants of colonial-era migrant workers and have difficulty obtaining citizenship and identity documentation.

Sudan

Polity: Military-civilian
Economy: Mixed
capitalist
Population: 28,500,000
PPP: $1,110
Life Expectancy: 51
Ethnic Groups: Black (52 percent), Arab (39 percent), Beja (6 percent), other (3 percent)
Capital: Khartoum

Political Rights: 7
Civil Liberties: 7
Status: Not Free

Overview:
An October appeal by humanitarian groups for UN action to bring peace to Sudan captured the grim reality of the country's 17-year civil war. According to the appeal, the conflict and human tragedy accompanying it "have now reached an unimaginable and extraordinary level of tragedy." It concludes that peace is the "only hope for progress and to prevent further humanitarian catastrophe."

There is little cause for optimism that a solution to the bloody war will soon be found. As many as two million people may have perished in fighting and famine in southern Sudan during the past 15 years. In November, the Islamist regime in Khartoum reached an accord with the Sudan People's Liberation Movement, the main southern rebel group, to allow increased delivery of relief supplies to millions of people threatened with starvation. The parties would not agree, however, to extend a partial July ceasefire beyond January 15, 1999. Severe human rights abuses by various contestants to power persisted, and government forces continued slave raids in the country's south. Sudan's conflict broadly pits the country's Arab Muslim north against the black African animist and Christian south. Some pro-democratic northerners, however, have allied with southern rebels to form the National Democratic Alliance (NDA), while northern rebels of the Sudan Allied Forces have staged attacks in northeastern Sudan. Some southern Sudanese groups have signed peace pacts with the government and southern militias have fought among themselves.

Both rebels and government forces launched repeated offensives during the year, and government aircraft indiscriminately bombed civilian targets. A general conscription to replenish serious government battlefield losses continued. In July, a new constitution was adopted after reportedly being approved by 97 percent of a nearly universal referendum turnout. In October, an ill-defined law allowing formation of "political associations' was enacted. The regime's campaign against secular and democratic forces in the Arab north continued with arrests, detention without trial, and severe pressure against media and the country's few remaining independent institutions.

The United States has identified Sudan as a sponsor of international terrorism, and in November renewed economic sanctions against the Khartoum regime. Sudan is also under UN sanctions as punishment for official Sudanese involvement in a 1995 assassination attempt against Egyptian President Hosni Mubarak in Addis Ababa. In August, the United States launched a cruise missile attack that destroyed a factory allegedly being used to manufacture chemical weapons and reportedly linked to Osman bin-Laden, the Saudi millionaire charged with planning the August bombings of the U.S. embassies in Nairobi and Dar-es-Salaam.

Sudan, Africa's largest country, has been embroiled in devastating civil wars for 32 of its 43 years as a modern state. It achieved independence in 1956 after nearly eight decades of British rule. The Anya Nya movement, representing mainly Christian and animist black Africans in southern Sudan, battled government forces from 1956 to 1972. The south gained extensive autonomy under a 1972 accord, and, for the next decade, an uneasy peace prevailed. In 1983, General Jafar Numeiri, who had toppled an elected government in 1969, restricted southern autonomy and introduced *Shari'a* law. These actions, along with pervasive racial and religious discrimination and fears of economic exploitation raised by government plans to pipe oil discovered in the south to northern Sudan, sparked renewed civil war. Numeiri was overthrown in 1985. Civilian rule was restored in 1986, but the war continued. Lieutenant General Omar Hassan Ahmed al-Bashir ousted the freely elected government in 1989. He now rules through a military-civilian regime strongly backed by senior Muslim clerics, including Hassan al-Turabi, who wields considerable power as leader of the National Islamic Front (NIF), the de facto, but undeclared ruling party. In December, Turabi announced that he would resign as speaker of the National Assembly and concentrate on work for the NIF.

Political Rights and Civil Liberties:

Sudanese President and Prime Minister al-Bashir claims electoral legitimacy from heavily manipulated March 1996 elections that cannot credibly be said to have reflected the will of the Sudanese people. Sudanese are unable to choose or change their government democratically. Elections were also held in 1996 for 264 members of the National Assembly. The remaining 136 seats in the parliament are filled by presidential appointment. A new constitution adopted in July and a law regulating political associations are unlikely to bring significant change, despite provisions for multiparty elections, direct election of the head of state, and religious freedom. The constitution also calls for an independence referendum in south Sudan in 2002.

Under the current regime, formal guarantees of basic civil and political rights mean little. The hardline Islamist-backed junta has zealously pursued military solutions to the civil war. Sudan is officially an Islamic state. There is little autonomous civil society, and few independent voices in media. Trade unions were heavily suppressed after the 1989 coup and operate today under tight control by the regime. The entire judiciary and security apparatus are controlled by the NIF, and officials and security forces act with impunity. Civil law has been supplanted by Shari'a law, which discriminates against women and provides for severe punishments, including floggings, amputations, crucifixion, and death. Two Roman Catholic priests are among 20 people who face execution by crucifixion if convicted of dubious charges of involvement in bombings in Khartoum in June.

Serious human rights abuses by nearly every faction involved in the war have been reported. "Ghost houses," secret detention and torture centers, are reportedly operated by secret police in several cities. Many thousands of southern Sudanese have been enslaved after being seized in raids by Arab militias and other government forces. Relief agencies have liberated numerous captives by purchasing slaves' freedom. The government has denied and denounced the widespread slavery, but has not acted to end the practice.

The war's devastation has been compounded by famine among the displaced populace. In southern Sudan, the conflict is complicated by ethnic clashes within rebel ranks. In 1991, the Sudan People's Liberation Army (SPLA), led by Colonel John Garang, was split when ethnic Nuer troops joined dissident Riak Machar in the Southern Sudan Independence Movement in protest over alleged ethnic Dinka domination of the SPLA. Machar defected to the government in 1996. Internecine strife within rebel ranks intensified in 1998. The NDA, a broad coalition of secular and religious groups from both northern and southern Sudan, enjoys support from Ethiopia, Uganda, and, most importantly, Eritrea, where it is headquartered. The rebels also receive American assistance.

The once vigorous print media have been steadily tamed by the closure of publications and harassment of journalists creating increasing self-censorship. A 1996 press law further eroded media freedom. The regime has tightened controls on international and domestic communication by confiscating fax and telex machines, typewriters, and copiers. Broadcast media are entirely state-controlled. Some newspapers still test the limits of regime tolerance. Editions of two newspapers criticizing the new constitution were seized in July.

Women face extensive societal discrimination and unequal treatment as stipulated under Shari'a law. Despite its legal prohibition, female genital mutilation is routine, although UN and government programs are campaigning against it. Rape is reportedly routine in war zones.

Sudan's people are mostly agriculturists. Trade, investment, and development have been severely limited by the civil war. Oil fields in the country's southwest could provide sizable revenues, but their exploitation will be difficult as long as the war continues. Rebels have warned foreign oil workers that they are subject to attack as the government seeks to complete a new 1,000-mile oil pipeline that would bring revenue crucially needed to prosecute the war.

↓ Suriname

Polity: Presidential-par-
liamentary democracy
Economy: Capitalist-
statist
Population: 400,000
PPP: $4,862
Life Expectancy: 70

Political Rights: 3
Civil Liberties: 3
Status: Partly Free

Ethnic Groups: East Indian (37 percent), Creole (31 percent),
Javanese (15 percent), other (13 percent)
Capital: Paramaribo
Trend arrow: Suriname receives a downward trend arrow due to politicization of
the country's judiciary.

Overview:

Europeans sought to use a private July 1998 visit by former military strongman Desi Bourterse to nearby Trinidad and Tobago to press for his extradition on international drug charges. But protected by President Jules Wijdenbosch, whom he both supports and advises, Bourterse, placed in 1998 on Interpol's most wanted list, remained one step ahead of Dutch police. The Bourterse affair came just a month after protesting opposition parties and striking oil workers shut down the capital city for several days. In late 1998, the Wijdenbosch government oversaw the takeover of Suriname's traditionally independent high court.

The Republic of Suriname achieved independence from the Netherlands in 1975. Five years later, a military coup brought strongman Bourterse to power as the head of a regime that brutally suppressed civic and political opposition, and initiated a decade of military intervention in politics. In 1987, Bourterse permitted elections under a constitution providing for a directly elected, 51-seat National Assembly, which serves a five-year term and selects the state president. If the Assembly is unable to select a president with the required two-thirds vote, a People's Assembly, comprised of parliament and regional and local officials, chooses the president. The Front for Democracy and Development, a three-party coalition, handily won the 1987 elections with the military-organized National Democratic Party (NDP) winning just three seats.

In 1990, the army ousted President Ramsewak Shankar, and Bourterse again took power. International pressure led to new elections in 1991. The New Front, a coalition of mainly East Indian, Creole, and Javanese parties, won a majority, although the NDP increased its share to 12. The Assembly selected the Front's candidate, Ronald Venetiaan, as president.

Bouterse quit the army in 1992 in order to lead the NDP. The Venetiaan government took some constitutional steps to curb military influence, and in late 1995 and early 1996, it purged several high-ranking pro-Bourterse military officials. The government's economic structural adjustment program led to social and labor unrest amidst an inflationary spiral and a collapse of the Surinamese guilder.

During the campaign for the May 23, 1996 parliamentary elections, the NDP pledged to reverse many of the economic programs of the Venetiaan government. The four-party New Front lost seats, winning 24, and entered into a coalition with the smaller Central Bloc, consisting of two opposition groups. The alliance proved insufficient to gain the necessary two-thirds parliamentary majority needed to return Venetiaan to office.

Bourterse's NDP, with 16 seats, joined with the Javanese-based Party of National Unity and Solidarity as well as dissident members of the East Indian-based United Reform Party to press the convening of the constitutionally mandated 869-member People's Assembly in September. The deadlock was broken when Wijdenbosch, a former deputy party leader under Bourterse, was elected president.

The Netherlands has sought international help in tracking down Bourterse, who it charges was involved in drug trafficking and money laundering. Despite unprecedented cooperation with international narcotics control efforts, the Trinidad and Tobago government does not have an extradition treaty with Holland, and in 1998, suffered significant embarrassment when it could not hand over the former dictator for lack of an extradition treaty. In contravention of the constitutional balance of powers requirements, Wijdenbosch chose a president of the high court as well as the attorney general in July 1988. The move was declared null and void by the court, after which officers of the Central Intelligence and Security Service occupied the court president's office in October.

Political Rights and Civil Liberties:

Citizens of Suriname can change their government democratically. The May 1996 elections were generally free and fair, and marked the first time since independence that one elected government transferred power to another. Political parties mostly reflect the cleavages of Surinam's ethnically-complex society, a factor contributing to parliamentary gridlock. Civic institutions are weak, and Bourterse's considerable influence seemed bolstered by his appointment in 1997 to the newly created position of Advisor of State, an effort to insulate him from the reach of Dutch justice.

The judiciary, already weak before Wijdenbosch's 1998 efforts at politicization, has been reluctant to handle cases involving human rights issues, the military, and supporters of Bourterse. In 1996, a lower court upheld a 1992 law granting amnesty to former rebels and soldiers for rights violations committed between 1985 and mid-1992. In January 1997, responding to the demands of human rights organizations, Wijdenbosch promised the imminent creation of a commission to create an institute to investigate the murders of more than 140 people during the 1980s. In October 1997, the Organization for Justice and Peace (*Organisatie voor Gerechtigheid en Vrede*, OGV) initiated a campaign for the establishment of a "truth commission" to investigate events of that period. However, a year later, the government had failed to prosecute any person responsible for the rights violations. Abuse of detainees by the civilian police is a problem, and prisons are dangerously overcrowded.

The government generally respects freedom of expression. Radio is both public and private, and a number of small commercial radio stations compete with the government-owned radio and television broadcasting system. State broadcast media generally offer pluralistic viewpoints. The private press practices some self-censorship, particularly concerning news about Bourterse. In June 1998, a Dutch journalist in Suriname was briefly abducted by unknown persons, who accused him of being a spy for the Netherlands.

Indigenous groups, although constituting 15 percent of the population, are geographically isolated and face social discrimination, political marginalization, and denial of land rights, including the dislocation from their lands by foreign mining interests.

Constitutional guarantees on gender equality are not enforced, and the Asian Marriage Act allows parents to arrange marriages. Human rights organizations function relatively freely, and several specifically address violence against women, trafficking of Brazilian women, and related issues.

Workers can join independent trade unions, and the labor movement is active in politics. Collective bargaining is legal and practiced fairly widely. Civil servants have no legal right to strike but do so in practice.

Swaziland

Polity: Traditional monarchy
Economy: Capitalist
Population: 1,000,000
PPP: $2,954
Life Expectancy: 39
Ethnic Groups: African (97 percent), European (3 percent)
Capital: Mbabane

Political Rights: 6
Civil Liberties: 4*
Status: Not Free

Ratings change: Swaziland's civil liberties rating changed from 5 to 4 due to a slight relaxation of political controls.

Overview:
In November, Swaziland appeared to teeter on the edge of serious trouble as several bombs exploded in Mbabane following October legislative elections that excluded political parties and most of the democratic opposition. The voting was marked by very low turnout and was neither open nor fair. It was based on the Swazi *tinkhundla* (local council) system of closely controlled nominations and voting that seeks to legitimatize the rule of King Mswati III and his Dlamini clan. Security forces arrested and briefly detained labor and other pro-democracy leaders before the elections and after the bomb blasts. Long an oasis of regional calm amid turmoil in neighboring Mozambique and South Africa, Swaziland is now the only southern African country without an elected government. A Constitutional Review Commission (CRC) appointed in 1996 has made little apparent progress in formulating a new charter that would extend democratic rights and limit the power of the dominant Dlamini clan.

King Mswati III is the latest monarch of the Dlamini dynasty, under which Swazi kingdom expanded and contracted in conflicts with neighboring groups. Britain declared the kingdom a protectorate to prevent Boer expansion in the 1880s and assumed administrative power in 1903. In 1968, Swaziland regained its independence, and an elected parliament was added to the traditional kingship and chieftaincies. Sobhuza II, Mswati's predecessor who died in 1983, ended the multiparty system in favor of the *tinkhundla* system in 1973.

Political Rights and Civil Liberties: Swazis are barred from exercising their right to elect their representatives or to change their government freely. All of Swaziland's citizens are subjects of absolute monarch Mswati III. Royal decrees carry the full force of law. The king rejected an official 1993 report suggesting multiparty elections, and the bicameral legislature of indirectly elected and appointed members is mostly window dressing to royal rule. The 55 members of the House of Assembly elected in October with low voter turnout were government-approved. They will be joined by ten direct royal appointees. The King also appoints 20 members of the Senate, with the remaining ten selected by the National Assembly.

The judiciary is generally independent in most civil cases, although the royal family and government can influence the courts. Traditional courts hear many cases. Prison conditions are poor, and overcrowding has increased since the adoption of the 1993 Non-Bailable Offenses Order. The decree covers serious crimes, including murder, robbery, rape, weapons violations, and poaching. The Swazi Law Society and international groups have protested that the decree effectively denies the presumption of innocence and convicts people without trial. There are regular reports of police brutality.

Freedom of expression is seriously restricted, especially regarding political issues or matters regarding the royal family. In November, a senior minister threatened to bar South African journalists after they generated critical coverage of the election process. Legislation bans publication of any criticism of the monarchy. The constitutional commission has broad authority to prosecute people who "belittle" or "insult" it. Self-censorship is widespread. The *Times of Swaziland,* the only independent newspaper, is routinely harassed by the government. State-run television and radio stations are closely controlled by the government. Broadcast and print media from South Africa are received in the country. A controversial new press law considered by parliament in November was strongly condemned by journalists in Swaziland and media watchdog groups in southern Africa and elsewhere. The bill would create a government-sponsored press council with regulatory and punitive powers, including licensing of journalists. Violations of an as yet undrafted media "code of ethics" could draw large fines against journalists and publishing houses.

Freedom of religion is respected, and a variety of Christian sects operate freely. Nongovernmental organizations not involved in politics are also permitted. Several political groupings operate openly despite their official prohibition, but members are harassed and sometimes detained.

Swazi women encounter discrimination in both formal and customary law. Married women are considered minors, requiring spousal permission to enter into almost any form of economic activity. Women are allowed only limited inheritance rights. Employment regulations requiring equal pay for equal work are obeyed unevenly. Violence against women is common, and discriminatory traditional values still great carry weight.

Unions are able to operate independently under the 1980 Industrial Relations Act, although the International Labor Organization sharply criticized the government's labor policies in a 1997 report. The Swaziland Federation of Trade Unions has been a leader in demands for democratization. Wage agreements are often reached by collective bargaining, and 75 percent of the private work force is unionized.

Swaziland's free market sector operates with little government interference, but most Swazis remain engaged in subsistence agriculture.

Sweden

Polity: Parliamentary democracy
Economy: Mixed capitalist
Population: 8,900,000
PPP: $19,297
Life Expectancy: 79
Ethnic Groups: Swede (89 percent), Finn (2 percent), Lapp [Saami]
Capital: Stockholm

Political Rights: 1
Civil Liberties: 1
Status: Free

Overview:

In September elections, Prime Minister Goran Persson won a second term in office after his Social Democratic Party (SDP) received a 36.6 percent plurality of the vote. It was the worst electoral performance ever by the SDP, which has dominated Swedish post-war politics. Persson had come to power when fellow SDP member Ingvar Carlson resigned in 1996.

In his new government, Persson formed a coalition with the Left and Green parties, which, unlike the SDP, oppose membership in the European Monetary Union (EMU). All political parties support a national referendum on the issue. With polls suggesting that the public would reject the EMU, however, Persson has not sought to schedule a vote.

Sweden is a constitutional monarchy and a multiparty parliamentary democracy. After monarchical alliances with Finland, Denmark, and Norway between the eleventh and nineteenth centuries, it emerged as a modern democracy. Although it has been non-aligned and neutral since World War I, Sweden is now an active member of NATO's Partnership for Peace program. It became a member of the European Union after a 1994 national referendum.

Political Rights and Civil Liberties:

Swedes can change their government democratically. The 310-member, unicameral *Riksdag* (parliament) is elected every four years through universal suffrage. To ensure absolute proportionality for all parties that secure more than four percent of the vote, an additional 39 representatives are selected from a national pool of candidates. Single-party majority governments are rare.

Citizens abroad are entitled to absentee votes in national elections, and non-nationals in residence for three years can vote in local elections. The Saami (Lappic) community elects its own local parliament with significant powers over educational and cultural issues. It serves as an advisory body to the government.

The role of King Carl Gustaf XVI, who was crowned in 1973, is ceremonial. The prime minister is appointed by the speaker of the house and confined by the Riksdag. The country's independent judiciary includes six Courts of Appeal, 100 district courts, a Supreme Court, and a parallel system of administrative courts. Freedom of assembly and association is guaranteed, as are the rights to strike and participate in unions. Strong and well-organized trade union federations represent 90 percent of the labor force. Despite historic ties with the SDP, the labor movement has become increasingly independent.

The media are independent. Most newspapers and periodicals are privately owned. The government subsidizes daily newspapers regardless of their political affiliation. In recent years, new satellite and ground-based commercial television channels and radio stations have ended the government's monopoly over broadcasting.

Citizens can freely express their ideas and criticize their government. The government can prevent publication of information related to national security. A quasi-governmental body censors extremely graphic violence from film, video, and television.

Religious freedom is constitutionally guaranteed. Approximately 90 percent of the population is Lutheran. In 1995, the government and the Lutheran church agreed to disestablish the state religion. By the year 2000, baptism will be required for membership in the church, and only baptized members will be required to pay the three percent income or "church" tax. Roman Catholics, Muslims, Buddhists, Hindus, Jews, and Mormons are represented among the population. Compulsory religion classes in schools now include surveys of various religious beliefs.

International human rights groups have criticized Sweden for its strict immigration policies, which have severely limited the number of refugees admitted annually. Nordic immigrants can become citizens after two years, while others must wait for a minimum of five years. The country does not systematically provide asylum-seekers with adequate legal counsel or access to the appeals process. Some asylum-seekers continue to be detained with criminals.

Dozens of violent incidents with anti-immigrant or racist overtones are reported annually, and the government supports volunteer groups that oppose racism. Human rights monitors operate without government restrictions.

Although the country's 17,000 Saami enjoy some political autonomy, Sweden was the last Nordic country to approve a parliament for its Lappic population. In 1994, the government ended the Saamis' control of hunting and fishing on their lands. Reports of housing and employment discrimination against Saami continue. In August, the government apologized to the Saami for abuses "carried out against them over the years" in connection with the country's "colonialization" of its northern territories.

In a 1994 effort to promote gender-based equality, the Riksdag passed a law requiring working fathers to take at least one month of state-subsidized leave for child care or lose one month's employment benefits. Women constitute approximately 45 percent of the labor force, but their wage levels lag behind those of men. They are well represented in government, including approximately 40 percent of the parliament — in part due to the SDP's pledge to appoint equal numbers of men and women to government positions at all levels.

In a UN study of countries' provision of equal rights for women, Sweden received the highest rating. The country's reputation was tarnished in 1997, however, with the revelation that, under leftist governments from 1935 to 1975, 62,000 Swedes, 90 percent of whom were women, were forcibly sterilized. In August, the government announced that it would begin payments to compensate victims in 1999.

Switzerland

Polity: Federal par-
liamentary democracy
Economy: Capitalist
Population: 7,100,000
PPP: $24,881
Life Expectancy: 79
Ethnic Groups: German (65 percent), French (18 percent),
Italian (10 percent), Romansch (1 percent), other (6 percent)
Capital: Bern (administrative), Lausanne (judicial)

Political Rights: 1
Civil Liberties: 1
Status: Free

Overview:

In August, Switzerland's two largest banks bowed to international pressure by agreeing to pay $1.25 billion in compensa-
tion for wartime losses by Holocaust survivors. Switzerland
had been severely criticized after it was revealed in 1997 that, during and after World
War II, Swiss banks traded in gold looted by the Nazis and did little to help Holocaust
survivors retrieve their bank deposits. The U.S. government concluded that these policies prolonged the war and shielded Nazi assets in the years thereafter.

Officially neutral and nonaligned, Switzerland is not a member of the United Nations or the European Union (EU). In a 1986 national referendum, voters rejected UN
membership by a three-to-one margin. In a 1992 referendum, a narrow majority of voters
rejected joining the European Economic Area, a grouping that is seen as a step toward
EU membership. Since then, the government has grown increasingly anxious to negotiate a pact with the EU to give Swiss industries and service sectors some benefits of
access to the single European market.

In 1996, Switzerland joined NATO's Partnership for Peace program, through which
it can participate in nonmilitary humanitarian and training missions. President and Foreign Minister Flavio Cotti, who supports UN and EU membership, has vowed to make
the country's neutrality policy sufficiently flexible to allow cooperation in international
peacekeeping missions and other security matters.

With the exception of a brief period of centralized power under Napoleonic rule,
Switzerland has remained a confederation of local communities as established in the
Pact of 1291. Most responsibility for public affairs rests at the local and cantonal levels. The 1815 Congress of Vienna formalized the country's borders and recognized its
perpetual neutrality.

Switzerland is often cited as a rare example of peaceful coexistence in a multiethnic
state. The republic is divided into 20 cantons and 6 half-cantons and includes German,
French, Italian, and Romansch communities.

Political Rights and Civil Liberties:

The Swiss can change their government democratically. Free
and fair elections are held at regular intervals. Initiatives and
referenda give citizens an additional degree of involvement
in the legislative process. The cantonal system allows considerable local autonomy,
and localities' linguistic and cultural heritages are zealously preserved.

At the national level, both houses of the Federal Assembly have equal authority.

After legislation has been passed in both the directly elected, 200-member National Council and the Council of States, which includes two members from each canton, it cannot be vetoed by the executive or reviewed by the judiciary. The seven members of the Federal Council (*Bundesrat*) exercise executive authority. They are chosen from the Federal Assembly according to a "magic formula" that ensures representation of each party, region, and language group. Each year, one member serves as president. The judicial system functions primarily at the cantonal level, with the exception of a federal Supreme Court that reviews cantonal court decisions involving federal law. Switzerland's judiciary is independent. The government's postal ministry operates broadcasting services, and the broadcast media enjoy editorial autonomy. Foreign broadcast media are readily accessible. In addition, there are many private television and radio stations. Privately owned daily, weekly, and monthly publications are available in each of the most common languages and are free from government interference.

Freedoms of speech, assembly, association, and religion are observed. While no single state church exists, many cantons support one or several churches. Taxpayers may opt not to contribute to church funds, yet, in many instances, companies cannot. Human rights monitors operate freely. The country's anti-racist law prohibits racist or anti-Semitic speech and actions, and is strictly enforced by the government. In November, the Federal Commission against Racism, the country's official human rights watchdog, warned that "latent anti-Semitism is again being increasingly expressed by word and by deed." It estimated in a major report that one tenth of the population holds anti-Semitic views. To remedy this, it proposed steps to foster closer ties to the country's Jewish community and called on the government to meet its special responsibility to stand up for Jewish citizens.

A 1994 Amnesty International report cited excessive police force used against persons—particularly foreigners—in custody. The report was issued, in an effort to curb the drug trade, shortly after the National Council increased police powers of search and detention of foreigners who lack identification.

In 1995, federal laws aimed at dissuading drug traffickers from entering Switzerland authorized pretrial detention of legal residents for as long as nine months. With 33,000 drug addicts in a population of seven million, the use of hard drugs has become one of the country's most pernicious social ailments.

Although a law on gender equality entered effect in 1996, women still face some barriers to political and social advancement. Some studies estimate women's earnings to be 15 percent lower than men's for equal work. Some charge that the army, from which women are excluded, creates networking opportunities for men, thus creating an economic disadvantage for women. Women were not granted federal suffrage until 1971, and the half-canton, Appenzell-Innerrhoden, did not relinquish its status as the last bastion of all-male suffrage in Europe until 1990. Until the mid-1980s, women were prohibited from participating in the Federal Council. In 1997, journalists revealed that hundreds of women had been forcibly sterilized under a cantonal law passed in 1928. A government critic demanded an official investigation after a historian claimed that the practice continued to this day.

Workers may organize and participate in unions and enjoy the right to strike and bargain collectively. Unions are independent of the government and political parties, and approximately one-third of the workforce belongs to unions.

Syria

Polity: Dominant party (military-dominated)
Economy: Mixed statist
Population: 15,600,000
PPP: $5,374
Life Expectancy: 67
Ethnic Groups: Arab (90 percent), other, including Kurd and Armenian (10 percent)
Capital: Damascus

Political Rights: 7
Civil Liberties: 7
Status: Not Free

Overview:

Syrian support for Kurdish rebels in Turkey brought the two countries to the brink of war in 1998. Tensions subsided in October when Syria agreed to stop aiding the Kurds. Despite this concession, President Hafez al-Assad used Arab fears of growing ties between Israel and Turkey, along with frustration over the stalled peace process, to boost his status as a regional player. He also took steps to end doubts about who will succeed him as leader of one of the region's most repressive regimes.

Following four centuries of rule under the Ottoman Empire, Syria came under French control after World War I and gained independence in 1941. A 1963 military coup brought the pan-Arab, Socialist Ba'ath party to power. As head of the Ba'ath military wing, Assad took power in a 1970 coup and formally became president of the secular regime in 1971. Members of the Alawite Muslim minority, which constitutes 12 percent of the population, were installed in most key military and intelligence positions.

The 1973 constitution vests executive power in the president, who must be a Muslim and who is nominated by the Ba'ath party to be elected through popular referendum. The 250-member People's assembly holds little independent legislative power. In the late 1970s, the fundamentalist Muslim Brotherhood, drawn from the Sunni majority, carried out anti-government attacks in several northern and central towns. In 1982, the government sent the army into the northern town of Hama to crush a Muslim Brotherhood rebellion. As many as 20,000 militants and civilians died in the resulting bloodshed, which decisively ended active opposition to the regime.

Assad last won re-election in 1991, running unopposed in a tightly controlled vote. The death of Major Basil al-Assad, the president's son and heir apparent, in a 1994 auto accident left the question of Assad's successor unclear. However, the president's clear grip on political power was evident at the late-1994 parliamentary elections, in which the ruling National Progressive Front, dominated by the Ba'ath party, took all 167 seats that it contested, with pro-regime "independents" winning the remaining 83 seats.

With his domestic credibility reliant on his hard line against Israel, Assad is in no rush to negotiate a settlement leading to the return of the Israeli-controlled Golan Heights, as this would likely require establishing full diplomatic relations with Jerusalem. Prior to losing the Golan in 1967, Syria had used the territory to shell northern Israeli towns.

Uneasiness over the stalled Middle East peace process and the strengthening of an Israeli-Turkish alliance prompted Syria to engage its Arab neighbors in unified opposition to the Israeli government. In June, Syria and Saudi Arabia issued a joint statement condemning Israeli-Turkish military cooperation. Syria also called for the formation of a pan-Arab organization to pressure Israel and to compete with economic blocs like NAFTA and ASEAN. During the year, the regime reached out to Iraq and Iran and released Muslim and Lebanese political prisoners. Assad balanced this regionalism by seeking a greater role for France and the EU in the Middle East peace process.

In February, Assad removed his brother, Rifaat Assad, as one of the country's three vice-presidents. Rifaat Assad was considered a possible opponent to the eventual succession of the President's son, Bashar. Following this dismissal, Assad replaced his Chief of Staff and Head of General Security in July with loyal aides who would not oppose Bashar al-Assad.

Political Rights and Civil Liberties:

Syrians cannot change their government democratically, though they ostensibly vote for the president and the People's assembly. President Assad maintains absolute authority in the military-backed regime. Tightly controlled elections in November resulted in Assad's National Progressive Front dominating parliament. The outlawed Muslim Brotherhood condemned the elections and called for true political pluralism in Syria.

The Emergency Law, in effect almost continuously since 1963, allows authorities to carry out preventative arrests and to supersede due process safeguards in searches, detentions, and trials in the military-controlled State Security courts, which handle political and security cases. Several independent security services operate independently of each other and without judicial oversight. Authorities monitor personal communications and conduct surveillance of suspected security threats.

The judiciary is subservient to the government. Defendants in ordinary civil criminal cases have some due process rights, though there are no jury trials. In State Security courts, confessions obtained through torture are generally admitted as evidence. Nevertheless, acquittals have been granted in political cases. Trials in the Economic Security Court, which hears cases involving currency violations and other financial offenses, are also conducted without procedural safeguards. In June, the government released approximately 250 political prisoners, including some members of banned Communist and left-wing parties as well as Lebanese and Muslim activists. However, hundreds of other political prisoners remain in jail.

Freedom of expression is sharply restricted. All media are owned and operated by the government and the Ba'ath party. Satellite dishes are illegal, although they are increasingly tolerated. In April, government ministries and universities were connected to the Internet. Private access, however, does not exist. In 1998, the media increased reporting on regional issues, including the Middle East peace process, and a number of articles as well as TV programs criticized official corruption and government inefficiency. Nonetheless, coverage of many topics can result in prosecution. At least ten journalists were imprisoned in Syria in 1998, according to Human Rights Watch and the Committee to Protect Journalists.

Freedom of assembly is nonexistent. The Interior Ministry must grant citizens permission to hold meetings, and most public demonstrations are organized by the government or Ba'ath party. Freedom of association is restricted. Private associations must register with the government, which usually grants registration to groups that are nonpolitical.

The state prohibits Jehovah's Witnesses and Seventh-Day Adventists from worshiping as a community and from owning property. The security apparatus closely monitors the Jewish community, and Jews are generally barred from government employment. They are also the only minority group required to have their religion noted in their passports and identity cards. Religious instruction is mandatory in schools, with government-approved teachers and curricula. Separate classes are provided for Christian and Muslim students.

Although the regime has supported Kurdish struggles abroad, the Kurdish minority in Syria faces cultural and linguistic restrictions, and suspected Kurdish activists are routinely dismissed from schools and jobs. Some 200,000 Kurdish Syrians are stateless and unable to obtain passports, identity cards, or birth certificates as a result of a policy some years ago under which Kurds were stripped of their Syrian nationality. The government never restored their nationality, though the policy ended after the 1960s. As a result, these Kurds are unable to own land, to gain government employment, or to vote. Traditional norms place Syrian women at a disadvantage in marriage, divorce, and inheritance matters. Women also face legal restrictions on passing citizenship on to children.

All unions must belong to the government-controlled General Federation of Trade Unions. By law, the government can nullify any private sector collective bargaining agreement. Strikes are prohibited in the agricultural sector, and rarely occur in other sectors due to previous government crackdowns.

Taiwan (Rep. of China)

Polity: Presidential-legislative democracy
Economy: Mixed capitalist
Population: 21,700,000
PPP: na
Life Expectancy: 75
Ethnic Groups: Taiwanese (84 percent), mainland Chinese (14 percent), aborigine (2 percent)
Capital: Taipei

Political Rights: 2
Civil Liberties: 2
Status: Free

Overview: Taiwan's ruling Nationalist Party (KMT) scored impressive victories in both local and national elections in December, including a successful bid to regain the mayor's post in Taiwan and a comfortable majority in the newly expanded parliament. The opposition Democratic Progressive Party (DPP), a proponent of Taiwan's independence from China, suffered its first major electoral setback in over a decade, although it controls key local governments and all of southern Taiwan. Contributing to the KMT's win were voters' fears of tenser relations with the mainland under a pro-independence leadership, the public's desire for political change, and the Nationalist's ability to cut across ethnic divisions by appealing to a united Taiwanese identity.

At an historic meeting in October, Koo Chen-fu, an influential member of the KMT, met with Chinese President Jiang Zemin in Beijing, representing the highest level contact between Taiwan and China on the mainland in almost 50 years. The two sides agreed to reopen formal negotiations stalled since 1995, although their marked differences over the future status of Taiwan remained unresolved. China has called for reunification under a "one country, two system" policy, while Taiwan insists that union with the mainland would be possible only when China adopts multiparty democracy.

Following the Communist victory on the mainland in 1949, KMT leader Chiang Kai-shek established a government-in-exile on Taiwan, located 100 miles off China. Both Beijing and Taipei officially consider Taiwan a province of China, although Taipei has abandoned its longstanding claim to be the legitimate government of mainland China. Native Taiwanese comprise 85 percent of the population, while mainlanders or their descendants are a minority.

After four decades of authoritarian KMT rule, Taiwan's democratic transition began with the lifting of martial law in 1987. Lee Teng-hui became the first native Taiwanese president in 1988. Since then, he has asserted native Taiwanese control of the KMT, marginalized its mainlander faction, and de-emphasized the party's commitment to eventual reunification with China.

Taiwan's first multiparty elections, in 1991, maintained the KMT's control of the National Assembly, but also established the DPP, which officially favors formal independence from China, as a viable opposition. In the 1992 legislative elections, the KMT won 96 of 161 seats.

In 1993, Lien Chan became the first native Taiwanese prime minister. But as the political space widened, the KMT faced increasing criticism for its factionalism, corruption, and alleged organized crime links. In the 1995 elections for an expanded 164-seat legislature, the KMT won just 85 seats; the DPP, 54; the pro-reunification New Party, 21; and independents, four. On March 23, 1996, Lee won the first direct presidential election with 54 percent of the vote against the DPP's Peng Ming-min with 21 percent and two other candidates. Days earlier, China had held missile tests near the island to underscore its longstanding threat to invade if Taiwan declared independence.

Premier Lin, who in May 1997 had been the target of massive demonstrations protesting rising violent crime rates and calling for greater government accountability, resigned in August. On September 1, the KMT's Vincent Siew became premier. At the November 29 local elections, the DPP, downplaying its independence platform and promising clean, responsive government, defeated the KMT for the first time both in terms of administrative posts and in the popular vote, at 43 percent versus 42 percent. In the election for mayor of Taiwan in December 1998, KMT candidate and former justice minister Ma Ying-jeou defeated DPP leader and incumbent Mayor Chen Sui-bian and the New Party's Wang Chien-shien with a slim 51 percent of the vote. The bitterly fought contest was widely regarded as a crucial testing ground for the presidential vote in the year 2000, as the capital city controls significant political and financial resources. In the mayoral race for Taiwan's second city of Kaohsiung, the DPP challenger Frank Hsieh won a surprise victory by a narrow margin over Nationalist incumbent Wu Den-yih.

In concurrent national legislative elections for an expanded 225-seat parliament, a race that was largely overshadowed by the closely followed mayoral elections, the KMT won a working majority of 123 seats, followed by the DPP with 70 seats. The New Party, which is the most supportive of unification with China, suffered a humiliating defeat, securing only 11 seats. There were few substantive issues discussed during the legislative and mayoral campaigns, which focused largely on personal character issues. Both the KMT and DPP avoided the sensitive topic of Taiwan's relations with mainland China; public opinion polls have indicated that the majority of Taiwanese oppose a formal declaration of independence, a fact widely believed to have contributed to the DPP's electoral defeats.

Political Rights and Civil Liberties: Taiwanese can change their government democratically, a process which was consolidated with the March 1996 presidential election. The constitution vests executive power in a president who appoints the premier without parliamentary confirmation and can dissolve the legislature. The National Assembly can amend the constitution and, until 1994, elected the president and vice president. The government has five specialized *yuan* (branches), including a legislature that, since 1992, is directly elected for a three-year term. The ruling KMT maintains political advantages through its influence over much of the broadcast media and its considerable business interests in Taiwan's industrial economy. Nevertheless, opposition parties, which have grown rapidly in recent years, contest elections freely and have an impact on national policy. The 1998 parliamentary and mayoral elections were generally regarded to have been free and fair.

Taiwan enjoys one of the most free media environments in Asia, despite some continuing legal restrictions and political pressures. Taiwanese law prohibits advocacy of formal independence from China or of communism and allows police to censor or ban publications considered seditious or treasonous. These provisions, however, are not enforced in practice. Courts occasionally convict journalists for criminal libel in cases brought by the government or politicians, but no such cases were reported during the year.

With the exception of Taiwan's four major television networks, which are owned or closely associated with the government, opposition political parties, or the military, most of the country's media are privately owned and express a wide variety of viewpoints. Taiwan boasts one of the world's highest penetrations of cable television stations, some of which broadcast programs which are openly critical of the ruling party. Controls over radio stations, already more limited than those over television, continue to be relaxed, and there is a vigorous independent press. The government respects constitutional provisions for freedom of religion.

In January, provisions of the Parade and Assembly Law prohibiting demonstrations which promote communism or advocate Taiwan's separation from mainland China were ruled unconstitutional. Authorities have refused to register some nongovernmental organizations with the word "Taiwan" in their titles, although such groups operate freely. Despite constitutional protections on the formation of trade unions, a number of regulations restrict the right of association in practice. The right to strike and bargain collectively are limited by laws which allow the authorities to impose mandatory dispute mediation and other restrictions. About 31 percent of the country's labor force belong to over 3,000 registered unions. However, the country's labor law maintains the pro-KMT Chinese Federation of Labor's monopoly by allowing only one labor federation. The lack of effective anti-union discrimination legislation has facilitated the dismissal of trade union activists in recent years.

The judiciary, which is not fully independent, is susceptible to corruption and political influence from the ruling KMT, although judges are being drawn increasingly from outside the party. There were a number of indictments of judges during 1998 for accepting bribes in exchange for favorable judgments. The Anti-Hoodlum Law allows police to detain alleged "hoodlums" on the basis of testimony by unidentified informants. In May, a new organization of prosecutors was established to promote ongoing judicial reform, including higher professional standards. Police continue to abuse suspects, conduct personal identity and vehicle checks with widespread discretion, and obtain evidence illegally with few ramifications. Prisons are overcrowded, and conditions are harsh in detention camps for illegal immigrants.

In a move expected to help reduce corruption and reform business contract procedures, legislators adopted a law in May 1998 which bans companies connected with political parties from bidding for public contracts and which prescribes life imprisonment for bid-riggers.

Taiwan considerably relaxed restrictions against travel by Taiwanese to the Chinese mainland in 1998, though many limits on the entry of Chinese from the mainland remain in force, ostensibly for security reasons. Women face employment discrimination, and rape and domestic violence remain serious problems. In a positive move, new legislation was adopted in June requiring all city and county governments to establish domestic violence prevention centers. The country's 357,000 aboriginal descendants of Malayo-Polynesians suffer from social and economic alienation and have limited influence over policy decisions regarding their land and natural resources.

⬇ Tajikistan

Polity: Presidential (transitional) (post conflict)
Economy: Statist
Population: 6,100,000
PPP: $943
Life Expectancy: 68
Ethnic Groups: Tajik (65 percent), Uzbek (25 percent), Russian (4 percent), other (6 percent)
Capital: Dushanbe

Political Rights: 6
Civil Liberties: 6
Status: Not Free

Trend arrow: Tajikistan receives a downward trend arrow due to renewed violence, armed insurrection, and assassinations.

Overview:　　　　In 1998, violent flare-ups threatened to undermine the fragile agreement reached the year before between the government, led by President Emomali Rakhmonov, and the United Tajik Opposition (UTO) which ended a five-year civil war that killed tens of thousands. Despite assassinations, sporadic fighting by renegade war lords, the killing of four United Nations observers in July, and a rash of kidnappings, they year saw slow but deliberate progress in implementing the internationally brokered accords. In March, Khodzhi Akbar Turadzhonzade, a major UTO leader was named first deputy prime minister in charge of relations with the Commonwealth of Independent States, and former opposition members were named to over 20 posts in October and December.

Among the poorest of the former Soviet republics, Tajikistan was carved out of the Uzbek Soviet Republic on Stalin's orders in 1929. Leaving Samarkand and Bukhara - the two main centers of Tajik culture - inside Uzbekistan, angered Tajiks, who trace their origins to Persia. The four leading regionally based tribes are the Leninabad and Kulyab in the north and northwest and the Gharm and the Badakhshan in the south.

In December 1992, after months of ethnic and political conflict, a governing coalition of Muslim activists from the Islamic Renaissance Party (IRP), secular democrats and nationalists who had replaced the Communists, was overthrown by former Communist hardliners backed by the Russians. Rakhmonov, a Communist and an ethnic Kulyab from Leninabad, was named head of state and launched an ethnic war in the Gharm, Badakhshan, and Pamiri regions which supported the democratic-Islamic opposition. Some 60,000 people fled across the Armu Daray River into Afghanistan, from which the opposition launched violent raids. Some 25,000 Russian troops were stationed along the Afghan border to discourage rebel incursions.

The February 1995 parliamentary vote was boycotted by the opposition, including the Party of Popular Unity led by former presidential candidate Abdumalik Abdulladjanov, who lost to Rakhmonov. Opponents blamed violations of election law and official pressure on their candidates. In early 1996, three former prime ministers, including former presidential candidate Abdulladjanov, established the National Rival Movement (NRM) in the spring, which was courted by the government and the UTO. All three ex-prime ministers were from the Leninabad region in northern Tajikistan, home to 40 percent of Tajikistan's population where more than half of the republic's Tajiks live. After months of intense negotiations, a National Reconciliation Commission was created in late December composed of 40 percent government, 40 percent UTO, and 20 percent other groups; leaders of the NRM were left out of the commission.

On June 27, 1997, President Rakhmonov and UTO leader Said Abdullo Nuri signed a formal peace agreement in Moscow. Opposition forces began returning from Afghanistan to be integrated into a national army, and the government agreed that one-third of government posts would be given to UTO representatives.

In 1998, incidents of renewed violence threatened to undermine a fragile stability. In March and April, police accused opposition forces of launching several attacks near Dushanbe. On May 2, government and UTO leaders agreed to end all armed conflicts. On July 20, four members of the UN observer mission (UNMOT) were murdered.

In September, Otakhon Latifi, a member of the National Reconciliation Commission, was killed. On September 29, after a meeting between President Rakhmonov and UTO Chairman Nuri, the government announced the formation of a joint commission to investigate the Latifi murder and said it was accelerating plans to bring UTO representatives into the government.

The most serious outbreak of violence occurred in November when forces loyal to renegade Col. Mahmaud Khudaberdiyev, former commander of the First Brigade of the Tajik army, launched a series of attacks near Khujand in the Leninabad region. After five days of fighting, rebel forces were scattered, many attempting to flee into neighboring Uzbekistan.

Tajikistan charged the Uzbek government with involvement in plotting the armed uprising, accusing Uzbek President Islam Karimov of supporting former prime minister and member of the NRM, Abdulladjanov, an alleged organizer of the rebellion.

Throughout the year, some progress was made in implementing the peace accords.

In June, a ban on religious parties was lifted. On October 26, President Rakhmonov agreed to give the UTO 19 seats in ministries and other government bodies. In December, he appointed five candidates nominated by the UTO to the posts of deputy prime ministers and first deputy chairmen of state committees. Thousands of former opposition fighters had moved into UN-monitored camps.

Political Rights and Civil Liberties:

Citizens cannot change their government democratically. The constitution, adopted by referendum in 1994, provides for a strong executive, who serves as head of parliament and has broad powers to appoint and dismiss officials. Parliamentary elections in 1995 were boycotted by the quasi-opposition parties and were not "free and fair."

Both the 1991 Law on the Press and the constitution guarantee press freedom. A 1996 law allowed for independent television. Penalties for libel and "irresponsible" journalism encourage self-censorship. There are some 200 newspapers and magazines published in Tajikistan, including some 50 newspapers that are either independent or affiliated with political parties. State-run Tajik Radio is the major radio service, and the only national television service is state-run Tajik Television. Television and radio service disrupted by war have yet to be restored to all parts of the country. There are some ten private television stations, but all must use state-owned facilities. The government's control of the printing presses and the supply of newsprint, as well as subsidies it provides for most publications and TV broadcasts, give it considerable leverage over press content. In July, correspondent Elena Masiuk of Russia's NTV had her accreditation revoked under Article 6 of the press law for reporting on attempts by the foreign ministry to discredit the Tajik leadership. In June, Meirkhaim Gavrielov, a journalist for 50 years, was killed by unknown assailants. Over 60 journalists have been killed in Tajikistan since 1992, according to Russia's Glasnost Defense Fund.

The constitution provides for freedom of religion, but under law, the Council of Ministers registers religious communities and monitors their activities. In June, the government lifted a ban on religious parties. In August, four Pakistani citizens were expelled from the country for preaching Muslim fundamentalism. While Islam is the dominant religion, the majority of those living in Gorno Badakhshan in the Pamir Mountains are Ismaili Shiites; most other Tajiks are Sunnis.

There are restrictions on freedom of assembly. While nonpolitical associations such as trade unions are allowed to meet, registered organizations must apply for a permit from the local executive committee in order to legally organize any public assembly or demonstration.

While political parties are nominally allowed, there are only six officially recognized groups, including the Communist Party, the Party of Political and Economic Revival, the Popular Party, the Party of Popular (People's) Unity, and the National Revival Movement. The IRP, the Democratic Party and the Lali Badakhshan are banned, as most of their top leaders reside outside the country. In April, the Party of Justice and Development was registered.

There are no independent trade unions. All workers belong to the official Confederation of Trade Unions, an umbrella organization of 20 separate labor unions, which controls access to pension funds, health-care benefits, and other social services. The separate, state-controlled Trade Unions of Private Enterprise Workers reportedly functions at over 3,400 smaller enterprises.

Judicial officials at all levels of the court system are heavily influenced by both the political leadership, local officials, and paramilitary organizations. The court system is largely unmodified from the Soviet era. Bribery of judges and prosecutors is widespread. In March 1998, the Supreme Court sentenced six people to death for their role in the 1997 assassination attempt against President Rakhmonov, including Abdulladjanov. Fifteen other people convicted of complicity in the attack received sentences ranging from one to 14 years. Earlier, a judge favorable to the defendants had been removed, and many defendants were subjected to beatings and ill treatment while detained.

Criminal organizations, war lords, and paramilitary groups continue to threaten to citizens. Corruption is also rampant in the civil service, government, and business. Insider privatization has been endemic, and many enterprises went to a newly emergent elite consisting of government officials and their relatives, leaders of armed groups who plundered wealth during the fighting.

The constitution provides for the right of citizens to choose their place of residence. There are restrictions on travel and movement, and traveling within a 25 kilometer zone along the borders of China and Afghanistan requires permission from the ministry of foreign affairs. After the signing of the 1997 peace accords, refugees from Afghanistan returned to Tajikistan, and those displaced by conflict in the Gono-Badakhshan region also sought to return. Many returnees' homes are occupied by members of progovernment militias, though the process of evicting them has begun.

Though property and land rights are guaranteed by law, the presence of militias and criminal organizations have undermined these rights. Farmland seized from refugees often has not been returned, but the establishment of a Higher Economic Court in 1997 and regional economic courts in 1998 was aimed at settling property and economic disputes. Barriers to private enterprise remain high, as entrepreneurs generally must pay bribes and extortion to authorities and criminal syndicates. Limited access to commercial real estate and other physical assets, the vast majority of which are controlled by state enterprises, also remains an obstacle to private enterprise, limiting economic freedom and equality of opportunity.

Women face traditional societal discrimination. Domestic violence often is not investigated, and the abduction of brides is widely reported. Under law, men and women have equal rights, and inheritance laws do not discriminate against women. Women are well represented in education, the workforce, and in urban areas, women can be found throughout government and business.

Tanzania

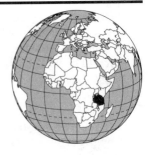

Polity: Dominant party   **Political Rights:** 5
Economy: Mixed statist   **Civil Liberties:** 4*
Population: 30,600,000   **Status:** Partly Free
PPP: $636
Life Expectancy: 47
Ethnic Groups: African (99 percent), other, including
Asian, European, and Arab (1 percent)
Capital: Dar-es-Salaam
Ratings change: Tanzania's civil liberties rating changed from 5 to 4 due
to a slight relaxation of political controls.

Overview: President Benjamin Mkapa and his ruling *Chama Cha Mapinduzi* (CCM, Party for the Revolution) appeared to be seeking to consolidate their power through pending constitutional changes that would strengthen the executive and provide for some appointed members of parliament. The actions revived lingering doubts over the legitimacy of Mpaka's 1995 election victory and the CCM's commitment to a genuine transition to an open polity and market economy. Opposition parties are firmly against the changes and are seeking electoral reform to provide independent, competent, and transparent conduct of presidential and legislative polls, which have been scheduled for 2000. Media restrictions and reports of security force abuses persist on the mainland, while the local government continued repressive practices on the federated semi-autonomous isles of Zanzibar and Pemba. Most international aid to Zanzibar remained suspended. There were signs of Islamic fundamentalism on Zanzibar and the mainland. The country was shaken by the August terrorist bombing of the U.S. Embassy in Dar-es-Salaam, but the attack, allegedly by Arab extremists, was unconnected to bilateral U.S.-Tanzanian relations, which remain cordial.

Despite numerous public pronouncements, the government has failed to take effective action to curb corruption. Tanzania ranked near the bottom on Transparency International's 1998 corruption perception index. Corruption and mismanagement have hindered growth and reduced confidence in the current administration. Interpol has warned that Tanzania has become a major center for the transport of drugs from Asia to Europe.

After the county gained independence from Britain in 1961, the CCM dominated Tanzania's political life under President Julius Nyerere's authoritarian rule. The Zanzibar and Pemba Islands were merged with then-Tanganyika to become the Union of Tanzania after Arab sultans who had long ruled the islands were deposed in a bloody 1964 revolution. The union agreement gave the islanders, who now number more than 700,000 and are 90 percent Muslim, limited autonomy. The mainland's population is mostly Christian and animist.

Nyerere retained strong influence after he officially retired in 1985. Opposition parties were legalized in 1992. The CCM continues to dominate the country's political life, and a genuine democratic transition and strong economic growth are unlikely until the party reforms itself.

Political Rights and Civil Liberties: While marred by administrative chaos and irregularities, legislative and presidential elections in 1995 were the most free on mainland Tanzania since independence. The voting in Zanzibar was plainly fraudulent, but the island's High Court summarily rejected opposition demands for fresh polls. President Mkapa at best boasts a tarnished mandate, while the CCM's landslide legislative victory was even less credible. Extensive use of state broadcasting and other government resources during the campaign favored the ruling party. The CCM won 80 percent of the 232 parliamentary seats. The CCM retains sizable self-awarded government subsidies based on parliamentary representation.

Tanzania's judiciary has displayed signs of autonomy after decades of subservience to the one-party CCM regime, but remains subject to considerable political influence. Constitutional protections for the right to free assembly are generally, but not always, respected. In November, opposition demonstrations were banned in Dar-es-Salaam. Laws allow rallies only by officially registered political parties, which may not be formed on religious, ethnic, or regional bases and cannot oppose the union of Zanzibar and the mainland. Freedom of religion is respected.

Arrest and pretrial detention laws are often ignored. Prison conditions are harsh, and police abuses are said to be common. Many nongovernmental organizations are active, but some human rights groups have experienced difficulties in receiving required official registration. The broad distribution of Tanzania's population among many ethnic groups has largely diffused potential ethnic rivalries that have wracked neighboring countries.

Media freedom has expanded markedly since 1992, but instances of repression continue, especially in Zanzibar, where the government controls all electronic media. In August, the mainland Kiswahili newspaper *Mtanzania* was banned on the island. The *Tingisha* and *Watu* newspapers were closed in Dar-es-Salaam in June. Some private radio and television stations operate on the mainland, but state broadcasting remains predominant. Numerous independent newspapers and magazines are published, but they circulate mostly in major cities.

Women's rights guaranteed by the constitution and other laws are not seriously protected. Especially in rural areas and in Zanzibar, traditional or Islamic customs discriminatory toward women prevail in family law, and women have fewer educational and economic opportunities. Domestic violence against women is reportedly common and rarely prosecuted. Human rights groups have sought laws to bar forced marriages, which are most common among Tanzania's coastal peoples. The employment of children as domestic servants is widespread.

Workers do not have the right to organize and join trade unions freely. Essential workers are barred from striking. Other workers' right to strike is restricted by complex notification and mediation requirements. Collective bargaining effectively exists only in the small private sector.

Approximately 85 percent of Tanzania's people survive through subsistence agriculture. Economic decline in Zanzibar continues to dim the entire country's prospects.

Thailand

Polity: Parliamentary
democracy
(military-influenced)
Economy: Capitalist-statist
Population: 61,100,000
PPP: $7,742
Life Expectancy: 69

Political Rights: 2*
Civil Liberties: 3
Status: Free

Ethnic Groups: Thai (75 percent), Chinese (14 percent), other (11 percent)
Capital: Bangkok
Ratings Change: Thailand's political rights rating changed from 3 to 2, and its status changed from Partly Free to Free, due to increased political transparency and accountability under the 1997 constitution.

Overview: In 1998, premier Chuan Leekpai's government won international praise for its efforts to bring Thailand out of its economic crisis by promoting official accountability, cleaning up the banking system, and adhering to an International Monetary Fund-mandated (IMF) austerity program. Yet at home, rising unemployment caused severe hardship for ordinary Thais.

Thailand is the only Southeast Asian nation never colonized by a European power. A 1932 bloodless coup, the first of 17 coups or coup attempts this century, led to a new constitution's curbing the monarch's powers. Today, King Bhumibol Alduyadej's duties are limited to approving the premier, but he is widely revered and exerts informal political influence.

In 1991, the army deposed a hugely corrupt, elected government that had tried to limit the military's powers. Following elections in 1992, parliament appointed coup leader General Suchinda Kraprayoon, who had not stood in the elections, as premier, leading to demonstrations in Bangkok in May. Soldiers killed more than 50 protesters. Suchinda resigned, the country returned to civilian rule, and parliament amended the constitution to require premiers to be MPs.

The 1996 elections brought to power a coalition headed by Chavalit Yongchaiyudh, a former army commander. Chavalit inherited an economy on the downturn after recording the world's fastest growth between 1984 and 1995, with exports slowing, banks and corporations saddled with $63 billion in mostly short-term foreign debt, and the weak, poorly supervised banking system burdened by bad property loans. Middle-class Thais blamed the economic troubles on a political system dominated by patronage-oriented rural politicians.

The government floated the currency, the *baht*, on July 2, and in August agreed to a $17.2 billion IMF-led loan package in return for financial austerity. Responding to middle-class street protests in Bangkok, parliament approved a reformist constitution in September that created a directly elected House of Representatives with 400 single-member constituencies and 100 party-list seats, as well as a 200-seat, directly elected Senate. Anti-corruption provisions include an independent election commission and a financial disclosure requirement for MPs. In November, further middle class protests brought to power a new six-party coalition headed by former premier Chuan Leekpai of the Democratic Party.

In 1998, Chuan's financial reforms drew international praise and domestic criticism. The opposition accused the government of not taking a harder stance against favored banks, and blamed the high interest rates demanded by the IMF for crippling the economy. As the year ended, the Senate continued to hold up passage of 11 reform bills, claiming the measures would allow the economy to be dominated by foreigners and lead to even greater job losses. The economic crisis caused the number of unemployed Thais to rise from one million to three million in 1998, as the economy contracted an estimated seven to eight percent.

In another development, in early 1998 authorities cracked down on a small, 30-year-old Muslim separatist movement in southern Thailand that had allegedly been responsible for recent bombings of trains, buses, schools, and police stations.

Political Rights and Civil Liberties:

Thai citizens can change their government through elections, but widespread corruption weakens institutions and contributes to civil liberties violations. In the 1996 elections, candidates spent an estimated $1 billion buying votes and reportedly hired off-duty police and soldiers to intimidate voters and stuff ballots. The campaign was the most violent ever, with partisan attacks killing seven people and wounding several others. Observers also reported extensive vote buying in the 1998 local elections. Criminality is penetrating politics; in recent years, several politicians have been implicated in land and banking scandals and drug trafficking schemes. The 1997 constitution included several safeguards against corruption. In January, the Counter Corruption Commission mandated by the constitution published the declared assets of every cabinet member. Yet many doubt whether such measures will be enough to reform this patronage-based political culture.

The military continues to be influential in politics, albeit generally in support of democratic institutions. The armed forces have accepted greater civilian control of the military through budgetary oversight and a civilian defense minister.

The judiciary is independent but is undermined by corruption. Courts may order closed trials in certain situations, although procedural safeguards are generally adequate. The police force is rife with corruption, is inadequately trained, and operates with relative impunity in a culture where criminal suspects are presumed guilty. Hundreds of detainees and prison inmates have died in custody in recent years. Security forces kill dozens of well-armed drug traffickers and other criminal suspects each year, many of whom reportedly had surrendered. Conditions at immigration detention centers, where female detainees say rape is common, worsened as Thailand's economic crisis resulted in an immigration crackdown. An amnesty protects soldiers responsible for killing 52 people (with 39 others missing and presumed dead) in the 1992 pro-democracy demonstrations.

Freedom of expression is restricted in specific areas, including advocating a Communist government and inciting disturbances. Laws against defaming the monarchy (*lese majeste*) are strictly enforced. The press criticizes government policies and publicizes human rights abuses, but journalists face occasional intimidation and exercise self-censorship regarding the military, judiciary, and other sensitive subjects. In January, unknown gunmen killed a journalist in the central city of Phichit who had investigated allegations of corruption related to a building project. Many newspapers responded to the economic crisis by focusing more on corruption scandals and financial mismanagement, but publishers were also forced to lay off hundreds of journalists. The government licenses radio and television (radio stations must renew licenses annually), and authorities censor and occasionally delete politically sensitive material. The government or military control all five national television networks, and news coverage favors the government. The army also owns the franchises of most radio stations. Rural officials occasionally falsely charge peaceful demonstrators with inciting unrest and intent to commit violence. Nongovernmental organizations (NGO) are active but are sometimes harassed by authorities. The 1997 constitution called for an independent National Human Rights Commission, with implementing legislation due by September 1999.

NGOs estimate that at least 250,000 female prostitutes work in Thailand, up to one-fifth of whom are under age 18. Many are trafficked from hill tribes and from neighboring Burma, and the system operates with the complicity of corrupt police and local officials. Girls sold into prostitution by their families become bonded laborers. The government has extended compulsory education and expanded an awareness campaign, but has barely enforced a 1996 anti-trafficking law. Domestic violence remains a problem. Women are frequently denied the minimum wage, and are underrepresented in parliament.

Religious freedom is respected. However, Muslims face societal and employment discrimination, and several activists are reportedly imprisoned for political views. Roughly half of the 500-700,000 members of hill tribes are not registered citizens, and thus cannot vote or own land and have difficulty in obtaining social services.

Thailand has for years sheltered hundreds of thousands of Southeast Asian refugees, including currently some 125,000 Burmese refugees. However, military officials reportedly occasionally harass refugees to get them to return to Burma. In recent years, a militia allied to the Burmese government has carried out cross-border raids and attacked refugees and burnt camps inside Thailand. Burmese refugees outside of camps are considered "illegal immigrants" and are frequently arrested and deported. By midyear, Thailand also hosted 87,000 Cambodian refugees.

Unions are independent, although there is no anti-discrimination protection for workers seeking to organize. State workers can only join "associations" which cannot negotiate wages or hold strikes. Child labor is widespread. Safety regulations are flouted at many factories and enforcement is lax.

Togo

Polity: Dominant party
(military-influenced)
Economy: Mixed statist
Population: 4,900,000
PPP: $1,167
Life Expectancy: 58
Ethnic Groups: Ewe, Mina, Kabye, 34 other tribes
(99 percent), European and Syrian-Lebanese (1 percent)
Capital: Lome

Political Rights: 6
Civil Liberties: 5
Status: Not Free

Overview:

President Gnassingbé Eyadéma was declared victor in a fraudulent June presidential contest that will prolong his rule of more than three decades. Interior Minister Senyi Mémène claimed that Eyadéma had won approximately 51 percent of the vote, thereby avoiding a runoff election against a single opposition candidate.

The United States and European Union (EU) announced that aid suspended since equally fraudulent 1993 presidential elections would not resume until respect for basic rights improved. France disagreed, again embracing its client Eyadéma, who has reportedly been a major contributor to French political parties.

The electoral process was neither free nor fair. Electoral rolls were suspect, and multiple voter cards were issued. The National Election Commission was not independent and was either incapable or unwilling to provide adequate logistical support. Hundreds of domestic, EU-trained observers were denied accreditation. Eyadéma spent lavishly and used state resources for his campaign. State media coverage was heavily biased in his favor and virtually ignored Gilchrest Olympio, the main opposition candidate. At a critical moment in the vote counting, Eyadéma's backers on the electoral commission resigned, thereby allowing the interior ministry to tally the votes and declare the results.

Olympio, the leader of the Union of Forces for Change party, declared from exile that he was the real winner with 59 percent of the vote. Olympio is the son of the country's founding president, who was murdered in 1963 as Eyadéma, then a demobilized sergeant who had served in France's colonial wars, led an army coup to topple the country's democratically elected government.

Eyadéma has ruled Togo with varying levels of repression and the strong support of successive French governments since he took direct power in 1967. Members of his Kabye ethnicity overwhelmingly dominate the security forces and, along with fellow northerners, Togo's civil administration.

Togoland was a German colony for more three decades until France seized it at the outset of World War I. It was held as French territory until its independence in 1960. After assuming direct power in 1967, Eyadéma suspended the constitution and extended his repressive rule through mock elections and a puppet political party.

In 1991, free political parties were legalized, and multiparty elections were promised. The transition faltered, however, as soldiers and secret police harassed, attacked, and killed opposition supporters. In the 1993 presidential election, which the opposition boycotted, Eyadéma claimed to have won 96 percent of the vote.

Violence and intimidation also marred the 1994 legislative elections. Opposition parties won a majority in the national assembly, but splits and flawed 1996 by-elections allowed Eyadéma's Rally of the Togolese People party to regain control of the legislature.

Political Rights and Civil Liberties: Eyadéma's 1998 re-election was blatantly fraudulent. The Togolese people cannot choose their representatives freely. Power in the country is overwhelmingly concentrated in the presidency. The judiciary is still heavily influenced by the president. All three constitutional court justices were appointed by Eyadéma before the transition to a multiparty system.

Killings, arbitrary arrest, and torture have continued. Security forces commit abuses with impunity, and illegal detention is common. Togo's criminal courts generally respect legal procedures, and traditional courts handle many minor matters. Courts are understaffed and inadequately funded. Pretrial detentions are lengthy, and prisons are severely overcrowded.

A number of private newspapers publish in Lomé, but independent journalists are subject to harassment and the perpetual threat of various criminal charges. Several journalists were arrested in 1998. Advertisers are also pressured to avoid the opposition press. Private radio and television stations now broadcast, but offer little independent local coverage. The government controls and allows little opposition assess to the broadcast media.

Constitutionally protected religious freedom is generally respected, but demonstrations are often banned or violently halted. Political parties operate openly, but under constant menace. Human rights groups are closely monitored and sometimes harassed.

Ethnic discrimination is rife. Political power is narrowly held by members of a few ethnic groups from northern Togo. Southerners dominate the country's commerce, and violence occasionally flares between the two groups.

Despite constitutional guarantees of equality, women's opportunities for education and employment are limited. A husband may legally bar his wife from working or receive her earnings. Customary law bars women's rights in divorce and inheritance rights to widows. Violence against women is common. Female genital mutilation is widely practiced by the country's northern ethnic groups. The Women, Democracy and Development Think Tank and Action Group, a new nongovernmental organization, has provided legal assistance to hundreds of women at two legal counseling centers.

Togo's constitution includes the right to form and join unions, but essential workers are excluded. Health care workers may not strike. Only 15 percent of the labor force is unionized. Unions have the right to bargain collectively, but most labor agreements are brokered by the government in tripartite talks with unions and management. Several labor federations are politically aligned.

Most of the country's people work in rural subsistence agriculture. Political instability and corruption deter significant international investment.

Tonga

Polity: Monarchy and
partly-elected
legislature
Economy: Capitalist
Population: 100,000
PPP: na
Life Expectancy: na
Ethnic Groups: Polynesian
Capital: Nuku'alofa

Political Rights: 5
Civil Liberties: 3
Status: Partly Free

Overview:

Despite ongoing calls from the country's pro-democracy movement for increased government accountability and transparency, as well as more balanced power sharing between the king and parliament, the king resisted calls for greater democracy, and the government continued its attempts to intimidate journalists and opposition politicians during 1998.

These 169 South Pacific islands, with a predominantly Polynesian population, were unified as a kingdom under King George Tupou I in 1845. Following 70 years of British influence, Tonga became an independent member of the Commonwealth in 1970. King Taufa Ahau Tupou IV has reigned since 1965.

The 30-seat Legislative Assembly serves a three-year term and consists of 12 ministers from the privy council, nine nobles selected by and from among Tonga's 33 noble families, and nine "People's Representatives" (commoners) elected by universal suffrage. The 1990 legislative elections saw the emergence of a pro-democracy bloc that won five commoner seats. In August 1992, reform-oriented commoner representatives, led by Akilisi Pohiva, formed the Pro-Democracy Movement (PDM). The PDM favored holding direct elections for all 30 parliamentary seats and having parliament rather than the king select the privy council, while retaining the king as a figurehead. In November, the PDM organized a seminal public conference on amending the constitution to introduce democratic reforms that was backed by the influential Roman Catholic and Free Wesleyan churches.

At the 1993 elections, pro-democracy candidates won six commoner seats. In 1994, the PDM organized Tonga's first political party, the Tonga Democratic Party, subsequently renamed the People's Party. In the January 1996 elections, pro-democracy candidates swept all nine commoner seats. The next legislative elections are scheduled for March 1999.

In 1998, a parliamentary committee investigated charges of financial mismanagement and abuse of power against Speaker of Parliament Noble Fusitu'a. The king ordered the investigation after receiving a petition with over 1,000 signatures describing the allegations and calling for Fusitu'a to be removed from office.

Political Rights and Civil Liberties:

Tongans lack the democratic means to change their government. The 1875 constitution, which is the product of an era in which chiefs had unlimited powers over the so-called commoners, grants the king and hereditary nobles a perpetual majority in parliament with a total of 21 out of 30 seats. This allows legislation to be passed without the assent of the popularly elected People's Representatives, whose nine seats represent roughly 95 percent of the population. Nevertheless, the commoner representatives have managed on occasion to reject legislation and the budget when joined by some noble representatives. The king has broad executive powers, appoints the prime minister, and appoints and heads the privy council (cabinet). The king and the nobility also hold a preeminent societal position through substantial land holdings.

Since 1985, when he was fired from a government post for disclosing that assemblymen had granted themselves pay increases, pro-democracy commoner MP Akilisi Pohiva has been harassed by the authorities. In the early 1990s, a court fined him $26,000 for allegedly defaming the crown prince. In March 1998, the supreme court acquitted Pohiva of criminal libel charges brought against him by the government over a 1994 interview with the *Wall Street Journal* and a statement in his own newsletter, *Kele'a* (Conch Shell), regarding the business dealings of the king's daughter. However, later that month, Pohiva was convicted on two defamation charges over comments about Police Minister Clive Edwards which were published in 1997 in *Kele'a* and the *Times of Tonga*, a pro-democracy weekly published in New Zealand and sold in Tonga.

In December, the Tonga-based editor of the *Times of Tonga* was found guilty of defaming Edwards and fined about U.S. $400. Michael Field, the New Zealand and Pacific correspondent for *Agence France Presse,* continued to be denied entry into Tonga in 1998. Although Tonga usually allows foreign journalists free entry, Field has been barred from the country since 1993 after publishing articles about Tonga's prodemocracy movement and allegations of government financial mismanagement.

Besides the government weekly *Tonga Chronicle*, which carries some opposition views, there are several private newspapers, including the *Times of Tonga, Kele'a*, and an outspoken Roman Catholic Church newsletter. Political coverage on the Tonga Broadcast Commission's Radio Tonga favors the government, and the state owns the country's one television station. Libel remains a criminal offense. Religious freedom is respected in this predominantly Christian society.

There are no significant restrictions on freedom of assembly. The 1964 Trade Union Act recognizes the right of workers to form independent unions. Most Tongans are engaged in subsistence agriculture and no unions have formed. The king appoints all judges, and the lower levels of the judiciary are not independent. The Supreme Court is independent and uses expatriate judges.

Citizens are free to travel domestically and abroad. Although nobles enjoy certain economic advantages, including control over much of the country's land, commoners can achieve financial success in the private sector. Women generally occupy a subordinate role in this male-dominated society. Few women participate in the formal labor force, and they cannot own land or hold noble titles. Several nongovernmental organizations work actively on women's rights and development issues.

⬇ Trinidad and Tobago

Polity: Parliamentary **Political Rights:** 1
democracy **Civil Liberties:** 2
Economy: Capitalist-statist **Status:** Free
Population: 1,300,000
PPP: $9,437
Life Expectancy: 71
Ethnic Groups: East Indian (41 percent), Black (40 percent),
mixed (14 percent), European (1 percent), Chinese (1 percent), other (3 percent)
Capital: Port-of-Spain
Trend arrow: Trinidad and Tobago receives a downward trend arrow due to greater
government hostility toward the press.

Overview:
Prime Minister Basdeo Panday´s cool relations with his
country´s media turned gelid in 1998, as journalists and their
supporters took to the streets to protest what they said were
attacks on them and threats to democracy. At the end of 1997, Panday, whose pro-
business United National Congress (UNC) government has been praised for its solid
economic management and for cooperation in fighting the region's growing drug trade,
had promised to curb his strident condemnations of the press.

Trinidad and Tobago, a member of the British Commonwealth, achieved independence in 1962. The 1976 constitution established the two-island nation as a republic
with a president, elected by a majority of both houses of parliament, replacing the former
governor-general. Executive authority remains vested in the prime minister. The bicameral parliament consists of a 36-member House of Representatives elected for five
years, and a 31-member Senate, with 25 senators appointed by the prime minister and
six by the opposition.

In the 1986 elections, the National Alliance for Reconstruction (NAR), a coalition
that bridges traditional political differences between black and East Indian communities, led by A.N.R. Robinson, soundly defeated the black-based People's National Movement (PNM), which had ruled for 30 years. The coalition unraveled when Basdeo
Panday, the country's most prominent East Indian politician, was expelled and then
formed the East Indian-based UNC.

In July 1991, a radical black Muslim group briefly seized parliament. Tensions increased between black and East Indian communities, each roughly 40 percent of the
population, as the latter edged towards numeric, and thus political, advantage. In December, Patrick Manning led the PNM to victory by taking 21 of 36 parliamentary
seats. Manning's government deregulated the economy and floated the currency, but
the social costs of these economic reforms caused the PNM's popularity to decline.
Manning called snap elections for November 6, 1995.

The election campaign focused on unemployment and the effects of the structural
adjustment program. Voting ran largely on ethnic lines, with East Indians voting overwhelmingly for the UNC and blacks for the PNM. Each party won 17 seats on Trinidad.
The NAR retained its two seats on Tobago, and entered into a coalition with the UNC
in exchange for a ministerial position for former premier Robinson and a promise of

greater autonomy for Tobago. UNC leader Panday became Trinidad's first prime minister of East Indian descent.

In March 1996, Robinson was elected president. A series of incidents with Venezuela involving maritime rights—revolving around oil exploration and fishing rights, and Venezuelan drug interdiction efforts—dominated the news. Internal divisions within the NAR, caused by strains of being the minority member of a governing coalition, threatened its disappearance. More recently, unemployment has fallen to its lowest level in a decade and a half.

In 1997, there were growing accusations about sweetheart contracts and patronage jobs, and Panday responded by assailing the "lies, half truths and innuendoes" of the opposition press. In 1998, Panday continued his campaign, as his government chose not to renew the work permit of Barbadian newsman Julian Rogers, in apparent reprisal for broadcasting telephone calls from government critics.

Political Rights and Civil Liberties: Citizens of Trinidad and Tobago can change their government democratically. Politics and party affiliations are largely polarized along ethnic lines.

The judiciary is independent, and the United Kingdom's Privy Council serves as the recourse of ultimate appeal. Due to rising crime rates, the court system is severely backlogged, in some cases up to five years, with an estimated 20,000 criminal cases awaiting trial. Prisons are grossly overcrowded, and there are more than 100 prisoners on death row.

Because of British pressure to regulate application of the death penalty, Trinidad and Tobago, together with Barbados, Guyana and Jamaica, plans to cut ties with the Privy Council and form a Caribbean Court of Justice. In May 1998, Panday announced that his government would withdraw from the American Convention on Human Rights, which prohibits countries from extending the death penalty beyond those crimes for which it was in effect at the time the treaty was ratified. However, in September, a government-sponsored bill to restrict appeals of convicted murderers was defeated in parliament.

High levels of drug-related violence and common crime continue to undermine the protection of civil liberties. Trinidad and Tobago are important transshipment points for cocaine, and an estimated 80 percent of all crimes are believed to involve narcotics. There have been more than a two-dozen drug related killings in recent years, including the still unsolved murder of former Attorney General Selwyn Richardson. Successive governments have also failed to enforce certain criminal laws. Corruption in the police force, often drug related, is endemic and inefficient law enforcement results in the dismissal of some criminal cases.

The Panday government has won some points for its anti-drug efforts and has been a principal proponent of a regional witness protection program. It has also signed several anti-narcotics accords with the United States.

The press is privately owned and vigorous, and it offers pluralistic views; however, in May 1997, the government floated a restrictive journalistic code of conduct that the Media Association of Trinidad and Tobago said led to instances in which reporters and other press workers were physically attacked. In 1998, Panday's refusal to allow the renewal of the work permit of a respected Barbadian broadcaster became a regional cause celebre. He also reiterated his refusal to sign the Inter-American Press Association's Chapultepec Declaration on press freedom until it addressed instances of media dissemination of "lies, half-truths and innuendoes." The broadcast media are both private and public, and freedom of association and assembly are respected.

Domestic violence and other violence against women is extensive and a low priority for police and prosecutors. Labor unions are well organized, powerful and politically active, although union membership has declined. Strikes are legal and occur frequently.

Tunisia

Polity: Dominant party
Economy: Mixed capitalist
Population: 9,500,000
PPP: $5,261
Life Expectancy: 68
Ethnic Groups: Arab and Berber (98 percent)
Capital: Tunis

Political Rights: 6
Civil Liberties: 5
Status: Not Free

Overview:

In July, Tunisian President Zine el-Abidine Ben Ali was selected by his ruling Constitutional Democratic Rally (RCD) party to stand for re-election in March 1999. The predetermined outcome of these polls will be a landslide victory for the incumbent. Tunisia's steady economic growth and promotion of social benefits and women's rights will garner the president significant support. Pervasive controls on all political activities ensures that there is no viable or even visible opposition. Since 1987, Ben Ali's rule has become increasingly autocratic and repressive. There is scant open political opposition, and freedom of expression is thoroughly suppressed. Trade unionists and human rights activists are special targets, but the most severe repression is reserved for Islamists, whose activities are entirely proscribed. President Ben Ali has escaped harsh criticism from Western powers, in part because much of the worst abuse is aimed at Islamic fundamentalists, but also because Tunisia is an important trading partner for several European countries.

For three decades after Tunisia's independence from France in 1956, President Habib Bourguiba pursued secular pro-Western policies and brooked little dissent. In 1987, then General Ben Ali ousted Bourguiba and offered a brief promise of an open, multiparty political system. Opposition parties have since been crippled by arrests and harassment or banned. In 1994, Ben Ali won a second five-year term with 99.9 percent of the vote in an election that barred credible challengers and defied credibility. Opposition parties have been prevented from seriously contesting local elections.

Political Rights and Civil Liberties:

Tunisians have never been allowed to exercise their constitutional right to elect their representatives freely. Presidential and legislative elections in 1994 were neither open nor competitive. The ruling RCD party, the successor to parties that have controlled Tunisia since its independence, used considerable state resources for campaigning. Opposition leaders were disqualified as candidates. The RCD won all 144 single-member districts in the legislative polls, although a facade of open debate and multipartyism was maintained through the allotment of 19 seats to other parties on a proportional basis. The RCD lost only 6 of 4,090 seats contested in 1996 municipal elections. For elections due in early 1999, Ben Ali has proposed that one-fifth of the parliamentary seats be reserved for the opposition, which appears unable to gain representation under the current dispensation.

No political party based on religion or region is permitted, and all must be licensed. The judiciary is controlled by the executive, and legal limits on detention without trial are flouted. There is little hope for redress in the courts, especially for political matters. Torture and other forms of mistreatment by police are reportedly commonplace, and security forces act with impunity. Many human rights activists have been harassed, briefly detained, or jailed.

The right to free information and expression is not respected. The government tightly controls domestic broadcast media and restricts rebroadcast of foreign programming. Severe new regulations and a stiff tax have limited ownership of satellite dishes, although many are used illegally. Considerable self-censorship constrains the independent print media, and the Press Code includes vaguely defined and threatening prohibitions against defamation and subversion. Official news guidelines shape coverage, and pre-publication submission requirements allow the government to seize publications without compensation. Printers are generally unwilling to risk government retribution by printing statements or reports by human rights groups. All foreign publications are censored. Visiting journalists are barred from meeting dissidents, and many citizens are unwilling to meet journalists, foreign academics, or activists for fear of official reprisals.

Complicated 1992 legislation inhibits independent nongovernmental organizations, which suffer from official harassment if they delve into human rights or other sensitive matters. Agendas, papers, and other details of meetings and conferences must be provided to the interior ministry in advance, and hotel managers must report on all gatherings on their premises. Meetings by human rights groups are routinely blocked.

Islam is the official state religion, but is practiced under intense government scrutiny. Muslim clergy receive official salaries, prayer leaders are appointed by the regime, and mosques are closely monitored. Proselytizing by all non-Muslims is forbidden. Other religious practice is tolerated, with the exception of Baha'i, whose adherents are sometimes harassed.

General equality for women has advanced more in Tunisia than elsewhere in the Arab world. Educational and employment opportunities have grown, and job rights are legally protected. This tendency is seen as both a challenge to and bulwark against radical Islamists.

Tunisia's sole labor federation, the Tunisian General Federation of Labor operates under severe restrictions. Several trade unionists were detained in 1997 for publishing appeals for respect of human rights. The rights to strike and bargain collectively are both nominally protected, although labor settlements can be imposed by arbitration panels.

In 1998, Tunisia's tourism earnings and industrial exports rose, and a broad privatization plan continued. Sixty-eight state corporations are scheduled to be sold during the next two years.

Turkey

Polity: Presidential-par- **Political Rights:** 4
liamentary democracy **Civil Liberties:** 5
(military-influenced) **Status:** Partly Free
(insurgency)
Economy: Capitalist-statist
Population: 64,800,000
PPP: $5,516
Life Expectancy: 68
Ethnic Groups: Turk (80 percent), Kurd (20 percent)
Capital: Ankara

Overview:

Prime Minister Mesut Yilmaz's Motherland (ANAP)-led coalition government fell in November over corruption charges, ending 16 months of political infighting that often involved the military. After the constitutional court banned the Islamist *Refah* (Welfare) party in January, army leaders stepped up pressure on the government to fight political Islam. The military's heavy political influence and the resulting crackdown on Islamic politicians, businesses, and students diminished international confidence in Turkish democracy and further soured already strained relations with Europe. Meanwhile, badly needed economic reform was impeded by conflicting agendas within and beyond the governing coalition.

Mustapha Kemal Ataturk, who launched a reform program under which Turkey abandoned much of its Ottoman and Islamic heritage, proclaimed Turkey a republic in 1923. His secular, nationalistic legacy has profoundly influenced Turkish politics through most of this century, notably in the post-World War II period. The doctrine of "Kemalism" has been used by the military to justify three coups since 1960. Turkey returned to civilian rule in 1983.

In 1995, Refah took advantage of discontent over corruption, high inflation, and unemployment to win 158 parliamentary seats in December elections. DYP took 135 seats, ANAP 132, Democratic Left 76, and the Republican People's Party (CHP), 49. A shaky coalition between DYP and ANAP collapsed in May 1996, and in June, Refah and DYP formed Turkey's first Islamist-led coalition government, with Necmettin Erbakan as prime minister and Tansu Ciller in charge of foreign affairs.

Erbakan almost immediately found himself at odds with the military-led National Security Council (NSC), which considers itself the guardian of Turkish secularism. Government policies such as allowing female civil servants to wear traditional headscarves led the generals to accuse the government of undermining the secular foundations of the state. Under intense pressure from the NSC, Erbakan resigned on June 18, 1997. Yilmaz was appointed prime minister two days later, and assembled a ruling coalition including the social Democratic Left and the conservative Democratic Turkey parties. Despite being an opposition party, the CHP provided 54 seats for support.

The constitutional court closed Refah in January 1998 for "conspiring against the secular order." Erbakan and five other Refah leaders lost their parliamentary seats and were banned from politics for five years. With over four million members, Refah was Turkey's largest political party. Over 100 of its remaining 147 MPs launched the Virtue party in February.

By March, the NSC publicly expressed dissatisfaction with Yilmaz's measures to curb Islamic activism. Yilmaz countered that the military need not interfere with political matters. But pressure intensified, and on March 23, the government presented a plan for an "all out war" on fundamentalism. In the following months, Recep Tayyip Erdogan, the Islamist mayor of Istanbul, was sentenced to ten months in jail for "inciting hatred" in a 1997 address. Erbakan was charged with slandering the constitutional court. Police raided businesses suspected of financing fundamentalist activities, arresting dozens. Students protesting the ban on headscarves met with violent reaction from riot police. In August, Turkey's chief prosecutor began legal action against 12 Refah politicians, including seven MPs, for misappropriation of party funds. And the military dismissed over 150 officers suspected to be Islamist sympathizers.

Calls for Yilmaz to resign came repeatedly from CHP leader Deniz Baykal over politically unpopular economic reform as well as enforcement of anti-Islamic codes. In an attempt to introduce a measure of economic reform, Yilmaz signed a pact with Baykal promising early elections in return for support of a tax plan to combat Turkey's 90 percent inflation. Other anti-inflationary measures and social security restructuring plans proved too difficult for this weak government to implement.

The 14-year-old conflict in southeastern Turkey between the army and the Marxist Kurdistan Workers' Party (PKK) continued in 1998, often crossing over into Iraq. As the Turkish army has gained ground, the PKK has softened its rhetoric, calling for a measure of autonomy within Turkey rather than a separate state. The conflict spilled over into relations with Syria late in the year, when Turkey threatened to invade Syria to eradicate Kurdish bases there. In October, Syria expelled PKK leader Abdullah Ocalan and promised to shut down Kurd rebel camps on its territory. Ocalan was arrested in Italy in November. Italy's refusal to extradite him to Turkey, where he faces the death penalty, created tensions between the two countries.

The suppression of Kurds and excessive military involvement in government have been the most problematic issues in relations between Turkey and the EU. Turkey's 34-year-old effort to join the EU suffered a setback in late 1997 when the country was omitted from a short list of EU applicants. Still infuriated by the snub, Yilmaz boycotted a March 1998 EU conference planned largely as a consolation prize for Turkey. To exacerbate the situation, the EU began accession talks with Cyprus. Tensions remained high at year's end despite attempts by Great Britain, holder of the EU presidency, to mediate.

In late November, the government lost a vote of confidence over accusations that Yilmaz tampered with the privatization of a state-owned bank and had ties to organized crime. President Demirel appointed Deputy Prime Minister Bulent Ecevit to assemble a temporary coalition government to lead Turkey until elections in April. By year's end, Ecevit had failed to win enough backing to secure a majority, and Demirel replaced him with Yalim Erez, minister for industry and trade.

Political Rights and Civil Liberties: Turkish citizens can change their government democratically, though the military wields considerable influence in political matters. The 1982 constitution provides for a Grand National

Assembly (currently 550 seats) that is directly elected to a five-year term. The Assembly elects the president, whose role is largely ceremonial, to a seven-year term.

Along with the Refah party, which was banned in January, the Kurdish People's Democracy Party (HADEP) suffered severe harassment at the hands of security forces in 1998. In mid-March, at least 100 members were arrested in overnight raids on their homes and party offices. Prosecutors charged them with links to the PKK and demanded prison sentences.

Turkey's bleak human rights record is largely related to the PKK insurgency. Kurds, who make up some 20 percent of the population, are not recognized as a national, racial, or ethnic minority. Security forces carry out extrajudicial killings of suspected PKK terrorists and are believed to be responsible for dozens of unsolved killings and disappearances of journalists, Kurdish activists, and suspected PKK members, either directly or through state-backed death squads. A government report in January confirmed years of accusations by human rights groups that an execution squad within the state killed as many as 5,000 Kurds between 1993 and 1996 under the DYP-led government of Tansu Ciller. Under emergency law in the southeastern provinces, the army has forcibly depopulated more than half the 5,000 villages and hamlets in the region, in many cases killing and torturing villagers. Five provinces currently remain under a state of emergency. Civil governors throughout the southeast may authorize military operations, expel citizens suspected of Kurdish sympathies, ban demonstrations, and confiscate publications. In June, the European Court of Human Rights ruled against Turkey in two cases involving Kurdish separatists and freedom of expression.

The PKK and smaller Kurdish groups also commit extrajudicial killings and kidnappings. They target individuals believed to be state sympathizers, such as government-sponsored "village guards" or civil defense forces, their families, local officials, and teachers who teach Turkish rather than Kurdish.

Although the judiciary is nominally independent, the constitutional court is seen as an arm of the military. In the 18 state security courts (SSCs), which try terrorist offenses, procedural safeguards are inadequate and the right to appeal is limited. Prison conditions are abysmal, characterized by widespread torture, sexual abuse, and denial of medical attention to inmates. Human Rights Watch reported that hundreds of ordinary detainees as well as security detainees were tortured or abused in 1998.

Freedom of expression in Turkey is limited by the Criminal Code, which forbids insulting state officials and incitement to racial or ethnic hatred. The Anti-Terror Law (ATL) assigns penalties for the dissemination of separatist propaganda. Writers and journalists are routinely jailed under the ATL and other similarly restrictive measures. According to Reporters Sans Frontiers, five journalists were tortured, 58 were threatened, attacked, or harassed, and 45 others were arrested between January and October 1998. Numerous arrests, raids, and seizures occurred later in the year. RSF also counted 118 cases of censorship or seizure by SSC prosecutors against 19 publications between January and September. Three daily newspapers were banned in March from covering the armed forces. The pro-Kurdish *Ulkede Gundem* was fined $12,000 and closed for 312 days. And in the first such conviction, an 18-year-old was given a ten-month suspended prison sentence for insulting police on the Internet.

Authorities may restrict freedom of association and assembly on the grounds of maintaining public order, and prior notice of gatherings is required. Human rights activists suffered severe harassment in 1998. Akin Birdal, chairman of the Human Rights

Association (IHD) was gunned down in May after a series of media reports linked him to the PKK. He survived only to be jailed in July for provoking hatred. In June, another IHD activist went missing; the left-wing Marxist Leninist Communist Party (MLKP) claimed responsibility for his death. In May, the government's campaign against Islamic activism led to the prosecution of Musiad, Turkey's leading pro-Islamic business group, on charges of inciting hatred.

Roughly 99 percent of Turks are Muslim. Religious freedom is restricted by limits on worship to designated sites, constraints on building houses of worship for minority religions, and the recent military-backed government crackdown on what it perceives as Islamic fundamentalism. After a 1997 law drastically reduced attendance in Islamic high schools, an administrative court in February raised the age of eligibility to attend religious schools from 12 to 15 and banned weekend and summer Koran courses. Also in February, the ministry of education renewed a longstanding but unenforced ban on traditional headscarves in schools, government offices, and state-run facilities. Hundreds of civil servants, teachers, governors, and mayors have been investigated for allegedly supporting fundamentalism, and suspected militants have been rounded up in raids on clubs and associations.

Women face discrimination in family matters such as inheritance and marital rights and obligations. Laws and social norms make it difficult to prosecute rape cases, and the penalty for rape may be reduced if a woman was not a virgin prior to her attack. The practice of "virginity testing" continued despite the introduction of legislation to ban it in police investigations. A law passed in January prohibits spousal abuse.

Workers, except members of security forces, may join independent trade unions. The right to strike is restricted to exclude workers engaged in the protection of life and property and those in the mining and petroleum industries, sanitation services, national defense, and education. Public sector employees demonstrated for several days in March over a draft law which does not allow for middle-ranking public workers to strike and bargain collectively.

Turkmenistan

Polity: Presidential
Economy: Statist
Population: 4,700,000
PPP: $2,345
Life Expectancy: 66
Ethnic Groups: Turkmen (77 percent), Uzbek (9 percent), Russian (7 percent), Kazakh (2 percent), other (5 percent)
Capital: Ashgabat

Political Rights: 7
Civil Liberties: 7
Status: Not Free

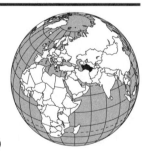

Overview: In 1998, President Saparmurad Niyazov, the absolute ruler of this oil- and gas-rich country, made his first official visit to the United States, meeting with President Bill Clinton, Vice President Al Gore as well as the presidents of the World Bank and International Monetary Fund. The high-level meetings highlighted the geostrategic importance of this

Caspian nation, which is believed to have the worlds fourth-largest reserves of natural gas, with Russia, Iran, and the U.S. vying for valuable pipeline projects.

President Niyazov, former first secretary of the Turkmen Communist Party, renamed himself Turkmenbashi, or Head of the Turkmen, in 1991, with the aim of uniting the country's many different clans. He has established a cult of personality that rivals Lenin and micromanages everything from the economy to the authorization of doctoral dissertations.

Turkmenistan, the former Soviet Central Asian republic bordering Afghanistan and Iran, was ruled by various local leaders until the thirteenth century, when the Mongols conquered it. In the late nineteenth century, Tsarist Russia seized the country. The Turkmen Soviet Socialist Republic was declared in 1924, after the Bolsheviks ousted the Khan of Merv.

Turkmenistan declared independence after a national referendum in October 1991; Niyazov won a one-man election in December. In 1992, after the adoption of a new constitution, Niyazov was re-elected, claiming 99.5 percent of the vote. The main opposition group, Agzybirlik, formed in 1989 by leading intellectuals, was banned and its leaders harassed. The country has two parliamentary bodies, the 50-member *Majlis* (Assembly)and the *Khalk Maslakhaty* (People's Council), which includes the members of the Assembly, 50 directly elected members and leading executives as well as judicial officials. Niyazov is president of the People's Council. In December 1994 parliamentary elections, only Niyazov's Democratic Party of Turkmenistan (DPT) was permitted to field candidates. The president has extensive powers and can prorogue the parliament if has passed two no-confidence motions within an 18-month period. In addition, he issues edicts that have the force of law, appoints and removes all judges, and names the state prosecutor. He is also prime minister and commander-in-chief. Parliament extended his term to the year 2002.

A highlight of his April 1998 official visit to the United States was a $750,000 grant from the Trade and Development Agency to pay for a feasibility study of alternative pipeline routes. In 1997, Iran and Turkmenistan had signed a memorandum of cooperation in exploiting oil and gas in the Caspian Sea. A year earlier, a strategic rail link was opened between Turkmenistan and Iran, providing Central Asian states access to Iran's warm-water ports. A small portion of an Iranian-Turkmen gas pipeline was completed in 1998.

In October, Turkmenistan signed two oil transportation deals with several countries. In December, President Niyazov gave permission for Lukoil, the huge Russian energy concern, to begin operations in the country. In October, the U.S. company Unocal said it would continue work on a project to lay a gas pipeline to Pakistan via Afghanistan.

Despite Turkmenistan's vast resources, there has been no reform of the Soviet command system, and the majority of citizens live in dire poverty. In December, the National Bank suspended free currency conversion as the country was in the midst of a cash and balance-of-payment crisis caused by a drop in gas revenue.

In 1998, President Niyazov continued his practice of routinely dismissing top officials to stop a potential power base from challenging his authority. In May, the oil minister was replaced, and in September Niyazov replaced the defense minister and sacked several top military officials, allegedly for their dismal response to an incident in which several servicemen deserted and took hostages.

Political Rights and Civil Liberties: Citizens of Turkmenistan do not have the means to change their government democratically. Power remains concentrated in the hands of the president. The one-party elections to a rubber-stamp parliament in 1994 were undemocratic.

While the constitution provides for freedom of the press and expression, the government controls and funds all electronic and print media, prohibits the media from reporting the views of opposition political leaders and critics, and rarely allows the mildest of criticism of the government and its policies. Only two newspapers, *Adalat* and *Galkynysh* are nominally independent, and they were created by presidential decree. President Niyazov has been declared the "founder" of all newspapers in Turkmenistan. Whereas cable TV existed in the late 1980s in all cities and three commercial TV stations existed in the early 1990s, they have been closed. The state controls all TV and radio broadcasts. In October, Turkmenistan clamped restrictions on Russian public TV, and announced that broadcasts would be shown "selectively."

The population is overwhelmingly Sunni Muslim. The government has kept a rein on religion to avert the rise of Islamic fundamentalism. Religious congregations are required to register with the government and religious organizations must have at least 500 adherents to register. This restriction has caused problems for minority religions, especially the Baha'i. The government discourages proselytizing and foreign missionaries.

The constitution allows for peaceful assembly and association, but the government restricts these rights. In 1995, authorities broke up the first peaceful demonstration in years, convicting 20 people.

The DPT is the only legal party. Opposition parties have been banned, and most leaders of Agzybirlik have fled, many to Moscow, Sweden, Norway, and the Czech Republic. Those still in the country face harassment and detention from the Committee on National Security (KNB), the successor to the Soviet-era KGB. There are several government controlled entities which attempt to fill the niche normally filled by NGOs, among them the Institute for Democracy and Human Rights, which is affiliated with the office of the president.

The central trade union, the Trade Union Federation of Turkmenistan, is the successor to the Soviet-era body. There are no legal guarantees entitling workers to form or join unions.

The judiciary is subservient to the regime; the president appoints all judges for a term of five years without legislative review. In December, the government declared a moratorium on the death penalty. In October, President Niyazov granted amnesty to 8,000 convicts and detainees, mostly women, minors, invalids, and the sick. In April, prior to President Niyazov's visit to the United States, several opposition figures were released, including Durdymurat Khojamukhammed, co-leader of the banned Democratic Progress Party, who had been confined in a mental hospital since 1995. Also released were two members of the so-called Ashgabat 8, Begmurat Khojayev, and Batyr Sakhetliyev, organizers of the 1995 anti-government demonstrations in the capital. Six organizers remain jailed.

Corruption continues to be pervasive. President Niyazov continued to complain publicly about corrupt officials, but no major prosecutions occurred. In the past, Niyazov has stated that he would allow officials to keep their illegal private gains if they proved they were working for the overall benefit of the country and people.

Citizens are required to carry internal passports, and while residence permits are not required, place of residence is registered and noted in passports.

A Soviet-style command economy diminishes equality of opportunity and leaves citizens dependent on bureaucrats, state managers, and the government for a livelihood.

Women face discrimination in education, business, and government, and social-religious norms restrict women's freedom.

Tuvalu

Polity: Parliamentary democracy
Economy: Capitalist
Population: 10,000
PPP: na
Life Expectancy: na
Ethnic Groups: Polynesian (96 percent)
Capital: Fongafale

Political Rights: 1
Civil Liberties: 1
Status: Free

Overview: Following general elections in March, parliament reelected incumbent Prime Minister Bikenbeu Paeniu.

This small, predominantly Polynesian country, formerly known as the Ellice Islands, consists of nine atolls stretching over 500,000 square miles of the western Pacific Ocean. The islands were proclaimed a British protectorate with the Gilbert Islands (now independent Kiribati) in 1892. Formally annexed by Britain in 1915-1916, when the Gilbert and Ellice Islands Colony was established, the Ellice Islands separated in October 1975 and were renamed Tuvalu. The country became an independent member of the British Commonwealth in 1978. In Tuvalu's first post-independence general election in September 1971, Dr. Tomasi Puapua was elected as prime minister.

Following the September 1993 elections, parliament was deadlocked between two candidates for premier after two rounds of voting. Then-Governor General Sir Toalipi Lauti used his constitutional powers to dissolve this new legislature, and the country held fresh elections in November. In December, parliament elected Kamuta Laatasi, a former general manager of BP Oil in Tuvalu, as prime minister.

Laatasi lost a vote of confidence on December 17, 1996, and on December 23, parliament elected Bikenibeu Paeniu as prime minister. After the country's last general election in March 1998, Paeniu was elected by the 12-member parliament to another term as prime minister. The instability in the tiny parliament has been cited by citizens who favor ending the country's link to the monarchy and adopting republican status under an ostensibly more stable presidential form of government.

The primarily subsistence economy consists mainly of coconuts, taros, and fishing. Much of the country's revenue comes from the sale of stamps and coins as well as from remittances by some 1,500 countrymen working abroad, mostly as merchant seamen or phosphate miners on Nauru and Kiribati. Interest from the Tuvalu Trust Fund, established in 1987 by major aid donors, covers one-fourth of the annual budget. Until recently, an estimated ten percent of the country's budget came from the controversial practice of leasing unused telephone numbers to international providers of sex telephone lines.

Political Rights and Civil Liberties: Citizens of Tuvalu can change their government democratically. The 1978 constitution vests executive power in a prime minister and a cabinet of up to four ministers. The 12-member parliament, *Fale I Fono*, is directly elected for a four-year term. The prime minister appoints and can dismiss the governor general, who is a Tuvalu citizen and represents the Queen of England, who is head of state, for a four-year term. The governor general appoints the cabinet members and can name a chief executive or dissolve parliament if its members cannot agree on a premier. Each of the country's nine islands is administered by directly elected six-person councils, which are influenced by village-based hereditary elders who wield considerable traditional authority. Political parties are legal, but no formal parties have been established. Most elections hinge on village-based allegiances rather than policy issues.

Freedom of speech and the press are respected. The government broadcasts over Radio Tuvalu and publishes the fortnightly newspaper *Tuvalu Echoes* in Tuvaluan and English, and there is a monthly religious newsletter. Although most of the population belongs to the Protestant Church of Tuvalu, all religious faiths practice freely.

The government respects freedom of assembly and association. Workers are free to join independent trade unions, bargain collectively, and stage strikes. Only the Tuvalu Seamen's Union, with about 600 members, has been organized and registered. No strikes have ever occurred, largely because most of the population is engaged outside the wage economy. Civil servants, teachers, and nurses, who total less than 1,000 employees, have formed associations which do not yet have union status.

The judiciary is independent. Citizens receive fair public trials with procedural safeguards based on English common law, with a right of ultimate appeal under certain circumstances to the Privy Council in London. The small police force is under civilian control.

Citizens are free to travel within the country and abroad. Traditional social restrictions limit employment opportunities for women, though many are securing jobs in education and health care and are becoming more politically active. Violence against women appears to occur rarely.

Uganda

Polity: Dominant party (military-influenced)
Economy: Capitalist-statist
Population: 21,000,000
PPP: $1,483
Life Expectancy: 40

Political Rights: 4
Civil Liberties: 4
Status: Partly Free

Ethnic Groups: Baganda (17 percent), Karamojong (12 percent), Basogo (8 percent), Iteso (8 percent), Langi (6 percent), Rwanda (6 percent), Bagisu (5 percent), Acholi (4 percent), Lugbara (4 percent), Bunyoro (3 percent), Batobo (3 percent), other (23 percent)
Capital: Kampala

Overview:

Worsening wars in three of Uganda's five neighboring states helped to fuel domestic rebel activity that threatened both internal security and the economic growth that has marked Yoweri Museveni's rule. Resources desperately needed for development were diverted as military spending rose sharply to meet insurgencies in the north and west. Uganda's army was also fighting in the Democratic Republic of Congo and was reportedly supporting rebels in southern Sudan. In return, Sudan's Islamist regime is backing the brutal Lord's Resistance Army, which has murdered thousands of civilians in northern Uganda and abducted thousands of young people in its avowed quest to create a separate state ruled in strict accordance with the ten commandments.

Parties formally banned since 1986 will now be allowed to campaign on the 2000 referendum that will decide whether Uganda will return to a multiparty system. Museveni and the current parliament were elected to five-year terms in 1996 elections conducted officially on a nonparty basis. Nevertheless, political parties that have their roots in Uganda's pre-independence period and that are largely divided along ethnic lines continue to operate and vigorously seek to revive party politics. The relative peace and prosperity that most of Uganda has enjoyed for the past decade could persuade many voters to maintain Museveni's formula. Growing insecurity and increasing corruption, as manifested in the December resignation as presidential advisor of Museveni's half brother Maj. Gen. Salim Saleh due to financial improprieties, will be used as arguments for a more open political system.

Ugandans began a 15-year national nightmare with Idi Amin's 1971 coup against Milton Obote. Amin's brutality and buffoonery made world headlines as hundreds of thousands of people were killed. Amin's 1978 invasion of Tanzania finally prompted his demise. Tanzanian forces and Ugandan exiles routed Amin's army and prepared for Obote's return to power in fraudulent 1980 elections. Obote and his backers from northern Uganda savagely repressed his critics, who were primarily from southern Ugandan ethnic groups. Approximately 250,000 people were killed as political opponents were tortured and murdered and soldiers terrorized the countryside. Obote was ousted for a second time in a 1985 army coup. Conditions continued to worsen until Museveni led his National Resistance Army into Kampala in January 1986.

Manipulation and exploitation of ethnic divisions pose the gravest threat to peace in Uganda. Baganda people in the country's south are demanding more recognition of their traditional kingdom, and northern ethnic groups are complaining of government neglect.

Political Rights and Civil Liberties: Uganda's only open multiparty elections were held in 1961 in preparation for the country's independence from Britain. Museveni's 1986 formal ban on political party activities will be tested by referendum in 2000. In 1996, Ugandans voted for their president and parliamentarians in elections without open party competition. State media and other official resources were mobilized in support of Museveni's candidacy, and the ban on formal party activities further hindered the opposition. Most observers believe that Museveni would have won handily in a multiparty contest and described the balloting and counting as largely transparent. Museveni won 74 percent of the vote for president, and his National Resistance Movement dominated the legislative elections. Only 20 opposition representatives won seats in the 276-seat parliament. Most of these were members of the formally banned Uganda People's Congress. War-torn districts in northern Uganda did not participate in local council elections in late 1997.

With parliamentary approval, the president names a judicial commission that oversees judicial appointments. The judiciary is still influenced by the executive despite increasing autonomy. It is also constrained by inadequate resources and the army's occasional refusal to respect civilian courts. Local courts are subject to bribery and corruption. Prison conditions are difficult, especially in local jails. More than 500 prisoners die annually due to poor diet, sanitation, and medical care. Serious human rights violations by rebel groups and the Uganda People's Defense Forces have been reported.

Freedom of assembly for banned political parties is formally proscribed, but such groups meet without interference. The Uganda Human Rights Activists, the Uganda Law Society, and the Foundation for Human Rights Initiatives are among nongovernmental organizations that focus directly on human rights issues. The official Human Rights Commission, which has limited legal powers, began hearings on alleged human rights violations in November and has received substantial international support.

There is no state religion, and freedom of worship is constitutionally protected and respected. Various Christian sects and the country's Muslim minority practice their creeds freely.

There is broad public debate as freedom of expression and the media is generally respected. The independent print media, which include more than two dozen daily and weekly newspapers, are often highly critical of the government and offer a full range of opposition views. Several private radio stations and two private television stations report openly on local political developments. The largest newspapers and broadcasting facilities that reach rural areas remain state-owned. Governmental corruption is reported. Opposition positions are also presented, but the coverage is often not balanced. Some direct restrictions on the media are in force. Provisions of 1995 and 1996 press laws have effectively barred some journalists from working by imposing educational and training requirements. The Uganda Journalists Safety Committee has sued the government for alleged use of sedition laws to arrest or intimidate journalists. Uncensored but expensive Internet access is available in the larger centers, and at least daily two newspapers are available on the World Wide Web. Rebel groups have also established websites from servers outside of Uganda.

Women experience discrimination based on traditional law, particularly in rural areas, and are treated unequally under inheritance, divorce, and citizenship statutes. A woman cannot obtain a passport without her husband's permission. Domestic violence against women is widespread.

The National Organization of Trade Unions, the country's largest labor federation, is independent of the government and political parties. An array of essential workers is barred from forming unions. Strikes are permitted only after a lengthy reconciliation process.

Most Ugandans are subsistence farmers. The country's economy has grown steadily due to pragmatic open market policies and the largesse of international aid donors.

Ukraine

Polity: Presidential-par- **Political Rights:** 3
liamentary democracy **Civil Liberties:** 4
Economy: Mixed statist **Status:** Partly Free
(transitional)
Population: 50,300,000
PPP: $2,361
Life Expectancy: 68
Ethnic Groups: Ukrainian (73 percent), Russian (22 percent),
Jewish (1 percent), other (4 percent)
Capital: Kiev

Overview: The Communist Party and its left-wing allies won the most seats in parliamentary elections on March 29, 1998, leading to a continuing deadlock with President Leonid Kuchma over the pace and scope of needed economic reforms.

While labeling the vote generally free and fair, international monitoring groups from the Organization for Security and Cooperation in Europe and the Council of Europe cited corruption scandals, killings, arrests, and the closing of a newspaper as marring the election campaign. The Communist Party won 123 seats in the 450-member uni-cameral Verkhovna Rada under an electoral system adopted in 1997 in which half the seats were decided by proportional representation according to national party lists, and half were allocated in single-mandate constituencies. The leftist Social-Peasant Bloc took 32 seats; the democratic Rukh party took 46; independents won 114; the govern-ment People's Democratic Party led by Prime Minister Valery Pustovoitenko took 28 seats; the progovernment Green Party, 19; and former Prime Minister Pavlo Lazarenko's Hromada party captured 23. Turnout was reported at 70 percent.

In other issues, the U.S. and the International Monetary Fund warned Ukraine that continued aid and assistance was contingent upon implementation of structural and fiscal reforms. The IMF suspended a tranche of $585 million in March after Ukraine exceeded a limit on growth in wage and pension arrears, and net international reserves fell. In December, former Prime Minister Lazarenko was arrested in Geneva and charged with money laundering before being released on $3 million bail.

Ukraine declared independence from a crumbling Soviet Union in 1991, when Leonid Kravchuk was elected president. In the 1994 presidential race, Kravchuk lost to Kuchma, an industrialist and former prime minister, in a runoff. The Communist Party and its allies dominated the parliamentary elections, but did not win a majority. In early 1996, Kuchma pressed a reluctant parliament to adopt a new national charter. After the president warned that he would call for a popular referendum, parliament voted in favor of the constitution. In July 1997, Prime Minister Lazarenko, who had replaced Yevhen Marchuk a year before, resigned amid stalled economic reforms and persistent allegations of cronyism and corruption.

The run-up to the March 1998 elections saw a series of charges and counter-charges concerning corruption between the pro-government forces of President Kuchma and Prime Minister Pustovoitenko, and former Prime Minister Lazarenko and his Hromada Party. In February, the Ministry of Information closed *Pravda Ukrainy*, linked to Lazarenko, for not filling out the right forms when registering a Ukrainian-Antiguan venture. Mykhailo Brodksy, owner of the anti-government *Kievskiye Vedomosti*, was arrested in mid-March and charged with illegal property deals. The election campaign also included violence, particularly in Odessa, long a hotbed of corruption and criminal activity.

Political wrangling also led to a protracted deadlock in choosing a parliamentary speaker, a key obstacle to an IMF agreement on granting a $2 billion three-year credit. Between the convening of the new parliament on May 12 and late June, parliament failed thirteen times to elect a speaker, thus holding up the budget and important tax legislation. As the crisis intensified, President Kuchma threatened to dissolve parliament and rule by decree. Critics accused the president of trying to discredit parliament, allowing him to rule by decree. On July 8, after 20 attempts, parliament elected Oleksander Tkachenko from the leftist Socialist-Peasant Bloc, as speaker. On December 15, President Kuchma said he might call a referendum to extend his right to issue economic decrees for five more years. The 1996 constitution initially granted the president three years to issue economic decrees on matters not covered by existing legislation.

In other issues, Ukrainian Foreign Minister Borys Tarasiuk made an official two-day visit to Russia in mid-November to discuss ratification by the Russian parliament of a broad treaty signed by Presidents Kuchma and Yeltsin in May 1997. Ukraine's parliament ratified the treaty in early 1998. Ukrainian-Russian tensions continued over Crimea, with its ethnic Russian majority and a key Russian naval base.

Political Rights and Civil Liberties: Ukrainians can change their government democratically. Presidential and parliamentary elections in 1994 were deemed generally "free and fair" by international observers, though there were reports of irregularities and pre-election intimidation as well as violence directed at democratic organizations and activists. Changes in the electoral law adopted in 1997 instituted a mixed system, where 50 percent of candidates were elected by majority vote and 50 by proportional representation. The 1998 elections were generally free and fair, though international organizations criticized the election campaign as being "marred by incidents of violence, arrests and actions against candidates, and abuse of public office." The OSCE report also pointed to many attempts by the government to manipulate the national media.

A 1991 press law purports to protect freedom of speech and press, but it only covers print media. The Constitution, the Law on Information (1992), and the Television and Radio Broadcasting Law (1994) protect freedom of speech, but there are laws banning attacks on the president's "honor and dignity." There are over 5,000 Ukrainian- and Russian-language newspapers, periodicals, and journals. Privately owned broadcasters include 1+ 1, financed by the U.S.-based Central European Communications Enterprise (CME), Inter, STB, and radio stations—Radio Kievski Vedomosti, Nashe Radio, Music Radio, and Radio Lux. There are 25 regional and two national state-owned television and radio stations. In 1998, the media faced pressure from entrenched political interests and criminal organizations. In January, a reporter working for a paper in Dnipropetrovsk had acid thrown in his face. Several days later, a grenade went off in the offices of a newspaper in Donetsk. In Odessa, reporters for ART Television have been threatened for exposing links between the mafia and the regional police.

Although the previously outlawed Ukrainian Catholic and Ukrainian Autocephalous Orthodox churches are legal, conflicts continue over churches and property between the two churches and the old Russian Orthodox Church. There are three Ukrainian Orthodox churches, two with allegiances to patriarchs in Kiev and one with allegiance to Moscow. In March, the patriarchs of the Autocephalous Church and the Orthodox Church (*Kiev Patriarchate*) signed a memorandum on unification. Ukraine's estimated 600,000 Jews have over 300 organizations and four national umbrella groups that maintain schools and social services. The large Russian minority enjoys full rights and protections. Hungarians in Subcarpathia continue to press for greater cultural rights.

Freedom of assembly is generally respected, but organizations must apply for permission to their respective local administration at least ten days before a planned event or demonstration, of which there were several in Kiev in 1998.

There are some 54 national political parties representing the political spectrum from far-left to far-right. Thirty parties and blocs contested the 1998 parliamentary elections. There are some 4,000 registered NGOs in Ukraine, including cultural, women's, sports, human rights, environmental, and public policy organizations.

The Federation of Trade Unions, a successor to the Soviet-era federation, claims 20 million members. The National Confederation of Trade Unions has three million members and includes some independent trade unions. Though the Association of Free Trade Unions of Ukraine dissolved due to internal conflicts in April 1996, its constituent unions, including miners, sailors, civil air dispatchers, aviation ground crews, scientists, and railroad workers, have a total membership of 150,000. In June, 1,000 striking mine workers marched to Kiev from eastern Ukraine to demand wage arrears.

The judiciary remains subject to political interference. The courts are organized on three levels: *rayon* (district) courts, *oblast* (regional) courts, and the Supreme Court. Parliament, the president, and the Congress of Judges each appoint six of the Constitutional Court's 18 members for nine-year terms. Judges are appointed by the president for an initial five-year term, after which they are subject to parliamentary approval for lifetime tenure. Shortages of qualified judges have led to delays in the court system and violations of the rights of detainees. Many judges on the subnational levels remain sensitive to pressures by the local administrations.

Corruption is pervasive at all levels of government. Bribery is common for services, education, and in the police forces. Former Prime Minister Pavlo Lazarenko, widely believed to have a stake in the lucrative gas company, United Energy Systems, was arrested in Switzerland in December and charged with money laundering. While several presidential decrees and laws deal with corruption, there have been no major trials or prosecutions.

Freedom of movement within the country is not restricted by law. However, regulations impose a nationwide requirement to register at the workplace and place of residence in order to be eligible for social benefits, thereby complicating freedom of movement by limiting access to certain social benefits to the place where one is registered.

Property rights are formally guaranteed by the constitution and the property laws. *De facto*, the right to private property remains ill-defined. Land reform is still in preliminary stages. Though under law citizens have the right to form businesses, these rights are hindered by taxation policies, bureaucratic hurdles, and growing crime and corruption. Many leading businessmen are former members of the *nomenklatura* who used contacts and lax laws to gain an advantage in the privatization of enterprises and economic sectors. These factors restrict equality of opportunity. Between 50 and 60 percent of GDP is believed generated by the "shadow economy" that operates outside business and tax regulations.

Women are well represented in education, government and in the professional classes, and there are numerous NGOs which focus on women's issues such as domestic violence.

United Arab Emirates

Polity: Federation of traditional monarchies
Economy: Capitalist-statist
Population: 2,700,000
PPP: $18,008
Life Expectancy: 74
Ethnic Groups: South Asian (50 percent), Arab and Iranian (42 percent), other (8 percent)
Capital: Abu Dhabi

Political Rights: 6
Civil Liberties: 5
Status: Not Free

Overview:　The United Arab Emirates' (UAE) GDP declined by 5.5 percent in 1998, reflecting the falling world oil prices which continue to threaten the region's economic prosperity. Overall, the UAE has fared well in comparison with its neighbors, in part because of its strong non-oil sector, and also because it possesses large cash reserves which help to cushion the oil price shock. In fact, the UAE was called upon in 1998 to bail out cash-strapped Saudi Arabia with a loan estimated at $5 billion.

The seven emirates which constitute the United Arab Emirates formed a unified federation after gaining independence from Britain in 1971. Under the 1971 provisional constitution, the emirate rulers make up the Federal Supreme Council, the highest legislative and executive body. The Council elects a state president and vice president from among its membership, and the president appoints the prime minister and cabinet. A 40-member consultative Federal National Council, composed of delegates appointed by the seven rulers, holds no legislative power. While there are separate consultative councils in several emirates, there are no political parties or popular elections.

Skeikh Zayed ibn Sultan al Nuhayyan of Abu Dhabi, the largest emirate and capital of the UAE, has served as president since independence and is considered largely responsible for the country's unification and economic success. The UAE has a free market economy based on oil and gas production, trade, and light manufacturing. The economy provides citizens with a high per capita income, but is heavily dependent on foreign workers, who comprise some 80 percent of the population.

The UAE has maintained a generally pro-Western foreign policy since the Persian Gulf War and continues to cooperate militarily with the United States, Great Britain, and France. The UAE in 1998 became a more vocal supporter of easing UN-imposed sanctions against Iraq and sought to provide humanitarian assistance for Iraq under the UN's oil-for-food program.

The UAE and Iran appeared to make progress in 1998 on resolving the status of three disputed Gulf islands. The UAE welcomed reports late in the year that the UN secretary general sought to mediate the dispute. Iran controls the three islands near the Strait of Hormuz in defiance of UAE claims to the territory. Although the islands had been ruled jointly by Iran and the emirate of Sharjah for two decades, the Iranian government expelled the emirate's citizens in 1992. In response to this and other Iranian threats, the UAE has spent over $60 million on arms purchases since the war.

Political Rights and Civil Liberties:

Citizens of the UAE cannot change their government democratically. There are no elections at any level, political parties are illegal, and executive and legislative authority is in the hands of the Federal Supreme Council. The seven emirate rulers, their extended families, and their allies by marriage or common interest wield political control in their respective emirates. Citizens may voice concerns to their leaders through open *majlis* (gatherings) held by the emirate rulers.

The judiciary is generally independent of the government, though its decisions are subject to review by the political leadership. There is a dual system of *Shari'a* (Islamic) and civil (secular) courts. Most of the courts, except those in Dubai and Ras al-Khaimah, are accountable to the Federal Supreme Court in Abu Dhabi. There are no jury trials. Military tribunals try only military personnel, and there is no separate state security court system. Police may enter homes without a warrant or probable cause, but their actions are subject to review and disciplinary action. The government investigates reports of maltreatment during detention. Authorities generally bring detainees to trial within reasonable time, and there is an appeals process. Sentences of amputation and death by firing squad have been handed down, but are rarely carried out. Flogging is frequently a punishment for violations of Islamic law.

Journalists routinely practice self-censorship when reporting on government policy, national security, and religion and refrain from criticizing the ruling families. The print media are largely privately owned but receive government subsidies. All publications must be licensed by the ministry of education. Foreign publications are censored before distribution. The broadcast media are government-owned and present only government views. Satellite dishes are widely owned and provide foreign broadcasting without censorship.

The government restricts freedom of assembly and association. Permits are required for public organized gatherings. Some emirates permit conferences where government policies are discussed, but all private associations must be non-political. Islam is the official religion in the UAE, and most citizens are Sunni Muslims. Shi'ite Muslims are free to maintain mosques, and non-Muslims are free to practice their religions. Major cities have Christian churches and Hindu and Sikh temples, some built on land donated by the ruling families.

There are no restrictions on internal travel, except near oil and defense facilities. The small, stateless Bedouin population is prohibited from receiving passports. Women must have permission from husbands or male relatives to leave the country. They also face discrimination in employment benefits, but they are free to hold government positions, though tradition has limited their political role. Under Shari'a law, Muslim women are forbidden to marry non-Muslims unless they convert to Islam. Rights groups have reported that offenders have received prison sentences.

Unions, strikes, and collective bargaining are illegal and do not occur.

United Kingdom

Polity: Parliamentary democracy
Economy: Mixed capitalist
Population: 59,100,000
PPP: $19,302
Life Expectancy: 77
Ethnic Groups: English (81.5 percent), Scottish (9.6 percent), Irish (2.4 percent), Welsh (1.9 percent), Ulster (1.8 percent), other, including West Indian, Indian, and Pakistani (2.8 percent)
Capital: London

Political Rights: 1
Civil Liberties: 2
Status: Free

Overview:

In 1998, Labour Prime Minister Tony Blair added a Northern Ireland peace agreement and progress on wide-ranging political reforms to his list of achievements. His government commands a 179-seat majority in parliament and enjoys the highest popularity ratings in British history. With the opposition Conservative party in disarray, the government has room to implement its political agenda. However, allegations of corruption, which sped the downfall of Conservatives in the 1997 election, have tainted numerous Labour politicians, including some close to the prime minister.

The United Kingdom of Great Britain and Northern Ireland encompasses the two formerly separate kingdoms of England and Scotland, the ancient principality of Wales, and the six counties of the Irish province of Ulster (see *Northern Ireland* under Related Territories). The British parliament has an elected House of Commons with 659 members chosen by plurality vote from single-member districts, and a House of Lords with some 1,100 hereditary and appointed members. A cabinet of ministers appointed from the majority party exercises executive power on behalf of the mainly ceremonial sovereign. Queen Elizabeth II nominates the party leader with the most support in the House of Commons to form a government.

After ruling the UK for 18 years, Conservatives succumbed to petty corruption, political infighting over European policy, and a series of sex scandals. Blair's "New Labour," so called because of its radical shift from its socialist past, adopted Conservative-style positions on a number of issues and swept general elections in May 1997.

The government continues to define itself as it goes along by blending traditional Labour and Conservative policies. Since taking office, Labour has abandoned tax-and-spend policies, devolved monetary policy to the Bank of England, and imposed strict spending limits. But it has also re-introduced the minimum wage and restored rights to trade unions.

With his sizeable parliamentary majority, Blair has successfully pushed through a number of reforms. Devolution of power to Scotland and Wales began in September 1997, when each territory voted to create its own legislature. General elections for the 129-member Scottish parliament and the 60-member Welsh assembly will be held in May 1999. In March 1998, the government announced the creation of a mayoral seat and a 25-member assembly for London. Voters approved of the measure in a May referendum, and elections are scheduled for 2000. Welfare reform fell short of the thorough restructuring anticipated, though a "New Deal" program of jobs for youths reportedly placed some 50,000 in the last seven months of 1998. The government also made progress on reforms of the electoral system and the House of Lords.

As holder of the European Union presidency during the first half of 1998, Blair called for an enhanced role for the EU in the Middle East peace process. In November, British farmers received a boost when the EU announced the lifting of its 32-month-old ban on British beef. The ban was imposed in 1996 after an outbreak of Bovine Spongiform Encephalopathy (BSE, or "Mad Cow Disease"). On European Monetary Union (EMU), the government still rules out joining the single currency during the current parliamentary term, which likely precludes a referendum until 2002.

Blair's active involvement in multiparty talks on the future of Northern Ireland helped secure an agreement on April 10, 1998 after months of deadlock. The "Good Friday Agreement" recognizes the principle that a united Ireland may not come about without the consent of a majority of people in both jurisdictions. It also creates a 108-member assembly elected by proportional representation, establishes a north-south ministerial council to consult on matters of mutual concern to Ireland and Northern Ireland, and establishes a British-Irish council of British, Irish, Northern Irish, Scottish, and Welsh representatives to discuss particular policy issues. The new assembly was elected on June 25 and spent the latter half of the year battling over the composition of executive and north-south institutions and disarmament.

Allegations of financial and political misconduct have multiplied since Labour's election. Most notably, trade and industry secretary and chief Blair ally Peter Mandelson resigned on December 23 after it was revealed that he had accepted a £373,000 loan from Paymaster General Geoffrey Robinson. At the time of the disclosure, Robinson was under investigation by Mandelson's office for corruption. Robinson also resigned. Earlier in the year, Blair was embarrassed by the disclosure that the head of Formula One racing had donated £1 million to influence government policy on tobacco advertising. Critics of the government say that internal investigations by Labour's National Executive Committee (NEC) are often inconclusive and serve only to give the appearance of action. However, allegations of impropriety have apparently not taken a toll on Blair's popularity; he ended 1998 with an approval rating of 65 percent.

Political Rights and Civil Liberties:

Citizens of the United Kingdom can change their government democratically. Voters are registered by government survey and include both Irish and Commonwealth (former British empire) citizens resident in Britain. British subjects abroad retain voting rights for 20 years after emigration. Welsh and Scottish legislatures to be elected in 1999 will have authority over matters of regional importance such as education, health, and some economic matters. The Scottish parliament will have limited power to raise taxes. Northern Ireland's assembly will assume power in 1999.

In June, the government proposed to make the House of Lords more representative by sacking hereditary peers. Critics argue that Lords reform must begin with arrangements for partial election, lest a government pack the house with cronies. Hereditary peers comprise over half the members of the Lords; the balance are government appointees.

A commission on electoral reform issued a report in October advocating a combination of additional-member and alternative-vote systems for the House of Commons. Analysts say that the new system would strengthen smaller parties and effectively end the current two-party system.

Britain does not have a written constitution, and civil libertarians have criticized legal attempts to combat crime and terrorism as dangerous to basic freedoms. Under the Prevention of Terrorism Act, which is renewed every two years, suspects may be detained without charge or legal representation for up to seven days. The Criminal Justice and Public Order Act of 1994 allows a jury to infer guilt from a defendant's silence. In the wake of a bombing that killed 28 people in Omagh, Northern Ireland in August 1998, the government called an emergency session of parliament to pass the toughest anti-terror laws in British history. The laws make it possible to jail suspected terrorists on the word of a senior police officer, and allow security forces to seize the property and money of known terrorists.

In November, the government passed the Human Rights Act of 1998, incorporating articles of the European Convention on Human Rights (ECHR) into British law. The act compels all public bodies to act in accordance with the convention, and allows British citizens to take alleged violations of the convention to British courts.

Home Secretary Jack Straw in March announced the introduction of measures to tackle corruption in Britain's police force. Beginning in April 1999, the level of proof necessary to take disciplinary action against an officer will be reduced; a fast-track dismissal procedure for the worst offenders will be implemented; disciplinary hearings may be held in the absence of the offending officer; and an officer's right to silence may be abridged during internal hearings.

Though uncensored and mostly private, the British press is subject to strict libel and obscenity laws. Print media are privately owned and independent, though many of the national daily newspapers are aligned with political parties. The BBC runs about half the electronic media in the country. It is funded by the government but editorially independent. In February, the bill incorporating the ECHR into British law was amended to prevent courts from using the convention to "hinder investigative journalism." The move is meant to protect British journalists from the convention's privacy codes. Legislation for a long-awaited freedom of information act was postponed again in 1998, and is anticipated in 1999.

British workers are free to form and join independent trade unions. A 1998 Fairness at Work bill proposes to boost worker rights and improve union recognition. It includes improvements in maternity and sick leave, provisions for equality between part-time and full-time workers, and higher rewards for unfair dismissal. It also grants unions automatic recognition where 50 percent of workers in a workplace are union members, or if 40 percent of workers support recognition.

Intense criticism of British asylum procedures proliferated in 1998. An investigation into the Campsfield center in southern England concluded that detention centers are "unsafe" for detainees. The number of asylum seekers in the UK has increased from 2,000 in the mid-1980s to 32,500 in 1997, creating a massive overload of the system. A broadly welcomed Immigration and Asylum Bill introduced in November proposes to address this problem.

United States of America

Polity: Federal presidential-legislative democracy
Economy: Capitalist
Population: 270,200,000
PPP: $26,977
Life Expectancy: 76

Political Rights: 1
Civil Liberties: 1
Status: Free

Ethnic Groups: White (73 percent), black (13 percent), hispanic (10 percent), Asian-Pacific (3 percent), native American (1 percent)
Capital: Washington, D.C.

Overview:

For only the second time in the history of the United States, a sitting president was impeached by a vote of the House of Representatives. In December, members of the House voted along strongly partisan lines to impeach President Bill Clinton on two of four counts brought against him: lying before a grand jury about a sexual affair with a White House intern, Monica Lewinsky, and obstruction of justice in subsequent attempts to investigate the matter.

Ironically, while the President devoted much of his attention to the political and public relations fallout from the Lewinsky affair, his public approval ratings remained high. Furthermore, the Democratic Party fared relatively well in the November mid-term elections. Although the Republicans retained control of both the House and Senate, they saw their margin of control in the House shrink, the first time a president's party had gained House seats in a mid-term election in over a half-century.

The U.S. federal government has three branches, executive, legislative, and judiciary. The American federal system gives substantial powers to state and local governments and the citizenry.

The president and vice president are elected by popular vote to four-year terms. The technical device for the election of a president is the electoral college. The voters in each state and Washington, D.C., cast their ballots for slates of electors who, in turn, cast ballots in the electoral college for the candidate who received the most votes in their particular state. In 1996, the ticket of incumbent President Bill Clinton and Vice President Al Gore won 379 electoral votes to 159 for the Republican ticket of Bob Dole and his running mate Jack Kemp. In the popular vote, the Clinton ticket received 49 percent, with Dole at 42 percent.

The U.S. Congress is bicameral. There are 435 members of the House of Representatives as well as nonvoting members from Washington, D.C., and several related territories. Each state is guaranteed at least one representative in the House. The rest are apportioned on the basis of population. In the 1998 mid-term elections, Republicans continued their domination of the House by winning 223 seats to 211 for the Democrats, with one independent. This result represented a net gain of five seats for the Democrats. The 100-member Senate has two members from each state, regardless of population. Each senator serves a six-year term. In the mid-term election, Republicans won 55 Senate seats; the Democrats won 45 seats.

Political Rights and Civil Liberties: Americans can change their government democratically. Voter turnout has been relatively low in recent years; in the 1998 midterm elections, voter turnout stood as just 36 percent of the voting age population, the lowest level since 1942. Elections are competitive, but congressional incumbents win in a majority of cases. In recent years, the cost of political campaigns has risen substantially. Much of a candidate's time is consumed with fund raising, and while Congress has periodically passed laws imposing limitations on political contributions, candidates have found ways to circumvent the spirit of the laws and court decisions have limited their effectiveness. Some critics have argued that generous contributions by business, labor unions, and other "special interests" have made it practically impossible for candidates to dislodge incumbents. Recent elections, however, have tended to weaken the thrust of that argument. In the 1994 midterm election, Republican challengers ousted a substantial number of Democratic incumbents, and in the 1998 elections, Democratic challengers defeated a significant number of sitting Republicans.

The American political system is overwhelmingly dominated by the two major parties. Various insurgent parties of the Left and Right have issued periodic challenges through the years, with little success. The most recent effort was spearheaded by Ross Perot, a Texas billionaire who sought the presidency on the Citizens Party line in both 1992 and 1996. In 1998, Jesse Ventura, a former professional wrestler, was elected governor of Minnesota on the Citizens' Party line. Nevertheless, at present, the party does not pose a significant challenge to the dominant position of the Republicans and Democrats.

The two parties choose their presidential candidates through a lengthy and expensive process during the winter and spring of election years. Party members vote for their preferred candidates either in primary elections or in local meetings of party members, called caucuses. The nominating process has been criticized for its cost, length, and for sometimes undue influence of unrepresentative minority factions. Defenders of the system claim that allowing rank-and-file party members to participate in the nominating process is more democratic than is the case in countries where a small group of party leaders selects the nominee.

A recent trend has been the increased use of initiative and referendum to determine issues of public policy. Some states, California most notably, permit public initiatives on almost any issue of public concern; in other states, strict limits are placed on the practice. In recent years, voters in various states have decided on such issues as whether to impose restrictions on illegal immigrants, the legality of assisted suicide, the use of marijuana for medicinal purposes, affirmative action for women and minorities, and casino gambling.

The American media are free and competitive. Some observers have expressed concern over the trend towards the ownership of the largest and most influential newspapers, magazines, and television networks by large corporate conglomerates. Another worrying trend is the enhanced role of television, where news is covered in a superficial and sensationalistic way, at the expense of newspapers. On the other hand, some point to the explosion of new, specialized journals as well as the Internet and public affairs programming on cable television in arguing that Americans have suffered no loss of alternative viewpoints or in-depth coverage of public issues.

Public and private discussion are very open in the United States. In recent years, concern has been expressed over the adoption by many universities of restrictive codes designed to prohibit speech that is deemed insulting to women, racial minorities, and homosexuals. Several of these codes have been struck down by the courts, but many remain in place, and are said to have a chilling effect on academic freedom.

The American court system has long been a subject of controversy. Some critics accuse judges of being overly "activist" by issuing rulings on issues which, critics contend, should be resolved through the legislative process. More recently, the courts have been at the center of controversial lawsuits which seek millions of dollars in damages from tobacco firms and handgun manufacturers. Some fear that such actions could establish a trend towards social regulation through lawsuit rather than by acts of Congress or state legislatures.

The past year has seen the continuation of a trend towards the decrease in crime throughout the country. Instances of violent crime are at their lowest level in years, especially in major cities like New York. The reason for the decrease is a source of debate, though some credit is given new strategies of community-based, zero-tolerance law enforcement adopted in a number of cities. These tactics, in turn, have elicited the criticism of civil liberties organizations, which claim that police abuse of civilians is on the increase.

The U.S. has freedom of association. Trade unions are free, but have been in decline for some years and today represent the lowest percentage of American workers in the postwar period. In 1995, the national labor federation, the AFL-CIO, elected a new president, John J. Sweeney, on a promise to institute sweeping changes in labor's political and organizing work. Although trade unions have made several organizational breakthroughs, labor suffered a major setback due to a scandal involving the election for the leadership of the Teamsters, the federation's largest union.

Despite the ripple effects of the Asian financial crisis, the American economy remained strong in 1998, with an official unemployment rate under 4.5 percent and one of the world's lowest rates of inflation. More so than in most other countries, the U.S. economy is well integrated in the world economy. This has brought a certain degree of disruption for workers in the private sector, with many high paying manufacturing jobs having been lost to countries in Latin America and Asia.

There is religious freedom in America. A persisting controversy involves the separation of church and state, in particular regarding whether federal money can be given to organizations or projects sponsored by religious groups. Although the courts have generally ruled in favor of strict separation of church and state, the Supreme Court in 1998 let stand a lower court decision which allowed students who attended church-sponsored schools in Milwaukee, Wisconsin to receive government tuition assistance.

Race relations remained one of America's most serious problems. Black Americans remain disproportionately poor, less likely to complete high school or college, more likely to have out-of-wedlock births, and more likely to suffer major health problems than other groups. Although a substantial degree of integration has been achieved in a number of American institutions, residential segregation is still high as is the tendency of blacks and Hispanics to predominate in the public schools of major cities. Blacks did, however, benefit from the high growth and low unemployment which characterized the economy in 1998.

Affirmative action programs remained a source of friction. Voters in the state of Washington approved a referendum which outlawed racial or gender preferences in public employment and the state university system. A federal court ruled that an affirmative action requirement adopted by the Federal Communications Commission for radio and television stations which gave preference to minorities and women was invalid. The year 1998 also saw a major setback for bilingual education. Voters in California overwhelmingly approved a measure outlawing the use of bilingual education for immigrant students in the public schools.

Civil rights organizations and homosexual groups called for the enactment of sweeping "hate crime" laws following the killings of a black man in Texas and a young gay man in Wyoming, crimes which were motivated by anti-Black and anti-gay prejudices.

America continued to permit high levels of legal immigration. At the same time, the U.S. has beefed up its patrols at the border with Mexico in an attempt to stem the flood of illegal immigrants, resulting in an increased number of clashes between the border patrol and illegal immigrants. The U.S. has also adopted stricter criteria for the approval of political asylum, and has raised concerns over the incarceration of some asylum seekers in prisons with regular criminals.

American women have made significant gains in recent years, and have benefited from affirmative action laws, anti-discrimination measures, and judicial decisions which have penalized corporations millions of dollars in discrimination cases.

American Indians continued to suffer a disproportionate level of poverty and social problems such as alcoholism. In recent years, some Indian reservations have experienced some economic progress through the development of gambling casinos on Indian property. But many have expressed doubts that casino gambling will lead to broad economic development for the majority of impoverished Indians.

Uruguay

Polity: Presidential-
legislative democracy
Economy: Capitalist-
statist
Population: 3,200,000
PPP: $6,854
Life Expectancy: 75
Ethnic Groups: European (88 percent), mestizo (8 percent),
black and mulatto (4 percent)
Capital: Montevideo

Political Rights: 1
Civil Liberties: 2
Status: Free

Overview:

Civil-military relations were front and center in Uruguayan politics in 1998, as President Julio Sanguinetti faced continued pressure from human rights groups and others to account fully for what happened during more than a decade of brutal military rule. Early in the year, Sanguinetti, who first achieved the presidency through a deal with the generals, received harsh criticism from the armed ranks after reincorporating 41 officers cashiered during the dictatorship for political reasons.

After gaining independence from Spain, the Oriental Republic of Uruguay was established in 1830. The Colorado Party dominated a relatively democratic political system throughout the 1960s. The 1967 constitution established a bicameral congress consisting of a 99-member Chamber of Deputies and a 31-member Senate, with every member serving a five-year term. The president is also directly elected for a five-year term.

An economic crisis, social unrest, and the activities of the Tupumaro urban guerrilla movement led to a right-wing military takeover in 1973, even though the Tupumaros had been largely crushed a year earlier. During the period of military rule, Uruguay had the largest number per capita of political prisoners in the world and was known as "the torture chamber of Latin America." Civilian rule was restored through negotiations between the regime and civilian politicians. Julio Sanguinetti won the presidential elections in 1984. In 1989, Luis Alberto Lacalle of the centrist National Party was elected president. His popularity plummeted, however, as he attempted to liberalize one of Latin America's most statist economies.

In the 1994 campaign, Sanguinetti ran as a social democrat. The other main contenders were the leftist Broad Front's Tabare Vasquez, the popular mayor of Montevideo, and the National Party's Alberto Volante. The 1994 election was the closest ever with the Colorado Party winning 31.4 percent of the vote, the National Party 30.2 percent, and the Broad Front 30 percent. In the Chamber of Deputies, the Colorado Party won 32 seats, the Nationals 31, and the Broad Front 28. In the Senate, the Colorados won 11 seats, the National Party ten, and the Broad Front nine.

Sanguinetti took office in March 1995 and enjoyed considerable congressional support, in part due to the inclusion of numerous National Party members in his cabinet. He won legislative support for an austerity package that partially dismantled the country's welfare state. A series of labor stoppages and a sharp decline in Sanguinetti's popularity followed.

In 1998, the Broad Front continued to be wracked by internal divisions that threatened its viability as a third national electoral option. Mutual accusations of corruption, particular during the time of the Lacalle government, added fuel to internal conflicts among the Blancos and threatened the orderly holding of party primaries in April 1999. Public safety continues to be a primary concern. In addition to new wrinkles in the civil-military relationship on issues left over from the time of armed forces rule, the generals floated a trial balloon to gain a greater role in internal security—this time under the guise of fighting crime.

Political Rights and Civil Liberties:

Citizens of Uruguay can change their government democratically. Constitutional guarantees regarding free expression, freedom of religion, and the right to form political parties, labor unions, and civic organizations are generally respected. The former Tupamaro guerrillas now participate in the system as part of the Broad Front. In May 1998, however, the commander of the Uruguayan army warned of dire consequences should the Broad Front win national elections and insist on investigating the fate of Uruguay's "disappeared."

The judiciary is relatively independent, but has become increasingly inefficient in the face of escalating crime, particularly street violence and organized crime. The court system is severely backlogged, and prisoners often spend more time in jail than they would were they to serve the maximum sentence for their alleged crime. Allegations of mistreatment, particularly of youthful offenders, have increased, and prison conditions do not meet international standards.

In 1991, a decision by the Inter-American Commission on Human Rights of the Organization of American States ruled that the 1985 law which granted the military amnesty from rights violations during the years of dictatorship violated key provisions of the American Convention on Human Rights. (During Sanguinetti's first government, a military commission he appointed cleared the armed forces of responsibility for hundreds of brutal detentions as well as the disappearance of more than 150 Uruguayans at home or in neighboring countries.) Sanguinetti has remained steadfast in refusing to concede to further investigations of the issue.

The press is privately owned, and broadcasting is both commercial and public. Numerous daily newspapers publish, many associated with political parties, and there are also a number of weeklies. In 1996, a number of publications ceased production due to the government's suspension of tax exemptions on the import of newsprint. In addition, a June 1996 decree requires government authorization to import newsprint.

Civic organizations have proliferated since the return of civilian rule. Numerous women's rights groups focus on violence against women, societal discrimination, and other problems. The small black minority continues to face discrimination. Uruguay's continuing economic crisis has forced thousands of formerly middle-class citizens to join rural migrants in the shantytowns ringing Montevideo.

Workers exercise their rights to join unions, bargain collectively, and hold strikes, and unions are well organized and politically powerful. Strikes are often marked by violent clashes and sabotage.

Uzbekistan

Polity: Presidential
Economy: Statist
Population: 24,100,000
PPP: $2,376
Life Expectancy: 70
Ethnic Groups: Uzbek (80 percent), Russian (5.5 percent), Tajik (5 percent), Kazakh (3 percent), Karakalpak (2.5 percent), Tatar (1.5 percent), other (2.5 percent)
Capital: Tashkent

Political Rights: 7
Civil Liberties: 6
Status: Not Free

Overview:

In 1998, authoritarian President Islam Karimov was faced with key issues concerning increasingly strained relations with neighboring Tajikistan, a crackdown on independent Muslim activists for alleged anti-government activities, and the consolidation of power by the extreme fundamentalist Taliban in neighboring Afghanistan.

Located along ancient trade routes and among the world's oldest civilized regions, Uzbekistan became part of the Russian empire in the 19th century. In 1920, it became part of the Turkistan Soviet Socialist Republic within the Russian republic. Separated from Turkmenia in 1924, it entered the USSR as a constituent republic in 1925. In 1929, its eastern Tajik region was detached and also made a constituent Soviet republic.

Karimov, former first secretary of the Communist Party, was elected president on December 29, 1991 as head of the People's Democratic Party (PDP), formerly the Communist Party. He received 86 percent of the vote, defeating well-known poet Mohammed Salih of the *Erk* Democratic Party, who received 12 percent. The largest opposition group, the nationalist *Birlik* (Unity), was barred from registering as a party, and the Islamic Renaissance Party (IRP) was banned entirely, as was the Islamic Adolat group. A February 1995 national referendum which Karimov ordered in order to extend his term to coincide with that of parliament's was allegedly approved by 99 percent of 11 million voters.

The 1992 constitution called for 1994 elections for a new, 250-member legislature, the *Ulu Majilis*, to replace the Communist-era, 500-member Supreme Soviet. Throughout 1993, the regime curtailed all opposition. The PDP took 179 seats; nominally non-party but pro-government candidates gained 20 seats; and the *Vatan Taraqioti* (Fatherland Progress Party), which is nominally oppositionist but created by the government as a businesspersons' party, gained 6. In 1995, the PDP and its allies filled the remainder in by-elections.

In early November 1998, Tajik President Imomali Rakhmonov accused the Uzbek government of helping plot an armed uprising and attempted coup, and said that President Karimov personally supported former Tajik Prime Minister Abdumalik Abdullodzanov, the alleged organizer of the mutiny. Despite Karimov's denials, relations were strained, and the growing antagonism had possible regional ramifications.

With the secular opposition severely repressed, President Karimov launched a campaign in 1998 against independent Islamic groups, particularly the so-called

Wahhabies, a Sunni sect. A new religion law passed in May called for strict registration requirements and placed restrictions on the activities of religious groups. Some 1,500 activists were arrested in the provincial city of Namangan in the Fergana Valley after the December 1997 killing of a policeman.

In other issues, Karimov replaced several cabinet members from the Samarkand region, including powerful deputy prime minister and agricultural minister Ismail Jorabekov, and dismissed the governor of Samarkand, Alisher Mardiyev, charging him with fostering tribalism, favoritism, and corruption. The move was widely seen as consolidating Karimov's control and discouraging potential rivals.

Meanwhile, the Uzbek economy continued to slump. As of November 1998, trade volume had dropped by 28 percent, privatization has lagged, and the value of the national currency, the *som*, was low.

Political Rights and Civil Liberties:

Uzbekistan is de facto a one-party state dominated by the former Communists, who have put severe restrictions on opposition political activity. The 1994 parliamentary elections were not free and fair, with only progovernment parties taking part.

Most media remains controlled by the government. A new media law signed in December 1997 purports to facilitate press freedom, but censorship and other pressures remain. Libel, public defamation of the president, and irresponsible journalism (spreading "falsehoods") are subject to financial penalties and possible imprisonment. In June, Samarkand regional radio journalist Shadi Mardiev was sentenced to 11 years in prison for defamation and extortion stemming from a satirical broadcast involving a prominent businessman. The Supreme Court upheld the sentence in August. In August, two Russian journalists were assaulted after a meeting with Marat Zakhidov, a well-known Uzbek human rights activist. The attack was believed to be connected to the journalists' visit to the Fergana Valley to collect information of religious repression. In December, the BBC's World Service protested a restriction of facilities. Uzbekistan has 471 newspapers and magazines, of which 328 are published by the government. Only 34 publications are commercial. There are independent television stations in Urgench, Smarkand, and Tashkent. Samarkand Independent Television (STV) has been severely criticized by the government.

While freedom of religion is nominally respected in this largely Sunni Muslim nation, the government continues to crackdown on Wahhabis and other independent Muslim activists. A new religion law adopted in May 1998 calls for strict registration procedures and puts restrictions on religious practices, proselytizing, and conversions. The government-funded Spiritual Directorate for Muslims funds progovernment Islamic activities. In 1998, over a thousand people were arrested, and several dozen were tried and sentenced for religious activities. The Russian Orthodox Church and the Jewish community face no serious restrictions. Ethnic Russians, along with Ukrainians, Tatars, Jews, and Kurds, continued to leave, citing fears of persecution.

While the constitution guarantees freedom of assembly, authorities have the right to suspend or ban rallies, meetings, and demonstrations on security grounds.

While enshrining a multi-party system, the constitution contains articles which undermine the rights of parties to organize. Article 62 forbids "organized activities leading...to participation in anti-government organizations." The president's People's Democratic Party continues to be the dominant party. A 1997 law prohibits parties based on ethnic or religious lines and those advocating war or subversion of the constitutional order. Prospective parties must submit a detailed list of at least 5,000 members, must register with the Justice Ministry, and may be banned by the Supreme Court if they are found guilty of persistent legal violations. Opposition parties such as Erk, Birlik, the Right Path is Justice Party, the Social Development Party, and others have been barred from registering, though activists have held meetings in people's apartments.

A 1992 law allows for the formation of trade unions. The Council of the Federation of Trade Unions, the successor to the Soviet-era federation, is subservient to the state. There are a small number of NGOs, including a human rights group, professional associations, and cultural groups, though their role, independence from the government, and strength remains uncertain.

The judiciary is subservient to the regime, with the president appointing all judges with no mechanisms to ensure their independence. The penal code contains many statutes intended to limit free expression and association. Article 60 bans "anti-state activities" and Article 204, aimed at "malicious delinquency," has been used to stifle opposition activity. In August, the Uzbek Human Rights Society, which had not been officially registered as of June 1998, called on President Karimov to free all political prisoners, estimated to be in the hundreds, including Birlik, Erk, and religious activists. Corruption in business and the civil service is believed to be pervasive. Karimov himself has ties to the largest cotton trading company in Uzbekistan. In November, senior officials from the tax committee, the internal affairs department, and the regional customs department in Samarkand were removed for bribery and abuse of power.

There are no significant restrictions on freedom of movement, emigration, and choice of residence. With limited mass privatization and a heavily agricultural economy, choices of employment are limited but not mandated by the government. Some two-thirds of the service sector has been privatized, though much is in the control of former Communist-era elites. Property rights are guaranteed by the constitution and a decree on private property. In the absence of a market system, citizens continue to be dependent, in large part, on the state sector, agricultural concerns, and bureaucrats for economic gains. Islamic traditions undermine the rights of women, and women are underrepresented in high-level positions throughout society.

Vanuatu

Polity: Parliamentary
democracy
Economy: Capitalist-
statist
Population: 200,000
PPP: $2,507
Life Expectancy: 63
Ethnic Groups: Melanesian (94 percent), French (4 percent),
other (2 percent)
Capital: Port Vila

Political Rights: 1
Civil Liberties: 3
Status: Free

Overview:

Political instability and allegations of corruption continued to plague Vanuatu in 1998, as a newly elected coalition government fell after just seven months, and widespread rioting following disclosures of financial improprieties by leading politicians led to a nationwide two-week state of emergency.

Located in the southwestern Pacific, this predominantly Melanesian archipelago, formerly the New Hebrides, was an Anglo-French condominium until achieving independence in 1980. The condominium arrangement divided the islands into English- and French-speaking communities, creating rifts that continue today.

The first post-independence government, led by Prime Minister Father Walter Lini's anglophone, Vanua'aku Pati (VP), largely excluded francophones from key posts. In 1991, a divided VP ousted premier Lini, who formed the National United Party (NUP). This split the anglophone vote and allowed the francophone Union of Moderate Parties (UMP) to win a plurality in the December elections and form a government under Maxime Carlot.

At the November 30, 1995, national legislative elections, a four-party opposition coalition headed by VP leader Donald Kalpokas won a plurality with 20 seats. But the UMP, itself now divided, formed a coalition government with the NUP headed by new UMP leader Serge Vohor. In February 1996, Carlot formed a government that fell after seven months in the wake of a report by Vanuatu's ombudsman, Marie Noelle Ferrieux Patterson, implicating Carlot in a banking scandal. In May 1997, Vohor reunited the UMP and formed the fourth government since the 1995 elections. On November 27, President Jean Marie Leye dissolved parliament, citing continued instability and corruption allegations, and called for elections in March 1998, a decision upheld by the Supreme Court in January 1998.

Throughout 1998, Ombudsman Patterson continued to expose alleged corruption and mismanagement by senior government officials, including reports that several high-ranking politicians had been involved in the illegal issuance of passports to foreign nationals. In January, Patterson issued a report charging that the Vanuatu National Provident Fund, a national retirement scheme for workers, had improperly issued loans to leading politicians. The disclosure sparked a protest on January 12 at the Fund's headquarters in the capital, Port Vila, as investors tried to withdraw their savings, and quickly escalated into widespread rioting and looting. Vanuatu's radio and television stations were forced off the air briefly by protestors who stormed the office of the Vanuatu Broadcasting and Television Corporation (VBTC) and warned staff not to broadcast news about the rioting. President Leye responded by declaring a nationwide two-week state of emergency, during which time the police questioned and arrested more than 500 people in connection with the riots.

At the March 6 parliamentary elections, Donald Kalpokas' VP won 18 seats; Serge Vohor's UMP, 12; Walter Lini's NUP, 11; and minor parties and independent candidates, the remaining 11 seats. Following intense negotiations, the VP and NUP agreed to form a coalition government, and parliament elected Kalpokas as prime minister with 35 votes over Vohor's 17. However, the coalition lasted only seven months, when Kalpokas ousted the NUP in October, saying that Lini could no longer be trusted, and formed a new coalition with the opposition UMP. Lini was subsequently replaced as deputy prime minister by UMP member Willie Jimmy. In December, the opposition's attempt to bring a no-confidence motion against Kalpokas was defeated.

As part of its Comprehensive Reform Program, which includes an overhaul of state administration and increased private sector development, the government began implementing plans to reduce the country's public service sector by about ten percent and enacted a strict leadership code of conduct. It also adopted legislation to establish a special unit to recover and manage more than US$25 million in debts for the Vanuatu National Provident Fund, the Development Bank of Vanuatu, and the National Bank of Vanuatu, which have been plagued by bad loans and political interference. The January riots and public loss of confidence had forced the government to make large payments to members of these three financial institutions, bringing the country near bankruptcy early in the year.

Political Rights and Civil Liberties:

Citizens of Vanuatu can change their government democratically. The constitution vests executive power in a prime minister. The unicameral, 52-member parliament is directly elected for a four-year term. A largely ceremonial president is elected for a five-year term by an electoral college consisting of the parliament and the six provincial council presidents. Although the 1998 national elections were regarded to have been generally free and fair, there were allegations of voting irregularities. In October, the Supreme Court ruled that a by-election for one seat would be held in July 1999 after a candidate's campaign workers were found to have campaigned inside a polling station, in breach of electoral laws.

Although the country's media covered politically sensitive issues with less government interference than in previous years, there were some setbacks in 1998. Early in the year, Ombudsman Ferrieux Patterson asserted that the state-owned Radio Vanuatu's Bislama language service, which is the main source of news outside of the country's capital, was no longer broadcasting her findings of misconduct by government officials; the station resumed airing Patterson's remarks shortly thereafter. There were also allegations that Radio Vanuatu journalists had been threatened by former cabinet minister and parliamentarian Willie Jimmy.

The government owns most of the country's media, including a television station serving the capital, Port Vila, two radio stations, and the *Vanuatu Weekly* newspaper. The smaller private press consists of a growing independent newspaper and political party newsletters. Religious freedom is respected in this predominantly Christian country.

While more than 80 percent of the population is engaged in subsistence agriculture and fishing, there are five active, independent trade unions operating under the umbrella of the Vanuatu Council of Trade Unions (VCTU). Unions exercise their right to organize and bargain collectively.

Although the judicial system is generally independent, the government has at times attempted to pressure the largely expatriate judiciary in politically sensitive cases. After the arrest of some 500 suspected rioters in January, there were credible reports that police assaulted or otherwise poorly treated prisoners, many of whom sought medical treatment for their injuries. A number of law enforcement officials have been charged with "intentional assault," and their trial was still pending at year's end. According to a report by Amnesty International, the mass arrests in January highlighted long-standing, serious deficiencies in Vanuatu's penal system, including buildings made unsafe by earthquakes and water seepage, insufficient food for prisoners, and a lack of safe accommodation for female inmates.

The country's small ethnic minority communities experience discrimination regarding land ownership. Women continue to face limited opportunities in education and politics, and domestic violence is reportedly common.

Venezuela

Polity: Presidential-legislative democracy
Economy: Capitalist-statist
Population: 23,300,000
PPP: $8,090
Life Expectancy: 72
Ethnic Groups: Mestizo (67 percent), European (21 percent), black (10 percent), Indian (2 percent)
Capital: Caracas

Political Rights: 2
Civil Liberties: 3
Status: Free

Overview:

In December 1998, a paratrooper-turned-politician who in 1992 staged a failed coup against a corrupt civilian government was elected president in a landslide. The victory by Hugo Chavez was a body blow to Venezuela's ailing, discredited two-party system that has presided over several oil booms for four decades but left eighty percent of Venezuelans impoverished. The rout of the two traditional parties was so complete that neither of their presidential candidates proved to be serious contenders. However, the choice of the *putschist* former lieutenant colonel created unease in a region with an unhappy history of military rule.

The Republic of Venezuela was established in 1830, nine years after gaining independence from Spain. Long periods of instability and military rule ended with the establishment of civilian rule in 1961. Under the 1961 constitution, the president and a bicameral Congress are elected for five years. The Senate has at least two members from each of the 21 states and the federal district of Caracas. The Chamber of Deputies has 189 seats.

Until 1993, the social democratic Democratic Action (AD) party and the Social Christian Party (COPEI) dominated politics. Former President Carlos Andres Perez (1989-93) of the AD was nearly overthrown by Chavez and other nationalist military officers in two 1992 coup attempts in which dozens were killed. In 1993, he was charged with corruption and removed from office by Congress.

Rafael Caldera, a former president (1969-1974) from COPEI and a populist, was elected president in late 1993 at the head of the 16-party National Convergence, which included Communists, other leftists, and right-wing groups. The octogenarian Caldera's term was marked by a national banking collapse in 1994, the suspension of a number of civil liberties, mounting violent crime and social unrest, and rumors of a military coup.

In 1995, Caldera's reputation for honesty was tarnished by allegations of corruption among his inner circle. With crime soaring, oil wealth drying up, and the country in the worst economic crisis in 50 years, popular disillusionment with politics continued to deepen. In April 1996, the government launched "Agenda Venezuela," a sweeping austerity-stabilization program to secure a $1.4 million IMF stand-by loan, removing many price and foreign exchange controls. In September 1997, the government admitted that it had made little progress in streamlining the notoriously corrupt and inefficient public sector, which employs one-sixth of the workforce, due to an "unfavorable political climate."

At the beginning of 1998, the early form presidential favorite was a former beauty queen whose appeal stemmed largely from her own roots outside the corrupt political establishment famous for its interlocking system of privilege and graft. Chavez's anti-establishment, anti-corruption populism also played well in a country whose elites considered politics their private preserve. Army leaders, however, signaled that a Chavez victory was a threat to military discipline and hierarchy. As victory appeared more likely, Chavez, the veteran coup plotter, moved toward the center, jettisoning rhetoric in which he criticized the free market and promised to "fry" opposition leaders.

Last-minute efforts to find a consensus candidate against Chavez were largely unsuccessful, and Yale-educated businessman Henrique Salas, the other leading presidential contender, steered away from association with the old political order. Salas, a respected two-term former state governor, won just 40 percent of the vote, to Chavez's 57 percent. After winning, Chavez moved quickly to reassure foreign investors. His plans to involve the Venezuelan military in "nation-building" tasks continued to worry observers concerned about the impact of his victory on regional democracies' civil-military relations.

Political Rights and Civil Liberties:

Citizens can change their government democratically. Despite the unusual degree of political polarization and a number of technical difficulties, the regional and presidential elections conducted in 1998 were free and fair. Computerized ballots designed to speed results and limit traditional fraud were the object of complaints in that they were too complex and difficult to read. On November 9, 1998, Venezuelans chose 237 Congressional representatives, 23 state governors, and 391 members of regional legislative assemblies in peaceful although somewhat chaotic circumstances. The December elections were considered to have been run much more effectively.

The constitution guarantees freedom of religion and the right to organize political parties, civic organizations, and labor unions. The judicial system is headed by a Supreme Court and is nominally independent. However, it is highly politicized, undermined by the chronic corruption that permeates the entire political system (including the growing influence of narcotics traffickers), and unresponsive to charges of rights abuses. The continued lack of independent courts has dampened the enthusiasm of foreign investors. Citizen security in general remains threatened by a drug-fueled crime wave that has resulted in hundreds of killings monthly in major cities and vigilante mob killings of alleged criminals. According to one recent study, Venezuela ranked second of the ten most violent nations in the Americas and Europe.

Widespread arbitrary detentions and torture of suspects continue as do dozens of extra-judicial killings by military security forces and the notoriously corrupt police. Since the 1992 coup attempts, weakened civilian governments have had less authority over the military and the police, and rights abuses overall are committed with impunity. Police brutality and murder are rampant as crime increases. The government's plans to use the armed forces in the fight against narcotics is worrisome as efforts to involve the military in internal security tends to politicize the generals and demoralize the police. A separate system of armed forces courts retains jurisdiction over members of the military accused of rights violations and common criminal crimes; decisions by these cannot be appealed in civilian court.

Venezuela's 32 almost medieval prisons, the most violent in the world, hold some 26,000 inmates—of whom less than one-third have been convicted of a crime—even though they were designed to hold no more than 14,000. Deadly prison riots are common and inmate gangs have a striking degree of control over the penal system. In 1997, some 336 inmates were murdered, and in 1998, scores of prisoners were killed.

The press is mostly privately owned, although the practice of journalism is supervised by an association of broadcasters under the government communication industry. Since 1994, the media in general have faced a pattern of intimidation. Congress has passed a series of restrictive laws involving the rights of reply and journalistic conduct.

In September 1997, the Justice Ministry decertified the Unification Church led by Korea's Sun Myung Moon, saying its activities violated Venezuelan laws and customs.

Indigenous communities trying to defend their legal land rights are subject to abuses by gold miners and corrupt rural police and are often killed. In 1998, the national guard was used to intimidate hundreds of Pemon Indians protesting encroachments by road and power lines onto their lands.

Labor unions are well organized but highly politicized and prone to corruption. Security forces frequently break up strikes and arrest trade unionists.

Vietnam

Polity: Communist one-party
Economy: Statist
Population: 78,500,000
PPP: $1,236
Life Expectancy: 67
Ethnic Groups: Vietnamese (85-90 percent), Chinese (3 percent), Muong, Tai, Meo, Khmer, Man, Cham
Capital: Hanoi

Political Rights: 7
Civil Liberties: 7
Status: Not Free

Overview:

In 1998, Vietnam struggled to cope with the Asian economic crisis, which has precipitated the country's worst economic downturn since Vietnam's Communist government launched landmark economic reforms a decade ago. Although Vietnamese officials have acknowledged the need for greater political and economic reform, real progress has been slow in coming, and in 1998, Vietnam remained one of the world's most closed and tightly-controlled societies.

Vietnam was colonized by France in the nineteenth century and was occupied by Japan during World War Two. It gained independence in 1954 and was divided between the Republic of South Vietnam and the Communist-ruled Democratic Republic of Vietnam in the north. After years of fighting, North Vietnam overtook the United States-backed south in 1975, and reunited the country under a Communist government in 1976.

In 1986, the government began decentralizing economic decision making, encouraging small-scale private enterprise, and dismantling collectivized agriculture. Economic reforms accelerated as Soviet aid dwindled after 1990, and Vietnam looked increasingly to Asia and the West. The 1992 constitution codified many economic reforms, although it retained the Vietnamese Communist Party (VCP) as the sole legal party. A collective state council was replaced by a president who is nominally elected by the National Assembly, although in practice, the VCP makes all key decisions.

By 1997, severe unrest had hit Vietnam's impoverished countryside. Farmers in northern Thai Binh province began demonstrations against corruption, bureaucratic abuse of authority, and falling prices for rice crops. Several thousand mainly Catholic demonstrators clashed with police in the southern Dong Nai province after authorities tried to break up protests against corruption and the confiscation of church land. The unrest and financial turmoil that swept other Southeast Asian countries in 1997 merely strengthened the hand of hardliners and military figures adverse to economic reform. On December 30, General Le Kha Phieu, the army's political commissar, became party leader.

In 1998, Vietnam released several thousand prisoners in two mass amnesties. Several political and religious dissidents were among those released. No official reasons were given for the event, but the Hanoi government, which continues to deny that it holds political prisoners, has permitted several such releases in recent years, often coinciding with national holidays. Numerous human rights groups and monitors have complained of government obstacles and harassment in attempts to observe or report on human rights practices in Vietnam. Observers have been routinely prevented from meeting dissidents.

The Asian crisis, weak economic management, and natural disasters that have hit Vietnam in recent years are threatening to undermine, and even reverse, the country's economic progress.

Vietnam's prime minister Phan Van Khai paid an official visit to China in October 1998, the first visit by a Vietnamese head of state since the two countries normalized relations in 1991. Vietnam has largely adhered to China's strategy of pursuing economic reform without enacting political reforms that threaten Communist control. Vietnam hosted the Association of Southeast Asian Nations (ASEAN) summit of leaders in December 1998, marking Vietnam's full integration into the regional group.

Political Rights and Civil Liberties: Vietnamese cannot change their government democratically. The VCP maintains tight control of all political, economic, religious, and social affairs. Policy and leadership issues are decided by the Politburo and its five-member Standing Committee. The Fatherland Front, a VCP mass organization, controls candidate selection for the National Assembly.

The judiciary is not independent. The president appoints judges, and the VCP instructs them on rulings. In 1996, the government established courts to address abuse and corruption by officials, but VCP control of the courts subordinates enforcement to political whim. Though somewhat less aggressively than in past years, authorities continue to monitor the population through mandatory household registrations, block wardens, surveillance of communications, informants, and official peasant associations.

The media are state owned, and in recent years, the government has shut down several newspapers for violating the narrow limits on permissible reporting. In a recent case, a prominent newspaper editor was detained for over a year for reporting on high-level corruption. The government has announced plans to regulate local Internet use, although it remains unclear how this will be carried out in practice. Assemblies require a permit, and are limited to occasional small demonstrations over non-political issues. Vietnamese have some latitude to criticize government corruption and inefficiency, but it is illegal to advocate political reform.

All clergy must belong to the official Vietnam Buddhist Church and must obtain government permission to hold meetings or training seminars, operate religious schools, appoint clergy, and repair places of worship. The Independent Unified Buddhist Church of Vietnam (UBCV) was banned in 1981, and much of the UCBV's leadership has since been arrested or placed under house arrest. The government similarly regulates Catholic activities through the Catholic Patriotic Association. In the central highlands, the government restricts the Protestant religious affairs of the ethnic Montagnards and has arrested clergy and worshippers. Authorities reportedly restrict exit permits for Muslims seeking to make the Hajj.

Local authorities impose internal travel, education, and employment restrictions on ethnic minorities. Women face violence, as well as social and employment discrimination. Child prostitution and international trafficking of minors are reportedly increasing. In early 1998, police in southern An Giang province arrested six people on charges of child trafficking. There were also reports in 1998 of women selling their babies at an underground market in Ho Chi Minh City.

The UNDP estimates that about half the Vietnamese population lives under the poverty line. More than 2 million members of Vietnam's ethnic minorities live in extreme poverty, subsisting on hunting, gathering, or slash-and-burn farming methods.

All unions must belong to the state-controlled Vietnam General Confederation of Labor and all union leaders are VCP members. The 1994 Labor Code recognizes only a limited right to strike.

Yemen

Polity: Dominant coalition (military-influenced)
Economy: Capitalist-statist
Population: 15,800,000
PPP: $856
Life Expectancy: 58
Ethnic Groups: Predominantly Arab, some Afro-Arab, South Asian
Capital: Sana'a

Political Rights: 5
Civil Liberties: 6
Status: Not Free

Overview: Yemen suffered setbacks in its efforts to achieve political stability and economic reform in 1998. The year was marked by an abrupt change in government, widespread and violent protest against economic reforms, and kidnappings of foreigners, which became increasingly deadly.

After hundreds of years of rule by autocratic Imams, or religious leaders, the northern Yemen Arab Republic came under military control in 1962. Field Marshall Ali Abdullah Saleh was elected president by a constituent assembly in 1978. The southern People's Republic of Yemen was under British control from 1839 to 1967. After the British withdrawal, hardline Marxist nationalists seized power in the southern capital of Aden. Through the unification of the north and south, the Republic of Yemen was formed in 1990, with Saleh of the General People's Congress (GPC) as president and southern Yemeni Socialist Party (YSP) leader Ali Salim al-Biedh as vice president.

In April 1993, parliamentary elections were held after a five-month delay due to civil unrest. Saleh and the GPC won the most seats and formed a coalition with Islah and the YSP. The parliament formally elected Saleh president and al-Biedh vice president in October. However, al-Biedh boycotted the new government and called for demilitarization of the former north/south border, decentralization of authority, and investigation into dozens of pre-election killings of YSP activists.

The south attempted to secede in April 1994, sparking a 70-day civil war. Northern troops triumphed, and al-Biedh and other secessionist leaders fled the country.

In September, parliament revised the 1991 constitution, broadening the powers of the chief executive and empowering itself to elect the next president. It elected Saleh to a fresh five-year term, after which the president will be directly elected. In October, the GPC and Islah formed a governing coalition. Thirteen opposition groups led by the YSP formed the Democratic Opposition Coalition in 1995.

Reports of fraud in the April 1997 parliamentary elections were few and came mostly from opposition members who denounced the elections as the government's attempt to legitimize the "unfair" outcome of the 1994 civil war. There was less violence than expected; the only major incident occurred when a soldier opened fire on a polling station, killing eight people. Other irregularities involved widespread public illiteracy and balloting mistakes.

With the help of the IMF and the World Bank, Saleh has pursued an economic restructuring program since 1995. Although the program made inroads on inflation and the country's budget deficit, its political and social costs began to emerge in 1998. First, Prime Minister Dr. Faraj Bin Ghanim resigned in April, and President Saleh appointed Foreign Minister Abd al-Karim al-Iryani to the post but made few other changes. Sources within Yemen attributed Ghanim's resignation not only to his declining health, but also to his reluctance to implement a new round of IMF-mandated reforms. Then, after the government increased the prices of basic goods 40 percent, rioting erupted in June and July in several cities. Dozens of people were killed and the disturbances did much to shatter Yemen's sought-after stability. World Bank officials have praised Yemen, one of the region's poorest countries, for implementing the painful measures, but also emphasized the need for civil service reforms and eliminating government corruption. In 1998, the country also suffered from a 40 percent fall in oil revenues, a 36 percent unemployment rate, and an estimated per capita annual income of $300.

Political Rights and Civil Liberties: The right of citizens to change their government is limited by the concentration of political power in the hands of a few leaders, particularly the president. While the parliament occasionally defied the president in 1998, it is still not an effective lawmaking body; it does little more than debate issues, and its power is subjugated by the president's *de facto* authority to rule by decree.

Central government authority is weak in some rural areas, which are governed by tribal leaders who command heavily armed militias. Yemen is a country of 16 million people and 50 million firearms. On occasion, tribal leaders take foreign hostages in order to gain leverage with the government in negotiations on matters such as infrastructure development. In 1998, the government made these kidnappings punishable by death. Yet the new penalties seemed to have had little effect. The year concluded with the highly publicized kidnapping of 16 foreign tourists, four of whom were killed during a shoot-out when the Yemeni authorities tried to rescue them. Such incidents pose a major threat to attracting foreign investment and developing Yemen's tourism industry.

The judiciary is not independent. Judges are susceptible to bribes and government influence. All courts are governed by *Shari'a* (Islamic law). There are no jury trials. Local tribal leaders adjudicate land disputes and criminal cases in areas under their authority. Arbitrary arrest and prolonged detention without charge are common practice. Enforcement of due process is arbitrary and often nonexistent in cases involving security offenses. Trials reportedly do not meet international standards of due process.

Authorities reportedly use force during interrogation, and Amnesty International did document several cases of prisoner abuse in 1998. Torture, however, is not systematic. Heavy leg-irons and shackles have been banned since 1997. Prisons are overcrowded and sanitary conditions poor. The government does not allow access to political prisoners. Security forces monitor personal communications and search homes and offices without warrants.

The press is allowed a certain degree of freedom to criticize government officials and policies. Yet the government obstructs freedom of the press by occasionally detaining journalists without charge and requiring licensing fees. In 1998, at least six journalists for opposition papers were detained or imprisoned. The government also substantially raised licensing fees for newspapers in June. Almost all of the country's printing presses and radio and television stations are government-owned.

Associations must register with the government. The independent Yemeni Human Rights Organization operates openly, and international human rights observers are allowed broad access. The government arbitrarily cracks down on demonstrations. On February, 15 pro-Iraqi demonstrators were arrested without explanation during a peaceful rally in Aden. And in July, government authorities arrested several political activists for organizing a march without official approval.

Islam is the state religion. The tiny Jewish population in the north faces discrimination in employment opportunities. There are several churches and Hindu temples in the south, but no non-Muslim places of worship in the north. Church services are regularly held without harassment in private homes or public facilities such as schools for the predominantly foreign Christian community.

Citizens with a non-Yemeni parent, and members of the tiny *Akhdam* (servant) minority face discrimination in employment. Women face legal discrimination in marriage and divorce matters. An estimated 80 percent of Yemeni women are illiterate, compared with 35 percent of men. Women enjoy the right to vote though only 20 percent of those eligible are registered. Women were active participants in the 1997 parliamentary elections, organizing voter drives and education programs and fielding candidates; yet, they are still underrepresented in Yemeni politics. In November, the Yemeni Socialist Party, a traditional advocate of women's issues, held its first congress in thirteen years. The presence of 132 women among the 1,357 delegates was considered an encouraging sign.

The 1996 labor law permits only one union per enterprise and only one trade union confederation. State employees in many sectors are prohibited from joining unions. Workers may bargain collectively and have the right to strike. In 1998, there were two documented cases in which the government used the Political Security Office to detain and intimidate union leaders during contract negotiations.

↓ Yugoslavia (Serbia & Montenegro)

Polity: Presidential   **Political Rights:** 6
(dominant parties)   **Civil Liberties:** 6
Economy: Mixed statist   **Status:** Not Free
Population: 10,600,000
PPP: na
Life Expectancy: 72
Ethnic Groups: Serbian (63 percent), Albanian (14 percent),
Montenegrin (6 percent), Hungarian (4 percent), other (13 percent)
Capital: Belgrade
Trend arrow: Yugoslavia receives a downward trend arrow due to the violent crackdown in Kosovo, a repressive media law, and purges in universities, police and the army.

Overview:

In 1998, President Slobodan Milosevic launched a massive offensive against ethnic Albanians in the formerly autonomous region of Kosovo, driving more than 250,000 people from their homes and resulting in the killings of hundreds of civilians. The campaign, in response to attacks on Serbian officials and Albanians by the separatist Kosovo Liberation Army (KLA), led to threats of international retaliation, but a last minute deal in October between U.S. special envoy Richard Holbrooke and President Milosevic averted NATO air strikes and led to a pullback of Belgrade forces. Nevertheless, by year's end, the return of KLA triggered more violence and civilian massacres, and led to renewed threats of Western intervention.

In other issues, President Milosevic consolidated his repressive hold on power by pushing through a rubber-stamp parliament a draconian media law that led to fines and the closing of several papers and radio stations for disseminating "anti-state" materials, to dismissing professors under a law tightening political control of universities, and to purging elements in the military and police deemed disloyal, including the army chief of staff, Gen. Momcilo Peris, and longtime state security chief, Jovica Stanisic. Both had questioned strategy in Kosovo and opposed any crackdown in Montenegro, Serbia's smaller partner within the Yugoslav federation led by pro-Western President Milo Djukanovic.

The reconstituted Federal Republic of Yugoslavia, formed in 1992 after Slovenia, Croatia, Macedonia, and Bosnia-Herzegovina seceded, leaving left Serbia—which had seized control of the autonomous provinces of Kosovo and Vojvodina—and Montenegro as the only republics. The Serbian and Montenegrin legislatures accepted a constitution declaring the FRY a "sovereign federal state based on the principles of equality of its citizens and member republics."

The bicameral Federal Assembly (parliament) consists of the 42-member Chamber of Republics (divided evenly between Serbia and Montenegro) and the 138-seat Chamber of Citizens. In November 1996 elections, despite growing public discontent, a media blockade of the opposition, a highly unfavorable election law, and fragmentation among the opposition helped the Socialists and the United Left, led by Milosevic's wife, win 64 seats with the Democratic Socialist Party (Montenegro's ruling party) winning 20. The Zajedno coalition, consisting of Vuk Draskovic's Serbian Renewal

Movement (SPO), the Democratic Party led by Zoran Djindjic, and the Civic Alliance headed by Vesna Pesic, took 22 seats, with 16 going to the nationalist Serbian Radical Party (SRS). The remainder was parceled out among six minor parties and coalitions. But the results of the local runoff elections on November 17 came as a shock to the government and the opposition, as the Zajedno alliance won 15 of 18 major cities, including Belgrade. After the government nullified the results, hundreds of thousands of demonstrators poured into the streets of Belgrade, Nis, and other major cities. The pro-government local election commissions ignored court decisions ordering them to turn control over to the opposition in several cities. As the crisis escalated, the government closed the independent radio station, B-92, setting off international condemnation and the threat of punitive measure; it was subsequently allowed back on the air. Eventually, Belgrade, Nis, and other cities were turned over to the opposition, but the central authorities often denied these municipalities funding and service.

In 1997, Milosevic reasserted his hold on power as the massive civil disobedience campaign petered out with the three-party Zajedno (Unity) opposition disintegrating amid political squabbling. In October, Zajedno leader Zoran Djindjic was ousted as mayor of Belgrade. Barred by the constitution from serving another term as Serb president, Milosevic was elected president of the Federal Republic of Yugoslavia (FRY) in July by the federal parliament dominated by members of his Socialist Party. His archrival, ultranationalist Vojislav Seselj of the SRS lost his bid for the Serb presidency in a fourth-round election in December which was widely viewed as fraudulent. The winner was Milan Milutanovic, the Yugoslav foreign minister and Milosevic ally. The Socialists lost their majority in the 250-seat Serbian parliament, and Milosevic foe Prime Minister Milo Djukanovic was elected president of Montenegro.

In addition to the Kosovo crisis, 1998 saw a continued deterioration in relations between Milosevic and Montenegro. In May, on the eve of Montenegro's parliamentary elections, Milosevic sacked federal Prime Minister Radoje Kontic, a Djukanovic ally, and replaced him with former Montenegrin President Momir Bulatovic, whom Djukanovic had defeated in 1997. Kontic had refused to clamp down on reformist leaders in Montenegro.

In June elections to Montenegro's 78-member parliament, Djukanovic's ruling coalition, For a Better Life, won over 50 percent of the vote (40 seats), with Bulatovic's Socialists winning 36 percent (30 seats). The secessionist Liberal Alliance and ethnic Albanian legislators, both pro-Djukanovic, took the rest. In November, the Montenegrin government adopted a decree endorsing full and unrestricted freedom of local and foreign media in response to Serbia's repressive media law. In December, Montenegro accused the Yugoslav leadership of foisting unwelcome economic policies on the republic after the federal parliament, from which Djukanovic's party as banned in favor of deputies loyal to Bulatovic, adopted an economic program for 1999.

The Yugoslav economy continued to be crippled by mismanagement and endemic corruption. During the year, there were sporadic shortages of food stables, the *dinar* was devalued by 45 percent, public spending was over 45 percent of GDP, the average monthly wage was $90, and over 25,000 companies were effectively bankrupt.

Political Rights and Civil Liberties:

Citizens of the Federal Republic of Yugoslavia can elect representatives to the federal and regional parliaments; both the federal president and prime minister are appointed by a parliament dominated by former Communists loyal to Serbian President Slobodan Milosevic. The 1996 federal and local elections were marred by the government's refusal to provide opposition airtime on state-run radio and television. In 1997, Serbian presidential elections were marred by irregularities, including ballot stuffing, leading to four rounds before a president was elected. The Serb parliamentary elections were generally "free and fair," and irregularities were reported in both rounds of Montenegro's presidential vote as well as the 1998 Montenegrin parliamentary election.

In 1998, the Serbian government imposed severe restrictions on the media in the wake of the crackdown in Kosovo. A law passed in October banned broadcasts in Serbo-Croatian by foreign media and criticism of the president or government as "anti-state," subjecting the media to heavy fines. On October 30, 600 judges signed a statement calling the law unconstitutional. Days earlier, police raided the offices of the dailies *Nasa Borba* and *Danas*. The publisher of the daily *Dnevni Telegraf* was fined $246,000 for an article accusing Milosevic of introducing "dictatorship" and leading the country into political and economic chaos. In November, issues of the paper were confiscated. Authorities also took over Radio Index, a student-run Belgrade station. Radio B-92, long an independent voice, was threatened with closure for carrying Radio Index programs. The state-run daily, *Politika,* was fined $15,000 for allegedly slandering opposition leader Zoran Djindjic. During the year, the federal Ministry of Communication set exorbitant fees for use of radio and television frequencies. The largest and most influential media in the country are state-owned and are strictly progovernment. Relations between Montenegro's republic-run media and the state-run media soured as the junior republic's TV was openly anti-Milosevic after Djukanovic's election as president. Montenegro passed a liberal media law. Albanian-language papers in Kosovo were closed by Serb authorities during the crackdown.

Freedom of religion is respected for the progovernment Serb Orthodox Church, while Muslims in Kosovo and the Sandzak region between Serbia and Montenegro face persecution and harassment.

Freedom of assembly is restricted by law. Political parties are allowed to organize, but Article 4 of the constitution forbids any organizations that advocate the violent overthrow of the constitutional order.

The independent Nezavisimost trade union has faced harassment and persecution, and most trade unions are directly or indirectly controlled by the government or the SPS. Despite restrictions and intimidation, workers have gone out on strike in several sectors over the last five years. Unions are often prohibited from busing their members to strikes or demonstrations held in different parts of the country.

The federal judiciary, headed by a Constitutional and a Federal Court, are subordinate to Serbia and staffed by Milosevic loyalists. The government has openly flouted rule of law, ignoring statutes that barred the forced mobilization of refugees into military units and decisions mandating the government recognize election results.

In 1998, the government intensified the campaign against Albanians who constitute 94 percent of the population of Kosovo.

Economic opportunity is circumscribed by widespread corruption and government control of large sectors of the economy. Lucrative smuggling operations are controlled by criminal organizations with connections to the government. Milosevic loyalists are in charge of the federal customs agency, and many are directors of state-run enterprises. Property rights are not secure.

Women and men are equal under the law, but discrimination in employment and advancement persists. In rural areas, societal norms have led to problems of domestic abuse.

Zambia

Polity: Dominant party **Political Rights:** 5
Economy: Mixed statist **Civil Liberties:** 4
Population: 9,500,000 **Status:** Partly Free
PPP: $986
Life Expectancy: 37
Ethnic Groups: African (99 percent), European (1 percent)
Capital: Lusaka

Overview:
Zambia continued to be ruled under a state of emergency that suspended many basic rights as 77 people faced trial for treason for alleged involvement in a short-lived coup attempt in October 1997. Charges against former president Kenneth Kaunda were dropped, and he was released from prison on June 1, immediately announcing his retirement from politics and his leadership of the previously sole legal party, the United National Independence Party (UNIP). Zambia Democratic Congress (ZDC) President Dean Mung'omba remained in detention. Long delayed local elections were finally held on December 30, despite opposition calls for a further postponement due to faulty voters lists. They were overwhelmingly won by President Frederick Chiluba's ruling Movement for Multiparty Democracy (MMD) party amidst the opposition's charges of fraud. The country was hit by a series of strikes as living standards continued to plummet. In November, former finance minister and potential 2001 presidential candidate Ronald Penza was murdered by gunmen whose motives will never be known. Wrapping up an unusually speedy, efficient investigation, Zambian police killed five of six of Penza's alleged assailants within a few hours of what appears to have been a political assassination. Zambia's democratic institutions are increasingly under threat. Dialogue between the President and the main opposition parties in December offered some hope for a renewal of the country's democratic space. A fiercely independent print media, a partially autonomous judiciary, and pressure from international donors continue to slow President Chiluba's slide towards authoritarianism, but their success is far from assured.

Zambia was ruled by President Kaunda and UNIP from its 1964 independence until the transition to a multiparty system in 1991. Kaunda's regime grew increasingly repressive and corrupt as it faced security and economic difficulties during the long guerrilla wars against white rule in the neighboring Rhodesia (now Zimbabwe) and Portuguese-controlled Mozambique. UNIP's socialist policies, combined with a crash in price of copper, Zambia's main export, precipitated an economic decline unchecked for two decades.

Kaunda permitted free elections in 1991 in the face of domestic unrest and international pressure. Former labor leader Chiluba and his MMD won convincingly. Economic liberalization and privatization have earned Zambia substantial external aid, but rampant corruption and narcotics has distorted the economy and blocked sustainable growth. The country is among those suffering most from the AIDS pandemic; it is estimated the country will need to care for over 600,000 AIDS orphans within a few years.

Political Rights and Civil Liberties: Zambia's president and parliament are elected to serve concurrent five-year terms by universal adult suffrage. Zambians' constitutional right to change their government freely was honored in 1991 elections. However, the November 1996 presidential and parliamentary polls were neither free nor fair. State resources and state media were mobilized extensively to support Chiluba and the ruling MMD. Serious irregularities plagued election preparations. Voters lists were incomplete or otherwise suspect; independent monitors reckon that over two million people were effectively disenfranchised. Court challenges to Chiluba's re-election to a second five-year term, which heard official admissions that over half a million people may have received voter registration cards with identical numbers, have been dismissed. The election was conducted under a new June 1996 constitution shaped to bar former president Kaunda, the most credible opposition candidate. Most opposition parties boycotted the polls, and the MMD also renewed its parliamentary dominance. Several international observer groups refused to monitor the polls. Those that did, along with independent domestic monitors and opposition parties, declared the process and the results as fraudulent. In December, a controversial contract with an Israeli company to update voter rolls was terminated.

Some of Zambia's jurists retain a stubborn independence while others are subservient to Chiluba and the MMD. The court system is severely overburdened. Pre-trial detainees are sometimes held for years under harsh conditions before their case reaches trial. Malnourishment and poor health care in Zambia's prisons cause many deaths. Criminal cases are heard in government courts, but many civil matters are decided by customary courts of variable quality and consistency whose decisions often conflict with both national law and constitutional protections. The state of emergency imposed in October 1997 after an ill-planned and abortive coup attempt suspends many constitutional protections. Official reports admit that several of the coup suspects were badly tortured, but their tormentors enjoy apparent impunity. Wiretapping both legal and illegal is reportedly routine. In December, Zambia forcibly returned Zimbabwean human rights activist Archbald Ngcobo to Zimbabwe after he had sought political asylum. His fate is unknown.

President Chiluba has dropped pledges to privatize the closely controlled state media. The government dominates broadcasting and the few independent radio stations offer little political reporting. In December, the Zambia Independent Media Association (ZIMA) charged that state media had launched a campaign to discredit potential opposition candidates for the 2001 presidential election, including charging one politician with satanism. The Preservation of Public Security Act of 1960 is among many statutes used to harass, intimidate, and even imprison journalists. Security forces surveil independent media and seek to deny them printing facilities. Tools of harassment include criminal libel suits and defamation suits brought by MMD leaders in response to stories on corruption. *Zambia Post* editor Fred M'membe publishes under threat of 100-years' imprisonment on assorted charges. In 1996, the government may have made cyber-history by ordering Zambia national server to delete a web edition of the *Post*, perhaps the first formal censorship of an Internet newspaper.

Constitutionally protected religious freedom has been respected in practice. New scrutiny of "fake" churches was announced in November, and a government minister said "homosexual" churches would be barred. Nongovernmental organizations engaged in human rights, such as the Zambian Civic Education Association and the Law Association of Zambia, operate openly. The government human rights commission investigated frequent complaints about police brutality, and denounced torture of coup suspects, but has no power to bring charges against alleged perpetrators.

Societal discrimination remains a serious obstacle to women's rights even when fair legislation exists. Women are denied full economic participation and are disfavored in rural lands allocation. Married women must have their husband's permission to obtain contraceptives. Discrimination against women is especially prevalent in traditional tribunals that are courts of first instance in most rural areas. Spousal abuse and other violence against women is reportedly common.

Zambia's trade unions remain among Africa's strongest, and union rights are constitutionally guaranteed. The Zambia Congress of Trade Unions (ZCTU), an umbrella for Zambia's 19 largest unions, operates democratically without government interference. Collective bargaining rights are protected by the 1993 Industrial and Labor Relations Act (ILRA), and unions negotiate directly with employers. About two-thirds of the country's 300,000 formal sector employees are union members.

Development is burdened by high levels of corruption and inflation. The official Anti-Corruption Commission has not taken on major figures, and large sums of underground drug money may be distorting the money supply. Privatization of state enterprises continued, but there was little progress on sale of immense state-owned copper mines. New business formation is slowed by the country's weak financial structures.

Zimbabwe

Polity: Dominant party
Economy: Capitalist-statist
Population: 11,000,000
PPP: $2,135
Life Expectancy: 40
Ethnic Groups: Shona (71 percent), Ndebele (16 percent), other African (11 percent), white (1 percent), mixed and Asian (1 percent)
Capital: Harare

Political Rights: 5
Civil Liberties: 5
Status: Partly Free

Overview: Zimbabwe President Robert Mugabe closed 1998 with his traditional pre-Christmas shopping trip to European capitals.
While his young wife Grace reportedly spent lavishly, perhaps to furnish the new mansions built back home for the first couple, Mugabe visited arms dealers in Italy after doing the same during an Egyptian stopover. On his list were said to be more helicopter gunships to support Zimbabwe's 8,000-strong expeditionary force propping Congolese dictator Laurent Kabila, as well as riot control equipment to suppress increasing domestic dissent among workers and students. Mugabe stepped up

pressure on trade unionists, independent media and oppositionists by invoking emergency and pressing restrictive new legislation through a rubber stamp parliament controlled by his Zimbabwe African National Union-Patriotic Front (ZANU-PF). Hoping to buttress support in rural areas where two-thirds of Zimbabwe's 12 million people live—most in abject poverty—Mugabe ordered the seizure of 841 white-owned farms in November. The land is to be redistributed to landless farmers, but few people believe this will be done on an honest or equitable basis in a country afflicted by cronyism and corruption. In any case, land pressure may soon lessen; about a quarter of Zimbabwe's adults are thought to be infected with HIV. The Mugabe regime has failed utterly to address the epidemic through the sort of strong awareness campaigns successful in Uganda and elsewhere.

Zimbabwe gained independence in 1980 after a bloody guerrilla war against a white minority regime that had declared unilateral independence from Britain in 1965 in what was then Northern Rhodesia. From 1983-87, a civil war suppressed resistance by the country's largest minority group, the Ndebele, to dominance by Mugabe's majority ethnic Shona group. Severe human rights abuses accompanied the struggle, which ended with an accord that brought Ndebele leaders into the government, although several senior Ndebele figures later died under suspicious circumstances.

Zimbabwe is facing its worse crisis since achieving independence in 1980. Mugabe holds only a seriously tarnished electoral mandate, and there is much speculation concerning whether he will be able to serve out his term until 2002. His March 1996 presidential election victory was largely the product of state patronage and repression, including electoral laws boosting the ruling party and restrictions on free expression. The country is arguably a *de facto* one-party state, reflecting ZANU-PF's firm grip on parliament, the security forces, and much of the economy. ZANU-PF has dominated Zimbabwe since independence, enacting numerous laws and constitutional amendments to strengthen its grip on power, including awarding itself millions of dollars in annual state subsidies for which no other party qualifies. This year, parliament passed extensive retirement benefits for Mugabe and his family. Yet Mugabe cannot yet exercise an outright dictatorship. The judiciary remains largely independent and trade unions powerful. Corruption among senior officials is reported by a small independent media. Massive protests by war veterans and trade unionists have challenged the regime and been met with deadly violence by security forces. In November, after two successful one-day strikes by the Zimbabwe Congress of Trade Unions (ZCTU), Mugabe used emergency powers to bar further labor actions.

Despite numerous obstacles including nearly complete state dominance of media, civil society groups are seeking to organize alternatives to Mugabe and ZANU-PF rule. The unofficial National Constitutional Assembly has been holding public forums on a new and more democratic constitution, but could be banned under tightened security legislation.

Political Rights and Civil Liberties: The constitutional right of Zimbabwe's citizens to elect their representatives and change their government through democratic means has not been honored. President Robert Mugabe won another six-year term of office in 1996, tallying nearly 93 percent of votes cast. Less than one-third of those eligible voted in an noncompetitive contest in which the opposition had no real hope of victory. His only two opponents withdrew to protest alleged harassment and intimidation of their supporters. Voter registration and identi-fication procedures and tabulation of results were highly irregular. ZANU-PF swept nearly all the seats contested in parliamentary elections and local polls in April and October 1995, entrenching its de facto one-party rule. The heavily state-controlled or influenced media offers very limited coverage of opposition viewpoints, and ZANU-PF uses state resources heavily in its campaigning. Twenty of the National Assembly's 150 members are presidential appointees, and ten others are traditional chiefs also beholden to the government. Only three oppositionists won seats in the 1995 parlia-ment. One of them, the 78-year-old Reverend Ndabaningi Sithole, president of ZANU-Ndonga party and for 30 years Mugabe's political rival, was expelled from parliament after his highly dubious December 1997 conviction of an unlikely 1995 plot to assassi-nate Mugabe; he remains free on bail. There is now the form but little substance of representative government, despite rising factionalism in ZANU-PF ranks.

The judiciary remains largely independent and has repeatedly struck down or dis-puted government actions. Its protection of basic rights, however, has been subverted by 13 constitutional amendments since 1980 that easily pass the ZANU-PF-controlled National Assembly. A new Public Order and Security Bill restricts rights further, lim-iting public assembly and allowing police to impose arbitrary curfews. Intelligence agencies are now included among law enforcement agencies empowered to disperse "illegal" assemblies or arrest participants. Another clause establishes as a criminal of-fense any individual or media uttering, publishing, or distributing news deemed by the state to be subversive. Security forces, particularly the Central Intelligence Organiza-tion, often ignore basic rights regarding detention, search, and seizure, and sometimes appear to act as an extension of the president's office or ZANU-PF. Prison conditions are reportedly harsh.

The right of free assembly is constitutionally guaranteed but generally respected only for groups that the government deems non-political. Union demonstrations were banned in November. Several groups focus on human rights, including the Catholic Commission for Justice and Peace, the Zimbabwe Human Rights Organization (Zimrights), and the Legal Relief Fund. The founder of the Southern African Human Rights Foundation, Archbald Ngcobo, escaped from Zimbabwe to Zambia in April, but was handed back to his country's authorities in December. His fate is unknown. Reli-gious practice is respected. A 1997 report detailed the officially sanctioned brutality of the repression of Ndebele rebels in the mid 1980s, in which thousands of people were murdered by government forces, but perpetrators of the violence still enjoy impunity. Mugabe has continued his verbal attacks on homosexuals, describing them as "worse than pigs." However, former President Cannan Banana, who fled to South Africa after his conviction for sodomizing a bodyguard, returned to the country in December and reportedly may receive a presidential pardon.

The government directly controls all broadcasting and several newspapers, includ-ing all dailies; it indirectly controls most others. A small independent print media is overshadowed by state-run media, and election media coverage is heavily slanted in the ruling party's favor. In December, a popular talk show which voiced the public's increasing disenchantment with Mugabe was canceled. Extensive self-censorship in government media is caused by official control over editorial policy and appointments, and promoted in the small independent press by a wide-ranging Official Secrets Act and threat of anti-defamation suits which forced the independent *Gazette* newspaper to close in 1995. The Parliamentary Privileges and Immunities Act has been used to force journalists to reveal their sources regarding reports on corruption before the courts and parliament.

Women's rights enjoy extensive legal protection, but de facto societal discrimination persists. Married women still cannot hold property jointly with their husbands. Especially in rural areas, access to education and employment for women is difficult, and few women are fully aware of their legal rights or possess the means to pursue them. Domestic violence against women is common; a 1997 survey by a women's organization found that over 80 percent of women had been subjected to some form of physical abuse.

The Labor Relations Act (LRA) broadly protects private sector workers' rights, but public sector workers are barred from joining unions. After massive demonstrations by trade unionists in December 1997, Zimbabwe Congress of Trade Unions (ZCTU) leader Morgan Tsvangirai was assaulted in an attack that union members blamed on the government and for which no one has been arrested. The ZCTU has announced it will defy Mugabe's November ban on strikes.

Zimbabwe's economy has floundered as inflation soared to over 40 percent and the country's fledging stock market plunged. Expropriation of over 800 white-owned farms could hurt maize production needed for domestic consumption and tobacco exports. The seizure of white-owned properties has also helped cause suspension of crucially needed IMF loans and sent the national currency tumbling further. Despite repeated pledges, the government has yet to privatize numerous loss-making state enterprises, reflecting Mugabe's belief in a command economy and state corporations' role as a source of patronage.

Armenia/Azerbaijan
Nagorno-Karabakh

Polity: Presidential   **Political Rights:** 5
Economy: Mixed statist   **Civil Liberties:** 5
Population: 150,000   **Status:** Not Free
Ethnic Groups: Armenian (95 percent), Assyrian, Greek, Kurd, others

Overview:
In 1998, efforts to mediate the ten-year conflict between Azerbaijan and this Armenian enclave by the Organization on Security and Cooperation in Europe's so-called Minsk Group, co-chaired by Russia, the United States, and France, were unsuccessful, as Karabakh President Arkady Gukasyan continued to reject autonomy within Azerbaijan and the return of six Azerbaijan districts seized in 1994.

In other issues, President Gukasyan, elected in 1997 after his predecessor, Robert Kocharian, was named prime minister of Armenia, reshuffled the government in June, replacing Prime Minister Leonard Petrosian with Deputy Prime Minster Zhirayr Pogosyan amid disagreements over economic policy. Local elections were held on September 27 for 199 community leaders and 1,500 members to councils of elders. Sporadic skirmishes between Karabakh and Azeri forces flared up throughout the year.

In 1921, Nagorno-Karabakh was transferred from Armenia and placed under Soviet Azerbaijaini jurisdiction by Josef Stalin. Subsequently, the Nagorno-Karabakh Autonomous Oblast (region) was created, with a narrow strip (the Lachin Corridor) bordering Armenia proper. In 1930, Moscow permitted Azerbaijan to establish and resettle the border areas between Nagorno-Karabakh and Armenia.

Azeri militia and special forces launched a violent crackdown in 1988 in response to Karabakh Armenians' demands for greater autonomy. In 1991, the legislatures of Nagorno-Karabakh and Shahumyan voted for secession. Multiparty elections were held and on January 6, 1992, parliament's inaugural session adopted a declaration of sovereignty. In much of 1993-94, parliament did not meet, as many parliamentarians were fighting on the front lines. At the end of 1993, which saw major military gains by the Karabakh Armenians, Azeri forces launched offensives in the northern, eastern, and southern parts of the enclave. Before a cease-fire was reached in 1994, Karabakh forces had established military control over six Azeri districts outside the enclave.

In 1995, then President Kocharian created a government structure consisting of nine ministries, seven state departments, and five state enterprises. Elections to the 33-member parliament were held in April and May, with 80 percent voter turnout. Prior to the vote, a public organization, *Democratia*, was formed to assist all political parties, unions, and other groups in preparation for the elections, which were generally free and fair.

In February 1998, President Gukasyan again rejected an OSCE proposal that he said would place Nagorno-Karabakh under Azerbaijani subordination. The plan, accepted by the Armenian and Azerbaijani presidents, called for the unilateral withdrawal of Karabakh forces from several key areas, the return of refugees to these areas, and the demilitarization of border regions as preconditions to an eventual negotiation over the future political and diplomatic status of the enclave. In March, an OSCE report expressed concern over the growing number of sporadic attacks in the border region. In June, President Gukasyan issued a decree modifying the governmental structure into a system of 11 ministries and four state departments.

In a December meeting of the Parliamentary Assembly of the Council of Europe, President Gukasyan accepted the possibility of creating a "common state" with Azerbaijan. The Azeri delegation did not attend the Paris meeting, however. Discussions continued about a "package" solution to address all facets of the issues rather than an earlier OSCE proposal for an incremental solution that enumerated several preconditions prior to a political settlement.

Political Rights and Civil Liberties: Residents of Nagorno-Karabakh have the means to change their government democratically, and the enclave has had what amounts to *de facto* independence since military victories in 1994. Parliamentary elections in 1995 were generally free and fair, as were the 1996 and 1997 presidential elections.

There are independent newspapers, though self-censorship is an issue, particularly on subjects dealing with policies related to Azerbaijan and the peace process. The government controls most broadcast media.

With Armenians comprising over 95 percent of the enclave, the Armenian Apostolic Church is the main religion, and years of conflict have constrained the religious rights of the few Muslims remaining in the region. With a state of emergency still technically in force, freedoms of assembly and association are restricted. Political parties and unions are allowed to organize and operate without significant impediments.

The judiciary is not independent and is influenced by the executive branch and powerful political and clan forces. In 1998, a land law was adopted, but the details and implementation of land privatization would be clarified in 1999. Azeri homes and businesses have been expropriated, confiscated, or destroyed. Economic activity remains mainly in the hands of powerful elites and clans.

China
Hong Kong

Polity: Appointed governor and partly-elected legislature
Economy: Capitalist
Population: 6,700,000
Ethnic Groups: Chinese (98 percent)

Political Rights: 5*
Civil Liberties: 3
Status: Partly Free

Ratings change: Hong Kong's political rights rating changed from 6 to 5 due to the replacement of an appointed body by a partially directly elected legislature.

Overview:
In 1998, Chief Executive Tung Chee-hwa's government continued to marginalize Hong Kong's democratic institutions and subtly erode the rule of law.

Hong Kong consists of Hong Kong Island and Kowloon Peninsula, both ceded in perpetuity to China by Britain in the mid-1800s following the Opium Wars; it also consisted of the mainland New Territories, "leased" for 99 years in 1898. As a colony, executive power rested with a British-appointed governor. The 60-seat Legislative Council (Legco) consisted of gubernatorial appointees, senior civil servants, and members chosen by "functional constituencies" representing bankers, industrialists, and trading houses. A strong rule of law, a free press, and the entrepreneurial spirit of mainland refugees and their children contributed to a post-War-era economic boom.

Under the 1984 Joint Declaration, Britain agreed to transfer sovereignty over the colony to China in 1997. China agreed to maintain Hong Kong's political, legal, and economic autonomy for 50 years. The 1989 Tiananmen Square massacre in Beijing raised Hong Kong residents' political consciousness and anxiety about the handover. In 1990, Britain and China agreed to introduce the first-ever direct elections for 18 Legco seats in 1991, followed by 20 in 1995, 24 in 1999, and 30 in 2003.

In 1992, Christopher Patten took office as the last colonial governor. Patten instituted electoral reforms that made the 1995 Legco elections the first in which all seats were either directly or indirectly elected. Most importantly, the reforms granted nearly 2.7 million workers a second vote for the 30 functional constituency seats. Pro-democracy candidates won 16 of the 20 directly elected seats, led by Martin Lee's Democratic Party with 12. China had rejected the proposals, and in 1994 announced it would dissolve all elected bodies after the handover.

In December 1996, a Beijing-organized selection committee chose shipping tycoon Tung Chee-hwa, China's preferred candidate, as the post-handover chief executive. The committee also appointed a 60-member, post-colonial Provisional Legislative Council (PLC) composed of probusiness and pro-China representatives.

In February 1997, China's rubber-stamp National People's Congress (NPC) approved plans to repeal or amend 24 Hong Kong laws which allegedly contravened the 1990 Basic Law, Hong Kong's Beijing-drawn, post-colonial constitution. They included several provisions of Hong Kong's 1991 Bill of Rights, including one placing the bill above other laws, and two laws, the Societies Ordinance and the Public Order Ordinance (POO), that Legco had previously amended to conform with the Bill of Rights.

Public pressure forced Tung to somewhat modify the plans before the PLC approved them in June.

Immediately after the handover, China dismantled Legco as well as the elected district boards and municipal councils. In September, the PLC approved arrangements for the 1998 Legco elections. Although 20 seats would again be directly elected, the PLC scrapped the single-member district, "first-past-the-post" system in favor of proportional balloting for five four-seat districts. Critics charged the new arrangements would make it easier for the smaller probusiness and pro-China parties to gain seats at the expense of pro-democracy parties. The PLC also reduced the franchise for the 30 functional constituency seats to 180,000 business and professional leaders, with an appointed electoral college choosing the remaining ten seats.

Despite torrential rains, 53 percent of the electorate turned out for the May 1998 elections. Pro-democracy candidates won more than 60 percent of the popular vote and took 16 of the 20 directly elected seats. However, overall, pro-democracy candidates won only 20 of Legco's 60 seats.

In October, Tung announced plans to scrap Hong Kong's municipal councils, which handle local issues such as health and cultural events, after their terms expire at the end of 1999. Analysts said the move would hamper the financing of the Democratic Party, since under party rules each legislator or municipal councilor must contribute a certain percentage of his salary to the party. Many Democratic Party members would also need to get full-time jobs if the councils are scrapped, hampering their ability to carry out grassroots organizing.

Most observers agree that Beijing does not directly influence policy decisions. However, many feel this is a moot point, because Tung and the business leaders that surround him largely agree with Beijing's notion of Hong Kong as a city for business, rather than politics. Tung's reactions to the regional economic crisis also reinforced a growing concern that business leaders have an inordinate input into policy decisions. In 1997, the PLC scrapped labor laws. As property prices plummeted, in spring 1998, authorities halted auctions of government-owned land indefinitely, a move largely supported by property developers.

Hong Kong's unemployment rate rose to a record 5.5 percent in the three months through November. In late December, tycoon Li Ka-shing blamed Hong Kong politicians for damaging the territory's business environment and making major new investments difficult.

Political Rights and Civil Liberties:

Hong Kong citizens cannot change their government democratically. Under the British, Legco became fully elected by 1995, albeit under a powerful, appointed governor. Legco is now only partially elected, and there are few institutional checks on the appointed chief executive. Legislators have limited ability to introduce bills. Although the Basic Law allows for all legislative seats and the chief executive to be elected by universal suffrage after 2007, this would have to be approved by two-thirds of the legislature (only half of which would be directly elected by then), and by the chief executive and China's NPC. Under the Basic Law, China's NPC can repeal Hong Kong laws which conflict with the Basic Law.

In 1997, an appeals court ruling held that although the Basic Law made no provisions for the appointed PLC to replace the elected Legco, the PLC was legal because it had been authorized by China's NPC. The nongovernmental Human Rights Monitor argued that the appeals court ruling rested on grounds that ran counter to the Basic Law; specifically, the ruling stated that Hong Kong courts cannot review decisions or bodies authorized by the NPC, and that the NPC and the bodies it creates have complete authority over Hong Kong. In June 1998, the outgoing PLC enacted an interpretive amendment mandating that where ordinances did not formerly bind the crown, they will not now bind the state. Pro-democracy politicians criticized the PLC for including in the definition of "state" ostensibly subordinate organizations such as the China-owned Xinhua news agency.

The judiciary is independent, and trials are fair. An independent commission nominates judges. The post-handover Court of Final Appeal is prohibited from hearing cases broadly involving "acts of state such as defense and foreign affairs," and under the Basic Law matters before the Court that affect the Chinese government must be referred to the NPC for interpretation, both of which critics say limits the Court's jurisdiction.

In 1998, several developments undermined confidence in the judiciary. Authorities declined to prosecute the China-run Xinhua news agency for breaching privacy laws by missing the deadline to respond to a request by a legislator as to whether it held a file on her. The Justice Secretary declined to prosecute Sally Aw, the politically connected owner of the Hong Kong Standard, in a case in which senior executives of her paper were put on trial for allegedly inflating circulation figures. In December, authorities in the southern Chinese city of Guangzhou executed convicted gangster Cheung "Big Spender" Tze-keung and four henchmen for kidnapping two Hong Kong tycoons and other violent crimes. Critics in Hong Kong said Cheung should have been tried in Hong Kong, where his most serious crimes occurred, and accused Hong Kong authorities of surrendering the territory's judicial independence to China by not seeking Cheung's extradition. Hong Kong authorities said they did not seek extradition because the victims had never filed charges. Police abuse of suspects is a continuing problem.

The Basic Law requires Hong Kong to enact laws on treason, secession, sedition, subversion, and theft of state secrets. Chinese authorities use such laws to imprison dissidents and journalists. The last Legco amended and liberalized existing laws on sedition and treason and passed a controversial Official Secrets Ordinance to comply with Basic Law requirements and pre-empt harsher post-handover legislation. Tung called the new legislation inadequate. In 1998, the government said new legislation on sedition and treason would be introduced, along with secession and subversion laws, but not until at least 1999. All are required under the Basic Law.

Hong Kong's dozens of newspapers and magazines practice some self-censorship regarding Beijing and Hong Kong tycoons. Radio Television Hong Kong (RTHK) is government funded but editorially independent. In March, senior pro-China politician Xu Simin stirred a debate on press freedom by attacking RTHK as a remnant of British colonialism, and calling on the station to stop criticizing the government and instead promote its policies. Chief Executive Tung defended freedom of speech but also said RTHK should present government policies in a positive light. Hong Kong has three privately owned television stations and a commercial radio station.

In 1997, the PLC approved amendments to the Societies Ordinance. The amendments require that all NGOs be registered (previously NGOs only had to inform authorities of their existence), allow authorities to deny registration or deregister existing societies on broad "national security" grounds, and bar political parties from receiving funds from foreign political organizations. The PLC also amended the POO to require police permission to hold demonstrations (previously organizers only had to notify police of a demonstration), which can now be banned on national security grounds. In 1997, authorities listed advocacy of Taiwanese or Tibetan independence as grounds for banning demonstrations. Organizers of some demonstrations, particularly those critical of Beijing, say police often impose last-minute restrictions. According to Amnesty International, police have sometimes used heavy-handed methods to keep protesters in "demonstration areas" that are often far from the targets of the protests.

Unions are independent. The Trade Union Ordinance places some restrictions on organizing and allows authorities to monitor union administration. In 1997, the PLC repealed five laws on collective bargaining, anti-union discrimination, and the right to associate internationally without first notifying the government. The amendments also prohibit the use of trade union funds for political purposes. Workplace anti-discrimination legislation is inadequate, and women are discriminated against in employment matters. In May, authorities closed the last detention center for Vietnamese refugees, with the 32 remaining detainees moved to mainstream prisons.

Tibet

Polity: Communist
one-party
Economy: Statist
Population: 4,590,000*
Ethnic Groups: Tibetan, Han Chinese

Political Rights: 7
Civil Liberties: 7
Status: Not Free

*This figure from China's 1990 census includes 2.096 million Tibetans living in the Tibet Autonomous Region (TAR), and 2.494 million Tibetans living in areas of eastern Tibet that beginning in 1950 were incorporated into four Chinese provinces. Independent observers estimate there are at least six million Tibetans under Chinese rule.

Overview:

Prior to the Chinese invasion in 1949, Tibet had been a sovereign state for the better part of 2,000 years, coming under modest foreign influence only during brief periods in the thirteenth and eighteenth centuries. China invaded Tibet with 100,000 troops in late 1949 and in 1951 formally annexed the country.

In 1959, popular uprisings against Chinese rule culminated in mass pro-independence uprisings in Lhasa, the capital. Over the next several months, China crushed the uprisings, killing an estimated 87,000 Tibetans in the Lhasa region alone. The Tibetan spiritual and temporal leader, the fourteenth Dalai Lama, Tenzin Gyatso, fled to Dharamsala, India, with 80,000 supporters.

In 1960, the International Commission of Jurists called the Chinese occupation genocidal and ruled that prior to the 1949 invasion, Tibet had possessed all the attributes of statehood as defined under international law. In 1965, China created a Tibet Autonomous Region encompassing only half the territory of pre-invasion Tibet. The rest of Tibet had, since 1950, been incorporated into four southwestern Chinese provinces. During the Cultural Revolution, China imprisoned thousands of monks and nuns, destroyed all but 11 of Tibet's 6,200 monasteries, and burned sacred texts in an effort to obliterate Tibetan culture. By the late 1970s, 1.2 million Tibetans had died as a result of the occupation.

Between 1987 and 1990 Chinese soldiers forcibly broke up peaceful demonstrations throughout Tibet, killing hundreds and arresting thousands more. In May 1995, the Dalai Lama identified six-year-old Gedhun Choekyi Nyima as the eleventh reincarnation of the Panchen Lama, Tibetan Buddhism's second highest religious figure. Chinese authorities detained the child and his family, and orchestrated the selection of another six-year-old boy as the eleventh Panchen Lama. Since the Panchen Lama identifies the reincarnate Dalai Lama, Beijing will be able to control the identification of the fifteenth Dalai Lama.

On May 1 and May 4, 1998, Tibetans in Drapchi prison in Lhasa held peaceful protests apparently motivated by the visit of a European Union delegation scheduled for May 4. According to the London-based Tibet Information Network (TIN), in the ensuing weeks a crackdown in the prison killed at least six nuns, four monks, and a layperson. During the year, authorities strengthened their already harsh campaign to erode support among Tibetans for the Dalai Lama and his exile government, and for independence from China. In November, TIN reported that authorities were now searching the homes of Tibetan officials in Lhasa for shrines and religious objects, and had renewed a requirement for Tibetan members of the Chinese Communist Party to withdraw their children from exile schools in India.

Political Rights and Civil Liberties:

Tibetans lack the right to self-determination and cannot change their government democratically. In a 1997 report, the International Commission of Jurists called for a United Nations supervised referendum on self-determination. China appoints compliant Tibetan officials to some largely ceremonial posts to provide a veneer of self-rule, but in reality controls all major policy decisions and sharply restricts basic rights and liberties. In 1997, TIN reported that only 44 percent of regional or higher level government department heads are Tibetan, and 62 of 72 county-level deputy heads are Chinese, who wield actual power behind Tibetan figureheads. Chinese officials also dominate the military and police.

Arrests of political dissidents and torture in prisons have increased since July 1994, when the Chinese government decided at a high-level Third Work Forum on Tibet in Beijing to tighten political control over the region. In 1997, the Dharamsala-based Tibetan Center for Human Rights and Democracy said there were 1,216 known Tibetan political prisoners, many of them monks and nuns, jailed for displaying Tibetan flags or symbols of cultural identity, for holding peaceful demonstrations, possessing a photograph of the Dalai Lama, forming prisoner lists, making political posters, and other nonviolent activities. In 1997, the Boston-based Physicans for Human Rights reported that of 258 Tibetan refugees surveyed in Dharamsala in 1996, 15 percent said they had been tortured in Tibet, including 94 percent of those who had been detained for political activities. Security forces routinely rape imprisoned nuns. Political prisoners are reportedly subjected to forced labor.

In 1996, Chinese-organized "re-education" teams began conducting forcible political indoctrination sessions in Lhasa's three main monasteries and several smaller ones aimed at discrediting the Dalai Lama and his selection of the reincarnate Panchen Lama. In October 1997, the New York-based Human Rights Watch/Asia reported that the refusal of monks and nuns to renounce their beliefs had resulted in more than 150 arrests, two known deaths, and 1,300 expulsions in a campaign that had reached 900 monasteries and nunneries by September 1997. Authorities replaced many purged monks and nuns with pro-China counterparts.

Authorities continued to monitor and control monasteries and nunneries through state-organized "management committees." In 1995, authorities placed a near-total moratorium on the building of new monasteries and nunneries, tightened limits on the number of monks and nuns permitted in monasteries, and limited the total number of clerics permitted in Tibet. Authorities have closed numerous monasteries and nunneries, demolished several others, and forced some senior monks to retire. Officials also generally prevent religious figures from giving large public teachings, and restrict the travel of some politically active monks. In 1996, China banned all photographs of the Dalai Lama from monasteries and residences, extending a 1994 ban on the sale of the Dalai Lama's photograph and displaying such photographs in state offices.

Although Beijing's draconian family planning policy ostensibly does not extend to Tibetans and other minorities, the one-child rule is generally enforced in Tibet. Authorities often use the threat of fines to coerce women into undergoing abortions and sterilizations.

Beijing's Sinification policy includes granting employment, education, healthcare, and housing incentives to lure ethnic Chinese into migrating to Tibet. This has altered the demographic composition of the region, displaced Tibetan businesses, reduced employment opportunities for Tibetans, and further marginalized Tibetan cultural identity. Since 1992, Beijing has expanded Tibet's road and air links with China, further facilitating the mass settlement of Han Chinese into Tibet.

Beijing's attempts to indoctrinate Tibetan primary- and middle-school students include daily ceremonies to raise the Chinese flag and sing the Chinese national anthem. Schools and universities are increasingly using Mandarin as well as Tibetan as the language of instruction. Tibetans are whipsawed between seeing their cultural autonomy undermined by the increasing use of Mandarin, and the need to learn Mandarin to gain preferences in government and factory employment as well as university admission.

India
Kashmir

Polity: Indian-administered   **Political Rights:** 6*
Economy: Capitalist-statist   **Civil Liberties:** 6*
Population: 7,719,000   **Status:** Not Free
Ethnic Groups: Muslim majority, Hindu minority
Ratings change: Kashmir's political rights and civil liberties ratings changed from 7 to 6 due to limited gains in political participation and freedom of expression since a return to home rule in 1996.

Overview: While India and Pakistan sharpened their rhetoric over Kashmir in the wake of tit-for-tat nuclear tests in May 1998, the new Hindu nationalist Bharatiya Janata Party government in New Delhi did little to address human rights abuses or other concerns in the disputed territory. Kashmiri militants carried out a series of massacres against Hindu civilians.

Following centuries of rule by Afghan, Sikh, and local strongmen, the British seized control of the Himalayan region of Kashmir in 1846 and sold it to the Hindu maharajah of the neighboring principality of Jammu. The maharajah subsequently incorporated Ladakh, Baltistan, and other distinct Himalayan areas into a new princely state of Jammu and Kashmir. At the partition of British India in August 1947, Maharajah Hari Singh attempted to preserve Jammu and Kashmir's independence. Pakistani tribesmen invaded, and in October, the maharajah agreed to Jammu and Kashmir's accession to India in return for autonomy and a promise of eventual self-determination. Indian Premier Jawaharlal Nehru immediately appointed Sheikh Abdullah of the secular National Conference as head of the Jammu and Kashmir government, and Indian troops engaged Pakistani forces in the first of three wars between the two countries.

A United Nations-brokered cease-fire in 1949 established the present-day boundaries. Pakistan retained control of roughly one-third of Jammu and Kashmir, including the western third of Kashmir. India's share of Jammu and Kashmir included two-thirds of Kashmir, predominantly Hindu Jammu, as well as Buddhist-majority Ladakh.

The present conflict centers around Kashmir, a Muslim-majority land with a distinct language and culture. The conflict has been exacerbated by New Delhi's failure to honor pledges of self-determination for the territory, which India claims it cannot do until Pakistan withdraws its troops from territory under Islamabad's control. Article 370 of India's 1950 constitution and a 1952 accord granted the territory substantial autonomy. But in 1953, Nehru dismissed Abdullah's government. Successive Indian-backed governments passed legislation largely annulling the autonomy guarantees, and in 1957, New Delhi formally annexed Jammu and Kashmir as India's only Muslim-majority state.

In 1959, China occupied a portion of Jammu and Kashmir, which it continues to hold. India and Pakistan fought a second, inconclusive war over the territory in 1965.

Mounting unrest over a rigged 1987 state election, continuing high unemployment, and persistent abuses by Indian security forces triggered an insurgency in December 1989. Militant groups divided into two broad camps—the Jammu and Kashmir Liberation Front, and other secular, pro-independence groups, and Islamist groups seeking incorporation into Pakistan and backed by Islamabad, which have gained control over the insurgency more recently. In 1990, New Delhi placed the state under federal rule.

Violence continued throughout the mid-1990s. The October 1996 state elections were held amidst calls for a boycott by militants and moderate groups, violence, and reports of soldiers coercing Kashmiris to vote. The National Conference, the only Kashmir-based party to contest the elections, won a majority of the 87-seat assembly behind Farooq Abdullah, the son of Sheikh Abdullah, who returned for a second term as chief minister.

After both India and Pakistan carried out nuclear tests in May 1998, observers increasingly feared that tensions over Kashmir could lead to a fourth war between the two countries. In July, Indian premier Atal Bihari Vajpayee met his Pakistani counterpart, Nawaz Sharif, at a regional meeting in Colombo. The two leaders failed to agree on a formula for resuming talks on Kashmir and other issues. India insisted that Kashmir could only be discussed in the context of a broader security dialogue, while Pakistan insisted that Kashmir be the focus of any talks.

Political Rights and Civil Liberties: India has never held a referendum on Kashmiri self-determination as called for in a 1948 United Nations resolution. Violence by militants and security forces has killed more than 25,000 people since 1989.

Prior to and during the 1996 national and state elections, militants urging a boycott threatened elections officials and candidates, and carried out terrorist attacks against candidates, their family members, campaign workers, Hindus, and other ordinary civilians, killing at least 20 people during the state vote. Soldiers and state-backed militias coerced Kashmiris into voting, and authorities detained leaders of the All Party Hurriyat Conference (APHC), a coalition of some 30 groups opposed to Kashmir's status as an Indian state, which had advocated a boycott.

The judiciary barely functions. Militants routinely threaten judges, witnesses, and the families of defendants. Security forces frequently ignore court orders regarding detainees and human rights petitions.

The 1990 Jammu and Kashmir Disturbed Areas Act and the Armed Forces (Jammu and Kashmir) Special Powers Act allow security forces to search homes, arrest suspects without a warrant, shoot suspects on sight, and destroy structures believed to house militants or arms. The latter act requires that the central government approve any prosecutions of members of the armed forces. In November, the Indian defense ministry said a court had sentenced a junior army officer to life imprisonment for murdering a man during an army night raid on a village in 1995. However, overall there have been few investigations and prosecutions of security forces for human rights violations, contributing to a climate of impunity. In 1997, the state government established an official human rights commission, although it will not be empowered to investigate alleged human rights abuses by the army or paramilitary forces.

Indian soldiers and paramilitary troops carry out arbitrary arrests and detentions of suspected militants and civilians, and in recent years have been responsible for hundreds of "disappearances," deaths in custody, and extrajudicial killings, which they often claim occurred during armed encounters with militants. In 1997, Amnesty International reported a sharp increase in custodial deaths and allegations of rape of Kashmiri women by armed forces. According to the New York-based Human Rights Watch, in September, the nongovernmental Association of Parents of Missing People stated that 2,000 people had disappeared since 1990 after being taken into custody in Kashmir, and that there were no legal remedies for discovering their fate.

Indian troops occasionally cordon off entire neighborhoods and conduct house-to-house searches, and in recent years have destroyed hundreds of homes of suspected militants and family members. In past years, soldiers have fired into crowds on several occasions, killing scores of civilians. More recently, the number of civilian deaths directly attributed to security forces appeared to be decreasing. However, Human Rights Watch/Asia reported that in 1998 Indian security forces carried out offensives in Doda district and border villages, in response to killings of Hindu civilians (see below), that "revived patterns of abuse by Indian forces that had abated in the Kashmir valley."

Kashmiri militant groups are responsible for kidnappings of government officials, politicians, and businessmen, and the torture and killings of politicians, party workers, public employees, suspected informers, members of rival factions, and civilians refusing to shelter militants. Since 1990, militants have raped or killed scores of Pandits, or Kashmiri Hindus. Some 300,000 Hindus have fled the Kashmir Valley. In 1998, militants massacred more than 90 Hindu civilians in at least five separate attacks in Doda district and border villages. In August, suspected Pakistani-backed militants also killed 35 construction workers in the neighboring Indian state of Himachal Pradesh. Human Rights Watch/Asia noted that the massacres, "appeared to represent a tactical shift for militant groups that had been largely driven out of major towns in the Kashmir valley."

Since 1995, progovernment militias, composed of former militants and operating with limited accountability, have carried out counterinsurgency operations and extrajudicial executions in the countryside against pro-Pakistani militants. These so-called "renegades" are also responsible for human rights violations against alleged militant sympathizers, journalists, and human rights monitors.

Indian and Pakistani troops conduct almost daily artillery exchanges across the 550-mile Line of Control separating the Indian- and Pakistani-held parts of Kashmir. In the months after both nations carried out nuclear tests in May 1998, artillery and shooting exchanges intensified, killing more than 100 civilians and causing hundreds of villagers to flee their homes.

Authorities pressure the private press through occasional beatings, detentions, and other harassment of journalists. India's 1971 Newspapers Incitements to Offenses Act (in effect only in Jammu and Kashmir) allows a district magistrate to order censorship in certain circumstances. Nevertheless, newspapers continued to publish accounts of alleged human rights abuses by security forces. In recent years, militant groups have detained, tortured, killed, or otherwise harassed and threatened journalists. Militants also occasionally coerce newspapers into suspending publication. According to the New York-based Committee to Protect Journalists, at least eight journalists have been murdered in Kashmir since 1989, four of whom were specifically targeted because of their work with the state-owned broadcast media.

Security forces and "renegades" threaten and occasionally attack human rights workers, and have killed several since 1989. In recent years, authorities have subjected APHC leaders to brief, arbitrary arrests either before or during peaceful protests.

Indonesia
East Timor

Polity: Dominant party (military-dominated)
Economy: Capitalist-statist
Population: 778,000
Ethnic Groups: Timorese, Javanese, others

Political Rights: 7
Civil Liberties: 6*
Status: Not Free

Ratings change: East Timor's civil liberties rating changed from 7 to 6 due to a slight easing of restrictions on freedom of expression which coincided with President Suharto's May 1998 ouster.

Overview:

Indonesian President Suharto's May 1998 ouster offered a brief window in East Timor during which independence, autonomy, or at least an improved human rights situation all seemed possible. By year's end, the human rights situation had improved only marginally, and new Indonesian President B.J. Habibie had offered only vague proposals for greater autonomy.

The Portuguese arrived on Timor around 1520, and in the nineteenth and early twentieth centuries took formal control of the island's eastern half. In 1974, Portugal agreed to hold a referendum on self-determination. In November 1975, the leftist Revolutionary Front for an Independent East Timor (Fretilin) declared an independent republic. Indonesia invaded in December, and in 1976 formally annexed East Timor as its twenty-seventh province. By 1979, Indonesian soldiers had killed up to 200,000 Timorese. Skirmishes between Indonesian forces and the poorly equipped armed resistance have since continued.

On November 12, 1991, Indonesian soldiers fired on a peaceful pro-independence march to the Santa Cruz Cemetery in the territorial capital of Dili. Between 150 and 270 civilians were killed. In 1992, courts-martial handed down light prison sentences ranging from 8 to 18 months to ten soldiers. Separately, courts sentenced 18 Timorese to terms ranging from six months to life imprisonment for allegedly organizing the Santa Cruz march. In November, Indonesian soldiers captured resistance leader Jose "Xanana" Gusmao. In 1993, a court sentenced Gusmao to life imprisonment, subsequently reduced to 20 years, in a sham trial.

The 1996 award of the Nobel Peace Prize to East Timor Roman Catholic Bishop Carlos Felipe Ximenes Belo and Jose Ramos Jorta, the leading East Timorese exile activist, brought renewed international attention to Indonesian abuses in the territory. During and after the May 1997 Indonesian parliamentary election period, attacks by East Timorese National Liberation Army (*Falintil*) guerrillas on military and civilian targets killed at least nine suspected collaborators and other civilians, as well as 33 soldiers, police, and guerrillas. The army responded by arbitrarily detaining and often torturing hundreds of civilians, and there were reports of killings and "disappearances." A September report by Human Rights Watch/Asia linked the recent violence to tensions caused by the army's effort, since mid-1995, to "Timorize" the security forces by creating paramilitary groups and counterinsurgency forces that rely heavily on unemployed East Timorese youths as informers. The report also blamed the continued influx of Indonesians to East Timor, a high unemployment rate, and development policies favoring non-Timorese.

In August 1998, the Indonesian military said it had completed a withdrawal of all combat troops from East Timor, leaving some 5,000 "territorial personnel." Yet by September, residents and church groups were reporting a new combat troop buildup. In October, the New York-based East Timor Action Network, publicized as credible, leaked Indonesian Ministry of Defense documents from August showing a total of more than 12,000 Indonesian troops in the territory, twice the number of soldiers Indonesia had said were based there. In the fall, the Habibie government offered to grant autonomy to East Timor, but ruled out a referendum on independence. Falintil attacks on Indonesian soldiers in southern Manufahi District in October and November brought reprisals from security forces. Some accounts reported that soldiers had massacred up to 50 people in Alas, although in December, Amnesty International put the confirmed death toll at two. The army reportedly detained more than 20 people from Manufahi District, many of whom were reportedly tortured.

Political Rights and Civil Liberties:

The United Nations does not recognize Indonesia's 1976 annexation of East Timor. A referendum on self-determination, promised by Portugal in 1974, has never been held. Suharto's ouster left the existing Indonesian power structure intact, and civil liberties improvements in East Timor were modest.

The judiciary is not independent, particularly for trials of dissidents. The trial of Jose "Xanana" Gusmao (see above) fell well short of international standards. While the Habibie government released 120 political prisoners throughout the archipelago, there are still several East Timorese political prisoners. Many are held for peaceful activities including participating in demonstrations advocating East Timorese independence or criticizing the Indonesian government.

Under Suharto, the army and police committed arbitrary arrests, detention, torture, "disappearances," extrajudicial killings, rape, and other abuses with near impunity. During security crackdowns, soldiers arbitrarily detained and often tortured civilians to extract information. Under Habibie, many of these practices have apparently continued. In December, Amnesty International reported that security forces were responsible for "unlawful killings, arbitrary arrests and ill treatment" in the context of military operations following Falintil attacks in October and November.

In recent years, army-organized gangs have harassed the local population, and kidnapped and beaten dozens of pro-independence East Timorese. In 1997, a paramilitary group, Gadapaksi, participated in army operations and committed abuses against civilians. Leaked Ministry of Defense documents publicized in October 1998 (see above) show that the Indonesian military counts among its ranks some 9,000 members of these pro-Jakarta local groups and militias, despite past government denials that such organizations were not army-linked.

The armed resistance is responsible for extrajudicial executions and other abuses against suspected civilian collaborators and informants.

In October, thousands of East Timorese demonstrated in Dili and Bacau demanding a referendum on independence, acts that would have brought a swift crackdown from security forces only a few months earlier. Yet overall, authorities continued to restrict freedoms of speech, press, assembly, and association. In recent years, authorities closed schools that refused to use the official Bahasa Indonesia as the language of instruction. In October, Jakarta-appointed governor Abilio Soares warned civil servants that they risked being fired if they opposed Indonesia's proposals on granting East Timor autonomy but not independence.

The predominantly Roman Catholic population can worship openly, but religious freedom must be seen in the context of East Timor's overall human rights situation. Authorities restrict access by foreign journalists and human rights organizations to East Timor. The Indonesian government's controversial transmigration program brought thousands of Indonesians to the territory in recent years despite charges that this reduced economic activity for East Timorese.

West Papua (Irian Jaya)

Polity: Dominant party (military-dominated)
Economy: Capitalist-statist
Population: 1,700,000
Ethnic Groups: Mainly Papuan
Ratings change: West Papua's civil liberties rating changed from 7 to 6 due to a slight easing of restrictions on freedom of expression which coincided with President Suharto's May 1998 ouster.

Political Rights: 7
Civil Liberties: 6*
Status: Not Free

Overview:

By 1848, the Dutch controlled the entire western half of the island of New Guinea. In 1963, Indonesia assumed administrative responsibility for the territory under a United Nations agreement mandating that a referendum on self-determination be held by 1969.

In the mid-1960s, the guerrilla Free Papua Movement (OPM) began fighting for independence. Rather than hold a popular referendum, in the summer of 1969, Indonesia convened a sham "Act of Free Choice." The predominantly Melanesian population apparently favored independence, but the councils voted unanimously for annexation by Indonesia. The Indonesian military had a heavy presence in the territory, and the UN special observer reported that "the administration exercised at all times a tight political control over the population." Nevertheless, the UN accepted the referendum. In 1973, Indonesia renamed the land, known locally as West Papua, as Irian Jaya.

In 1984, an army offensive against the OPM drove hundreds of villagers into neighboring Papua New Guinea, and security forces murdered prominent intellectual Arnold Ap. In 1989, the army conducted further anti-OPM offensives.

In recent years, the army has committed human rights violations in the area around the giant Grasberg copper and gold mine in the central highlands owned by Freeport Indonesia, the local subsidiary of the United States-based Freeport McMoRan. In 1995, Indonesia's official National Commission on Human Rights confirmed that the army had killed 16 civilians and caused four "disappearances" since October 1994, shortly after the killing of a Freeport employee by suspected OPM guerrillas. The Australian Council for Overseas Aid had earlier attributed some responsibility to Freeport for allowing the army use of its vehicles and facilities.

In 1996, residents rioted in the mining town of Timika and nearby Tembagapura after a vehicle driven by a Freeport employee injured a man. Freeport drew up a plan to contribute one percent of its annual gross revenues from the mine to a trust fund for community works. Several tribes protested that the money would be dispersed through the government. During the year, OPM guerrillas abducted and killed several civilian hostages.

In August 1997, security forces near Timika fired rubber bullets at Ekari tribesmen, some of whom were allegedly armed with traditional weapons, killing two. According to *Agence France-Presse*, the tribesmen were protesting the deaths of two youths whom they alleged had fallen from a Freeport company truck, a charge Freeport denied. Freeport agreed to postpone disbursements from the trust fund after church groups said payments to the Amungme and Kamoro tribes were insufficient, and warned the disbursement process could inflame communal tensions.

According to Human Rights Watch/Asia, the May 1998 ouster of Indonesian President Suharto and signs of support for a dialogue on Irian Jaya's political future from members of the United States Congress, encouraged church leaders, intellectuals, and nongovernmental activists in the territory to push for a "national dialogue" that would discuss possible political solutions ranging from autonomy to federalism to independence. The Habibie government initially accepted the idea. By late November, as more organizations pushed for independence, the government, which wanted to restrict the dialogue to autonomy, pushed it back until after the Indonesian elections in June 1999.

According to HRW, in early July, troops shot several protesters in separate incidents in Sorong and Jayapura after pro-independence demonstrations turned violent, killing one person. On July 6, security forces opened fire in the town of Biak on independence supporters who had gathered for several days around a West Papuan flag that had been illegally hoisted atop a water tower. The death toll is unknown. While one person died in a local hospital and two others died shortly after their release from prison, more than 30 bodies washed up on the shore of East Biak in subsequent weeks. Authorities claimed the bodies were from the tidal wave that struck neighboring Papua New Guinea around the same time, but buried the bodies before autopsies could be carried out.

In October 1998, the military ended the designation of Irian Jaya as a combat area, although this has apparently not yet led to a diminished troop presence.

Political Rights and Civil Liberties: West Papuans lack the right to self-determination. As Indonesia's 26 province, residents can participate in Indonesia's tightly-controlled political process. The independence movement in the territory is kept alive by grievances over human rights violations, the loss of ancestral land for development projects, and underrepresentation of Papuans in the local government

The judiciary is not independent. Several OPM guerrillas and suspected supporters are incarcerated under Indonesia's harsh anti-subversion laws.

Indonesian authorities sharply restrict freedoms of speech, press, assembly, and association in the territory. In recent years, authorities have arrested and convicted independence supporters of subversion and rebellion for peaceful attempts to raise the West Papuan flag. According to HRW, as the year ended, trials were underway or expected to begin for 30 people accused of raising the West Papuan flag in separate incidents in Wamena in July and Maokwari in October, and for six people accused of organizing demonstrations in Jayapura in July and October. Trials of suspects in the Biak demonstrations (see above) began in October.

In 1995, Indonesia's National Commission on Human Rights accused the Indonesian military of extrajudicial killings, torture, arbitrary arrest and detentions, "disappearances," widespread surveillance of the local population, and destruction of property in the territory, often around Timika, near Freeport's Grasberg mine (see Overview). Most violations have gone unpunished, and the few sentences and convictions have been relatively lenient.

The U.S. State Department has reported that, at various times, authorities closed certain areas in the central highlands to nonresidents due to army counterinsurgency operations. Soldiers reportedly occupied villages and restricted internal movement, and in some cases, beat and raped villagers, destroyed homes and crops, and were responsible for forced labor.

In 1997, the *Far Eastern Economic Review* (FEER) reported that Freeport is paying $35 million for barracks and other facilities for an 800-strong military task force that the government brought in following the 1996 Timika-Tembagapura riots.

The population follows either indigenous beliefs or Christianity, and residents can generally worship freely. Since the 1970s, Indonesian authorities have resettled more than 170,000 residents of Java and other overcrowded islands into West Papua under a controversial transmigration program that critics charge jeopardizes local employment opportunities, expropriates traditional lands, and threatens to marginalize the indigenous culture. Other migrants have arrived on their own. Violent clashes have occasionally erupted between the economically dominant migrants and indigenous groups. Special permits are required to visit certain areas, and the government limits access to West Papua for foreign journalists. The constant loss of ancestral land to development projects has been one of the factors contributing to what is believed to be fairly widespread support among the population for independence.

Iraq
Kurdistan

Polity: Dual leadership
Economy: Capitalist-statist
Population: 4,000,000
Ethnic Groups: Kurdish majority, Assyrian

Political Rights: 6
Civil Liberties: 6
Status: Not Free

Overview:　　　　Leaders of the Kurdistan Democratic Party (KDP) and the Patriotic Union of Kurdistan (PUK) signed an agreement in

Washington, D.C., on September 17 in hopes of ending four years of intermittent military clashes. Part of a U.S.-sponsored effort to unite Kurdish leaders against Iraqi President Saddam Hussein, the agreement provides for the establishment of an elected government after a transitional period of power sharing, arrangements for the equitable distribution of revenues from cross-border trade with Turkey, and guarantees of U.S. military protection of the Kurdish provinces against Iraqi attack.

In April 1991, the United States, Britain, France, and Turkey established a secure region with a U.S.-enforced no-fly zone north of the 36th parallel in Iraq. The 105-member Iraqi Kurdistan National Assembly was created following the collapse of an autonomy agreement with the Iraqi government in 1991. After a 1992 vote produced no clear winner, the KDP and the PUK agreed to fill 50 seats each. The remaining five seats were reserved for Christian Assyrians. Disputes between the two militias over power and revenue sharing erupted into full-scale civil war in 1994, precluding the operation of the government and any further elections. Frequent clashes have occurred since 1994, and the two sides have remained at odds despite occasional ceasefires.

Particular terminology in the September agreement referring to "Kurdistan" and "autonomy" aroused anxiety within neighboring Turkey. Turkey has been fighting its own Kurdish insurgency for the past 14 years, and opposes the establishment of a Kurdish state in northern Iraq on the grounds that it might further provoke secessionist-minded Kurds in southeastern Turkey. In November, KDP and PUK leaders held meetings with Turkish officials in Ankara to provide reassurances that they do not intend to establish an independent state.

Political Rights and Civil Liberties:

Iraqi Kurds cannot change their government democratically. Though reasonably free and fair elections were held in 1992, the post of president was never filled, and factional violence has precluded parliamentary activity since 1995.

No independent judiciary exists in Kurdistan. Hearings are conducted, adjudicated, and enforced by local officials of the KDP and PUK. The two groups run separate prisons and detention centers where human rights violations occur. The Kurdish administration of northern Iraq has been accused of arbitrary arrest and detention, torture of detainees, summary trials, and extrajudicial executions of prisoners of war, political opponents, and demonstrators. Iraqi laws passed prior to 1991 remain in effect in Kurdistan, save for those judged to be "against Kurdish interests."

Political chaos has allowed the Kurdistan Workers' Party (PKK) to continue using Iraqi Kurdistan as a base for its military insurgency against Turkey. Efforts by the PKK to maintain control of territorial bases have led to political killings, terrorist actions, and the deaths of local residents. In turn, Turkish operations against the PKK in Iraqi Kurdistan resulted in civilian deaths and destruction of residences.

Observers report a generally open climate for dialogue on political issues. Many independent newspapers as well as opposition radio and television broadcasts are widely available. The absence of a governing authority has allowed free expression to flourish, though many journalists have ties to political organizations. Numerous political parties, social organizations, and cultural associations operate freely, and their members may assemble without harassment.

Amnesty International and other human rights groups reported that 1,468 Kurdish families were scheduled to be expelled from the oil-rich northern city of Kirkuk between April and June 1998 as part of a forcible campaign of "Arabization" of particular northern areas. Regional Kurdish authorities report that some 400 families were actually relocated, creating an influx of refugees into the Sulemaniyah province of Iraqi Kurdistan. Deportation procedures include punitive measures such as detention of at least one member of each deported family and confiscation of property and ration cards.

Israel
Israeli-Administered Territories[a]
& Palestinian Authority-Administered Territories [b]

Polity: Military and PLO administered
Economy: Capitalist
Population: 2,184,000
Ethnic Groups: Palestinian, Jewish, Bedouin

Political Rights: 6 [a]
Civil Liberties: 5 [a]
Status: Not Free

Political Rights: 5 [b]
Civil Liberties: 6 [b]
Status: Not Free

Overview:

Accusations of autocratic leadership, mismanagement, and rampant corruption plagued Palestinian leader Yassir Arafat throughout 1998, and led the marginalized Palestinian Legislative Council (PLC) to threaten its first no-confidence vote against his government. As his popularity wanes, support for the militant Islamic Hamas grows and presents a creeping challenge to Arafat's authority. Hamas' increasing political influence presents a dilemma for Arafat, who has promised to crack down on its activists as part of peace negotiations with Israel. The Middle East peace process remains deadlocked despite a breakthrough agreement in October. Israeli leaders refused to implement the terms of the agreement, calling Palestinian efforts to guarantee Israeli security inadequate.

The West Bank, Gaza, and East Jerusalem came under the British Mandate in 1920. Jordan seized East Jerusalem and the West Bank in 1948, while Egypt took control of Gaza. In the 1967 Six Day War, Israel took the West Bank, Gaza, East Jerusalem, and the Golan Heights, which had been used by Syria to shell towns in northern Israel. Israel annexed East Jerusalem in 1967, and the Golan Heights in 1981.

Palestinians living in the West Bank and Gaza began attacking mainly military targets in 1987 to protest Israeli rule in what became known as the *intifada* (uprising). A series of secret negotiations between Israel and Arafat's Palestinian Liberation Organization (PLO) conducted in Oslo, Norway, produced an agreement in August 1993. The Declaration of Principles provides for three Israeli troop withdrawals and gradual Palestinian autonomy in the West Bank and Gaza before mid-1998, and negotiations on the final status of East Jerusalem and the fate of refugees by May 1999.

Elections for the first Palestinian Legislative Council and head of the Council's executive authority were held in January 1996, and were considered to be generally free and fair. Independents won 35 of the 88 Council seats, while Arafat's Fatah movement won the remainder. Arafat won the leadership of the executive authority with 88 percent of the vote.

The Oslo agreement has languished since the election of Netanyahu's conservative Likud government in 1996. Dependent on the votes of ultra-conservatives who oppose the peace process, Netanyahu has stalled implementation of Oslo by continuing to build Jewish settlements in disputed territories while accusing Arafat of reneging on promises to combat terrorism. Under the provisions of Oslo implemented so far, the Palestinians have full autonomy in three percent of the West Bank, with another 24 percent jointly controlled. Most of Gaza and the West Bank town of Jericho were turned over to the Palestinian National Authority (PNA) in May 1994, and in late 1995, Israel began redeploying its forces in the West Bank. An interim agreement concluded in January 1997 provided for Israeli redeployment in Hebron, a West Bank town with Jewish and Muslim holy sites.

After months of pressure from the U.S., Netanyahu and Arafat met for nine days of intense negotiations at Wye River Plantation, Maryland. On October 23, they signed an interim agreement for a second Israeli redeployment, from 13.1 percent of the West Bank, in exchange for Palestinian security guarantees. The Wye agreement also provides for the transfer of 14.2 percent of jointly controlled land to Palestinian control; CIA monitoring of Palestinian anti-terrorism measures; the revocation of clauses in the Palestinian National Charter deemed hostile to Israel; an Israeli guarantee of two safe passages between the West Bank and Gaza; the release of 750 Palestinian prisoners; and the opening of a Palestinian airport at Gaza. However, Netanyahu formally suspended implementation of the agreement in December after the beating of an Israeli soldier by Palestinians in the West Bank.

Allegations of corruption and abuse of power have been increasingly problematic for Arafat's government. His autocratic tendencies have put him at odds with the PLC. In early 1998, he announced an indefinite freeze on local elections. In late April, Attorney General Fayez Abu Rahma resigned after just nine months in office, citing government interference in the judicial process. In May, the PLC threatened a no-confidence vote against the government, but Arafat sidestepped the motion by agreeing to a cabinet reshuffle. The announcement of a "new" cabinet in August drew harsh criticism; Arafat had simply added ten ministers to the original lineup.

Government corruption and popular disaffection with the peace process have benefited Hamas, an Islamic group whose military wing is largely responsible for terrorist attacks against Israel. Vocal opposition to Israel and to Oslo has turned Hamas into a political alternative to Arafat's Fatah even as the Palestinian leader, under western pressure, routinely jails Hamas activists. Sheikh Ahmad Yassin, founder and spiritual leader of Hamas, was warmly received as he toured the Middle East in 1998, capitalizing on the deadlock in the peace process and denouncing Arafat for undermining Palestinian unity.

In what is seen by Palestinians as a major diplomatic victory, the United Nations General Assembly in July voted 124-4 to upgrade Palestinian status to "nonvoting member." The new status allows Palestinian representatives to raise issues, cosponsor draft resolutions on Middle East peace, and reply on record to speeches made in the chamber. Palestinians had been granted observer status in the UN in 1974.

Political Rights and Civil Liberties: Palestinian residents of the West Bank, Gaza, and Jerusalem chose their first popularly elected government in 1996. Despite some irregularities, international observers regarded the vote as reasonably reflective of the will of the voters. The PLC has complained of being marginalized by executive authority; though it has debated hundreds of draft laws, only one has been signed into law. The Palestinian government indefinitely postponed local elections in May, citing the threat of Israeli interference. However, most believe that democratic municipal elections would reflect widespread Palestinian disillusionment with Oslo and Arafat's leadership.

Although the PLC passed a Basic Law in 1997, the government has not approved it. Such a law would outline the separation between legislative and executive authority, and presumably curtail Arafat's authority.

The PNA judiciary, consisting of criminal, civil, and state security courts, is not independent. Attorney General Fayez Abu Rahma resigned in April because of what he called continuous intervention by the minister of justice and the security services in judicial matters. The Palestinian Society for the Protection of Human Rights and the Environment (LAW) described a "precarious situation…in which the judiciary has been seriously undermined, its decisions disregarded, and the Attorney General's position eroded." The post remained unfilled at year's end.

Palestinian judges lack proper training and experience. Israeli demands for a Palestinian crackdown on terrorism have given rise to state security courts, which lack almost all due process rights. Suspected Islamic militants are rounded up en masse and often held without charge or trial. There are reportedly some 1,200 administrative detainees currently in the PNA. Trials are conducted in secret and sentences are often issued only hours after arrest. Human Rights Watch reported that judges who complained about judicial abuses faced retaliation. Of 23 death sentences issued since 1994, only two have been carried out. Brothers Mohammad and Ra'id Abu Sultan, both military intelligence agents, were executed on August 30 for murdering two brothers in a dispute.

Palestinian security forces routinely abuse, and sometimes torture, detainees. This practice is not prohibited under Palestinian law. Two Palestinians died in custody during 1998, at least one from torture.

Palestinians accused by Israel of security offenses in Israeli-controlled areas are tried in Israeli military courts. Security offenses are broadly defined. Some due process protections exist in these courts, though there are limits on the right to counsel, bail, and the right to appeal. Administrative detention is widely used. Most convictions in military courts are based on confessions, which are often obtained through torture. Confessions are usually spoken in Arabic and translated into Hebrew for official records. Palestinian detainees seldom read Hebrew and thus sign confessions that they cannot read.

Human Rights Watch reported widespread and systematic torture and ill treatment during interrogation by the Israeli General Security Services (GSS). Israeli authorities investigate allegations of torture, but the results of such investigations are generally not made public. At least three Palestinians died in Israeli custody in 1998. Pursuant to the Wye accord, Israel released some 250 Palestinian prisoners in November. However, those released were mostly common criminals rather than political prisoners.

Israel continued to destroy Palestinian homes built without permits throughout 1998, displacing hundreds. Building permits are nearly impossible for West Bank Palestinians to obtain. In addition, Israel revoked permanent residency permits of Palestinian residents of East Jerusalem who could not prove that their "center of life" was within the city's municipal boundaries. Along with residency rights, these Palestinians lost health insurance and other social benefits. Meanwhile, the Israeli government approved the vast expansion and construction of Jewish settlements in the West Bank and East Jerusalem, offering economic incentives to prospective Jewish settlers.

Israeli soldiers shoot rubber-coated bullets indiscriminately at Palestinian demonstrators. Clashes between Palestinians, who often throw stones, and Israeli soldiers resulted in the deaths of at least 16 Palestinians in 1998, including a 13-year-old boy. Four Palestinians were killed by Israeli security forces at military checkpoints and roadblocks, and Israeli officers killed several other Palestinians whom they claimed were involved in acts of terrorism. A 1997 draft law limits the right of Palestinians to claim compensation for wrongful injury or death caused by Israeli soldiers.

Under a 1995 press law, journalists may be fined and jailed and newspapers closed for publishing "secret information" on Palestinian security forces or news that might harm national unity or incite violence. Several small private radio and television stations are pressured by authorities to provide favorable coverage of Arafat and the PNA. Official Palestinian radio and television are government mouthpieces. In 1998, a Reuters office and a television station were shut down. Late in the year, dozens of journalists were arrested and numerous news offices were temporarily closed for covering pro-Iraqi demonstrations.

Newspapers are subject to Israeli censorship on security matters, though such control has eased since 1993. Israeli authorities prohibit expressions of support for Hamas and other groups that call for the destruction of Israel. Numerous journalists were injured by Israeli security forces while covering clashes with Palestinians during 1998.

The Israeli government limits freedom of assembly; military orders ban public gatherings of ten or more persons without a permit, though they are generally only enforced with regard to Palestinians. The PNA requires permits for rallies and demonstrations, and prohibits violence and racist sloganeering. Private Palestinian organizations must register with Israeli authorities. In the PNA, Palestinian and pro-Islamic organizations that oppose Arafat's government have been harassed and detained.

Freedom of movement is heavily restricted by Israeli authorities. All West Bank and Gaza residents must have identification cards in order to obtain entry permits into Israel and Jerusalem. Israel often denies permits to applicants with no explanation. Even senior Palestinian officials are subject to long delays and searches at Israeli West Bank checkpoints. Residents of Gaza are rarely given permission to enter the West Bank, and vice versa. Israel continued to impose curfews in areas of the West Bank during Israeli and religious holidays, which are considered high risk periods. During curfews, Israelis are generally free to move about while Palestinians are confined to their homes. Israel frequently seals off the West Bank and Gaza in response to terrorist attacks, preventing tens of thousands of Palestinians from traveling to their jobs in Israel and causing economic hardship.

Palestinian women are underrepresented in most professions, and encounter discrimination in employment. Under *shari'a* (Islamic) law, women are disadvantaged in marriage, divorce, and inheritance matters. Rape, domestic abuse, and "honor killings," in which unmarried women thought not to be virgins are murdered by male relatives, continue. Since societal pressures prevent reporting of such incidents, the exact frequency of attacks is unknown.

Labor affairs in the West Bank and Gaza are governed by a combination of Jordanian law and PNA decisions pending the enactment of new Palestinian labor codes. Workers may establish and join unions without government authorization. Palestinian workers seeking to strike must submit to arbitration by the PNA ministry of labor. There are no laws in the PNA-ruled areas to protect the rights of striking workers. Palestinian workers in Jerusalem are subject to Israeli labor law.

Moldova
Transdniester

Polity: Presidential
Economy: Statist (transitional)
Population: 700,000
Ethnic Groups: Ukrainian and Russian (60 percent),
Moldovan-Romanian (40 percent)

Political Rights: 6
Civil Liberties: 6
Status: Not Free

Overview: In 1998, international efforts continued to mediate the status of the self-proclaimed republic of Transdniester, the largely ethnically Slavic sliver of land in Moldova bordering Ukraine. Despite a 1997 socio-economic cooperation agreement signed by Moldova's Prime Minister Ion Ciubuc and Transdniester's President Igor Smirnov, there was little momentum in Chisinau for a political settlement as Moldova's government appeared content to accept the region's *de facto* independence for the time being.

In 1990, Slavs in the Transdniester, a narrow strip of land that was part of Ukraine until 1940 and joined to Moldova after Soviet annexation, proclaimed the Dniester Moldovan Republic (DMR). Fighting in Transdniester, where local Slavs were supported by Russian mercenaries and elements of Russia's 14th Army, ended with a cease-fire in mid-1992. In 1994, Russia and Moldova agreed to a three-year timetable for withdrawing the 14th Army. In 1996, President Smirnov was re-elected to another five-term.

Throughout 1998, high-level officials from Moldova, Transdniester, and the international community met, but there was little progress. In March, the presidents of Moldova and Transdniester met in Odessa with Ukrainian President Leonid Kuchma and Russian Prime Minister Viktor Chernomyrdin acting as intermediaries. It was agreed to send Ukrainian peacekeepers into a security zone already patrolled by Moldovan, Russian, and Transdniester forces.

In November, Moldovan President Petru Lucinschi asked the Parliamentary Assembly of the Council of Europe to help mediate the Transdniester situation. In December, Transdniester authorities announced that they would not participate in scheduled negotiations in Kiev that month with mediators from Ukraine, Russia, and the OSCE.

Transdniester remained a key center of smuggling which cost the Moldovan economy millions in custom's revenues and duties. President Smirnov's son was put in charge of a custom's sector rife with corruption. By year's end, elements of the 14th Army remained in the region despite Moscow's commitment to remove those forces.

Political Rights and Civil Liberties: Residents of Transdniester can elect their leaders democratically. In the 1996 presidential elections, incumbent Igor Smirnov defeated challenger Vladimir Malakhov, a businessman, 72 percent to 20 percent. Turnout was 57 percent, the lowest for the republic since its proclamation of sovereignty. In 1994, local authorities forbade residents in voting in Moldova's parliamentary election, though a similar stricture was not specified for the 1998 vote.

The print and local electronic media are progovernment, though citizens have access to Moldovan, Ukrainian, and Russian radio as well as television broadcasts and print media. Freedom of religion is generally respected, though there are restrictions on assembly. There are a number of political parties coalesced around the left-wing Bloc of Patriotic Forces as well as the moderate Movement for the Development of Dniester, which has backed the ruling Labor Movement of Dniester. Unions are remnants of Soviet-era labor organizations. The United Council of Labor Collectives works closely with the government.

The local judiciary is based on the Soviet-era model and is not independent. Economic rights have been circumscribed by lack of reform, high-level corruption, and criminal activity.

Morocco
Western Sahara

Polity: Appointed governors
Economy: Capitalist
Population: 228,000
Ethnic Groups: Arab, Sahrawi

Political Rights: 7
Civil Liberties: 6
Status: Not Free

Overview: United Nations Secretary General Kofi Annan traveled to the disputed and sparsely populated territory of Western Sahara, as well as to Morocco and Algeria, in November and December in hopes of reaching final agreement on an oft-postponed referendum on the territory's future. A September 1997 agreement reached at UN-sponsored talks between the Moroccan government and the Popular Front for the Liberation of Saguia el-Hamra and Rio de Oro (Polisario) scheduled a now-postponed December 1998 referendum on the territory's future. The central issue of who is entitled to Sahrawi citizenship, and thus will be allowed to vote in the referendum, remains the principal stumbling block.

The former Spanish Sahara was seized by Morocco after Spain withdrew from its colony in 1975. The United Nations Mission for a Referendum in Western Sahara (Minurso) has been seeking to conduct a referendum on nationhood or integration into Morocco for the territory since a 1991 peace pact ended 15 years of bloody guerrilla war, but Moroccan obstruction has continually blocked its efforts. The UN Security

Council has sent landmine clearing teams to the territory early in 1998 and repeatedly extended Minurso's mandate, and a new referendum deadline of December 1999 is pending.

A Spanish colonial census of 1974 will be the base for voter registration rolls, but intense arguments over additions to that list continues to impede the process and raises fears of a return to the costly desert war of 1975-1991. Secretary General Kofi Annan ordered Minurso personnel to accept on an individual basis registration by members of three clans whose Sahrawi identity have been questioned.

The coastal strip of the Western Sahara was claimed by Spain in 1888. The nomadic residents of the "Spanish Sahara" who ranged over its vast desert interior were only gradually subdued over the next five decades. Both Morocco and Mauritania laid claim to parts of the region after achieving their own independence from French rule in 1956 and 1960, respectively. When Spain withdrew from the colony in early 1976, local Sahrawis in the Polisario Front proclaimed the Saharan Arab Democratic Republic and launched a war against Morocco and Mauritania with support and sanctuary provided by neighboring Algeria.

Morocco has ignored the International Court of Justice's 1975 finding against its claim to the territory and affirmation of the Sahrawi people's right to self-determination. Mauritania abandoned the costly conflict in 1979, leaving Morocco its third of the disputed territory. Moroccan security forces replied ferociously to Polisario's hit-and-run attacks, quelling political opposition through arbitrary detention, torture, and extrajudicial killings. In 1984, the Organization of African Unity (OAU) recognized the Saharan Arab Democratic Republic, provoking Morocco's withdrawal from the OAU.

Political Rights and Civil Liberties: Sahrawis have never enjoyed the right to elect their own government. Spain and then Morocco have administered the territory by force. Morocco has settled thousands of people there with economic inducements. Western Sahara residents recognized by Morocco elect representatives to Morocco's parliament, but Polisario rejects integration into Morocco.

Morocco controls over 80 percent of Western Sahara and severely restricts civil liberties. Widespread human rights abuses have been reported. Several hundred Sahrawis detained by Moroccan security forces were released in 1994, but a similar number remain unaccounted for. Many may have been murdered, and sporadic arrests continue. Torture and other abuses by Polisario forces is also reported, but scant access to areas they control makes verification difficult.

Portugal
Macao

Polity: Appointed
governor and partially
elected legislature

Political Rights: 6
Civil Liberties: 4
Status: Partly Free

Economy: Capitalist-statist
Population: 447,000
Ethnic Groups: Chinese, Macanese, Portuguese

Overview:
Since the first Portuguese traders settled here in 1557, Macao, located at the mouth of the Canton River, has been an entrepot for trade with China and more recently has become a gambling Mecca. Since 1974, Portugal and China have officially considered Macao a "Chinese territory under Portuguese administration." The 1976 Organic Statute, or local constitution, vests executive power in a governor appointed by Lisbon, and grants legislative power to both the Portuguese government (acting through the governor) and Macao's legislative assembly. The assembly has eight directly elected members, eight members named by businesses and other interest groups, and seven appointed by the governor, all for four-year terms.

The 1987 Sino-Portuguese Joint Declaration calls for China to assume sovereignty over Macao on December 20, 1999, with the enclave maintaining its legal system and capitalist economy for 50 years. More recently, Beijing has agreed that the legislature elected in 1996 will serve through the handover. The current governor, General Vasco Rocha Viera, took office in 1991. In 1993, China finalized the Basic Law, Macau's post-1999 constitution.

Featured prominently in the last election before the handover, which 12 groups contested in September 1996, were a depressed property market, the need to secure a regional role for an economy dominated by gambling, real estate, and tourism, and other economic concerns. Pro-Chinese businessmen defeated leftist union and neighborhood association candidates to win seven directly elected seats, with democratic activist Ng Kuok-cheong winning the eighth.

In April 1998, China's National People's Congress approved the 100 members of the Preparatory Committee, which is charged with establishing rules for the election of Macau's post-handover chief executive and legislative council. Organized crime violence continued to rock the territory. In early May, police arrested several allegedly senior members of one of Macao's most powerful triad gangs, the 14-K, including reputed leader Wan "Broken Tooth" Kuok-koi. By then, gang related violence had already killed eight people since the beginning of the year. In September, Beijing announced it would station troops in Macau after the handover in response to security problems, even though the Basic Law stipulates that the local government should be in charge of law and order.

There are continuing concerns that mechanisms to safeguard Macau's autonomy after the handover are inadequate. The "localization" of the 17,000-member civil service, which involves replacing Portuguese expatriates and Macanese (people of mixed

Chinese and Portuguese descent) with ethnic Chinese has proceeded slowly. More-over, the status of the Macanese, who also play a leading economic role, remains un-certain; most hold Portuguese passports, but Chinese law forbids dual nationality. An exodus of experienced Macanese and expatriate judges and civil servants is expected. Progress has also been slow in adapting and translating Portuguese-language court pro-cedures and statutes.

Political Rights and Civil Liberties:

Citizens of Macao lack the democratic means to change their government and had no voice in the 1987 Joint Declaration's ceding control to China in 1999. The governor is appointed by Portugal, and only one-third of the legislature is directly elected. Due to the dearth of legal and political experience among MPs, and Portugal's practice of deferring to China on key policy decisions, the legislature holds little power. The governor initiates most laws, which the legislature rarely contest. China maintains a dominant influence through its business interests and control of two key entities: the General Association of Workers and the General Association of Residences, a civic group.

The legal system is based on Portuguese Metropolitan Law, and citizens are ex-tended the rights granted by the Portuguese constitution. The governor appoints judges and prosecutors for three-year terms. The United States State Department has noted that the Judiciary Council, which recommends lower court judges and prosecutors to the governor, has strong ties to the executive and China. Critics charge that judges and prosecutors might have to compromise their independence to win support from the Council for renewal of their terms. The right of ultimate appeal to Portugal is being phased out in favor of a new local Superior Court.

The government owns a controlling interest in the television and radio stations, although opposition views are generally aired. The press is private. As the handover approaches, self-censorship regarding China and the territory's future is increasing. Most newspapers are, in any case, pro-Chinese, including Beijing's *Macao Daily*; alterna-tive views receive limited coverage.

Women increasingly hold administrative posts but are underrepresented in poli-tics. The United Nations has raised concern over the trafficking of women from China, often by criminal gangs, into Macao for prostitution.

Nearly all private sector workers belong to the pro-Beijing General Association of Workers, a confederation which is more a political organization than a labor advocate. A few private sector unions are independent of Beijing, as are two of the four public sector unions. Legislation protecting striking workers from dismissal is inadequate. Foreign workers often work for less than half the wages of Macao citizens, live in con-trolled dormitories, and owe substantial money to proxies for the purchase of their jobs.

Russia
Chechnya

Polity: Presidential
Economy: Mixed statist
Population: 500,000-1,000,000
[accurate figures unavailable
since 1994-96 conflict]
Ethnic Groups: Chechen majority [accurate demographic
data unavailable]

Political Rights: 6
Civil Liberties: 6
Status: Not Free

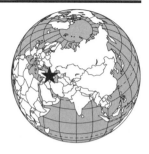

Overview:

Kidnappings and hostage taking of foreign nationals (including Russian servicemen and a special envoy of Russia's President Boris Yeltsin), assassination attempts against Chechnya President Aslan Maskhadov, and the murder and decapitation of three Britains and a New Zealander in December, underscored the pervasive lawlessness that marked 1998 in this secessionist Caucasus republic in Russia.

The year also saw an ongoing power struggle between President Maskhadov, radical field commander Salman Raduyev, and former acting prime minister Shamil Basayev, who accused the president of being too conciliatory to Moscow. In September, Basayev, Raduyev, and a third former field commander, Khunkar-Pasha Israpilov, called on parliament to impeach the president. When parliament declined to do so, the field commanders referred their appeal to the Chechen Supreme Sharia court. Maskhadov retaliated by calling for Raduyev's arrest, and on November 4, the Supreme Sharia Court sentenced him *in abstentia* to four years' imprisonment. He was stripped of his rank of general, but security forces did not apprehend him.

Throughout the year, states of emergencies were imposed, then lifted, then re-imposed, as kidnappings, political murders, and hostage taking pervaded.

Chechnya declared sovereignty in November 1991 in the final days of the Soviet Union. In 1992, under the leadership of Dzhokhar Dudayev, Chechnya declared independence. When Dudayev clashed with parliament in June 1992, he announced the introduction of direct presidential rule. Parliament was dissolved in June 1993, sparking a battle between parliamentary supporters and Dudayev's national guard. Dudayev's rule was marked by corruption and the rise of powerful clans and criminal gangs.

In 1994, Russia began to overtly assist the opposition with the hope of overthrowing Dudayev. Low-intensity conflicts developed in July, and fighting escalated in September. In December, Russian President Boris Yeltsin issued a decree authorizing the army and security forces to attack Chechnya. In 1995, as Chechen resistance stiffened, Russian forces intensified the shelling of Grozny and other population centers, and civilians became targets. The war was marked by brutality and gross human rights violations. Some 500,000 people were displaced. Chechen forces regrouped, and made significant gains against ill-trained, undisciplined, and demoralized Russian troops. In 1996, President Dudayev was killed by a Russian missile.

In May 1997, Russia and Chechnya agreed to a cease-fire, similar to the one brokered by Russia's Gen. Alexander Lebed and Maskhadov in August 1996. Maskhadov, who was elected in January, sought to maintain Chechen sovereignty while pressing Moscow to help rebuild the economy and infrastructure destroyed by war. More than 120,000 civilians were killed in the conflict.

In 1998, the situation in Chechnya remained unstable. In July, Maskhadov survived an assassination attempt by a car bomb, believed to be the fifth attempt on his life since he became president. Kidnappings of foreigners became endemic, some by criminal gangs and others by militia groups hoping to discredit Maskhadov. In November, President Maskhadov announced that Chechnya was building a Muslim state with Islamic ideology. He said the *Shari'a* courts would supersede the constitutional court. In December, parliament voted to introduce a state of emergency, but turned down the president's request for partial mobilization of reservists. The move was aimed at curbing crime and at militant warlords opposed to the government.

Political Rights and Civil Liberties: Residents of Chechnya have the political means to change the government. The 1997 presidential elections were reasonably free and fair. Parliament remains weak and ineffectual. In 1993, then President Dudayev suspended parliament, and though it was eventually restored, power remains in the hands of the president, and there were indications in late 1998 that President Maskhadov would dissolve the body again.

The media is subject to government control and persecution. Newspapers have been arbitrarily closed. In December, the government announced that Russian and foreign journalists had to re-register. In November, the Kavkaz independent TV company was banned by the prosecutor-general's office, but the ban was suspended by the Shari'a Court. According to the republican law on mass media, TV, radio, and newspapers may only be closed by court order, though the government has flouted the law. In August, the first issue of *Sotechestvennik*, the republican newspapers for the Russian-speaking population, was released.

There are serious restrictions on freedom of assembly and association, though several demonstrations took place in 1998.

Political parties are allowed to form and several have coalesced around popular leaders. Most have no broad popular base. The few trade unions that exist are small and powerless.

The lack of rule of law remains a serious problem. In October, the Shari'a Court said it was opposed to the return of a constitutional court, which was disbanded in 1993 after it sided with parliament in its conflict with President Dudayev. The Shari'a Court has shown some independence from the executive. Lower courts are corrupt. Citizens face threats from government forces, criminal gangs, powerful clans, and warlords, many of whom operate with impunity.

Only about 50,000 ethnic Russians remain in Chechnya, most of them pensioners or the infirm. Most face severe financial hardship as well as intimidation and harassment.

Muslims enjoy religious freedom, though the Wahhabi sect was banned in July. In March, Chechen lawmakers extended women's suffrage to bring women's voting rights closer to men's. However, women face societal discrimination in a traditionally male-dominant cultural milieu.

Turkey
Cyprus (T)

Polity: Presidential par- **Political Rights:** 4
liamentary democracy   **Civil Liberties:** 2
(Turkish-occupied)   **Status:** Partly Free
Economy: Mixed capitalist
Population: 178,000
Ethnic Groups: Turkish Cypriot, Turk, Greek Cypriot, Maronite

Note: See Cyprus (Greek) under country reports

Overview: The Cypriot Republic received independence from Britain in 1960. Throughout the 1960s and early 1970s, violence flared between the island's Greek and Turkish communities. In July 1974, following an abortive coup attempt organized by Greece's military junta, Turkey invaded Cyprus, seized 37 percent of the territory, and expelled 200,000 Greek Cypriots from the north. The Turkish Republic of Northern Cyprus (TRNC) declared its independence in 1982, but so far has only been recognized by Turkey, which maintains more than 35,000 troops in the territory and provides an estimated $200 million in annual assistance. Nevertheless, the North is less prosperous than the South; it suffers from constant shortages and high unemployment, and is almost totally reliant on the Cypriot Republic for a free, but insufficient, power supply that is responsible for frequent outages of 12 to 14 hours per day. A 1,200-strong United Nations force controls the island's 103-mile demarcation line, which runs through Nicosia, the world's last divided capital.

The launch of European Union (EU) assession talks with the Cypriot Republic in late 1998 provided new urgency for a political settlement for the divided island. Turkish Cypriots have refused to participate in the talks, which Turkey strongly opposes. As the talks began, TRNC President Rauf Denktash vowed not to renew bi-communal settlement talks unless the talks were suspended. At the same time, France, Germany, Italy, and the Netherlands warned that Cyprus should not be admitted to the EU without a political solution to the island's division. For its part, Greece vowed to block any expansion of EU membership if the Cypriot Republic is not admitted.

The Cypriot government's 1996 purchase of Russian-made air defense missiles has added to the pressure for a political solution. Greece opposed the purchase and has offered to deploy the S-300 missiles on its island of Crete, while Turkey has threatened a preemptive strike to prevent the missiles' use. Nevertheless, Greek Cypriot leaders have vowed to deploy the weaponry on their own territory in 1999.

While prospects for a settlement remained bleak on the political front, businessmen from Greece, Turkey, and the two Cypriot communities held talks in Turkey in late 1998. The meeting, which was designed to end mistrust in the region, followed a similar gathering in Brussels in 1997.

Political Rights   Citizens of the Turkish Republic of Northern Cyprus can
and Civil Liberties: change their government democratically. The TRNC has a

presidential-legislative system of government with elections held at least every five years. Turkish immigrants who settled in the North after the 1974 Turkish invasion have the right to vote in TRNC elections. The Greek and Maronite communities, with a combined population of approximately 1,000 people, are disenfranchised in the North but maintain the right to vote in Cypriot Republic elections. Ankara has considerable influence over the TRNC's policies, and, after the EU rejected Turkey's membership application in 1997, Turkey and the TRNC responded by announcing plans to further integrate their economic and security policies. In 1998, they again vowed to achieve greater integration because, in their view, Greece and the Cypriot Republic are being integrated through the latter's anticipated accession to the EU.

The judiciary is independent, and trials are fair. Civilians deemed to have violated military zones are subject to trial in military courts, which provide due process rights. In 1995, the TRNC allowed for the first time an investigation into the whereabouts of five American citizens of Greek Cypriot descent who disappeared during the 1974 invasion. Ethnic violence in 1996 killed four unarmed Greek Cypriots in the UN-controlled buffer zone. Three of the victims were killed by Turkish troops; one was beaten to death by armed demonstrators.

The private press includes newspapers and periodicals that carry a range of viewpoints. Broadcast media are government-owned and offer some pluralistic views. Authorities control the content of Greek Cypriot textbooks, and many titles are rejected on the grounds that they "violate the feelings" of Turkish Cypriots.

Advocates for Greek Cypriots living in the Northern city of Karpassia claim these "enslaved" individuals are denied freedom of movement, speech, property and access to the Greek press. Outstanding property claims arising from the division and population exchange in 1974 remain an obstacle to peace and demilitarization on the island. Approximately 85 percent of the land in the north continues to be claimed by its original Greek Cypriot owners. In 1996, the European Court for Human Rights at Strasbourg held Turkey directly responsible for denying a Greek Cypriot refugee unconditional access to her property in the North since 1974. In 1998, the Court ruled that Turkey must pay the refugee approximately $574,000 in compensation. In these rulings, the Court recognized Ankara, not the TRNC, as having control of the North and treated the internationally recognized Cypriot Republic as the sole legitimate government on the island. According to the Financial Times, property fights are weak within the TRNC itself, and some residents accuse politically connected persons of illegally appropriating land.

The majority Sunni Muslims, the minority Greek, and the Maronite Orthodox Christians worship freely. Restrictions exist on travel to and from the South. Trade unions are independent.

↑ United Kingdom
Northern Ireland

Polity: British adminis-   **Political Rights:** 3
tration and elected local   **Civil Liberties:** 3
councils   **Status:** Partly Free
(military-occupied)
Economy: Mixed capitalist
Population: 1,630,000
Ethnic Groups: Protestant [mostly Scottish and English],
(57 percent), Irish Catholic (43 percent)
Trend arrow: Northern Ireland receives an upward trend arrow due to a Catholic-Protestant power-sharing agreement which provides for a devolved legislature with multiparty representation.

Overview: On April 10, eight unionist and nationalist parties successfully concluded 22 months of negotiations on the future of Northern Ireland with a power-sharing agreement that devolves executive power from London to Belfast. Continuing efforts by splinter paramilitary groups on both sides to disrupt the peace effort grew intensely violent at times, but only exacerbated popular weariness of the conflict. Indeed, public opinion, along with the personal involvement of British and Irish Prime Ministers Tony Blair and Bertie Ahern, helped promote cooperation among longstanding opponents.

Northern Ireland comprises six of the nine counties of the Irish province of Ulster. At the insistence of the locally dominant Protestants, these counties remained part of the United Kingdom after the other 26 predominantly Catholic Irish counties gained independence in 1921. Catholics now constitute a majority in four of the six counties. The demographic trends have aroused anxiety within the Protestant population, which is largely descended from seventeenth-century Scottish and English settlers. Britain's 1920 Government of Ireland Act set up the Northern Irish parliament, which functioned until the British imposed direct rule in 1972.

Disorder resulting from a nonviolent Catholic civil rights movement in the 1960s prompted the deployment of British troops that have occupied Northern Ireland ever since. Amid sectarian violence beginning in the 1970s, division grew within both the primarily Protestant unionist and Catholic nationalist communities. In addition to numerous political factions including the conservative Ulster Unionist Party (UUP), the hardline Democratic Unionist Party (DUP), the interdenominational unionist Alliance Party, the moderate pro-nationalist Social Democratic and Labour Party (SDLP), and the pro-nationalist Sinn Fein, there are also paramilitary groups on both sides that continue to engage in terrorism.

Negotiations for a peace settlement began in June 1996, with Sinn Fein banned by then Prime Minister John Major pending a cessation and renunciation of violence by the Irish Republican Army (IRA). British general elections in May 1997 brought significant gains for republicans and a new Labour government with a mandate to bolster the peace process. Sinn Fein took 17 percent of the Northern Ireland vote, while Tony Blair's Labour party won an overwhelming majority in the Commons, and thus the freedom to make concessions to republicans in the interests of peace. He immediately began to undertake confidence-building measures, such as reinstating official contacts between his government and Sinn Fein and repatriating republican prisoners from Northern Irish to Irish prisons. His efforts helped secure an IRA cease-fire in July 1997.

Intense determination by Blair and Ahern kept negotiations on track despite numerous incidents of sectarian violence. Paramilitary groups that had not declared ceasefires carried out car bombings, mortar attacks, and shootings, killing at least ten people between Christmas 1997 and March 1998. Blair intervened personally when talks hit crisis proportions, appealing for a settlement before the summer marching season, when Protestant parades through predominantly Catholic neighborhoods have in the past sparked violent unrest. Former U.S. Senator George Mitchell, who chaired the talks, presented an urgent compromise plan on April 7. A marathon negotiating session including Blair, Ahern, and phone calls from President Bill Clinton, produced a settlement on April 10.

The "Good Friday Agreement" provides for a democratically elected, 108-member legislature in Belfast with full executive and legislative authority and a weighted voting system giving Catholics substantial power; a north-south council of Irish and Northern Irish officials to develop consultation, cooperation, and action on matters of mutual interest; and a council of British, Irish, Northern Irish, Scottish, and Welsh representatives to meet twice a year to discuss particular policy issues. Perhaps most significantly, the agreement recognizes the "principle of consent;" that is, that a united Ireland will not come about without the consent of a majority of people in both jurisdictions. In a May 22 referendum, 71 percent of Northern Irish voters supported the settlement.

Elections to the new assembly took place on June 25. Of almost 300 candidates representing 12 political parties, pro-agreement moderates and nationalists were the big winners. The UUP took 28 seats, while the Progressive Unionists, aligned with the UUP, took 2. The SDLP took 24 and Sinn Fein 18. Anti-agreement parties took 28 seats, not enough to hinder political progress. The Alliance party won six seats. Women candidates, including the Women's Coalition party, won just 12 seats. At the first session of the new legislature on July 1, David Trimble of the UUP and Seamus Mallon of the SDLP were elected first minister and deputy first minister, respectively.

Beginning in September, sessions of the new assembly were beset by intense infighting over IRA disarmament and the composition of the institutions set up by the agreement. In late November, Blair again stepped in to defuse a crisis. A compromise was reached in mid-December allowing for ten ministerial departments and outlining formal and informal areas of cooperation with Ireland. The transfer of powers from London to Belfast is scheduled for 1999.

As feared, the summer marching season brought widespread bloodshed from groups opposed to the peace agreement. Protestants stage about 2,500 marches every year to observe ancient military victories against Catholics. About 12 of the parades have been disputed because their routes take them through Catholic neighborhoods. A decision by the new Northern Ireland Parades Commission to reroute a contentious parade led to rioting and firebombings in July. Related violence included hundreds of attacks against security forces and the firebombing of ten churches throughout the North. The two most disturbing incidents were an arson attack in July that killed three young Catholic boys and an August bombing in Omagh by the extremist "Real IRA," which killed 28 people and injured over 200. Despite fears of a breakdown in the peace agreement, many argue that the widespread revulsion triggered by the attacks has helped isolate splinter groups by undermining their support.

Political Rights and Civil Liberties: The people of Northern Ireland elected a 108-member legislature in June, the first since the 1972 suspension of a regional parliament and the imposition of direct British rule. The new assembly will have full executive and legislative power, though Britain will maintain responsibility for defense and security.

The Good Friday Agreement specifically addresses a number of human rights issues. It requires that the British government incorporate the European Convention on Human Rights (ECHR) into Northern Irish law, so that aggrieved parties may take alleged violations of the ECHR to Northern Irish courts. It also requires Britain to promote equality in employment, to preserve and promote the Irish language, to reduce the number of British soldiers deployed in Northern Ireland to peacetime levels, to establish an independent commission on police reform, and to appoint a body to review the criminal justice system. Human Rights Watch expressed satisfaction about the inclusion of such provisions, but cautioned that some of them are too vague to be effective.

The Prevention of Terrorism Act (PTA), which is renewed every two years, allows the police to arrest without a warrant persons believed to be involved in terrorism, and to detain and interrogate such persons for up to 48 hours without legal representation or judicial review. The Northern Ireland Emergency Provisions Act (EPA) allows for the arrest and detention for up to four hours of an individual suspected of committing or believed about to commit any offense. Under the EPA, individuals suspected of terrorist offenses are tried in "Diplock courts" without a jury. Diplock courts have been widely criticized by human rights groups for compromising internationally recognized standards for due process. Anti-terror laws passed in the wake of the Omagh bombing make it possible to jail suspected terrorists on the word of a senior police officer and allow security forces to seize the property and money of known terrorists.

In June, the British government named a panel to assess policing structures and arrangements for Northern Ireland. The commission is to report in mid-1999, recommending measures to ensure that policing is representative of the community as a whole. On April 1, a UN special rapporteur issued a report citing evidence of systematic harassment of lawyers representing republican and loyalist terrorist suspects by the Royal Ulster Constabulary (RUC). A report by the UN Committee Against Torture in November called for a ban on plastic bullets, the closure of certain detention centers, and an end to the continuing state of emergency. In February, video recording equipment was introduced in interrogation sessions at all three holding centers.

According to the Good Friday Agreement, prisoners convicted of paramilitary offenses could be free within two years if their affiliate groups maintain a ceasefire. A number of prisoners were released in 1998, and several were transferred to Irish prisons, a longstanding demand of the IRA. The releases of some 400 paramilitary inmates are scheduled to be completed by July 2000.

Paramilitaries, particularly extremist splinter groups on both sides, engaged in terrorist acts with the intention of derailing the peace process. According to the U.S. State Department, such attacks led to 55 deaths, 210 shootings, and 126 bombings in 1998.

So-called punishment beatings (and shootings) by republican and loyalist paramilitaries also continued. According to the RUC, there were 34 shootings and 86 assaults by loyalists, and 38 shootings and 51 assaults by republicans in 1998.

In January, the British government launched an inquiry into the 1972 Bloody Sunday massacre in Londonderry, in which 14 unarmed Catholic civil rights marchers were shot to death by British paratroopers. The inquiry is chaired by three judges, and has the power to subpoena witnesses and compel the disclosure of documents. It intends to satisfy demands for accountability, and thus will not protect the identities of soldiers involved in the incident.

United States
Puerto Rico

Polity: Elected governor and legislature
Economy: Capitalist
Population: 3,613,000
Ethnic Groups: Hispanic

Political Rights: 1
Civil Liberties: 2
Status: Free

Overview:
Puerto Ricans were given yet another opportunity to change the island's status as a commonwealth in free association with the United States. And once again, in a plebiscite held on December 13, Puerto Ricans voted in favor of retaining commonwealth status.

Puerto Rico acquired the status of a commonwealth in free association with the U.S. following approval by plebiscite in 1952. Under its terms, Puerto Rico exercises approximately the same control over its internal affairs as do the 50 U.S. states. Though U.S. citizens, residents cannot vote in presidential elections and are represented in the U.S. Congress by a delegate to the House of Representatives who can vote in committee but not on the floor.

The Commonwealth constitution, modeled after that of the U.S., provides for a governor and a bicameral legislature, consisting of a 28-member Senate and a 54-member House of Representatives, elected for four years. A Supreme Court heads an independent judiciary and the legal system is based on U.S. law.

Pedro Rosello of the pro-statehood New Progressive Party (PNP) was elected governor in 1992, defeating Victoria Munoz Mendoza of the incumbent Popular Democratic Party (PPD). The PNP also won majorities in the House and Senate.

The election reflected anti-incumbency sentiment and immediate concerns over rising crime, high unemployment, government corruption, and education. Still, the island's relationship with the U.S. remains a fundamental issue. In a nonbinding 1993 referendum, voters narrowly opted to retain commonwealth status. Commonwealth status received 48.4 percent of the vote, statehood 46.3 percent, and independence 4.4 percent. The vote indicated significant gains for statehood, which in the last referendum, in 1967, received only 39 percent of the vote.

In the 1998 referendum, 75 percent of the voting age population turned out at the polls. Many politicians and community leaders had urged Puerto Ricans to vote in favor of a statehood option. In the end, voters chose the status quo by a solid margin, although many more chose statehood than opted for national independence.

Any vote to change the island's status would have to be approved by the U.S. Congress.

At the November 5, 1996 elections, Rosello won re-election with 51.2 percent of the vote, defeating the PPD's Hector Luis Acevedo, who took 44.4 percent; the Puerto Rico Independence Party's (PIP) David Noriega Rodriguez took 3.8 percent. In the House the PNP won 37 seats, the PPD, 16, and the PIP, 1. In the Senate, the PNP won 19 seats, the PPD, 8, and the PIP, 1.

As Washington seeks to cut the federal deficit, the benefits the island receives under Section 936 of the Internal Revenue Code will be phased out over the next ten years. This fundamental change in U.S.-Puerto Rican economic relations means the eventual end to a system in which income tax and wage credits to subsidiaries of U.S. companies operating on the island will be eliminated, as will the tax-free status of interest earned on income.

Political Rights and Civil Liberties:

As U.S. citizens, Puerto Ricans are guaranteed all civil liberties granted in the U.S. The press and broadcast media are well developed, highly varied, and critical. In recent years, the Puerto Rican Journalists' Association (ASPRO) has charged successive governments with denying complete access to official information. During 1998, a major controversy broke out between the Rosello administration and the island's largest newspaper, *El Nuevo Dia*. In a federal lawsuit, the newspaper accused the administration of harassment. Some journalists went so far as to question Rosello's commitment to press freedom. Labor unions are well organized and have the right to strike.

The greatest cause for concern is the steep rise in criminal violence in recent years, much of which is drug related, and the Rosello government's response to it. Puerto Rico is now the Caribbean's main drug transshipment point. Since mid-1993, about 80 public housing projects, or about two-fifths of the total, have been under the control of the National Guard, the first time U.S. military units have been routinely deployed to fight crime.

In 1997, island residents were shocked by a U.S. District Court report that found that many elected officials were actively currying the favor of incarcerated gang members in order to court votes among inmates. The report said that violent narcotics gangs were in virtual control of Puerto Rico's 36 prisons, and had the ability to decide who received goods ranging from toothpaste to cocaine. According to the report, a "shadow governing body" led by the strongest of several competing prison gangs—the *Asociacion Neta*, which dominates the drug trade inside the corrections system—had taken control of prison functions from corrections staff.

The Rosello government claims the projects have been "liberated" from drug traffickers. Critics point to civil rights abuses including unlawful search and seizure and other transgressions. The policy appears to have reduced crime in some categories, including homicide. Corruption and criminal activity within the police force are continuing concerns.

Yugoslavia
Kosovo

Polity: Serbian   **Political Rights:** 7
administration   **Civil Liberties:** 7
Economy: Mixed-statist   **Status:** Not Free
Population: 2,018,000
Ethnic Groups: Albanian (90 percent), Serb, Montenegrin

Overview:
In 1998, the government in Serbia launched a massive counteroffensive against the Kosovo Liberation Army (KLA) in this overwhelmingly ethnic-Albanian enclave within Serbia, burning scores of villages, massacring civilians, and driving more than 250,000 civilians from their homes.

A last-minute deal between U.S. special envoy Richard Holbrooke and Yugoslav President Slobodan Milosevic in October averted NATO air strikes and led to a pullback of Serb forces. But before year's end, as 2,000 unarmed monitors moved in to consolidate the cease-fire, the KLA had moved back into regions it had controlled in the summer, and violence continued.

For Serbs, Kosovo is the historic cradle of the Serbian medieval state and culture. It was the site of the Battle of Kosovo Fields in 1389 between Serbian Prince Lazar and the Turks, which solidified Ottoman control over the Serbs for the next 500 years. Serbian President Slobodan Milosevic rose to power in 1987 over the issue of Kosovo's status. Central to his platform was the subjugation of the then autonomous Yugoslav province (established by the 1974 constitution) to Serbian authority. Persecution by ethnic Albanians caused some 50,000 Serb and Montenegrin residents to flee Kosovo after the 1980 death of Yugoslav strongman Josip Broz "Tito."

In 1989-1990, Milosevic abolished the provincial government and legislature and introduced a series of amendments to the Serbian constitution that effectively removed the legal basis for Kosovo's autonomy. Albanians elected a shadow president, Ibrahim Rugova, leader of the Democratic League of Kosovo (LDK), and a 130-member parliament in 1992 to underscore the illegitimacy of Serb rule. Bujar Bukoshi, based in Bonn, was named prime minister whose key task is to raise funds from the large Albanian diaspora in Europe.

Since the Serb takeover, hundreds of thousands of Albanians lost their jobs, and over 200,000 left for other parts of Europe and the United States. Serbs were placed in control of hospitals, universities, businesses, schools, and government. While Albanian resistance has officially been nonviolent, several Serbian policemen and militiamen were murdered in the last six years.

In 1996, President Milosevic and President Rugova signed an agreement for the return of ethnic Albanians to schools and the university, thus ending the parallel school system set up by Albanians after the abolition of the region's autonomy. But by the end of 1997, the agreement had not been implemented, largely because of resistance from Serb academics and nationalist leaders in Kosovo. Some 200 schools continued to operate in private homes.

In 1997, the KLA, a shadowy group armed with Chinese-made weapons, launched a string of attacks on Serb police stations and Albanians seen to be collaborating with the state. The attacks increasingly undermined President Rugova, whose adherence to passive resistance and civil disobedience came under increased criticism from opposition parties and members of the shadow government. Among the critics is Adem Demaci, a highly respected former political prisoner and head of the Kosovo Human Rights Council and a leader of the Parliamentary Party (PPK), an LDK rival. The United States and Europe have proposed a new federation that would give Kosovo, the Muslim Sandjak region, and Vojvodina a constitutional status equal to that of Serbia and Montenegro, but without the right to secede from Yugoslavia. Both Serbia and the Kosovars have rejected the plan.

In 1998, the violent crackdown delayed elections for the president of Kosovo. Though President Rugova remained at his post, support for KLA militants grew after the Serb counteroffensive.

Political Rights and Civil Liberties: Kosovars cannot change democratically the *de jure* government imposed by Serbia. The Parliamentary Party and the Social Democrats are technically outlawed, while the LDK and its leaders have been targets of harassment and detention. Kosovo's democratically elected legislature and government were forced underground after the 1992 elections, which were not recognized by Serbia.

Albanian TV and radio have been abolished. A Belgrade-based conglomerate took over the newspaper, *Rilindja*. The weekly *Zeri* continues to be published. The Serb crackdown led to the temporary shutdown of Albanian-language papers. Serb authorities have closed mosques and have harassed Albanian-Muslim clergy and believers. The Serb Orthodox Church gets government support. Over the last ten years, Albanian monuments have been destroyed, streets have received Serbian names, and signs in Cyrillic have replaced those in the Latin script. Serbian has supplanted Albanian as the official language. Since 1991, some 8,000 Albanian teachers have been dismissed. In 1993, Serb authorities shut down all Albanian-language secondary schools, denying schooling to an estimated 63,000 children. The crackdown shut all 58 Albanian-language secondary schools and 21 of the 350-odd Albanian-language primary schools. A network of clandestine, underground schools have been established in Albanian households.

The Independent Trade Unions of Kosovo (BSPK), an outlawed Albanian-language confederation, has been the subject of repression for refusing to affiliate with the official Serbian unions or sign collective agreements approved by these unions.

There is no independent judiciary, as courts and judges are appointed by Belgrade. The fighting in 1998 led to the massacre of hundreds of civilians, and a policy of "ethnic cleansing" forced some 250,000 ethnic Albanians to flee.

The economy is largely controlled by ethnic Albanians and is buttressed by remittances from ethnic Albanians abroad. Organized crime has engaged in gun-running and drug-trafficking. In addition to these factors, normal economic activity has been disrupted by the Serb crackdown.

The Comparative Survey of Freedom—1998-1999 Survey Methodology

Since its inception in the 1970s, Freedom House's *Freedom in the World* survey has provided an annual evaluation of political rights and civil liberties throughout the world. The *Survey* attempts to judge all countries and territories by a single standard and to emphasize the importance of democracy and freedom. At a minimum, a democracy is a political system in which the people choose their authoritative leaders freely from among competing groups and individuals who were not designated by the government. Freedom represents the opportunity to act spontaneously in a variety of fields outside the control of the government and other centers of potential domination.

The *Survey* rates countries and territories based on real world situations caused by state and nongovernmental factors, rather than on governmental intentions or legislation alone. Freedom House does not rate governments per se, but rather the rights and freedoms enjoyed by individuals in each country or territory. The *Survey* does not base its judgment solely on the political conditions in a country or territory (i.e., war, terrorism, etc.), but by the effect which these conditions have on freedom.

Freedom House does not maintain a culture-bound view of democracy. The *Survey* demonstrates that, in addition to countries in Europe and the Americas, there are free states with varying forms of democracy functioning among people of all races and religions in Africa, the Pacific, and Asia. In some Pacific islands, free countries can have political systems based on competing family groups and personalities rather than on European- or American-style political parties. In recent years, there has been a proliferation of democracies in developing countries, and the *Survey* reflects their growing numbers. To reach its conclusions, the *Survey* team employs a broad range of international sources of information, including both foreign and domestic news reports, NGO publications, think tank and academic analyses, and individual professional contacts.

Definitions and Categories of the *Survey*

The *Survey's* understanding of freedom encompasses two general sets of characteristics grouped under political rights and civil liberties. Political rights enable people to participate freely in the political process, which is the system by which the polity chooses authoritative policy makers and attempts to make binding decisions affecting the national, regional, or local community. In a free society, this represents the right of all adults to vote and compete for public office, and for elected representatives to have a decisive vote on public policies. Civil liberties include the freedoms to develop views, institutions, and personal autonomy apart from the state.

The *Survey* employs two series of checklists, one for questions regarding political rights and one for civil liberties, and assigns each country or territory considered a numerical rating for each category. The political rights and civil liberties ratings are then averaged and used to assign each country and territory to an overall status of "Free," "Partly Free," or "Not Free." (See the section below, "Rating System for Political Rights and Civil Liberties," for a detailed description of the *Survey's* methodology.)

Freedom House rates both independent countries and their territories. For the purposes of the *Survey*, countries are defined as internationally recognized independent states whose governments are resident within their officially claimed borders. In the case of Cyprus, two sets of ratings are provided, as there are two governments on that divided island. In no way does this imply that Freedom House endorses Cypriot division. We note only that neither the predominantly Greek Republic of Cyprus, nor the Turkish-occupied, predominantly Turkish territory of the Republic of Northern Cyprus, is the *de facto* government for the entire island.

This year, Freedom House has divided the previously single related territory category into two parts: related territories and disputed territories. Related territories consist mostly of colonies, protectorates, and island dependencies of sovereign states which are in some relation of dependency to that state and whose relationship is not currently in serious legal or political dispute. Puerto Rico, Hong Kong, and French Guiana are three examples of related territories. Since most related territories have a broad range of civil liberties and some form of self-government, a higher proportion of them have the "Free" designation than do independent countries. Disputed territories represent areas within internationally recognized sovereign states which are usually dominated by a minority ethnic group and whose status is in serious political or violent dispute. This group also includes territories whose incorporation into nation-states is not universally recognized. In some cases, the issue of dispute is the desire of the majority of the population of that territory to secede from the sovereign state and either form an independent country or become part of a neighboring state. Tibet, East Timor, and Abkhazia are examples falling within this category. Freedom House added Chechnya to its *Survey* this year as a disputed territory of Russia, reflecting the decline of effective Russian central authority over this secessionist region.

Freedom House assigns only designations of "Free," "Partly Free," and "Not Free" for the eight related territories with populations under 5,000, designated as "microterritories," without corresponding category numbers. However, the same methodology is used to determine the status of these territories as for larger territories and independent states. The microterritories in the *Survey* are Cocos (Keeling) Islands, Rapanui (Easter Island), Falkland Islands, Niue, Norfolk Island, Pitcairn Islands, Svalbard, and Tokelau. The *Survey* excludes from its consideration uninhabited territories and such entities as the U.S.-owned Johnston Atoll, which has only a transient military population and no native inhabitants.

Political Rights Checklist

1. Is the head of state and/or head of government or other chief authority elected through free and fair elections?
2. Are the legislative representatives elected through free and fair elections?
3. Are there fair electoral laws, equal campaigning opportunities, fair polling, and honest tabulation of ballots?
4. Are the voters able to endow their freely elected representatives with real power?
5. Do the people have the right to organize in different political parties or other competitive political groupings of their choice, and is the system open to the rise and fall of these competing parties or groupings?
6. Is there a significant opposition vote, de facto opposition power, and a realistic possibility for the opposition to increase its support or gain power through elections?

7. Are the people free from domination by the military, foreign powers, totalitarian parties, religious hierarchies, economic oligarchies, or any other powerful group?

8. Do cultural, ethnic, religious, and other minority groups have reasonable self-determination, self-government, autonomy, or participation through informal consensus in the decision-making process?

Additional discretionary Political Rights questions:

A. For traditional monarchies that have no parties or electoral process, does the system provide for consultation with the people, encourage discussion of policy, and allow the right to petition the ruler?

B. Is the government or occupying power deliberately changing the ethnic composition of a country or territory so as to destroy a culture or tip the political balance in favor of another group?

To answer the political rights questions, Freedom House considers the extent to which the system offers the voter the chance to make a free choice among candidates, and to what extent the candidates are chosen independently of the state. Freedom House recognizes that formal electoral procedures are not the only factors that determine the real distribution of power. In many Latin American countries, for example, the military retains a significant political role, and in Morocco the king maintains considerable power over the elected politicians. The more that people suffer under such domination by unelected forces, the less chance the country has of receiving credit for self-determination in our *Survey*.

The Civil Liberties Checklist

A. Freedom of Expression and Belief

1. Are there free and independent media and other forms of cultural expression? (Note: In cases where the media are state-controlled but offer pluralistic points of view, the *Survey* gives the system credit.)

2. Are there free religious institutions and is there free private and public religious expression?

B. Association and Organizational Rights

1. Is there freedom of assembly, demonstration, and open public discussion?

2. Is there freedom of political or quasi-political organization? (Note: this includes political parties, civic organizations, ad hoc issue groups, etc.)

3. Are there free trade unions and peasant organizations or equivalents, and is there effective collective bargaining? Are there free professional and other private organizations?

C. Rule of Law and Human Rights

1. Is there an independent judiciary?

2. Does the rule of law prevail in civil and criminal matters? Is the population treated equally under the law? Are police under direct civilian control?

3. Is there protection from political terror, unjustified imprisonment, exile, or torture, whether by groups that support or oppose the system? Is there freedom from war and insurgencies? (Note: Freedom from war and insurgencies enhances the liberties in

a free society, but the absence of wars and insurgencies does not in and of itself make a not free society free.)

4. Is there freedom from extreme government indifference and corruption?

D. Personal Autonomy and Economic Rights

1. Is there open and free private discussion?

2. Is there personal autonomy? Does the state control travel, choice of residence, or choice of employment? Is there freedom from indoctrination and excessive dependency on the state?

3. Are property rights secure? Do citizens have the right to establish private businesses? Is private business activity unduly influenced by government officials, the security forces, or organized crime?

4. Are there personal social freedoms, including gender equality, choice of marriage partners, and size of family?

5. Is there equality of opportunity, including freedom from exploitation by or dependency on landlords, employers, union leaders, bureaucrats, or other types of obstacles to a share of legitimate economic gains?

When analyzing the civil liberties checklist, Freedom House does not mistake constitutional guarantees of human rights for those rights in practice. For states and territories with small populations, particularly tiny island nations, the absence of trade unions and other types of association is not necessarily viewed as a negative situation unless the government or other centers of domination are deliberately blocking their formation or operation. In some cases, the small size of these countries and territories may result in a lack of sufficient institutional complexity to make them fully comparable to larger countries. The question of equality of opportunity also implies a free choice of employment and education. Extreme inequality of opportunity prevents disadvantaged individuals from enjoying full exercise of civil liberties. Typically, very poor countries and territories lack both opportunities for economic advancement and other liberties on this checklist. The question on extreme government indifference and corruption is included because when governments do not care about the social and economic welfare of large sectors of the population, the human rights of those people suffer. Government corruption can pervert the political process and hamper the development of a free economy.

For this year's *Survey*, Freedom House reorganized the existing questions in the civil liberties checklist into four subsets. A new question on personal autonomy was added under section D, resulting in an increase in the total number of possible points that could be awarded in the civil liberties category.

Rating System for Political Rights and Civil Liberties

The *Survey* rates political rights and civil liberties separately on a seven-category scale, 1 representing the most free and 7 the least free. A country is assigned to a particular numerical category based on responses to the checklist and the judgments of the *Survey* team at Freedom House. According to the methodology, the team assigns initial ratings to countries by awarding from 0 to 4 raw points per checklist item, depending on the comparative rights or liberties present. (In the *Surveys* completed from 1989-90 through 1992-93, the methodology allowed for a less nuanced range of 0 to 2 raw points

Political Rights	
Category Number	Raw Points
1	28-32
2	23-27
3	19-22
4	14-18
5	10-13
6	5-9
7	0-4

Civi Liberties	
Category Number	Raw Points
1	50-56
2	42-49
3	34-41
4	26-33
5	17-25
6	9-16
7	0-8

per question.) The only exception to the addition of 0 to 4 raw points per checklist item is additional discretionary question B in the political rights checklist, for which 1 to 4 raw points are subtracted depending on the severity of the situation. The highest possible score for political rights is 32 points, based on up to 4 points for each of eight questions. The highest possible score for civil liberties is 56 points, based on up to 4 points for each of fourteen questions.

After placing countries in initial categories based on checklist points, the *Survey* team makes minor adjustments to account for factors such as extreme violence, whose intensity may not be reflected in answering the checklist questions. These exceptions aside, in the overwhelming number of cases, the results of the checklist system reflect the real world situation and are adequate for placing countries and territories into the proper comparative categories.

At its discretion, Freedom House assigns up or down trend arrows to countries and territories to indicate general positive or negative trends that may not be apparent from the ratings. Such trends may or may not be reflected in raw points, depending on the circumstances in each country or territory. Only countries or territories without ratings changes since the previous year warrant trend arrows. Distinct from the trend arrows, the triangles located next to the political rights and civil liberties ratings (see accompanying tables of comparative measures of freedom for countries and related and disputed territories) indicate changes in those ratings caused by real world events since the last *Survey*.

Without a well-developed civil society, it is difficult, if not impossible, to have an atmosphere supportive of democracy. A society that does not have free individual and group expressions in nonpolitical matters is not likely to make an exception for political ones. There is no country in the *Survey* with a rating of 6 or 7 for civil liberties and, at the same time, a rating of 1 or 2 for political rights. Almost without exception in the *Survey*, countries and territories have ratings in political rights and civil liberties that are within two ratings numbers of each other.

Explanation of Political Rights and Civil Liberties Ratings

Political Rights

Countries and territories which receive a rating of 1 for political rights come closest to the ideals suggested by the checklist questions, beginning with free and fair elections. Those who are elected rule, there are competitive parties or other political groupings, and the opposition plays an important role and has actual power. Citizens enjoy self-determination or an extremely high degree of autonomy (in the case of territories), and minority groups have reasonable self-government or can participate in the government through informal consensus. With the exception of such entities as tiny island states, these countries and territories have decentralized political power and free subnational elections.

Countries and territories rated 2 in political rights are less free than those rated 1. Such factors as gross political corruption, violence, political discrimination against minorities, and foreign or military influence on politics may be present and weaken the quality of democracy.

The same conditions which undermine freedom in countries and territories with a rating of 2 may also weaken political rights in those with a rating of 3, 4, and 5. Other damaging elements can include civil war, heavy military involvement in politics, lingering royal power, unfair elections, and one-party dominance. However, states and territories in these categories may still enjoy some elements of political rights, including the freedom to organize quasi-political groups, reasonably free referenda, or other significant means of popular influence on government.

Countries and territories with political rights rated 6 have systems ruled by military juntas, one-party dictatorships, religious hierarchies, and autocrats. These regimes may allow only a minimal manifestation of political rights, such as competitive local elections or some degree of representation or autonomy for minorities. Some countries and territories rated 6 are in the early or aborted stages of democratic transition. A few states are traditional monarchies that mitigate their relative lack of political rights through the use of consultation with their subjects, toleration of political discussion, and acceptance of public petitions.

For countries and territories with a rating of 7, political rights are absent or virtually nonexistent due to the extremely oppressive nature of the regime or severe oppression in combination with civil war. States and territories in this group may also be marked by extreme violence or warlord rule which dominates political power in the absence of an authoritative, functioning, central government.

Civil Liberties

Countries and territories which receive a rating of 1 come closest to the ideals expressed in the civil liberties checklist, including freedom of expression, assembly, association, and religion. They are distinguished by an established and generally equitable system of rule of law and are comparatively free of extreme government indifference and corruption. Countries and territories with this rating enjoy free economic activity and tend to strive for equality of opportunity.

States and territories with a rating of 2 have deficiencies in three or four aspects of civil liberties, but are still relatively free.

Countries and territories which have received a rating of 3, 4, and 5 range from those that are in at least partial compliance with virtually all checklist standards to those with a combination of high or medium scores for some questions and low or very low scores on other questions. The level of oppression increases at each successive rating level, particularly in the areas of censorship, political terror, and the prevention of free association. There are also many cases in which groups opposed to the state engage in political terror that undermines other freedoms. Therefore, a poor rating for a country is not necessarily a comment on the intentions of the government, but may reflect real restrictions on liberty caused by nongovernmental terror.

Countries and territories rated 6 are characterized by a few partial rights, such as some religious and social freedoms, some highly restricted private business activity, and relatively free private discussion. In general, people in these states and territories experience severely restricted expression and association, and there are almost always political prisoners and other manifestations of political terror.

States and territories with a rating of 7 have virtually no freedom. An overwhelming and justified fear of repression characterizes these societies.

Free, Partly Free, Not Free

The *Survey* assigns each country and territory the status of "Free," "Partly Free," or "Not Free" by averaging their political rights and civil liberties ratings. Those whose ratings average 1-2.5 are generally considered "Free," 3-5.5 "Partly Free," and 5.5-7 "Not Free." The dividing line between "Partly Free" and "Not Free" usually falls within the group whose ratings numbers average 5.5. For example, countries that receive a rating of 6 for political rights and 5 for civil liberties, or a 5 for political rights and a 6 for civil liberties, could be either "Partly Free" or "Not Free." The total number of raw points is the definitive factor which determines the final status. Countries and territories with combined raw scores of 0-30 points are "Not Free," 31-59 points are "Partly Free," and 60-88 are "Free." Based on raw points, this year there are several unusual cases: Mali's and Argentina's ratings average 3.0, but they are "Free," and Chad, Cote d'Ivoire, and Swaziland are rated 5.0, but they are "Not Free."

It should be emphasized that the "Free," "Partly Free," and "Not Free" labels are highly simplified terms that each cover a broad third of the available raw points. Therefore, countries and territories within each category, especially those at either end of each category, can have quite different human rights situations. In order to see the distinctions within each category, one should examine a country's or territory's political rights and civil liberties ratings.

The differences in raw points between countries in the three broad categories represent distinctions in the real world. There are obstacles which "Partly Free" countries must overcome before they can be called "Free," just as there are impediments which prevent "Not Free" countries from being called "Partly Free." Countries at the lowest rung of the "Free" category (2 in political rights and 3 in civil liberties, or 3 in political rights and 2 in civil liberties) differ from those at the upper end of the "Partly Free" group (e.g., 3 for both political rights and civil liberties). Typically, there is more violence and/or military influence on politics at 3, 3 than at 2, 3.

The distinction between the least bad "Not Free" countries and the least free "Partly Free" may be less obvious than the gap between "Partly Free" and "Free," but at "Partly Free," there is at least one additional factor that keeps a country from being assigned to the "Not Free" category. For example, Lebanon, which was rated 6, 5, "Partly Free" in 1994, was rated 6, 5, but "Not Free," in 1995 after its legislature unilaterally extended the incumbent president's term indefinitely. Though not sufficient to drop the country's political rights rating to 7, there was enough of a drop in raw points to change its category.

Freedom House does not view democracy as a static concept, and the *Survey* recognizes that a democratic country does not necessarily belong in our category of "Free" states. A democracy can lose freedom and become merely "Partly Free." Sri Lanka and Colombia are examples of such "Partly Free" democracies. In other cases, countries that replaced military regimes with elected governments can have less than complete transitions to liberal democracy. Guatemala fits the description of this kind of

"Partly Free" democracy. Some scholars use the term "semi-democracy" or "formal democracy," instead of "Partly Free" democracy, to refer to countries that are democratic in form but less than free in substance.

The designation "Free" does not mean that a country enjoys perfect freedom or lacks serious problems. As an institution which advocates human rights, Freedom House remains concerned about a variety of social problems and civil liberties questions in the U.S. and other countries that the *Survey* places in the "Free" category. An improvement in a country's rating does not mean that human rights campaigns should cease. On the contrary, the findings of the *Survey* should be regarded as a means to encourage improvements in the political rights and civil liberties conditions in all countries.

Tables and Ratings

Table of Countries
Comparative Measures of Freedom

Country	PR	CL	Freedom Rating	Country	PR	CL	Freedom Rating
Afghanistan	7	7	Not Free	Dominica	1	1	Free
Albania	4	5▼	Partly Free	Dominican Republic	2▲	3	Free
Algeria	6	5▲	Not Free				
Andorra	1	1	Free	Ecuador	2▲	3	Free
Angola	6	6	Not Free	Egypt	6	6	Not Free
Antigua and Barbuda	4	3	Partly Free	El Salvador	2	3	Free
				Equatorial Guinea	7	7	Not Free
Argentina	3▼	3	Free	Eritrea	6	4	Partly Free
Armenia	4▲	4	Partly Free	Estonia	1	2	Free
Australia	1	1	Free	Ethiopia	4	4▲	Partly Free
Austria	1	1	Free	Fiji	4	3	Partly Free
⬇ Azerbaijan	6	4	Partly Free	Finland	1	1	Free
Bahamas	1	2	Free	France	1	2	Free
Bahrain	7	6	Not Free	Gabon	5	4	Partly Free
Bangladesh	2	4	Partly Free	The Gambia	7	5▲	Not Free
Barbados	1	1	Free	Georgia	3	4	Partly Free
Belarus	6	6	Not Free	Germany	1	2	Free
Belgium	1	2	Free	Ghana	3	3	Partly Free
Belize	1	1	Free	Greece	1	3	Free
Benin	2	2	Free	Grenada	1	2	Free
Bhutan	7	6▲	Not Free	⬇ Guatemala	3	4	Partly Free
Bolivia	1	3	Free	Guinea	6	5	Not Free
Bosnia-Herzegovina	5	5	Partly Free	Guinea-Bissau	3	5▼	Partly Free
Botswana	2	2	Free	Guyana	2	2	Free
Brazil	3	4	Partly Free	Haiti	5▼	5	Partly Free
Brunei	7	5	Not Free	Honduras	2	3	Free
Bulgaria	2	3	Free	Hungary	1	2	Free
Burkina Faso	5	4	Partly Free	Iceland	1	1	Free
Burma	7	7	Not Free	India	2	3▲	Free
Burundi	7	6▲	Not Free	Indonesia	6▲	4▲	Partly Free
Cambodia	6▲	6	Not Free	Iran	6	6▲	Not Free
Cameroon	7	5	Not Free	Iraq	7	7	Not Free
Canada	1	1	Free	Ireland	1	1	Free
Cape Verde	1	2	Free	Israel	1	3	Free
Central African Republic	3	4▲	Partly Free	Italy	1	2	Free
				Jamaica	2	2▲	Free
Chad	6	4▲	Not Free	Japan	1	2	Free
Chile	3▼	2	Free	Jordan	4	5▼	Partly Free
China (P.R.C.)	7	6▲	Not Free	⬇ Kazakhstan	6	5	Not Free
Colombia	3▲	4	Partly Free	Kenya	6	5▲	Not Free
Comoros	5	4	Partly Free	Kiribati	1	1	Free
Congo (Brazzaville)	7	5	Not Free	Korea, North	7	7	Not Free
⬇ Congo (Kinshasa)	7	6	Not Free	Korea, South	2	2	Free
Costa Rica	1	2	Free	Kuwait	5	5	Partly Free
Côte d'Ivoire	6	4	Not Free	Kyrgyz Republic	5▼	5▼	Partly Free
⬇ Croatia	4	4	Partly Free	Laos	7	6	Not Free
⬆ Cuba	7	7	Not Free	⬆ Latvia	1	2	Free
Cyprus (G)	1	1	Free	Lebanon	6	5	Not Free
Czech Republic	1	2	Free	Lesotho	4	4	Partly Free
Denmark	1	1	Free	⬇ Liberia	4	5	Partly Free
Djibouti	5	6	Not Free	Libya	7	7	Not Free

Country	PR	CL	Freedom Rating
Liechtenstein	1	1	Free
Lithuania	1	2	Free
Luxembourg	1	1	Free
Macedonia	3▲	3	Partly Free
Madagascar	2	4	Partly Free
⬇Malawi	2	3	Free
Malaysia	5▼	5	Partly Free
Maldives	6	5▲	Not Free
Mali	3	3	Free
Malta	1	1	Free
Marshall Islands	1	1	Free
Mauritania	6	5▲	Not Free
Mauritius	1	2	Free
Mexico	3	4	Partly Free
Micronesia	1	2	Free
Moldova	2▲	4	Partly Free
Monaco	2	1	Free
Mongolia	2	3	Free
Morocco	5	4▲	Partly Free
Mozambique	3	4	Partly Free
Namibia	2	3	Free
Nauru	1	3	Free
⬇Nepal	3	4	Partly Free
Netherlands	1	1	Free
New Zealand	1	1	Free
Nicaragua	2▲	3	Free
Niger	7	5	Not Free
Nigeria	6▲	4▲	Partly Free
Norway	1	1	Free
Oman	6	6	Not Free
⬇Pakistan	4	5	Partly Free
Palau	1	2	Free
⬆Panama	2	3	Free
Papua New Guinea	2	3▲	Free
Paraguay	4	3	Partly Free
Peru	5	4	Partly Free
Philippines	2	3	Free
Poland	1	2	Free
Portugal	1	1	Free
⬆Qatar	7	6	Not Free
Romania	2	2	Free
Russia	4▼	4	Partly Free
Rwanda	7	6	Not Free
St. Kitts and Nevis	1	2	Free
St. Lucia	1	2	Free
⬇St. Vincent and the Grenadines	2	1	Free
Samoa	2	3▼	Free
San Marino	1	1	Free
Sao Tome and Príncipe	1	2	Free
Saudi Arabia	7	7	Not Free
Senegal	4	4	Partly Free
Seychelles	3	3	Partly Free

Country	PR	CL	Freedom Rating
Sierra Leone	3▲	5▲	Partly Free
Singapore	5	5	Partly Free
Slovakia	2	2▲	Free
Slovenia	1	2	Free
Solomon Islands	1	2	Free
Somalia	7	7	Not Free
South Africa	1	2	Free
Spain	1	2	Free
Sri Lanka	3	4	Partly Free
Sudan	7	7	Not Free
⬇Suriname	3	3	Partly Free
Swaziland	6	4▲	Not Free
Sweden	1	1	Free
Switzerland	1	1	Free
Syria	7	7	Not Free
Taiwan (Rep. of China)	2	2	Free
⬇Tajikistan	6	6	Not Free
Tanzania	5	4▲	Partly Free
Thailand	2▲	3	Free
Togo	6	5	Not Free
Tonga	5	3	Partly Free
⬇Trinidad and Tobago	1	2	Free
Tunisia	6	5	Not Free
Turkey	4	5	Partly Free
Turkmenistan	7	7	Not Free
Tuvalu	1	1	Free
Uganda	4	4	Partly Free
Ukraine	3	4	Partly Free
United Arab Emirates	6	5	Not Free
United Kingdom*	1	2	Free
United States	1	1	Free
Uruguay	1	2	Free
Uzbekistan	7	6	Not Free
Vanuatu	1	3	Free
Venezuela	2	3	Free
Vietnam	7	7	Not Free
Yemen	5	6	Not Free
⬇Yugoslavia (Serbia and Montenegro)	6	6	Not Free
Zambia	5	4	Partly Free
Zimbabwe	5	5	Partly Free

PR and CL stand for Political Rights and Civil Liberties. 1 represents the most free and 7 the least free category.

⬆⬇ up or down indicates a general trend in freedom.

▲▼ up or down indicates a change in Political Rights or Civil Liberties since the last *Survey*.

The Freedom Rating is an overall judgment based on *Survey* results. See the essay on Survey methodology for more details.

* Excluding Northern Ireland.

Table of Related Territories
Comparative Measures of Freedom

Country	PR	CL	Freedom Rating	Country	PR	CL	Freedom Rating
Australia	3	2	Free	Cayman Islands	1	1	Free
Christmas Island				Channel Islands	2	1	Free
Cocos (Keeling) Islands*			Free	Falkland Islands*			Free
Norfolk Island*			Free	Gibraltar	1	1	Free
Chile			Free	Isle of Man	1	1	Free
Rapanui (Easter Island)*				Montserrat	1	2	Free
China				Northern Ireland	3	3	Partly Free
Hong Kong	5▲	3	Not Free	Pitcairn Island*			Free
Denmark				St. Helena and Dependencies	2	1	Free
Faeroe Islands	1	1	Free	Turks and Caicos	1	1	Free
Greenland	1	1	Free	United States of America			
Finland				American Samoa	1	1	Free
Aland Islands	1	1	Free	Guam	1	1	Free
France				Northern Marianas	1	3▼	Free
French Guiana	1	2	Free	Puerto Rico	1	2	Free
French Polynesia	1	2	Free	U.S. Virgin Islands	1	1	Free
Guadeloupe*			Free	Yugoslavia			
Martinique	1	2	Free	Kosovo	7	7	Not Free
Mayotte (Mahore)	1	2	Free				
New Caledonia	3	2	Free				
Reunion	2	2	Free				
St. Pierre and Miquelon	1	1	Free				
Wallis and Futuna Islands	2	2	Free				
Iraq							
Kurdistan	6	6	Not Free				
Netherlands							
Aruba	2	1	Free				
Netherlands Antilles	1	2	Free				
New Zealand							
Cook Islands	1	2	Free				
Niue*			Free				
Tokelau*			Free				
Norway							
Svalbard*			Free				
Portugal							
Azores	1	1	Free				
Macao	6	4	Partly Free				
Madeira	1	1	Free				
Spain							
Canary Islands	1	1	Free				
Ceuta	1	2	Free				
Melilla	1	2	Free				
United Kingdom							
Anguilla	2	1	Free				
Bermuda	1	1	Free				
British Virgin Islands	1	1	Free				

* Micro-territories have populations of under 5,000. These areas are scored according to the same methodology used in the rest of the *Survey*, but are listed separately due to their very small populations.

Table of Disputed Territories
Comparative Measures of Freedom

Country	PR	CL	Freedom Rating
Armenia/Azerbaijan	5	6	Not Free
Nagorno-Karabakh			
China			
Tibet	7	7	Not Free
Georgia			
Abkhazia	6	5	Not Free
India			
Kashmir	6▲	6▲	Not Free
Indonesia			
East Timor	7	6▲	Not Free
West Papua	7	6▲	Not Free
(Irian Jaya)			
Israel			
Israeli-Administered	6	5	Not Free
territories			
Palestinian Authority-	5	6	Not Free
Administered			
territories			
Moldova			
Transdniester	6	6	Not Free
Morocco			
Western Sahara	7	6	Not Free
Russia			
Chechnya	6	6	Not Free
Turkey			
Cyprus (T)	4	2	Parlty Free

Table of Social and Economic Indicators

Country	Real GDP Per Capita (PPP$)	Life Expectancy	Country	Real GDP Per Capita (PPP$)	Life Expectancy
Afghanistan	na	46	Ecuador	4,602	69
Albania	2,853	72	Egypt	3,829	67
Algeria	5,618	67	El Salvador	2,610	69
Andorra	na	79	Equatorial Guinea	1,712	48
Angola	1,839	47	Eritrea	983	54
Antigua and Barbuda	9,131	74	Estonia	4,062	68
Argentina	8,498	72	Ethiopia	455	42
Armenia	2,208	73	Fiji	6,159	63
Australia	19,632	78	Finland	18,547	77
Austria	21,322	77	France	21,176	78
Azerbaijan	1,463	70	Gabon	3,766	54
Bahamas	15,738	72	The Gambia	948	45
Bahrain	16,751	69	Georgia	1,389	73
Bangladesh	1,382	59	Germany	20,370	77
Barbados	11,306	75	Ghana	2,032	56
Belarus	4,398	68	Greece	11,636	78
Belgium	21,548	77	Grenada	5,425	71
Belize	5,623	72	Guatemala	3,682	65
Benin	1,800	54	Guinea	1,139	45
Bhutan	1,382	66	Guinea-Bissau	811	43
Bolivia	2,617	60	Guyana	3,205	66
Bosnia-Herzegovina	na	72	Haiti	917	51
Botswana	5,611	41	Honduras	1,977	68
Brazil	5,928	67	Hungary	6,793	70
Brunei	31,165	71	Iceland	21,064	78
Bulgaria	4,604	71	India	1,422	59
Burkina Faso	784	47	Indonesia	3,971	62
Burma	1,130	61	Iran	5,480	67
Burundi	637	46	Iraq	3,170	59
Cambodia	1,110	52	Ireland	17,590	75
Cameroon	2,355	55	Israel	16,699	78
Canada	21,916	78	Italy	20,174	78
Cape Verde	2,612	70	Jamaica	3,801	71
Central African Republic	1,092	46	Japan	21,930	80
Chad	1,172	48	Jordan	4,187	68
Chile	9,930	75	Kazakhstan	3,037	65
China	2,935	71	Kenya	1,438	49
Colombia	6,347	69	Kiribati	na	na
Comoros	1,317	59	Korea, North	4,058	66
Congo (Brazzaville)	2,554	47	Korea, South	11,594	74
Congo (Kinshasa)	355	49	Kuwait	23,848	72
Costa Rica	5,969	76	Kyrgyz Republic	1,927	67
Cote d'Ivoire	1,731	52	Laos	2,571	54
Croatia	3,972	72	Latvia	3,273	70
Cuba	3,100	75	Lebanon	4,977	70
Cyprus (Greek)	13,379	78	Lesotho	1,290	56
Czech Republic	9,775	74	Liberia	na	59
Denmark	21,983	75	Libya	6,309	65
Djibouti	1,300	48	Liechtenstein	na	72
Dominica	6,424	na	Lithuania	3,843	71
Dominican Republic	3,923	70	Luxembourg	34,004	76

Table of Social and Economic Indicators

Country	Real GDP Per Capita (PPP$)	Life Expectancy	Country	Real GDP Per Capita (PPP$)	Life Expectancy
Macedonia	4,058	71	Solomon Islands	2,230	70
Madagascar	673	52	Somalia	na	47
Malawi	773	36	South Africa	4,334	58
Malaysia	9,572	72	Spain	14,789	77
Maldives	3,540	62	Sri Lanka	3,408	72
Mali	565	46	Sudan	1,110	51
Malta	13,316	77	Suriname	4,862	70
Marshall Islands	na	62	Swaziland	2,954	39
Mauritania	1,622	52	Sweden	19,297	79
Mauritius	13,294	70	Switzerland	24,881	79
Mexico	6,769	72	Syria	5,374	67
Micronesia	na	66	Taiwan		
Moldova	1,547	66	(Rep. of China)	na	75
Monaco	na	na	Tajikistan	943	68
Mongolia	3,916	57	Tanzania	636	47
Morocco	3,477	72	Thailand	7,742	69
Mozambique	959	44	Togo	1,167	58
Namibia	4,054	42	Tonga	na	na
Nauru	na	na	Trinidad and Tobago	9,437	71
Nepal	1,145	55	Tunisia	5,261	68
Netherlands	19,876	78	Turkey	5,516	68
New Zealand	17,267	72	Turkmenistan	2,345	66
Nicaragua	1,837	66	Tuvalu	na	na
Niger	765	47	Uganda	1,483	40
Nigeria	1,270	50	Ukraine	2,361	68
Norway	22,427	78	United Arab Emirates	18,008	74
Oman	9,383	70	United Kingdom	19,302	77
Pakistan	2,209	58	United States	26,977	76
Palau	na	67	Uruguay	6,854	75
Panama	6,258	74	Uzbekistan	2,376	70
Papua New Guinea	2,500	56	Vanuatu	2,507	63
Paraguay	3,583	69	Venezuela	8,090	72
Peru	3,940	69	Vietnam	1,236	67
Philippines	2,762	66	Yemen	856	58
Poland	5,442	72	Yugoslavia		
Portugal	12,674	75	(Serbia and		
Qatar	19,772	71	Montenegro)	na	72
Romania	4,431	69	Zambia	986	37
Russia	4,531	67	Zimbabwe	2,135	40
Rwanda	na	43			
St. Kitts and Nevis	10,150	67			
St. Lucia	6,530	71			
St. Vincent and Grenadines	5,969	73			
Samoa	2,948	65			
San Marino	na	76			
Sao Tome and Principe	1,744	64			
Saudi Arabia	8,516	70			
Senegal	1,815	49			
Seychelles	7,697	70			
Sierra Leone	625	34			
Singapore	22,604	77			
Slovakia	7,320	73			
Slovenia	10,594	75			

Combined Average Ratings: Independent Countries

FREE

1.0

Andorra
Australia
Austria
Barbados
Belize
Canada
Cyprus (G)
Denmark
Dominica
Finland
Iceland
Ireland
Kiribati
Liechtenstein
Luxembourg
Malta
Marshall Islands
Netherlands
New Zealand
Norway
Portugal
San Marino
Sweden
Switzerland
Tuvalu
United States

1.5

Bahamas
Belgium
Cape Verde
Costa Rica
Czech Republic
Estonia
France
Germany
Grenada
Hungary
Italy
Japan
Latvia
Lithuania
Mauritius
Micronesia
Monaco
Palau
Poland
St. Kitts and Nevis
St. Lucia
St. Vincent and
Grenadines
Sao Tome and
Principe
Slovenia

Solomon Islands
South Africa
Spain
Trinidad and Tobago
United Kingdom
Uruguay

2.0

Benin
Bolivia
Botswana
Greece
Guyana
Israel
Jamaica
Korea, South
Nauru
Romania
Slovakia
Taiwan
Vanuatu

2.5

Bulgaria
Chile
Dominican Republic
Ecuador
El Salvador
Honduras
India
Malawi
Mongolia
Namibia
Nicaragua
Panama
Papua New Guinea
Philippines
Samoa
Thailand
Venezuela

3.0

Argentina
Mali

PARTLY FREE

3.0

Bangladesh
Ghana
Macedonia
Madagascar
Moldova
Seychelles
Suriname

3.5

Antigua and Barbuda

Brazil
Central African
Republic
Colombia
Fiji
Georgia
Guatemala
Mexico
Mozambique
Nepal
Paraguay
Sri Lanka
Ukraine

4.0

Armenia
Croatia
Ethiopia
Guinea-Bissau
Lesotho
Russia
Senegal
Sierra Leone
Tonga
Uganda

4.5

Albania
Burkina Faso
Comoros
Gabon
Jordan
Liberia
Morocco
Pakistan
Peru
Tanzania
Turkey
Zambia

5.0

Azerbaijan
Bosnia-Herzegovina
Eritrea
Haiti
Indonesia
Kuwait
Kyrgyz Republic
Malaysia
Nigeria
Singapore
Zimbabwe

NOT FREE

5.0

Chad

Cote d'Ivoire
Swaziland

5.5

Algeria
Djibouti
Guinea
Kazakhstan
Kenya
Lebanon
Maldives
Mauritania
Togo
Tunisia
United Arab Emirates
Yemen

6.0

Angola
Belarus
Brunei
Cambodia
Cameroon
Congo (Brazzaville)
Egypt
The Gambia
Iran
Niger
Oman
Tajikistan
Yugoslavia

6.5

Bahrain
Bhutan
Burundi
China (PRC)
Congo (Kinshasa)
Laos
Qatar
Rwanda
Uzbekistan

7.0

Afghanistan
Burma
Cuba
Equatorial Guinea
Iraq
Korea, North
Libya
Saudi Arabia
Somalia
Sudan
Syria
Turkmenistan
Vietnam

Combined Average Ratings: Related Territories

FREE
1.0
Aland Islands (Finland)
American Samoa (US)
Azores (Portugal)
Bermuda (UK)
British Virgin Islands (UK)
Canary Islands (Spain)
Cayman Islands (UK)
Faeroe Islands (Denmark)
Gibraltar (UK)
Greenland (Denmark)
Guam (US)
Isle of Man (UK)
Madeira (Portugal)
St. Pierre and Miquelon
(France)
Turks and Caicos (UK)
U.S. Virgin Islands (US)

1.5
Anguilla (UK)
Aruba (Netherlands)

Ceuta (Spain)
Channel Islands (UK)
Cook Islands
(New Zealand)
French Guiana (France)
French Polynesia
(France)
Martinique (France)
Mayotte [Mahore]
(France)
Melilla (Spain)
Montserrat (UK)
Netherlands Antilles
(Netherlands)
Puerto Rico (US)
St. Helena and
Dependencies (UK)

2.0
Northern Marianas (US)
Reunion (France)
Wallis and Futuna
Islands (France)

2.5
Christmas Island
(Australia)
New Caledonia (France)

PARTLY FREE
3.0
Northern Ireland (UK)

4.0
Hong Kong (China)

5.0
Macao (Portugal)

NOT FREE

6.0
Kurdistan (Iraq)

7.0
Kosovo (Yugoslavia)

MICRO-TERRITORIES
(ALL FREE)
Cocos (Keeling)
Islands (Australia)
Falkland Islands (UK)
Guadeloupe (France)
Niue (New Zealand)
Norfolk Island
(Australia)
Pitcairn Island (UK)
Rapanui [Easter Island]
(Chile)
Svalbard (Norway)
Tokelau (New Zealand)

Micro-territories have
populations of under
5,000. These areas are
scored according to the
same methodology used
in the rest of the *Survey,*
but are listed separately
due to their very small
populations.

Combined Average Ratings: Disputed Territories

PARTLY FREE
3.0
Cyprus (Turkey)

NOT FREE
5.5
Abkhazia (Georgia)

Israeli-Administered
Territories (Israel)
Nagorno-Karabakh
(Armenia/Azerbaijan)
Palestinian Authority-
Administered Territories
(Israel)

6.0
Chechnya (Russia)
Kashmir (India)
Transdniester (Moldova)

6.5
East Timor (Indonesia)

West Papua [Irian Jaya]
(Indonesia)
Western Sahara
(Morocco)

7.0
Tibet (China)

Electoral Democracies (117)

Albania
Presidential-parliamentary democracy

Andorra
Parliamentary democracy

Argentina
Federal presidential-legislative democracy

Australia
Federal parliamentary democracy

Austria
Federal parliamentary democracy

Bahamas
Parliamentary democracy

Bangladesh
Parliamentary democracy

Barbados
Parliamentary democracy

Belgium
Federal parliamentary democracy

Belize
Parliamentary democracy

Benin
Presidential-parliamentary democracy

Bolivia
Presidential-legislative democracy

Bosnia-Herzegovina
Presidential-parliamentary democracy

Botswana
Parliamentary democracy and traditional chiefs

Brazil
Federal presidential-legislative democracy

Bulgaria
Parliamentary democracy

Canada
Federal parliamentary democracy

Cape Verde
Presidential-parliamentary democracy

Central African Republic
Presidential-parliamentary democracy

Chile
Presidential-legislative democracy

Colombia
Presidential-legislative democracy
(insurgencies)

Costa Rica
Presidential-legislative democracy

Croatia
Presidential-parliamentary democracy

Cyprus
Presidential-legislative democracy

Czech Republic
Parliamentary democracy

Denmark
Parliamentary democracy

Dominica
Parliamentary democracy

Dominican Republic
Presidential-legislative democracy

Ecuador
Presidential-legislative democracy

El Salvador
Presidential-legislative democracy

Estonia
Presidential-parliamentary democracy

Fiji
Parliamentary democracy and native chieftains

Finland
Presidential-parliamentary democracy

France
Presidential-parliamentary democracy

Georgia
Presidential-parliamentary democracy

Germany
Federal parliamentary democracy

Ghana
Presidential-parliamentary democracy

Greece
Parliamentary democracy

Grenada
Parliamentary democracy

Guatemala
Presidential-legislative democracy

Guinea-Bissau
Presidential-parliamentary democracy
(military-influenced) (transitional)

Guyana
Parliamentary democracy

Haiti
Presidential-parliamentary democracy

Honduras
Presidential-legislative democracy

Hungary
Parliamentary democracy

Iceland
Parliamentary democracy

India
Parliamentary democracy   (insurgencies)

Ireland
Parliamentary democracy

Israel
Parliamentary democracy

Italy
Parliamentary democracy

Jamaica
Parliamentary democracy

Japan
Parliamentary democracy

Kiribati
Parliamentary democracy

Korea, South
Presidential-parliamentary democracy

Kyrgyz Republic
Presidential-parliamentary democracy

Latvia
Presidential-parliamentary democracy

Liberia
Presidential-parliamentary democracy

Liechtenstein
Principality and parliamentary democracy

Lithuania
Presidential-parliamentary democracy

Luxembourg
Parliamentary democracy

Macedonia
Parliamentary democracy

Madagascar
Presidential-parliamentary democracy

Malawi
Presidential-parliamentary democracy

Mali
Presidential-parliamentary democracy

Malta
Parliamentary democracy

Marshall Islands
Parliamentary democracy

Mauritius
Parliamentary democracy

Micronesia
Federal parliamentary democracy

Moldova
Presidential-parliamentary democracy

Monaco
Principality and legislative democracy

Mongolia
Presidential-parliamentary democracy

Mozambique
Presidential-legislative democracy

Namibia
Presidential-legislative democracy

Nauru
Parliamentary democracy

Nepal
Parliamentary democracy

Netherlands
Parliamentary democracy

New Zealand
Parliamentary democracy

Nicaragua
Presidential-legislative democracy

Norway
Parliamentary democracy

Pakistan
Presidential-parliamentary democracy
(military-influenced)

Palau
Presidential-legislative democracy

Panama
Presidential-legislative democracy

Papua New Guinea
Parliamentary democracy

Paraguay
Presidential-legislative democracy

Philippines
Presidential-legislative democracy

Poland
Presidential-parliamentary democracy

Portugal
Presidential-parliamentary democracy

Romania
Presidential-parliamentary democracy

Russia
Presidential-parliamentary democracy

St. Kitts and Nevis
Parliamentary democracy

St. Lucia
Parliamentary democracy

St. Vincent and the Grenadines
Parliamentary democracy

Samoa
Parliamentary democracy and family heads

San Marino
Parliamentary democracy

Sao Tome and Principe
Presidential-parliamentary democracy

Seychelles
Presidential-legislative democracy

Sierra Leone
Presidential-legislative democracy
(rebel insurgencies)

Slovakia
Parliamentary democracy

Slovenia
Presidential-parliamentary democracy

Solomon Islands
Parliamentary democracy

South Africa
Presidential-legislative democracy

Spain
Parliamentary democracy

Sri Lanka
Presidential-parliamentary democracy (insurgency)

Suriname
Presidential-parliamentary democracy

Sweden
Parliamentary democracy

Switzerland
Federal parliamentary democracy

Taiwan
Presidential-legislative democracy

Thailand
Parliamentary democracy (military-influenced)

Trinidad and Tobago
Parliamentary democracy

Turkey
Presidential-parliamentary democracy (military-
influenced) (insurgency)

Tuvalu
Parliamentary democracy

Ukraine
Presidential-parliamentary democracy

United Kingdom
Parliamentary democracy

United States of America
Federal presidential-legislative democracy

Uruguay
Presidential-legislative democracy

Vanuatu
Parliamentary democracy

Venezuela
Presidential-legislative democracy

Sources

Publications

Africa Confidential
Africa News Online
Africa Recovery Magazine (United Nations)
Agence France Presse
Armenian Information Service
Asian Bulletin
Asian Survey
Associated Press
The Atlantic Monthly
Azerbaijan International (U.S.)
Balkan Medja (Bulgaria)
The Baltic Times
Baltic News Service
British Broadcasting Corporation (BBC)
Cable News Network (CNN)
Caretas (Lima)
Carib News
Caribbean Insight
Caribbean Review
Catholic Standard (Guyana)
Central America Report
Christian Science Monitor
Columbia Journalism Review
Dawn News Bulletin (All Burma Students Democratic Front)
Deutsche Presse Agentur
Eastern European Constitutional Review
The Economist
The Economist Intelligence Unit
Editor & Publisher
EFE Spanish News Agency
El Financiero (Mexico City)
El Nuevo Herald (Miami)
EPOCA (Mexico)
Ethiopian Review
Far Eastern Economic Review
Foreign Broadcast Information Service (FBIS)
The Financial Times
Free Labour World
The Free Press (Ghana)
The Globe & Mail (Toronto)
The Guardian
Gulf Times
Hemisfile
Hemisphere
Himal
Hong Kong Digest
Hornet Online
The Hungarian Quarterly
HuriNet
Index on Censorship
Index of Economic Freedom (Heritage Foundation)
Indian Ocean Newsletter
InterPress News Service
The Irish Echo
The Irish Times
Jerusalem Post
Jordan Times
Journal of Commerce
Journal of Democracy
La Jornada (Mexico)
Kathmandu Post
Latin American Regional Reports
Latin American Weekly Report

Le Soleil (Dakar)
Lettre du Continent
Los Angeles Times
Mail & Guardian Weekly (Johannesburg)
Miami Herald
The Middle East
Middle East International
The Middle East Times
Miist (Ukraine)
Monitor (Kampala)
Monthly Digest of News from Armenia
The Nation
New African
The New Republic
New Vision (Kampala)
New York Newsday
New York Times
New Yorker
North-South Magazine
Oman Daily Observer
The Other Side of Mexico (Equipo Pueblo)
Pacific Islands Monthly
Pacific Islands News Agency
Pan African News Agency
The Post (Zambia)
Proceso (Mexico City)
Radio Australia
Radio Free Europe-Radio Liberty
Reforma (Mexico)
La Repubblica
Sources UNESCO
Sposterihach (Ukraine)
The Standard (Nairobi)
State Department Country Reports on Human Rights
    Practices for 1997
The Statesman (Calcutta)
Swiss Press Review
The Tico Times (Costa Rica)
Times of London
Transition
Ukrainian Press Agency
Ukrainian Weekly
Uncaptive Minds (Institute for Democracy in Eastern Europe)
UNDP Human Development Report
U.S. News and World Report
Voice of America Online
Vuelta (Mexico)
Wall Street Journal
Washington Post
Washington Times
The Week in Germany
West Africa
World Population Data Sheet 1998 (Population Reference Bureau)
Xinhua News Agency
Yemen Times

Organizations

AFL-CIO
Africa Policy Information Center (APIC)
Africa Rights (London)
American Anti-Slavery Group
American Institute for Free Labor Development
Amnesty International
Andean Commission of Jurists
Anti-Slavery International
Article 19 (London)
Association Pour La Fondation Mohsen Hachtroudi
Baltic Media Centre
Bangladesh National Women Lawyers Association

Caribbean Institute for the Promotion of Human Rights
Caribbean Rights
The Carter Center
Center for Free Speech (Lagos)
Center for Strategic and International Studies
Centers for Pluralism (Poland)
Central Statistical Office, Warsaw (Poland)
Chadian Association for the Protection of Human Rights
Child Workers in Nepal
Chilean Human Rights Commission
Civic Alliance (Mexico)
Committee of Churches for Emergency Help (Paraguay)
Committee to Protect Journalists
Constitutional Rights Project (Lagos)
Council for Democracy (Mexico)
Croatian Democracy Project (Croatia)
Cuban Committee for Human Rights
Democracy After Communism Foundation (Hungary)
Democratic Initiatives (Ukraine)
Elections Canada
Equal Access Committee (Ukraine)
Estonian Institute for Human Rights
Ethnic Federation of Romani (Romania)
Fray Bartocome de Las Casas Center for Human Rights (Mexico)
Free Africa Foundation
Free and Democratic Bulgaria Foundation
Free Trade Union Institute
Group for Mutual Support (Guatemala)
Guyana Human Rights Group
Haitian Center for Human Rights
Helsinki Committee for Human Rights in Serbia
Honduran Committee for the Defense of Human Rights
Hong Kong Human Rights Monitor
Human Rights Commission (El Salvador)
Human Rights Commission of Pakistan
Human Rights Organization of Bhutan
Human Rights Organization of Nepal
Human Rights Watch
Immigration and Refugee Board of Canada
Indian Law Resource Center
Inform (Sri Lanka)
Instate for Free Expression (Johannesburg)
Institute for Legal Research and Resources (Nepal)
Institute for the Study of Conflict, Ideology and Policy
Inter-American Commission on Human Rights
Inter-American Dialogue
Inter-American Press Association
International Campaign for Tibet
International Commission of Jurists
International Federation of Journalists
International Foundation for Electoral Systems (IFES)
International Freedom of Expression Exchange (IFEX)
International Human Rights Law Group

International Press Institute
International Republican Institute
International Research and Exchange Board (IREX)
Jaan Tonisson Institute
Jamaica Council for Human Rights
Latin American Association for Human Rights
Latin American Association for Human Rights and Freedoms
    of the Workers
Latin American Ombudsmen Institute
Latvian Centre for Human Rights and Ethnic Studies
Latvian Human Rights Institute
Lawyer to Lawyer Network (Lawyers Committee for Human Rights)
Lawyers Committee for Human Rights
Lawyers for Human Rights and Legal Aid (Pakistan)
Media Institute of South Africa (MISA)
Mexican Human Rights Academy
Milan Simecka Foundation (Slovakia)
National Bank of Hungary
National Coalition for Haitian Refugees
National Coordinating Office for Human Rights (Peru)
National Democratic Institute for International Affairs
National Endowment for Democracy (U.S.)
Network for the Defense of Independent Media in Africa
North-South Center (Miami)
Operation Lifeline Sudan
Organization for Security and Cooperation in Europe
Organization of American States
Panamanian Committee for Human Rights
Peoples Forum for Human Rights, Bhutan
Permanent Commission on Human Rights (Nicaragua)
Permanent Committee for the Defense of Human Rights (Columbia)
Physicians for Human Rights
Reporters Sans Frontieres
Runejel Junam Council of Ethnic Communities (Guatemala)
Tibet Information Network
Tibetan Center for Human Rights and Democracy
Tutela Legal (El Salvador)
Uganda Journalists' Safety Committee
Ukrainian Center for Independent Political Research
UNICEF
Union of Councils for Soviet Jews
U.S. Committee for Refugees
Venezuelan Human Rights Education Action Program
Vicaria de la Solidaridad (Chile)
Vietnam Committee on Human Rights
Voice of Bahrain
Washington Office on Africa
Washington Office on Latin America
West Africa Journalists Association
Women Acting Together for Change (Nepal)
Women's Commission for Refugee Women and Children
World Press Freedom Committee
Zambia Independent Monitoring Association